Lecture Notes in Computer Science 16216

Founding Editors

Gerhard Goos
Juris Hartmanis

The series Lecture Notes in Computer Science (LNCS), including its subseries Lecture Notes in Artificial Intelligence (LNAI) and Lecture Notes in Bioinformatics (LNBI), has established itself as a medium for the publication of new developments in computer science and information technology research, teaching, and education.

LNCS enjoys close cooperation with the computer science R & D community, the series counts many renowned academics among its volume editors and paper authors, and collaborates with prestigious societies. Its mission is to serve this international community by providing an invaluable service, mainly focused on the publication of conference and workshop proceedings and postproceedings. LNCS commenced publication in 1973.

Erkay Savas · Amir Moradi · Gregor Leander
Editors

Lightweight Cryptography for Security and Privacy

6th International Workshop, LightSec 2025
Istanbul, Türkiye, September 1–2, 2025
Revised Selected Papers

 Springer

Editors
Erkay Savas (ID)
Sabancı University
Tuzla, Türkiye

Amir Moradi (ID)
Technische Universität Darmstadt
Darmstadt, Germany

Gregor Leander (ID)
Ruhr-Universität Bochum
Bochum, Germany

ISSN 0302-9743   ISSN 1611-3349 (electronic)
Lecture Notes in Computer Science
ISBN 978-3-032-15540-5   ISBN 978-3-032-15541-2 (eBook)
https://doi.org/10.1007/978-3-032-15541-2

Preface

LightSEC 2025 was the sixth International Workshop on Lightweight Cryptography for Security & Privacy, which was held at the Conrad İstanbul Bosphorus, Beşiktaş, Istanbul, Türkiye during September 1–2, 2025.

The LightSEC 2025 Workshop was co-chaired by Erkay Savas (Sabanci University), Amir Moradi (Technical University of Darmstadt), and Gregor Leander (Ruhr University Bochum). The workshop serves as a platform to promote and initiate novel research on cryptographic solutions for security, privacy, and trust, with a particular emphasis on efficient algorithms, techniques, and implementations. This year's edition placed special focus on advancing cutting-edge cryptographic paradigms such as homomorphic encryption, zero-knowledge proofs, and post-quantum cryptography. The technical program featured sessions on Post-Quantum Cryptography, Efficient Implementation of Post-Quantum Cryptography, Advanced Cryptographic Algorithms: Fully Homomorphic Encryption and Zero-Knowledge, Hardware and Architecture Security, and Security, Cryptanalysis, and Attacks, comprising a total of 18 accepted papers.

The Program Committee (PC) was composed of distinguished experts from around the world dedicated to maintaining the highest scientific quality, and consisted of 35 members representing 30 distinguished institutions spanning 13 countries. A notable number of members represented leading research institutions such as Ruhr University Bochum, Katholieke Universiteit Leuven, Sabanci University, and the National Research Council Canada, each contributing multiple reviewers. The committee included scholars from both academia and industry, with participation from organizations such as Intel AI, NVIDIA, and the Technology Innovation Institute, ensuring a balance between theoretical research and practical innovation. This diverse and experienced committee played a crucial role in maintaining the scientific rigor and high standards of the review process.

A total of 31 submissions were received for this year's workshop, of which 16 papers were accepted, resulting in an acceptance rate of 52%. Each submission underwent a rigorous double-blind peer-review process, comprising 98 reviews conducted by 12 external reviewers, who collectively contributed 13 additional external reviews. Every paper received at least three reviews, with some evaluated by four or five reviewers, ensuring a balanced and thorough assessment. Contributions were submitted from 19 countries, reflecting the international scope of the workshop. The highest number of submissions came from Türkiye, followed by the Netherlands, Germany, Norway, and the UK, each demonstrating strong participation.

This broad participation and rigorous review process together highlight the workshop's commitment to academic excellence, fairness, and global collaboration.

LightSEC 2025 featured two invited papers and one invited talk. On the first day, Mark M. Tehranipoor, Distinguished Professor and Intel Charles E. Young Preeminence Endowed Chair at the University of Florida, delivered an invited talk on a multi-agent assistant system leveraging large language models (LLMs) to automate and enhance system-on-chip (SoC) security verification. This innovative approach integrates specialized LLM agents to perform tasks such as verification question answering, security asset identification, threat modeling, test plan and property generation, vulnerability detection, and simulation-based bug validation. The invited papers included "Stealthy Hardware Trojan Attacks on MQ-Based Post-Quantum Digital Signatures" by Aikata et al., presented on the first day, and "Protecting AES-128 Against First-Order Side-Channel Analysis in Micro-Architectures by Enforcing Threshold Implementation Principles" by De Paepe et al., presented on the second day.

As a side note, the workshop was organized within the scope of the enCRYPTON project, supported by the European Union under the Twinning Project No. 101079319.

We would like to express our sincere gratitude to everyone who contributed to the success of LightSEC 2025. We deeply appreciate the valuable efforts of the authors for submitting their high-quality manuscripts and sharing their research with the community. Our heartfelt thanks go to the Program Committee members and external reviewers whose diligent evaluations ensured the scientific rigor and excellence of the program. We are also grateful to our invited speakers for their insightful contributions and willingness to participate. Finally, we extend our warmest thanks to the organizing team from the enCRYPTON project for their exemplary management, dedication, and commitment throughout the preparation and execution of the event.

October 2025

Erkay Savas
Amir Moradi
Gregor Leander

Organization

General Chairs

Erkay Savas	Sabanci University, Türkiye
Cihangir Tezcan	Middle East Technical University, Türkiye

Program Committee Chairs

Erkay Savas	Sabanci University, Türkiye
Amir Moradi	Technical University of Darmstadt, Germany
Gregor Leander	Ruhr University Bochum, Germany

Steering Committee

Aydin Aysu	North Carolina State University, USA
Reza Azarderakhsh	Florida Atlantic University, USA
Orhun Kara	Izmir Institute of Technology, Türkiye
Amir Moradi	Technical University of Darmstadt, Germany
Sujoy Sinha Roy	Graz University of Technology, Austria
Igor Semaev	University of Bergen, Norway

Program Committee

Sedat Akleylek	University of Tartu, Estonia
Erdem Alkim	Dokuz Eylul University, Türkiye
Aydin Aysu	North Carolina State University, USA
Lejla Batina	Radboud University, Netherlands
Christof Beierle	Ruhr University Bochum, Germany
Emad Heydari Beni	Katholieke Universiteit Leuven, Belgium
Rosario Cammarotta	Intel AI, USA
Yarkin Doroz	NVIDIA, USA
Kris Gaj	George Mason University, USA
Shibam Ghosh	National Institute for Research in Digital Science and Technology, France
Lorenzo Grassi	Eindhoven University of Technology, Netherlands

Orhun Kara	Izmir Institute of Technology, Türkiye
Koray Karabina	National Research Council Canada & University of Waterloo, Canada
Elif Bilge Kavun	Barkhausen Institut, Germany
Mehran Mozaffari Kermani	University of South Florida, USA
Ayesha Khalid	Queen's University Belfast, UK
Gregor Leander	Ruhr University Bochum, Germany
Amir Moradi	Technical University of Darmstadt, Germany
Koksal Mus	Worcester Polytechnic Institute, USA
Berna Ors	Istanbul Technical University, Türkiye
Elisabeth Oswald	University of Klagenfurt, Austria***University of Birmingham, UK
Kamil Otal	TUBITAK Informatics and Information Security Research Center, Türkiye
Svetla Petkova-Nikova	Katholieke Universiteit Leuven, Belgium
Rachel Player	Royal Holloway, University of London, UK
Shahram Rasoolzadeh	Ruhr University Bochum, Germany
Francisco Rodriguez-Henriquez	Technology Innovation Institute, United Arab Emirates
Kurt Rohloff	Duality Technologies, USA
Sujoy Sinha Roy	Graz University of Technology, Austria
Sadegh Sadeghi	Institute for Advanced Studies in Basic Sciences, Iran
Erkay Savas	Sabanci University, Türkiye
Patrick Schaumont	Worcester Polytechnic Institute, USA
Meltem Sonmez Turan	National Institute of Standards and Technology, USA
Cihangir Tezcan	Middle East Technical University, Türkiye
Ingrid Verbauwhede	Katholieke Universiteit Leuven, Belgium
Melek Önen	EURECOM – Digital Security, France

Additional Reviewers

Can Balikci	Arsalan Ali Malik
Ahmet Calikus	Giuseppe Manzoni
Muhammed Said Gundogan	Ali Alper Sakar
Kubra Kaytanci	Martin Schmid
Jean Belo Klamti	Kubra Seyhan
Onur Kocak	Elmar Tischhauser

Sponsoring Institutions

European Union – Twinning Project, enCRYPTON Project No. 101079319
Sabanci University

Powered by

New Innovation Frontiers with Large Language Models for SoC Security (Invited Talk)

Mark M. Tehranipoor

Distinguished Professor, the Intel Charles E. Young Preeminence Endowed Chair Professor and the Sachio Semmoto Chair of the Department of Electrical and Computer Engineering (ECE) at the University of Florida

Ensuring the security of system-on-chips (SoCs) and edge devices is a critical imperative, yet traditional verification techniques struggle to keep pace due to significant challenges in automation, scalability, comprehensiveness, and adaptability. The advent of large language models (LLMs), with their remarkable capabilities in natural language understanding, code generation, and advanced reasoning, presents a new paradigm for tackling these issues. Moving beyond monolithic models, an agentic approach allows for the creation of multi-agent systems where specialized LLMs collaborate to solve complex problems more effectively. This keynote address will present a multi-agent assistant system designed to automate and enhance SoC security verification by integrating specialized agents for tasks like verification question answering, security asset identification, threat modeling, test plan and property generation, vulnerability detection, and simulation-based bug validation.

Contents

Post-quantum Cryptography

HAPPIER: Hash-Based, Aggregatable, Practical Post-quantum Signatures
Implemented Efficiently with Risc0 3
    Arda Saygan, Muhammed Said Gündoğan, Atakan Arslan,
    and Mehmet Emin Gönen

Isotropic Quadratic Forms, Diophantine Equations and Digital Signatures,
DEFIv2 23
    Martin Feussner and Igor Semaev

Stealthy Hardware Trojan Attacks on MQ-Based Post-quantum Digital
Signatures 39
    Aikata Aikata, Anisha Mukherjee, and Sujoy Sinha Roy

Efficient Implementation of Post-quantum Cryptography

LightNTT: A Tiny NTT/iNTT Core for ML-DSA Featuring
a Constant-Geometry Pipelined Design 57
    Bardia Taghavi, Reza Azarderakhsh, and Mehran Mozaffari Kermani

A Comparison of Unified Multiplier Designs for the FALCON Post-quantum
Digital Signature: A Case Study of Baseline, Tiling, Comba and Karatsuba
Approaches for FPGA and ASIC 77
    Rahul Magesh, Modini Ayyagari, Sharath Pendyala, and Aydin Aysu

An Optimized FrodoKEM Implementation on Reconfigurable Hardware 97
    Giuseppe Manzoni, Shekoufeh Neisarian, and Elif Bilge Kavun

**Advanced Cryptographic Algorithms: Fully Homomorphic
Encryption, Zero-Knowledge**

Optimized FPGA Architecture for Modular Reduction in NTT 117
    Tolun Tosun, Selim Kırbıyık, Emre Koçer, and Ersin Alaybeyoğlu

Leveraging Smaller Finite Fields for More Efficient ZK-Friendly Hash
Functions 138
    Gökçe Düzyol and Kamil Otal

Hardware and Architecture Security

ARCHER: Architecture-Level Simulator for Side-Channel Analysis
in RISC-V Processors 157
  *Asmita Adhikary, Abraham Basurto-Becerra, Lejla Batina,
  Ileana Buhan, Durba Chatterjee, Senna van Hoek,
  and Eloi Sanfelix Gonzalez*

MIDSCAN: Investigating the Portability Problem for Cross-Device
DL-SCA 178
  Lizzy Grootjen, Zhuoran Liu, and Ileana Buhan

Protecting AES-128 Against First-Order Side-Channel Analysis
in Micro-Architectures by Enforcing Threshold Implementation Principles 198
  *Charles-Antoine De Paepe, John Gaspoz, Dilara Toprakhisar,
  and Svetla Nikova*

On Advancing Pre-silicon Hardware Trojan Detection Against Lightweight
Block Ciphers 212
  *Charilaos Memeletzoglou, Evangelia Konstantopoulou,
  and Nicolas Sklavos*

Hardware Circuits for the Legendre PRF 231
  Subhadeep Banik and Francesco Regazzoni

Lightweight Fault Detection Architecture for Modular Exponentiation
in Cryptography on ARM and FPGA 244
  *Saeed Aghapour, Kasra Ahmadi, Mehran Mozaffari Kermani,
  and Reza Azarderakhsh*

Security, Cryptanalysis and Attacks

Cube-Attack-Like Cryptanalysis of Keccak-Based Constructions
Exploiting State Differences 263
  Mohammad Vaziri and Vesselin Velichkov

Differential and Linear Analyses of DIZY Through MILP Modeling 285
  Murat Burhan İlter, Onur Koçak, Orhun Kara, and Fatih Sulak

Automated Tool for Meet-in-the-Middle Attacks with Very Low Data
and Memory Complexity 306
  Mohammad Vaziri

JWT Back to the Future on the (Ab)use of JWTs in IoT Transactions 328
*Alberto Battistello, Guido Bertoni, Filippo Melzani,
and Maria Chiara Molteni*

Author Index 345

Post-quantum Cryptography

HAPPIER: Hash-Based, Aggregatable, Practical Post-quantum Signatures Implemented Efficiently with Risc0

Arda Saygan[1,2], Muhammed Said Gündoğan[1(✉)], Atakan Arslan[1], and Mehmet Emin Gönen[1]

[1] TÜBİTAK BİLGEM National Research Institute of Electronics and Cryptology, Kocaeli, Turkey
`{arda.saygan,said.gundogan,atakan.arslan,mehmet.gonen}@tubitak.gov.tr`
[2] Boğaziçi University, İstanbul, Turkey

Abstract. The adoption of NIST's post-quantum cryptographic standards has accelerated the shift toward quantum-resistant systems. While many protocols like TLS, IKEv2, and Signal can integrate these standards, others still rely on primitives lacking efficient post-quantum replacements. One such primitive is the BLS signature scheme, widely used in proof-of-stake (PoS) blockchains for its ability to aggregate multiple signatures into a single compact one, reducing communication and verification overhead.

Recent research has proposed post-quantum aggregate signatures to replace BLS, but existing schemes remain impractical due to high memory usage and slow aggregation. While prior solutions produce smaller signatures (hundreds of KB), they require hundreds of gigabytes of RAM to aggregate 2^{10} signatures. In contrast, our scheme generates slightly larger signatures (2–3 MB) but drastically reduces aggregation time and can handle up to 2^{16} signatures on a standard laptop, making it significantly more practical.

In addition to improved scalability, our design is grounded in strong security principles, relying on minimal assumptions—specifically, the use of secure hash functions. For the signature primitive, we employ XMSS, a stateful hash-based signature scheme that is already standardized by NIST.

To the best of our knowledge, no previous post-quantum aggregation schemes have implemented multi-level aggregation. We have implemented this capability, enabling incremental aggregation of signatures across the network. This is particularly relevant to Ethereum's Beam chain roadmap, which emphasizes modular zk-rollup architectures and the integration of post-quantum primitives. Moreover, by enabling multi-level signature aggregation, our approach provides a practical solution for secure validator coordination and signature verification in future post-quantum Ethereum consensus mechanisms.

Keywords: Aggregate Signatures · Post-quantum Cryptography · Zero-Knowledge Proofs · Recursive SNARK · zkVM · hash-based

E. Savas et al. (Eds.): LightSec 2025, LNCS 16216, pp. 3–22, 2026.
https://doi.org/10.1007/978-3-032-15541-2_1

1   Introduction

Over the past decade, the growing practicality of quantum computing technologies has reignited concerns within the cryptographic community about the risks posed by quantum-capable algorithms. The security of widely deployed asymmetric cryptosystems such as RSA and Diffie-Hellman is fundamentally based on the hardness of problems like integer factorization and discrete logarithms. However, with Shor's groundbreaking quantum algorithms in 1994, which solve these problems in polynomial time on a quantum computer [32], future quantum machines pose a serious threat to these cryptosystems. Anticipating this risk, researchers have long explored post-quantum (or quantum-resistant) cryptographic schemes under the assumption that adversaries may possess quantum capabilities.

Since NIST's 2016 call for post-quantum standardization [1], global efforts to develop secure alternatives have intensified—especially for digital signatures, where the standardization process is still underway. For quantum resistant signatures, the following has been concluded:

- Stateful hash-based signatures XMSS and LMS were standardized in 2020 [14].
- Stateless hash-based signature SPHINCS+ was selected as a standard [26].
- MLWE-based signatures Crystals-Dilithium and Falcon were selected as standards [26].

With the standards introduced by NIST, post-quantum solutions for public-key encryption and digital signatures have now been established. However, certain cryptographic primitives still lack well-established quantum-resistant counterparts, and remain active areas of research. One such primitive is aggregate signatures, which are particularly relevant given that state-of-the-art consensus protocols—such as Ethereum and Algorand [16]—rely heavily on aggregatable signature schemes, most notably BLS signatures [9]. In this context, there is a growing body of research focused on developing post-quantum alternatives to BLS to ensure long-term security against quantum adversaries. An aggregate signature scheme is a cryptographic primitive that enables n distinct parties to each sign a different message and subsequently allows all individual signatures to be combined into a single compact signature σ [8]. This aggregated signature must ensure that a verifier can be convinced that each signer indeed signed their respective message, preserving both authenticity and efficiency.

The construction of post quantum aggregate signature schemes has witnessed significant progress, particularly those grounded in lattice-based techniques [3,19,33]. Unlike hash based constructions [22,36], lattice-based schemes benefit from rich underlying algebraic structures. However, despite their relatively efficient performance, the precise security guarantees of lattice-based schemes remain somewhat ambiguous. This uncertainty is reflected in NIST's selection of SPHINCS+ [6,26] for standardization—an approach that, while less efficient than its lattice-based counterparts, addresses both practical and theoretical demands for cryptographic constructions rooted in diverse hardness assumptions. Consequently, the exploration of hash based aggregate signatures is important.

The first practical aggregate signature scheme based on symmetric-key primitives was introduced in [22]. This scheme compresses hash-based one-time signatures (i.e., Lamport+) using STARKs [9], a variant of SNARKs, thereby enabling aggregation. The Loquat scheme was proposed [36] as a symmetric primitive-based aggregate signature construction that supports many-time signing. However, despite its novel design, the performance of Loquat has been shown to be insufficient for practical deployment.

As a remedy, in this work, we propose a new approach to hash-based aggregate signatures by leveraging XMSS-based signatures in combination with STARKs to achieve efficient aggregation. Unlike Loquat, our scheme supports multi-level aggregation, enabling more scalable and flexible signature compression. Our construction achieves superior performance compared to Loquat while introducing the first aggregate signature scheme that satisfies the following properties:

- Hash-based,
- Not limited to one-time use,
- Supports multi-level aggregation.

The improved performance of our scheme compared to Loquat can be attributed to several key factors:

- Instead of relying on stateless signatures, we employ the stateful XMSS signature scheme, which offers significantly better performance in practice.
- The implementation was carried out using RISC Zero (RISC0) zkVM, enabling an optimized realization of the protocol with improved efficiency and practical viability.

The practical implications of secure and efficient post-quantum aggregate signatures extend notably to blockchain systems like Ethereum. As detailed in Sect. 7, Ethereum's roadmap—particularly the Beam initiative—emphasizes zk-rollup modularity and the integration of post-quantum cryptography. However, existing post-quantum aggregate signature schemes often demand excessive RAM and prover time, making them unsuitable for real-world deployment in platforms like Ethereum where thousands of signatures may need to be aggregated efficiently.

In contrast, our scheme offers a practical alternative. We were able to benchmark up to 2^{16} signatures on a standard laptop with 16 GB RAM, achieving reasonable prover times and resource usage. This level of scalability and efficiency suggests that our approach can serve as a viable solution to Ethereum's needs for post-quantum secure and scalable signature aggregation.

The remainder of this paper is structured as follows. In Sect. 2, we review related work on post-quantum signature aggregation and provide an overview of existing signature aggregation schemes across different cryptographic foundations, including elliptic curve-based, lattice-based, and symmetric primitive-based constructions. We then offer a feature-level comparison to highlight how our approach differs from and improves upon prior work. In Sect. 3, we provide the preliminaries. Section 4 presents our design, detailing the architecture, cryptographic components, and aggregation strategy. In Sect. 5, we present the implementation details. In Sect. 6, we provide our benchmark results and compare them with existing work. In Sect. 7, we explore potential applications of our scheme in consensus protocols, emphasizing its benefits for decentralized systems. Finally, Sect. 8 concludes the paper with a summary of our contributions.

2   Related Work

In the literature, studies on aggregate signatures are typically categorized into three main groups: elliptic curve-based schemes (e.g., BLS and related constructions), lattice-based schemes, and hash-based schemes.

2.1   Elliptic Curve-Based Schemes

BLS signatures enable aggregation through the use of bilinear pairings [9]. A body of research has focused on improving the efficiency of BLS-based schemes under various security assumptions related to elliptic curves and pairings. To the best of our knowledge, the current state-of-the-art in this line of work is represented by KZH-Fold [21]. For this reason, we include only BLS and KZH-Fold as elliptic curve-based schemes in the comparison presented in Table 1.

Kadianakis et al. [21] propose KZH-Fold, a novel polynomial commitment scheme combined with an accumulation mechanism achieving sublinear verification complexity and proof sizes. This approach substantially reduces communication and verifier time compared to traditional BLS signature aggregation and existing accumulation methods such as Nova. KZH-Fold's effectiveness is particularly evident in large-scale blockchain consensus protocols, where minimizing communication overhead and verifier complexity is paramount.

2.2   Lattice-Based Schemes

Several recent works have addressed the challenges associated with post-quantum resistant signature aggregation, focusing particularly on lattice-based and hash-based constructions due to their promising quantum resistance.

Tomita and Shikata [33] and Aardal et al. [3] have both used the LaBRADOR proof system to aggregate lattice-based signatures. Specifically, [3] aggregates Falcon-512 signatures, while [33] modifies the Dilithium signature to reduce proof size. Both papers formulate the proof sizes analytically, but neither has implemented their schemes. As a result, performance metrics such as RAM usage, proof time, and verification time are not available. In comparison to the NIST-standard-based [3,33] achieves a smaller proof size. For 1024 signatures, [3] results in a proof size of 122 KB, whereas [33] results in 63 KB.

Hsiang et al. [10,19] propose PQScale, a post-quantum signature aggregation scheme specifically tailored for Falcon signatures, utilizing Aurora, a zk-SNARK proving system. For 1000 aggregated signatures, the reported proof size is approximately 105 KB. Additionally, they report that aggregating 1487 signatures takes 33 min on a machine with 512 GB of RAM. Although the implementation code has not been made publicly available, these figures suggest that the aggregation process is computationally intensive and resource demanding.

2.3   Symmetric Primitive Based Schemes

To the best of our knowledge, Khaburzaniya et al. [22] presents the first attempt at constructing a hash-based aggregate signature scheme. Their work explores the compression of Lamport signatures using STARK proofs. To improve performance and ensure better compatibility with STARK-friendly arithmetic, the authors instantiate Lamport one-time signatures using the Rescue-Prime hash function. Since the proposed scheme fundamentally relies on one-time signatures, it requires each participant to generate a new key pair for every aggregated signature. This constraint limits the practicality of the approach in real-world applications.

Loquat [36] introduces a SNARK-friendly signature scheme based on the Legendre pseudorandom function (PRF), with low R1CS constraint costs. The authors aggregate this signature using various SNARK systems, including Aurora, Fractal, and Recursive Fractal. Their benchmarks show that aggregating 16 signatures takes approximately 1 minute with Aurora and 10 min with Fractal. Due to a 28 GB RAM constraint, the maximum number of signatures that could be aggregated was limited to 64 with Aurora and 16 with Fractal. For 1024 signatures, aggregation was not feasible due to memory limitations, and performance metrics such as prover time were only provided as estimates. Additionally, the aggregation using Recursive Fractal was not implemented; the reported results are based solely on estimation. Despite the relatively small proof sizes, the resource requirements for the aggregator render the scheme impractical in its current form for large-scale use.

2.4   Feature-Level Comparison with Existing Work

Our proposed design advances beyond existing work by providing implemented support for multi-level aggregation, a feature that has not been realized in prior hash-based aggregate signature schemes. Furthermore, it is built upon a NIST-approved post-quantum signature scheme, offering a more conservative and reliable security foundation through the use of hash-based primitives. While the proof sizes are relatively larger compared to some lattice-based approaches, our scheme demonstrates superior aggregation efficiency in terms of prover time. Thanks to its efficient proving performance, it can be benchmarked for up to 2^{16} signatures using a standard laptop with 16 GB of RAM, eliminating the need for high-end server infrastructure. A feature-level comparison of existing work and our construction is presented in Table 1, while detailed performance comparisons and benchmarks are provided in Sect. 6.

Table 1. Feature-Level Comparison of Aggregation Signature Schemes

Properties	BLS [9]	KZH25 [21]	TS23 [33]	AAB24 [3]	PQS23 [19]	KCL22 [22]	LOQ24 [36]	Our work
Many Time Signature Scheme	✓	✓	✓	✓	✓	×	✓	✓
Multi-Level Aggregation Support	✓	✓	×	×	×	×	×	✓
Post-quantum (PQ) Secure	×	×	✓	✓	✓	✓	✓	✓
NIST Approved PQ Signature	×	×	×	✓	✓	×	×	✓
Transparent Setup	✓	×	✓	✓	✓	✓	✓	✓
Implemented	✓	✓	×	×	✓	✓	✓	✓
Cryptographic Assumptions	Elliptic Curve	Elliptic Curve	Lattice	Lattice	Lattice	Hash	LPRF & Hash	Hash

3 Prelimineries

3.1 STARK

We define a STARK [5] protocol as consisting of three algorithms: STARK = (Setup, Prove, Verify), detailed as follows. We modified the definition slightly to match with RISC0 zkVMs interface, by making **Prove** algorithm return the output of the program to be proved.

- $\mathsf{pp} \leftarrow$ **Setup**$(1^\lambda, \mathrm{Prog})$:
  Given a security parameter λ and a program description $\mathrm{Prog} : \{0,1\}^* \to \{0,1\}^*$, this algorithm outputs public parameters pp.
- $(\pi, \mathsf{z}) \leftarrow$ **Prove**$(\mathsf{pp}, \mathsf{x}, w)$:
  Given public parameters pp, a statement x, and a witness w, such that $\mathrm{Prog}(\mathsf{x}\|w) = \mathsf{z}$, this algorithm produces a proof π and returns the output z of the program.
- $b \leftarrow$ **Verify**$(\mathsf{pp}, \pi, \mathsf{x}, \mathsf{z})$:
  Given public parameters pp, a proof π, and a statement x, and program output z, this algorithm returns a bit b, where $b = 1$ denotes acceptance and $b = 0$ denotes rejection.

Out modification is only a slight change and it can easily be shown that it's identical to the well-known definition.

3.2 ZkVMs

SNARKs are cryptographic proof systems that verify the integrity of arbitrary computations. Each SNARK involves an arithmetization step, which transforms a computational statement into a mathematical representation, typically referred to as a circuit. Notable arithmetization techniques include Quadratic Arithmetic Programs (QAP), used in Groth16 [18], and Algebraic Intermediate Representations (AIR), used in STARKs [5]. However, converting a program into its corresponding circuit is often non-trivial and can require significant manual effort. Zero-Knowledge Virtual Machines (zkVMs) alleviate this burden by translating a program's low-level assembly code into an arithmetic circuit, relying on predefined arithmetizations for each instruction provided by the zkVM framework. As a result, there has been an increasing variety of zkVMs for various instruction sets, such as RISC-V [4,24,30], Ethereum Virtual Machine [25,27,31] and others [17,23].

4 Our Design

In this section, we will present our design choices, on various methods we have used in our post-quantum aggregate signature scheme.

4.1 Using STARK for Post-Quantum Signature Aggregation

SNARKs can be used to construct signature aggregation schemes in a natural way. A program that verifies a group of signatures can be proven using a SNARK, and the resulting proof certifies the correctness of individual signature verifications—thus serving as an aggregate signature. In particular, post-quantum secure SNARKs, referred to as pqSNARKs, can be utilized to build post-quantum aggregate signature schemes.

In this work, we select STARKs [5] as our underlying pqSNARK framework for several reasons. First, STARKs are hash-based, aligning with our goal of minimizing security assumptions. Second, they offer high scalability, with a proving time of $O(n \log n)$ relative to the size of the program. Finally, STARKs do not require a trusted setup, making them especially suitable for deployment in decentralized or distributed environments.

4.2 XMSS for Post-Quantum Signatures

Hash-based signature schemes are considered post-quantum secure as they rely solely on the well-studied assumption of hash function preimage resistance. This minimal reliance on cryptographic assumptions distinguishes them from other post-quantum approaches, such as those based on lattices or codes, and makes them an robust choice. Motivated by these properties, our design adopts a hash-based signature as its foundation.

Among hash-based options, we selected the Extended Merkle Signature Scheme (XMSS) due to its balance of performance and security. XMSS is a stateful, many-time signature scheme that provides efficient signing and verification compared to alternatives. It was first introduced in [11], later published as RFC 8391 in 2018 [20], and subsequently standardized by NIST in 2020 [14], further reinforcing its credibility and maturity as a practical post-quantum solution. In our implementation, we instantiate the XMSS signature scheme using the NIST-recommended parameter set `XMSS-SHAKE256_16_192` [14].

4.3 Multi-level Aggregation and Recursive SNARKs

As discussed in the previous section, individual signatures can be aggregated into a succinct proof using zk-SNARKs—a technique adopted in several prior works [3,19,22,33,36]. However, this method comes with key limitations. In particular, once a group of signatures is aggregated, incorporating a new signature requires re-aggregating the entire set. This is known as single-level aggregation, where all signatures must be collected at a single aggregator before the aggregation process can begin. Such a centralized requirement is highly impractical in decentralized environments like blockchain systems, as it leads to latency from global communication, scalability issues, and linear aggregation time relative to the number of signatures.

A more scalable alternative is multi-level aggregation [21], where previously aggregated signatures can themselves be re-aggregated into a new aggregate proof. This model enables distributed aggregators to perform partial aggregation in parallel, with intermediate aggregate proofs being recursively combined into a final proof. The result is a significant reduction in aggregation time, from linear to logarithmic in the number of total signatures—ideal for large-scale and decentralized settings.

Our design achieves multi-level aggregation through the use of recursive SNARKs. In this paradigm, a SNARK proof can be verified inside another instance of the same SNARK system. Crucially, enabling recursion requires that the prover has access to the SNARK verifier code as part of the circuit input. This allows a proof to validate previous proofs within the same circuit, and produce a new proof attesting to the correctness of all prior verifications. By iteratively applying this mechanism, aggregate proofs can be continuously merged, allowing the construction of deeply nested and scalable aggregate signature structures.

4.4 Formal Specification of Our Design

In this section, our scheme will be formally described, and details on how we use STARK for aggregation will be explained.

We assume that, prior to the aggregation procedure, the public keys of the designated signers (e.g., validators) are already known. In our setting, only signatures from these parties are eligible for aggregation—that is, only votes from validators are aggregated. To reference this set of public keys efficiently, we assume that the vector of public keys is committed via a Merkle tree and indexed starting from 1, reserving index 0 to represent a null public key. Using a commitment scheme, we decrease the size of the inputs and improve the efficiency of our algorithm.

Given

- signature scheme XMSS $=$ (KeyGen, Sign, Verify) [20],
- proving system STARK $=$ (Setup, Prove, Verify)
- set commitment scheme MT $=$ (Commit, Open, Check)

we define our multi-level aggregate signature scheme $\mathsf{SA}^{S,k,r} = (\mathsf{T}, \mathsf{G}, \mathsf{S}, \mathsf{V}, \mathsf{A}, \mathsf{VA}, \mathsf{M})$ with parameters number of signers (e.g. validators) S, maximum number k of signatures aggregated in A, and maximum number r of aggregate signatures merged in M as following:

- **Transparent Set-up** $\mathsf{pp} \leftarrow \mathsf{SA.T}(1^\lambda)$:
  Takes input parameter λ, returns $\mathsf{pp} \leftarrow \mathsf{STARK.Setup}(1^\lambda, \mathrm{Prog}_{\mathsf{agg}})$ where $Prog_{agg}$ is the program that verifies given signatures and aggregate signatures, defined in Sect. 5.3.
- **Key Generation** $(pk, sk) \leftarrow \mathsf{SA.G}(1^\lambda)$:
  Takes security parameter λ, returns $(pk, sk) \leftarrow \mathsf{XMSS.KeyGen}(1^\lambda)$
- **Signing** $(\sigma, sk') \leftarrow \mathsf{SA.S}(sk, m)$:
  Takes a private key sk and a message m, returns $(\sigma, sk') \leftarrow \mathsf{XMSS.Sign}(sk, m)$
- **Signature Verification** $b \leftarrow \mathsf{SA.V}(pk, m, \sigma)$:
  Takes a public key pk, a message m and a signature σ. Returns $b \leftarrow \mathsf{XMSS.Verify}(pk, m, \sigma)$
- **Signature Aggregation** $(\sigma^{ag}, \mathbf{b}) \leftarrow \mathsf{SA.A}(\boldsymbol{pk}, m, \boldsymbol{\sigma}, \rho^{pk}, \boldsymbol{\pi}^{MT}, \boldsymbol{i}, \mathsf{pp})$:
  Takes vectors of k public keys $\boldsymbol{pk} = (pk_1, \ldots, pk_k)$, k signatures $\boldsymbol{\sigma} = (\sigma_1, \ldots, \sigma_k)$, a message m, a Merkle tree root of validator public keys ρ^{pk}, a vector of k Merkle inclusion proofs $\boldsymbol{\pi}^{MT} = (\pi_1^{MT}, \ldots, \pi_k^{MT})$, a vector of k indices of given public keys in the Merkle tree $\boldsymbol{i} = (i_1, i_2, \ldots, i_k)$ and public parameters pp. Initializes r many empty bitvectors $[\mathbf{0}]^r$ where $\mathbf{0} \in \{0,1\}^S$ and r many dummy aggregate signatures $\boldsymbol{\sigma}^{ag}$ for the $Prog_{agg} interface$.
  Returns $(\sigma^{ag}, \mathbf{b}) \leftarrow \mathsf{STARK.Prove}(\mathsf{pp}, (\rho^{pk}, m), ([\mathbf{0}]^r, \boldsymbol{pk}, \boldsymbol{\sigma}, \boldsymbol{\pi}^{MT}, \boldsymbol{i}, \boldsymbol{\sigma}^{ag}))$
- **Aggregate Verification** $b \leftarrow \mathsf{VA}(\rho^{pk}, m, \sigma^{ag}, \mathbf{b}, \mathsf{pp})$:
  Takes a Merkle tree root of validator public keys ρ^{pk}, a message m, aggregate signature σ^{ag}, a bitfield $\mathbf{b}$ and public parameters pp.
  Returns boolean $b \leftarrow \mathsf{STARK.Verify}(\mathsf{pp}, \sigma^{ag}, (\rho^{pk}, m), \mathbf{b})$
- **Aggregate Signature Merging** $(\sigma^{ag}, \mathbf{b}) \leftarrow \mathsf{M}(\rho^{pk}, m, \boldsymbol{\sigma}^{ag}, \mathbf{b}, \mathsf{pp})$:
  Takes a Merkle tree root ρ^{pk} of validator public keys, a message m, a vector of r aggregate signatures $\boldsymbol{\sigma}^{ag} = (\sigma_1^{ag}, \ldots, \sigma_r^{ag})$, a vector of r bitfields $\mathbf{b} = (\mathbf{b}_1, \ldots, \mathbf{b}_r)$, where $\mathbf{b_i} \in \{0,1\}^S$ for $i \in [r]$, and public parameters pp. Initializes dummy public key vector $\boldsymbol{pk}$, signature vector $\boldsymbol{\sigma}$, Merkle inclusion proofs $\boldsymbol{\pi}^{MT}$ and indices $\boldsymbol{i}$ for the $Prog_{agg} interface$. $(\sigma^{ag}, \mathbf{b}) \leftarrow \mathsf{STARK.Prove}(\mathsf{pp}, (\rho^{pk}, m), (\mathbf{b}, \boldsymbol{pk}, \boldsymbol{\sigma}, \boldsymbol{\pi}^{MT}, \boldsymbol{i}, \boldsymbol{\sigma}^{ag}))$

5   Implementation

In this section, we describe the practical realization of our scheme, detailing the critical design choices and underlying technologies.

5.1   Using RISC0 ZkVM

In this work, we chose to implement our scheme using a zkVM due to its practical advantages in prototyping. The abstraction and modularity provided by zkVMs significantly streamline the development of proof-of-concept systems, making them an ideal choice for demonstrating the feasibility of our recursive aggregation scheme.

We utilized the RISC Zero zkVM primarily because it employs STARKs as its underlying zero-knowledge proof system[1], thus considered post-quantum secure. Moreover, RISC0 claims to have optimized its internal proof verification circuits—an important factor in the efficient implementation of recursive SNARKs.

In addition to these advantages, RISC0 offers precompiled implementations of certain hash functions from the SHA family. These precompiles are optimized for improved proving and verification times. Given that our scheme is based on hash-based signatures, where hashing is one of the primary performance bottlenecks, such optimizations are especially beneficial in reducing overall performance.

We adopted a modular zk-proof development architecture leveraging Risc0, which allows us to generate proofs efficiently and re-use components flexibly. This modularity simplifies the integration of recursive proof techniques and accelerates development by enabling isolated implementation and testing of individual logic units. This modular environment not only improves scalability and maintainability but also aligns well with modern zero-knowledge system design principles, where composability and abstraction are key to building complex proof systems efficiently.

Although our prototype instantiation uses XMSS as the underlying signature scheme, the construction is modular and can be adapted to support alternative digital signature schemes. The flexibility of the RISC Zero zkVM plays a key role in this extensibility, allowing the recursive aggregation logic to remain unchanged while swapping out the signature primitive. This makes our approach broadly applicable to various post-quantum and classical schemes, depending on application needs. We selected RISC Zero due to its general-purpose execution environment and rapid prototyping capabilities, which significantly streamlined development and experimentation.

---

[1] Although STARK is the primary proof system used in RISC0-zkVM, it incorporates proof composition with Groth16 to reduce proof sizes [29]. In our implementation, we disabled the Groth16 composition to maintain post-quantum security.

Terminology in RISC0 ZkVM. We introduce some terminology specific to the RISC0-zkVM framework, as these concepts will be used consistently throughout the paper. In RISC0's architecture, three key terms are crucial:

- **Guest Program**: This is the program to be proven, and it corresponds to the program Prog in the stament $Prog(x\|w) = z$, described in the STARK definition at 3.1 . Designing the guest program is a central component of our scheme and will be discussed in detail in the following section.
- **Image ID**: This identifier uniquely represents a specific guest program. It must be supplied whenever a proof is verified to ensure that the proof is correctly associated with the guest program from which it was generated. It corresponds to the public parameters pp at 3.1.
- **Receipt**: This refers to the proof object produced by the host program. A receipt contains both the cryptographic proof attesting to the correct execution of the guest program and the output data produced by it. This encapsulation allows verifiers to validate both the integrity of the computation and its result within a single object.

5.2   Data Types and Components

Our design relies on the following core data types:

- **Public Key Merkle Tree:** Implemented via the `merkle_light` crate [28], this data structure encodes a list of signers' public keys in a succinct and verifiable manner.
- **Bitfield:** A binary vector of length equal to the number of signers. It tracks which participants have submitted valid signatures by setting the corresponding index to one.
- **Signature Scheme Data Types:** Includes `Signature`, `PublicKey`, `PrivateKey`, and `SignatureScheme`, all derived from the `hash-sig` library [34]. These structures encapsulate the components required for hash-based digital signing.
- **Receipt:** The native term used in RISC0 for the proof object. A receipt contains both the STARK proof and the output data returned by the guest program. It is generated by the RISC0-zkVM during runtime.

5.3   The Guest Program

Algorithm 1. Prog$_{\mathrm{agg}}$: Guest Program for Aggregate Signature Verification

---

1: **public parameter:** $image\_id$
2: **inputs:** $merkle\_root, message$
3: **witness:** $bitfields = [bitfield_1, bitfield_2, \ldots, bitfield_r]$, $pks = [pk_1, pk_2, \ldots, pk_k]$, $sigs = [sig_1, sig_2, \ldots, sig_k]$, $merkle\_proofs = [\pi_1, \pi_2, \ldots, \pi_k]$, $indices = [i_1, i_2, \ldots, i_k]$, $agg\_sigs = [agg\_sig_1, agg\_sig_2, \ldots, agg\_sig_r]$
4: **Constants:** $zero\_bitfield = [0]^S$
5:
6: **for all** $(pk_j, sig_j, \pi_j, i_j) \in (pks, sigs, merkle\_proofs, indices)$ **do**
7:    **if** $i_j \neq 0$ **then**
8:        **if** XMSS.Verify$(pk_j, message, sig_j) = $ **false then**
9:            **fail**
10:       **end if**
11:       **if** MT.Check$(merkle_root, pk_j, i_j, \pi_j) = $ **false then**
12:            **fail**
13:       **end if**
14:    **end if**
15: **end for**
16:
17: **for all** $(bitfield_j, agg\_sig_j) \in (bitfields, agg\_sigs)$ **do**
18:    **if** $bitfield_j \neq zero\_bitfield$ **then**
19:        STARK.Verify$(image_id, agg_sig_j, (merkle_root, message), bitfield_j)$
20:    **end if**
21: **end for**
22:
23: $final\_bitfield \leftarrow zero\_bitfield$
24: **for all** $i_j \in indices$ **do**
25:    **if** $i_j \neq 0$ **then**
26:        $final\_bitfield[i_j - 1] \leftarrow 1$
27:    **end if**
28: **end for**
29: **for all** $bitfield_j \in bitfields$ **do**
30:    $final\_bitfield \leftarrow final\_bitfield \vee bitfield_j$
31: **end for**
32:
33: **return** $final\_bitfield$

The pseudo-code for the guest program is given in the Algorithm 1. The guest program verifies the following claims for the given inputs:

- The provided public key is a valid member of the public key Merkle tree.
- The given signature is valid with respect to the provided public key and message.
- Each supplied proof is a valid STARK proof of a guest program with image id, $image\_id$.

– The outputs of each provided proof are consistent with the claimed bitfields, Merkle root, and message.

If all verifications succeed, the bitfields are merged using a logical OR operation, and the bit corresponding to the current signer's index is updated. The program outputs the updated bitfield.

The guest program's functionality can be logically grouped into two independent tasks:

1. Verifying an individual signature,
2. Merging multiple existing aggregate signatures.

However, these two types of inputs, signatures and proofs, are not always available at the same time. For instance, in the initial round of aggregation, no prior proofs exist; only individual signatures are available. In contrast, an aggregator may later need to merge multiple existing proofs without introducing any new signature.

To accommodate such cases, the guest program supports conditional execution: it skips certain verification steps when the input indicates their irrelevance. Specifically:

– If the signer index is set to zero, the program interprets this as an absence of a new signature and bypasses signature verification.
– If a bitfield containing all zeros is provided, it is treated as an empty claim, i.e., no prior signers are asserted, allowing the proof verification for that input to be skipped.

These conditional skips not only improve expressiveness but also result in tangible performance improvements. As shown in Table 3, the time and proof size required for running the program vary significantly between signature verification and proof merging phases.

5.4   Aggregation Procedure

In our aggregation scheme, we assume a distributed setting where both signers and aggregators are spread across a network. Prior to aggregation, a fixed Merkle root (corresponding to the public key Merkle tree) is generated, and a common message to be signed is selected. Each signer uses their private key to sign the message and produces an individual signature.

The aggregation process proceeds in multiple phases:

1. **Signature-to-Proof Conversion:** Each individual signature is passed as input to the guest program, along with a zero-initialized bitfield. The guest program verifies the signature and updates the corresponding index in the bitfield. The resulting proof and its output constitute the first-level aggregation artifact.

2. **Proof Merging:** Each proof and its associated output (bitfield, Merkle root, and message) is distributed over the network. Aggregators receive these proofs and merge them by running the guest program again—this time skipping the signature verification step (by setting index $i = 0$) and providing multiple bitfields as input. The result is a new proof representing an aggregated claim over multiple signers, which itself can be further aggregated.

This recursive, multi-level aggregation model enables efficient and scalable signature compression in decentralized networks.

5.5   Code Repository

Our implementation is publicly available in the following GitHub repository: PQ-Aggregation-via-Recursive-SNARKs[2]. The commit history of the repository can be used to verify that the referenced commit was pushed prior to the submission deadline.

6   Performance and Comparison

In this section, we evaluate the performance of our signature scheme by two tables: comparing it with similar constructions in the literature and presenting benchmark results obtained from a series of tests conducted on a standard personal computer.

Table 2 provides a performance comparison between our proposed scheme and existing post-quantum aggregate signature constructions in the literature. Among lattice-based schemes, only PQScale [19] includes reported benchmarking results based on an actual implementation. Although its implementation is not open-sourced, it remains the only lattice-based scheme with concrete performance evaluations in the literature. PQScale was benchmarked on a server equipped with 512 GB of RAM, yet was only able to aggregate a maximum of 1,483 signatures, with an aggregation time of approximately 33 min. In our work, we successfully aggregated up to 2^{16} signatures on a standard laptop with only 16 GB of RAM, demonstrating significantly improved scalability and efficiency.

While lattice-based schemes generally produce smaller aggregated signature sizes, they suffer from impractical RAM usage and aggregation time. Our approach, despite producing aggregate signatures in the range of a few megabytes, offers a far more practical solution in real-world settings. Transmitting a few megabytes over the network is considerably more feasible than tolerating excessive memory and time requirements, which become untenable as the number of signatures increases.

Compared to other hash-based constructions, our design exhibits significantly improved practicality. For example, the Loquat scheme [36] was only able to aggregate a maximum of 64 signatures on a 24 GB RAM machine, highlighting

---

[2] https://github.com/ArdaSaygan/PQ-Aggregation-via-Recursive-SNARKs.

its limited scalability in terms of memory usage. Furthermore, its recursive aggregation results—for larger numbers such as 1024 signatures—are based solely on performance estimates rather than actual implementation and benchmarking. [22] remains the only other scheme in the literature that demonstrates relatively practical prover time and RAM consumption. However, it relies exclusively on one-time signature instantiations, requiring each signer to generate a new key pair for every aggregated signature. This requirement introduces considerable overhead and limits the feasibility of [22] in real-world applications.

In conclusion, our construction is the only aggregate signature scheme that combines post-quantum security with practical implementability, making it a strong candidate for real-world adoption.

Table 2. Performance comparison of post-quantum aggregate signature schemes based on key metrics including the number of signatures, signature size, total system RAM used during experiments, aggregation time, verification time, underlying cryptographic assumptions, and security levels. NI: Not Implemented

Schemes	# Sign.	Sig. Size	RAM	Aggr. Time	Ver. Time	Assumption
KCL22 [22]	2^9	77 KB	3.7 GB	10.5 sec	0.1 sec	Hash
KCL22 [22]	2^9	155 KB	4.8 GB	13.6 sec	0.1 sec	Hash
PQS23 [19]	783	98 KB	<512 GB	966 sec	108 sec	Hash
TS23 [33]	2^{10}	63.48 KB	NI	NI	NI	Lattice
AAB24 [3]	2^{10}	88 KB	NI	NI	NI	Lattice
KCL22 [22]	2^{10}	83 KB	7.4 GB	19.7 sec	0.1 sec	Hash
KCL22 [22]	2^{10}	165 KB	9.5 GB	25.7 sec	0.1 sec	Hash
Loquat/Aurora [36]	2^{10}	235 KB	>28 GB	7000 sec	487 sec	LPRF + Hash
This Work	2^{10}	2.34 MB	<16 GB	220.6 sec	0.14 sec	Hash
AAB24 [3]	2^{10}	252 KB	NI	NI	NI	Lattice
AAB24 [3]	2^{10}	417 KB	NI	NI	NI	Lattice
PQScale	1483	108 KB	<512 GB	1992 sec	192 sec	Hash
TS23 [33]	2^{12}	65.02 KB	NI	NI	NI	Lattice
AAB24 [3]	2^{12}	252 KB	NI	NI	NI	Lattice
This Work	2^{12}	2.36 MB	<16 GB	286.79 sec	0.13 sec	Hash
TS23 [33]	2^{16}	77.46 KB	NI	NI	NI	Lattice
This Work	2^{16}	2.89 MB	<16 GB	795 sec	0.16 sec	Hash

In the Table 3, we benchmark our signature scheme in number of signatures, and present data on aggregation time, proof size and verification. All benchmarks of our implementation were conducted on a MacBook running macOS Sequoia, equipped with an Apple M1 chip (8-core CPU) and 16 GB of unified memory. The system was plugged in (not battery-powered) to avoid performance throttling. Code was compiled using the `rustc` version 1.85.0 and the `cargo-risczero` toolchain version 1.2.5, with builds executed in release mode.

Table 3. Benchmark results of our proposed scheme with different batch sizes and merging factors.

# Signatures S	Merge r proofs	Signature-to-Proof Conversion Time T_c	Proof Merging Time T_r	Aggregation Time T_a	Proof Size	Verification Time
2^{10}	2	167.22 sec	5.39 sec	220.64	2.24 MB	0.14 sec
2^{10}	4	151.62 sec	10.82 sec	205.23 sec	4.45 MB	0.25 sec
2^{10}	8	160.12 sec	11.27 sec	200.42 sec	8.64 MB	0.49 sec
2^{11}	2	166.26 sec	12.43 sec	301.84 sec	2.35 MB	0.13 sec
2^{11}	4	161.35 sec	10.94 sec	222.35 sec	4.45 MB	0.25 sec
2^{11}	8	165.36 sec	12.18 sec	209.44 sec	8.64 MB	0.49 sec
2^{12}	2	171.92 sec	10.36 sec	286.79 sec	2.36 MB	0.13 sec
2^{12}	4	165.95 sec	12.36 sec	247.87 sec	4.47 MB	0.25 sec
2^{12}	8	154.50 sec	20.32 sec	233.43 sec	8.65 MB	0.51 sec
2^{13}	2	180.47 sec	10.12 sec	304.39 sec	2.36 MB	0.14 sec
2^{13}	4	168.01 sec	11.02 sec	249.74 sec	4.47 MB	0.27 sec
2^{13}	8	188.58 sec	22.25 sec	284.02 sec	8.76 MB	0.51 sec
2^{14}	2	180.47 sec	10.12 sec	304.39 sec	2.36 MB	0.14 sec
2^{14}	4	168.01 sec	11.02 sec	249.74 sec	4.47 MB	0.27 sec
2^{14}	8	188.58 sec	22.25 sec	284.02 sec	8.76 MB	0.51 sec
2^{15}	2	189.55 sec	21.61 sec	512.91 sec	2.39 MB	0.14 sec
2^{15}	4	172.78 sec	38.53 sec	457.73 sec	4.52 MB	0.26 sec
2^{15}	8	209.01 sec	44.69 sec	441.20 sec	10.96 MB	0.63 sec
2^{16}	2	180.92 sec	38.12 sec	795.03 sec	2.89 MB	0.16 sec
2^{16}	4	210.84 sec	38.02 sec	513.73 sec	5.64 MB	0.35 sec
2^{16}	8	245.74 sec	78.23 sec	664.25 sec	13.73 MB	0.77 sec

We want to point out the algebraic relation about the aggregation time T_a, to allow the reader to interpret the table better. For this, we again repeat the aggregation process. At the beginning of the aggregation, the signatures are distributed across the network. These signatures are converted into proofs in parallel, this operation takes time T_c. After conversion, the proofs are broadcast on the network, aggregators gather r proofs and merge them into a single proof in time T_r. This merging occurs $\lceil \log_r S \rceil$ times for all S signatures to be aggregated. Then, the time T_a to aggregate S signatures can be expressed as

$$T_a = T_c + T_r \lceil \log_r S \rceil$$

where T_c is the time to convert a signature into proof and T_r is the time to merge r proofs. Both of these variables depend on S and r.

7 Applications on the Consensus Protocols

Proof of Stake (PoS) systems can be viewed as open ballot voting mechanisms in which validators must reach consensus. In this context, cryptographic signatures serve as ballots, with validators expressing their agreement by signing a common message that represents the decision being finalized.

Ethereum's transition from Proof of Work (PoW) to Proof of Stake (PoS) brought new challenges, particularly in handling the verification of validator signatures efficiently. With thousands of validators participating, verifying individual ECDSA signatures became a bottleneck, slowing down consensus processes.

To tackle this, [2] introduced BLS signature aggregation, leveraging the compact multi-signature approach described in [7]. By adopting this method, [2] optimized signature verification by enabling multiple signatures to be combined into a single, efficient representation. This drastically reduces verification time and computational costs, making Ethereum's PoS mechanism more scalable and efficient. Similar to Ethereum 2.0, many blockchain protocols employ BLS signatures [12, 16, 35].

The Ethereum community has placed increasing emphasis on the transition to post-quantum security, particularly in identifying alternatives to BLS signatures within the Ethereum protocol. Several initiatives reflect this strategic direction.

- A recent effort has focused on formally proving the security of a generalized variant of XMSS to facilitate the development of pqSNARK-friendly hash-based signature schemes [15].
- Under the broader Beam roadmap, Ethereum has actively supported, accelerated, and coordinated both hash-based and lattice-based cryptographic research.
- To assess and promote the suitability of Poseidon as a secure hash function for post-quantum hash-based signatures, the Ethereum Foundation launched a dedicated cryptanalysis initiative with a $500,000 bounty, encouraging rigorous public analysis.
- In its recurring academic grant calls, the Foundation has explicitly included post-quantum aggregate signatures in its wishlist, underlining the importance and urgency of advancing research in this area.

Existing post-quantum aggregate signature schemes typically require substantial RAM and prover time even for aggregating as few as 1024 signatures. In contrast, our design enables efficient aggregation of thousands of signatures using only standard laptops, demonstrating its practicality and scalability in resource-constrained environments. This is especially important for Ethereum, which currently aggregates up to 32,768 validator signatures per epoch to finalize blocks—a process that can take several minutes due to the cost of aggregation and verification [13]. By applying our construction, signature verification could be offloaded to zkVM-based recursive SNARKs, reducing the on-chain cost of finality, accelerating consensus, and improving scalability. Moreover, the use of standardized primitives like XMSS ensures compatibility with NIST recommendations, addressing regulatory and interoperability concerns in future Ethereum upgrades.

8   Conclusion

In the literature, post-quantum aggregate signature schemes primarily fall into two categories: hash-based and lattice-based constructions [3, 19, 22, 33, 36]. Among these, only three schemes—two hash-based and one lattice-based—have been implemented and evaluated with actual performance metrics such as RAM usage and aggregation time [19, 22, 36]. One of the hash-based schemes, [22], is instantiated using one-time signatures, which require all signers to regenerate key pairs for each aggregate signature. This introduces substantial overhead and limits practical deployment. The remaining two schemes also exhibit scalability constraints. The hash-based Loquat scheme aggregates at most 64 signatures using a 24 GB machine and was unable to produce results for 1024 signatures, instead providing only estimated runtimes of around two hours. The lattice-based PQScale, while achieving aggregation of up to 1483 signatures, did so using a 512 GB RAM server and reported an aggregation time of 33 min.

In contrast, our proposed construction achieves significant performance improvements. We demonstrate the ability to aggregate up to 2^{16} signatures on a standard laptop with just 16 GB of RAM. For 1024-signature aggregation, our scheme achieves practical runtimes as low as 4 min, made possible by our multi-level aggregation design, which enables parallelization across distributed aggregators. Benchmarks conducted on standard hardware demonstrate that our approach achieves competitive aggregation times and significantly lower memory requirements, making it practically deployable in decentralized blockchain settings like Ethereum. We believe that our work brings post-quantum aggregate signatures significantly closer to practical deployment. In particular, it presents a viable and scalable candidate to replace BLS signatures in Ethereum's ongoing transition to post-quantum cryptography.

References

1. Call for Proposals - Post-Quantum Cryptography | CSRC. https://csrc. nist.gov/Projects/post-quantum-cryptography/post-quantum-cryptography-standardization/Call-for-Proposals. Accessed 23 Jan 2024
2. Pragmatic signature aggregation with BLS — ethresear.ch. https://ethresear.ch/t/pragmatic-signature-aggregation-with-bls/2105?u=benjaminion. Accessed 05 Mar 2025
3. Aardal, M.A., Aranha, D.F., Boudgoust, K., Kolby, S., Takahashi, A.: Aggregating falcon signatures with labrador. In: Reyzin, L., Stebila, D. (eds.) Advances in Cryptology - CRYPTO 2024 - 44th Annual International Cryptology Conference, Santa Barbara, CA, USA, August 18-22, 2024, Proceedings, Part I. Lecture Notes in Computer Science, vol. 14920, pp. 71–106. Springer (2024). https://doi.org/10. 1007/978-3-031-68376-3_3
4. Arun, A., Setty, S., Thaler, J.: Jolt: snarks for virtual machines via lookups. In: Joye, M., Leander, G. (eds.) Advances in Cryptology - EUROCRYPT 2024, pp. 3–33. Springer Nature Switzerland, Cham (2024)
5. Ben-Sasson, E., Bentov, I., Horesh, Y., Riabzev, M.: Scalable, transparent, and post-quantum secure computational integrity. Cryptology ePrint Archive, Paper 2018/046 (2018). https://eprint.iacr.org/2018/046
6. Bernstein, D.J., Hülsing, A., Kölbl, S., Niederhagen, R., Rijneveld, J., Schwabe, P.: The SPHINCS$^+$ signature framework. In: Cavallaro, L., Kinder, J., Wang, X., Katz, J. (eds.) Proceedings of the 2019 ACM SIGSAC Conference on Computer and Communications Security, CCS 2019, London, UK, November 11-15, 2019, pp. 2129–2146. ACM (2019). https://doi.org/10.1145/3319535.3363229

7. Boneh, D., Drijvers, M., Neven, G.: Compact multi-signatures for smaller blockchains. In: International Conference on the Theory and Application of Cryptology and Information Security, pp. 435–464. Springer (2018)
8. Boneh, D., Gentry, C., Lynn, B., Shacham, H.: Aggregate and verifiably encrypted signatures from bilinear maps. In: Biham, E. (ed.) EUROCRYPT 2003. LNCS, vol. 2656, pp. 416–432. Springer, Heidelberg (2003). https://doi.org/10.1007/3-540-39200-9_26
9. Boneh, D., Lynn, B., Shacham, H.: Short signatures from the weil pairing. J. Cryptol. **17**(4), 297–319 (2004). https://doi.org/10.1007/S00145-004-0314-9
10. BTQ: Introducing PQScale - A scaling solution for post-quantum signatures. https://www.btq.com/blog/introducing-pqscale-a-scaling-solution-for-post-quantum-signatures. Accessed 26 Feb 2024
11. Buchmann, J., Dahmen, E., Hülsing, A.: XMSS - a practical forward secure signature scheme based on minimal security assumptions. In: Yang, B.Y. (ed.) Post-Quantum Cryptography, pp. 117–129. Springer, Berlin Heidelberg, Berlin, Heidelberg (2011)
12. Camenisch, J., Drijvers, M., Hanke, T., Pignolet, Y.A., Shoup, V., Williams, D.: Internet computer consensus. In: Proceedings of the 2022 ACM Symposium on Principles of Distributed Computing, pp. 81–91. PODC'22, Association for Computing Machinery, New York, NY, USA (2022). https://doi.org/10.1145/3519270.3538430
13. Community, E.R.: Signature merging for large-scale consensus. https://ethresear.ch/t/signature-merging-for-large-scale-consensus/17386 (2023). Accessed 17 Apr 2025
14. Cooper, D.A., Apon, D.C., Dang, Q.H., Davidson, M.S., Dworkin, M.J., Miller, C.A.: Recommendation for stateful hash-based signature schemes (Oct 2020). https://doi.org/10.6028/NIST.SP.800-208. Accessed April 18 2025
15. Drake, J., Khovratovich, D., Kudinov, M., Wagner, B.: Hash-based multi-signatures for post-quantum ethereum. IACR Commun. Cryptol. **2**(1) (2025). https://doi.org/10.62056/aey7qjp10
16. Gilad, Y., Hemo, R., Micali, S., Vlachos, G., Zeldovich, N.: Algorand: Scaling byzantine agreements for cryptocurrencies. In: Proceedings of the 26th Symposium on Operating Systems Principles, Shanghai, China, October 28-31, 2017. pp. 51–68. ACM (2017). https://doi.org/10.1145/3132747.3132757, https://doi.org/10.1145/3132747.3132757
17. Goldberg, L., Papini, S., Riabzev, M.: Cairo – a turing-complete STARK-friendly CPU architecture. Cryptology ePrint Archive, Paper 2021/1063 (2021). https://eprint.iacr.org/2021/1063
18. Groth, J.: On the size of pairing-based non-interactive arguments. In: Fischlin, M., Coron, J.-S. (eds.) EUROCRYPT 2016. LNCS, vol. 9666, pp. 305–326. Springer, Heidelberg (2016). https://doi.org/10.1007/978-3-662-49896-5_11
19. Hsiang, J.H., Fu, S., Kuo, P.C., Cheng, C.M.: PQScale: a post-quantum signature aggregation algorithm. https://uploads-ssl.webflow.com/642374103c1677f8f335c581/64771752dbe6933ceb1d712b_PQScale.pdf (2023). online
20. Huelsing, A., Butin, D., Gazdag, S.L., Rijneveld, J., Mohaisen, A.: XMSS: eXtended Merkle Signature Scheme. RFC 8391 (May 2018). https://doi.org/10.17487/RFC8391, https://www.rfc-editor.org/info/rfc8391
21. Kadianakis, G., Zapico, A., Hafezi, H., Bünz, B.: KZH-fold: Accountable voting from sublinear accumulation. Cryptology ePrint Archive, Paper 2025/144 (2025). https://eprint.iacr.org/2025/144

22. Khaburzaniya, I., Chalkias, K., Lewi, K., Malvai, H.: Aggregating and thresholdizing hash-based signatures using starks. In: Proceedings of the 2022 ACM on Asia Conference on Computer and Communications Security, pp. 393–407. ASIA CCS '22, Association for Computing Machinery, New York, NY, USA (2022). https://doi.org/10.1145/3488932.3524128

23. Liu, T., Zhang, Z., Zhang, Y., Hu, W., Zhang, Y.: Ceno: Non-uniform, segment and parallel zero-knowledge virtual machine. J. Cryptol. 38(2), 17 (2025). https://doi.org/10.1007/S00145-024-09533-2

24. Marin, D., Abdalla, M., Govereau, P., Groth, J., Judson, S., Sosnin, K., Vamsi, G.: Nexus 1.0: Enabling verifiable computation. https://nexus-xyz.github.io/assets/nexus_whitepaper.pdf (2024)

25. Matter Labs: zkSync protocol: zkSync virtual machine (zkvm). https://docs.zksync.io/zksync-protocol/vm (2024). Accessed Apr 18 2025

26. NIST: NIST Announces First Four Quantum-Resistant Cryptographic Algorithms — nist.gov. https://www.nist.gov/news-events/news/2022/07/nist-announces-first-four-quantum-resistant-cryptographic-algorithms. Accessed 23 Feb 2024

27. Polygon Labs: Polygon zkEVM documentation. https://docs.polygon.technology/zkEVM/ (2024). Accessed Apr 18 2025

28. Prisyazhnyy, I.: merkle_light: Lightweight merkle tree implementation in rust. https://crates.io/crates/merkle_light (2023). Accessed 18 Apr 2024

29. RISC Zero: RISC zero proof system documentation. https://dev.risczero.com/proof-system/ (2024). Accessed 18 Apr 2024

30. RISC Zero: RISC zero proof system in detail. https://dev.risczero.com/proof-system-in-detail.pdf (2024). Accessed 17 Apr 2025

31. Scroll Team: Scroll: A native zkEVM layer 2 solution for Ethereum. https://scroll.io/files/whitepaper.pdf (2023). Accessed Apr 18 2025

32. Shor, P.W.: Algorithms for quantum computation: Discrete logarithms and factoring. In: 35th Annual Symposium on Foundations of Computer Science, Santa Fe, New Mexico, USA, 20-22 November 1994, pp. 124–134. IEEE Computer Society (1994). https://doi.org/10.1109/SFCS.1994.365700

33. Tomita, T., Shikata, J.: Compact aggregate signature from module-lattices. Cryptology ePrint Archive, Paper 2023/471 (2023). https://eprint.iacr.org/2023/471

34. Wagner, B., Coratger, T., Khovratovich, D., Han: hash-sig: A rust library for hash-based signature schemes. https://github.com/b-wagn/hash-sig/commit/05fdfe5ee3cca789082d2c86556dba103dd67678 (2023), commit: 05fdfe5. Accessed 18 May 2024

35. Zcash Team: Zcash protocol specification. https://zips.z.cash/protocol/protocol.pdf (2024). Accessed 18 May 2025

36. Zhang, X., Steinfeld, R., Esgin, M.F., Liu, J.K., Liu, D., Ruj, S.: Loquat: a snark-friendly post-quantum signature based on the legendre prf with applications in ring and aggregate signatures. In: Reyzin, L., Stebila, D. (eds.) Advances in Cryptology - CRYPTO 2024, pp. 3–38. Springer Nature Switzerland, Cham (2024)

Isotropic Quadratic Forms, Diophantine Equations and Digital Signatures, DEFIv2

Martin Feussner[ID] and Igor Semaev[✉]

Selmer Center, University of Bergen, Bergen 5006, Norway
{martin.feussner,igor.semaev}@uib.no

Abstract. This work introduces DEFIv2 - an efficient hash-and-sign digital signature scheme based on isotropic quadratic forms over a commutative ring of characteristic 0. The form is public, but the construction is a trapdoor that depends on the scheme's private key. For polynomial rings over integers and rings of integers of algebraic number fields, the cryptanalysis is reducible to solving a quadratic Diophantine equation over the ring or, equivalently, to solving a system of quadratic Diophantine equations over rational integers. It is still an open problem whether quantum computers will have any advantage in solving Diophantine problems.

Keywords: Digital signatures · Isotropic quadratic forms · Diophantine equations

1 Introduction

1.1 Motivation

Subset sum problem is usually treated as finding $0, 1$-solutions to a linear Diophantine equation in n variables. More precisely, given positive integers $a_1, \ldots, a_n$ and a, the goal is to decide whether there exist $x_i \in \{0, 1\}$ such that

$$x_1 a_1 + \ldots + x_n a_n = a.$$

This problem is known to be NP-complete [7]. Obviously, the subset sum problem is equivalent to solving (or deciding) the system of multivariate quadratic Diophantine equations

$$x_1 a_1 + \ldots + x_n a_n = a, \quad x_1^2 - x_1 = 0, \ldots, x_n^2 - x_n = 0.$$

To decide whether or not a more general system of multivariate quadratic Diophantine equations

$$f_1(x) = 0, \ldots, f_m(x) = 0, \tag{1}$$

where $x = (x_1, \ldots, x_n)$, $f_i \in \mathbb{Z}[x]$, and $\deg f_i \leq 2$, is solvable in rational integers is therefore at least NP-hard. Finding explicit integer solutions to (1) is generally difficult.

© The Author(s), under exclusive license to Springer Nature Switzerland AG 2026
E. Savas et al. (Eds.): LightSec 2025, LNCS 16216, pp. 23–38, 2026.
https://doi.org/10.1007/978-3-032-15541-2_2

1.2 Related Work

Several cryptographic schemes have been claimed to be constructed upon the hardness of the subset sum problem and Diophantine equations. The most famous one is the Merkle-Hellman public key cryptosystem, in which a super-increasing vector, the scheme's private key, is hidden using a modular linear transformation to derive the public key. The scheme was broken in [18], and its variations were also broken; see [13] for a survey. A digital signature scheme proposed in [14] based on a quadratic congruence modulo a composite integer and its extensions were broken; see [2]. A number of key exchange protocols built on the difficulty of solving general Diophantine equations and on finding equivalences for binary quadratic forms over rational integers were published in [8,17], respectively; see also the references therein. The cryptographic schemes above differ from the current proposal.

1.3 Our Contribution

In this work, a new hash-and-sign digital signature scheme called DEFIv2 is presented. The security of the scheme is based on the hardness of computing isotropic vectors over commutative rings of characteristic 0 for quadratic forms with a trapdoor. Given a message, one may construct an isotropic vector for the form, where one of the entries is its digest and the remaining entries serve as a signature.

For polynomial rings R over $\mathbb{Z}$ and rings of integers of algebraic number fields the cryptanalysis is reducible to solving quadratic Diophantine equations over R or equivalently to solving systems of quadratic Diophantine equations over $\mathbb{Z}$ such as (1). For the parameters defined in Sect. 4 (NIST security level 1), forging a signature is equivalent to finding a relatively small solution to a nonhomogeneous quadratic Diophantine equation in 4 variables over $R = \mathbb{Z}[X]/(q)$, where (q) is the ideal in $\mathbb{Z}[X]$ generated by an irreducible polynomial $q = q(X)$ of degree $m = 28$. It is well known [11] that given one solution to a homogeneous quadratic equation over a ring, all other solutions can be obtained via parametrisation. However, this method is not applicable to nonhomogeneous equations. Additionally, there is a restriction on the solution size. Hence, one must find a relatively small solution to a system of 28 multivariate quadratic Diophantine equations over $\mathbb{Z}$ in 84 variables to forge a signature for a given message.

No modular transforms are used in the digital signature algorithm proposed in this work. All calculations are performed in the ring of integers. Therefore, the security of the proposed algorithm does not rely on solving multivariate polynomial equations over finite fields, as with the Matsumoto-Imai scheme [10], the Hidden Field Equations (HFE) cryptosystem [15], and their derivatives. Furthermore, advances in solving common lattice problems such as SVP (Shortest Vector Problem) and CVP (Closest Vector Problem) do not appear to undermine the security of the new scheme; see Sects. 4 and 5.6 below.

The idea of using isotropic forms for signatures and the design of the new scheme is due to Semaev, the choice of numerical parameters and implementation are due to Feussner.

2   Isotropic Quadratic Forms

Suppose R is any commutative ring of characteristic 0 with unity and without zero divisors, a module over $\mathbb{Z}$ with a finite or infinite basis $\alpha_0, \alpha_1, \ldots, \alpha_{m-1}, \ldots$ For $a \in R$, where $a = a_0\alpha_0 + a_1\alpha_1 + \ldots + a_{m-1}\alpha_{m-1}$ and $a_i \in \mathbb{Z}$, the function $|a| = \max_{0 \leq i < m} |a_i|$ defines a norm on R. For $y = (y_1, y_2, \ldots, y_n) \in R^n$, we set $|y| = \max_{1 \leq i \leq n} |y_i|$. Let

$$f(x_1, \ldots, x_n) = \sum_{1 \leq i \leq n} c_{ii}x_i^2 + \sum_{1 \leq i < j \leq n} 2c_{ij}x_ix_j$$

be a quadratic form over R. Denote $x = (x_1, \ldots, x_n)$. Then $f(x) = x^T C x$, where $C \in R^{n \times n}$ is a symmetric matrix with entries $c_{ij} \in R$. The quadratic form is called *isotropic* if it represents 0. That is, $f(z) = 0$ for a nonzero vector $z \in R^n$. The vector z is then called an *isotropic vector*.

The security of the proposed digital signature scheme is based on the hardness of computing isotropic vectors $z \in R^n$ for the form $f(x)$. It is well known that given one solution to the homogeneous quadratic equation $f(x) = 0$ it is possible to compute all other solutions over R via parametrisation [11]. However, in the proposed digital signature scheme some entries of the target isotropic vector $z \in R^n$ are prescribed by the hash value of a message. That makes the method inefficient for forgery.

The approach to construct an isotropic quadratic form $f(x)$ over R is described below within this section. In Sect. 3.7, we present a way to construct such an isotropic vector z for $f(x)$. To verify a signature in the scheme, one checks that $f(z) = 0$ in R.

When $R = \mathbb{Z}[X]/(q)$, where (q) is the ideal in $\mathbb{Z}[X]$ generated by a monic irreducible polynomial $q(X) \in \mathbb{Z}[X]$, the cryptanalysis of the scheme is presented in Sect. 5. Numerical parameters are proposed in Sect. 4 and provide 128-bit security corresponding to NIST security category 1 according to [12].

Let r, s, n be positive integers such that $s \geq 2$ and $n = r + s$. Let J be a diagonal matrix of size $n \times n$ with diagonal entries ± 1 as

$$J = \mathrm{Diag}\,(\pm 1, \ldots, \pm 1, \pm 1),$$

where both 1 and -1 may occur. The choice of the diagonal entries match a known identity used to construct isotropic vectors. This ensures that J is indefinite and admits isotropic vectors. Suppose $B \in R^{n \times n}$ is a matrix of rank n (the rows of B are linearly independent over R). Then the matrix $C = B^T J B \in R^{n \times n}$ defines an indefinite quadratic form

$$f(x) = (Bx)^T J (Bx) = x^T C x, \tag{2}$$

which is isotropic by construction. For matrices B specified in Sect. 3, isotropic vectors can be computed efficiently.

3 Signature Scheme

This section outlines the structure of the signature scheme. While the core equations are presented in general terms, we also include example constructions that are suitable for practical use. Specific parameter choices and constructions are provided in Sect. 4.

3.1 Private Key

The private key of the signature scheme is a matrix $B \in R^{n \times n}$, where $n = r + s$, constructed with blocks as

sizes	r	s
r	B_{11}	0
s	B_{21}	B_{22}

,

where B_{ij} are matrices over R of sizes according to the definition above and the matrix B_{22} is invertible in $R^{s \times s}$. For efficiency, the entries of $B_{11}, B_{21}, B_{22}, B_{22}^{-1}$ may be taken of relatively small norms. To construct B_{22}, formulae in Sect. 3.6 may be used.

3.2 Public Key

The public key of the signature scheme is the matrix $C = B^T J B \in R^{n \times n}$, which defines the quadratic form (2). The matrix $J \in R^{n \times n}$ is also public and is fixed to ensure that isotropic vectors can be constructed efficiently. One such choice is described in Sect. 3.7.

3.3 Signature Generation

Let M be a message and let $h \in R^r$ encode its hash value. The entries of h may be chosen to have relatively small norms.

1. Given M, compute $h \in R^r$.
2. Set $Z' = B_{11}h \in R^r$. Generate randomly $Z'' \in R^s$ such that $Z^T J Z = 0$, where $Z = (Z'|Z'') \in R^n$. See Sect. 3.7, where the construction is specified for $r = 1, s = 3$.
3. Compute $y \in R^s$ by
$$y = B_{22}^{-1}(Z'' - B_{21}h).$$

4. The signature for M is y.

In the instantiation of the scheme presented in Sect. 4, a bound parameter γ_y is used. The generated signature y is valid if additionally $|y| < \gamma_y$.

3.4   Signature Verification

Let M, y be a signed message.

1. If $y \notin R^s$, then reject. Otherwise, compute $h \in R^r$.
2. Set $z = (h|y) \in R^n$. If
$$f(z) = z^T C z = 0,$$
then accept the signature, otherwise reject.

In the instantiation of the scheme presented in Sect. 4, the signature is also rejected if $|y| \geq \gamma_y$.

3.5   Verification Proof

Let M, y be a correctly generated signature. For $z = (h|y)$ we have
$$B_{21}\, h + B_{22}\, y = Z''$$
and
$$Bz = \begin{pmatrix} B_{11} & 0 \\ B_{21} & B_{22} \end{pmatrix} \begin{pmatrix} h \\ y \end{pmatrix} = \begin{pmatrix} Z' \\ Z'' \end{pmatrix} = Z.$$
Therefore,
$$f(z) = z^T C z = [Bz]^T J [Bz] = Z^T J Z = 0.$$

3.6   Constructing B_{22}, B_{22}^{-1} with Small Entries

Let R be a ring of integers in an algebraic number field and $s > 1$ be a positive integer. It seems a rather difficult problem to construct a matrix $M \in R^{s \times s}$ invertible in $R^{s \times s}$ such that the entries of both M and M^{-1} are of small norms (small coefficients in the polynomial representation of the elements of R). The matrix M must look randomly generated in appearance so neither permutation nor elementary matrices may work. In the current version of DEFI we set

$$B_{22} = (\prod_{i=1}^{k} P_i E_i)\, F, \tag{3}$$

where k is a parameter that increases the entropy and complexity of the construction, E_i is a randomly generated elementary matrix, P_i is a randomly generated permutation matrix, and $F \in R^{s \times s}$ is a randomly generated unimodular matrix that is easy to invert but hard to guess; see explicit constructions in Sect. 4. Using some other constructions for B_{22} may reduce the parameters of the scheme as signature and public key sizes. Then

$$B_{22}^{-1} = F^{-1}(\prod_{i=1}^{k} E_{k-i+1}^{-1} P_{k-i+1}^{-1}).$$

A matrix $E \in R^{s \times s}$ is called elementary if

$$E = \mathrm{Diag}(1, \ldots, 1) + V_{ij}, \ 1 \leq i, j \leq s, \ i \neq j,$$

where $V_{ij} \in R^{s \times s}$ is such that

$$V_{ij}[u, v] = \begin{cases} b & \text{if } (u, v) = (i, j), \\ 0 & \text{if } (u, v) \neq (i, j) \end{cases}$$

for some $b \neq 0$. Then

$$E^{-1} = \mathrm{Diag}(1, \ldots, 1) - V_{ij}.$$

3.7   Constructing Vector Z Such that $Z^T J Z = 0$

In this section, we set $r = 1, s = 3, n = 4$. The construction may be easily extended to larger parameters. We also set $B_{11} = 1$ in the definition of B and let $J = \mathrm{Diag}(1, 1, -1, -1)$. Then

1. Let $(v_1, v_2, v_3, v_4) = \mathrm{HASH}(M) \in R^4$ and compute $h = v_1 v_4 - v_2 v_3 \in R$. In another variation of the scheme, we set $v_2 = v_3 = 0$ and let $(v_1, v_4) = \mathrm{HASH}(M) \in R^2$, then compute $h = v_1 v_4 \in R$.
2. Randomly generate $(a_1, a_2, a_3, a_4), (d_1, d_2, d_3, d_4) \in R^4$ such that

$$a_1 a_4 - a_2 a_3 = \det \begin{pmatrix} a_1 & a_2 \\ a_3 & a_4 \end{pmatrix} = 1,$$

$$d_1 d_4 - d_2 d_3 = \det \begin{pmatrix} d_1 & d_2 \\ d_3 & d_4 \end{pmatrix} = 1.$$

Similar to (3), the matrices $A = \begin{pmatrix} a_1 & a_2 \\ a_3 & a_4 \end{pmatrix}$ and $D = \begin{pmatrix} d_1 & d_2 \\ d_3 & d_4 \end{pmatrix}$ may be formed as products of randomly generated elementary and permutation matrices.

3. Compute

$$\begin{pmatrix} V_1 & V_2 \\ V_3 & V_4 \end{pmatrix} = \begin{pmatrix} d_1 & d_2 \\ d_3 & d_4 \end{pmatrix} \begin{pmatrix} v_1 & v_2 \\ v_3 & v_4 \end{pmatrix} \begin{pmatrix} a_1 & a_2 \\ a_3 & a_4 \end{pmatrix}.$$

4. Set

$$Z_1 = V_1 V_4 - V_2 V_3 = h,$$
$$Z_2 = V_1 V_2 + V_3 V_4,$$
$$Z_3 = V_1 V_2 - V_3 V_4,$$
$$= V_1 V_4 + V_2 V_3,$$

then

$$Z = (Z_1, Z_2, Z_3, Z_4).$$

Therefore,

$$Z^T J Z = Z_1^2 + Z_2^2 - Z_3^2 - Z_4^2$$
$$= (V_1 V_4 - V_2 V_3)^2 + (V_1 V_2 + V_3 V_4)^2 - (V_1 V_2 - V_3 V_4)^2 - (V_1 V_4 + V_2 V_3)^2$$
$$= 0.$$

4   Proposed Parameters and Performance

In this section, we propose parameters to provide instantiations of the 2 variations (see 1. of Sect. 3.7) of our scheme targeting NIST security level 1 [12]. We refer to them as DEFIv2-1a and DEFIv2-1b. The latter requires only half as many hash bits. Implementation details and performance benchmarks are also presented.

4.1   Scheme Setup and Ring Definition

Let $r = 1, s = 3, n = 4$ and $m = 28$. We set $q = q(X) = X^m + X + 1$ which is an irreducible polynomial in $\mathbb{Z}[X]$. This defines the ring $R = \mathbb{Z}[X]/(q)$, which corresponds to a ring of integers in the algebraic number field $K = \mathbb{Q}(\alpha)$, where α is a root of $q(X)$.

4.2   Bounding Parameters

We introduce bound parameters $\gamma_{C_1}, \gamma_{C_2}, \gamma_{C_3}, \gamma_{B_{22}}, \gamma_{B_{22}^{-1}}, \gamma_y$. These are upper bounds on the absolute values of the polynomial coefficients in the blocks of the public key matrix C, the secret matrices B_{22} and B_{22}^{-1}, and the signature y, respectively. The matrix $C \in R^{n \times n}$ is partitioned into blocks as follows

sizes	r	s
r	C_1	C_2
s	C_2	C_3

If any coefficient in C, B_{22}, B_{22}^{-1}, or y exceeds its bound, it is regenerated. The bound γ_y also imposes the additional rejection condition during signature verification: if $|y| \geq \gamma_y$, the signature is rejected.

4.3   Construction of B_{21}, B_{22}, A, D

Entries of $B_{21} \in R^{3 \times 1}$ have randomly generated coefficients from $[-\delta_{B_{21}}, \delta_{B_{21}}] \setminus \{0\}$. The matrix $B_{22} \in R^{3 \times 3}$ is constructed as in (3). That is, as a product of k_B randomly generated elementary (each with exactly one non-zero off-diagonal entry from $\{\pm 1\}$) and permutation matrices, and a randomly generated matrix F. Our choice of F is defined using $u, v \in R$ with randomly generated coefficients from $[-\delta_F, \delta_F] \setminus \{0\}$. It is expressed as

$$F = \begin{pmatrix} 1 & -v & 0 \\ u & 1 & v \\ 0 & u & 1 \end{pmatrix} = \begin{pmatrix} 1 & 0 & 0 \\ u & 1 & 0 \\ 0 & 0 & 1 \end{pmatrix} \begin{pmatrix} 1 & 0 & 0 \\ 0 & 1 & v \\ 0 & 0 & 1 \end{pmatrix} \begin{pmatrix} 1 & 0 & 0 \\ 0 & 1 & 0 \\ 0 & u & 1 \end{pmatrix} \begin{pmatrix} 1 & -v & 0 \\ 0 & 1 & 0 \\ 0 & 0 & 1 \end{pmatrix}.$$

The construction of A and D follows similarly as a product of only k_{AD} randomly generated elementary and permutation matrices and no F.

4.4 Guessing Complexity for B_{22}

To generate a valid B_{22}, we require that all of its entries have a minimum guessing complexity denoted by 2^{Ω_B}. If this criterion is not met, the matrix is regenerated. By construction, the coefficients of each polynomial entry in B_{22} lie within the range $[-\gamma_{B_{22}}+1, \gamma_{B_{22}}-1]$. We estimate the guessing complexity of an entry by computing the inverse of its probability of occurrence. This is done by multiplying the inverse probabilities of its individual coefficients, using a precomputed likelihood table. For efficiency, these likelihoods are stored as rounded-down base-2 integers. For example, a probability of $\frac{1}{123}$ is stored as 6. To construct these tables, we randomly generated 2^{25} valid B_{22} at each iteration. Since the use of a newly generated table influences the acceptance of entries (and thereby the distribution used for the next table), this process was repeated until the distributions converged and the tables stabilized.

4.5 Hash Size and Encoding

We denote by d the parameter that specifies the output size (in bits) of the message digest produced by FIPS202-SHAKE256. In DEFIv2-1a, d is a multiple of $4m$, allowing coefficients of $(v_1, v_2, v_3, v_4) = \mathrm{HASH}(M) \in R^4$ to belong in $[-2^{d/(4m)-1}, 2^{d/(4m)-1} - 1]$ from which we compute $h = v_1 v_4 - v_2 v_3 \in R$. Similarly for DEFIv2-1b, d is a multiple of $2m$, allowing coefficients of $(v_1, v_4) = \mathrm{HASH}(M) \in R^2$ to belong in $[-2^{d/(2m)-1}, 2^{d/(2m)-1} - 1]$ from which we compute $h = v_1 v_4 \in R$.

4.6 Parameter Set

The parameter values were chosen to support efficient implementation and minimize public key and signature sizes, while also satisfying minimum security requirements against the attacks discussed in Sect. 5. The full parameter set is provided in Table 1.

Table 1. DEFIv2-1a and DEFIv2-1b parameters

Variation	m	n	s	r	k_B	k_{AD}	δ_F	$\delta_{B_{21}}$	Ω_B	γ_{C_1}	γ_{C_2}	γ_{C_3}	$\gamma_{B_{22}}$	$\gamma_{B_{22}^{-1}}$	γ_y	d
DEFIv2-1a	28	4	3	1	13	10	4	8	112	2^{11}	2^{12}	2^{15}	2^7	2^{11}	2^{49}	560
DEFIv2-1b	28	4	3	1	13	10	4	8	112	2^{11}	2^{12}	2^{15}	2^7	2^{11}	2^{49}	280

4.7 Implementation and Performance

In Table 2 we summarize the performance of the reference implementation for DEFIv2-1a and DEFIv2-1b. The secret key consists of a seed used to reconstruct the matrix B_{21} and a byte-packed representation of the matrix B_{22}^{-1}. All timing measurements (in milliseconds) are averaged over 10^4 iterations, compiled with the -O3 optimization flag on a Windows 10 64-bit laptop with a 12th Gen Intel(R) Core(TM) i7-12800H @ 2.40 GHz processor and 16 GB RAM.

The implementation follows the submission guidelines in [12] and is available at [3]. While further optimization is ongoing, the current performance (even with just the -O3 optimization flag) is already comparable to some of the fastest secure digital signature schemes proposed to date [16].

Table 2. Performance of DEFIv2-1a and DEFIv2-1b

	DEFIv2-1a	DEFIv2-1b
Public key	515 bytes	515 bytes
Private key	426 bytes	426 bytes
Signature	525 bytes	525 bytes
Public key + signature	1040 bytes	1040 bytes
Key generation	0.896 ms	0.896 ms
Signature generation	0.124 ms	0.115 ms
Signature verification	0.054 ms	0.054 ms
Average trials for valid B	2.708	2.708
Average trials for valid C	2.095	2.095
Average trials for valid signature	1.003	1.002
Expected maximum trials for valid signature	3	3

4.8 Variant With Smaller Signatures

To further reduce the size of the signature, the construction of B_{22} and B_{22}^{-1} can be interchanged. This would result in a larger public key, a smaller secret key, and a slightly smaller signature. The sizes resulting from a quick construction with comparable time performance as in Table 2 are presented in Table 3.

Table 3. Current vs Variant

	Current	Variant	Change	Relative Change
Public key	515 bytes	742 bytes	+227 bytes	+44%
Private key	426 bytes	300 bytes	-126 bytes	-30%
Signature	525 bytes	483 bytes	-44 bytes	−8%
Public key + signature	1225 bytes	1040 bytes	+185 bytes	+18%

5 Cryptanalysis

The security of the scheme relies on the basis ring R not counting the parameters r, s, n. In what follows, we set $R = \mathbb{Z}[X]/(q)$, where (q) is the ideal in $\mathbb{Z}[X]$ generated by a monic irreducible polynomial $q = q(X)$ of degree m with integer coefficients. Let $|a|, a \in R$ be the maximum in absolute values of the coefficients of a polynomial of degree $< m$ which represents a modulo $q(X)$. We call that a max-norm. To simplify some arguments below, we may assume that R is the ring of integers of the algebraic number field $K = \mathbb{Q}(\alpha)$, where α is a root of $q(X)$. All experimental results and observations in the following subsections are based on the DEFIv2-1a parameter set (see Table 1).

5.1 Collision Resistance of the Hash Representation

The message hash representation $h = v_1 v_4 - v_2 v_3 \in R$, where $(v_1, v_2, v_3, v_4) = \mathrm{HASH}(M) \in R^4$, admits more possibilities for collision due to the non-injectivity of the mapping from (v_1, v_2, v_3, v_4) to h. In particular, two distinct messages M_1 and M_2 may yield different tuples (v_1, v_2, v_3, v_4), and yet result in the same value of h. This non-injectivity may stem from algebraic symmetries in the bilinear as negating or permuting certain entries (e.g., swapping (v_1, v_4) with (v_2, v_3) and changing signs) can leave h unchanged. These invariances, which can also occur even among structurally unrelated or seemingly random tuples, lead to multiple preimages mapping to the same h, increasing the collision surface.

For DEFIv2-1a, each v_1, v_2, v_3, v_4 is a polynomial of degree less than 28 with coefficients in the range $[-16, 15]$, resulting in 2^{560} possible input tuples. While this is large, security depends not only on the number of distinct possible values of h, but also on their distribution. Empirical experiments using Pollard's rho algorithm with $m = 4, 6, 8, 10$ and v_i having coefficients in the range $[-4, 3]$ suggest that collisions in h occur after approximately $2^{d/4}$ iterations. With $d = 560$, this provides a conservative safety margin consistent with 128-bit collision resistance.

For DEFIv2-1b, $v_1, v_4 \in R$ are represented by polynomials of degree < 28 with coefficients in $[-16, 15]$ too. This results in 2^{280} possible input tuples v_1, v_4. The security mostly depends on the number of distinct possible values of $h = v_1 v_4 \in R$. Similarly to rational integers, the number of distinct possible values of h is asymptotically $2^{280-\lambda}$ for some relatively small $\lambda > 2$ as one may permute v_1, v_4 and change signs while keeping the product h intact. Otherwise, $v_1 v_4 = v_1' v_4'$ has low probability in the algebraic number ring R. That provides 128-bit collision resistance.

5.2 Private Key Recovery

Given the public matrix C, an adversary may attempt to recover a matrix $B \in R^{n \times n}$ such that $C = B^T J B$. This equation can be written as a system of $(n^2 + n)/2$ quadratic Diophantine equations over R in $n(n-r)$ unknowns—the entries of B_{21} and B_{22}. Solving such a system is generally hard.

However, if the entries of B are represented by very sparse polynomials, a brute-force or guessing strategy might succeed. To prevent this, we enforce a minimum guessing complexity per entry. For B_{21}, this is straightforward: each entry has 2^{112} possible values. For B_{22}, our metric (Sect. 4.4) similarly ensures more than 2^{112} possibilities per entry.

Suppose the adversary correctly guesses one entry in a column of B (say b_{22}). They might then attempt to recover b_{32} and b_{42} from $c = b_{22}^2 - c_{22} = b_{32}^2 + b_{42}^2$ by solving an instance of SVP in a lattice of rank $2m$ and volume $V = \mathrm{Norm}_{K/\mathbb{Q}}(c)$. The complexity to solve this SVP problem can be conservatively estimated as $(2m)^3 \log_2^2 V$ bit operations.

In our experiments with over 2^{20} randomly generated c, we observed that $V > 2^{132}$. Thus, recovering b_{22}, b_{32}, b_{42} from such an attack would require more than 2^{143} bit operations.

5.3   Forgery Attack over $\mathbb{Z}$

One may write the form (2) as

$$f(x) = x^T C x = f_0(\bar{x}) + f_1(\bar{x})\alpha + \ldots + f_{m-1}(\bar{x})\alpha^{m-1}, \tag{4}$$

where $f_i(\bar{x})$ are quadratic forms over $\mathbb{Z}$ the variables of which are the coefficients of the polynomials $x_i = x_{i0} + x_{i1}\alpha + \ldots + x_{im-1}\alpha^{m-1}$ and

$$\bar{x} = (x_{10}, x_{11}, \ldots, x_{nm-1}).$$

Forging the signature for a message M with the hash $h = (x_1, \ldots, x_r)$ is thus equivalent to solving the system of quadratic Diophantine equations

$$f_0(\bar{x}) = 0, \ldots, f_{m-1}(\bar{x}) = 0,$$

where the variables

$$x_{ij}, \ 1 \le i \le r, \ 0 \le j < m$$

are fixed by the entries of h. That is a system of m Diophantine equations in $(n - r)m$ variables. Such equations are generally hard to solve as discussed in Sect. 1.

5.4   Forgery Attack over R

Let M be a message with the hash $h \in R^r$. In order to forge a signature one sets $(x_1, \ldots, x_r) = h$, and randomly chooses $x_{r+1}, \ldots, x_{n-1}$ from R with bounded max-norms. One may try to calculate $z \in R$ such that $f(x) = 0$, where $x = (x_1, \ldots, x_r, x_{r+1}, \ldots, x_{n-1}, z)$. That is

$$f(x) = c_{nn}z^2 + 2(c_{n1}x_1 + c_{n2}x_2 + \ldots + c_{nn-1}x_{n-1})z + g(x_1, \ldots, x_{n-1}) = 0.$$

Denote $a = 2(c_{n1}x_1 + c_{n2}x_2 + \ldots + c_{nn-1}x_{n-1})$ and $b = g(x_1, \ldots, x_{n-1})$. If $c_{nn} \ne 0$, then z satisfies the quadratic equation

$$c_{nn}z^2 + az + b = 0 \tag{5}$$

with roots $(-a \pm \sqrt{a^2 - 4bc_{nn}})/2c_{nn}$. One of the roots is in R if and only if

$$v = a^2 - 4bc_{nn} = u^2 \tag{6}$$

for some $u \in R$, and

$$2c_{nn}|a - u \quad \text{or} \quad 2c_{nn}|a + u. \tag{7}$$

We estimate the probability of these conditions with a heuristic argument. Let $D = \max |a^2 - 4bc_{nn}|$, where the maximum is taken over all possible values of $x_1, \ldots, x_{n-1}$ with bounded max-norms as above. Condition (6) implies that $\text{Norm}_{K/\mathbb{Q}}(v)$ is a square. The maximum of that norm is of magnitude D^m. The probability that an integer of such magnitude is a square is $D^{-m/2}$.

To estimate D, we generated 2^{10} public keys and, for each, sampled 2^{10} tuples $(h, x_{r+1}, \ldots, x_{n-1})$ with x_i having randomly generated coefficients in $[-1, 1]$. The minimum observed value of $|a^2 - 4bc_{nn}|$ was $2^{12.69}$. Thus, we conservatively estimate $D^{-m/2} \ll 2^{-177.66}$, indicating that this forgery is computationally infeasible.

The probability of (7) is around $2\,|\text{Norm}_{K/\mathbb{Q}}(2c_{nn})|^{-1}$, that is of magnitude $|2c_{nn}|^{-m}$. From experiments, using 2^{16} randomly generated public keys, this was at most $2^{-201.20}$. We conclude that this forgery is not efficient for $c_{nn} \neq 0$. If $c_{nn} = 0$, then (5) has a root in R if and only if $a|b$ in R which happens with exponentially small probability too. Similar holds for other c_{ii}.

More generally, for a parameter l such that $1 \leq l \leq n - r - 1$ one randomly chooses $x_{r+1}, \ldots, x_{n-l}$ from R with bounded max-norms. One then tries to calculate $z_1, \ldots, z_l \in R$ such that $f(x) = 0$, where $x = (x_1, x_2, \ldots, x_{n-l}, z_1, \ldots, z_l)$. The unknowns $z_1, \ldots, z_l$ must satisfy

$$g(z_1, \ldots, z_l) = 0 \tag{8}$$

for a quadratic polynomial $g(z_1, \ldots, z_l)$ in l variables with coefficients from R. Since the problem is Diophantine, it is difficult to decide whether (8) is solvable or not and calculate the solutions. Even for $R = \mathbb{Z}$ an efficient algorithm to solve a general binary quadratic Diophantine equation may not exist as the minimal solution size in bits may depend exponentially in the size of input as with negative Pell equation, see [9].

5.5 Adapting Attack

Given signed message M, y, one may try to construct another signature y' for M. Let $x = (h|y) = (x_1, \ldots, x_{n-1}, x_n)$. Therefore $z = x_n$ is a root in R of the quadratic equation (5). If another root

$$x_n' = -a/c_{nn} - x_n \in R,$$

then one constructs another signature M, y' as $f(x_1, \ldots, x_{n-1}, x_n') = 0$. However, $x_n' \in R$ if and only if c_{nn} divides a in R. For random a this happens with probability $|\text{Norm}_{K/\mathbb{Q}}(c_{nn})|^{-1}$. This probability is of order $|c_{nn}|^{-m}$, and is very small even for moderate m. One may try to modify at least one of x_i, $r+1 \leq i \leq n$ in a similar way. The success probability is

$$1 - \prod_{i=r+1}^{n} \left(1 - |\mathrm{Norm}_{K/\mathbb{Q}}(c_{ii})|^{-1}\right). \tag{9}$$

It is easy to compute $\mathrm{Norm}_{K/\mathbb{Q}}$ numerically given the roots of the polynomial $q(X)$. The probability (9) is therefore easy to compute and the maximum probability obtained using 2^{16} randomly generated C was $2^{-165.48}$.

The adapting attack may be extended to modifying several entries of the signature. One has to solve a Diophantine equation in $l \geq 2$ variables similar to (8), where one solution is given. The parametrisation produces solutions from the field K and generally does not work for the ring R.

5.6   Lattice Attack

Suppose $r = 1, s = 3$ and $Z'' \in R^3$ is constructed by Sect. 3.7 formulae. Every signature $y \in R^3$ results in one equation

$$\left(B_{21}|B_{22}\right) \binom{h}{y} = Z'',$$

where h is constructed from the hash of the message and $\left(B_{21}|B_{22}\right) \in R^{3\times 4}$ is the scheme secret key. Given N signatures $M_i, y_i, i = 1, \ldots, N$, one may form a matrix

$$H = \begin{pmatrix} h_1 & h_2 & \ldots & h_N \\ y_1 & y_2 & \ldots & y_N \end{pmatrix} \in R^{4\times N},$$

where h_i are constructed from the hash of M_i. Let here

$$Z = \left(Z_1'' \ \ldots \ Z_N''\right) \in R^{3\times N}.$$

Then $\left(B_{21}|B_{22}\right) H = Z$ and so $\left(B_{21}|B_{22}|Z\right) = \left(B_{21}|B_{22}\right)\left(I_4|H\right)$, where I_4 is a unity (4×4)-matrix. The rows of $\left(B_{21}|B_{22}|Z\right)$ belong to a module generated over R by the rows of $\left(I_4|H\right)$. One may construct an integer $(4\,m \times (4+N)\,m)$-matrix the rows of which represent over $\mathbb{Z}$ the rows of $\left(I_4|H\right)$. Let L be a lattice of rank $4m$ generated by the rows of that matrix. Since the rows of $\left(B_{21}|B_{22}|Z\right)$, after transforming into a $(3\,m \times (4+N)\,m)$-matrix over $\mathbb{Z}$, have relatively small entries compared with the rows of $\left(I_4|H\right)$ and they belong to L, one may try to apply a lattice reduction algorithm to recover some or all of them.

However, experimentally, with 2^8 randomly generated secret keys used to sign $1 \leq N \leq 2^5$ randomly generated messages, the largest vector v_l in a LLL reduced basis of L was significantly shorter than the shortest row-vector v_s in the target matrix $\left(B_{21}|B_{22}|Z\right)$. More precisely, $\frac{\|v_s\|}{\|v_l\|} > 3.34$, where $\|\cdot\|$ denotes the Euclid norm of a vector. So, the rows of $\left(B_{21}|B_{22}|Z\right)$ should be impossible to recover directly from the reduced basis. Using BKZ generally makes the reduced basis even smaller and therefore won't help to recover the secret, rendering the complexity of lattice attacks irrelevant in this context.

5.7   Bambury and Nguyen Attack on DEFIv1

In May 2024, the first version of the scheme was published in [5] and shared on the pqc-forum [6], where it was broken by Henry Bambury and Phong Nguyen. A detailed description of the attack was later published in [1].

The attack targeted the construction of the secret vector Z, which is different in DEFIv1 compared to DEFIv2. The construction in version 1 ensured that

$$Z = (Z_1, Z_2, Z_3, Z_4) = (h, v + u_2 u_1^2 - hu_1, v + hu_1, u_1 u_2 - h).$$

So Z satisfies $Z^T J Z = 0$ with $J = \mathrm{Diag}(1, 1, -1, -1)$. Here $h = \mathrm{HASH}(M) \in R$ and $u_1, u_2 \in R$ of relatively small norm such that $u_2 = 2v_2$ for some $v_2 \in R$ and $v = v_2(1 - u_1^2) \in R$ (see Section III.G of [5]). It is easy to see that $Z_2 + Z_3 = u_2$ and $Z_1 + Z_4 = u_1 u_2$.

Bambury and Nguyen observed that the lattice attack described within [5] (Section IV.E) was not exhaustive as it only exploited information considering a single signature. They describe a heuristic attack that exploits some k signatures under the same secret key. To this end they define a lattice L_1 of rank $4m$ in $\mathbb{R}^{(k+4)m}$, whose basis can be constructed from public components $(h^{(i)}, y_2^{(i)}, y_3^{(i)}, y_4^{(i)})$. The key insight is that the vector

$$\mathbf{s}_1 = \left(b_{21} + b_{31},\, b_{22} + b_{32},\, b_{23} + b_{33},\, b_{24} + b_{34},\, u_2^{(1)},\, \ldots,\, u_2^{(k)}\right)$$

is unusually short and lies in L_1 due to the structure of the signature equations and the design of B (small coefficients). Lattice reduction techniques such as BKZ can be used to recover $\mathbf{s}_1$, thereby revealing the values $b_{2j} + b_{3j}$ for $j = 1, \ldots, 4$ and all $u_2^{(i)}$, effectively breaking the scheme. The feasibility of the attack arises from the algebraic dependencies introduced by the construction of Z and the constrained parameter choices, which together yield short vectors with sufficient structure to be distinguishable and recoverable via lattice reduction.

The difference with the present version is in how vector Z is constructed when the signature is generated, see Sect. 3.7. This is immune to such lattice attacks as secret vectors are significantly larger than the vectors in L produced with BKZ, see Sect. 5.6 for details.

6   DEFI Challenge

We introduce a publicly available 90-bit security challenge for both variations of the scheme, which we refer to as DEFIv2-0a and DEFIv2-0b (as in Sect. 4). The parameters used in these challenges are summarized in Table 4. In particular, we define the base ring as $R = \mathbb{Z}[X]/(X^{16} + X + 1)$.

The challenge is to devise an attack that requires fewer than 2^{90} binary operations to recover any secret entry of the matrix B or to forge a valid signature for a given message hash.

The challenge datasets consist of signatures generated using a single key pair on 2^{14} randomly generated messages. It is available at [4] and includes the following files, formatted as JSON arrays:

Table 4. DEFIv2-0a and DEFIv2-0b parameters

Variation	m	n	s	r	k_B	k_{AD}	δ_F	$\delta_{B_{21}}$	Ω_B	γ_{C_1}	γ_{C_2}	γ_{C_3}	$\gamma_{B_{22}}$	$\gamma_{B_{22}^{-1}}$	γ_y	d
DEFIv2-0a	16	4	3	1	9	9	4	8	63	2^9	2^{10}	2^{11}	2^5	2^8	2^{45}	384
DEFIv2-0b	16	4	3	1	9	9	4	8	63	2^9	2^{10}	2^{11}	2^5	2^8	2^{45}	192

- `C.txt` - contains a public key matrix $C \in R^{4 \times 4}$ in its uncompressed form.
- `v.txt` - contains the hash of a message as $(v_1, v_2, v_3, v_4) \in R^4$ or .
- `h.txt` - contains the hash value representation $h = v_1 v_4 - v_2 v_3 \in R$.
- `y.txt` - contains the signature $y \in R^3$ in its uncompressed form.
- `z.txt` - contains $z = (h|y) \in R^4$ from the signature verification step.

Acknowledgments. The authors have no acknowledgments to make.

Disclosure of Interests. The authors have no competing interests to declare that are relevant to the content of this article.

References

1. Bambury, H., Nguyen, P.Q.: Cryptanalysis of an Efficient Signature Based on Isotropic Quadratic Forms. Cryptology ePrint Archive, Paper 2025/133 (2025). https://eprint.iacr.org/2025/133
2. Estes, D., Adleman, L.M., Kompella, K., McCurley, K.S., Miller, G.L.: Breaking the Ong-Schnorr-Shamir signature scheme for quadratic number fields. In: Williams, H.C. (ed.) CRYPTO 1985. LNCS, vol. 218, pp. 3–13. Springer, Heidelberg (1986). https://doi.org/10.1007/3-540-39799-X_1
3. Feussner, M.: DEFIv2. GitHub repository (2025). https://github.com/martinfeussner/DEFIv2/tree/main
4. Feussner, M.: DEFIv2 Challenge Files. GitHub repository (2025). https://github.com/martinfeussner/DEFIv2/tree/main/challenge-files
5. Feussner, M., Semaev, I.: Isotropic Quadratic Forms, Diophantine Equations and Digital Signatures. Cryptology ePrint Archive, Paper 2024/679 (2024). https://eprint.iacr.org/archive/2024/679/20240503:175841
6. Feussner, M., Semaev, I.: New Digital Signature Scheme - DEFI. pqc-forum mailing list (2024). https://groups.google.com/a/list.nist.gov/g/pqc-forum/c/x7-nf3NuYTs/m/dGvflCePAQAJ
7. Garey, M.R., Johnson, D.S.: Computers and Intractability: A Guide to the Theory of NP-Completeness. Series of Books in the Mathematical Sciences, W. H. Freeman and Company, New York (1979)
8. Harry, Y.: The key exchange cryptosystem used with higher order diophantine equations. Int. J. Netw. Secur. Appl. **3**(2) (2011). https://doi.org/10.5121/ijnsa.2011.3204
9. Lagarias, J.C.: On the computational complexity of determining the solvability or unsolvability of the equation $X^2 - DY^2 = -1$. Trans. Am. Math. Soc. **260**(2), 485–508 (1980). https://doi.org/10.2307/1998017

10. Matsumoto, T., Imai, H.: Public quadratic polynomial-tuples for efficient signature-verification and message-encryption. In: Barstow, D., et al. (eds.) EUROCRYPT 1988. LNCS, vol. 330, pp. 419–453. Springer, Heidelberg (1988). https://doi.org/10.1007/3-540-45961-8_39
11. Mordell, L.J.: Diophantine Equations. Academic Press, London and New York (1969)
12. National Institute of Standards and Technology (NIST): Post-Quantum Cryptography Standardization (2024). https://csrc.nist.gov/projects/post-quantum-cryptography/post-quantum-cryptography-standardization
13. Odlyzko, A.M.: The rise and fall of knapsack cryptosystems. in: cryptology and computational number theory. In: Proceedings of Symposia in Applied Mathematics, vol. 42, pp. 75–88. American Mathematical Society (1991). https://doi.org/10.1090/psapm/042/1095552
14. Ong, H., Schnorr, C.P., Shamir, A.: An Efficient Signature Scheme Based on Quadratic Equations. In: Proceedings of the Sixteenth Annual ACM Symposium on Theory of Computing (STOC '84). pp. 208–216. Association for Computing Machinery, New York, NY, USA (1984). https://doi.org/10.1145/800057.808683
15. Patarin, J.: Hidden Fields Equations (HFE) and Isomorphisms of Polynomials (IP): two new families of asymmetric algorithms. In: Maurer, U. (ed.) EUROCRYPT 1996. LNCS, vol. 1070, pp. 33–48. Springer, Heidelberg (1996). https://doi.org/10.1007/3-540-68339-9_4
16. PQShield: NIST Signature Zoo (2024). https://pqshield.github.io/nist-sigs-zoo/
17. Prasamsa, K.V., Kameswari, P.A., Raju, K.N., Surendra, T., Devi, D.M.: A key exchange algorithm with binary quadratic forms to design complex security framework. Adv. Math.: Sci. J. **10**(1), 589–595 (2021). https://doi.org/10.37418/amsj.10.1.58
18. Shamir, A.: A polynomial-time algorithm for breaking the basic Merkle - Hellman cryptosystem. IEEE Trans. Inf. Theory **30**(5), 699–704 (1984). https://doi.org/10.1109/TIT.1984.1056964

Stealthy Hardware Trojan Attacks on MQ-Based Post-quantum Digital Signatures

Aikata Aikata, Anisha Mukherjee, and Sujoy Sinha Roy[(✉)]

University of Technology Graz, Graz, Austria
{aikata,anisha.mukherjee,sujoy.sinharoy}@tugraz.at

Abstract. We investigate the risk of embedding stealthy hardware Trojans in implementations of multivariate quadratic (MQ) based post-quantum signature schemes that use the Keccak-based hashing module. Our study reveals that MAYO and UOV are more vulnerable due to the predictable interaction of message and secret seed within the Keccak module, while SNOVA and QR-UOV exhibit inherent resilience by deviating from this structure. We demonstrate how minimal hardware Trojans, occupying merely 0.03% of the circuit area, can be inserted into MAYO implementations to leak critical internal secrets such as the seed, potentially enabling key recovery under suitable conditions. Our results underscore the need for thorough hardware security evaluation of PQC implementations before they are deployed.

Keywords: Trojan Horses · MAYO · UOV · SNOVA · QR-UOV · Key-Recovery

1 Introduction

The emergence of quantum computing poses a significant challenge to the foundations of classical cryptographic algorithms such as RSA and ECC, primarily due to Shor's algorithm [36] which can efficiently solve integer factorization and discrete logarithm problems. As quantum computers continues to advance, the urgency to develop cryptographic systems that can withstand quantum attacks has become increasingly evident. Post-quantum cryptography (PQC) is the area of cryptographic research and development that focuses on designing algorithms secure against both classical and quantum attackers. These algorithms rely on mathematical problems such as lattice problems, multivariate polynomial equations, error-correcting codes, isogenies which are assumed to be infeasible even by quantum computers. Recognizing the need for standardized quantum-safe primitives, the National Institute of Standards and Technology (NIST) initiated an international effort to standardize PQC algorithms with several rounds of cryptanalysis, performance evaluation, and community feedback.

E. Savas et al. (Eds.): LightSec 2025, LNCS 16216, pp. 39–54, 2026.
https://doi.org/10.1007/978-3-032-15541-2_3

Following the NIST calls, these emerging PQC algorithms have initiated numerous research trajectories, especially in the areas of security and implementation analysis. These two domains often converge when addressing physical attacks on dedicated hardware implementations, such as side-channel [4,39,40] and fault analysis [14,23]. These operate under the assumption that the hardware implementations of PQC are developed in a trusted supply chain. This assumption is increasingly unrealistic in the modern hardware ecosystem, where design, fabrication, and deployment are often distributed across multiple, globally dispersed stakeholders.

Thus, in this work, we question the integrity of this trust boundary and focus on a more critical, yet practical, threat model – one where the *supply chain has been compromised*. Specifically, we explore the possibility that adversaries may embed malicious modifications, commonly referred to as **Hardware Trojan Horses (HTH)**, into the PQC hardware implementations during any stage of the design or manufacturing pipeline. These Trojans can be stealthy yet harmful, capable of leaking secret keys.

We focus on digital signature schemes submitted to NIST's call for additional post-quantum digital signatures that have progressed into Round 2 [2], specifically those based on the hardness of the Multivariate Quadratic (MQ) problem, namely, MAYO [8], QR-UOV [15], SNOVA [37], and UOV [22]. These schemes represent a critical class of candidates where implementation-level security is tightly coupled with complex algebraic structures, making them both promising and uniquely susceptible to low-level attacks.

1.1 Related Works

Research into subverting cryptographic systems through HTHs has rapidly evolved into a critical field at the intersection of hardware security and adversarial modeling. The researchers adopt an offensive security model and simulate powerful attackers to better understand the realistic risks facing cryptographic implementations. [33] was one of the earliest works in this space targeting lattice-based post-quantum Key Exchange Mechanism- Kyber and Saber. Their work, however, focused solely on a Third-Party Intellectual Property (3PIP) threat model, in which the PQC hardware block is procured from an untrusted vendor with the backdoor already hardwired into the design.

Subsequent efforts broadened the landscape. In [25,32], researchers adopted a "red-team vs blue-team" methodology. However, the adversarial insertion was emulated rather than physically realised, while [25] involved actual chip analysis. The authors in [16] approached the problem differently, crafting an HTH that subtly undermines a masked implementation of the PRESENT block cipher [10]. Their Trojan selectively disables masking countermeasures, making the implementation vulnerable to side-channel attacks under specific trigger conditions.

Hepp et al. extended the field further in multiple directions. In [17], they proposed a generic HTH insertion strategy that targets functionally critical ASIC gates identified via reverse engineering. Later, in [18], they demonstrated four distinct HTH attack vectors against a PQC accelerator- two of which depend on software-based triggers, while all four were manually inserted. This practical work culminated in validating the attacks on an actual fabricated chip. Similarly, the authors in [29,30] exploited the Engineering Change Order (ECO) capabilities in commercial chip design tools to covertly introduce hardware Trojans, again demonstrating their efficacy on real silicon.

Another recent prior work by Pagliarini et al. [26] has laid important groundwork in this direction. In this study, the authors targeted the hardware implementation of Dilithium [1], the lattice-based digital signature scheme standardized by NIST. The Trojan was embedded within the Keccak [28] sponge construction, commonly used in SHA-3 and SHAKE for hashing and pseudo-random number generation. Notably, the authors developed an automated tool capable of identifying Keccak logic in RTL designs by analyzing its unique fan-in/fan-out signature. This tool enables precise localization and modification of the Keccak module, effectively streamlining the HTH insertion process for attackers. Our work builds upon this attack vector by similarly targeting the Keccak module as the insertion point for the Hardware Trojan, to facilitate stealthy key recovery.

1.2 Our Contribution

We observe that the Trojan insertion technique presented by Pagliarini et al. [26] exploits the fact that both the message (M) and the secret (e.g., $seed_{sk}$) are inputs to the Keccak function during Dilithium signature generation, in this particular order. This allows a user-controlled message to act as a trigger, while the secret can be exfiltrated through the Trojan payload. In this work, we generalize this Trojan insertion technique, noting that this use of Keccak ($c = H(M\|salt)$) is not unique to Dilithium; it is, in fact, a universal non-interactive challenge generation mechanism inspired by the FiatShamir transform [13]. It underpins unforgeability and soundness in post-quantum signatures, regardless of the underlying hardness assumption. The lack of this could result in unsound/unextractable proofs [5]. Thus, it is commonly utilized across various post-quantum secure digital signature schemes.

As a case study, we examine post-quantum digital signature schemes based on the MQ problem, focusing on how the Trojan insertion technique can exploit the challenge mechanism in MAYO [8] and UOV [22]. In contrast, we demonstrate that the remaining two MQ-based schemes SNOVA [37] and QR-UOV [15] are not susceptible to this attack. In SNOVA, the secret seed is processed before the message, causing the trigger to activate too late. In QR-UOV, the message is never combined with a secret seed at all. These deviations from the conventional design effectively protect them from such Trojan-based exploits.

We go beyond theory by analyzing how a Trojan occupying just 0.03% of the area [19] can be embedded into MAYO to leak the secret seed. While we do not perform a full key recovery attack experiment, prior cryptanalytic works [20,26] suggest that recovering the seed could potentially lead to full key reconstruction under realistic assumptions. The minimal area footprint enhances the Trojan's stealth, making it difficult to detect. This highlights a pressing risk, especially as these MQ-based PQC schemes have advanced to Round 2 of NIST's additional signature call [2], and hardware Trojans are an increasingly serious concern in both cybersecurity and warfare [38].

Paper Organization. Relevant background on post-quantum multivariate-based digital signature schemes and hardware trojan horses is provided in Sect. 2. Our Trojan insertion techniques leading to key recovery are detailed in Sect. 3, for multiple schemes as case studies. The corresponding results are discussed in Sect. 4, and the work is concluded in Sect. 5.

2   Background

We briefly discuss the relevant concepts necessary to understand the technical contributions of this work.

2.1   Post-quantum Cryptography and Digital Signatures

The field of PQC seeks to develop cryptographic schemes that remain secure against quantum adversaries, based on problems assumed to be mathematically hard to solve even for quantum computers. Post-quantum public-key cryptographic primitives can be broadly categorized into two main branches: Key Encapsulation Mechanisms (KEM) and Digital Signature Algorithms (DSA). While KEMs are used for establishing shared keys for en(de)cryption in communication protocols, DSAs ensure authenticity and integrity of the communicated messages through verifiable signatures. NIST launched a multi-round PQC standardization project in 2016 that sought to identify secure and efficient candidates for both KEMs and DSAs, leading to a diverse set of submissions such as those based on hard problems in lattices, codes and multivariate quadratic maps. After several rounds of evaluation, NIST announced in 2022 that the lattice-based schemes Kyber [35] (for KEM) and Dilithium [12] (for DSA) would be standardized, with Falcon [31] and SPHINCS+ [6] also retained as backup signature algorithms. However, despite the selection of these strong candidates, in order to increase algorithmic diversity of signature algorithms, NIST initiated a separate call for additional digital signatures in 2023, with the goal of identifying signature schemes that offer compact key and signature sizes, fast signing and verification and do not rely on mathematical hardness assumptions of structured lattices. Among the submissions, a set of four multivariate-based signature schemes: UOV [22], MAYO [8], QR-UOV [15], and SNOVA [37], were selected to advance to the second round. We discuss these schemes in the following sub-section.

Unbalanced Oil and Vinegar Schemes. The unbalanced oil-and-vinegar (UOV) signature scheme is a multivariate signature scheme whose security is based on the hardness of the multivariate quadratic (MQ) problem which asks to solve systems of multivariate quadratic equations over finite fields.

Multivariate Quadratic Maps: Let $\mathbb{F}_q$ be a finite field. The multivariate quadratic map $\mathcal{P}$ over $\mathbb{F}_q$ is defined as a vector of m multivariate quadratic polynomials: $\mathcal{P} = (p_1(\mathbf{x}), p_2(\mathbf{x}), \cdots, p_m(\mathbf{x})) \in \mathbb{F}_q^m$, such that each $p_k : \mathbb{F}_q^n \to \mathbb{F}_q$ is a polynomial in n variables, $\mathbf{x} = (x_1, \cdots, x_n) \in \mathbb{F}_q^n$. In cryptographic UOV schemes, the map $\mathcal{P} : \mathbb{F}_q^n \to \mathbb{F}_q^m$ serves as a trapdoor one-way function that vanishes on a linear subspace $O \subset \mathbb{F}_q^n$ of dimension m, referred to as the oil space, that is, $\mathcal{P}(\mathbf{o}) = 0$ for all $\mathbf{o} \in O$. While computing $\mathcal{P}(\mathbf{x})$ is efficient, recovering a basis of the subspace O (i.e., inverting $\mathcal{P}$) is believed to be computationally hard when $m \approx n$.

More precisely, the Multivariate Quadratic (MQ) problem is to find a solution $\mathbf{s} \in \mathbb{F}_q^n$ such that $\mathcal{P}(\mathbf{s}) = \mathbf{t}$ for a given target vector $\mathbf{t} \in \mathbb{F}_q^m$. This problem is NP-hard and forms the basis of security for UOV-based signature schemes. For a legitimate party possessing the trapdoor information which is a basis of the oil subspace O, this inversion problem becomes efficiently solvable. To compute a pre-image $\mathbf{s} \in \mathbb{F}_q^n$ such that $\mathcal{P}(\mathbf{s}) = \mathbf{t}$, one samples a random vector $\mathbf{v} \in \mathbb{F}_q^n$ and attempts to solve: $\mathcal{P}(\mathbf{v} + \mathbf{o}) = \mathbf{t}$ for $\mathbf{o} \in O$. Due to the structure of $\mathcal{P}$ and its vanishing property on O, this amounts to solving a linear system in the variables of $\mathbf{o}$ whose coefficients depend on the choice of $\mathbf{v}$. This system has a unique solution $\mathbf{o} \in O$ with probability approximately $1 - 1/q$. If $\mathcal{P}'$ is not invertible, one simply selects a new random $\mathbf{v}$ and repeats the process until a solution is found. The final pre-image is then $\mathbf{s} = \mathbf{v} + \mathbf{o}$. This principle forms the basis of the signature generation algorithm in multivariate UOV-based signature schemes such as the Round 2 multivariate-based candidates for NIST call for "additional digital signatures", namely, UOV [22], MAYO [8], QR-UOV [15], and SNOVA [37]. In MAYO [8], the authors propose a 'whipping' technique to construct compact public keys while preserving the structure of traditional UOV signature schemes. MAYO chooses a smaller oil space, of dimension $o < m$, which greatly reduces the number of coefficients required to describe the public map $\mathcal{P}$. To ensure that signatures can still be generated efficiently, MAYO defines a new public map $\mathcal{P}^*$ by combining multiple evaluations of the original map $\mathcal{P}$ and its derivatives on k separate input vectors. This "whipped-up" map is constructed so that it vanishes on a structured subspace derived from the smaller oil space, letting the signer to generate valid signatures using only $ko > m$ oil variables. As a result, the size of the public key, which is determined primarily by the number of non-zero coefficients in $\mathcal{P}^*$ is reduced by roughly a factor of m^2/o^2 making MAYO public keys more than an order of magnitude smaller than in classical UOV schemes, but at the cost of larger signatures. We provide their pseudo-codes in Algorithms 1,2,3.

Notice that in these schemes, the vinegar variables v_i act as ephemeral masks for the secret oil space elements $\mathbf{O}x_i$, with each signature component constructed as $s_i = v_i + \mathbf{O}x_i$. If an adversary can recover (or partially recover) the vinegar vectors $v_1, \cdots, v_k$ during the signing process, this directly yields linear equations of the form $\mathbf{O}x_i = s_i - v_i$ over the secret matrix $\mathbf{O}$. Accumulating such equations over multiple signatures enables an attacker to reconstruct $\mathbf{O}$ using standard linear algebra techniques. Cryptanalytic works such as [7,11,27] have described algebraic attacks against UOV-like schemes. Recent works such as [3,20] have shown that full or even partial leakage of $\mathbf{v}$ can be exploited to reconstruct $\mathbf{O}$, leading to full key recovery. We highlight (in red) the exact generation steps of the vinegar vector $\mathbf{v}$ during the signing procedure. In the context of UOV and MAYO, the generation of $\mathbf{v}$ occurs in line 4 of Algorithm 2 and lines 8,11 of Algorithm 1 as the output of SHAKE256 hash of the message M and the secret $\mathsf{seed}_\mathsf{sk}$ along with the salt. In the case of UOV, the salt and $\mathsf{seed}_\mathsf{sk}$ are 128 and 256 bits respectively for NIST security levels-1, 3, 5, whereas MAYO has the same salt and $\mathsf{seed}_\mathsf{sk}$ sizes, namely: 24, 32 and 40 bytes for NIST levels-1 (MAYO$_1$ or MAYO$_2$), 3 (MAYO$_3$) and 5 (MAYO$_5$). A leakage-based attack that targets this operation either through side-channels, faults or an inserted hardware Trojan can therefore expose the seed-dependent randomness underlying the vinegar variables. Since $\mathbf{v}$ is deterministically decoded into $v_1, \cdots, v_k$, any leakage of its bits propagates to the effective exposure of the masking terms used in signature construction.

Algorithm 1. MAYO.Sign(sk, M) [8]

Input: Secret key sk, message M
Output: Signature σ

1: $(\mathsf{seed}_\mathsf{sk}, \mathbf{O}) \leftarrow \mathsf{sk}$
2: $\mathsf{seed}_\mathsf{pk} \leftarrow \mathsf{SHAKE256}(\mathsf{seed}_\mathsf{sk})$
3: **for** i from 1 to m **do**
4:      $\mathbf{P}_i^{(1)} \leftarrow \mathsf{Expand}(\mathsf{seed}_\mathsf{pk}\|P1\|i)$
5:      $\mathbf{P}_i^{(2)} \leftarrow \mathsf{Expand}(\mathsf{seed}_\mathsf{pk}\|P2\|i)$
6: **end for**
7: $R \leftarrow \{0,1\}^r$ ▷ *For deterministic variant:* $R \leftarrow \{0\}^r$
8: $\mathrm{salt} \leftarrow \mathsf{SHAKE256}(M\|R\|\mathsf{seed}_\mathsf{sk})$
9: $\mathbf{t} \leftarrow \mathsf{SHAKE256}(M\|\mathrm{salt})$
10: **for** ctr from 0 to 255 **do**
11:      $\mathbf{v} \leftarrow \mathsf{SHAKE256}(M\|\mathrm{salt}\|\mathsf{seed}_\mathsf{sk}\|ctr)$
12:      $v_1, \cdots, v_k \leftarrow \mathsf{Decode}(\mathbf{v})$
13:      $(\mathbf{A}, \mathbf{y}) \leftarrow \mathsf{BuildLinearSystem}(\{v_1, \cdots, v_k\}, \mathbf{O}, \mathbf{P}^{(1)}, \mathbf{P}^{(2)}, \mathbf{t})$
14:      $x \leftarrow \mathsf{SampleSolution}(\mathbf{A}, \mathbf{y})$ ▷ *Try to find $Ax = y$ (i.e. $\mathcal{P}^*(s) = t$)*
15:      **if** $x \neq \bot$ **then break**
16:      **end if**
17: **end for**
18: $\mathbf{s} \leftarrow \{v_i + \mathbf{O}x_i \mid x_i\}_{1 \leq i \leq k}$
19: **return** $\sigma = (\mathbf{s}, \mathrm{salt})$

2.2   Hardware Trojan Horses

Over the past few decades, the Integrated Circuit (IC) industry has transformed into a highly globalized and fragmented supply chain. Modern IC design and fabrication workflows typically span multiple entities, including design houses,

---

Algorithm 2. UOV.Sign(esk, M)

Input: Extended secret key esk $= (\mathsf{seed}_{\mathsf{sk}}, \mathbf{O}, \{\mathbf{P}_i^{(1)}, \mathbf{S}_i\}_{i \in [m]})$, message M
Output: Signature σ

1: salt $\leftarrow \{0,1\}^{\mathsf{salt\_len}}$
2: $\mathbf{t} \leftarrow \mathsf{SHAKE256}(M\|\mathsf{salt})$ $\qquad\qquad\qquad\qquad\qquad\qquad \triangleright \mathbf{t} \in \mathbb{F}_q^m$
3: **for** $ctr = 0$ upto 255 **do**
4: $\quad$ $\mathbf{v} \leftarrow \mathsf{SHAKE256}(M\|\mathsf{salt}\|\mathsf{seed}_{\mathsf{sk}}\|ctr)$ $\qquad\qquad\qquad \triangleright \mathbf{v} \in \mathbb{F}_q^v$
5: $\quad$ $\mathbf{L} := \mathbf{0}_{m \times m}$
6: $\quad$ **for** $i = 1$ upto m **do**
7: $\quad\quad$ Set i-th row of $\mathbf{L}$ to $\mathbf{v}^\top \mathbf{S}_i$.
8: $\quad$ **end for**
9: $\quad$ **if** $\mathbf{L}$ is invertible **then**
10: $\quad\quad$ $\mathbf{y} \leftarrow \left[\mathbf{v}^\top \mathbf{P}_i^{(1)} \mathbf{v} \right]_{i \in [m]}$
11: $\quad\quad$ Solve $\mathbf{L}\mathbf{x} = \mathbf{t} - \mathbf{y}$ for $\mathbf{x}$
12: $\quad\quad$ $\mathbf{s} := \begin{bmatrix} \mathbf{v} \\ \mathbf{0}_m \end{bmatrix} + \begin{bmatrix} \mathbf{O} \\ \mathbf{I}_m \end{bmatrix} \cdot \mathbf{x}$ $\qquad\qquad\qquad\qquad \triangleright \mathbf{s} \in \mathbb{F}_q^n$
13: $\quad\quad$ $\sigma := (\mathbf{s}, \mathsf{salt})$
14: $\quad\quad$ **return** σ
15: $\quad$ **end if**
16: **end for**
17: **return** $\perp$

---

third-party IP vendors, and offshore foundries. Crucially, the IP owners often lack direct control over the fabrication process, creating an ideal attack surface for HTH insertion.

A fundamental feature of most HTHs is the presence of a *trigger*, a carefully designed control mechanism (e.g., a comparator) that ensures the Trojan remains dormant under normal operation and activates only under specific, attacker-controlled conditions. This delayed activation significantly complicates detection, as the device continues to behave normally unless the correct trigger input is provided. To reduce the likelihood of accidental activation, triggers are often long, ranging from 16 to 64 bits, as demonstrated in [26]. Moreover, well-designed HTHs ensure that the trigger does not remain active across subsequent executions unless explicitly re-supplied, further minimizing their footprint.

Once activated, an HTH can leak secret information either by directly manipulating output data or through more covert means. Direct output manipulation, such as embedding secret information into signature outputs, can be risky, as malformed signatures may fail verification and alert the user, prompting a key rotation or system audit. To avoid such detection, a more sophisticated alternative is the use of side-channel HTHs [24,26,30], which uses physical power consumption leakage without altering functional outputs. These Trojans are inherently stealthier, as they bypass traditional output-based monitoring mechanisms and exploit side channels to leak sensitive information bit by bit.

Algorithm 3. QRUOV.Sign(M, sk)

Input: message $M \in \mathbb{B}^*$ and private key $\mathsf{sk} \in \{0,1\}^{2\lambda}$
Output: signature $\sigma \in \{0,1\}^{\lambda} \times \mathbb{F}_q^m$

1: $(\mathsf{seed}_{\mathsf{sk}}, \mathsf{seed}_{\mathsf{pk}}) \leftarrow \mathsf{sk}$
2: $\bar{S}' \leftarrow \mathsf{Expand}_{sk}(\mathsf{seed}_{\mathsf{sk}})$
3: $\mathbf{y} = (y_1, \cdots, y_v)^\top \xleftarrow{\$} \mathbb{F}_q^v$
4: **for** i from 1 to m **do**
5:     $(\bar{P}_{i,1}, \bar{P}_{i,2}) \leftarrow \mathsf{Expand}_{\mathsf{pk}}(\mathsf{seed}_{\mathsf{pk}}, i)$
6:     $\bar{\mathbf{y}} \leftarrow W^{(V)} \phi^{-1}\left(\bar{P}_{i,1}\right) \mathbf{y}$ $\qquad\qquad\qquad\qquad\qquad\qquad \rhd\, \bar{\mathbf{y}} \in \mathbb{F}_q^v$
7:     $\mathbf{L}_i \leftarrow -2\phi^{-1}\left(\bar{S}'\right)^\top \bar{\mathbf{y}} + 2W^{(V)}\phi^{-1}\left(\bar{P}_{i,2}^\top\right)\mathbf{y}$ $\qquad\quad \rhd\, \mathbf{L}_i \in \mathbb{F}_q^m$
8:     $u_i \leftarrow \mathbf{y}^\top \bar{\mathbf{y}}$ $\qquad\qquad\qquad\qquad\qquad\qquad\qquad\qquad\quad \rhd\, u_i \in \mathbb{F}_q$
9: **end for**
10: $L \leftarrow (\mathbf{L}_1, \cdots, \mathbf{L}_m)^\top$ $\qquad\qquad\qquad\qquad\qquad\qquad\quad \rhd\, L \in \mathbb{F}_q^{m \times m}$
11: $\mathbf{u} \leftarrow (u_1, \cdots, u_m)^\top$ $\qquad\qquad\qquad\qquad\qquad\qquad\quad \rhd\, \mathbf{u} \in \mathbb{F}_q^m$
12: $\mu \leftarrow \mathsf{SHAKE256}(\mathsf{seed}_{\mathsf{pk}} \| \mathrm{BytesToBits}(M), 512)$
13: **repeat**
14:     $r \xleftarrow{\$} \{0,1\}^{\lambda}$
15:     $\mathbf{t} \leftarrow \mathrm{Hash}(\mu, r)$ $\qquad\qquad\qquad\qquad\qquad\qquad\qquad\quad \rhd\, \mathbf{t} \in \mathbb{F}_q^m$
16: **until** $L\mathbf{x} = \mathbf{t} - \mathbf{u}$ has solutions for $\mathbf{x}$.
17: Choose one solution $(y_{v+1}, \cdots, y_n)^\top \in \mathbb{F}_q^m$ of $L\mathbf{x} = \mathbf{t} - \mathbf{u}$ randomly.
18: $\mathbf{s} \leftarrow (y_1, \cdots, y_v, y_{v+1}, \cdots, y_n)^\top - (\phi^{-1}(\bar{S}')) \cdot (y_1, \cdots, y_v)^\top \| \mathbf{0}_m)$ $\quad \rhd\, \mathbf{s} \in \mathbb{F}_q^n$
19: **return** $\sigma = (r, \mathbf{s})$

Thus, in this work, we also adopt the side-channel HTH paradigm, leveraging its proven effectiveness and intrinsic stealth to mount a practical and evasive key recovery attack on post-quantum digital signature implementations.

Another critical component of an HTH is its *payload*– the logic that defines the malicious behavior once the trigger is activated. The payload determines how the HTH interacts with the system, whether by modifying control signals, altering data paths, or leaking sensitive information. In our case, the payload is designed to leak secret inputs to the Keccak module. Payloads can take a variety of forms depending on the attack objective and side-channel vector. For example, ring oscillators [30], or on-chip antennas [21] have been employed as payloads due to their ability to modulate power consumption. Thus, payload serves as the medium through which the HTH leaks the secret data.

3 Key Recovery and Hardware Trojan Insertion

As outlined in Sect. 2.2, an HTH typically comprises two primary components: a **trigger** and a **payload**. In our work, we closely follow the HTH construction proposed by Pagliarini et al. [26], reusing their power-based side-channel payload. This payload relies on a ring oscillator to modulate the chip's power consumption according to the secret bits to be leaked. In addition to the trigger and payload, the complete Trojan architecture also includes auxiliary components: a finite state machine (FSM) for the control logic, a short shift register to buffer the secret bits for sequential leakage, and a multi-bit comparator serving as the activation for the trigger.

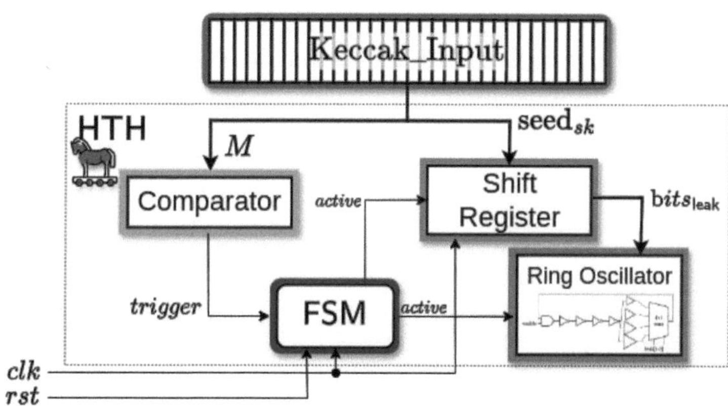

Fig. 1. Illustration of the HTH inserted into the 64-bit Keccak input buffer. The buffer receives the message M-used as part of the trigger mechanism, and the secret seed$_{sk}$, which is leaked via a power side channel. The leakage is orchestrated using a combination of ring oscillators and shift registers, enabling controlled and covert transmission of sensitive data following [26].

Crucially, the Trojan in [26] targets the Keccak function within the Dilithium signature routine. This choice is deliberate: both the trigger inputs and the sensitive data to be leaked are processed by the Keccak function invocation. The Dilithium signing operation repeatedly invokes Keccak with user-controllable inputs (i.e., the message to be signed), making it an attractive and realistic Trojan insertion point. The beauty and the risk of this approach lies in its simplicity: identifying the Keccak logic in the hardware netlist alone suffices for surgical Trojan placement, with no need to analyze the broader control or data flow, as shown in Fig. 1.

In this work, our goal is to investigate whether a similar class of HTH can be adapted and deployed in the context of the new MQ-based signature scheme. Specifically, we aim to analyze whether an analogous insertion point exists, where the secret-dependent values and the trigger conditions converge within a single core function, thus enabling the Trojan to be both stealthy and effective.

3.1   Case Study 1: MAYO

In Sect. 2.1 we outlined how leakage of the vinegar variables can effectively unmask the oil space components and lead to complete recovery of the secret key. Building on this observation, we consider a scenario where the same class of HTH is inserted into the SHAKE256 invocation in lines 8, 11 of MAYO's signing

Algorithm 1. This hash input includes the secret $\mathsf{seed_{sk}}$ along with attacker-controllable values such as the message M. Such a structure makes the hash function an attractive trojan insertion point with the message M serving as a natural trigger under adversarial control. Once triggered, it can leak $\mathsf{seed_{sk}}$ (and the salt in line 8) using which the attacker can re-compute the SHAKE256 instance themselves to obtain the vector $\mathbf{v}$ in line 11. After this, the attacker deterministically runs the Decode procedure on $\mathbf{v}$ to recover the vinegar variables v_i. Next, taking inspiration from [20], we now detail the key recovery procedure that exploits the leakage of vinegar variables during the signature generation process. Note that we refer to the signing algorithm of MAYO as given in [8]. The signing algorithm in MAYO's most recent Round 2 NIST specification [9] generates the oil space directly from the seed, making it much easier for the attacker to recover the oil space, as the attacker can simply run the key generation algorithm instead of a more complex key recovery.

Recall that each signature in the MAYO scheme consists of k vectors of the form $s_i = v_i + \mathbf{O}x_i$, where $v_i \in \mathbb{F}_q^{n-o}$ is a vinegar vector deterministically derived from $\mathsf{seed_{sk}}$, and $x_i \in \mathbb{F}_q^o$ are components of a solution $\mathbf{x}$ to the linear system defined by the trapdoor in line 13 of Algorithm 1. Notice from line 18 that subtracting v_i from the publicly known signature components s_i reveals the masked contribution $\mathbf{O}x_i$. More specifically, using the known s_i and the recovered v_i, an attacker constructs a linear system with unknowns corresponding to $\mathbf{O}$. To formalize this, suppose the attacker selects o such vectors $(v_1, x_1), \cdots, (v_o, x_o)$ and forms the matrix $\mathbf{X} \in \mathbb{F}_q^{o \times o}$ by using $x_1^\top, \cdots, x_o^\top$ as its rows. The attacker then constructs a stacked matrix $\mathbf{X}' \in \mathbb{F}_q^{(n-o)o \times o(n-o)}$ consisting of $n - o$ block-diagonal copies of $\mathbf{X}$. Simultaneously, the corresponding oil-space contributions $\mathbf{O}x_1, \cdots, \mathbf{O}x_o$ are extracted as $s_i - v_i = v_i + \mathbf{O}x_i - v_i$ with $1 \leq i \leq o$, by subtracting the known vinegar components from the signature vectors. These are then concatenated to form a target vector $\mathbf{z} \in \mathbb{F}_q^{o(n-o)}$. Thus, solving the linear system,

$$\mathbf{X}' \cdot \mathbf{o} = \mathbf{z}$$

$$\implies \begin{bmatrix} \mathbf{X} & & \\ & \ddots & \\ & & \mathbf{X} \end{bmatrix} \cdot \mathbf{o} = \begin{bmatrix} \mathbf{O}x_1 \\ \vdots \\ \mathbf{O}x_o \end{bmatrix},$$

where $\mathbf{X}' \in \mathbb{F}_q^{o(n-o) \times o(n-o)}$ and $\mathbf{z} \in \mathbb{F}_q^{o(n-o)}$ gives the required secret oil space $\mathbf{O}$ as a matrix with entries from $\mathbf{o}$. This approach is effective under the condition that the matrix $\mathbf{X}$ has full rank, which holds with high probability due to the linear independence of the x_i vectors selected during signing.

Additionally, the authors of [3] propose utilizing a combination of *reconciliation* and *Kipnis-Shamir* attack strategies to recover the secret key. In particular, they first explain that if a single oil vector $o_1 \in \mathbf{O}$ is known via a reconciliation attack then it can be used to derive a system of m linear equations in the entries of a second oil vector o_2 which can be solved using system solvers, although the cost may still be exponential for large parameter sizes. To reduce complexity, the authors therefore propose a combined use of the Kipnis-Shamir subspace attack with the reconciliation techniques. The idea is to fix certain coordinates of the obtained oil variable o_1 which restricts the search space for additional vectors in $\mathcal{O}$ and yields a residual MQ system that resembles a balanced oil-and-vinegar instance. This balanced structure is then suitable for applying the classical Kipnis-Shamir attack efficiently. Once a second oil vector o_2 is obtained, the remaining oil space can be reconstructed using the reconciliation attack. The authors show that this combined method succeeds with high probability and remains practically efficient for all NIST security levels.

3.2   Case Study 2: UOV

Like in the case of MAYO, the HTH is inserted into the SHAKE256 invocation in line 4 of UOV's signing Algorithm 2 which includes the secret $\mathsf{seed}_{\mathsf{sk}}$ preceded by the attacker-controllable message M. As mentioned in the previous section, such schemes where key generation is only dependent on $\mathsf{seed}_{\mathsf{sk}}$, the attacker can simply perform a key generation instead of backtracking. Otherwise, similar approaches for key recovery techniques from [3, 20] as for MAYO could also be utilized to obtain the secret oil variables by observing the signature.

3.3   Case Study 3: QR-UOV and SNOVA

In SNOVA, the Keccak input is not the raw message M, but rather its hash (i.e., a digest). This complicates the use of a user-controlled trigger, as the attacker cannot directly inject M to activate the HTH. However, since the attacker is assumed to know M, they can precompute and fix the trigger to the corresponding hash value. Despite this, the core challenge remains: the $\mathsf{seed}_{\mathsf{sk}}$ required for recovering the vinegar variables, is consumed prior to the digest being input to Keccak (for generation of the vinegar variables). As a result, the HTH activates after the secret seed has already been processed, rendering it incapable of leaking $\mathsf{seed}_{\mathsf{sk}}$. While the Trojan may still leak the ephemeral *salt*, this is insufficient for full key recovery, as reconstructing the vinegar variables without $\mathsf{seed}_{\mathsf{sk}}$ is infeasible.

In contrast, QR-UOV adopts a fundamentally different approach. It generates vinegar variables using a pseudo-random number generator that is independent of the message M. The message digest is used only to construct the target vector for the linear system, which is then solved to form the signature. Consequently, Keccak does not process any secret values that could be targeted for leakage. As a result, the Keccak-based Trojan [26] is not exploitable in QR-UOV, as no valuable secrets flow through the Keccak module that would be accessible to the HTH via the Trigger.

4   Results

To experimentally evaluate the conceptual HTH attack of the last section, we would require hardware implementations of MQ-based post-quantum digital signature schemes. However, implementing all MQ candidate schemes in hardware from scratch is beyond the scope of this work. Therefore, we selectively focus on representative implementations that capture the core design patterns and security-critical components relevant to our analysis.

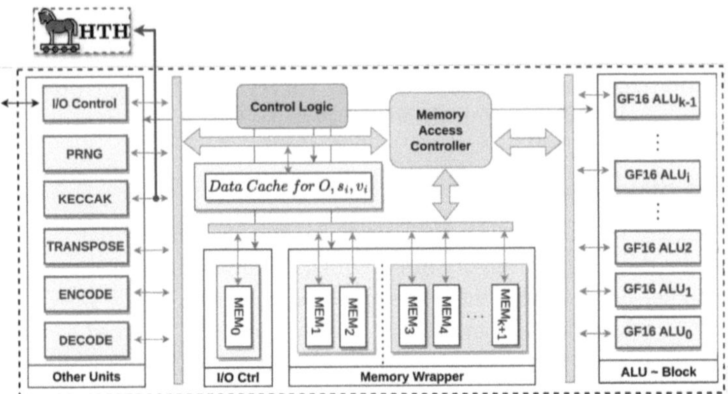

Fig. 2. Hardware architecture diagram for MAYO [19] with Hardware Trojan described in [26]. The architecture diagram is borrowed from [19].

We leverage an existing hardware implementation of the MAYO digital signature scheme [19], which integrates the same Keccak module as used in [26], specifically the implementation from [34]. The authors of [19] provide ASIC synthesis results using the Cadence toolchain, reporting the area overhead on a TSMC 28nm technology node. The reported area for the cryptoprocessors targeting the three security levels is at least $1.02mm^2$ for MAYO$_1$, $1.71mm^2$ for MAYO$_3$, and $3.09mm^2$ for MAYO$_5$.

In contrast, the HTH described in [26] occupies only 0.1% of the unified KaLi cryptoprocessor [1], which supports all Dilithium security levels within a single design and consumes just $0.263mm^2$. Applying the same HTH to the larger MAYO designs yields significantly lower relative area overheads: approximately 0.026% for MAYO$_1$, 0.015% for MAYO$_3$, and 0.008% for MAYO$_5$. A depiction of this is provided in Fig. 2. While we do not perform full key recovery, our analysis shows that the Trojan can leak secret values such as the seed, which prior works [20] have shown may be sufficient for key reconstruction. These findings emphasize that such Trojans can remain extremely stealthy, especially when embedded in higher-area designs.

5 Discussion and Conclusion

A generic way to prevent Hardware Trojan insertion is by trying to hide the Keccak input via duplication (multiple copies of Keccak). It prevents attackers from easily grouping Keccak's input registers. A similar effect can also be achieved via decoy flip-flops. These are not proven defence techniques and will only slow down the attack. As discussed in [26], the changing synthesis via retiming or rearranging the circuit logic does not impact the security against hardware trojan insertion.

To conclude, in this work, we investigated the applicability of hardware trojan insertion attacks on multivariate post-quantum digital signature schemes, with a particular focus on those employing the FiatShamir transform. We generalized a Trojan insertion technique previously proposed for Dilithium [26], which exploits the ordering of secret and message-dependent inputs to the Keccak hash function.

We observed that this vulnerability arises from the universal structure of Fiat-Shamir-based challenge generation, and demonstrated that similar weaknesses could appear in other schemes using the same paradigm. Specifically, we examined the impact of this Trojan technique on the signature generation procedures of the NIST Additional Signatures Round 2 candidates MAYO, UOV, SNOVA and QR-UOV. In the case of MAYO and UOV, we showed that the input to the hash function contains both attacker-controlled values (e.g., the message) and secret-dependent values (e.g., seed_{sk}), enabling trojan insertion. However, this procedure did not extend to SNOVA and QR-UOV due to structural differences and the order of the inputs in the hash function.

We also estimated the area overhead of inserting a hardware Trojan into real implementations, such as the MAYO hardware design from [19]. Our analysis indicates that the Trojan logic could occupy as little as 0.003% of the total area, highlighting the feasibility of highly stealthy leakage channels. With this work, we aim to motivate further investigation into hardware trojan insertion and leakage-based threats for the other NIST PQC additional digital signature candidates, encouraging a more comprehensive evaluation of their resilience in real-world deployment contexts.

Acknowledgement. Anisha Mukherjee was supported by FWF (Austrian Science Fund) grant PAT6402023. Texts of this paper were edited using AI to improve grammatical issues.

References

1. Aikata, A., Mert, A.C., Imran, M., Pagliarini, S., Roy, S.S.: Kali: a crystal for post-quantum security using kyber and dilithium. IEEE Trans. Circuits Syst. I Regul. Pap. **70**(2), 747–758 (2023). https://doi.org/10.1109/TCSI.2022.3219555
2. Alagic, G., et al.: Status report on the first round of the additional digital signature schemes for the nist post-quantum cryptography standardization process. In: National Institute of Standards and Technology, Gaithersburg, MD, pp. 1–30. NIST (2024)
3. Aulbach, T., Campos, F., Krämer, J., Samardjiska, S., Stöttinger, M.: Separating oil and vinegar with a single trace side-channel assisted kipnis-shamir attack on UOV. IACR Trans. Cryptogr. Hardw. Embed. Syst. **2023**(3), 221–245 (2023). https://doi.org/10.46586/TCHES.V2023.I3.221-245

4. Beirendonck, M.V., D'anvers, J.P., Karmakar, A., Balasch, J., Verbauwhede, I.: A side-channel-resistant implementation of saber. J. Emerg. Technol. Comput. Syst. **17**(2) (Apr 2021). https://doi.org/10.1145/3429983

5. Bernhard, D., Pereira, O., Warinschi, B.: How not to prove yourself: pitfalls of the fiat-shamir heuristic and applications to helios. In: Wang, X., Sako, K. (eds.) ASIACRYPT 2012. LNCS, vol. 7658, pp. 626–643. Springer, Heidelberg (2012). https://doi.org/10.1007/978-3-642-34961-4_38

6. Bernstein, D.J., Hülsing, A., Kölbl, S., Niederhagen, R., Rijneveld, J., Schwabe, P.: The SPHINCS$^+$ signature framework. In: Cavallaro, L., Kinder, J., Wang, X., Katz, J. (eds.) ACM CCS 2019, pp. 2129–2146. ACM Press (Nov 2019).https://doi.org/10.1145/3319535.3363229

7. Beullens, W.: Improved cryptanalysis of UOV and rainbow. In: Canteaut, A., Standaert, F. (eds.) Advances in Cryptology - EUROCRYPT 2021 - 40th Annual International Conference on the Theory and Applications of Cryptographic Techniques, Zagreb, Croatia, October 17-21, 2021, Proceedings, Part I. Lecture Notes in Computer Science, vol. 12696, pp. 348–373. Springer (2021). https://doi.org/10.1007/978-3-030-77870-5_13

8. Beullens, W.: MAYO: practical post-quantum signatures from oil-and-vinegar maps. In: AlTawy, R., Hülsing, A. (eds.) Selected Areas in Cryptography - 28th International Conference, SAC 2021, Virtual Event, September 29 - October 1, 2021, Revised Selected Papers. Lecture Notes in Computer Science, vol. 13203, pp. 355–376. Springer (2021). https://doi.org/10.1007/978-3-030-99277-4_17

9. Beullens, W., Campos, F., Celi, S., Hess, B., Kannwischer, M.J.: MAYO: Round 2 version. National Institute for Standards and Technology (2025)

10. Bogdanov, A., et al.: PRESENT: an ultra-lightweight block cipher. In: Paillier, P., Verbauwhede, I. (eds.) CHES 2007. LNCS, vol. 4727, pp. 450–466. Springer, Heidelberg (2007). https://doi.org/10.1007/978-3-540-74735-2_31

11. Ding, Y.Z.: Oblivious transfer in the bounded storage model. In: Kilian, J. (ed.) CRYPTO 2001. LNCS, vol. 2139, pp. 155–170. Springer, Heidelberg (2001). https://doi.org/10.1007/3-540-44647-8_9

12. Ducas, L., et al.: Crystals-dilithium: a lattice-based digital signature scheme. IACR Trans. Cryptogr. Hardw. Embed. Syst. **2018**(1), 238–268 (2018). https://doi.org/10.13154/tches.v2018.i1.238-268

13. Fiat, A., Shamir, A.: How to prove yourself: practical solutions to identification and signature problems. In: Odlyzko, A.M. (ed.) CRYPTO 1986. LNCS, vol. 263, pp. 186–194. Springer, Heidelberg (1987). https://doi.org/10.1007/3-540-47721-7_12

14. Fouque, P.-A., Guillermin, N., Leresteux, D., Tibouchi, M., Zapalowicz, J.-C.: Attacking RSA–CRT signatures with faults on montgomery multiplication. In: Prouff, E., Schaumont, P. (eds.) CHES 2012. LNCS, vol. 7428, pp. 447–462. Springer, Heidelberg (2012). https://doi.org/10.1007/978-3-642-33027-8_26

15. Furue, H., Ikematsu, Y., Kiyomura, Y., Takagi, T.: A new variant of unbalanced oil and vinegar using quotient ring: QR-UOV. In: Tibouchi, M., Wang, H. (eds.) Advances in Cryptology - ASIACRYPT 2021 - 27th International Conference on the Theory and Application of Cryptology and Information Security, Singapore, December 6-10, 2021, Proceedings, Part IV. Lecture Notes in Computer Science, vol. 13093, pp. 187–217. Springer (2021). https://doi.org/10.1007/978-3-030-92068-5_7

16. Ghandali, S., Moos, T., Moradi, A., Paar, C.: Side-channel hardware trojan for provably-secure sca-protected implementations. IEEE Trans. Very Large Scale Integr. (VLSI) Syst. **28**(6), 1435–1448 (2020). https://doi.org/10.1109/TVLSI.2020.2982473

17. Hepp, A., Perez, T., Pagliarini, S., Sigl, G.: A pragmatic methodology for blind hardware trojan insertion in finalized layouts. In: Proceedings of the 41st IEEE/ACM International Conference on Computer-Aided Design. ICCAD '22, Association for Computing Machinery, New York, NY, USA (2022). https://doi.org/10.1145/3508352.3549452

18. Hepp, A., Sigl, G.: Tapeout of a risc-v crypto chip with hardware trojans: a case-study on trojan design and pre-silicon detectability. In: Proceedings of the 18th ACM International Conference on Computing Frontiers, pp. 213–220. CF '21, Association for Computing Machinery, New York, NY, USA (2021). https://doi.org/10.1145/3457388.3458869

19. Hirner, F., Streibl, M., Krieger, F., Mert, A.C., Roy, S.S.: Whipping the multivariate-based mayo signature scheme using hardware platforms. In: Proceedings of the 2024 on ACM SIGSAC Conference on Computer and Communications Security, pp. 3421–3435. CCS '24, Association for Computing Machinery, New York, NY, USA (2024). https://doi.org/10.1145/3658644.3690258

20. Jendral, S., Dubrova, E.: MAYO key recovery by fixing vinegar seeds. IACR Commun. Cryptol. 1(4), 17 (2024). https://doi.org/10.62056/AB0LJBKRZ

21. Jin, Y., Makris, Y.: Hardware trojans in wireless cryptographic ICS. IEEE Design Test Comput. 27(1), 26–35 (2010). https://doi.org/10.1109/MDT.2010.21

22. Kipnis, A., Patarin, J., Goubin, L.: Unbalanced oil and vinegar signature schemes. In: Stern, J. (ed.) Advances in Cryptology - EUROCRYPT '99, International Conference on the Theory and Application of Cryptographic Techniques, Prague, Czech Republic, May 2-6, 1999, Proceeding. Lecture Notes in Computer Science, vol. 1592, pp. 206–222. Springer (1999). https://doi.org/10.1007/3-540-48910-X_15

23. Krämer, J., Loiero, M.: Fault attacks on UOV and rainbow. In: Polian, I., Stöttinger, M. (eds.) COSADE 2019. LNCS, vol. 11421, pp. 193–214. Springer, Cham (2019). https://doi.org/10.1007/978-3-030-16350-1_11

24. Lin, L., Burleson, W., Paar, C.: Moles: malicious off-chip leakage enabled by side-channels. In: Proceedings of the 2009 International Conference on Computer-Aided Design, pp. 117–122. ICCAD '09, Association for Computing Machinery, New York, NY, USA (2009). https://doi.org/10.1145/1687399.1687425

25. Muehlberghuber, M., Gürkaynak, F.K., Korak, T., Dunst, P., Hutter, M.: Red team vs. blue team hardware trojan analysis: Detection of a hardware trojan on an actual asic. In: Proceedings of the 2nd International Workshop on Hardware and Architectural Support for Security and Privacy. HASP '13, Association for Computing Machinery, New York, NY, USA (2013). https://doi.org/10.1145/2487726.2487727

26. Pagliarini, S., Aikata, Imran, M., Roy, S.S.: REPQC: reverse engineering and backdooring hardware accelerators for post-quantum cryptography. In: Zhou, J., Quek, T.Q.S., Gao, D., Cárdenas, A.A. (eds.) Proceedings of the 19th ACM Asia Conference on Computer and Communications Security, ASIA CCS 2024, Singapore, July 1-5, 2024. ACM (2024). https://doi.org/10.1145/3634737.3657016

27. Pébereau, P.: One vector to rule them all: Key recovery from one vector in UOV schemes. In: Saarinen, M.O., Smith-Tone, D. (eds.) Post-Quantum Cryptography - 15th International Workshop, PQCrypto 2024, Oxford, UK, June 12-14, 2024, Proceedings, Part II. Lecture Notes in Computer Science, vol. 14772, pp. 92–108. Springer (2024). https://doi.org/10.1007/978-3-031-62746-0_5

28. Peeters, G.B.J.D.M., Assche, G.V.: The Keccak reference. Round 3 submission to NIST SHA-3 (2011). http://keccak.noekeon.org/Keccak-reference-3.0.pdf

29. Perez, T., Imran, M., Vaz, P., Pagliarini, S.: Side-channel trojan insertion - a practical foundry-side attack via eco. In: 2021 IEEE International Symposium on Circuits and Systems (ISCAS), pp. 1–5 (2021). https://doi.org/10.1109/ISCAS51556.2021.9401481
30. Perez, T.D., Pagliarini, S.: Hardware trojan insertion in finalized layouts: From methodology to a silicon demonstration. IEEE Trans. Comput. Aided Des. Integr. Circuits Syst. **42**(7), 2094–2107 (2023). https://doi.org/10.1109/TCAD.2022.3223846
31. Prest, T., et al.: FALCON. Proposal to NIST PQC Standardization, Round3 (2021). https://csrc.nist.gov/Projects/post-quantum-cryptography/round-3-submissions
32. Puschner, E., Moos, T., Becker, S., Kison, C., Moradi, A., Paar, C.: Red team vs. blue team: a real-world hardware trojan detection case study across four modern cmos technology generations. In: 2023 2023 IEEE Symposium on Security and Privacy (SP), pp. 56–74. IEEE Computer Society, Los Alamitos, CA, USA (May 2023). https://doi.org/10.1109/SP46215.2023.00044
33. Ravi, P., Deb, S., Baksi, A., Chattopadhyay, A., Bhasin, S., Mendelson, A.: On threat of hardware trojan to post-quantum lattice-based schemes: A key recovery attack on saber and beyond. In: Batina, L., Picek, S., Mondal, M. (eds.) Security, Privacy, and Applied Cryptography Engineering, pp. 81–103. Springer International Publishing, Cham (2022)
34. Roy, S.S., Basso, A.: High-speed instruction-set coprocessor for lattice-based key encapsulation mechanism: Saber in hardware. IACR Trans. Crypt. Hardw. Embed. Syst. **2020**(4), 443–466 (2020). https://doi.org/10.13154/tches.v2020.i4.443-466
35. Schwabe, P., et al.: CRYSTALS-KYBER. Proposal to NIST PQC Standardization (2021). https://csrc.nist.gov/Projects/post-quantum-cryptography/round-3-submissions
36. Shor, P.W.: Polynomial-time algorithms for prime factorization and discrete logarithms on a quantum computer. SIAM J. Comput. **26**(5), 1484–1509 (oct 1997). https://doi.org/10.1137/S0097539795293172
37. Wang, L.C., et al.: SNOVA specification document. https://csrc.nist.gov/csrc/media/Projects/pqc-dig-sig/documents/round-1/spec-files/SNOVA-spec-web.pdf (2023). available from NIST PQC Digital Signatures Project
38. Xue, M., Gu, C., Liu, W., Yu, S., O'Neill, M.: Ten years of hardware trojans: a survey from the attacker's perspective. IET Comput. Digit. Tech. 14(6), 231–246 (2020). https://doi.org/10.1049/IET-CDT.2020.0041
39. Zhang, Y.: Cache side channels: State of the art and research opportunities. In: Thuraisingham, B.M., Evans, D., Malkin, T., Xu, D. (eds.) ACM CCS 2017, pp. 2617–2619. ACM Press (Oct / Nov 2017). https://doi.org/10.1145/3133956.3136064
40. Zhang, Y., Juels, A., Reiter, M.K., Ristenpart, T.: Cross-VM side channels and their use to extract private keys. In: Yu, T., Danezis, G., Gligor, V.D. (eds.) ACM CCS 2012, pp. 305–316. ACM Press (Oct 2012). https://doi.org/10.1145/2382196.2382230

Efficient Implementation
of Post-quantum Cryptography

LightNTT: A Tiny NTT/iNTT Core
for ML-DSA Featuring
a Constant-Geometry Pipelined Design

Bardia Taghavi[1]([✉])[iD], Reza Azarderakhsh[1][iD],
and Mehran Mozaffari Kermani[2][iD]

[1] Florida Atlantic University, Boca Raton, FL, USA
{staghavi2024,razarderakhsh}@fau.edu
[2] University of South Florida, Tampa, FL, USA
mehran2@usf.edu

Abstract. The Number Theoretic Transform (NTT) is a foundation
of Module-Lattice-Based Cryptography (MLBC), yet its implementation can be resource-intensive, posing challenges for deployment on low-
power and constrained devices. This paper introduces LightNTT, a high-
efficiency NTT/iNTT core specifically architected for ML-DSA, emphasizing minimal resource utilization and optimal performance. LightNTT
leverages a constant-geometry dataflow combined with a deeply pipelined
single butterfly unit and an optimized Barrett modular multiplier to
achieve a compact footprint. Implemented on an Artix-7 FPGA, the
design consumes only 590 LUTs, 158 FFs, 2 DSPs, and 2.5 BRAMs. It
computes a full 256-point NTT/iNTT in 1056 clock cycles, achieving
a latency of $3.49\mu s$ at a clock frequency of $300\,$MHz. Critically, Light-
NTT demonstrates a superior Area-Time Product (ATP) of 5.82, which
is approximately 29% better than comparable state-of-the-art implementations of small designs. This work underscores the effectiveness of synergistic architectural and modular arithmetic optimizations in developing
practical PQC accelerators for resource-limited environments.

Keywords: Post-Quantum Cryptography · Lightweight Hardware
Security · Number Theoretic Transform · ML-DSA · FPGA

1 Introduction

The rapid advancement of quantum computing poses a significant threat to traditional cryptographic systems, which rely on the computational hardness of
problems like integer factorization and discrete logarithms. As quantum algorithms, such as Shor's algorithm [26], threaten to undermine these foundations,
the cryptographic community has turned to post-quantum cryptography (PQC)
to develop algorithms resistant to quantum attacks. Among the most promising
candidates is Module-lattice-based Cryptography (MLBC), which offers robust
security guarantees and computational efficiency for a wide range of applications.

E. Savas et al. (Eds.): LightSec 2025, LNCS 16216, pp. 57–76, 2026.
https://doi.org/10.1007/978-3-032-15541-2_4

A critical operation in many MLBC schemes, such as ML-KEM [20], ML-DSA [19], and FALCON [21], is polynomial multiplication, which is the most computationally intensive block and often represents a performance bottleneck in practical implementations.

The Number Theoretic Transform (NTT) has emerged as a pivotal tool for addressing this challenge in the implementation of PQC schemes. NTT is the generalization of the well-established discrete Fourier transform (DFT) and its efficient counterpart, the FFT. Unlike the traditional Discrete Fourier Transform, which operates over complex numbers and introduces round-off errors due to floating-point arithmetic, NTT performs the arithmetics over a finite field or a finite ring, typically the integers modulo a prime, ensures exact computations, a property essential for maintaining the integrity and security of cryptographic algorithms [12]. Using NTT, efficient polynomial multiplication can be done through pointwise operations in the transform domain. By leveraging fast Fourier transform algorithms like Cooley-Tukey [3] (CT) and Gentleman-Sande [6] (GS), NTT achieves a quasi-linear computational complexity of $\mathcal{O}(n \log_2 n)$ for a degree-n polynomial, making it highly efficient for high-degree polynomial operations.

Despite its computational advantages, implementing NTT, particularly in hardware, can be resource-intensive, requiring significant memory, power, and computational resources. This poses a challenge for deploying MLBC schemes on resource-constrained devices, such as embedded systems, Internet of Things (IoT) devices, mobile platforms, and smart cards, which are increasingly integral to modern computing ecosystems. These platforms typically have limitations in terms of processing power, available memory, and energy consumption, necessitating careful optimization of cryptographic primitives. As these devices become ubiquitous, the demand for compact and efficient NTT implementations has grown, driven by the need to balance security, performance, and resource utilization. Compact NTT designs aim to minimize area, power consumption, and computational overhead while preserving the efficiency required for real-time cryptographic operations.

However, translating the theoretical efficiency of NTT into a compact and practical hardware implementation presents a formidable engineering challenge. Designers must navigate a series of intertwined trade-offs, where optimizing one aspect often compromises another. The central conflict lies between performance (latency and throughput) and resource utilization (area and power). For instance, a straightforward approach to boost speed is to use multiple parallel butterfly units, but this dramatically increases the hardware footprint (LUTs, FFs, DSPs) and power draw, rendering it unsuitable for constrained devices. This fundamental trade-off is compounded by the specific implementation hurdles of the NTT algorithm itself. The reliance on modular arithmetic makes the choice of a reduction algorithm—such as Barrett, Montgomery, Plantard, etc.—a critical decision that profoundly impacts area, speed, and design complexity. This is coupled with the challenge of managing data flow and memory, as the algorithm must efficiently process large vectors of coefficients and twiddle factors (TFs) with potentially irregular access patterns that can complicate control logic, especially when on-chip memory is scarce. Furthermore, the intricate data dependencies between butterfly stages demand sophisticated but simple control logic to keep the hardware footprint minimal. Successfully addressing these intertwined challenges of arithmetic, memory, and control requires a holistic approach, where architectural choices, algorithmic optimizations, and arithmetic circuits are developed in synergy. This paper investigates this design space with the explicit goal of creating a highly efficient NTT core for resource-constrained environments.

This paper investigates the design space of compact NTT implementations, with a focus on optimization strategies that reduce resource utilization while maintaining computational efficiency. We explore a range of architectural approaches, algorithmic improvements, and hardware-specific optimizations, including making benefits of constant-geometry architecture in computing NTT to simplify the FSM, reducing the overall complexity of the design, and lowering the required number of logic gates to control the computations. By systematically analyzing the trade-offs between performance, area, and power consumption, we aim to provide comprehensive insights into designing NTT implementations that are both efficient and practical for deployment in resource-constrained environments. Our work builds on recent advances in the field, offering a detailed examination of how compact NTT designs can facilitate the widespread adoption of lattice-based cryptography in the post-quantum era. We try to design the smallest possible module that can compute both NTT and inverse NTT (iNTT) for the ML-DSA scheme while the performance is still acceptable.

1.1 Related Work

The field of hardware acceleration for post-quantum cryptography, particularly for lattice-based schemes like CRYSTALS-Dilithium and its underlying Number Theoretic Transform (NTT) operations, has seen significant research interest. This section reviews existing literature relevant to the FPGA implementation of NTT and related cryptographic primitives.

Authors in [9] introduce an FPGA-based NTT architecture for CRYSTALS-Kyber that prioritizes both compactness and low latency. By employing novel DSP-free butterfly units and an optimized coefficient access pattern, the design achieves significant hardware efficiency, indicated by its low LUT and FF count, suggesting a small and potentially low-power footprint. In another work, [5] proposes a "high-low interactive memory access pattern" that supports configurable parallelism within a constant-geometry NTT (CG NTT) framework. The design emphasizes area efficiency through flexible memory selection (LUTs or BRAMs based on parameters), aiming for a smaller hardware footprint and high memory utilization, which can contribute to lower power consumption. Their quantitative analysis of parallelism versus cycle count further aids in optimizing for minimal computing resources. Another work in paper [2] explores FPGA implementations of K^2-RED and Plantard modular multiplication, crucial for NTT operations in post-quantum cryptography, and performs a comparative analysis of their area, speed, and latency. The proposed design in [13] describes a flexible

FPGA-based NTT accelerator that explicitly uses a constant-geometry approach to simplify memory addressing. It allows for a configurable trade-off between computational speed and resource usage, enabling optimization for resource-conservative, smaller designs. Constant-geometry architectures are also explored in [11], when the authors give the details of compact FPGA implementations of Dilithium, featuring an NTT core optimized for minimal LUT/FF usage through efficient DSP utilization. The design leverages memory access patterns consistent with constant-geometry flows to reduce hardware footprint, targeting low-cost and area-constrained applications.

2 Background

2.1 Notation

Throughout this paper, we will use the ring of polynomials $\mathcal{R}_q = \mathbb{Z}_q[x]/(x^n+1)$, where q is a prime number, and n is a power of 2. Every arithmetic is done modulo $\mathcal{R}_q$, i.e., the coefficients of the polynomials are in the range of $[0, q-1]$, and all polynomials have a degree less than n. Polynomials are represented as vectors of their coefficients, i.e., $\mathbf{a} = (a_0, a_1, \ldots, a_{n-1})$ represents the polynomial $\mathbf{a}(x) = a_0 + a_1 x + \ldots + a_{n-1} x^{n-1}$. Bold-faced letters are used to denote vectors. The number of bits in q is represented by t, i.e., $t = \lceil \log_2 q \rceil$.

In this paper, NTT refers to the negacyclic NTT, which computes the multiplication of two polynomials $\pmod{x^n + 1}$ in the NTT domain, which is the irreduce polynomial in PQC schemes.

If the ring $\mathcal{R}_q$ is NTT-friendly, i.e., there exists a primitive $2n$-th root of unity ζ in $\mathbb{Z}_q$ such that $\zeta^{2n} \equiv 1 \pmod{q}$ and $\zeta^n \equiv -1 \pmod{q}$ (like in ML-DSA), we can compute the full NTT and iNTT of a polynomial $a(x)$ in $\mathcal{R}_q$, and $\mathrm{NTT}(\mathbf{a})$ is referred as $\hat{\mathbf{a}}$. If the ring is not NTT-friendly, but there exists an $n-$th root of unity ζ in $\mathbb{Z}_q$ such that $\zeta^n \equiv 1 \pmod{q}$ and $\zeta^{n/2} \equiv -1 \pmod{q}$ (like in ML-KEM), we can compute the NTT of a polynomial $a(x)$ in $\mathcal{R}_q$ by using incomplete NTT trick. As a result, ζ is used for both cases as the root of unity.

2.2 MLBC Schemes

Two MLBC schemes, ML-KEM and ML-DSA, formerly known as CRYSTALS-KYBER and CRYSTALS-DILITHIUM, are two finalists in the NIST PQC standardization process. ML-KEM is a key encapsulation mechanism based on the Module Learning With Error (MLWE) problem, and ML-DSA is a digital signature algorithm based on MLWE and the Selftarget (Inhomogeneous) Module Short Integer Solutions (IMSIS) problem. The MLWE problem is to find the secret key $\mathbf{s}$ from the public key $(\mathbf{A}, \mathbf{t})$ in the equation $\mathbf{t} = \mathbf{A} \cdot \mathbf{s} + \mathbf{e}$, where $\mathbf{A}$ is a random $k \times l$ matrix of polynomials, $\mathbf{s}$ is a length l vector of polynomials, and $\mathbf{e}$ is a small vector of error.

The IMSIS problem in ML-DSA is to find a short vector $[\mathbf{z}, -\mathbf{w}_0]^T$ from the public key $\mathbf{A}$ and publicly known values c, $\mathbf{t}$, γ_2, and $\mathbf{w}_1$ in the equation $\mathbf{A} \cdot \mathbf{z} - \mathbf{w}_0 = c \cdot \mathbf{t} + 2\gamma_2 \mathbf{w}_1$, where $\mathbf{w} = 2\gamma_2 \mathbf{w}_1 + \mathbf{w}_0$. The mentioned vector has to be short to prevent the adversary from finding the trivial solution, such that $||\mathbf{z}||_\infty < \gamma_1 - \beta$ and $||\mathbf{w}_0||_\infty \leq \gamma_2$. Both methods perform the arithmetics over the ring of $\mathcal{R}_q$. For ML-KEM, $\lceil \log_2 q \rceil = 12$, and for ML-DSA, $\lceil \log_2 q \rceil = 23$. ML-KEM and ML-DSA use the NTT to perform the polynomial multiplications in the ring of $\mathcal{R}_q$, and NIST constrained every multiplication to be done in the ring of $\mathcal{R}_q$ *only using NTT*. Figure 1 illustrates the required multiplications in MLBC schemes, and all of them have to be done using NTT, PWM, and iNTT.

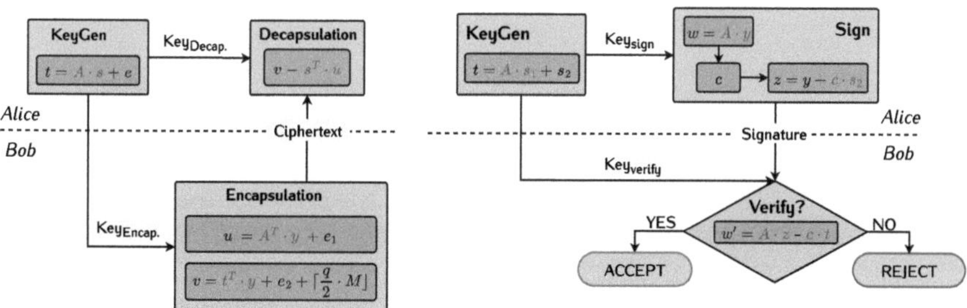

Fig. 1. High-Level Overview of ML-KEM (left) and ML-DSA (right). This figure illustrates that the NTT computation is used in the polynomial multiplication of both schemes multiple times, denoted by the dot product.

2.3   NTT

NTT is the core of many MLBC schemes, and it is used to compute the polynomial multiplication in the NTT domain. To compute the multiplication of two polynomials modulo $x^n + 1$, one can use negative-wrapped convolution (NWC) or NTT. To compute the product of two polynomials $\mathbf{a}$ and $\mathbf{b}$ in $\mathcal{R}_q$ using NWC, we can use the following equation:

$$c_j = \sum_{i=0}^{k} a_i b_{j-i} - \sum_{i=k+1}^{n-1} a_i b_{j-i+n} \pmod{q}, \tag{1}$$

where c_j is the j-th coefficient of the product polynomial $\mathbf{c}$. This method is simple and straightforward, but it has a time complexity of $\mathcal{O}(n^2)$, which can be inefficient for large polynomials, or when we need the fast computation of polynomial multiplication.

To improve efficiency, the NTT method is proposed. In NTT method, we first compute their NTTs, $\hat{\mathbf{a}} = \text{NTT}(\mathbf{a})$ and $\hat{\mathbf{b}} = \text{NTT}(\mathbf{b})$. Then, we compute the pointwise multiplication (PWM) of the two NTTs, i.e., $\hat{\mathbf{c}} = \hat{\mathbf{a}} \odot \hat{\mathbf{b}}$, where $\odot$ is the pointwise multiplication. Finally, we compute the iNTT of $\hat{\mathbf{c}}$ to obtain the product polynomial $\mathbf{c} = \text{iNTT}(\hat{\mathbf{c}})$. Similar to NWC, the naive NTT has the same asymptotic complexity of $\mathcal{O}(n^2)$. The equation to compute NTT($\mathbf{a}$) is as follows:

$$\hat{a_j} = \sum_{i=0}^{n-1} \zeta^{2ij+i} \cdot a_i \quad (\text{mod } q), \tag{2}$$

where $\hat{a_j}$ is the j-th coefficient of the NTT polynomial $\hat{\mathbf{a}}$. The equation to compute iNTT($\hat{\mathbf{c}}$), which is obtained after the trivial PWM, is as follows:

$$c_i = n^{-1} \sum_{j=0}^{n-1} \zeta^{-2ij-i} \cdot \hat{c}_j \quad (\text{mod } q). \tag{3}$$

However, NTT is much faster in practice, because it can make use of the fast Fourier transform (FFT) algorithms to compute the NTT and iNTT. The NTT algorithm is based on the divide-and-conquer approach, which recursively divides the polynomial into smaller polynomials until the base case is reached. The base case is when the polynomial has a degree of 1 (in case of full NTT), and degree of 2 (in case of incomplete NTT). To compute NTT and iNTT, CT and GS algorithms are used, respectively. The CT and GS algorithms are both efficient and have a time complexity of $\mathcal{O}(n \log_2 n)$. Both algorithms uses butterfly structure to compute the NTT and iNTT. The butterfly structure is a hardware-friendly structure, which consists of two inputs and two outputs. In the Cooley-Tukey algorithm, Eq. 2 is computed by recursively dividing the polynomial into two smaller polynomials and then combining the results using the periodicity and symmetry properties of the roots of unity. The butterfly unit (BFU) for CT performs the following operations:

$$\begin{bmatrix} x_i \\ x_{i+k} \end{bmatrix} = \begin{bmatrix} (x_i + x_{i+k} \cdot \zeta^{brv(i)}) & (\text{mod } q) \\ (x_i - x_{i+k} \cdot \zeta^{brv(i)}) & (\text{mod } q) \end{bmatrix}, \tag{4}$$

where x_i and x_{i+k} are the inputs to the CT BFU, and $brv(i)$ is the bit-reversed index of i. The output of the BFU is two new values, which are used as inputs to the next stage of the NTT computation. The BFU for GS performs the following operations:

$$\begin{bmatrix} \hat{x}_i \\ \hat{x}_{i+k} \end{bmatrix} = \begin{bmatrix} 2^{-1} \cdot (\hat{x}_{i+k} + \hat{x}_i) & (\text{mod } q) \\ 2^{-1} \cdot (\hat{x}_{i+k} - \hat{x}_i) \cdot \zeta^{brv(i)} & (\text{mod } q) \end{bmatrix}. \tag{5}$$

By looking at the Eqs. 4 and 5, we can see that the same operations are required for both CT BFU and GS BFU, but in different order. This means that we can use the same hardware for both BFUs, by just changing the input to the BFU. This is a very important point in our design because it will help us to reduce the area of our design. The factor 2^{-1} is applied here to consider n^{-1} factor of Eq. 3 at each stage, instead of applying it at the end, since n is a power of two, and we have $\log_2 n$ stages.

2.4 Modular Reduction

Equations 4 and 5 illustrate that modular reduction is a crucial part of butterfly structures. Three types of modular reduction are required for NTT/iNTT computations: (1) modular addition, (2) modular subtraction, and (3) modular multiplication. Modular addition and subtraction are straightforward operations, but modular multiplication is more complex. For modular multiplication, several algorithms were proposed to reduce the time complexity and area usage of the multiplication. Among them, Montgomery reduction, Barrett reduction, Plantard reduction, and K-RED reduction (and some modified versions of it, like K^2-RED [1]) are the most common ones in NTT computations. Although there are some other algorithms and optimizations for modular reduction that have been proposed for efficient computations of RSA/ECC/DH, they are not suitable for MLBC schemes because they are efficient for large moduli. In this paper, we will make a comparison between different modular reduction algorithms, and we will show that Barrett is the best choice for our design.

Barrett Reduction. Algorithm 1 shows the Barrett modular multiplication algorithm, which is used in our design, based on the algorithm in [22]. All multiplications are done by shifting and adding/subtracting, which is very efficient in hardware [16]. The important point in Barrett reduction is that by feeding a and b to the inputs, the output would be $a \cdot b \pmod{q}$, without any scaling factor, which is one of the problems in other algorithms. This algorithm requires the pre-computation of factor μ in this equation:

$$\mu = \lfloor \frac{2^{2t}}{q} \rfloor, \tag{6}$$

which is equal to $2^{23} + 2^{13} + 2^3 - 1$ in ML-DSA, and $q = 2^{23} - 2^{13} + 1$.

Algorithm 1: Hardware-friendly Optimized Barrett Modular Multiplication [22]

    Input: $a, b \in \mathbb{Z}_q, t = \lceil \log_2 q \rceil = 23$
    Output: $out = a \cdot b \pmod{q}$
1 $product \leftarrow a \cdot b$
2 $x_1 \leftarrow product \gg (t - 2)$
3 $x_2 \leftarrow (x_1 \ll 23) + (x_1 \ll 13) + (x_1 \ll 3) - x_1$
4 $s \leftarrow x_2 \gg (t + 2)$
5 $out \leftarrow product - ((s \ll 23) - (s \ll 13) + s) - q$
6 **if** $out < 0$ **then**
7 $\lfloor \quad out \leftarrow out + q$

K^2-RED Reduction K^2-RED reduction is a modified version of K-RED reduction, which is used in some MLBC schemes [1]. This algorithm works on any prime ring or prime field that the prime modulo q can be represented as $q = m \cdot 2^k + 1$. In this reduction algorithm, K^2-RED$(a, b) = a \cdot b \cdot k^2 \pmod{q}$, so to compute $a \cdot b \pmod{q}$, if b is known beforehand, i.e., b is constant, we can pre-compute $b \cdot k^{-2}$ (mod q) and use it in the computation to cancel out the k^2 factor.

$$\text{K}^2\text{-RED}(a, b \cdot k^{-2}) = a \cdot b \cdot k^{-2} \cdot k^2 \pmod{q} = a \cdot b \pmod{q}. \qquad (7)$$

The K^2-RED reduction algorithm is shown in Algorithm 2.

Algorithm 2: Hardware-friendly K^2-RED Modular Multiplication [1]

    Input: $a \in \mathbb{Z}_q, b = \zeta^j \cdot k^{-2}$ (mod q), $q = m \cdot 2^k + 1$
    Output: $out = a \cdot \zeta^j$ (mod q)
1   $product \leftarrow a \cdot b$
2   $cl_1 \leftarrow product[m-1:0]$
3   $ch_1 \leftarrow product \gg m$
4   $result_1 \leftarrow (cl_1 \ll 10) - cl_1 - ch_1$
5   $cl_2 \leftarrow result_1[m-1:0]$
6   $ch_2 \leftarrow result_1 \gg m$
7   $out \leftarrow (cl_2 \ll 10) - cl_2 - ch_2$
8   **if** $out \geq q$ **then**
9      $\lfloor$ $out \leftarrow out - q$
10 **else if** $out < 0$ **then**
11     $\lfloor$ $out \leftarrow out + q$

Montgomery Reduction. Montgomery reduction is another modular multiplication algorithm that is widely used in cryptography [17] [4]. The Montgomery reduction algorithm requires a pre-computed value of $R = 2^l$, where $l > t$, and $\bar{q}$, which is the inverse of $-q$ modulo R. The reduction function is Montgomery(a, b) $= a \cdot b \cdot R^{-1}$ (mod q), so to compute $a \cdot b$ (mod q), we can pre-compute $b \cdot R$ (mod q) and use it as the input to cancel out the R^{-1} factor, in case that b is constant. In ML-DSA, $\bar{q} = 2^{23} - 2^{13} - 1$, so we can compute the multiplication by shift and addition/subtraction. The Montgomery reduction algorithm is shown in Algorithm 3.

Plantard Reduction. Plantard reduction is another modular multiplication algorithm that is introduced in recent years [24], and it's an improved version of Montgomery reduction [8]. The Plantard reduction algorithm requires a pre-computed value of $R = 2^{2l}$, when $l \geq \lceil \log_2(q \cdot \frac{1+\sqrt{5}}{2}) \rceil$, and $\bar{q} = (q^{-1})$ (mod 2^{2l}). This reduction function computes Plantard$(a, b) = -a \cdot b \cdot R^{-1}$ (mod q). In order to compute $a \cdot b$ (mod q), we can pre-compute $-b \cdot R$ (mod q) if b is a constant number. In addition, the first step of Plantard reduction is to multiply $a \cdot b$ by $\bar{q}$, which is again a constant number. $\bar{q}$ can be very large (up to $2l$-bit), and the number of bits in $a \cdot b \cdot \bar{q}$ is at most $(2l + 2t)$-bit. To save space, we can compute the first step before the main computation. The Plantard reduction algorithm is shown in Algorithm 4.

Algorithm 3: Hardware-friendly Montgomery Modular Multiplication [17]

> **Input:** $a \in \mathbb{Z}_q, b = \zeta^j \cdot R \pmod{q}, l = 24, R = 2^l, \bar{q} = (-q^{-1}) \pmod{R}$
> **Output:** $out = a \cdot \zeta^j \pmod{q}$

1   $product \leftarrow a \cdot b$
2   $m \leftarrow (product \ll 23) - (product \ll 13) - product$
3   $qm \leftarrow (m \ll 23) - (m \ll 13) + m$
4   $out \leftarrow (product + qm) \gg l$
5   **if** $out \geq q$ **then**
6      $out \leftarrow out - q$

Algorithm 4: Hardware-friendly Plantard Modular Multiplication [24]

> **Input:** $a \in \mathbb{Z}_q, b = (((-\zeta^j \cdot 2^{2l}) \pmod{q})) \cdot \bar{q}) \pmod{2^{2l}}, l = 24, \bar{q} = (-q^{-1})$
> $\pmod{2^{2l}}$
> **Output:** $out = a \cdot \zeta^j \mod q$

1   $product \leftarrow a \cdot b$
2   $t_1 \leftarrow product[2 \cdot l - 1 : 0]$
3   $t_2 \leftarrow (t_1 \gg l) + 1$
4   $t_3 \leftarrow (t_2 \ll 23) - (t_2 \ll 13) + t_2$
5   $out \leftarrow t_3 \gg l$
6   **if** $out = q$ **then**
7      $out \leftarrow 0$

Solinas Reduction. Solinas reduction is a less explored modular multiplication in NTT applications, and it works on the modulus of special form, called Solinas prime or generalized Mersenne prime, which has the form of $f(2^m)$ [28]. When the modulus q is of the form $q = 2^k - 2^l + 1$, we can use Solinas reduction described in algorithm 5 to compute the modular multiplication.

The advantage of Solinas reduction is that no scaling factor exists in the output (like Barrett), so there is no need of changing input b to cancelling out the scaling factor.

3   Proposed Design

The proposed design is a compact NTT/iNTT architecture that can be used in MLBC schemes. The design is based on the constant-geometry (CG) architecture, or Pease architecture [23], which is a well-known architecture for FFT computations and can be trivially adapted to compute NTT/iNTT. In the normal NTT architecture, the distance between inputs of each BFU is not constant, starting from $\frac{n}{2}$, and it gets halved in each stage. To compute iNTT, the distance between inputs of each BFU starts from 1, and it gets doubled in each stage. This variability in the distance between inputs of each BFU makes the control logic more complex, and it requires more hardware resources. Moreover,

---

Algorithm 5: Hardware-friendly Solinas Modular Multiplication [7]

Input: $a, b \in \mathbb{Z}_q, q = 2^k - 2^l + 1, k = 23, l = 13,$
$q8 = q << 3, q4 = q << 2, q1 = q << 1$
Output: $out = a \cdot b \mod q$

1   $product \leftarrow a \cdot b$
2   $q_{1H} \leftarrow product \gg k$
3   $q_{1L} \leftarrow product[k - 1 : 0]$
4   $t_2 \leftarrow (q_{1H} \ll l) - q_{1H} + q_{1L}$
5   $q_{2H} \leftarrow t_2 \gg k$
6   $q_{2L} \leftarrow t_2[k - 1 : 0]$
7   $t_3 \leftarrow (q_{2H} \ll l) - q_{2H} + q_{2L}$
8   $t_4 \leftarrow (t_3 \geq q8)\ ?\ t_3 - q8 : t_3$
9   $t_5 \leftarrow (t_4 \geq q4)\ ?\ t_4 - q4 : t_4$
10   $t_6 \leftarrow (t_5 \geq q1)\ ?\ t_5 - q1 : t_5$
11   $out \leftarrow (t_6 \geq q)\ ?\ t_6 - q : t_6$

---

as the memory access pattern changes in each stage, the design is more prone to side-channel attacks (SCA).

On the other hand, in CG architecture, the distance between inputs of each BFU is constant, and it is equal to $\frac{n}{2}$ for NTT and 1 for iNTT, in all stages. The CG architecture is shown in Fig. 2 for an 8-point NTT/iNTT. The CG architecture has a simple control logic, making it more suitable for a small design. In addition, since the memory access pattern is constant in all stages, the power consumption of RAM usage will be reduced, and it will be potentially more secure against a number of the SCAs.

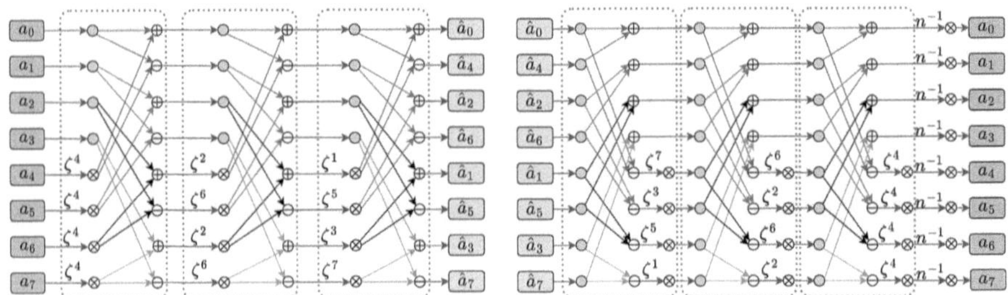

Fig. 2. Constant-geometry NTT (left) and iNTT (right) architecture for a degree-8 polynomial.

In the CG architecture, unlike the normal NTT architecture, the computations are out-of-place, i.e., the outputs of each BFU are not stored in the same location as the inputs. Figure 3 shows the data flow of CT BFU (for NTT) and GS BFU (for iNTT) in CG architecture [29].

As it can be seen in Fig. 3, for each BFU, three modular blocks are needed: (1) modular addition, (2) modular subtraction, and (3) modular multiplication.

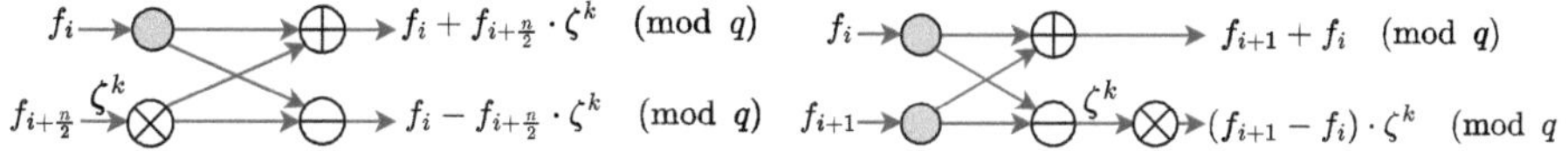

Fig. 3. Data flow for CT BFU (left) and GS BFU (right) in CG architecture.

As a result, using one butterfly unit with three modular blocks for each BFU, we can compute the NTT and iNTT of a polynomial $\mathbf{a}(x)$ in $\mathcal{R}_q$.

While techniques such as constant-geometry dataflows and pipelining have been used in prior NTT accelerators, the primary contribution of this work lies in their synergistic integration and optimization toward a singular goal: minimizing the area utilization for resource-constrained applications. Our design philosophy diverges from approaches that seek to maximize raw speed through high parallelism. Instead, we demonstrate how a deeply pipelined single butterfly unit (BFU), when paired with the simplified control logic inherent to the constant-geometry architecture, can achieve highly competitive performance with a minimal hardware footprint. The selection of the Barrett modular multiplier is also a critical and deliberate choice in this methodology, as its lack of scaling factors simplifies the overall design and allows for a unified multiplier for all phases of polynomial multiplication, a key advantage over other common reduction algorithms.

3.1   Modular Addition/Subtraction

Modular addition and subtraction are straightforward operations, and they can be implemented using a simple adder/subtractor. The final multiplication in iNTT by n^{-1} (mod q) is embedded in each stage of addition/subtraction, by multiplying the output of each BFU by 2^{-1} (mod q). This multiplication is done by a simple algorithm in Algorithm 6, which is a simple shift or add and shift operation. The algorithm is very efficient in hardware, instead of multiplying by 2^{-1} (mod q) at the end of each BFU, and helps to complete the operation in a single cycle.

Algorithm 6: Multiply by 2^{-1} (mod q)

  Input: $a \in \mathbb{Z}_q$
  Output: $out = 2^{-1} \cdot a$ (mod q)
1   $out \leftarrow a[0] \; ? \; a \gg 1 : (a + q) \gg 1$

The presented modular addition/subtraction architecture for this design is shown in Fig. 4. In this figure, $x[23]$ means the 23-th bit of x, which is the output of the first subtractor, and $y[0]$ means the 0-th bit of y, which is the output of the first multiplexer, and both of them serves as the select bit of the shown multiplexers.

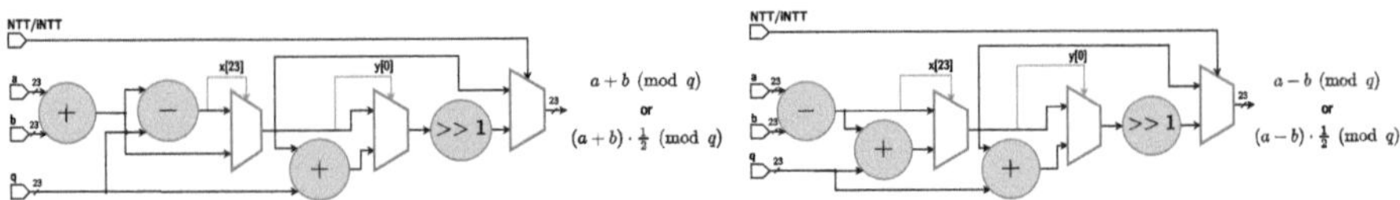

Fig. 4. Modular addition/subtraction architecture to support NTT/iNTT.

3.2 Modular Multiplication

As mentioned in Sect. 2.4, there are several modular multiplication algorithms that can be used in NTT/iNTT computations. In this design, we have implemented Barrett, Montgomery, Plantard, K^2-RED, and Solinas modular multipliers. As can be seen in Fig. 3, in the computation of NTT and iNTT, the multiplication is always done by the twiddle factors (TFs), which are the powers of ζ, and they are constant numbers. This means that in the Montgomery, K^2-RED, and Plantard multipliers, we can pre-compute the multiplication of ζ and the scaling factor of each algorithm, and instead of storing the TFs in the read-only memory (ROM), we can store the pre-computed values of $\zeta^{brv(i)} \cdot k^{-2} \pmod{q}$, $\zeta^{brv(i)} \cdot 2^l \pmod{q}$, and $(-\zeta^{brv(i)} \cdot 2^{2l} \pmod{q}) \cdot \bar{q} \pmod{2^{2l}}$ in the i-th element of ROM for K^2-RED, Montgomery, and Plantard, respectively. This will help to reduce the area of the design since one multiplication inside these algorithms is done in the pre-computation phase. For the Barrett and Solinas multipliers, we pre-compute the TFs without any scaling factor, and we store them in the ROM, i.e., in the i-th element of ROM, $\zeta^{brv(i)}$ is stored. This strategy will help to reduce the area of the design and the delay in the NTT computation significantly, and we can use the pre-computed values instead. All of these multipliers are implemented in a single cycle, and by performing all the multiplications (except the first one, $a \cdot b$) in the reduction part by shifting and adding/subtracting, we can reduce the area of the design, and make it faster by reducing the critical path. The multiplication of $a \cdot b$ is done by DSP48E, which has 18×25-bit inputs. As a result, to feed 23×23-bit inputs to the DSP48E, we need to use two DSPs.

However, this advantage will help only in NTT/iNTT converter, and for the PWM phase, when none of the inputs are constant, two strategies can be used: (1) using another multiplier for the PWM phase, or (2) using the same multiplier inside the BFU for the PWM phase, but with two cycles. In the second cycle, the result will be multiplied by the squared inverse of the constant scaling factor. It is clear that the first option is less area-efficient, but it will be faster. This makes the Barrett and Solinas multipliers more suitable for the smallest NTT/iNTT converter, as one can use the same multiplier of the converter for the PWM phase as well, and it will be still fast (Fig. 5 and Fig. 6).

3.3 Memory Management

In this design, to achieve fast and conflict-free memory access, a ping-pong memory architecture is used. Two Dual-port Block RAMs (BRAMs), DRAM-A and

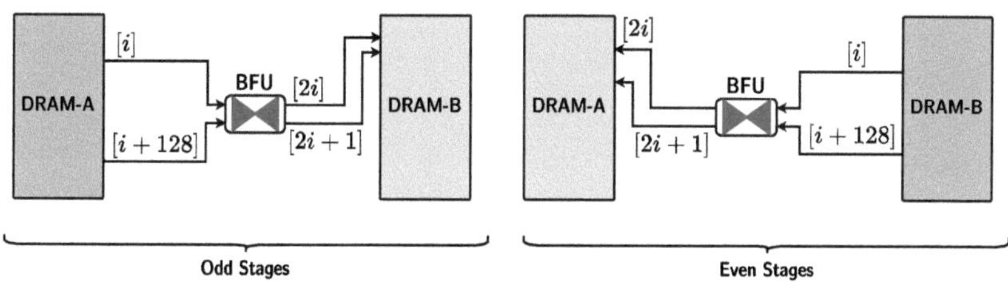

Fig. 5. Ping-Pong RAM architecture during NTT.

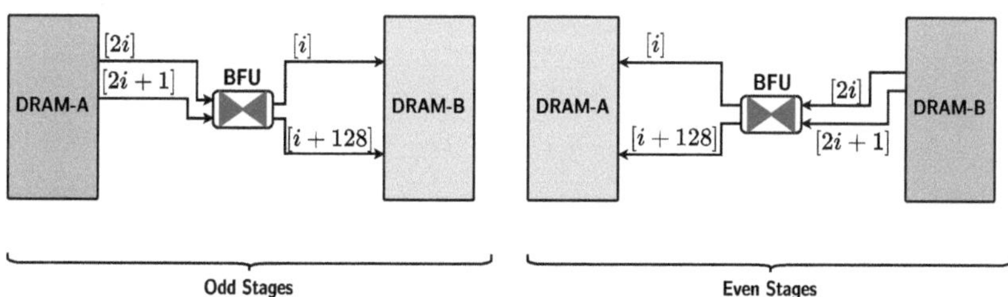

Fig. 6. Ping-Pong RAM architecture during iNTT.

DRAM-B are used to store the input and output data of the NTT/iNTT computation. In the first step, the vector of coefficients is stored in DRAM-A. Then, the NTT/iNTT computation is started, and for the first stage, each BFU reads the inputs from DRAM-A, and writes the outputs to DRAM-B. For the second stage, the BFUs read the inputs from DRAM-B, and write the outputs to DRAM-A. This process continues until the NTT/iNTT computation is finished. This architecture helps to reduce the memory access time, and it makes the design more efficient. Note that the memory access pattern is constant in all stages, and the memory access is done in a round-robin fashion. This means that while one BRAM is being read, the other BRAM is being written, and vice versa. The only difference in the stages is the twiddle factor used in each BFU, which is read from the ROM. The complete architecture of the design is shown in Fig. 8, which can compute both NTT/iNTT.

3.4 Pipeline Architecture

To improve the performance of the design, we have used a pipelined architecture for the NTT/iNTT computation. The pipeline architecture is shown in Fig. 7. In each cycle, four blocks are working in parallel: (1) the data that is going to be used in the next stage cycle is fetched from one BRAM, (2) the data that is computed in the previous stage is written to the other BRAM, (3) in NTT: the data that is fetched in the previous cycle is multiplied by the TF, in iNTT: the addition/subtraction, in addition to multiplying by 2^{-1} (mod q) of two data that are fetched in the previous cycle are computed, and (4) in NTT: the addition/subtraction of one fetched data and the multiplication by TF in

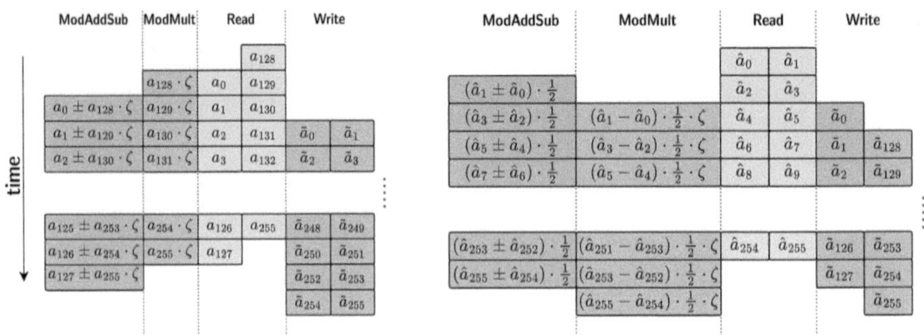

Fig. 7. Pipeline diagram for NTT (left) and iNTT (right).

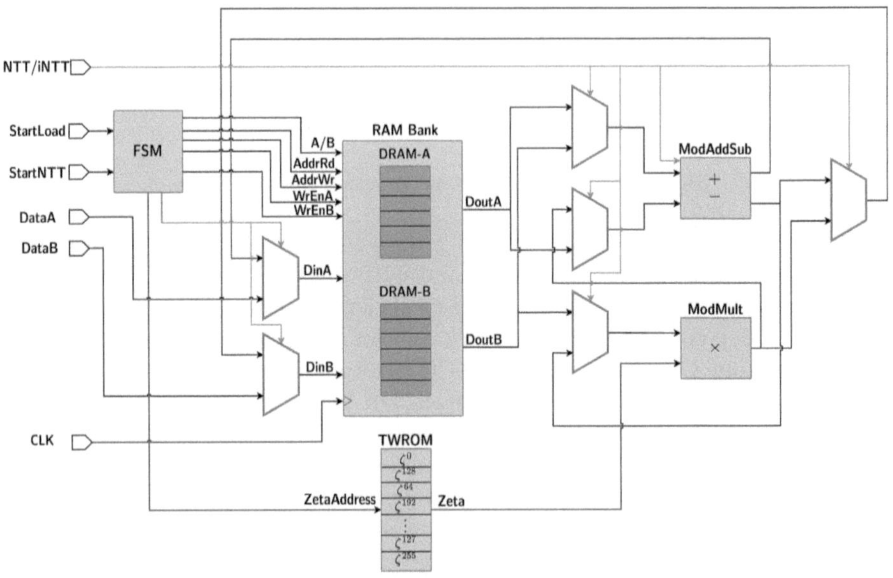

Fig. 8. Hardware architecture for NTT/iNTT computation.

the previous cycle is computed, in iNTT: the multiplication of one fetched data by 2^{-1} (mod q) and the subtraction result of the previous cycle is computed. The pipeline architecture is shown in Fig. 7, where the left side shows the NTT pipeline, and the right side shows the iNTT pipeline. As can be seen in this figure, in each cycle, four blocks are working in parallel, and they are all working on different data. This helps to improve the performance of the design, and compute the NTT/iNTT with only one BFU in the least amount of time. In the proposed architecture, considering 4 cycles for pipeline delay, the total clock cycles (CCs) for NTT/iNTT computation is $CCs = (\frac{n}{2} + 4) \cdot \log_2 n = 1056$.

4   Results and Discussion

The proposed lightweight NTT architecture was implemented on an Artix-7 XC7A100CSG324 FPGA using Vivado 2024.2 with default implementation settings. All pre-computations of Twiddle Factors (TFs) were performed in Python and subsequently stored in Read-Only Memory (ROM), tailored to the specific modular multiplier utilized. This section presents the performance and resource utilization of our design, alongside a comparative analysis with existing state-of-the-art (SOTA) implementations. Note that this architecture is designed for the ML-DSA scheme, which has a larger modulus than the ML-KEM scheme. As a result, the area utilization of the proposed design will be smaller in ML-KEM implementations.

Table 1 provides a detailed comparison of various modular reduction algorithms implemented within our NTT core framework. In this table, *Power* denotes to the dynamic power related to the NTT/iNTT converter using the mentioned modular multiplier. Note that the numbers in the table are related to the whole NTT/iNTT converter, not just the modular multiplier. The area utilization is measured in Look-Up Tables (LUTs), Flip-Flops (FFs), Digital Signal Processors (DSPs), and Block RAMs (BRAMs). The latency is measured in microseconds (μs) for a 1056-cycle NTT/iNTT computation, while the power consumption is measured in milliwatts (mW). The ATP formula used here is as follows [25]:

$$\text{ATP} = \frac{\text{LUT} + 0.5 \cdot \text{FF} + 250 \cdot \text{DSP} + 200 \cdot \text{BRAM}}{1000} \cdot \text{Latency}. \tag{8}$$

The results highlight discernible differences in resource utilization, latency, and power consumption across the evaluated multipliers. The Barrett reduction-based design utilizes 590 LUTs, 158 FFs, 2 DSPs, and 2.5 BRAMs, achieving a latency of 3.49μs and a power consumption of 77mW. The Montgomery-based multiplier shows a slightly higher LUT count (616) and a latency of 3.81μs, but consumes less power at 66mW. The Solinas Prime multiplier consumes more LUTs (692) with a latency of 3.77μs and power consumption of 74mW. The Plantard-based multiplier demonstrates the lowest LUT count (525) but requires an additional DSP and BRAM (3 DSPs, 3 BRAMs) due to the larger size of the scaled twiddle factors, resulting in a latency of 3.96μs and an ATP of 7.73. The K^2-RED algorithm, while competitive in LUTs (581), demands significantly more DSPs (7), leading to the highest latency of 4.11μs and the highest ATP of 11.96.

Based on the results, Barrett reduction emerges as the most efficient for our specific design goals, achieving the lowest ATP of 5.82. This favorable outcome for Barrett reduction is attributed to its balanced resource utilization, competitive latency, and the absence of scaling factors that would require pre-computation of adjusted TFs for the Pointwise Multiplication (PWM) phase, making it suitable for a unified multiplier design.

A broader comparison with other ML-DSA NTT implementations on FPGA is presented in Table 2. Our work, utilizing the Barrett modular multiplier,

Table 1. Area comparison of NTT/iNTT converter for ML-DSA utilizing different modular reduction algorithms in our design.

Modular Reduction	# LUTs	# FFs	# DSPs	# BRAMs	# CCs	Freq. (MHz)	Latency (μs)	Power (mW)	ATP
Barrett	590	158	2	2.5	1056	302	3.49	77	5.82
Montgomery	616	158	2	2.5		277	3.81	66	6.46
Solinas Prime	692	158	2	2.5		280	3.77	74	6.68
Plantard	525	158	3	3		266	3.96	62	7.73
K^2-RED	581	158	7	2.5		257	4.11	68	11.96

demonstrates compelling results in terms of resource efficiency, i.e., low resource utilization, yet fast enough. The design achieves a clock frequency of 300 MHz, resulting in a latency of 3.49μs for a 1056-cycle NTT/iNTT computation. Notably, our proposed architecture achieves an ATP of 5.82, which is the lowest among the compared implementations, even on higher-level FPGAs, and highly competitive overall. For instance, the work by Mandal et al. [14] on the same Artix-7 platform reports 690 LUTs, 771 FFs, 2 DSPs, and 2.5 BRAMs with a latency of 3.75μs and an ATP of 7.93. Land et al. [11], also on Artix-7, achieve a very low latency of 1.7μs but with significantly higher DSP usage (17 DSPs), leading to an ATP of 9.1. While designs on more advanced FPGAs like Zynq UltraScale+ (e.g., [10,27]) or Virtex UltraScale+ (e.g., [13]) may offer lower latencies or different resource trade-offs, our design distinguishes itself with its minimal resource footprint on a low-power device, making it particularly suitable for resource-constrained applications. The important aspect of a small design is that if the area usage is small enough, we can make the throughput higher simply by using multiple of these designs in parallel. For example, if we use 4 of these designs in parallel, we can achieve a throughput of 6.76 Gbps, which is very competitive with other designs.

$$\text{Throughput} = \frac{t \times n}{\text{Latency}} = \frac{23 \times 256}{3.48 \times 10^{-6}} = 1.69 \text{ Gbps}$$

In contrast, this is not true for a larger design, as the area utilization is already high, and we cannot make them smaller with lower throughput. As a result, a small design is not only suitable for a resource-constrained environment but also can be used in applications where high throughput is required, and we can use multiple of them in parallel to achieve higher throughput. The metrics for comparing this small design with larger designs to compare the throughput is the area-time product (ATP), and this design shows a 29% improvement in terms of ATP compared to the SOTA small designs.

The constant-geometry architecture and efficient pipeline design contribute significantly to these results, simplifying control logic and enabling high throughput with a single Butterfly Unit (BFU). The ping-pong memory architecture further ensures conflict-free memory access, sustaining the pipeline's efficiency.

Table 2. Area comparison of NTT implementations for ML-DSA on different FPGAs.

Paper	FPGA Platfrom	# LUTs	# FFs	# DSPs	# BRAMs	# CCs	Freq. (MHz)	Latency (μs)	ATP
[27]	ZUS+[1]	2287	1924	6	5	624	420	1.56	8.97
[15]	A7[2]	1302	571	9	3.5	1074	275	3.91	17.74
[13]	VUS+[3]	1601	699	10	5	603	142.8	4.22	23.00
[10]	ZUS+	3821	2970	20	5	258	322	0.80	9.06
[14]	A7	690	771	2	2.5	1024	273	3.75	7.93
[5]	V7[4]	1.2k	640	4	0	1034	246	4.2	10.59
[11]	A7	524	759	17	1	183	311	1.7	9.1
[18]	A7	13804	11019	0	0	64	163	0.39	7.53
This Work	A7	**590**	**158**	**2**	**2.5**	**1056**	**300**	**3.49**	**5.82**

1: Zynq UltraScale+
2: Artix-7
3: Virtex UltraScale+
4: Virtex-7

5   Conclusion and Future Work

This paper presented LightNTT, a lightweight and efficient NTT/iNTT hardware architecture tailored for ML-DSA, specifically targeting low-power and resource-constrained devices. By leveraging a constant-geometry dataflow, a deeply pipelined single butterfly unit, and an optimized Barrett modular multiplier, our design achieves a compelling balance between area, speed, and power consumption. Implemented on an Artix-7 FPGA, the proposed architecture utilizes only 590 LUTs, 158 FFs, 2 DSPs, and 2.5 BRAMs, while performing a full NTT/iNTT operation in $3.49\mu s$ at 300 MHz. The resulting ATP of 5.82 is highly competitive, particularly among implementations on similar FPGA families. The systematic comparison of different modular multiplication algorithms further validated the choice of Barrett reduction for achieving minimal ATP in our design context.

For future work, beginning with extensions related to performance and applicability. First, the compact nature of LightNTT makes it an ideal building block for high-throughput systems. As noted in our results, the design's small footprint allows for multiple cores to be instantiated in parallel. Future work could focus on implementing and evaluating a multi-core LightNTT architecture to quantify the throughput scaling and efficiency for server-side applications. Second, a promising direction is to evolve the architecture into a more flexible, parameterized core. While this work was optimized for ML-DSA, adapting the design to support other lattice-based schemes like ML-KEM, which use different parameters, would significantly broaden its applicability.

In addition to performance enhancements, investigating the security of the hardware is a critical next step. A primary concern for cryptographic hardware is its resilience against side-channel attacks (SCAs). The constant-geometry architecture used in LightNTT inherently provides a regular and predictable memory access pattern across all computation stages, which may offer some resistance to certain timing or memory-based SCAs. However, a thorough investigation is necessary to quantify this resilience and assess its security against power and electromagnetic analysis. Therefore, future security-focused research should involve implementing and testing countermeasures, such as masked modular arithmetic units or butterfly units resistant to differential power analysis (DPA), to create a hardened version of LightNTT for deployment in sensitive applications.

Acknowledgments. The authors are grateful to the reviewers for their time and feedback. This work is supported by NSF RINGS 214796.

References

1. Bisheh-Niasar, M., Azarderakhsh, R., Mozaffari-Kermani, M.: High-speed NTT-based polynomial multiplication accelerator for post-quantum cryptography. In: 2021 IEEE 28th Symposium on Computer Arithmetic (ARITH), pp. 94–101 (2021). https://doi.org/10.1109/ARITH51176.2021.00028
2. Can, F., Ustun, A., Ors, B., Alaybeyoglu, E., Savas, E.: Hardware implementation of K2RED and plantard modular multiplication algorithms in post-quantum cryptography. In: 2024 Panhellenic Conference on Electronics & Telecommunications (PACET), pp. 1–6 (2024). https://doi.org/10.1109/PACET60398.2024.10497033
3. Cooley, J.W., Tukey, J.W.: An algorithm for the machine calculation of complex Fourier series. Math. Comput. **19**(90), 297–301 (1965)
4. Du, G., Chen, Z., Li, Z., Wang, X., Zhang, D.: A low-latency polynomial multiplier accelerator for crystals-dilithium digital signature. In: Partin-Vaisband, I., Katkoori, S., Peng, L., Vaisband, B., Nikoubin, T. (eds.) Proceedings of the Great Lakes Symposium on VLSI 2024, GLSVLSI 2024, Clearwater, FL, USA, June 12-14, 2024, pp. 258–262. ACM (2024). https://doi.org/10.1145/3649476.3658794
5. Geng, Y., Hu, X., Li, M., Wang, Z.: Rethinking parallel memory access pattern in number theoretic transform design. IEEE Trans. Circuits Syst. II Express Briefs **70**(5), 1689–1693 (2023). https://doi.org/10.1109/TCSII.2023.3260811
6. Gentleman, W.M., Sande, G.: Fast Fourier transforms: for fun and profit. In: Proceedings of the November 7-10, 1966, Fall Joint Computer Conference. AFIPS Conference Proceedings, vol. 29, pp. 563–578. AFIPS / ACM / Spartan Books, Washington D.C. (1966). https://doi.org/10.1145/1464291.1464352
7. Greuet, A., Montoya, S., Vermeersch, C.: Quotient approximation modular reduction. In: 29th IEEE Symposium on Computer Arithmetic, ARITH 2022, Lyon, France, September 12-14, 2022, pp. 103–110. IEEE (2022). https://doi.org/10.1109/ARITH54963.2022.00028
8. Huang, J., et al.: Improved plantard arithmetic for lattice-based cryptography. IACR Trans. Cryptogr. Hardw. Embed. Syst. **2022**(4), 614–636 (2022). https://doi.org/10.46586/TCHES.V2022.I4.614-636
9. Kieu-Do-Nguyen, B., Binh, N.T., Pham-Quoc, C., Nghi, H.P., Tran, N., Hoang, T., Pham, C.: Compact and low-latency fpga-based number theoretic transform architecture for CRYSTALS kyber postquantum cryptography scheme. Inf. **15**(7), 400 (2024). https://doi.org/10.3390/INFO15070400
10. Kundi, D., Mera, J.M.B., Strub, P., Hutter, M.: High-performance NTT hardware accelerator to support ml-kem and ml-dsa. In: Proceedings of the 2024 Workshop on Attacks and Solutions in Hardware Security. pp. 100–105. ASHES '24, Association for Computing Machinery (2024). https://doi.org/10.1145/3689939.3695785

11. Land, G., Sasdrich, P., Güneysu, T.: A Hard Crystal - Implementing Dilithium on Reconfigurable Hardware, Lecture Notes in Computer Science, vol. 13173, pp. 210–230. Springer (2021). https://doi.org/10.1007/978-3-030-97348-3_12
12. Liang, Z., Zhao, Y.: Number theoretic transform and its applications in lattice-based cryptosystems: a survey (2022). https://doi.org/10.48550/ARXIV.2211.13546, https://doi.org/10.48550/arXiv.2211.13546
13. Malal, A.: Designing efficient and flexible NTT accelerators (2023). https://eprint.iacr.org/2023/1617
14. Mandal, S., Roy, D.B.: Kid: A hardware design framework targeting unified NTT multiplication for crystals-kyber and crystals-dilithium on fpga. In: 2024 37th International Conference on VLSI Design and 2024 23rd International Conference on Embedded Systems (VLSID), pp. 455–460. IEEE (2024). https://doi.org/10.1109/VLSID60093.2024.00082
15. Matteo, S.D., Sarno, I., Saponara, S.: Cryphtor: a memory-unified NTT-based hardware accelerator for post-quantum crystals algorithms. IEEE Access **12**, 25501–25511 (2024). https://doi.org/10.1109/ACCESS.2024.3367109
16. Miteloudi, K., Bos, J.W., Bronchain, O., Fay, B., Renes, J.: PQ.V.ALU.E: post-quantum RISC-V custom ALU extensions on dilithium and kyber. In: Bhasin, S., Roche, T. (eds.) Smart Card Research and Advanced Applications - 22nd International Conference, CARDIS 2023, Amsterdam, The Netherlands, November 14-16, 2023, Revised Selected Papers. Lecture Notes in Computer Science, vol. 14530, pp. 190–209. Springer (2023). https://doi.org/10.1007/978-3-031-54409-5_10
17. Montgomery, P.L.: Modular multiplication without trial division. Math. Comput. **44**, 519–521 (1985). https://api.semanticscholar.org/CorpusID:119574413
18. Nguyen, T.H., Kieu-Do-Nguyen, B., Pham, C.K., Hoang, T.T.: High-speed NTT accelerator for CRYSTAL-Kyber and CRYSTAL-Dilithium. IEEE Access **12**, 34918–34930 (2024). https://doi.org/10.1109/ACCESS.2024.3371581
19. NIST, F.: Module-lattice-based digital signature standard. National Institute of Standards and Technology (U.S.) (08 2024). https://doi.org/10.6028/nist.fips.204
20. NIST, F.: Module-lattice-based key-encapsulation mechanism standard. National Institute of Standards and Technology (U.S.) (08 2024). https://doi.org/10.6028/nist.fips.203
21. NIST, F.: Stateless Hash-Based Digital Signature Standard. National Institute of Standards and Technology (U.S.) (08 2024). https://doi.org/10.6028/NIST.FIPS.205
22. Özerk, Ö., Elgezen, C., Mert, A.C., Öztürk, E., Savaş, E.: Efficient number theoretic transform implementation on gpu for homomorphic encryption. J. Supercomput. **78**(2), 2840–2872 (2 2022). https://doi.org/10.1007/s11227-021-03980-5
23. Pease, M.C.: An adaptation of the fast Fourier transform for parallel processing. J. ACM **15**(2), 252–264 (Apr 1968). https://doi.org/10.1145/321450.321457
24. Plantard, T.: Efficient word size modular arithmetic. IEEE Trans. Emerg. Top. Comput. **9**(3), 1506–1518 (2021)
25. Sheet, S.F.D.: 7 Series fpgas Data Sheet: Overview. CA, USA, San Jose (2020)
26. Shor, P.W.: Algorithms for quantum computation: discrete logarithms and factoring. In: 35th Annual Symposium on Foundations of Computer Science, Santa Fe, New Mexico, USA, 20-22 November 1994, pp. 124–134. IEEE Computer Society (1994). https://doi.org/10.1109/SFCS.1994.365700
27. Shrivastava, R., Ratnala, C.P., Puli, D.M., Banerjee, U.: A unified hardware accelerator for fast Fourier transform and number theoretic transform. In: ICASSP 2025 - 2025 IEEE International Conference on Acoustics, Speech and Signal Processing (ICASSP), pp. 1–5 (2025). https://doi.org/10.1109/ICASSP49660.2025.10889132

28. Solinas, J.A.: Generalized mersenne prime. In: van Tilborg, H.C.A., Jajodia, S. (eds.) Encyclopedia of Cryptography and Security, 2nd Ed, pp. 509–510. Springer (2011). https://doi.org/10.1007/978-1-4419-5906-5_32
29. Taghavi, B., Azarderakhsh, R., Mozaffari Kermani, M.: ParallelNTT: Maximizing performance of forward and inverse NTT on FPGA for ML-DSA and ML-KEM. In: Proceedings of the Great Lakes Symposium on VLSI 2025, pp. 372–378. GLSVLSI '25 (2025). https://doi.org/10.1145/3716368.3735214

A Comparison of Unified Multiplier Designs for the FALCON Post-quantum Digital Signature
A Case Study of Baseline, Tiling, Comba and Karatsuba Approaches for FPGA and ASIC

Rahul Magesh$^{(\boxtimes)}$, Modini Ayyagari, Sharath Pendyala, and Aydin Aysu

HECTOR Research Lab, Department of Electrical and Computer Engineering, NC State University, Raleigh, USA
{rmagesh,mayyaga2,spendya,aaysu}@ncsu.edu

Abstract. This paper presents a comprehensive comparison of algorithmic-level design approaches for implementing unified multiplier hardware tailored for FALCON—an emerging post-quantum digital signature standard. A key requirement for FALCON is a 64-bit multiplier with a throughput of one multiplication per cycle that supports floating-point operations. While several multiplication techniques exist, their suitability depends on bit size, target technology, throughput, energy, and latency requirements. Our key novelty lies in conducting, for the first time, a systematic analysis and comparison of these techniques specifically for FALCON's multiplier needs across both FPGA (Virtex-7 Series Xilinx) and ASIC (SkyWater 130nm node) platforms. We evaluate four approaches: a baseline design without optimizations, an asymmetric Tiling approach optimized for FPGA multiplier block utilization, Comba, and the Karatsuba algorithm. Surprisingly, on FPGAs, Karatsuba achieves the highest area efficiency (19.2% smaller than the baseline) despite pipelining and more operations, while Tiling outperforms in energy efficiency (35.9% improvement). For ASICs, Karatsuba remains the most area-efficient, but Comba exhibits unexpected energy efficiency advantages (51.5% better than Karatsuba and 22.8% better than baseline). These findings represent the first direct comparison of these techniques under these conditions, providing designers with actionable insights for optimizing FALCON hardware for specific applications and technologies.

Keywords: 64-bit Multiplier, FALCON, FPGA, ASIC, Post-Quantum Cryptography, High-Throughput Arithmetic

1 Introduction

Capable of factorizing large integers within polynomial time, Shor's algorithm [1] when deployed on a quantum computer could compromise current public key cryptosystems that rely on the computational hardness of integer factorization

E. Savas et al. (Eds.): LightSec 2025, LNCS 16216, pp. 77–96, 2026.
https://doi.org/10.1007/978-3-032-15541-2_5

[2] and discrete logarithm problems [3]. This drives the pursuit of next-generation quantum-resilient cryptographic algorithms. FALCON (Fast Fourier Lattice-based Compact Signatures over NTRU) [4] is a candidate algorithm selected by the National Institute of Standards and Technology (NIST) for the post-quantum digital signature standard [5]. It is based on the hash-and-sign paradigm [6] and relies on the hardness of Ring-Short Integer Solution (SIS) [7] problem for quantum security. Compared to the other two NIST post-quantum digital signature standards [8,9], FALCON generates the smallest signatures making it suitable for resource-constrained systems.

Current hardware implementations of FALCON [10–15] identify the recursive Fast Fourier Sampling (`FFSampling`) subroutine, which uses 53-bit mantissa[1] multiplications, as the primary bottleneck due to its fixed execution order and limited scope for large-scale parallelization. Additionally, FALCON requires 64-bit integer multiplications for the `SamplerZ` subroutine. Since `FFSampling` subroutine follows a sequential execution order, these multiplications across various subroutines are not performed concurrently, thus enabling substantial hardware reuse through unified multipliers. Implementing the right **unified** multiplier fitting the design goals is thus critical.

This paper presents a comprehensive analysis and comparison of various algorithmic-level design approaches for implementing a **64-bit unified multiplier** for FALCON. Prior work [16,17] on multiplier implementations primarily focuses on larger operand sizes, typically ranging from 192 to 512 bits, aimed at accelerating homomorphic encryption [18]. These studies lack a detailed 64-bit metric comparison and **fail to meet one-multiplication-per-cycle requirement** of FALCON. While it is well established that algorithms like Karatsuba have a lower theoretical time complexity $(n^{1.58})$ than basic schoolbook multiplication splitting (n^2), the specific bit widths at which these algorithms become faster, more area efficient, or more energy friendly for FPGA or ASIC designs remain to be determined.

Table 1. Operation Summary Across Various Multiplication Algorithms

Operation Type	Baseline	Tiling	Comba	Karatsuba
Multiplication	1	12	16	10
Addition	0	11	15	11
Subtraction	0	0	0	18

Table 1 summarizes the operations of three 64-bit integer multiplication algorithms: Asymmetric Tiling [19], Comba [20], and Karatsuba [21], compared to a baseline multiplier. Determining the best algorithm for a specific technology

---

[1] The term "53-bit mantissa multiplication" refers to the straightforward integer multiplication aspect of the overall 64-bit floating-point multiplication. Further note that FALCON does not implement the full IEEE-754 floating point specification.

and design metric is challenging from the operation breakdown alone. In FPGAs, efficient implementations depend on operation mapping to DSP & LUT Slices. By contrast, ASIC technology allows more flexible designs based on design metrics and available arithmetic units. Additionally, pipelining strategies and design optimizations can significantly impact results in both FPGA and ASIC.

Despite the higher number of total operations, our results demonstrate that the Karatsuba algorithm is area-efficient on both FPGA and ASIC platforms. However, in average energy consumption per multiplication, Tiling outperforms others and achieves a 35.9% improvement in FPGAs, while Comba outperforms others and achieves a 22.8% improvement in ASICs compared to the baseline implementation.

These findings underscore the intricate balance of factors that highlight the non-trivial nature of implementing multipliers in hardware. In summary, the main contributions of this paper include:

- **Unified Multiplier for FALCON**:
  We propose a 64-bit unified hardware multiplier design for FALCON, efficiently handling both 53-bit mantissa multiplications in the `FFSampling` subroutine and 64-bit integer multiplications in the `SamplerZ` subroutine.
- **DSP-level FPGA Optimizations**:
  Our design optimizes FPGA performance by mapping the multipliers to DSP Slices and utilizing their **pre-adders, accumulators, and pipeline registers**, rather than LUTs and Registers. We also introduce algorithmic-level pipelining for both FPGA and ASIC to achieve **one-multiplication-per-cycle**, improving area and energy efficiency over previous designs.

- **In-Depth Multiplication Algorithm Comparison**:
  We provide a detailed comparison of **64-bit integer multiplication** algorithms (Baseline, Tiling, Comba, and Karatsuba) focused on **performance, power, and utilization**, offering valuable insights into hardware optimization for FALCON across both FPGA and ASIC platforms.

2 Related Works

Previous studies [16,17] on multiplier implementations have largely focused on larger operand sizes (192–512 bits) for cryptographic algorithms like elliptic curve cryptography (ECC) [22], and homomorphic encryption [18]. However, these studies lack a detailed comparison of design metrics for **64-bit integer** multipliers.

The study by [16] provides a graphical analysis of DSP and LUT utilization for 64-bit Karatsuba multiplication, while [17] presents only preliminary FPGA results for 64-bit Comba and Baseline multipliers, **without addressing the one-multiplication-per-cycle requirement of FALCON**. Furthermore, these studies omit critical metrics such as **latency and energy consumption**, which are necessary for optimizing 64-bit multipliers for FALCON hardware.

Furthermore, these works focus solely on FPGA implementations and **do not explore ASIC designs**. They also fail to consider FPGA DSP Slice features like **pipelining, pre-adders, and accumulators**, which can reduce LUT and register utilization. The role of algorithmic-level optimizations such as pipelining, which are vital for achieving one-multiplication-per-cycle, is not explored in the existing literature.

3   Background

This section provides an overview of the FALCON signature scheme, the `FFSampling` subroutine and its multiplication requirements, the applicability of our work to FALCON, various multiplication strategies, and the design methodologies adopted for FPGA and ASIC implementations.

3.1   FALCON Signature Scheme

Digital signature schemes are cryptographic mechanisms that ensure the authenticity, integrity, and non-repudiation of digital messages or documents. These schemes are widely used in secure communication protocols, such as SSL/TLS to prevent forgery and tampering.

FALCON (Fast Fourier Lattice-based Compact Signatures over NTRU) is a lattice-based digital signature scheme designed for post-quantum cryptography, offering resistance against attacks from quantum computers.

It comprises of three main processes which leverage the NTRU lattice [23] and rely on the Fast Fourier Transform (FFT) [24]: **key generation, signature generation,** and **signature verification**. FALCON is highly efficient for embedded systems and is designed to meet the small signature sizes of constrained applications. There exist two versions of **FALCON**:

- **FALCON-512** with an NTRU polynomial degree of 512, targeting **NIST Security Level I**.
- **FALCON-1024** with an NTRU polynomial degree of 1024, targeting **NIST Security Level V**.

Our proposed multiplier architecture is designed to support both variants.

3.2   FFSampling Overview

`FFSampling` is the principal computational subroutine invoked during signature generation in the FALCON digital signature scheme. It performs recursive lattice sampling over an NTRU lattice by traversing a binary tree of precomputed basis elements.

The algorithm primarily operates in the FFT domain and has two computational phases, each with distinct data characteristics and arithmetic behavior:

Algorithm 1. FFSAMPLING$_n(t, T)$

Require: $t = (t_0, t_1) \in \mathrm{FFT}\left((\mathbb{Q}[x]/(x^n + 1))^2\right)$, a FALCON tree T
Ensure: $z = (z_0, z_1) \in \mathrm{FFT}\left((\mathbb{Z}[x]/(x^n + 1))^2\right)$
1: *All polynomials are in FFT representation.*
2: **if** $n = 1$ **then**
3:     $\sigma' \leftarrow T.\text{value}$ $\triangleright$ It is always the case that $\sigma' \in [\sigma_{\min}, \sigma_{\max}]$
4:     $z_0 \leftarrow \texttt{SamplerZ}(t_0, \sigma')$ $\triangleright$ Base case: scalar sampling
5:     $z_1 \leftarrow \texttt{SamplerZ}(t_1, \sigma')$
6:     **return** $z = (z_0, z_1)$
7: **end if**
8: $(\ell, T_0, T_1) \leftarrow (T.\text{value}, T.\text{leftchild}, T.\text{rightchild})$
9: $(t_1, t_1') \leftarrow \texttt{splitfft}(t_1)$ $\triangleright$ Red: SPLIT
10: $z_1 \leftarrow \texttt{FFSampling}_{n/2}(t_1, T_1)$
11: $t_0 \leftarrow t_0 + (t_1 - z_1) \odot \ell$ $\triangleright$ MAC operation
12: $(t_0, t_0') \leftarrow \texttt{splitfft}(t_0)$
13: $z_0 \leftarrow \texttt{FFSampling}_{n/2}(t_0, T_0)$
14: $z \leftarrow \texttt{mergefft}(z_0, z_1)$ $\triangleright$ Black: MERGE
15: **return** $z = (z_0, z_1)$

---

1. **Phase 1: Recursive Tree Traversal (Lines 8–15 in Algorithm 1)**
   This phase initiates at the root of the binary sampling tree and continues until reaching the leaves. At each level, `FFSampling` recursively processes the left and right subtrees using polynomial inputs of decreasing size, halving the degree at each recursion level. Computationally, this phase consists primarily of FFT-based arithmetic operations such as `splitfft`, `mergefft`, and a multiply-accumulate (`MAC`) step involving the Gram-Schmidt orthogonalization coefficients. As a result, this phase is well-suited to vectorized/pipelined architectures at higher branches of the FALCON Tree.

2. **Phase 2: Base Case Discrete Sampling (Lines 2–8 in Algorithm 1)**
   Upon reaching the base of the tree (i.e., when the polynomial degree reduces to 1), the algorithm terminates the recursion and invokes `SamplerZ` to produce discrete Gaussian samples over the integers. Each coefficient of the target polynomial is individually sampled using integer arithmetic.

Phase 1 is characterized by operations on polynomial structures in the FFT domain with varying input sizes, whereas Phase 2 reduces the problem to discrete Gaussian sampling. The two phases exhibit fundamentally different computational behaviors: Phase 1 benefits from parallel FFT-friendly architectures, while Phase 2 can leverage scalar arithmetic units optimized for discrete sampling.

3.3   Fixed Sequence of `FFSampling`

The `FFSampling` algorithm is defined recursively, thus, its execution has a fixed, sequential order. This transformation is illustrated in Fig. 1, which shows the execution schedule for an input polynomial of degree 8. As we progress deeper into the FALCON tree—corresponding to smaller polynomial degrees—we observe an increasing number of FFSampling blocks.

This conversion reveals that the structure of the algorithm inherently prevents parallel execution across multiple blocks. This limitation is due to strict data dependencies, which enforce a top-down and bottom-up traversal pattern. These dependencies and their architectural implications are discussed in greater detail in the next subsection.

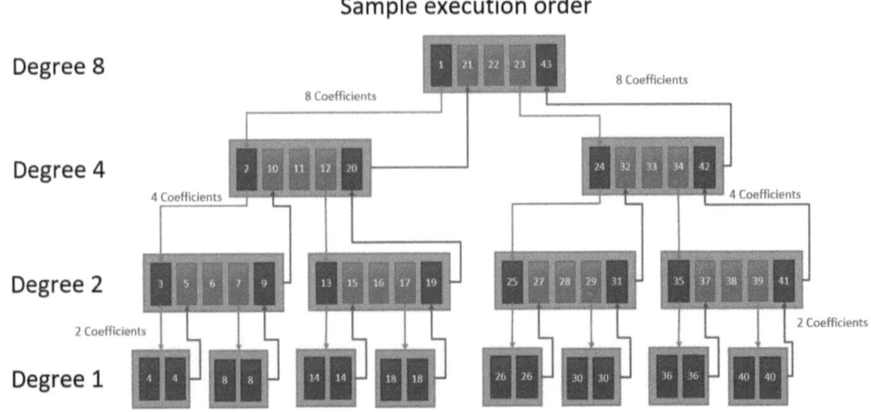

Fig. 1. Iterative execution order of FFSampling for a polynomial of degree 8.

3.4 Dataflow in FFSampling

Figure 2 illustrates the dataflow of FFSampling for an input polynomial of degree 8 (representative of the recursive pattern applied for actual degrees of 512 or 1024). A critical observation is that computations higher up in the FALCON tree hierarchy cannot be initiated until all dependent computations in the subtrees are complete.

As shown in Fig. 2, execution begins with a series of splitfft operations corresponding to Phase 1 (see Algorithm 1, Lines 8–10). These operations recursively divide the input polynomials until the base case (degree 1) is reached. At this point, Phase 2 begins, where two calls to SamplerZ are executed (Algorithm 1, Lines 2–5).

Once both samples are computed, the algorithm transitions back to Phase 1 to perform a mergefft and a multiply-accumulate (MAC) operation (Algorithm 1, Line 11). This completes one FFSampling block at degree 2. The process continues in this pattern until all nodes and branches of the FALCON tree have been evaluated.

This sequential traversal, governed by the data dependencies of the algorithm, enforces a strict computation order that is captured by the static schedule shown in Fig. 1.

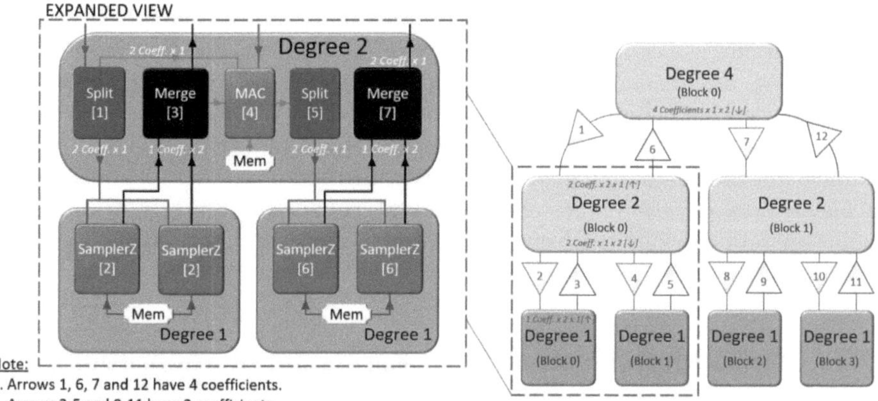

Note:
1. Arrows 1, 6, 7 and 12 have 4 coefficients.
2. Arrows 2-5 and 8-11 have 2 coefficients.
3. Red Lines represent data going down (i.e. input to lower degree block from higher degree block)
4. **Black** Lines represent data going up (i.e. **output** from lower degree block to higher degree block).
5. Mem contains the floating point value from the Falcon Tree **T**(Public Key) corresponding to each block.
6. Data Buswidth for the right figure is shown as *Size of Polynomial* x *No. of Polynomials* x *No. of Inputs/Outputs*
7. The Number N in [N] and inside arrows represents execution order.
8. Blocks with Degree > 1 have the same execution units

Fig. 2. Dataflow of `FFSampling` for an example input polynomial of degree 8.

3.5 Need for Unified Multipliers for FALCON

One key bottleneck in existing FALCON implementations [10–15] targeting resource-constrained systems is the aforementioned recursive `FFSampling` subroutine, which uses 53-bit mantissa multiplications. Additionally, FALCON requires 64-bit integer multiplications for the `SamplerZ` subroutine. Although the recursive nature of `FFSampling` can be transformed into an iterative form [25] as explained in Figs. 1 and 2, the fixed execution order across varying polynomial sizes limits large-scale parallelization. As such, improving throughput at the operation level becomes essential.

Crucially, the floating-point multiplications of `FFSampling` and the integer multiplications of `SamplerZ` are not executed concurrently due to FALCON's inherently serial structure. **This enables the reuse of a single high-throughput multiplier across both subroutines.** While our focus is on signature generation, similar reuse potential exists during the key-generation phase due to its FFT-based operations.

3.6 Applicability of This Work to FALCON

FALCON's signature generation requires traversing a binary tree (the FALCON Tree which is a part of the Public Key) composed of branches and leaves. At the branches, FALCON performs FFT-based polynomial multiplications across a range of degrees—512 for NIST Security Level I, 1024 for Level V, recursively down to 2—while at the leaves, the operations primarily involve integer multiplications. The number and size of these operations vary with the depth of the tree (i.e., polynomial size), making throughput optimization a critical design consideration.

A naïve design may allocate multiple dedicated multipliers to handle the required workload, but this increases area and power consumption with significant underutilization at lower branches (degrees). Instead, our approach emphasizes the design of a high-throughput, **unified** multiplier architecture that achieves area efficiency through **temporal reuse**. Importantly, the floating-point operations along the branches and integer operations at the nodes do not execute in parallel, making this reuse strategy particularly effective.

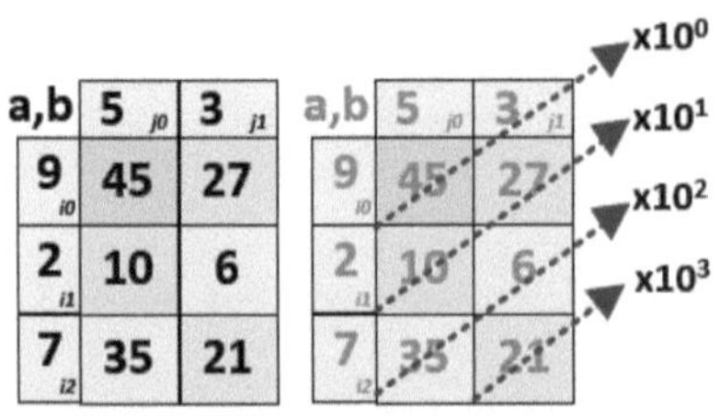

Fig. 3. Example for Multiplication Algorithm, A = 729 and B = 35: Comba multiplication (left) uses a matrix of partial products arranged diagonally, summed with shifts indicated by the arrows to yield the final product. 2-Split Karatsuba multiplication (right) splits the numbers into two parts (at the tens place) for efficient computation.

3.7   Multiplication Strategies

This subsection outlines state-of-the-art algorithms for integer multiplication while excluding techniques like Number Theoretic Transforms (NTT) [26] and Montgomery multiplication [27], as these are specifically designed for modular rather than integer multiplication.

Karatsuba multiplication, utilized in this study, can be considered a special case of the more general Toom-Cook algorithm [28], employing a split factor of 2. Higher split factors of Toom-Cook are excluded due to their increased computational complexity [17], which stems from operations that are inefficient for hardware implementation, such as division. These characteristics make Toom-Cook unsuitable for efficient 64-bit multiplication hardware.

Our designs include the following multiplication strategies:

1. **SchoolBook Multiplication:** Schoolbook multiplication is the traditional method where each digit of one number is multiplied by each digit of the other, with intermediate results shifted and added to produce the final product. We refer to this as the baseline multiplication.

2. **Comba Multiplication:** Comba is an optimized algorithm for multiplying multi-digit numbers, ideal for computer arithmetic [20]. Unlike traditional schoolbook multiplication, which processes digits sequentially, Comba organizes the computation into a matrix-like structure, as shown in Fig. 3. Summing partial products along diagonals with appropriate shifts enhances efficiency by reducing intermediate carry operations. Consider two n-digit numbers A and B, where A is represented as $A = \sum_{i=0}^{n-1} a_i \times 10^i$ and B as $B = \sum_{j=0}^{n-1} b_j \times 10^j$. Using Comba, the product $C = A \times B$ is described by Eq. 1.

$$C = \sum_{i=0}^{n-1}\sum_{j=0}^{n-1} (a_i \times b_j) \times 10^{i+j} \tag{1}$$

Eq. 1 depicts the following steps:

(a) Each digit of A is multiplied with each digit of B, and results are assigned positional weights based on the sum $i + j$.

(b) Products with the same total exponent $i + j$ are grouped along diagonals in a conceptual matrix.

(c) Intermediate carries are managed locally within each diagonal, improving accumulation efficiency.

(d) This layout allows better pipelining and register reuse in hardware implementations.

3. **Karatsuba Algorithm:** Karatsuba multiplication [29] is an efficient algorithm for multiplying large numbers. It reduces the complexity of multiplying two n-digit numbers from the traditional $O(n^2)$ to $O(n^{\log_2 3}) \approx O(n^{1.585})$, making it particularly useful for large numbers. The algorithm employs a divide-and-conquer strategy, splitting the two n-digit numbers A and B into smaller parts. For conceptual explanation, consider the 2-split approach: let $A = A_1 \cdot 10^m + A_0$ and $B = B_1 \cdot 10^m + B_0$, where m is approximately $n/2$. The product $C = A \times B$ is then represented as a sum of partial products as shown in Eq. 2 [30]. Figure 3 highlights the advantage of the Karatsuba algorithm, which requires only 3 multiplications compared to 6 in the Schoolbook method. However, this comes at the cost of 4 additions in Karatsuba versus just 1 in the Schoolbook method.

$$C = P_1 \times 10^{2m} + (P_3 - P_1 - P_2) \times 10^m + P_2 \tag{2}$$

$$P_1 = A_1 \times B_1 \quad ; \quad P_2 = A_0 \times B_0 \tag{3}$$

$$P_3 = (A_1 + A_0) \times (B_1 + B_0) \tag{4}$$

Eqs. 2-4 depict the following steps:

(a) Inputs A and B are split into high and low parts, each of roughly half the original length.

(b) Three key multiplications are performed: P_1, P_2, and P_3 as shown.
(c) The cross-term $(P_3 - P_1 - P_2)$ efficiently computes the middle coefficient.
(d) The final result is constructed from these three terms using appropriate powers of ten.
(e) Recursive application of this strategy enables further reductions in total multiplication count for large operands.

3.8 Hardware Implementation Methodologies

1. **ASIC Methodology:** For the ASIC implementation, we used the SkyWater 130nm Process Development Kit (PDK) [31] and leveraged the OpenLane methodology [32] on the Efabless ChipIgnite platform. We selected this platform due to the maturity of the SKY130A process node and the open-source nature of the PDK and OpenLane flow.
2. **FGPA Methodology:** We synthesized and implemented our designs for Xilinx Virtex-7 series FPGA XQ7VX980T-2L, which supports the DSP48E1 Slice [33], since this variant allows comparison alongside prior work [17]. The DSP48E1 features an asymmetrical 25×18-bit signed multiplier and supports pre-adder, accumulator, and pipelining functionalities. The recombination of partial products and summations in the multiplication algorithms can be mapped to pre-adders and accumulators to reduce FPGA LUT utilization. Additionally, the DSP Slices can be configured to include pipelining to achieve higher operating frequencies (up to 650MHz on XQ7VX980T-2L compared to 267.81Mhz for its single-cycle implementation [34]).

4 Hardware Design

Our optimized designs use bit-splitting on input operands, which are then recombined to yield the final product. This requires conversion to unsigned operands at the input stage, sign propagation at intermediate stages, and signed conversion at the final stage. These conversions are not needed in the baseline multiplier because the synthesis tool handles them automatically.

4.1 Baseline Multiplier

The Baseline Multiplier implementation directly infers multiplication in existing FALCON architectures using the '*' operator as interpreted by the synthesis tool for the platform (Xilinx Vivado for FPGAs and Yosys for ASICs). In FPGA, it is auto-mapped to DSP Slices (DSP48E1 for ZQ7VX980T-2L) by Vivado, configured for single-cycle latency. Vivado implements this 64-bit multiplication across 16 DSPs in single-cycle mode. However, this straightforward design does not fully leverage the capabilities and speed of the DSPs.

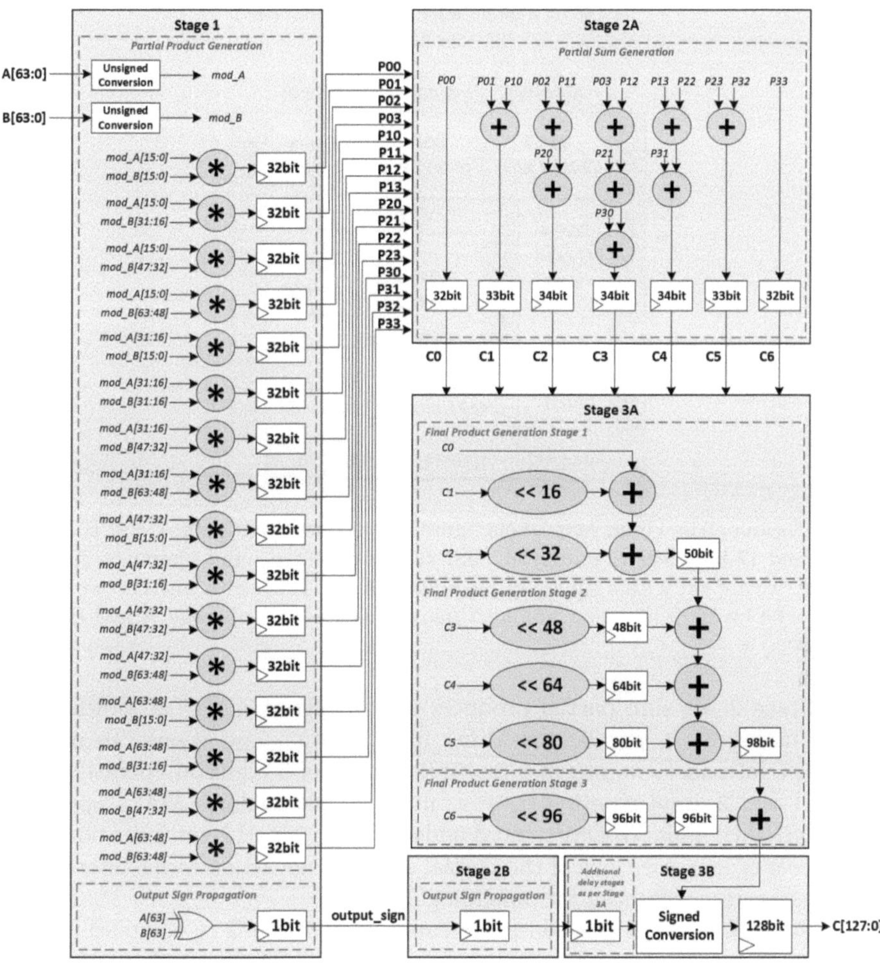

Fig. 4. Block Diagram for 3-Stage Pipeline Comba Multiplier: Stage 1 generates partial products from 16-bit input slices, Stage 2 adds partial products with the same shift, and Stage 3 shifts and adds these sums to produce the final result.

4.2   Comba Multiplier

Figure 4 illustrates the 3-stage pipelined implementation of our Comba Multiplier. In Stage 1, we divide the inputs into 16-bit slices, producing 16 partial products (32-bit unsigned). The choice of 16-bit slices ensures symmetric bit splitting, which aligns with the signed 25×18-bit input operand widths of the DSP48E1.

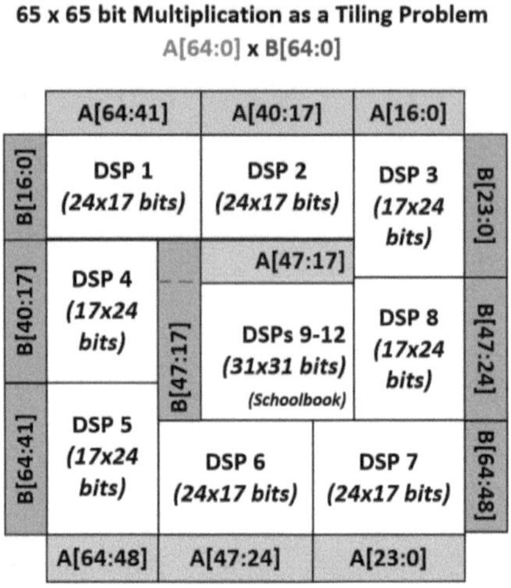

65 x 65 bit Multiplication as a Tiling Problem
A[64:0] x B[64:0]

	A[64:41]	A[40:17]	A[16:0]	
B[16:0]	DSP 1 (24x17 bits)	DSP 2 (24x17 bits)	DSP 3 (17x24 bits)	B[23:0]
B[40:17]	DSP 4 (17x24 bits)	A[47:17] / DSPs 9-12 (31x31 bits) (Schoolbook) B[47:17]	DSP 8 (17x24 bits)	B[47:24]
B[64:41]	DSP 5 (17x24 bits)	DSP 6 (24x17 bits)	DSP 7 (24x17 bits)	B[64:48]
	A[64:48]	A[47:24]	A[23:0]	

Fig. 5. Asymmetric Tiling Map. This figure shows how the inputs A and B are split into 24 and 17-bit slices to match the DSP48E1's expected input operands. After this mapping, we are left with a square in the middle of size 31*31 bits. Further, we perform only 64×64 bit multiplication leaving 1 unused bit for each operand A and B.

In Stage 2, we sum partial products with identical shifts (as shown by the arrows in Fig. 3) in parallel, resulting in 9 addition operations. To optimize FPGA performance, we merge 6 multiplication and 3 addition operations from Stages 1 and 2, implementing them as multiply-accumulate (MAC) operations using DSP48E1 units (6 DSPs and 3 adders). However, this optimization comes at the cost of increased size of the partial sums. Stage 2B performs intermediate sign propagation, essential for pipelining.

In Stage 3, we shift and add partial sums from Stage 2 to compute the final product. Due to carries exceeding 1 bit, each adder in Stage 3A, except the first, requires an additional adder, totaling 11 adders. This reflects a known limitation of the Comba algorithm. Optionally, Stage 3A can be configured with additional pipeline stages between each adder to achieve higher clock frequencies. In particular, our implementation uses 2 such pipeline stages. Finally, we perform unsigned to signed conversion in Stage 3B.

4.3 Asymmetric Tiling Multiplier

Given the asymmetric input operand widths supported by Xilinx's DSP48E1 i.e. signed 25×18-bit or unsigned 24×17-bit multiplications—we designed a high-throughput asymmetric tiling multiplier that maximizes DSP utilization. Our design follows the tiling methodology outlined in [19], which decomposes larger multiplications into smaller operand slices.

Figure 5 illustrates the tiling strategy applied to a 65-bit operand. Specifically, the operand is split into two 24-bit segments and one 17-bit segment,

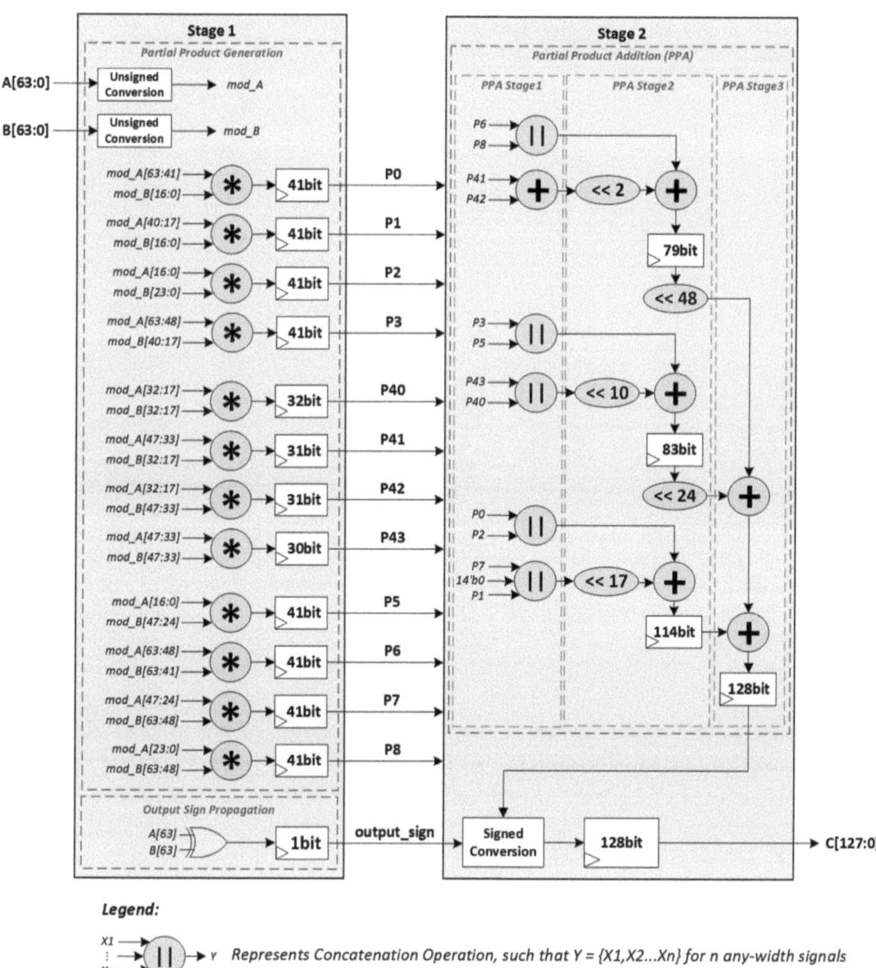

Fig. 6. Block Diagram for 2-Stage Pipeline Asymmetric Tiling Multiplier: Stage 1 generates partial products from asymmetric input slices, Stage 2 shifts and adds these sums to produce the final result.

satisfying the relationship $65 = 2 \times 24 + 17$. This decomposition allows the primary multiplication region to be covered using eight DSP blocks operating at full utilization. However, this tiling leaves a 31-bit square region in the center of the operand space, computed as $65 - 2 \times 17$, which does not map directly to the available DSP operand widths.

To efficiently compute this residual 31-bit region, we employ a Comba-style multiplication scheme implemented using four additional DSP blocks. The resulting architecture is depicted in Fig. 6, which shows the datapath of the full multiplier.

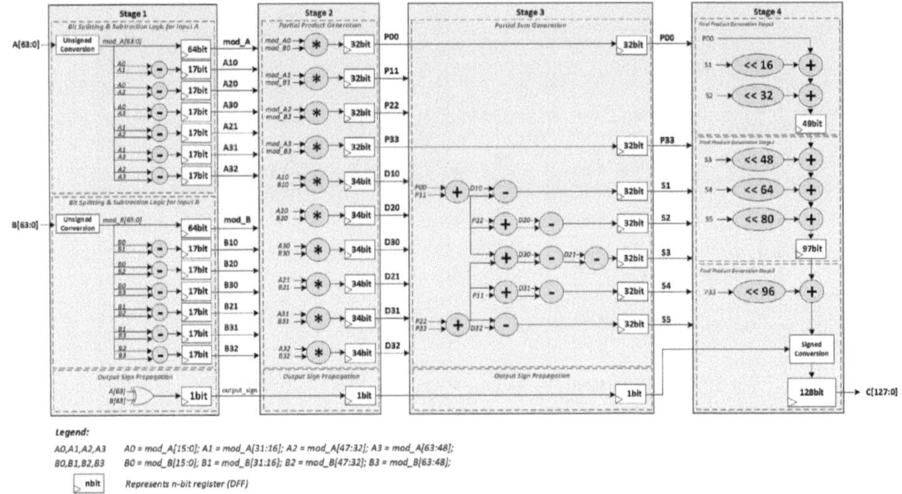

Fig. 7. Block Diagram for 4-Stage Pipeline 4-Split Karatsuba Multiplier: Stage 1 splits the input into 16-bit slices and performs the pre-subtractions, Stage 2 computes the partial products, Stages 3 and 4 handle the partial product additions and final product generation.

In Stage 1, the input operands are partitioned into asymmetric tiles corresponding to the DSP input widths, and each tile pair is processed independently to generate a total of 12 partial products. Among these, eight originate from the fully utilized tiling (P0–P3 and P5–P8), while four additional partial products (P40–P43) are derived from the Comba-based region. These partial results are then passed to Stage 2, where they are aligned and summed.

Stage 2 follows a structure similar to Schoolbook multiplication: the partial products are bit-shifted according to their respective positions and summed to produce the final product. To increase clock frequencies, Stage 2 can be configured with additional pipeline stages between each adder stage. In our design, we incorporated 4 extra pipeline stages.

4.4 Karatsuba Multiplier

In the Karatsuba multiplication algorithm, input operands are recursively divided using binary partitioning. However, too many partitions can increase addition operations, diminishing area and latency benefits, especially for small operand sizes, where the overhead from additional additions can outweigh the reduction in multiplication complexity.

A 4-way split is optimal for 64-bit multiplicands because it aligns with the DSP48E1 slice's asymmetric input size of 24×17 bits. Since symmetric multiplication requires multiplicands to fit within 17-bit widths, splitting into 4 parts approximates 16 bits per operand, ensuring efficient DSP resource utilization. Figure 7 depicts our 4-stage pipelined implementation of the multiplier. This

Table 2. FPGA QoR Comparison Across Multiplier Designs

Metric Category	Baseline	Tiling	Comba	Karatsuba
DSP	16	12	16	10
LUT	146	593	667	797
Registers	102	986	1555	1132
Area Cost[a]	1687.65	1500.3	1999.53	1364.75
Frequency *(MHz)*	142.8	300	300	300
Highest Logic Delay *(ns)*	5.508	2.099	2.289	2.18
Worst Negative Slack *(ns)*	0.011	0.146	0.251	0.114
Static Power *(mW)*	0.37	0.37	0.37	0.37
Dynamic Power *(mW)*	0.134	0.308	0.336	0.319
Avg. Energy per Mul. *(pJ)*	3.529	2.26	2.353	2.297
Latency *(#cycles)*	1	7	13	9
Throughput *(#cycles)*	1	1	1	1
Maximum frequency *(MHz)*	142.8	335	365	317
Throughput *(Million IOPs)*[b]	142.8	335	365	317

[a] The "Area Cost" calculation, as described in Eq. 5, is based on [34], which states that 1 FPGA Slice contains 4 LUTs and 8 Regs, and [35], which provides the conversion of a single DSP to an equivalent number of slices.
[b] Throughput (Million IOPs) of all the designs are equal to their Maximum frequency in MHz as their throughputs are 1 mult. per cycle

design achieves **one-multiplication-per-cycle** and improves upon the implementation presented in [21]. In Stage 1, we split the inputs into 16-bit segments and perform pre-subtractions (12 subtractions in total). In Stage 2, we compute the partial products through 10 multiplication operations. For FPGA implementation, we optimized resource utilization by moving 6 pre-subtractions (B10-B32) from Stage 1 to Stage 2, taking advantage of the pre-adder capabilities of the DSP48E1 Slices. Consequently, Stage 2 contains 4 unsigned multiplications (P00-P33) and 6 signed multiplications with pre-subtractions (D10-D32).

Stage 3 (5 additions and 6 subtractions) and Stage 4 (6 additions) handle the partial product summation and final product generation. Unlike the Comba multiplier, we do not use the DSP48E1 units for MAC operations in this design, as both the multiplication and MAC outputs are required within the same clock cycle. Similar to other multiplier architectures, additional pipeline stages can be added to the final stage to achieve higher clock frequencies.

5 Results

This section presents the post-implementation results of the multiplier designs described in Section III. The goal is to evaluate each design's performance independently on FPGA and ASIC platforms, avoiding direct comparisons between the two. The designs were synthesized for the Virtex-7 Series FPGA (28nm) and the SkyWater 130nm node (SKY130), representing the FPGA and ASIC implementations, respectively.

5.1 FPGA Results

Table 2 presents post-implementation utilization and power reports for our multiplier designs, synthesized using Xilinx Vivado v2023.2. These results are evaluated at 300MHz clock to standardize the Area Cost metric. While the synthesis tool adjusts LUTs and registers for higher frequencies, the **DSP count remains fixed**, dictated by the algorithm's partial product requirements.

$$\text{Area Cost} = \left(\frac{\text{LUTs}}{4} + \frac{\text{Registers}}{8}\right) + (\text{DSPs} \times 102.4) \tag{5}$$

- **Resource Utilization: Karatsuba** has the lowest overall area cost of 1364.75, which is about 19.2% lower than the baseline. Despite using the most LUTs (797) compared to Comba (667), Tiling (593), and Baseline (146), it achieves the reduced area cost by using fewer DSPs (10).
- **Performance** Pipelined implementations of Karatsuba, Comba, and Tiling outperform Baseline by 112.8% or greater due to better usage of the DSP48E1. We observe that **Comba** is the fastest (365 MHz) at the cost of the highest resource utilization. The improved throughput over baseline comes at the cost of added latency, which is acceptable due to the large number of multiplications expected in the design of FALCON-centric Hardware.
- **Power and Energy Efficiency:** The **Tiling** multiplier exhibits the highest energy efficiency, consuming 36% less energy per multiplication compared to the Baseline. However, all pipelined implementations show comparable energy efficiency, with only variance of 4%. In terms of dynamic power, the **Baseline** design is the most efficient largely due to its lower clock frequency. It is important to note that the power reports in Table 2 are based on activity estimates from Xilinx Vivado and not gate-level power analysis.

5.2 ASIC Results

Table 3 presents the comparison of the quality of results (QoR) for our various multiplier designs, evaluated across different PVT (Process, Voltage, Temperature) corners (TT: 1.8V, 25° C; SS: 1.6V, 100° C; FF: 1.95V, -40° C) at 75 MHz clock. Additionally, based on maximum operating frequency analysis, our pipelined multiplier designs meet timing requirements up to 120 MHz.

- **Resource Utilization: Karatsuba** is the most area-efficient design achieving 11.3% improvement against Baseline. Despite the highest register utilization, it achieves a reduced area due to better optimizations inferred by the synthesis tool from its pipelined design, compared to the Baseline multiplier. Additionally, it benefits from smaller combinatorial logic between pipeline stages compared to other pipelined designs.

Table 3. ASIC QoR Comparison Across Multiplier Designs

Metric Category	Baseline	Tiling	Comba	Karatsuba
Synthesis Area (mm^2)	229.11	259.51	231.50	203.17
GC *(Kgates)*	36.62	41.48	37.01	32.47
Registers	257	1236	1232	1281
Total Power *(mW)*	57.4	48.3	44.3	91.4
Worst Setup Slack *(ns)*	1.17	1.42	1.14	2.12
Worst Hold Slack *(ns)*	1.03	0.46	0.47	0.11
Latency *(#cycles)*	1	4	5	6
Throughput *(#cycles)*	1	1	1	1

- **Performance** We observed that the **Karatsuba** design exhibited the highest setup slack, indicating its potential to operate at the highest frequency among all evaluated designs. The pipelined implementations of Karatsuba, Tiling, and Multiplier successfully operated till 120 MHz, while the Baseline design encountered timing violations at the same frequency due to routing congestion.
- **Power and Energy Efficiency:** The **Comba** multiplier demonstrated unexpected power efficiency, achieving a 22.8% improvement over the Baseline. Surprisingly, despite its area-efficiency, **Karatsuba** consumed the most power, primarily due to switching power in the combinational logic, particularly from subtraction in Stage 1 and signed multiplication in Stage 2. Additionally, its higher register utilization further increased power consumption. These unexpected results highlight that, for energy-constrained systems, the Comba multiplier is the optimal choice, offering a 51.5% lower average power consumption than Karatsuba.

5.3 FPGA Results Discussion

On FPGA, we exploit the architectural features of DSP48E1 slices by aligning operand slices with their asymmetric input widths (unsigned 24×17), and leverage built-in pre-adders, post-adders, and pipeline registers. This DSP-aware mapping enables 64-bit multiplications to be distributed across multiple DSPs, achieving high throughput while also reducing overall area consumption. All proposed methods provide a notable improvement in throughput (up to 2.56x) compared to the baseline single-cycle latency multiplier, which is anticipated due to the suboptimal utilization of the DSP48E1 block in its unpipelined configuration (limited to a theoretical maximum of 267.81 MHz [34])

Among the designs, **Karatsuba achieves the lowest area cost** (1364.75), due to using the lowest number of DSPs (10). **Comba achieves the highest frequency** (365 MHz), benefiting from a balanced summation tree and fine-grained pipelining. **Tiling demonstrates the best energy efficiency** (2.26

pJ), by paralleling small segments mapped neatly to the DSP blocks, resulting in minimized switching activity per operation.

5.4 ASIC Results Discussion

The same multiplier designs were synthesized for an ASIC platform to evaluate their portability and efficiency in a standard-cell context. Despite the absence of dedicated multiplier blocks, our pipeline-centric architecture translated effectively to ASIC providing algorithmic perspective.

Karatsuba achieved the smallest area $(203.17\,\mathrm{mm}^2)$ across all designs, reaffirming its efficiency due to its reduced number of full-width multipliers. However, this came at the cost of higher dynamic power (91.4 mW), attributed to higher switching activity from subtraction and signed arithmetic in its partial summation stages.

In contrast, **Comba exhibited the best power efficiency**, reducing power by 22.8% compared to the baseline. Its structured partial-product accumulation resulted in balanced load and minimal logic transitions per stage. **Tiling**, which performed well on FPGA due to DSP-aware mapping, showed limited advantage on ASIC, as its reliance on mapping to asymmetric multiplier units increased area and switching power.

6 Conclusion

This paper evaluates four multiplier architectures—Baseline, Tiling, Comba, and Karatsuba—tailored for FALCON, a post-quantum digital signature scheme. The results demonstrate that the 4-split Karatsuba multiplier is the most area-efficient across both FPGA and ASIC platforms, while the Tiling approach provides the best energy efficiency for FPGA designs. Comba delivers superior energy efficiency for ASIC implementations.

The study also incorporates FPGA-specific architectural optimizations, such as efficient DSP utilization and pipelining, which improve performance and energy efficiency. These findings provide valuable insights for optimizing FALCON hardware for different design goals, offering designers guidance on selecting the appropriate multiplier architecture based on the target platform's requirements.

Acknowledgements. This paper is supported in part by the National Science Foundation (NSF) Award No. 2350142.

References

1. Shor, P.W.: Polynomial-Time algorithms for prime factorization and discrete logarithms on a quantum computer. SIAM J. Comput. **26**(5), 1484–1509 (1997). https://doi.org/10.1137/S0097539795293172

2. Rivest, R.L., Shamir, A., Adleman, L.: A method for obtaining digital signatures and public-key cryptosystems. Commun. ACM **21**(2), 120–126 (1978). https://doi.org/10.1145/359340.359342
3. Diffie, W., Hellman, M.: New directions in cryptography. IEEE Trans. Inf. Theor. **22**(6), 644–654 (1976). https://ieeexplore.ieee.org/document/1055638
4. Fouque, P.A., et al.: Falcon: Fast-Fourier Lattice-based Compact Signatures over NTRU.
5. I. T. L. Computer Security Division, "Post-Quantum Cryptography | CSRC | CSRC," (2017). https://csrc.nist.gov/projects/post-quantum-cryptography
6. National Institute of Standards and Technology (NIST), "SHA-3 Standard: Permutation-Based Hash and Extendable-Output Functions," U.S. Department of Commerce. Technical report. FIPS PUB 202, August 2015. https://doi.org/10.6028/NIST.FIPS.202
7. Ajtai, M.: Generating hard instances of lattice problems (extended abstract) In: Proceedings of the twenty-eighth annual ACM symposium on Theory of Computing, ser. STOC '96. New York, NY, USA: Association for Computing Machinery, pp. 99–108 (1996). https://doi.org/10.1145/237814.237838
8. Bos, J.P.B., et al.: CRYSTALS-Dilithium: Algorithm Specifications and Supporting Documentation (Round 3 Submission) (2022). https://csrc.nist.gov/projects/post-quantum-cryptography/round-3-submissions, Accessed 22 Sep 2024
9. Bernstein, D., et al.: SPHINCS+: Submission to the NIST Post-Quantum Cryptography Standardization Project (Round 3) (2022). https://csrc.nist.gov/projects/post-quantum-cryptography/round-3-submissions, Accessed 22 Sep 2024
10. Karabulut, E., Aysu, A.: A hardware-software co-design for the discrete gaussian sampling of FALCON digital signature. In: 2024 IEEE International Symposium on Hardware Oriented Security and Trust (HOST) (2024). https://ieeexplore.ieee.org/document/10545399/
11. Kim, Y., Song, J., Seo, S.C.: Accelerating Falcon on ARMv8. IEEE Access **10**, 44 446–44 460 (2022). https://ieeexplore.ieee.org/document/9762260
12. Lee, Y., et al.: An efficient hardware/software co-design for FALCON on low-end embedded systems. IEEE Access **12**, 57 947–57 958 (2024). https://ieeexplore.ieee.org/document/10496572
13. Schmid, M., Amiet, D., Wendler, J., Zbinden, P., Wei, T.: Falcon Takes Off - A Hardware Implementation of the Falcon Signature Scheme IACR Cryptol. ePrint Arch. (2023). https://www.semanticscholar.org/paper/Falcon-Takes-Off-A-Hardware-
14. Yu, X., Sun, Y., Zhao, Y., Kuang, H., Han, J.: RVCE-FAL: A RISC-V Scalar-vector custom extension for faster FALCON digital signature. In: 2024 Design, Automation and Test in Europe Conference and Exhibition (DATE), pp. 1–6 (2024) iSSN: 1558-1101. https://ieeexplore.ieee.org/document/10546713
15. Qiu, J., Aysu, A.: SHIFT SNARE: uncovering secret keys in FALCON via single-trace analysis. Cryptology ePrint Archive, Paper 2025/146, (2025). https://eprint.iacr.org/2025/146
16. Ustun, E., San, I., Yin, J., Yu, C., Zhang, Z.: IMpress: large integer multiplication expression rewriting for FPGA HLS. In: 2022 IEEE 30th Annual International Symposium on Field-Programmable Custom Computing Machines (FCCM), pp. 1–10. New York City, NY, USA: IEEE (2022). https://ieeexplore.ieee.org/document/9786123/
17. Rafferty, C., O'Neill, M., Hanley, N.: Evaluation of Large Integer Multiplication Methods on Hardware. In: IEEE Transactions on Computers, vol. 66, no. 8, pp. 1369–1382 (2017). https://ieeexplore.ieee.org/document/7869256/

18. Gentry, C.: Fully homomorphic encryption using ideal lattices. In: Proceedings of the forty-first annual ACM symposium on Theory of computing, ser. STOC '09, pp. 169–178. New York, NY, USA: Association for Computing Machinery (2009). https://doi.org/10.1145/1536414.1536440

19. Roy, D.B., Mukhopadhyay, D., Izumi, M., Takahashi, J.: Tile before multiplication: an efficient strategy to optimize DSP multiplier for accelerating prime field ECC for NIST curves. In: Proceedings of the 51st Annual Design Automation Conference, pp. 1–6. San Francisco CA USA: ACM (2014). https://doi.org/10.1145/2593069.2593234

20. Comba, P.G.: Exponentiation cryptosystems on the IBM PC. IBM Syst. J. **29**(4), 526–538 (1990). https://ieeexplore.ieee.org/document/5387492

21. Khan, S., Javeed, K., Shah, Y.A.: High-speed FPGA implementation of full-word Montgomery multiplier for ECC applications. Microprocess. Microsyst. **62**, 91–101 (2018). https://www.sciencedirect.com/science/article/pii/S0141933117302843

22. Miller, V.S.: Use of elliptic curves in cryptography. In: Advances in Cryptology – CRYPTO '85, pp. 417–426. Springer (1986)

23. Hoffstein, J., Pipher, J., Silverman, J.H.: NTRU: a ring-based public key cryptosystem. In: Buhler, J.P. (ed.) ANTS 1998. LNCS, vol. 1423, pp. 267–288. Springer, Heidelberg (1998). https://doi.org/10.1007/BFb0054868

24. Ducas, L., Prest, T.: Fast Fourier Orthogonalization. In: Proceedings of the 2016 ACM International Symposium on Symbolic and Algebraic Computation, ser. ISSAC '16, pp. 191–198. New York, NY, USA: Association for Computing Machinery (2016). https://doi.org/10.1145/2930889.2930923

25. Lee, W.K., Zhao, R.K., Steinfeld, R., Sakzad, A., Hwang, S.O.: High throughput lattice-based signatures on GPUs: comparing Falcon and Mitaka. IEEE Trans. Parallel Distrib. Syst. **35**(4), 675–692 (2024). https://ieeexplore.ieee.org/document/10440463

26. Schönhage, A., Strassen, V.: Schnelle multiplikation großer zahlen. Computing **7**(3–4), 281–292 (1971)

27. Montgomery, P.L.: Modular multiplication without trial division. Math. Comput. **44**(170), 519–521 (1985)

28. Toom, A.: The complexity of multiplication. Sib. Math. J. **4**, 214–216 (1963)

29. Karatsuba, A., Ofman, Y.: Multiplication of multidigit numbers on automata. Soviet Physics Doklady, vol. 7, pp. 595–596 (1963) originally published in Russian in 1962

30. Karatsuba algorithm for fast multiplication using Divide and Conquer algorithm section: Divide and Conquer (2013). https://www.geeksforgeeks.org/karatsuba-algorithm-for-fast-multiplication-using-

31. Skywater SKY130 PDK documentation. https://skywater-pdk.readthedocs.io/en/main/index.html

32. Shalan, M., Edwards, T.: Building OpenLANE: a 130nm openroad-based tapeout-proven flow: invited paper. In: IEEE/ACM International Conference On Computer Aided Design (ICCAD), pp. 1–6 (2020)

33. 7 Series DSP48E1 Slice User Guide (UG479) (2018)

34. 7 Series FPGAs Data Sheet: Overview (DS180) (2020)

35. Tu, Y., He, P., Koç, K., Xie, J.: LEAP: Lightweight and efficient accelerator for sparse polynomial multiplication of HQC. IEEE Trans. Very Large Scale Integr. (VLSI) Syst. **31**(6) 892–896 (2023). https://ieeexplore.ieee.org/document/10068178/

An Optimized FrodoKEM Implementation on Reconfigurable Hardware

Giuseppe Manzoni[1(✉)] [iD], Shekoufeh Neisarian[1] [iD], and Elif Bilge Kavun[1,2] [iD]

[1] Barkhausen Institut, Schweriner Straße 1, 01067 Dresden, Germany
{giuseppe.manzoni,shekoufeh.neisarian,elif.kavun}@barkhauseninstitut.org,
elif_bilge.kavun@tu-dresden.de
[2] TU Dresden, Nöthnitzer Straße 46, 01187 Dresden, Germany

Abstract. FrodoKEM is a Post-Quantum (PQ) Key Encapsulation Mechanism (KEM) built on the Learning with Errors (LWE) problem. Unlike other lattice-based approaches, it avoids using structured lattices to enhance its resilience against attacks. FrodoKEM is selected as a Round 3 alternate candidate in the US National Institute of Standards and Technology (NIST) Post-Quantum Cryptography (PQC) Standardization competition, recommended/accepted by several information security agencies in the world, and currently being reviewed for adoption by the International Organization for Standardization (ISO), which calls for efficient real-world implementations of the algorithm. This paper introduces an optimized Field Programmable Gate Array (FPGA)-based architecture for FrodoKEM that achieves up to a factor of 3.5 reduction in resource utilization compared to existing studies, eliminates the need for Digital Signal Processing (DSP) blocks in FPGA implementations, reduces the number of required BRAMs, and delivers up to 9.7 times the throughput. The architecture benefits from parallelization, which results in faster performance, and it integrates key generation, encapsulation, and decapsulation into a single unified implementation that supports all three parameter sets; FrodoKEM-640, FrodoKEM-976, and FrodoKEM-1344.

Keywords: Post-Quantum Cryptography (PQC) · Lattice-based · FrodoKEM · Multiplication · Reconfigurable Hardware · Field Programmable Gate Array (FPGA)

1 Introduction

Public-key cryptography relies heavily on mathematical problems such as factoring large integers or computing discrete logarithms, which are computationally difficult to solve in a reasonable time using classical computers [14]. The security of conventional cryptographic algorithms is fundamentally based on the assumption that these problems remain unsolvable. However, the emergence of quantum computers threatens this assumption. With their ability to solve certain problems, such as factoring in polynomial time, quantum computers pose a

E. Savas et al. (Eds.): LightSec 2025, LNCS 16216, pp. 97–113, 2026.
https://doi.org/10.1007/978-3-032-15541-2_6

significant risk to the security of traditional cryptographic systems [15,16]. This breakthrough would allow attackers to break public-key encryption schemes and compute secret keys. Since the arrival of quantum computers is inevitable, new ways of securing data are necessary.

This has led agencies and scientists all over the world to invest in research projects to prevent quantum computers from becoming a threat to the data that are currently transmitted on conventional computers [11]. The developments for this are grouped under the term Post-Quantum Cryptography (PQC) [10]. The goal of PQC is to develop systems that are secure on normal computers and quantum computers while simultaneously working on existing communication protocols and networks [12]. Since the mathematical problems of discrete logarithm and integer factorization can be feasibly broken by quantum computers, other problem classes have to be used as a means of achieving security. Some examples currently being researched are code-based cryptography, lattice-based cryptography, and hash-based cryptography [4].

To standardize PQC algorithms, the US National Institute of Standards and Technology (NIST) started its PQC project in February 2016 [13]. In addition to NIST, there are other national institutions that recommend different PQC algorithms to achieve security. Although not solely focused on the task of PQC, the German Federal Office for Information Security (BSI), without influencing the NIST process, gives its recommendation on algorithms to use to secure against quantum attacks. While the standardized algorithms presented by NIST are also part of the BSI's recommendations, their exact recommendations differ. BSI has published its own recommendations for cryptographic mechanisms in the 2024 technical guideline, called "Cryptographic Mechanisms: Recommendations and Key Lengths" [3]. In this guideline, BSI outlines recommendations in several areas, including asymmetric encryption schemes and key agreement, symmetric encryption schemes, hash functions, data authentication, instance authentication, random number generators, and secret sharing. Even though PQC is not the only focus of the guideline, it includes recommendations for PQC algorithms and emphasizes the importance of starting the migration process as early as possible. Although no specific evaluation criteria are provided for PQC algorithms, the guideline sets a minimum security level of 120 bits as the basis for its recommendations.

FrodoKEM [1] is the first Key Encapsulation Mechanism (KEM) recommended by BSI. It is based on the Learning with Errors (LWE) problem using unstructured grids. Similarly to Module-LWE (ML)-KEM, this LWE problem is utilized to construct a Public-Key Encryption (PKE) scheme, with the FujisakiâĂŞOkamoto (FO) transform applied to ensure Indistinguishability under Chosen-Ciphertext Attack (IND-CCA) security. FrodoKEM is considered the more conservative option, as unstructured grids are generally better understood than modules [1]. While NIST decided not to standardize FrodoKEM due to ML-KEM being more efficient, the BSI recommends using FrodoKEM with the parameter sets FrodoKEM-976 and FrodoKEM-1344. This recommendation reflects BSI's preference for schemes with fewer algebraic assumptions and a stronger security margin, particularly for long-term security use cases. These parameter sets correspond to security levels 3 and 5 of the NIST security levels, respectively, and result in the private key size, public key size, and signature size as shown in Table 1.

Table 1. Resulting key and signature sizes for the different parameter sets for FrodoKEM [1]

Parameter Set	Private Key Size	Public Key Size	Ciphertext Size	Security Level
FrodoKEM-640	19888	9616	9752	1
FrodoKEM-976	31296	15632	15792	3
FrodoKEM-1344	43088	21520	21696	5

The contributions of the paper are as follows.[1]

- We developed an optimized FPGA-based architecture for FrodoKEM, a BSI-recommended Post-Quantum (PQ) PKE scheme.
- Our architecture eliminates the need for Digital Signal Processing (DSP) units by utilizing Look-Up Tables (LUTs) for $16\times$ 5-bit multiplications to avoid the inefficiencies of DSP blocks that are typically designed for $25\times$ 18-bit operations. As we only use a fraction of DSPs' full capabilities, they would be under-utilized resources. If the FrodoKEM module is used as part of a larger design, we would leave the DSPs free to be utilized by another module that needs their full capabilities. Additionally, not all FPGAs have the same number of DSPs; for instance, some FPGAs, such as Lattice Semiconductor's iCE40, do not include DSPs at all. Furthermore, DSPs are large and area-consuming units that could be better utilized for other purposes or saved to reduce costs by opting for a more affordable FPGA.
- Our implementation benefits from 32-way parallel multiplication, which enhances the speed of matrix operations.
- A unified architecture is designed that combines key generation, encapsulation, and decapsulation, to simplify integration and reduce design overhead. This module can simultaneously configure all three functions, with shared resources such as the Keccak module, multiplier, and BRAMs.

This paper is organized as follows. Section 2 provides a detailed overview of FrodoKEM and FPGAs. Section 3 reviews related work in the literature. Section 4 details the optimized architecture and its implementation in FPGAs. Section 5 presents the results. Finally, Sect. 6 concludes the paper with a summary of the findings.

---

[1] It's possible to find the verilog implementation described in this paper at https://github.com/bi-tud-sds/lightsec_25_frodokem.

2   Background

This section presents details of the lattice-based FrodoKEM scheme and introduces reconfigurable hardware specifics.

2.1   FrodoKEM

FrodoKEM [1] is a lattice-based PQC algorithm based on the LWE problem. Unlike other schemes of this type, FrodoKEM avoids using structured lattices, which provides a more conservative security against quantum attacks, as FrodoKEM will remain secure even if there is a new cryptanalytic development against more structured lattices. The scheme is designed to provide different levels of security, in line with the standards set by NIST for PQC: FrodoKEM-640 offers a level of security similar to AES-128, FrodoKEM-976 provides security comparable to AES-192, and FrodoKEM-1344 has a security level similar to AES-256 [1]. Key generation, encapsulation, and decapsulation are presented in Algorithm 1, Algorithm 2, and Algorithm 3, respectively. The key generation function outputs the keypair $(pk, sk) = (seed_A \parallel b, s \parallel seed_A \parallel b \parallel S^T \parallel pkh)$. The Encapsulation takes as input a public key $pk = seed_A \parallel b$ and outputs a ciphertext $c = c_1 \parallel c_2 \parallel salt$ and a shared secret ss. The decapsulation function takes as input a ciphertext $c = c_1 \parallel c_2 \parallel salt$ and a secret key $sk = s \parallel seed_A \parallel b \parallel S^T \parallel pkh$, and outputs a shared secret ss. A key component in all three algorithms is the generation of the pseudorandom matrix $A \in \mathbb{Z}_q^{n \times n}$. As FrodoKEM avoids algebraic structures, it requires larger matrices, which makes directly storing and transmitting the public matrix A inefficient and resource-heavy. To solve this problem, a seed is included in the key pair and used to generate matrix A at the beginning of each algorithm execution. The function $\mathtt{Gen}(seed_A)$ is used to generate this matrix from a seed s of length l_A, which can be derived using either AES-128 or SHAKE-128. AES-128 is typically preferred for software-based implementations, while SHAKE-128 is more efficient and thus commonly used in hardware. It also employs the function $\mathtt{SampleMatrix}$ to obtain a matrix in $\mathbb{Z}_q^{n \times \bar{n}}$ whose values have a quantized Gaussian sampling distribution, using a pseudorandom array of 16-bit integers r, one per element of the matrix [1].

2.2   Field Programmable Gate Arrays (FPGAs)

FPGAs are reprogrammable logic devices that combine hardware performance with software flexibility. These electronic circuits, composed of an array of programmable logic gates, can be dynamically reshaped to perform various tasks, which distinguishes them from conventional computer chips, which have static functionality. To configure these devices, hardware description languages, such as Verilog, VHDL, or SystemVerilog, are used. These languages allow for the precise definition and implementation of digital circuits by specifying the interactions and functions of the logic gates within the FPGA. Furthermore, design

---

Algorithm 1. Key Generation for FrodoKEM

1: **Input:** None (the random seeds $s, seed_{SE}, z$ are chosen internally)

2: **Output:** Public key $pk = (seed_A \parallel b)$, Secret key $sk = (s \parallel seed_A \parallel b \parallel S^T \parallel pkh)$

3: Choose uniformly random seeds $s, seed_{SE}$ and z with bit lengths $len_{sec}, len_{SE}, len_A$ (respectively)

4: Generate pseudorandom seed $seed_A \leftarrow \text{SHAKE}(z, len_A)$

5: Generate matrix $A \leftarrow \text{Gen}(seed_A)$

6: Generate bit string $(r^{(0)}, r^{(1)}, \ldots, r^{(2n\bar{n}-1)}) \leftarrow \text{SHAKE}(0x5F \parallel seed_{SE}, 32n\bar{n})$

7: Sample error matrix $S^T \leftarrow \text{SampleMatrix}((r^{(0)}, r^{(1)}, \ldots, r^{(n\bar{n}-1)}), \bar{n}, n)$

8: Sample error matrix $E \leftarrow \text{SampleMatrix}((r^{(n\bar{n})}, r^{(n\bar{n}+1)}, \ldots, r^{(2n\bar{n}-1)}), n, \bar{n})$

9: Compute $B \leftarrow A \cdot S + E$

10: Compute $b \leftarrow \text{Pack}(B)$

11: Compute $pkh \leftarrow \text{SHAKE}(seed_A \parallel b, len_{sec})$

12: **Return:** Public key $pk = seed_A \parallel b$, Secret key $sk = s \parallel seed_A \parallel b \parallel S^T \parallel pkh$

Note: The matrix S^T is encoded row-by-row from $S_{0,0}^T$ to $S_{\bar{n}-1,n-1}^T$, where each matrix coefficient $S_{i,j}^T$ is a signed integer encoded as a 15 or 16-bit string in little-endian byte order. The encoding of $S_{i,j}^T$ is given by:

$$(s_0, s_1, \ldots, s_{15}) \leftarrow S_{i,j}^T = -s_{15} \cdot 2^{15} + \sum_{k=0}^{14} s_k \cdot 2^k$$

Algorithm 2. Encapsulation for FrodoKEM

1: **Input:** Public key $pk = seed_A \parallel b$

2: **Output:** Ciphertext $c = c_1 \parallel c_2 \parallel salt$, Shared secret ss

3: Choose uniformly random values u and $salt$ with bit lengths len_{sec} and len_{salt} (respectively)

4: Compute $pkh \leftarrow \text{SHAKE}(pk, len_{sec})$

5: Generate values $seed_{SE} \parallel k \leftarrow \text{SHAKE}(pkh \parallel u \parallel salt, len_{SE} + len_{sec})$

6: Generate $(r^{(0)}, r^{(1)}, \ldots, r^{(2\bar{n}n+\bar{n}^2-1)}) \leftarrow \text{SHAKE}(0x96 \parallel seed_{SE}, 16(2\bar{n}n + \bar{n}^2))$

7: Sample error matrix $S' \leftarrow \text{SampleMatrix}((r^{(0)}, r^{(1)}, \ldots, r^{(n\bar{n}-1)}), \bar{n}, n)$

8: Sample error matrix $E' \leftarrow \text{SampleMatrix}((r^{(n\bar{n})}, r^{(n\bar{n}+1)}, \ldots, r^{(2n\bar{n}-1)}), \bar{n}, n)$

9: Generate the matrix $A \leftarrow \text{Gen}(seed_A)$

10: Compute $B' \leftarrow S' \cdot A + E'$

11: Compute $c_1 \leftarrow \text{Pack}(B')$

12: Sample error matrix $E'' \leftarrow \text{SampleMatrix}((r^{(2\bar{n}n)}, r^{(2\bar{n}n+1)}, \ldots, r^{(2\bar{n}n+\bar{n}^2-1)}), \bar{n}, \bar{n})$

13: Compute $B \leftarrow \text{Unpack}(b, n, \bar{n})$

14: Compute $V \leftarrow S' \cdot B + E''$

15: Compute $C \leftarrow V + \text{Encode}(u)$

16: Compute $c_2 \leftarrow \text{Pack}(C)$

17: Compute $ss \leftarrow \text{SHAKE}(c_1 \parallel c_2 \parallel salt \parallel k, len_{sec})$

18: **Return:** Ciphertext $c = c_1 \parallel c_2 \parallel salt$, Shared secret ss

---

tools/suites accompanying FPGAs offer software that is used to design and program FPGA tasks sequentially.

Algorithm 3. Decapsulation for FrodoKEM

1: **Input:** Ciphertext $c = c_1 \parallel c_2 \parallel salt$, Secret key $sk = s \parallel seed_A \parallel b \parallel S^T \parallel pkh$
2: **Output:** Shared secret ss
3: Compute $B' \leftarrow \text{Unpack}(c_1, \bar{n}, n)$
4: Compute $C \leftarrow \text{Unpack}(c_2, \bar{n}, \bar{n})$
5: Compute $M \leftarrow C - B' \cdot S$
6: Compute $u' \leftarrow \text{Decode}(M)$
7: Generate values $seed'_{SE} \parallel k' \leftarrow \text{SHAKE}(pkh \parallel u' \parallel salt, len_{SE} + len_{sec})$
8: Generate $(r^{(0)}, r^{(1)}, \ldots, r^{(2\bar{n}n + \bar{n}^2 - 1)}) \leftarrow \text{SHAKE}(0x96 \parallel seed'_{SE}, 16(2\bar{n}n + \bar{n}^2))$
9: Sample error matrix $S' \leftarrow \text{SampleMatrix}((r^{(0)}, r^{(1)}, \ldots, r^{(n\bar{n}-1)}), \bar{n}, n)$
10: Sample error matrix $E' \leftarrow \text{SampleMatrix}((r^{(n\bar{n})}, r^{(n\bar{n}+1)}, \ldots, r^{(2n\bar{n}-1)}), \bar{n}, n)$
11: Generate the matrix $A \leftarrow \text{Gen}(seed_A)$
12: Compute $B'' \leftarrow S' \cdot A + E'$
13: Sample error matrix $E'' \leftarrow \text{SampleMatrix}((r^{(2\bar{n}n)}, r^{(2\bar{n}n+1)}, \ldots, r^{(2\bar{n}n + \bar{n}^2 - 1)}), \bar{n}, \bar{n})$
14: Compute $B \leftarrow \text{Unpack}(b, n, \bar{n})$
15: Compute $V \leftarrow S' \cdot B + E''$
16: Compute $C' \leftarrow V + \text{Encode}(u')$
17: (**In constant time**) $\bar{k} \leftarrow k'$ if $B' \parallel C = B'' \parallel C'$ else $k' \leftarrow s$
18: Compute $ss \leftarrow \text{SHAKE}(c_1 \parallel c_2 \parallel salt \parallel \bar{k}, len_{sec})$
19: **Return:** Shared secret ss

Their reprogrammable nature allows FPGAs to adapt to different tasks without replacement, which makes them different from Application-Specific Integrated Circuits (ASICs), which are designed for specific purposes. Inside an FPGA, there is a grid-like structure comprised of Configurable Logic Blocks (CLBs). These CLBs contain basic building blocks, such as Lookup Tables (LUTs), Multiplexors (MUXs), Full Adders (FAs), and D-Flip Flops (D-FFs). They can be thought as individual puzzle pieces that can be rearranged to create different circuits. The interconnections between these blocks enable communication and cooperation.

LUTs are employed in FPGAs as an alternative to conventional logic gates. LUTs serve as highly configurable, programmable memory units capable of executing a wide range of logical functions. In particular, FPGAs such as Zynq UltraScale+ and Artix-7 typically support configurations with either five input bits and two output bits or six input bits and one output bit [2]. Each LUT can be programmed to store a truth table, mapping each of the $2^5 = 32$ input combinations to one of the $2^2 = 4$ possible output states in a 5-input, 2-output configuration. This capability enables a LUT to implement up to 4^{32} different functions based on various input and output configurations. The architecture of an LUT comprises memory cells equal to 2^n, where n is the number of inputs. The exponential growth in memory capacity as the number of inputs increases generally limits practical FPGA applications to LUTs with two to five inputs. These configurations allow FPGAs to handle significantly more complex digital designs using fewer resources. In addition, LUTs can be interconnected to create small blocks of Random Access Memory (RAM) and execute complex functions or algorithms, which highlights their essential role in supporting customizable digital circuits within FPGAs.

FPGAs also feature Input-Output (I/O) blocks that act as gateways for signals entering and exiting the FPGA. Additionally, there are Fixed Functional Logic Blocks (FFLBs) like multipliers or Digital Signal Processing (DSP) blocks, as well as Block Random Access Memory (BRAM) for data storage. BRAMs are distinct components within FPGAs, separate from the individual LUTs that are typically used for logic operations. Unlike LUTs, BRAMs serve as dedicated memory blocks designed to store large amounts of data. This includes read-only data, temporary data, and data read from external devices. DSPs are more resource-intensive than LUTs and consume more power and area, especially for simple logic tasks. Additionally, LUTs are better in parallel designs, whereas DSPs are optimized for specific tasks and may not handle parallelism as effectively.

3   Related Work

Several works have explored FrodoKEM from both hardware and software perspectives, each with distinct trade-offs in performance, area, and design strategy. The first hardware implementation of FrodoKEM was introduced by Howe et al. [8], targeting the FrodoKEM-640 and FrodoKEM-976 parameter sets. Although it demonstrated the feasibility of hardware acceleration for lattice-based cryptography, the design was limited in terms of parallelism and resource efficiency. A subsequent hardware implementation was proposed by Howe et al. [7], also focusing on FrodoKEM-640 and 976. However, this design used Trivium to generate the large matrix A instead of the SHAKE128 or AES functions recommended by NIST. This deviation from the standard FrodoKEM specification reduces the comparability and applicability of the implementation in standardized settings.

Gu et al. [6] accelerated FrodoKEM on the Zynq Ultrascale+ FPGA platform by proposing a new architecture for the SHAKE128 function. They designed a high-throughput SHA-3 structure by optimizing combinational logic calculations and utilizing pipelining techniques, but the different FPGA platform makes it difficult to compare with existing results.

In the software domain, the work from Fiho et al. [5] investigated matrix multiplication optimizations and introduced strategies similar to the AMX accelerator found in Apple processors. Notably, our Mode 2 multiplier architecture closely aligns with the approach described in this work, although we implement it fully on hardware instead of using an accelerator.

4   Implementation

This section describes the architecture of our implementation, which integrates all three key generation, encapsulation, and decapsulation of FrodoKEM into a single module. First, we detail the sub-modules responsible for data handling, followed by those that manage command processing. Finally, we discuss general design considerations and optimization techniques.

4.1 Data Modules

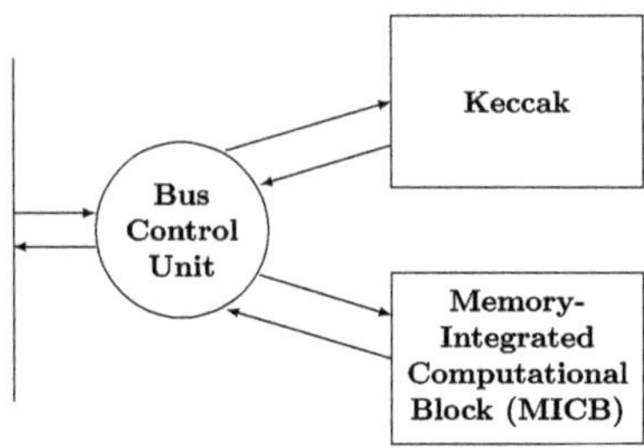

Fig. 1. High-level design architecture.

From a high-level perspective, the architecture consists of two primary sub-modules: the `Keccak` module, which handles the SHAKE128 and SHAKE256 computations, and the `Memory-Integrated Computational Block (MICB)` module, which stores the remaining variables and performs all other necessary operations. Each of these sub-modules interfaces with the peripherals through two ports, one for input and one for output. The connections between the sub-modules and the peripherals are managed by a `Bus Control Unit`, as illustrated in Fig. 1.

The ports have 64-bit data wires for unidirectional data transmission. Additionally, there is a `canReceive` wire, which operates in the opposite direction of the data and indicates whether the destination port is capable of receiving data. An `isReady` wire signals when data has been sent, and it can only be set if the `canReceive` wire is also active. Furthermore, a `isLast` wire is used to specify whether the current element is the final item in the data stream. This `isLast` wire may be driven either by the data source or the destination, with the goal of minimizing the need for additional counters and reducing the size of the control buses. With the exception of the `isLast` wire, this is the same port that our implementation uses to communicate with the peripherals. For these two ports, the `isLast` wire is managed by two small sub-modules located between the peripherals and the `Bus Control Unit`.

The `Bus Control Unit` is responsible for connecting three pairs of ports and routing the data between them, and it supports one multicast communication at a time. The unit uses the `isLast` wire of the ports to determine when a data flow has ended and when it can schedule a new connection between a set of ports.

Keccak Module. As shown in Fig. 2, the `Keccak` module can be divided into three parts: the `Keccak Core` module, which performs the main operation; the

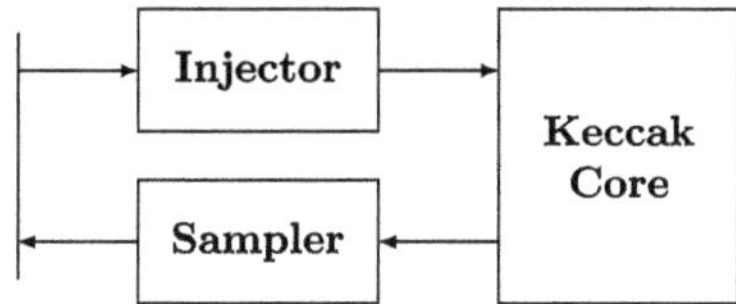

Fig. 2. Architecture of the `Keccak` module.

`Sampler` module, which optionally performs FrodoKEM's sampling on the output received from the `Keccak Core`; and the `Injector` module, which can inject into the data fed into the `Keccak Core` either an arbitrary number of 64-bit zeros, an arbitrary byte, or the $Seed_A$, which it stores internally. To allow sending bytes, the input port of the `Keccak Core` includes an additional `isByte` wire, which differentiates between 8-bit and 64-bit values.

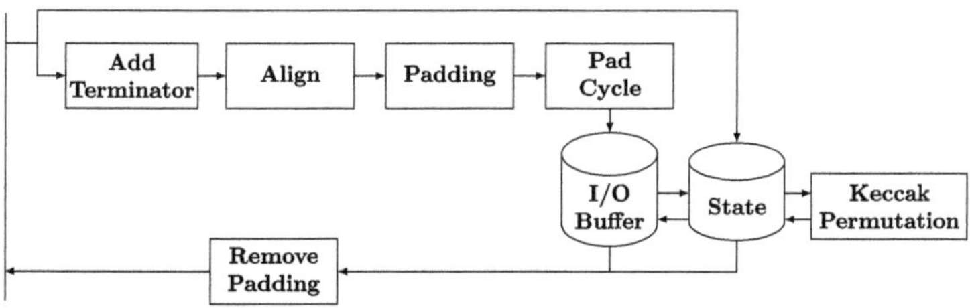

Fig. 3. Architecture of the `Keccak Core` module.

In Fig. 3, the structure of the `Keccak Core` is shown. This module can perform both the SHAKE128 and SHAKE256 operations, with the option to save and load the internal state. The `State` is implemented as a circular buffer, allowing for state I/O, and is used by the `Keccak Permutation` module every clock cycle to perform one round of the Keccak permutation on the 1600-bit state. Each round takes one clock cycle, and a total of 24 cycles are required to complete the full permutation. Additionally, the module includes a `I/O buffer`, which is another circular buffer for a 1344-bit value, corresponding to the data rate of SHAKE128. This buffer is kept separate from the `State` because reading and writing the I/O of the SHAKE128 function with a 64-bit bus takes 21 clock cycles. Keeping the buffers separate allows the Keccak permutation to be applied while the I/O operations are ongoing. The input to the `I/O buffer` is processed in multiple stages. First, the `Add Terminator` module appends the $0x1F$ SHAKE terminator at the end of the input (indicated by the `isLast` wire), by injecting a single byte into the bus and delaying the `isLast` signal. The `Align` bus converts the 8-bit or 64-bit bus into a 64-bit-only bus. The `Padding` module applies the Keccak padding to fill the input block to either 1088 or 1344 bits, and adds the last terminator bit required by Keccak's padding scheme. Finally, the `Pad Cycle` module adds zero words to fill the `I/O buffer` in the case of using SHAKE256, which has a smaller data rate than SHAKE128. The final sub-module of the `Keccak` module is the `Remove Padding` module, which removes the data from the `I/O buffer` that should not be sent as output. This occurs either when the data rate is smaller than the full buffer size or when the destination of the data flow sets the `isLast` wire.

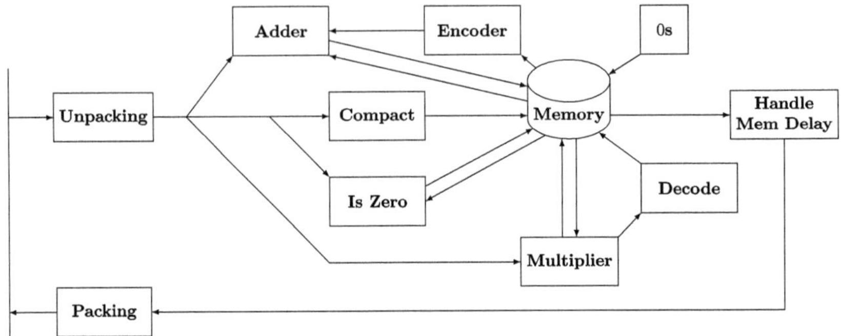

Fig. 4. Architecture of the `MICB` module.

MICB Module. The internal architecture of the `MICB` module is shown in Fig. 4. It consists of two main sub-modules: the `Memory` and `Multiplier` sub-modules, along with several smaller operations and multiplexers. The buses in the module are composed solely of data wires of varying sizes, and the entire module is centrally controlled. The `0 s` produces zeros to erase secret information from memory. The `Is Zero` verifies whether the input consists of zeros and then outputs either a value from the memory or the input. The `Encode`, `Decode`, `Pack`, and `Unpack` modules perform the corresponding FrodoKEM operations on buses of 4, 8, 4, and 4 values in parallel, respectively. The `Adder` operates on 4 pairs of values in parallel and is capable of both addition and subtraction. The `Handle Mem Delay` compensates for the 2-cycle delay of the BRAM's read operation. Finally, the `Compact` module either leaves the input unchanged or converts the 16-bit standard encoding of matrix S into a compact format with 4-bit values plus a sign, 4 values at a time. This transformation is possible because the values of S fall within the range $[-12, 12]$.

The `Multiplier` consists of 32 multipliers that operate on 5-bit and 16-bit operands, along with internal storage for temporary values and two modes of operation. In the first mode, it multiplies an input matrix of size 8×4 containing 5-bit values by an input vector of size 4×1 containing 16-bit values, accumulating the resulting 8×1 values in the internal storage. In the second mode, it multiplies a vector of size 8×1 containing 5-bit values from the internal storage by an input vector of size 1×4 containing 16-bit values, producing an output matrix of size 8×4.

Lastly, the `Memory` module consists of 8 BRAMs, organized as an 8×512 matrix of 64-bit words, and stores all variables of the FrodoKEM algorithms, except for $seed_A$. The non-matrix values are stored column-wise across the BRAMs. The 16-bit matrices are stored with 4 values in each word, while S is stored differently depending on the FrodoKEM variant: for FrodoKEM-1344, eight 4-bit values are stored per word, and for other variants, four 5-bit values are stored per word, depending on the range of the sampling distribution. Lastly, matrices with asymmetric dimensions may be stored in a transposed format to optimize memory usage.

4.2   Control Modules

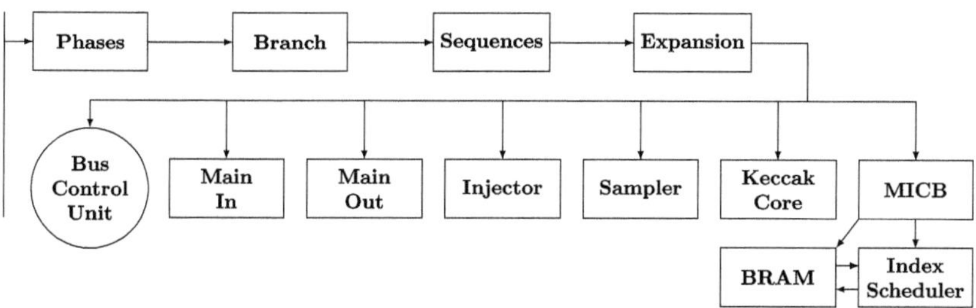

Fig. 5. Architecture of the control modules.

The implementation accepts multiple input commands: Key Generation, Encapsulation, Decapsulation, Add Entropy, and Setup Test. The first three commands are based on the FrodoKEM specification. The Add Entropy command is used to inject entropy into the Pseudo Random Number Generator (PRNG), for example, after startup. The Setup Test command disables the PRNG for the subsequent execution and loads values that would otherwise be generated by it. The input commands are sent to a `Phases` module, which breaks them down into a sequence of code blocks, ensuring that branches are fully contained within each phase. The output is then passed to a `Branch` module, which manages the loop to generate the matrix A and handles branches depending on whether the execution is a test or not, such as deciding whether to run the PRNG. These commands are subsequently sent to `Sequences`, which expands each input command into a series of individual instructions. Finally, `Expansion` converts each instruction into a command for the corresponding module, as illustrated in Fig. 5. In that figure, the `Main-in` and `Main-out` control the primary input and output of the implementation, while the `Bus Control Unit`, `Injector`, and `Sampler` modules serve as the controllers for the components described in the previous section. It is worth noting the `Keccak Core` controller, which includes an internal scheduler that enables partial overlapping of two consecutive executions of the SHAKE function. This feature is crucial to prevent noticeable slowdowns during the generation of the matrix A. Each row of A is generated with an independent SHAKE128 call, and a purely sequential execution would waste cycles to complete the last output before beginning the first input of the next execution. Instead, the scheduler allows the first input of the next execution to be processed during the final execution of the Keccak Permutation module. The last output is then computed while performing the first execution of the next Keccak Permutation. In this way, the Keccak Core continuously computes the Keccak permutation without idle cycles. Lastly, the control modules of the MICB module are introduced. The main control module breaks the 35 commands into multiple phases, if necessary, and determines which value or matrix is being operated on, as well as the type of operation to be performed. For each operation, the Index Scheduler manages the timing of the current index update, deciding which index to send data to or receive data from. The BRAM module handles the low-level details of storage, such as managing the offset and size of values, and rearranging the 512-bit parallel output from the 8 BRAMs into smaller buses for the output of the Memory module. It also performs the reverse operation for the input.

4.3   Inter Modules

In this section, we describe implementation details that are transversal to the individual modules.

Not Storing the Ciphertext in the Decapsulation. The decapsulation algorithm uses the ciphertext both at the beginning and at the end, but we will show here that both the latter usages can be moved ahead of time. This allows us to avoid saving the ciphertext, which can be up to 21,696 bits in size, and storing it would require an additional BRAM, increasing the area of the implementation.

The first operation that we need to move is the comparison between the matrices generated internally (B'', C') and those received as part of the ciphertext (B', C). This use can be moved ahead by initializing B'' with $-B'$ and C' with $-C$. In this way, at the end of the decapsulation we only need to compare the matrices with zero.

The second operation is the final hash of the decapsulation, which is given by $ss = \mathrm{SHAKE}(c \parallel \bar{k})$, where c represents the ciphertext. In this case we can not move the invocation of the hash function to an earlier point because $\bar{k}$ is available only at the end. Our solution was to store the 1,600-bit state of the Keccak module mid-operation in the BRAMs of the Memory module. This approach splits the input operation at a point that is not aligned with SHAKE's data rate, necessitating a division of the SHAKE operation in the middle of an input block. To address this, the Injector module is used to append zero-padding after the ciphertext to complete the input block, and subsequently, zero-padding is prepended before $\bar{k}$ to position it correctly within the input block.

Multiplication. FrodoKEM involves various multiplications in its algorithms, utilizing the two types of multiplication described previously. Specifically, in key generation, the expression $B = A \cdot S + E$ is transformed into $B^T + = S^T \cdot A^T$ to employ the first multiplier mode, with B initialized as E. In the encapsulation algorithm, the multiplications $B' = S' \cdot A + E'$ use the second multiplier mode, while $V = S' \cdot B + E''$ uses the first mode. In decapsulation, this last multiplication uses the second mode of operation as the intialization of B'' with $-B'$ means we can not store B in memory. As the packing restricts how the matrix B can be accessed, we need to use the second mode of operation of the multiplier. Lastly, the decapsulation has the additional multiplication $M = C - B' \cdot S$, which utilizes the first multiplier mode.

As with most existing implementations, we generate the matrix A on the fly, and in our case, we do so row-by-row. The operations involving the multiplications with the matrix A will now be detailed, as these are the slowest parts of the FrodoKEM algorithms and, therefore, the most time-sensitive.

During the $B^T + = S^T \cdot A^T$ operation, the `MICB` module manages the loading and storing of a column of B^T for each row of A, and loads an 8×4 sub-matrix of S for each block of 4×1 values of A, which are provided row-by-row from the `Keccak` module. As the processing of a row nears completion, the scheduler of the `Keccak` module facilitates the reception of the input for the next SHAKE128 invocation, signaling through the `canReceive` wire to the `Injector` to transmit the two bytes representing the row number and then the $seed_A$. Overall, this operation accesses A row-wise, while S is accessed once per row of A. Each row of B is updated once during the operation. The $B' + = S' \cdot A$ operation is similar, with the matrix A being accessed row-by-row. The key difference is that S' is accessed only once, with a column vector being loaded before each row of A. The matrix B' is fully updated once for every row of A, and for each block of 4×1 values of A, a sub-matrix of 8×4 values of B' is updated.

PRNG. The key generation and encoding algorithms of FrodoKEM require pseudo-random inputs. To generate these, the `Keccak` module is used in conjunction with a pool of 512-bit values stored in the `Memory` module. The entropy in the pool can be increased through an explicit command from the main module of the implementation. Additionally, the pool is automatically updated using the inputs processed by other commands. At the beginning of the key generation, the required pseudorandom variables are generated using SHAKE256($0x00 \parallel$ pool), and the entropy is subsequently updated with pool = SHAKE256($0x01 \parallel$ pool). Near the start of the encapsulation process, the required pseudorandom values are generated using SHAKE256($0x02 \parallel$ pool), and the pool is updated with SHAKE256($0x03 \parallel$ pool $\parallel$ pkh). Here, pkh refers to the hash of the public key, which serves to introduce additional entropy. The hash typically contains entropy from an independent entropy pool, and if an adversary misses a single public key, they would need to guess the entire hash in order to derive the next state of the pool. Finally, while decapsulation does not require any pseudorandom values, the entropy is still updated with SHAKE256($0x04 \parallel$ pool $\parallel ss$), where ss represents the shared secret. This value is inaccessible to an adversary who either failed to intercept the incoming message or did not possess the private key, making it a valuable source of entropy. The explicit command for adding entropy executes pool = SHAKE256($0x05 \parallel$ pool $\parallel$ IN), where the input IN is 512 bits.

5   Results

This section presents the results of our proposed implementation and compares them with existing FPGA-based implementations, more specifically with Howe et al.'s work from 2018 [8]. We believe that Howe et al.'s work from 2021 [7] is not a fair comparison because its goal is to help the standardization process explore different alternatives, and so they generate the matrix A with Trivium, a lightweight cryptosystem, instead of the standard Shake128 or AES. Comparing the two would be like comparing the time of an implementation that uses RSA and one that uses ECC, the result is meaningful to compare variations of the standard, but it is not a fair comparison between implementations. This deviation from the standard is particularly relevant when in Sect. 1, paragraph 5, the authors say "To be parallelised, however, the matrix multiplication requires the use of a smaller and more performant pseudo-random number generator. We propose to achieve the performance required for the randomness generation by using Trivium" which we believe hints that their architecture would not be feasible with the regular Shake128 function.

We benchmark our results using the Xilinx Artix-7 XC7A35T FPGA using Vivado Design Suite 2024.2, while Howe et al. [8] uses the same FPGA but with Vivado Design Suite 2019.1. Also, we measured the overall area consumption in equivalent slices, which we estimate using the formula [2,9]:

$$\text{AREA} = 0.25 * \text{LUT} + 0.125 * \text{FF} + 102.4 * \text{DSP} + 116.2 * \text{BRAM} \qquad (1)$$

In Fig. 6 and Table 2 we show the comparison of our results with [8]'s. More specifically, we show both a comparison with the individual modules, and with a set of modules to achieve a given functionality.

If we compare a single algorithm of a single parameter set of FrodoKEM, we see that our module has $9.0\times$ to $9.7\times$ the throughput of [8]. On the other hand, comparing the area is more nuanced as our module does more than any individual module of [8]. The biggest module of [8] that is functionally included in ours is the FrodoKEM-976 decapsulation, and our implementation is 21% bigger, but the area to throughput ratio is reduced by a factor of 8. We want to point out that while we do have an increase in size, we also support the higher 1344 parameter set, which Howe et al.'s work [8] does not as it had not been standardized yet.

The other case is if the user needs a full implementation of FrodoKEM. In ASICs, it is common practice to create a single mask that contains all the functionalities to reduce costs. Yet this is still relevant for FPGAs, as a common use case is a server, which needs to be able to generate keys and perform the decapsulation to allow clients to connect to it, but it also needs to support the

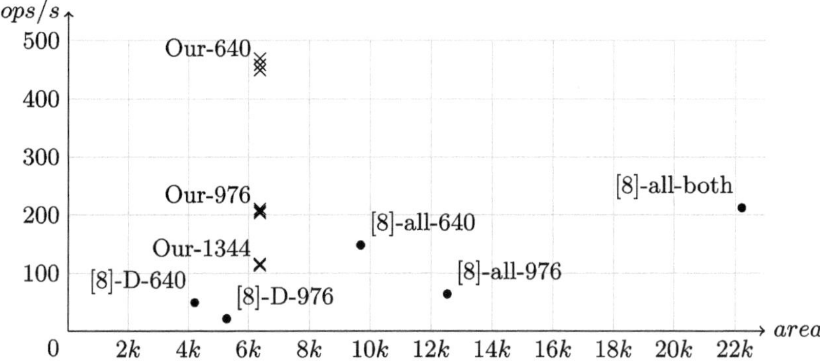

Fig. 6. Comparisons of area and throughput. For our results, we only use one label for each parameter set as the three data points are really close. Legend: Decapsulation (-D-), All three algorithms (-all-), both parameter sets supported by [8] (-both).

Table 2. Comparison of the implementations. Legend: Key generation (K), Encapsulation (E), Decapsulation (D). 'Both' and 'all' mean multiple modules together. A/T is the Area to Throughput Ratio. All works use the XC7A35T FPGA.

Ref.	Param.	Alg.	# of LUTs	# of FFs	# of BRAMs	# of DSPs	Freq. (MHz)	# of Slices	Op/s	A/T
[8]	640	K	3771	1800	6	1	167	1967	51	38.56
		E	6745	3528	11	1	167	3507	51	68.76
		D	7220	3549	16	1	162	4210	49	85.91
	976	K	7139	1800	8	1	167	3042	22	138.27
		E	7209	3537	16	1	167	4206	22	191.18
		D	7773	3559	24	1	162	5279	21	251.38
	640	all	17736	8877	33	3	162	9685	148	65.43
	976		22121	8896	48	3	162	12527	64	195.73
	both		39857	17773	81	6	162	22212	212	104.77
Ours	640	K	19082	5331	8	0	62.5	6367	469	13.59
		E							458	13.90
		D							449	14.18
	976	K							210	30.38
		E							206	30.92
		D							203	31.31
	1344	K							116	54.98
		E							114	55.71
		D							113	56.25

encapsulation too for whenever it needs to access external resources, for example, a database. Lastly, a server should support multiple parameter sets as it does not know what the other endpoint will support. In this case, we need to consider the set of all modules from [8]. The area of our module is a factor of 3.5 smaller than that of this set. The throughput depends on which operations we need to execute, as the set of [8]'s 6 modules can execute six operations at a time only for different operations. In the best case, their throughput is of 212 operations per second. For the same distribution of operations, our module computes 335 operations per second, which is 58% higher. Of course, if the operations are all of the same type, for example due to a Denial of Service attack, then our throughput is 798% to 868% higher, which shows the advantages of the higher flexibility of our unified module. This flexibility is further enhanced by our module's ability to execute operations for the 1344 parameter set.

6   Conclusion

This paper presents a novel hardware architecture optimized for FrodoKEM, a lattice-based PQC algorithm that is included in the BSI's recommended cryptographic algorithms. The proposed FPGA-based implementation has a novel architecture that allows it to reduce the number of BRAMs, eliminate the need for DSP blocks, and increase throughput and flexibility. The evaluation results, conducted on an Artix-7 FPGA, demonstrate a significant throughput improvement of nearly an order of magnitude over existing state-of-the-art FrodoKEM implementations. Additionally, the design benefits from a unified architecture that integrates key generation, encapsulation, and decapsulation into a single, streamlined module that can run either of them, and that can execute any of the three parameter sets of FrodoKEM.

Acknowledgements. This work is supported in part by DFG Project No. 543352068 and the AMD University Program.

References

1. Alkim, E., et al.: FrodoKEM: learning with errors key encapsulation algorithm specifications and supporting documentation. Tech. rep., FrodoKEM Project (2021). https://frodokem.org/files/FrodoKEM-specification-20210604.pdf. Accessed 30 Apr 2025
2. AMD: 7 series FPGAs data sheet: overview (DS180) (2020). https://docs.amd.com/v/u/en-US/ds180_7Series_Overview
3. Federal office for information security (BSI): Cryptographic mechanisms: recommendations and key lengths. Tech. Rep. BSI TR-02102-1, Federal Office for Information Security, Bonn, Germany (2024). https://www.bsi.bund.de/SharedDocs/Downloads/EN/BSI/Publications/TechGuidelines/TG02102/BSI-TR-02102-1.pdf. Accessed 30 Apr 2025

4. Federal office for information security (BSI): Post-quantum cryptography (2024). https://www.bsi.bund.de/EN/Themen/Unternehmen-und-Organisationen/ Informationen-und-Empfehlungen/Quantentechnologien-und-Post-Quanten-Kryptografie/Post-Quanten-Kryptografie/post-quanten-kryptografie_node.html. Accessed 30 Apr 2025
5. Filho, D.L.G., Brandão, G., Adj, G., Alblooshi, A., Canales-Martínez, I.A., Chávez-Saab, J., López, J.: PQC-AMX: accelerating saber and FRODOKEM on the apple M1 and M3 socs. In: 2024 IEEE 31st Symposium on Computer Arithmetic (ARITH), pp. 9–16 (2024). https://doi.org/10.1109/ARITH61463.2024.00012
6. Gu, S., et al.: A low latency and high throughout hardware design of random matrix number generator for Frodokem. In: 2024 IEEE 17th International Conference on Solid-State & Integrated Circuit Technology (ICSICT), pp. 1–3 (2024). https://doi.org/10.1109/ICSICT62049.2024.10831677
7. Howe, J., Martinoli, M., Oswald, E., Regazzoni, F.: Exploring parallelism to improve the performance of FrodoKEM in hardware. J. Cryptogr. Eng. **11**(4), 317–327 (2021). https://doi.org/10.1007/s13389-021-00258-7
8. Howe, J., Oder, T., Krausz, M., Güneysu, T.: Standard lattice-based key encapsulation on embedded devices. IACR Tran. Cryptographic Hardware Embed. Syst. **2018**(3), 372–393 (2018). https://doi.org/10.13154/tches.v2018.i3.372-393
9. Liu, W., Fan, S., Khalid, A., Rafferty, C., O'Neill, M.: Optimized schoolbook polynomial multiplication for compact lattice-based cryptography on FPGA. IEEE Trans. Very Large Scale Integration (VLSI) Syst. **27**(10), 2459–2463 (2019). https://doi.org/10.1109/TVLSI.2019.2922999
10. Moody, D., Perlner, R., Regenscheid, A., Robinson, A., Cooper, D.: Transition to post-quantum cryptography standards. NIST Internal Report NIST IR 8547 IPD, National Institute of Standards and Technology, Gaithersburg, MD (2024). https://nvlpubs.nist.gov/nistpubs/ir/2024/NIST.IR.8547.ipd.pdf. Accessed 30 Apr 2025
11. Mosca, M., Piani, M.: Quantum threat timeline report 2023. Tech. rep., Global Risk Institute (2023). https://globalriskinstitute.org/publication/2023-quantum-threat-timeline-report/. Accessed30 Apr 2025
12. National Institute of Standards and Technology: What is post-quantum cryptography? (2024). https://www.nist.gov/cybersecurity/what-post-quantum-cryptography, Last modified: 2025-06-11. Accessed 5 Aug 2025
13. NIST information technology laboratory, computer security resource center: post-quantum cryptography (2017). https://csrc.nist.gov/Projects/post-quantum-cryptography. Accessed 30 Apr 2025
14. Paar, C., Pelzl, J.: Understanding Cryptography: A Textbook for Students and Practitioners. Springer, Heidelberg, Germany (2010). https://doi.org/10.1007/978-3-642-04101-3
15. Shor, P.W.: Polynomial-time algorithms for prime factorization and discrete logarithms on a quantum computer. SIAM Rev. **41**(2), 303–332 (1999). https://doi.org/10.1137/S0036144598347011
16. Trend Micro: Quantum computing attacks on classical cryptography (2023). https://www.trendmicro.com/vinfo/us/security/news/security-technology/post-quantum-cryptography-quantum-computing-attacks-on-classical-cryptography. Accessed 30 Apr 2025

Advanced Cryptographic Algorithms: Fully Homomorphic Encryption, Zero-Knowledge

Optimized FPGA Architecture for Modular Reduction in NTT

Tolun Tosun[1]([✉]) [ID], Selim Kırbıyık[1]([✉]) [ID], Emre Koçer[1] [ID],
and Ersin Alaybeyoğlu[1,2] [ID]

[1] Sabancı University, Istanbul, Türkiye
{tosun,selimkirbiyik,kocer,ersin.alaybeyoglu}@sabanciuniv.edu,
ealaybeyoglu@bartin.edu.tr
[2] Bartın University, Bartın, Türkiye

Abstract. In this paper, we present a comprehensive analysis of various modular multiplication methods for Number Theoretic Transform (NTT) on FPGA. NTT is a critical and time-intensive component of Fully Homomorphic Encryption (FHE) applications while modular multiplication consumes a significant portion of the design resources in an NTT implementation. We study the existing modular reduction approaches from the literature, and implement particular methods on FPGA. Specifically Word-Level Montgomery (WLM) for NTT friendly primes [20] and K^2RED [4]. For improvements, we explore the trade-offs between the number of available primes in special forms and hardware cost of the reduction methods. We develop a DSP multiplication-optimized version of WLM, which we call WLM-Mixed. We also introduce a subclass of Proth primes, referred to as Proth-l primes, characterized by a low and fixed signed Hamming Weight. This special class of primes allows us to design multiplication-free shift-add versions of K^2RED and naive Montgomery reduction [21], referred to as K^2RED-Shift and Montgomery-Shift. We provide in-depth evaluations of these five reduction methods in an NTT architecture on FPGA. Our results indicate that WLM-Mixed is highly resource-efficient, utilizing only 3 DSP multiplications for 64-bit coefficient moduli. On the other hand, K^2RED-Shift and Montgomery-Shift offer DSP-free alternatives, which can be beneficial in specific scenarios.

Keywords: Modular Reduction · FPGA · Montgomery · K^2RED · DSP · FHE · NTT

1 Introduction

FHE is an advanced encryption technique that allows computations on encrypted data without needing to decrypt it first. FHE emerged in recent years by pioneering work from Gentry [14]. With FHE, data can remain secure even when processed by third-party data centers.

Several FHE algorithms exist in the literature such as BFV [5,11], CKKS [15] and TFHE [6]. Existing FHE algorithms are lattice-based schemes which is

---

T. Tosun and S. Kırbıyık—Equal contribution.

E. Savas et al. (Eds.): LightSec 2025, LNCS 16216, pp. 117–137, 2026.
https://doi.org/10.1007/978-3-032-15541-2_7

based on polynomial ring arithmetic. The core operation is the polynomial multiplication in the ring of polynomials. For FHE, the degrees of these polynomials range from 2^{12} to 2^{16}. Given the computational expense associated with operating on polynomials of such high degrees, there has been substantial research in the literature focused on accelerating FHE using FPGAs.

The state-of-art algorithm for polynomial multiplication is the well-known NTT, which reduces the complexity from $O(n^2)$ to $O(n \log n)$ compared to the naive school-book approach. The core component of the NTT is the butterfly unit, which primarily involves modular multiplication. There exists a variety of modular multiplication methods in the literature, such as Montgomery [21], Barrett [3], Plantard [26], and Montgomery-based methods like WLM [20], K^{2}RED [4]. These methods have different characteristics in terms of hardware complexity, latency, and throughput. In this paper, we study different modular reduction methods in the context of NTT implementations. Our contributions are outlined below.

- We evaluate existing modular reduction algorithms from the literature, focusing on their implementation in NTT for FHE applications on FPGAs. We propose an efficient architecture for K^{2}RED.
- We propose a novel variant of the WLM reduction algorithm [20], referred to as WLM-Mixed. This approach is particularly effective for 64-bit coefficient modulus, as it significantly reduces the number of DSP multiplications.
- We propose runtime configurable shift-add versions of the K^{2}RED and naive Montgomery reduction algorithms. These multiplication-free reduction algorithms are achieved by introducing a special subclass of Proth primes, referred to as Proth-l primes.
- We investigate the range of special primes utilized in this study, particularly in relation to the number of primes required for RNS representation in FHE applications. We analyze the trade-offs between the number of primes and the hardware cost of reduction algorithms.
- We implement the proposed modular reduction methods on AMD-Xilinx Alveo U280 (XCU280) FPGA, as well as the state-of-the-art techniques from the literature. We provide a comprehensive analysis of the performances of different modular multiplication methods studied in this paper on FPGA. According to characteristics of these algorithms, we present a general analysis for which modular multiplication suits the given parameter set. An example analysis provided in the paper is the trade-off between DSP and distributed logic use for a given algorithm.

2   Background

2.1   Notation

Lowercase italic letters, such as a, represent integers. The logarithm function (log) is base-2 and returns the ceiling integer. Values of individual bits of integers are shown using square brackets, e.g., $a[i]$. Bold lowercase letters, such as a, denote vectors. Elements of vectors are accessed using sub-indices, e.g., $\mathbf{a}_i$. q denotes the integer modulus and β is an alias for $\log q$. The cyclotomic ring of polynomials $\mathbb{Z}_q[x]/(x^n + 1)$ is denoted by $\mathcal{R}_{q,n}$. Polynomials are represented by bold lowercase italic letters, such as $\boldsymbol{a}(x)$. To simplify the narration, indeterminate x of polynomials are sometimes omitted. Polynomial coefficients are represented by sub-indices, such as $\boldsymbol{a}_i$.

2.2 Number Theoretic Transform (NTT)

NTT is the state-of-the-art method for polynomial multiplication. For two polynomials $\boldsymbol{a}(x), \boldsymbol{b}(x) \in \mathcal{R}_{q,n}$, multiplication using the NTT algorithm is performed as follows:

$$\boldsymbol{a}(x) \cdot \boldsymbol{b}(x) = \mathrm{iNTT}\Big(\mathrm{NTT}\big(\boldsymbol{a}(x)\big) \odot \mathrm{NTT}\big(\boldsymbol{b}(x)\big)\Big) \tag{1}$$

where $\odot$ represents element-wise multiplication of vectors in NTT domain. For NTT to be defined over $\mathcal{R}_{q,n}$, it is required that $q \equiv 1 \pmod{2n}$. In this context, there exists a primitive $2n$-th root of unity in $\mathbb{Z}_q$, denoted as ψ, such that $\psi^n \equiv -1 \pmod{q}$. For this condition to be satistifed, q must be in the form of $q_h 2^\omega + 1$ where $\omega \geq \log n + 1$. The forward NTT corresponds to the evaluation $\hat{\mathbf{a}}[i] = \boldsymbol{a}(\psi^{2i+1})$ for every coefficient $i < n$. The NTT can be efficiently implemented using butterfly circuits. Forward NTT is usually implemented with *Cooley-Tukey* (CT) [7] butterflies while the inverse NTT is implemented with *Gentleman-Sande* (GS) [13] butterflies. For two coefficients $\boldsymbol{a}_i$ and $\boldsymbol{a}_j$, the CT butterfly is defined as follows:

$$(\mathbf{a}_i', \ \mathbf{a}_j') = (\boldsymbol{a}_i + \boldsymbol{a}_j\zeta, \ \boldsymbol{a}_i - \boldsymbol{a}_j\zeta) \qquad (\mathrm{mod}\ q) \tag{2}$$

where ζ is the twiddle factor, which is a power of ψ. NTT with CT or GS butterflies have $\log n$ stages and performs $n/2$ butterflies at each stage, resulting in a time complexity of $O(n \log n)$.

2.3 Residue Number System (RNS)

FHE applications require performing large integer arithmetic due to security needs of the underlying computationally expensive Learning With Errors (LWE) problem. RNS improves the efficiency of arithmetic operations in FHE, by representing large integers as a set of relatively smaller integers, called residues. Handling smaller integers reduces the complexity of modular arithmetic significantly. Let $a \in \mathbb{Z}_{\tilde{q}}$ and $\tilde{q} = \prod_i^{\lambda-1} q_i$. Then, the set of residues is defined as $\{a_i\}_i^{\lambda-1}$ where $a_i = a \pmod{q_i}$. By utilizing Chinese Remainder Theorem (CRT), addition and multiplication between two integers $a, b \in \mathbb{Z}_{\tilde{q}}$ can be performed in the RNS domain element-wise. Multiplication is performed as follows:

$$ab = \{a_i\}_{i=0}^{\lambda-1} \odot \{b_i\}_{i=0}^{\lambda-1} = \{a_i b_i \bmod q_i\}_{i=0}^{\lambda-1} \tag{3}$$

Naturally, the isomorphism extends to the polynomials, $\mathcal{R}_{\tilde{q},n} \simeq \prod_i^{\lambda-1} \mathcal{R}_{q_i,n}$. The polynomial arithmetic involving the NTT is performed in the RNS domain,

Table 1. The relationship between $\tilde{q}$ and n for 128-bit security [1], showing the number of 32-bit and 64-bit primes q_i required with RNS.

$\log n$	$\log \tilde{q}$	λ	
		$\log q_i = 32$	$\log q_i = 64$
12	109	4	2
13	218	7	4
14	438	14	7
15	881	28	14
16	1761	55	28

operating in each $\mathcal{R}_{q_i,n}$ independently. In practice, q_i are usually around 32 to 64 bits, depending on the implementation choices and requirements of FHE schemes. Table 1 illustrates the number of distinct q_i required for the RNS representation in both 32-bit and 64-bit configurations.

2.4   Modular Reduction Algorithms

Montgomery Reduction. [21] is a widely used method for modular reduction in cryptographic applications, detailed in Algorithm 1. It requires two $\beta \times \beta$ multiplications and eliminates the division by using a modulus-dependent pre-computed factor, q'. The key idea is that by adding tq to the input a in Line 2, the lower β bits of $a + tq$ become 0. As a result, shifting it right by β bits reduces the bit-length of the result to β bits. The Montgomery reduction requires a final correction, as illustrated in Line 3. Note that the result of the Montgomery reduction includes a constant factor of $2^{-\beta}$.

Word-Level Montgomery (WLM) Reduction for NTT Friendly Primes. Instead of performing the reduction entirely at once, a word-by-word reduction approach also exists. In this case, the word size ω-bit is reduced from the input operand at each iteration while $\lceil \beta/\omega \rceil$ iterations are performed. The pre-computed factor q' is computed as $-q^{-1} \pmod{2^\omega}$. This approach is particularly advantageous for the NTT friendly primes, as the pre-computed factor q' becomes -1. Consider the case $\omega = \log n + 1$ where $q = 1 \pmod{2^\omega}$. As a result,

---

Algorithm 1. Naive Montgomery Reduction [21]

Input: modulus $q < 2^\beta$, pre-computed factor $q' = -q^{-1} \pmod{2^\beta}$, operand $a < q^2$
Output: $b = a2^{-\beta} \pmod{q}$
  1: $t \leftarrow q'a \pmod{2^\beta}$
  2: $b \leftarrow (a + tq) \gg \beta$
  3: **if** $b \geq q$ **then** $b \leftarrow b - q$
  4: **return** b

Algorithm 2. WLM; Word-Level Montgomery Reduction for NTT-friendly primes [20]

Input: modulus $q < 2^\beta$, word-size ω such that $q = 1 \pmod{2^\omega}$ and $q_h = q \gg \omega$, $\lambda = \lceil \frac{\beta}{\omega} \rceil$, operand $a < q^2$
Output: $b = a2^{-\omega\lambda} \pmod{q}$
 1: $t \leftarrow a$
 2: **for** $i = 0 \rightarrow \lambda - 1$ **do**
 3:     $t_l \leftarrow t \pmod{2^\omega}$, $t_h \leftarrow t \gg \omega$
 4:     $t' \leftarrow -t_l \pmod{2^\omega}$
 5:     $c \leftarrow t'[\omega - 1] \vee t[\omega - 1]$
 6:     $t \leftarrow t_h + q_h t_l + c$
 7: **if** $t \geq q$ **then** $b \leftarrow t - q$
 8: **else** $b \leftarrow t$
 9: **return** b

Algorithm 3. K^2RED [4]

Input: a Proth prime modulus $q < 2^\beta$ where $q = 1 \pmod{2^\omega}$ for $\omega \geq \beta/2$ and $q_h = q \gg \omega$, operand $a < q^2$
Output: $b = a2^{-2\omega} \pmod{q}$
 1: $a_l \leftarrow a \pmod{2^\omega}$, $a_h \leftarrow a \gg \omega$
 2: $t \leftarrow q_h a_l - a_h$
 3: $t_l \leftarrow t \pmod{2^\omega}$, $t_h \leftarrow t \gg \omega$
 4: $t' \leftarrow q_h t_l - t_h$
 5: **if** $t' \geq q$ **then** $b \leftarrow t' - q$
 6: **else if** $t' < 0$ **then** $b \leftarrow t' + q$
 7: **else** $b \leftarrow t'$
 8: **return** b

---

the multiplication by q' is eliminated. The word-level Montgomery reduction for NTT friendly primes [20] is detailed in Algorithm 2.

K^2RED. [4] is a reduction algorithm originally developed for Crystals-Kyber. K^2RED requires the modulus to be a Proth prime, which are in the form of $q = q_h 2^\omega + 1$ where $\omega \geq \log q/2$. For Kyber, the multiplications by q_h in (Algorithm 3) Lines 2 and 4 can be efficiently performed by fixed shifts and summations as the modulus q is known in design time [23]. Either the input operand needs to be pre-processed or the result needs to be post-processed to correct the $2^{-2\omega}$ term.

Barrett Reduction. [3] is another classical reduction algorithm widely used in cryptographic applications, detailed in Algorithm 4. Similar to Montgomery reduction, it requires 2 multiplication and uses a pre-computed factor. Note that the multiplication in Line 1 is $2\beta \times \beta$, making the overall multiplication cost for Barrett reduction $(2\beta \times \beta) + (\beta \times \beta)$. Also, the output of the Barrett reduction does not involve a constant factor compared to the Montgomery reduction.

Plantard Reduction. [26] is a relatively newer reduction algorithm, detailed in Algorithm 5. Similar to Barrett and Montgomery, Plantard reduction also uses

---

Algorithm 4. Barrett Reduction [3]

Input: modulus $q < 2^\beta$, pre-computed factor $q' = \lfloor 2^{2\beta}/q \rfloor$, operand $a < q^2$
Output: $b = a \pmod q$
1: $t \leftarrow (aq') \gg (2\beta)$
2: $b \leftarrow (a - tq)$
3: **if** $b \geq q$ **then** $b \leftarrow b - q$
4: **return** b

Algorithm 5. Plantard Modular Multiplication [26]

Input: modulus $q < 2^\beta$, pre-computed factor $q' = q^{-1} \pmod{2^{2\beta}}$, operands $a, b < q$
Output: $c = ab(-2^{-2\beta}) \pmod q$
1: $c' \leftarrow (abq' \pmod{2^{2\beta}}) \gg \beta$
2: $c \leftarrow ((c' + 1)q) \gg \beta$
3: **if** $c = q$ **then** $c = 0$
4: **return** c

---

a pre-computed factor q'. However, the multiplication bq' in Line 1 can be pre-computed, making Plantard reduction particularly advantageous for constant multiplications, such as those involving twiddle factors in butterfly circuits. As a drawback, the multiplication $(a) \cdot (bq')$ needs to be performed with double-word precision, a $2\beta \times \beta$ multiplication. The overall multiplication complexity for the case of multiplication by a constant is $(2\beta \times \beta) + (\beta \times \beta)$.

3   Proposed Modular Reduction Algorithms

3.1   Proth-*l* Primes

In this section, we introduce Proth-*l* primes, which are a subset of Proth primes. Recall that Proth primes are in the form of $q_h 2^\omega + 1$ where $\log q_h \leq \omega$. Proth-*l* primes require that the number of non-zero terms in the signed binary representation of q_h is small. To clarify the number of non-zero terms, we provide the following definitions:

Definition: Proth-2*l* prime. A Proth prime q is also a Proth-2*l* prime if $q = 2^{\beta-1} + (2^{l_1} - 2^{l_2})2^\omega + 1$ where $0 \leq l_2 \leq l_1 < \beta - \omega - 1$.

Definition: Proth-3*l* prime. A Proth prime q is also a Proth-3*l* prime if $q = 2^{\beta-1} + (2^{l_1} - 2^{l_2} + 2^{l_3})2^\omega + 1$ where $0 \leq l_2 \leq l_1 < \beta - \omega - 1$ and $0 \leq l_3 < \beta - \omega - 1$.

We write Proth-*l* to refer both Proth-2*l* or Proth-3*l* primes. Recall that the RNS representation requires use of multiple primes of relatively smaller sizes (in practice, usually 32-bit or 64-bit). Therefore, it is essential to know the number of Proth-*l* primes that can be found for these parameters. As shown in Table 2, the number of Proth-*l* primes is sufficient for FHE applications that employ 32-bit or 64-bit RNS arithmetic. For instance, consider the ring dimension $n = 2^{16}$ which requires $\log \tilde{q} \approx 1800$ for 128-bit security level. This case can be achieved by Proth-3*l* primes and 32-bit RNS arithmetic, as 80 such primes are found

Table 2. Number of proth-l primes for different bit-widths.

$\log q$	$\log q_h$	Proth-	#primes
64	32	$3l$	469
64	17	$3l$	53
64	32	$2l$	16
64	17	$2l$	5
32	16	$3l$	95
32	15	$3l$	80
32	16	$2l$	7
32	15	$2l$	7

(when $\log q_h = 15$) and $80 \times 32 > 1800$. Also, recall from Sect. 2.2 that NTT with $n = 2^{16}$ requires $\omega \geq 17$ as a $2n$-th root of unity is needed. In the next two sections, we present modular reduction algorithms that replace multiplications with shift-adds using Proth-l primes.

3.2 Montgomery with Barrel Shifters

In this section, we present a shift-add variant of naive Montgomery reduction algorithm (Algorithm 1) for Proth-l primes, referred to as Montgomery-Shift.

For a β-bit Proth prime q which is of the form $q = q_h 2^\omega + 1$, the Montgomery factor q' is $q_h 2^\omega - 1$:

$$q'q = (q_h 2^\omega + 1)(q_h 2^\omega - 1) = q_h^2 2^{2\omega} - 1 = -1 \quad (\mathrm{mod}\ 2^\beta) \tag{4}$$

Recall that $2^{2\omega} \geq 2^\beta$ is satisfied for Proth primes. For a Proth-$3l$ prime q:

$$q' = 2^{\beta-1} + (2^{l_1} - 2^{l_2} + 2^{l_3})2^\omega - 1 \tag{5}$$

As a result, the multiplications in Line 1 and Line 2 of Algorithm 1 can be implemented with 3 barrel shifters for Proth-$3l$ primes. Algorithm 6 presents the revised Montgomery reduction algorithm. Similarly, for Proth-$2l$ primes, the multiplications can be achieved using two barrel shifters. We would like to note that the shifts with l_1, l_2 and l_3 are run-time configurable while the shift with β and ω are known at the design-time. The bit-lengths of l_1, l_2, and l_3 are $\log(\log(q_h - 1))$, which is a critical factor for the hardware cost of the shifts in Line 2 and Line 3. For example, when $9 < \log q_h \leq 17$, $\log l_i = 4$. Similarly, when $17 < \log q_h \leq 33$, $\log l_i = 5$. Recall from Sect. 3.1 that the number of Proth-l primes increase with $\log q_h$, which is a trade-off between the number of primes and the hardware cost of the shifts. When $\log q_h = 2^x + 1$ the number of primes is maximized for $\log l_i = x$.

Algorithm 6. Montgomery-Shift; Montgomery Reduction with Shift-Adds

---

Input: a proth-l prime modulus $q = 2^{\beta-1} + (2^{l_1} - 2^{l_2} + 2^{l_3})2^{\omega} + 1$, operand $a < q^2$
Output: $b = a2^{-\beta} \pmod{q}$
1: $a_l \leftarrow a_l \pmod{2^{\beta}}$, $a_h \leftarrow a \gg \beta$
2: $t \leftarrow \left(a_l \ll (\beta - 1)\right) + \left(\left(\left(a_l \ll l_1\right) - \left(a_l \ll l_2\right) + \left(a_l \ll l_3\right)\right) \ll \omega\right) - a_l \pmod{2^{\beta}}$
3: $t' \leftarrow \left(t \ll (\beta - 1)\right) + \left(\left(\left(t \ll l_1\right) - \left(t \ll l_2\right) + \left(t \ll l_3\right)\right) \ll \omega\right) + t$
4: $t'_h \leftarrow t' \gg \beta$, $c \leftarrow t'[\beta - 1] \vee a_l[\beta - 1]$
5: $b' \leftarrow (a_h + t'_h + c)$
6: **if** $b' \geq q$ **then** $b \leftarrow b' - q$
7: **else** $b \leftarrow b'$
8: **return** b

Further Discussion on Barrett and Plantard. We would like to note that the optimization presented in this section does not apply to the Barrett and Plantard algorithms. For Plantard reduction, q' is computed modulo $2^{2\beta}$ which will avoid disappearance of the term $q_h^2 2^{2\omega}$ in Equation (4). For Barrett reduction, although the factor q' is approximately β-bit, the result of the division by a Proth-l modulus q does not lead to a term with low signed Hamming weight.

3.3 K²RED with Barrel Shifters

In this section, we present the shift-add variant of the run-time configurable version of the K²RED algorithm (Algorithm 3) for Proth-l primes, referred to as K²RED-Shift.

The trade-off between the number of primes and the hardware cost, through $\log q_h$ and using l_3, directly applies to K²RED-Shift. In Algorithm 7 the terms l_1, l_2, l_3 are run-time configurable and terms β and $\log q_h$ are design-time configurable, as in Montgomery-Shift. Recall that this flexibility allows for efficient reduction using barrel shifters with a specified range of primes which we can utilize in NTT. Although Algorithm 7 explicitly uses Proth-$3l$ primes, it trivially applies to Proth-$2l$ primes by removing l_3 terms. Using Proth-$3l$ provides

---

Algorithm 7. K²RED-Shift; K²RED with Shift-Adds

Input: proth-l prime modulus $q = 2^{\beta-1} + (2^{l_1} - 2^{l_2} + 2^{l_3})2^{\omega} + 1$, operand $a \leq (q-1)^2$
Output: $b = a2^{-2\omega} \pmod{q}$
1: $a_l \leftarrow a \pmod{2^{\omega}}$, $a_h \leftarrow a \gg \omega$
2: $t \leftarrow \left(\left(a_l \ll (\beta - 1 - \omega)\right) + \left(a_l \ll l_1\right) + \left(a_l \ll l_3\right)\right) - \left(\left(a_l \ll l_2\right) + a_h\right)$
3: $t_l \leftarrow t \pmod{2^{\omega}}$, $t_h \leftarrow t \gg \omega$
4: $t' \leftarrow \left(\left(t_l \ll (\beta - 1 - \omega)\right) + \left(t_l \ll l_1\right) + \left(t_l \ll l_3\right)\right) - \left(\left(t_l \ll l_2\right) + t_h\right)$
5: **if** $t' \geq q$ **then** $b \leftarrow t' - q$
6: **else if** $t' < 0$ **then** $b \leftarrow t' + q$
7: **else** $b \leftarrow t'$
8: **return** b

---

additional primes at the cost of increased area. Algorithm 7 requires six barrel shifters for Proth-$3l$ primes and four barrel shifters for Proth-$2l$ primes.

3.4   Mixed-Radix Word-Level Montgomery Reduction

In this section, we present an improved word-level Montgomery reduction algorithm that significantly reduces the number of DSP multiplications compared to Algorithm 2. This is achieved by using a mixed-radix approach with two reduction iterations and the regular Proth primes. The term mixed-radix indicates that the iterations are performed with varying word sizes. Algorithm 8 details the approach, referred to as WLM-Mixed. The word sizes for each iteration, ω_0 and ω_1, are determined based on the DSP operand sizes and $\log q_h$. Notice that the assignments in Line 1 aims to fit the multiplication in the second iteration into a single DSP by selecting the appropriate word size ω_1. Then, ω_0 is set accordingly. Lines 3–8 perform the reduction iterations as in Algorithm 2. The shift by δ_i is needed to align the multiplication output with the one in Line 6 of Algorithm 2. Note that for Algorithm 2, $\omega + \log q_h = \beta$. Similarly, for Algorithm 8, the relationship $\omega_i + \log q_h + \delta_i = \omega + \log q_h = \beta$ holds.

The requirement for q to be a Proth prime ensures that $\omega_0 \leq \omega$ (see Line 1 of Algorithm 8). Otherwise, the first iteration would require explicit computation of the Montgomery factor q' and therefore the existing algorithm definition would be incorrect.

Algorithm 8. WLM-Mixed; DSP-Optimized Mixed-Radix Word-Level Montgomery Reduction with two iterations

---

Input: a Proth prime modulus $q < 2^\beta$; DSP operand bit-lengths Γ_A, Γ_B such that
$\quad$ $\Gamma_A \geq \Gamma_B$; $\log q_h$ such that for $\omega = \beta - \log q_h$, $q = 1 \pmod{2^\omega}$, $\log q_h \leq \Gamma_B$, $\omega \geq \beta/2$
$\quad$ and $q_h = q \gg \omega$; operand $a < q^2$

Output: $b = a2^{-\beta} \pmod q$

1: $\omega_1 \leftarrow \min(\Gamma_A, \omega)$, $\omega_0 \leftarrow \beta - \omega_1$
2: $t \leftarrow a$
3: **for** $i = 0 \rightarrow 2$ **do**
4: $\quad$ $\delta_i \leftarrow \omega - \omega_i$
5: $\quad$ $t_h \leftarrow t \gg \omega_i$, $t_l \leftarrow t \pmod{2^{\omega_i}}$
6: $\quad$ $t' \leftarrow -t_l \pmod{2^{\omega_i}}$
7: $\quad$ $c \leftarrow t'[\omega_i - 1] \vee t[\omega_i - 1]$
8: $\quad$ $t \leftarrow t_h + \left((q_h t_l) \ll \delta_i\right) + c$
9: **if** $t \geq q$ **then** $b \leftarrow t - q$
10: **else** $b \leftarrow t$
11: **return** b

As an example, consider 26×17-bit DSP multipliers ($\Gamma_A = 26$, $\Gamma_B = 17$), and a 64-bit Proth prime q where $\log q_h = 17$. Then, the first reduction iteration is performed with $\omega_1 = 26$ and the second iteration is performed with $\omega_1 = 38$. Notice that both are feasible since $\log q - \log q_h = 47 \geq 26, 38$. The first iteration involves a 17×38-bit multiplication, which can be executed using 2 DSPs, while the second iteration involves a 17×26-bit multiplication, utilizing 1 DSP. Consequently, the total number of DSP multiplications is 3. The number of DSP multiplications is significantly greater for the classical WLM reduction (Algorithm 2) using general NTT-friendly primes. Consider the case of $n = 2^{16}$, continuing the above example with $\log q = 64$. Recall that WLM supports NTT-friendly primes without imposing constraints on their form; thus, $\omega = \log n + 1 = 17$. Then, four iterations are needed where a 47×17-bit multiplication is performed in each iteration, resulting in 8 DSP multiplications in total. For lower ring dimensions, the difference in the number of DSP multiplications becomes even more significant.

Naturally, the WLM-Mixed approach limits the range of primes. Specifically, the non-zero bits in the prime modulus q are constrained by the DSP operand sizes. However, there are still enough Proth primes that satisfy these constraints for FHE applications. For example, when $\log q = 64$ and $\log q_h = 17$, there are 2986 such primes available, which is far more than what is needed for FHE applications.

4   Implementation

In this section, we provide implementation details for the proposed algorithms, WLM-Mixed (Algorithm 8), K^2RED-Shift (Algorithm 7) and Montgomery-Shift (Algorithm6). We also implement WLM (Algorithm 2) and K^2RED (Algorithm 3) from the literature and provide the architectural details in this section. We do not implement the naive Montgomery reduction, Barrett reduction, and Plantard reduction, as these algorithms are theoretically more costly than the algorithms implemented, as detailed in Sect. 5.1. The implementations are developed using SystemVerilog (and Verilog) HDL, designed with a high degree of parameterization. Parameters such as $\log q$, $\log q_h$, and the option to enable l_3 for shift-add designs, can be specified at design time to generate the corresponding hardware. The complete implementations are publicly accessible at https://github.com/cisec-su/modmul-hdl.

In WLM, K^2RED, and WLM-Mixed, the multiplications are performed using a multiply-accumulate approach. Initially, the operands are partitioned according to the DSP word sizes to generate partial products. These partial products are then accumulated along with the corresponding terms specific to each algorithm. For example, in WLM-Mixed (Algorithm 8), the partial products from $q_h t_l$ are summed together with t_h and the carry c. Architectures implemented for WLM-Mixed and K^2RED for $\log q = 64$ are detailed in Figs. 1 and 2, respectively. The architecture implemented for WLM follows [20].

The implementations are pipelined[1]. Note that the pipeline steps are not illustrated in Figs. 1 and 2. We place Flip-Flops (FFs) to the partial products from the computation of $q_h t_l$ in Line 6, the output of summation t in Line 6,

---

[1] Indeed, the pipeline steps are fully configurable in our implementation; however, we report the most notable configurations in the paper.

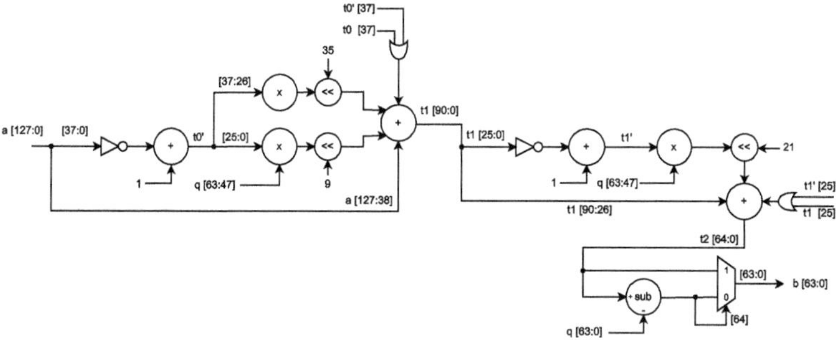

Fig. 1. WLM-Mixed Architecture for $\log q = 64$ and $\log q_h = 17$. DSP operand sizes are $\Gamma_A = 26$, $\Gamma_B = 17$.

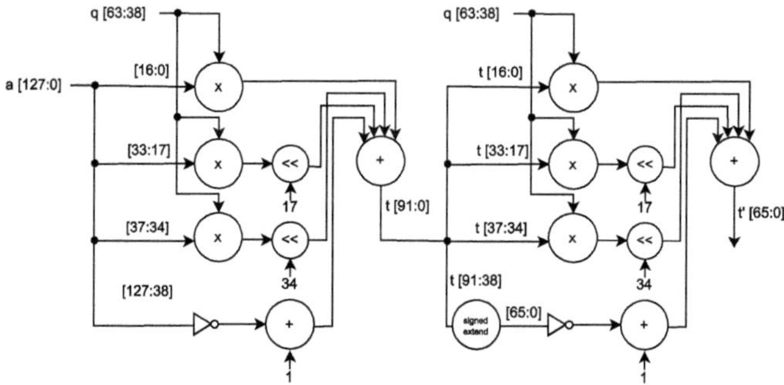

Fig. 2. K²RED Architecture for $\log q = 64$ and $\log q_h = 26$. DSP operand sizes are $\Gamma_A = 26$, $\Gamma_B = 17$. The correction step in Lines 5–7 of Algorithm 3 is skipped.

and b in Lines 7–8 of Algorithm 2 for WLM. As a result, the latency of WLM is $2\lceil \beta/\omega \rceil + 1$ clock cycles (ccs). We use the same pipeline strategy for WLM-Mixed and the latency is equal to 5 ccs. Similarly, for K²RED, we put FFs to the partial products from $q_h a_l$ and the output of summation t in Line 2; the partial products from $q_h t_l$ and the output of summation t' in Line 4; and b in Lines 6–8 of Algorithm 3, resulting in 5 ccs latency. For K²RED-Shift and Montgomery-Shift, we implement two pipeline configurations. ρ_A, ρ_B. For ρ_A, the shifts and additions are performed in different ccs while these are performed in single cc for ρ_B. This leads to a trade-off between speed and area. For Montgomery-Shift and ρ_A, we put FFs for t in Line 2; t' in Line 3; b' in Line 4; and b in Lines 6–7 of Algorithm 6, resulting in 4 ccs latency. Due to additional FFs, Latency of Montgomery-Shift is increased to 6 cc by using ρ_A. Similarly, for K²RED-Shift and ρ_B we put FFs for t in Line 2; t' in Line 4; b' in Line 4; and b in Lines 5–7 of Algorithm 7, resulting in 3 ccs latency. Using ρ_A increases the latency of K²RED-Shift to 5.

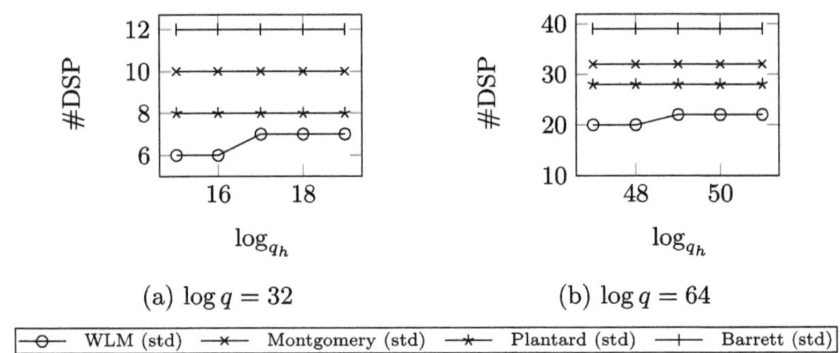

(a) $\log q = 32$ (b) $\log q = 64$

Fig. 3. DSP multiplication counts compared for Montgomery (Algorithm 1), Barrett (Algorithm 4), Plantard (Algorithm 5), and WLM (Algorithm 2).

5   Evaluation

In this section, we evaluate the resource efficiency of the proposed reduction algorithms in addition to the studied ones from the literature. First, we provide a theoretical analysis of the DSP usage by naive Montgomery (Algorithm 1), Barrett (Algorithm 4) and Plantard (Algorithm 5). Then, we provide practical results for the implemented reduction algorithms, namely WLM (Algorithm 2), WLM-Mixed (Algorithm 8), K^{2}RED (Algorithm 3), K^{2}RED-Shift (Algorithm 7) and Montgomery-Shift (Algorithm 6). We use the Area-Time-Product (ATP) as our assessment metric, which is widely used in the literature [27]. ATP is calculated as Average Latency $(\mu s) \times$ (LUT+FF/2+100$\times$ DSP + 300 $\times$ BRAM). We target the AMD-Xilinx Alveo U280[2] (XCU280) FPGA for our evaluations, using Vivado 2023.2[3] for synthesis and implementation. The XCU280 FPGA features 1303680 Look-Up Table (LUT)s, 2607360 FFs, 9024 DSPs[4], and 2016 BRAM36E1s. The DSP48E2 unit supports 26×17 unsigned multiplication with accumulation ($\Gamma_A = 26$, $\Gamma_B = 17$).

5.1   Theoretical Analysis of Montgomery, Barrett and Plantard

Figure 3 shows that the required number of DSP multiplications are significantly smaller for WLM compared to naive Montgomery, Barrett and Plantard. Recall that it eliminates the multiplication by a pre-computed factor such as q' which is the main reason behind its superiority. The number of DSP multiplications are counted by assuming standard tiling. In particular, to perform a $\beta \times \beta$-bit multiplication, $\lceil \beta/\Gamma_A \rceil \lceil \beta/\Gamma_B \rceil$ DSP multiplications are needed. Moreover, for multiplications involving q, only q_h is considered as an operand as the lower bits of NTT friendly primes is fixed. For instance, the multiplication tq in Line 2

---

[2] https://www.xilinx.com/products/boards-and-kits/alveo/u280.html.

[3] https://www.xilinx.com/products/design-tools/vivado.html.

[4] https://docs.amd.com/r/en-US/ug958-vivado-sysgen-ref/DSP48E2.

of Algorithm 1 is considered as a $\beta \times \log q_h$-bit multiplication. Also note that we report the DSP usage for a modular multiplication, involving the multiplication part as well. Recall that the Plantard reduction is particularly effective for multiplication by a constant situation, such as in a butterfly circuit of NTT. Therefore, to make a fair comparison, we include the cost of integer multiplication. For instance, for Montgomery, the total cost of modular multiplications is the summation of $\beta \times \beta$-bit multiplication for the integer multiplication part, and $(\beta \times \beta)$-bit and $(\beta \times \log q_h)$-bit multiplications for the reduction part which is based on Algorithm 1. In this case, the integer multiplication requires 12 DSP multiplications while the reduction part requires $12 + 8$ DSP multiplications, leading to 32 DSPs in total for $\beta = 64$. The DSP usage is counted in the same manner for the compared algorithms. There is an exception for the Barrett reduction. Observe from Algorithm 4 Line 2 that the multiplication tq does not have to be fully computed. Specifically, only the lower $\beta + 1$-bit of tq are required, since the output of the subtraction b, is at most $\beta + 1$-bit. We take this observation into account for counting the DSP usage of the Barrett reduction. Note that we did not include K^2RED and WLM-Mixed in the theoretical analysis, as a practical analysis is provided in the next section. This section aims to provide a rationale for comparing these algorithms with WLM. Additionally, we consider the case in which a non-standard tiling approach is employed for mapping DSPs to multiplications. Adapting the method of [9] to the DSP operand sizes considered here, a 60×60-bit multiplication can be implemented using 8 DSPs along with a small LUT-based multiplier. Applying this optimization, both Plantard and naive Montgomery multiplications for $\log q = 60$ can be realized using 24 DSPs, as each requires three 60×60-bit multiplications. In contrast, modular multiplication using WLM requires only 16 DSPs in this scenario: 8 DSPs for the 60×60-bit integer multiplication with non-standard tiling, and 8 DSPs for the WLM reduction (as described above). Consequently, adopting a non-standard tiling strategy does not alter the overall conclusions of our analysis.

5.2   Parameter Selection

In this section, we explain the parameter selection for evaluated algorithms. Since WLM supports general NTT-friendly primes, we always set $\omega = \log n + 1$ which is necessary for finding a primitive $2n$-th root of unity, resulting in $\log q_h = \log q - \log n - 1$. For WLM-Mixed, we set $\log q_h = 17$ ($\omega = 47$) as $\Gamma_B = 17$. As a result, the reduction requires only 3 DSPs while a sufficient number of primes are available as discussed in Sect. 3.4. For the 32-bit case, we set $\log q_h = 15$ to cover ring dimensions up to $n = 2^{16}$. The WLM-Mixed implementation also supports $\log q_h = 16$, but we skip it as the ATP results would be theoretically very similar to the previous case, with no effective difference in the number of primes.

For K^2RED, we employ a classical configuration where $\log q_h = 32$ for 64-bit as well as a DSP-optimized parameter selection where $\log q_h = 26$. With the latter, the number of DSPs is reduced to 6 from 8. Note that, $\log q_h = 26 \leq \Gamma_A$ and $\lceil (\log q - \log q_h), / \Gamma_B \rceil = 3$, leading to 3 DSP multiplications for Line 2 and

Line 4 of Algorithm 3. For the 32-bit case, we set $\log q_h = 15$ which corresponds to $n = 2^{16}$ and $\log q_h = 16$ to cover $n \leq 2^{15}$. Recall that $\log q_h$ must satisfy $\log q_h \leq \beta/2$ with respect to the definition of Proth primes.

For the K^{2}RED-Shift and Montgomery-Shift, we set $\log q_h = 17$ and $\log q_h = 32$ for 64-bit. Recall from Sect. 3 that the cost of shift operations as well as the number of available primes for both algorithms directly depends on $\log q_h$. For the 32-bit case, same with the K^{2}RED, we set $\log q_h = 15$, which corresponds to $n = 2^{16}$, and $\log q_h = 16$ to cover $n \leq 2^{15}$. We include both Proth-$2l$ and Proth-$3l$ primes, as it also leads to a trade-off between the available primes and resource consumption. Recall from Table 1 that the number of available primes is a crucial factor for the RNS representation.

Table 3. Implementation results for DSP-based reduction Algorithms.

$\log q$	$\log q_h$	# primes	max. $\log n$	LUT	FF	DSP	Freq. (MHz)	ATP
WLM (Algorithm 2)								
64	47	*	16	487	1177	8	416	4.5
64	48	*	15	518	1195	8	416	4.59
64	49	*	14	566	1450	10	434	5.26
64	50	*	13	579	1478	10	434	5.33
64	51	*	12	583	1506	10	434	5.37
32	15	*	16	136	226	2	526	0.85
32	16	*	15	130	210	2	526	0.82
32	17	*	14	152	315	3	526	1.15
32	18	*	13	156	320	3	526	1.17
32	19	*	12	160	325	3	526	1.18
WLM-Mixed (Algorithm 8)								
64	17	2986	≥ 16	315	522	3	476	1.83
32	15	1540	16	131	211	2	526	0.82
K^{2}RED (Algorithm 3)								
64	26	1522110	≥ 16	411	424	6	476	2.56
64	32	97482212	≥ 16	432	483	8	476	3.09
32	15	1540	16	151	201	2	588	0.76
32	16	3020	15	154	210	2	588	0.78

*: All NTT primes w.r.t. max. $\log n$.

5.3 Standalone Implementation Evaluations

Next, we evaluate the resource-efficiency of implemented reduction algorithms in a standalone manner. Tables 3 and 4 presents the ATP results for DSP-based and shift-add-based approaches, respectively. We report the maximum frequency that

Table 4. Implementation results for shift-add-based reduction algorithms.

ρ	$\log q$	$\log q_h$	l_3 en.	# primes	max. $\log n$	LUT	FF	DSP	Freq. (MHz)	ATP
K^2RED-Shift (Algorithm 7)										
ρ_A 64	17	✓	53	16	1259	979	0	476	3.67
ρ_B 64	17	✓	53	16	1295	409	0	370	4.04
ρ_B 64	17	✗	5	13	1079	397	0	454	2.81
ρ_A 64	32	✓	469	$\geq$16	1287	1071	0	500	3.64
ρ_B 64	32	✓	469	$\geq$16	1340	465	0	344	4.56
ρ_A 64	32	✗	16	15	945	953	0	588	2.41
ρ_B 64	32	✗	16	15	1048	449	0	416	3.05
ρ_A 32	15	✓	80	16	611	537	0	588	1.49
ρ_B 32	15	✓	80	16	617	245	0	434	1.7
ρ_B 32	15	✗	7	13	510	232	0	555	1.12
ρ_A 32	16	✓	80	15	595	537	0	555	1.55
ρ_B 32	16	✓	95	15	598	248	0	416	1.73
ρ_A 32	16	✗	7	13	462	466	0	714	0.97
ρ_B 32	16	✗	7	13	488	235	0	526	1.15
Montgomery-Shift (Algorithm 6)										
ρ_A 64	17	✓	53	16	1114	954	0	526	3.02
ρ_B 64	17	✓	53	16	1002	591	0	416	3.11
ρ_B 64	17	✗	5	13	671	583	0	416	2.31
ρ_A 64	32	✓	469	$\geq$16	1545	1101	0	500	4.19
ρ_B 64	32	✓	469	$\geq$16	1391	642	0	416	4.1
ρ_B 64	32	✗	16	15	945	632	0	416	3.02
ρ_A 32	15	✓	80	16	665	558	0	625	1.49
ρ_B 32	15	✓	80	16	603	329	0	434	1.76
ρ_B 32	15	✗	7	13	411	321	0	476	1.2
ρ_A 32	16	✓	95	15	667	564	0	588	1.61
ρ_B 32	16	✓	95	15	639	332	0	454	1.77
ρ_B 32	16	✗	7	13	420	324	0	476	1.22

ρ: Pipeline configuration. l_3 en.: ✓Proth-$3l$, ✗Proth-$2l$.

can be implemented using Vivado. Observe that the proposed WLM-Mixed leads to the lowest ATP scores for the 64-bit class, as it is designed for minimizing the number of DSP multiplications. It achieves $2.45\times$ and $1.39\times$ lower ATP compared to WLM and K^2RED. On the other hand, for 32-bit class, K^2RED and WLM-Mixed leads to comparable results while K^2RED slightly performs better. The performance of WLM is aligned with these two algorithms for $\log q_h = 15$ and $\log q_h = 16$. However, with $\log q_h \geq 17$, the number of iterations for WLM increases to 3 (see Algorithm 2), increasing its ATP.

It is worth noting that while the shift-add methods, Montgomery-Shift and K^2RED-Shift, result in higher ATPs, they can be advantageous in scenarios where the system has a limited number of available DSPs and the implementer prefers to trade DSPs for LUTs. The ATP performances of Montgomery-Shift and K^2RED-Shift are comparable.

Tables 3 and 4 also presents the maximum supported ring dimension n for each algorithm and parameter, which is particularly important for Montgomery-Shift and K^2RED-Shift to minimize the hardware cost for the desired n. It is computed based on the number of available primes considering the RNS representation (see Table 1) and the availability of the $2n$-th root of unity (see Sect. 2.2).

5.4 NTT Evaluations

We also evaluated the reduction algorithms within an NTT architecture, which follows the design presented in [2]. Specifically, we provide ATP results from the NTT implementation using different modular reduction algorithms inside the butterfly modules. Tables 5 and 6 presents the results for $\log q = 32$ and $\log q = 64$, respectively. The implementations are performed using various numbers of processing elements (PEs), n and q. Note that the number of PEs defines the number of parallel executed butterfly circuits. BRAM is not included in ATP computation as it is equivalent for all designs. For algorithm-specific configurations such as $\log q_h$, using Proth-$2l$ or Proth-$3l$, or the pipeline configurations, we selected the best set from Tables 3 and 4. For instance, for Montgomery-Shift $\log n = 12$ and $\log q = 64$, we employed Proth-$2l$ and $\log q_h = 17$ as it is the best configuration regarding resource consumption based on Table 4. For Montgomery-Shift, we opted for the ρ_B pipeline configuration. Although ρ_A yielded better results, the performance of the two configurations was comparable. Similar to the previous section, we report the smallest frequency that can be implemented for each design. Observe that the NTT implementation statistics mainly align with our initial observation from the previous section. Notably, Montgomery-Shift exhibits low ATP scores for $\log n = 12$. This is primarily due to the reduced hardware cost associated with this ring dimension, as fewer primes are required. Additionally, NTT with Montgomery-Shift achieves higher operating frequencies compared to the DSP-based reductions, WLM-Mixed and K^2RED. For ring dimensions $\log n = 14$ and $\log n = 16$ multiplication-based methods become the superior choice as WLM-Mixed leads to the lowest ATP scores for $\log q = 64$.

5.5 Comparison with Literature

We also compare our results with those reported in the literature, as shown in Table 7. We should note that FPGA devices VU37P, U250, and U280 belong to the Virtex Ultrascale+ family, while ZCU106 is a Zynq Ultrascale+ FPGA. The main goal in presenting this comparison is to demonstrate that the employed

Table 5. NTT Implementation results for $\log q = 32$ with different reductions.

Reduction	$\log n$	PE	$\log q_h$	ρ	l_3 en.	LUT $\cdot 10^3$	FF $\cdot 10^3$	DSP	BR	Freq. (MHz)	Lat. (μs)	ATP $\cdot 10^3$
WLM	12	16	19			14	10	112	17	434	3.60	113.71 (**1.07**$\times$)
WLM-M.	12	16	15			14	9	96	17	434	3.59	105.78 (**1.00**$\times$)
K^{2}RED	12	16	15			14	11	96	17	416	3.75	111.73 (**1.06**$\times$)
K^{2}RED-S.	12	16	16	ρ_A	✗	17	13	64	17	400	3.91	119.51 (**1.13**$\times$)
Mont.-S.	12	16	16	ρ_B	✗	17	10	64	17	400	3.91	115.56 (**1.09**$\times$)
WLM	12	32	19			26	22	224	32.5	357	2.23	135.24 (**1.17**$\times$)
WLM-M.	12	32	15			25	19	192	32.5	370	2.15	117.62 (**1.02**$\times$)
K^{2}RED	12	32	15			25	21	192	32.5	384	2.07	115.52 (**1.00**$\times$)
K^{2}RED-S.	12	32	16	ρ_A	✗	34	26	128	32.5	384	2.07	125.37 (**1.08**$\times$)
Mont.-S.	12	32	16	ρ_B	✗	34	20	128	32.5	384	2.06	120.39 (**1.04**$\times$)
WLM	12	64	19			42	39	448	64.5	312	1.32	142.89 (**1.20**$\times$)
WLM-M.	12	64	15			40	34	384	64.5	312	1.32	127.55 (**1.07**$\times$)
K^{2}RED	12	64	15			41	39	384	64.5	333	1.23	123.47 (**1.03**$\times$)
K^{2}RED-S.	12	64	16	ρ_A	✗	57	49	256	64.5	357	1.15	124.9 (**1.05**$\times$)
Mont.-S.	12	64	16	ρ_B	✗	58	39	256	64.5	357	1.15	119.46 (**1.00**$\times$)
WLM	14	16	17			14	11	112	50	400	18.01	565.49 (**1.10**$\times$)
WLM-M.	14	16	15			13	10	96	50	384	18.72	530.5 (**1.03**$\times$)
K^{2}RED	14	16	15			15	12	96	50	434	16.56	514.18 (**1.00**$\times$)
K^{2}RED-S.	14	16	15	ρ_A	✓	20	14	64	50	303	23.76	824.72 (**1.60**$\times$)
Mont.-S.	14	16	15	ρ_B	✓	21	11	64	50	370	19.44	657.52 (**1.28**$\times$)
WLM	16	16	15			13	11	96	65	416	78.73	2233.78 (**1.01**$\times$)
WLM-M.	16	16	15			13	9	96	65	400	82.01	2275.68 (**1.03**$\times$)
K^{2}RED	16	16	15			14	11	96	65	434	75.45	2214.43 (**1.00**$\times$)
K^{2}RED-S.	16	16	15	ρ_A	✓	19	14	64	65	370	88.57	2973.24 (**1.34**$\times$)
Mont.-S.	16	16	15	ρ_B	✓	17	10	64	65	400	82.01	2403.14 (**1.09**$\times$)

PE: Processing Elements, ρ: pipeline configuration, BR: BRAM. l_3 en.: ✓Proth-$3l$, ✗Proth-$2l$.

NTT architecture, which we benchmark the reduction algorithms, is comparable with existing designs in the literature, rather than claiming superiority. The reductions used in the referenced works generally employ the reduction techniques studied in this paper. Additionally, [12,16] utilize a specialized reduction method called eDARM. This technique uses primes of the form $q = 2^\beta - \delta$, where $\delta \leq 2^{\lfloor 2\beta/3 \rfloor}$ and β is even. To illustrate the efficiency of the proposed WLM-Mixed method compared to eDARM, consider the case where $\log q = 64$ and $\log n = 16$, resulting in $\delta \leq 2^{24}$. The eDARM method requires $3 \log \delta' \times \beta$-bit multiplications, where $\delta' \leq 2^{24 - \log n - 1} = 2^7$ that takes the advantage of the fact that lower $\log n + 1$ bits of q is fixed for NTT friendly primes. This can be

Table 6. NTT Implementation results for $\log q = 64$ with different reductions.

Reduction	$\log n$	PE	$\log q_h$	ρ	l_3 en.	LUT $\cdot 10^3$	FF $\cdot 10^3$	DSP	BR	Freq. (MHz)	Lat. (μs)	ATP $\cdot 10^3$
WLM	12	16	51			34	32	352	34	333	4.71	402.81 (**1.35**$\times$)
WLM-M.	12	16	17			28	22	240	34	322	4.85	310.58 (**1.04**$\times$)
K^{2}RED	12	16	26			30	22	288	34	333	4.70	330.71 (**1.11**$\times$)
K^{2}RED-S.	12	16	17	ρ_A	✗	38	27	192	34	333	4.70	334.79 (**1.12**$\times$)
Mont.-S.	12	16	17	ρ_B	✗	35	22	192	34	344	4.54	299.09 (**1.00**$\times$)
WLM	12	32	51			67	61	704	65	270	2.97	502.89 (**1.37**$\times$)
WLM-M.	12	32	17			57	43	480	65	270	2.95	376.2 (**1.03**$\times$)
K^{2}RED	12	32	26			60	43	576	65	263	3.03	421.92 (**1.15**$\times$)
K^{2}RED-S.	12	32	17	ρ_A	✗	75	53	384	65	263	3.03	427.1 (**1.16**$\times$)
Mont.-S.	12	32	17	ρ_B	✗	70	44	384	65	285	2.79	366.71 (**1.00**$\times$)
WLM	12	64	51			139	123	1408	129	238	1.76	601.5 (**1.36**$\times$)
WLM-M.	12	64	17			120	86	960	129	238	1.73	450.55 (**1.02**$\times$)
K^{2}RED	12	64	26			121	87	1152	129	250	1.65	463.03 (**1.04**$\times$)
K^{2}RED-S.	12	64	17	ρ_A	✗	155	107	768	129	250	1.65	471.71 (**1.06**$\times$)
Mont.-S.	12	64	17	ρ_B	✗	142	86	768	129	243	1.69	443.63 (**1.00**$\times$)
WLM	14	16	49			36	33	352	113.5	344	20.90	1849.13 (**1.22**$\times$)
WLM-M.	14	16	17			31	24	240	113.5	322	22.32	1512.35 (**1.00**$\times$)
K^{2}RED	14	16	26			32	24	288	113.5	333	21.60	1601.42 (**1.05**$\times$)
K^{2}RED-S.	14	16	32	ρ_A	✗	38	29	192	113.5	303	23.76	1720.62 (**1.37**$\times$)
Mont.-S.	14	16	32	ρ_B	✗	41	23	192	113.5	285	25.20	1819.62 (**1.20**$\times$)
WLM	16	16	47			31	30	320	129	333	98.43	7759.74 (**1.16**$\times$)
WLM-M.	16	16	17			30	22	240	129	322	101.70	6664.72 (**1.00**$\times$)
K^{2}RED	16	16	26			30	22	288	129	333	98.42	6945.1 (**1.04**$\times$)
K^{2}RED-S.	16	16	17	ρ_A	✓	44	30	192	129	333	98.42	7812.04 (**1.17**$\times$)
Mont.-S.	16	16	17	ρ_B	✓	41	22	192	129	303	108.25	7777.88 (**1.16**$\times$)

PE: Processing Elements, ρ: pipeline configuration, BR: BRAM. l_3 en.: ✓Proth-$3l$, ✗Proth-$2l$.

implemented using 9 DSPs, as $\lceil \log \delta' / \Gamma_B \rceil \times \lceil \beta / \Gamma_A \rceil = 3$. All of the works shown in Table 7 support run-time configurability of the prime modulus and allow for a sufficient number of primes to meet the requirements of the RNS representation.

Table 7. Comparison to NTT implementations from Literature

Work	Reduction	Device	$\log n$	$\log q$	PE	LUT $\cdot 10^3$	FF $\cdot 10^3$	DSP	BR	Freq. (MHz)	Lat. cc/μs	ATP $\cdot 10^3$
[20]	WLM	VC707	12	32	-	80	-	952	325.5	200	-/0.18	49.5
[8]	Barrett	ZCU106	12	32	-	3.3	1.5	42	29.5	180	-/136.58	2335.5
[22]	Mont.	Virtex-7	12	24	16	14.6	6.5	80	12	121	1543/12.8	377
[17]	Barrett	Virtex-7	12	32	8	6.8	6.4	88	24	228	3081/13.5	351
[25]	Mont.	VU37P	12	28	8	7.9	3.9	32	24	272	-/11.34	229.6
TW	WLM-M.	U280	12	32	16	14.9	9.6	96	17	434	1565/3.6	124.14
[16]	eDARM	VU37P	12	60	-	74.5	61.4	288	697.5	250	951/3.8	1304.4
[19]	WLM	Virtex-7	12	60	32	99.3	-	992	176	125	972/7.7	1935
[27]	K^2RED	Virtex-7	12	60	-	17	11	286	24.5	150	-/27.5	1607.4
TW	Mont.-S.	U280	12	64	16	35.5	22.5	192	34	344	1564/4.54	141.78
[16]	eDARM	VU37P	14	60	-	74.5	61.4	288	697.5	250	4340/17.3	5938.2
[24]	Barrett	U250	14	60	-	36.4	3.6	336	60	200	-/29.3	2631.1
[12]	eDARM	U250	14	60	-	99.7	56.6	384	135	388	8267/21.8	4510.4
TW	WLM-M.	U280	14	64	16	31	24	240	113.5	322	7201/22.32	2272.44
[10]	Barrett	U250	16	60	32	148.5	90.9	564	137	200	536832/2684	782251.8
[16]	eDARM	VU37P	16	60	-	74.5	61.4	288	697.5	264	16628/66.51	22829.6
[18]	Barrett	U250	16	60	-	274.4	83.1	630	1084	250	16552/66.2	46614.7
TW	WLM-M.	U280	16	64	16	30.4	22.4	240	129	322	32805/101.70	10600.33

TW: this work, PE: Processing Elements, BR: BRAM.

6   Conclusion

In this paper, we studied the resource efficiency of various modular reduction algorithms, targeting NTT implementations on FPGA. Particularly, we explored the optimization opportunities through the trade-offs between the number of primes available in special forms and the hardware costs. Our proposed WLM-Mixed outperformed WLM [20] and K^2RED [4] significantly in 64-bit modulus, as it only requires 3 DSP multiplications by design. On the other hand, we introduced multiplication-free variants of the Naive Montgomery algorithm and K^2RED, termed Montgomery-Shift and K^2RED-Shift, respectively. These algorithms demonstrated low ATP scores for small ring dimensions, such as $n = 2^{12}$. This is because reducing the number of required primes directly impacts the hardware cost. Our study reveals that significant improvements are possible by reducing the number of free bits in the modulus while leaving sufficient number of free bits to meet the requirements of RNS representation. Although we concentrated on FPGA implementations, our methodology applies to ASICs as well. We leave the in-depth analysis of ASIC implementations of our proposed algorithms for future work.

References

1. Albrecht, M.R., Player, R., Scott, S.: On the concrete hardness of learning with errors. J. Math. Crypt. **9**(3), 169–203 (2015)
2. Ayduman, C., Koçer, E., Kırbıyık, S., Can Mert, A., Savaş, E.: Efficient design-time flexible hardware architecture for accelerating homomorphic encryption. In: 2023 IFIP/IEEE 31st International Conference on Very Large Scale Integration (VLSI-SoC), October 2023, pp. 1–7 (2023). https://doi.org/10.1109/VLSI-SoC57769.2023.10321943
3. Barrett, P.: Implementing the Rivest Shamir and Adleman public key encryption algorithm on a standard digital signal processor. In: Odlyzko, A.M. (ed.) CRYPTO 1986. LNCS, vol. 263, pp. 311–323. Springer, Heidelberg (1987). https://doi.org/10.1007/3-540-47721-7_24
4. Bisheh-Niasar, M., Azarderakhsh, R., Mozaffari-Kermani, M.: High-speed NTT-based polynomial multiplication accelerator for post-quantum cryptography. In: 2021 IEEE 28th Symposium on Computer Arithmetic (ARITH), pp. 94–101. IEEE (2021)
5. Brakerski, Z.: Fully homomorphic encryption without modulus switching from classical GapSVP. In: Safavi-Naini, R., Canetti, R. (eds.) CRYPTO 2012. LNCS, vol. 7417, pp. 868–886. Springer, Heidelberg (2012). https://doi.org/10.1007/978-3-642-32009-5_50
6. Chilotti, I., Gama, N., Georgieva, M., Izabachène, M.: TFHE: fast fully homomorphic encryption over the torus. J. Cryptol. **33**, 34–91 (2019). https://doi.org/10.1007/s00145-019-09319
7. Cooley, J.W., Tukey, J.W.: An algorithm for the machine calculation of complex Fourier series. Math. Comput. **19**(90), 297–301 (1965)
8. Di Matteo, S., Gerfo, M.L., Saponara, S.: VLSI design and FPGA implementation of an NTT hardware accelerator for homomorphic seal-embedded library. IEEE Access **11**, 72498–72508 (2023)
9. de Dinechin, F., Pasca, B.: Large multipliers with fewer DSP blocks. In: 2009 International Conference on Field Programmable Logic and Applications, pp. 250–255. IEEE (2009)
10. Duong-Ngoc, P., Kwon, S., Yoo, D., Lee, H.: Area-efficient number theoretic transform architecture for homomorphic encryption. IEEE Trans. Circ. Syst. I Regul. Pap. **70**(3), 1270–1283 (2022)
11. Fan, J., Vercauteren, F.: Somewhat practical fully homomorphic encryption. Cryptology ePrint Archive (2012)
12. Geng, Y., Hu, X., Wang, Z.: GS-MDC: High-speed and area-efficient number theoretic transform design. IEEE Trans. Circ. Syst. II Exp. Briefs **71**(12), 4974–4978 (2024)
13. Gentleman, W.M., Sande, G.: Fast Fourier transforms: for fun and profit. In: Proceedings of the November 7–10, 1966, Fall Joint Computer Conference, pp. 563–578 (1966)
14. Gentry, C.: Fully homomorphic encryption using ideal lattices. In: Proceedings of the Forty-First Annual ACM Symposium on Theory of Computing, pp. 169–178 (2009)
15. Cheon, J.H., Kim, A., Kim, M., Song, Y.: Homomorphic encryption for arithmetic of approximate numbers. In: Takagi, T., Peyrin, T. (eds.) ASIACRYPT 2017. LNCS, vol. 10624, pp. 409–437. Springer, Cham (2017). https://doi.org/10.1007/978-3-319-70694-8_15

16. Kurniawan, S., Duong-Ngoc, P., Lee, H.: Configurable memory-based NTT architecture for homomorphic encryption. IEEE Trans. Circ. Syst. II Exp. Briefs **70**(10), 3942–3946 (2023)
17. Liu, S.H., Kuo, C.Y., Mo, Y.N., Su, T.: An area-efficient, conflict-free, and configurable architecture for accelerating NTT/INTT. IEEE Trans. Very Large Scale Integr. (VLSI) Syst. **32**(3), 519–529 (2023)
18. Mareta, R., Satriawan, A., Duong, P.N., Lee, H.: A bootstrapping-capable configurable NTT architecture for fully homomorphic encryption. IEEE Access **12**, 52911–52921 (2024)
19. Mert, A.C., Karabulut, E., Öztürk, E., Savaş, E., Aysu, A.: An extensive study of flexible design methods for the number theoretic transform. IEEE Trans. Comput. **71**(11), 2829–2843 (2020)
20. Mert, A.C., Öztürk, E., Savaş, E.: Design and implementation of encryption/decryption architectures for BFV homomorphic encryption scheme. IEEE Trans. Very Large Scale Integr. (VLSI) Syst. **28**(2), 353–362 (2019)
21. Montgomery, P.L.: Modular multiplication without trial division. Math. Comput. **44**(170), 519–521 (1985)
22. Mu, J., et al.: Scalable and conflict-free NTT hardware accelerator design: methodology, proof and implementation. IEEE Trans. Comput. Aided Des. Integr. Circ. Syst. **42**(5), 1504–1517 (2022)
23. Nguyen, D.N., et al.: HyperNTT: a fast and accurate NTT/INTT accelerator with multi-level pipelining and an improved K2-RED module. In: 2024 International Technical Conference on Circuits/Systems, Computers, and Communications (ITC-CSCC), pp. 1–6. IEEE (2024)
24. Nguyen, T.T., Kim, J., Lee, H.: CKKS-based homomorphic encryption architecture using parallel NTT multiplier. In: 2023 IEEE International Symposium on Circuits and Systems (ISCAS), pp. 1–4. IEEE (2023)
25. Paludo, R., Sousa, L.: NTT architecture for a Linux-ready RISC-V fully-homomorphic encryption accelerator. IEEE Trans. Circ. Syst. I Regul. Pap. **69**(7), 2669–2682 (2022)
26. Plantard, T.: Efficient word size modular arithmetic. IEEE Trans. Emerg. Top. Comput. **9**(3), 1506–1518 (2021). https://doi.org/10.1109/TETC.2021.3073475
27. Ye, Z., Cheung, R.C., Huang, K.: PipeNTT: a pipelined number theoretic transform architecture. IEEE Trans. Circ. Syst. II Exp. Briefs **69**(10), 4068–4072 (2022)

Leveraging Smaller Finite Fields for More Efficient ZK-Friendly Hash Functions

Gökçe Düzyol[1,2] and Kamil Otal[1(✉)]

[1] National Research Institute of Electronics and Cryptology, TÜBİTAK BİLGEM UEKAE, Gebze, Kocaeli, Turkey
[2] Boğaziçi University, Bebek, Istanbul, Turkey
{gokce.duzyol,kamil.otal}@tubitak.gov.tr

Abstract. Maximum distance separable (MDS) matrices are the main building blocks that provide the maximum possible diffusion in several block ciphers and cryptographic hash functions. In addition to using MDS matrices directly, there are also some indirect but simple and efficient methods that provide the maximum possible diffusion property. In particular, the subfield construction introduced by Barreto et al. in [DCC 56 (2–3) 141–162 (2010)] and its generalization examined by Otal in [IJISS 11 (2) 1–11 (2022)] make use of MDS matrices over smaller finite fields to provide the maximum possible diffusion property over larger finite fields.

ZK-friendly hash functions, in contrast to the classical cryptographic hash functions, use higher-dimensional MDS matrices over larger finite fields.

In this paper, we examine the applicability of the generalized subfield construction and the possibility of improvements on ZK-friendly hash functions. As a case study, we focus on a recent ZK-friendly hash function Vision Mark-32 presented by Ashur et al. in [IACR Preprint 2024/633]. In particular, instead of using a 24×24 MDS matrix over $\mathbb{F}_{2^{32}}$ for a 24×1 column input over $\{0,1\}^{32}$, we suggest separating the 24×1 column input over $\{0,1\}^{32}$ into four 24×1 subcolumns over $\{0,1\}^8$ and then using a 24×24 MDS matrix over $\mathbb{F}_{2^8}$ for each subcolumn. This method still keeps the maximum diffusion property without any compromise and provides simplicity and efficiency. For example, it is possible to significantly decrease the required LUT values to 265 from about 9200 and FF values to 102 from about 4600 for the hardware implementation. We also highlight that we do not need any additional tricks such as NTT for field multiplications.

We also push the theoretical boundaries of the generalized subfield construction to see how much small finite fields we can use, examine the arithmetization complexity, and discuss its applicability to other ZK-friendly hash functions.

Keywords: ZK-friendly hash functions · Arithmetization-oriented hash functions · MDS matrices · Generalized subfield construction

© The Author(s), under exclusive license to Springer Nature Switzerland AG 2026
E. Savas et al. (Eds.): LightSec 2025, LNCS 16216, pp. 138–153, 2026.
https://doi.org/10.1007/978-3-032-15541-2_8

1   Introduction

Zero-knowledge (ZK) proof systems are among the most popular and practical privacy-enhancing technologies. They have several applications in blockchains, cryptocurrencies, and web3 technologies. In particular, SNARKs (Succinct Non-Interactive Argument of Knowledge) have a special place due to their efficiency in verification and compact proof size.

A key challenge in ZK systems is the computational cost of hash functions. While traditional hash functions over binary fields, such as [6,12], are optimised for computational efficiency, they impose high arithmetization costs, leading to inefficient performance in ZK applications. To address this, ZK-friendly (a.k.a. arithmetization-oriented) hash functions such as Poseidon [14], Rescue [2], Monolith [13], MiMC [1], Vision [2], Vision Mark-32 [4], Tip5 [34], XHash [3], and Polocolo [16] have been developed. In such designs, finite fields are generally chosen as either a large prime field or a large binary tower field of sizes around 2^{64}.

1.1   Motivation and Related Work

Sponge construction is preferred by many ZK-friendly hash functions and contains mainly the following round profile: The input is considered as an m-tuple of elements from a finite field $\mathbb{F}_q$ of size q. Then we apply the following steps in one round.

1. S-box layer: We apply the $x \mapsto x^d$ mapping for each entry x from the m-tuple, where d is a special small positive integer or -1. Then we evaluate x^d in a linearised or affine polynomial over $\mathbb{F}_q$.
2. MDS matrix multiplication layer: The m-tuple is then multiplied by an $m \times m$ MDS (maximum distance separable) matrix over $\mathbb{F}_q$.
3. Addition: We add a suitable m-tuple over $\mathbb{F}_q$.

The most costly part in this construction is the S-box layer, whereas the second one is the MDS matrix multiplication layer. For example, for Vision Mark-32 [4] which takes the parameters $q = 2^{32}$, $m = 24$, and $d = -1$ we can illustrate and compare the hardware implementation complexities in Table 1 below.

Table 1.   [4, Table 3] Vision Mark-32 permutation round circuit complexity, implemented at 250 MHz.

Component	LUT	FF
S-box layer	41k	8.4k
MDS matrix multiplication	9.2k	4.6k
Total	50.0k	13.0k

Since the most costly part is the S-box layer, most of the performance-enhancing endeavours are focused on the S-box layer. However, as seen from Table 1, nearly 20% of the required LUTs and 35% of FFs are consumed by the MDS matrix multiplication process; hence, the optimization for the MDS matrix multiplication layer has significant importance. In this paper, we focus on the efficient solutions for the MDS matrix multiplication process.

Historically, MDS matrices and, in general, MDS transformations have always been of interest since their usage in the Advanced Encryption Standard [11]. As a result of this interest, the last few decades have comprised intense research studies on the design and implementation of efficient MDS transformations, see for example [19,20,24,27,33].

However, cryptographically significant MDS matrices have been of dimensions mostly $m \times m$ where $4 \leq m \leq 8$ and over the finite fields of size mostly between $16 \leq q \leq 256$. Therefore, the research on MDS matrices has been dedicated to such lower dimensions and small fields.

On the other hand, for higher-dimensional MDS matrices over larger finite fields, there are only some generic methods such as the MDS matrices derived from Reed-Solomon (RS) codes (see, for example [30] for further details on RS codes). Other types, such as the circulant MDS matrices, are not very available for higher dimensions. Therefore, for higher dimensions and larger finite fields, it is not easy to systematically produce the most efficient MDS matrices. Instead, MDS matrices are randomly produced, and some implementation tricks such as Number Theoretic Transformation (NTT) are preferred for finite field multiplications (as in [4], for example).

Note that the motivation behind choosing MDS matrices comes from their maximum possible diffusion capability. However, the maximum possible diffusion property can be provided by various methods, direct usage of MDS matrices is not the only way. For example, there are some nonlinear [25] and additive [5,27] MDS diffusion methods. We emphasize that especially the "generalized subfield construction" presented in [27] can be quite efficient for several ZK-friendly hash functions.

1.2 Our Contribution

In this paper, we examine the efficiency of the generalized subfield construction [5,27] by studying Vision Mark-32 [4].

In particular, instead of using a 24×24 MDS matrix over $\mathbb{F}_{2^{32}}$ for a 24×1 column input over $\{0,1\}^{32}$, we suggest separating the 24×1 column input over $\{0,1\}^{32}$ into four 24×1 subcolumns over $\{0,1\}^{8}$ and then using a 24×24 MDS matrix over $\mathbb{F}_{2^{8}}$ for each subcolumn. This method still keeps the maximum diffusion property without any security and performance compromise (i.e., we do not need to increase the number of rounds or do anything else). Also, it is possible to significantly decrease the required LUT and FF numbers for the hardware implementation, for example, we implemented our idea with 265 LUTs and 102 FFs at clock frequency operating at 220 MHz (recall Table 1 which includes numbers about 9200 LUTs and 4600 FFs for the hardware implementation). We also emphasize that we do not need any additional tricks such as NTT for finite field multiplications.

We also push the theoretical boundaries of the generalized subfield construction to see how much small finite fields we can use, examine the arithmetization complexity, and discuss its applicability to other ZK-friendly hash functions.

As a result, we show that the generalized subfield construction can be quite efficient; also, it provides simplicity and versatility.

1.3 Paper Organization

The rest of the paper is organized as follows: The next section gives preliminary information about MDS matrices and their efficiency, the generalized subfield construction, the round structure of the Vision Mark-32 ZK-friendly hash function, and basic information about FPGAs. Section 3 presents improvements based on the generalized subfield construction and regarding analysis. The last section contains some concluding remarks and future work.

2 Preliminaries

In this section, we give some basic information and fix our notation on MDS matrices and our target ZK-friendly hash function Vision Mark-32 [4].

2.1 MDS Transformations and Matrices

Let $\mathbb{F}_q$ denote the finite field of size q and $\mathbb{F}_q^l$ represent the set of l-tuples of $\mathbb{F}_q$. The function $d : \mathbb{F}_{2^n}^l \times \mathbb{F}_{2^n}^l \to \mathbb{R}$ given by $d(u, v) := |\{i : i \in \{1, 2, \ldots, l\}, u_i \neq v_i\}|$ satisfies the metric properties and is called the *Hamming distance*. A subset C of $\mathbb{F}_{2^n}^l$ endowed with the Hamming metric is called a *code*. We define the *minimum (Hamming) distance* of a code C by $d(C) := \min\{d(u, v) : u, v \in C, u \neq v\}$. There is an upper bound on $d(C)$ given by $d(C) \leq l + 1 - \log_{2^n}(|C|)$ and called the *Singleton bound*. A subset C of $\mathbb{F}_{2^n}^l$ satisfying the Singleton bound is called an *MDS code*.

The main parameters of a code C in $\mathbb{F}_{2^n}^l$ is denoted by $(l, |C|, d(C))_{2^n}$. In particular, if C is an m-dimensional subspace of $\mathbb{F}_{2^n}^l$ over $\mathbb{F}_{2^n}$, then we denote the main parameters of C by $[l, m, d(C)]_{2^n}$. MDS codes exist for many but not all parameters. In particular, the *MDS Conjecture*, which is stated below, formulates the existence of linear MDS codes for their parameters (see also [30, Conjecture 11.16] for example).

Conjecture 1 (The MDS Conjecture). The parameters of a linear MDS code $[l, m, l - m + 1]_{2^n}$ of length l and dimension $m > 1$ over $\mathbb{F}_{2^n}$ satisfy the following:

$$l \leq \begin{cases} 2^n + 1 & \text{if } m \in \{2\} \cup \{4, 5, \ldots, 2^n - 2\}, \\ 2^n + 2 & \text{if } m \in \{3, 2^n - 1\}, \\ m + 1 & \text{if } m \geq 2^n. \end{cases}$$

A linear code corresponds to a rowspace of an $m \times l$ matrix over $\mathbb{F}_{2^n}$. Such a matrix is called a *generator matrix* of the code. In particular, linear MDS codes can be uniquely represented by a $m \times l$ matrix $[I : M]$, which is a concatenation of the $m \times m$ identity matrix I and $m \times (l - m)$ matrix M over $\mathbb{F}_{2^n}$. Here, the redundancy (check) part M of the generator matrix is called an *MDS matrix*. The minimum distance of a given linear MDS code equips the corresponding MDS matrix as in the following well-known result.

Proposition 1. *Let u be a nonzero $m \times 1$ matrix and M be a $m \times m$ MDS matrix over $\mathbb{F}_{2^n}$. Then the number of minimum total nonzero entries in both u and Mu is at least $m + 1$.*

Construction of MDS matrices is an important and intensely studied area in mathematics and cryptography. We refer the reader to [15], which is a recent and comprehensive survey in this area. We now give an important and generic construction method in the following proposition.

Proposition 2. *[26] For distinct $x_0, x_1, \ldots, x_{m-1}, y_0, y_1, \ldots, y_{m-1}$ from $\mathbb{F}_{2^n}$, the $m \times m$ matrix $A = (a_{i,j})$, where*

$$a_{i,j} = \frac{1}{x_i + y_j},$$

is an MDS matrix.

Remark 1 (Some Definitions and Facts). The matrix constructed in Proposition 2 is called *Cauchy matrix* of $x_0, x_1, \ldots, x_{m-1}, y_0, y_1, \ldots, y_{m-1}$. We remark that if $A = (a_{i,j})$ is a Cauchy matrix in this form, then for any two nonsingular diagonal matrices $D_1 = \mathrm{diag}(c_0, c_1, \ldots, c_{m-1})$ and $D_2 = \mathrm{diag}(d_0, d_1, \ldots, d_{m-1})$, the matrix

$$D_1 A D_2 = \left(\frac{c_i d_j}{x_i + y_j} \right)$$

is called a *generalized Cauchy matrix*. We emphasize the fact that if A is MDS, then $D_1 A D_2$ is MDS.

A generalization of the construction in Proposition 2 and its relation to Reed-Solomon codes are available below.

Proposition 3. *[31,32] An $m \times 2m$ matrix G of the form $G = [I|A]$ over a finite field generates a generalized Reed-Solomon code if and only if $A = (a_{i,j})$ is a generalized Cauchy matrix, i.e.,*

$$a_{i,j} = \frac{c_i d_j}{x_i + y_j}$$

for $0 \leq i, j \leq m-1$, where the x_i, y_j are $2m$ distinct elements such that $x_i + y_j \neq 0$ for all i and j, and $c_i, d_j \neq 0$.

2.2   Efficiency of MDS Matrices

The efficiency of an MDS matrix is generally measured by the number of XORs that the mapping needs. In particular, we focus on the finite field multiplication between a constant finite field element and a variable. The number of XORs that the multiplication needs is determined by the irreducible polynomial which defines the finite field.

For example, consider the finite field $\mathbb{F}_{2^3} = \mathbb{F}(\alpha)$ where α is a root of $x^3 + x + 1 \in \mathbb{F}_2[x]$, the multiplication of $\alpha + \alpha^2$ and the arbitrary element $y = y_0 + y_1\alpha + y_2\alpha^2$ ($y_i \in \mathbb{F}_2$ for $0 \leq i \leq 2$) is given by

$$\begin{aligned}
(\alpha + \alpha^2)y &= (\alpha + \alpha^2)(y_0 + y_1\alpha + y_2\alpha^2) \\
&= (y_1 + y_2) + (y_0 + y_1)\alpha + (y_0 + y_1 + y_2)\alpha^2,
\end{aligned}$$

which corresponds to the mapping

$$(y_0, y_1, y_2) \mapsto (y_1 + y_2,\ y_0 + y_1,\ y_0 + y_1 + y_2). \tag{1}$$

Here, the addition corresponds to the XOR operation, and hence we need to apply $1 + 1 + 2 = 4$ XORs to execute the multiplication by $\alpha + \alpha^2$. The XOR counting procedure given above is also called the *direct XOR (d-XOR) counting* [18].

It is possible to define the number of XORs in a slightly different way. Let $f(x) = f_n x^n + f_{n-1}x^{n-1} + \cdots + f_1 x + f_0$ be an irreducible polynomial of degree n over $\mathbb{F}_2$, let α be a root of f, and define $\mathbb{F}_{2^n} = \mathbb{F}(\alpha)$. Here, considering α, define

$$M_\alpha = \begin{bmatrix} 0\,0 \ldots 0 & f_0 \\ 1\,0 \ldots 0 & f_1 \\ 0\,1 \ldots 0 & f_2 \\ \vdots\,\vdots\,\ddots\,\vdots & \vdots \\ 0\,0 \ldots 1 & f_{r-1} \end{bmatrix}.$$

We call M_α the *companion matrix* of α over $\mathbb{F}_2$. There is a field isomorphism between $\mathbb{F}_{2^n}$ and $\{0\} \cup \{M_\alpha^i : 0 \leq i \leq 2^n - 2\} \subseteq \mathbb{F}_2^{n \times n}$. Here, the number of ones in M_{α^i} for some $\alpha^i \in \mathbb{F}_2(\alpha)$ and $0 \leq i \leq 2^n - 1$ is equal to n plus the d-XOR of α^i. For instance, taking $\mathbb{F}_{2^3} = \mathbb{F}(\alpha)$ where α is a root of $x^3 + x + 1 \in \mathbb{F}_2[x]$, we see that

$$M_\alpha = \begin{bmatrix} 0\,0\,1 \\ 1\,0\,1 \\ 0\,1\,0 \end{bmatrix}.$$

Also, see that the companion matrix of $\alpha^2 + \alpha$ is

$$M_{\alpha^2+\alpha} = M_\alpha^2 + M_\alpha = \begin{bmatrix} 0\,1\,1 \\ 1\,1\,1 \\ 1\,0\,1 \end{bmatrix}.$$

Here, the number of ones in $M_\alpha^2 + M_\alpha$ is 7 and $n = 3$, hence the number of d-XORs of $\alpha^2 + \alpha$ is $7 - 3 = 4$ (recall the d-XOR of Eq. (1)).

The d-XOR counting process can be directly extended to matrices in $\mathbb{F}_{2^n}^{m \times m}$: Let $A \in \mathbb{F}_{2^n}^{m \times m}$ and M_A denote the $nm \times nm$ companion matrix of A over $\mathbb{F}_2$ which is constructed by taking $(M_A)_{i,j} = M_{A_{i,j}}$ for all $1 \le i, j \le m$. Then the number of XORs of A is equal to the number of ones in M_A minus nm. An MDS matrix with fewer XORs is considered more efficient than the others. In general, an MDS mapping with fewer XORs provides similar efficiency benefits.

We refer the reader to [7–10, 17, 21, 28, 35] for various types of optimization techniques.

2.3   Subfield Construction

Now we define a sample bijection between vector spaces $\mathbb{F}_{2^8}$ and $\mathbb{F}_{2^3} \times \mathbb{F}_{2^5}$ over $\mathbb{F}_2$: Let $\mathbb{F}_{2^8} = \mathbb{F}_2(\theta)$ where θ is a root of an irreducible polynomial of degree 8, $\mathbb{F}_{2^3} = \mathbb{F}_2(\alpha)$ where α is a root of an irreducible polynomial of degree 3, and $\mathbb{F}_{2^5} = \mathbb{F}_2(\beta)$ where β is a root of an irreducible polynomial of degree 5 over $\mathbb{F}_2$. Then, for

$$u = u_{0,0} + u_{0,1}\theta + u_{0,2}\theta^2 + \cdots + u_{0,7}\theta^7$$

where $u_{0,i} \in \mathbb{F}_2$ for $0 \le i \le 7$, we define

$$u_1 = u_{0,0} + u_{0,1}\alpha + u_{0,2}\alpha^2$$
$$u_2 = u_{0,3} + u_{0,4}\beta + u_{0,5}\beta^2 + u_{0,6}\beta^3 + u_{0,7}\beta^4$$

and hence construct a bijection

$$u \leftrightarrow (u_1, u_2).$$

(We sometimes use notation $u_1 \| u_2$ to denote (u_1, u_2).) In that way, we obtain

$$1 + \theta^2 + \theta^3 + \theta^4 + \theta^6 \quad \leftrightarrow \quad (1 + \alpha^2, 1 + \beta + \beta^3)$$

for example. This bijection idea can be easily extended from $\mathbb{F}_{2^8} \leftrightarrow \mathbb{F}_{2^3} \times \mathbb{F}_{2^5}$ to

$$\mathbb{F}_{2^{n_1 + n_2 + \cdots + n_s}} \leftrightarrow \mathbb{F}_{2^{n_1}} \times \mathbb{F}_{2^{n_2}} \times \cdots \times \mathbb{F}_{2^{n_s}}$$

for arbitrary positive integers n_i $(1 \le i \le s)$, and to matrices directly. (Remark that there always exists an irreducible polynomial of any degree over $\mathbb{F}_2$, see [22] for further details.)

We now give another method, first introduced in [5] and called the *subfield construction*, to satisfy the maximum byte-wise branching like in Proposition 1.

Proposition 4. *[5] Let n be an even integer, u be a nonzero $m \times 1$ matrix over $\mathbb{F}_{2^n}$, u_1 and u_2 be $m \times 1$ matrices over $\mathbb{F}_{2^{n/2}}$ such that $u = u_1 \| u_2$, and M be an $m \times m$ MDS matrix over $\mathbb{F}_{2^{m/2}}$. Then the minimum total nonzero entries in both u and $Mu_1 \| Mu_2$ is at least $m + 1$.*

In the subfield construction introduced in Proposition 4, we multiply the number of XORs by 2, since the matrix is applied on two separate semi-columns.

2.4   Generalized Subfield Construction

In this section, we generalize Proposition 4 and then investigate the efficiency of this generalization with respect to the XOR counting.

Proposition 5. *[27] Let u be a nonzero $m \times 1$ matrix over $\mathbb{F}_{2^{n_1+n_2+\cdots+n_s}}$, u_i be a $m \times 1$ matrix over $\mathbb{F}_{2^{n_i}}$ for $1 \leq i \leq s$, and $u = u_1\|u_2\| \ldots \|u_s$. Let also M_i be a $m \times m$ MDS matrix over $\mathbb{F}_{2^{n_i}}$ for $1 \leq i \leq s$ and $v := M_1u_1\|M_2u_2\| \ldots \|M_su_s$ be the $m \times 1$ matrix obtained by concatenating $M_1u_1, M_2u_2, \ldots, M_su_s$. Then the number of total nonzero entries in u and v is at least $m + 1$.*

We would like to highlight the differences between Proposition 5 and Proposition 4:

– We do not have to use the same MDS matrix M to multiply with u_1 and u_2 as in Proposition 4; we can use different MDS matrices M_1 and M_2 to satisfy the MDS branching.
– Similarly, M as in Proposition 4 does not have to be over $\mathbb{F}_{2^{n/2}}$, it can be over just a smaller field. That is, n does not have to be even (or a multiple of a certain fixed number).
– Additionally, we do not have to split u into two as u_1 and u_2, we can split it into more pieces.

The following example illustrates Proposition 5.

Example 1. Let $m = 2$, $s = 3$, $n_1 = 2$, $n_2 = 3$, $n_3 = 3$, $\alpha \in \mathbb{F}_{2^{n_1}}$ be a root of $x^2 + x + 1 \in \mathbb{F}_2[x]$ and $\beta \in \mathbb{F}_{2^{n_2}} = \mathbb{F}_{2^{n_3}}$ be a root of $x^3 + x + 1 \in \mathbb{F}_2[x]$. Let also

$$M_1 = \begin{bmatrix} \alpha & 1 + \alpha \\ 1 & 1 \end{bmatrix}, \quad M_2 = \begin{bmatrix} \beta + 1 & \beta^2 \\ 1 & \beta \end{bmatrix}, \quad M_3 = \begin{bmatrix} 1 & \beta \\ 1 & 1 \end{bmatrix}.$$

Note that M_1, M_2 and M_3 are MDS matrices. Remark that we can separate each nonzero $u \in \mathbb{F}_{2^8}^2$ by $u = u_1\|u_2\|u_3$ for some $u_1 \in \mathbb{F}_{2^2}^2, u_2 \in \mathbb{F}_{2^3}^2$, and $u_3 \in \mathbb{F}_{2^3}^2$. The transformation

$$u \mapsto v = M_1u_1\|M_2u_2\|M_3u_3$$

is an MDS diffusion, i.e. the number of nonzero bytes in both u and v is at least 3.

2.5   Vision Mark-32 and Its MDS Matrix

Vision [2] is a keyed permutation based on the Marvellous design strategy. Vision operates over $\mathbb{F}_{2^n}$ and each round consists of two steps that differ only in the linearized affine polynomial. Main input is an m-tuple from $\mathbb{F}_{2^n}$. We denote the input state of the ith round by $S_i = (s_{i,0}, \ldots, s_{i,m-1})$ where $s_{i,j} \in \mathbb{F}_{2^n}$. Each step in one round of Vision consists of three operations on the state:

– **Inverse function:** $\pi(s_{i,j}) = s_{i,j}^{-1}$.
– **Linearized affine polynomial:** $B(s_{i,j}) = \sum_{k=0}^{n-1} \beta_j s_{i,j}^{2^k} + \beta_n$.

– **MDS matrix:** $L(S_i) = M \cdot S_i$.

The only difference between the two steps is the linearized affine polynomial. The linearized affine polynomial of the second step has the form:

$$B(x) = \beta_0 x + \beta_1 x^2 + \beta_2 x^4 + \beta_3,$$

which is a sparse polynomial. The linearized affine polynomial of the first step is B^{-1}, which is dense with a high degree. The round function of Vision is depicted in Fig. 1.

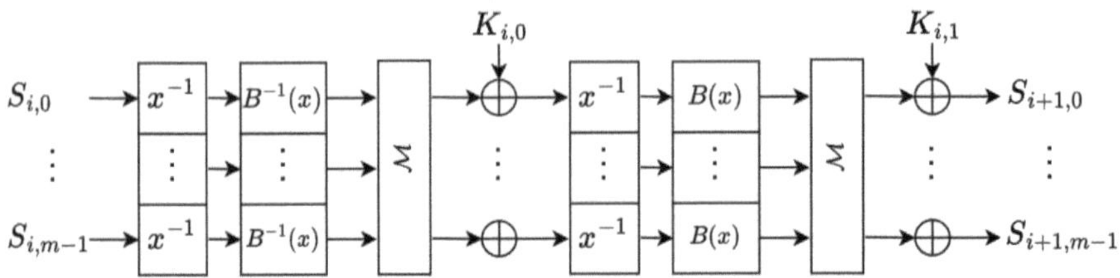

Fig. 1. [4] One round of Vision with two steps

Vision Mark-32 is a hash function instantiating a Sponge construction using the Vision permutation. Vision Mark-32 has 8 rounds and operates over $\mathbb{F}_{2^{32}}$, with state size of $m = 24$.

In [23], a novel basis of polynomials over a finite field of characteristic 2 is introduced for efficient encoding and decoding of Reed-Solomon erasure codes [29]. The same basis is used in Vision Mark-32 to generate the MDS matrix.

2.6   Field Programmable Gate Arrays

A Field Programmable Gate Array (FPGA) is a reconfigurable integrated circuit that can be programmed post-manufacturing, unlike Application-Specific Integrated Circuits (ASICs), which are fixed at fabrication time. This flexibility makes FPGAs ideal for prototyping, design testing, iterative development and small-scale production, whereas ASICs are more suited for finalized, large-scale production.

FPGAs are categorized into families that share architectural characteristics but differ in performance and capacity. For instance, the Xilinx Artix-7 family offers a low-cost, resource-efficient platform suitable for embedded applications, while higher-end families like Virtex-7 cater to performance-intensive use cases. Each FPGA contains a variety of configurable resources—such as logic blocks, DSP slices, and memory—that enable implementation of custom hardware functionality.

Modern FPGAs consist of various configurable resources, each tailored to perform specific tasks efficiently. Understanding these resources is essential for designing optimized hardware architectures, particularly in cryptographic applications.

- **Flip-Flops (FFs):** FFs are fundamental storage elements used to hold single-bit values. While they offer the fastest data access times, their limited quantity makes them unsuitable for storing large datasets.
- **Look-Up Tables (LUTs):** LUTs are the primary logic elements in FPGAs, capable of realizing arbitrary Boolean functions by storing truth tables. Typically supporting 5 to 6 input bits, multiple LUTs can be combined for complex operations. They can also be repurposed as distributed memory (LUTRAM), though with slower access than FFs. Due to resource constraints, LUTRAMs are less efficient for storing large data structures like cryptographic keys.
- **Block RAMs (BRAMs):** BRAMs are specialized memory blocks integrated into FPGAs, designed for efficient storage of large data sets. In Xilinx devices, a typical BRAM has a capacity of 36 Kbits, which can either function as a single memory unit or be split into two 18 Kbit blocks. These blocks support various configurations for data width and depth, enabling flexible use—from storing thousands of single-bit values to handling wider data elements (e.g., 64 or 128 bits) by combining multiple BRAMs.
  BRAMs support several access modes that determine the number of simultaneous read and write operations. In single-port mode, one read and one write can occur sequentially in a clock cycle. Simple dual-port mode adds a second read port, while true dual-port mode allows two reads, two writes, or one read and one write per cycle. This versatility makes BRAMs highly suitable for performance-critical applications like post-quantum cryptography, where both speed and storage capacity are crucial.
- **DSP Blocks:** Digital Signal Processing (DSP) units enable high-speed arithmetic operations, particularly multiply-accumulate (MAC) computations. These are crucial for operations like matrix or polynomial multiplication and offer significant performance advantages over LUT-based implementations.

The availability and capacity of these resources vary significantly across FPGA families. While entry-level devices typically offer limited logic and memory, high-performance families provide substantially greater capabilities.

3   Improving the Performance of Vision Mark-32 by Leveraging the Generalized Subfield Construction

Vision Mark-32 [4] makes use of a 24×24 MDS matrix over $\mathbb{F}_{2^{32}}$. In general, it is not easy to find efficient MDS matrices in this form since:

- The dimension is too high. For example, there is no generic method to construct 24×24 circulant MDS matrices, probabilistic methods to produce circulant MDS matrices can be cumbersome. Therefore, there are only some systematic constructions such as generalized Cauchy matrices mentioned in Proposition 3. However, we can not successfully control the number of XORs for all entries even if we can freely select the parameters c_i, d_i, x_i, and y_i in Proposition 3. Therefore, we suppose that each entry contains $\frac{n^2}{2} = 512$ ones and hence the matrix comprises $m^2 \cdot \frac{n^2}{2} - m \cdot n = 294144$ XORs on average.

- Also note that the finite field is too large. Therefore, the multiplication process requires some additional optimization ideas, such as NTT.

Instead of using a 24×24 MDS matrix over $\mathbb{F}_{2^{32}}$, we can apply the subfield construction given in Sect. 2.3. This time, the average number of XORs is

$$2 \cdot \left(24^2 \cdot \frac{16^2}{2} - 24 \cdot 16 \right) = 146688.$$

Note that the expected number of XORs decreases to half.

3.1 Improvement 1

As observed and emphasized in [27], applying the generalized subfield construction by separating into more subcolumns may be more efficient. A direct idea is to use a 24×24 MDS matrix over $\mathbb{F}_{2^8}$ for each quarter column. In this way, the average number of XORs is

$$4 \cdot \left(24^2 \cdot \frac{8^2}{2} - 24 \cdot 8 \right) = 72960.$$

See Fig. 2 for an illustration of this method.

Note that this $8 + 8 + 8 + 8$ separation can be implemented by one matrix whose XOR complexity is 18240. In this way, the complexity of the implementation can decrease further. In reality, the complexity is much more smaller than we expected; we implemented a 24×24 MDS matrix over $\mathbb{F}_{2^8}$ by using Proposition 2 by only 265 LUTs and 102 FFs (recall the numbers in Table 1) at clock frequency of 220 MHz, achieving an execution time of 3.08 μs for a single matrix multiplication. In our implementation, no explicit optimization tricks such as NTT are required for the finite field multiplications, although the total execution time can be further reduced by increasing parallelism at the cost of slightly higher resource utilization.

It is, of course, possible to implement the matrix twice or four times and hence gain speed by compromising the area. In other words, the $8 + 8 + 8 + 8$ separation provides a performance gain in hardware implementation and a time-memory trade-off.

3.2 Improvement 2

The most aggressive separation is the $6 + 6 + 6 + 7 + 7$ version, since:

- There are no MDS matrices over binary finite fields of size smaller than 64 according to Conjecture 1.
- The Cauchy construction given in Proposition 2 is applicable for all binary fields of size $\mathbb{F}_{2^n}$, where $n \geq 6$.

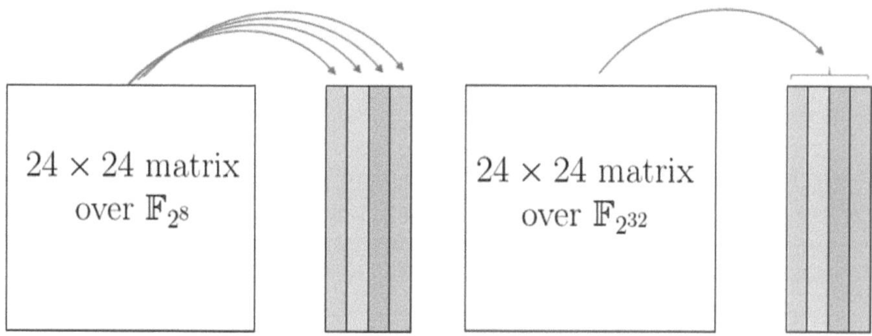

Fig. 2. Comparison of MDS diffusion methods

By the $6 + 6 + 6 + 7 + 7$ separation, the average number of XORs is

$$3 \cdot \left(24^2 \cdot \frac{6^2}{2} - 24 \cdot 6\right) + 2 \cdot \left(24^2 \cdot \frac{7^2}{2} - 24 \cdot 7\right) = 58560.$$

It is possible to implement such a transformation by using about 1000 LUTs and 500 FFs at clock frequency operating at 220 MHz.

3.3   Additional Advantages and Comparisons

Another advantage of both improvements is that the time required for a multiplication in $\mathbb{F}_{2^8}$ (or $\mathbb{F}_{2^7}$ or $\mathbb{F}_{2^6}$) is much shorter than a multiplication in $\mathbb{F}_{2^{32}}$, hence we surely gain speed. So, we do not need special methods such as NTT for the multiplication, i.e. we also get the simplicity gain.

MDS matrices over $\mathbb{F}_{2^8}$ can be easy to apply since the MDS matrix of AES is over $\mathbb{F}_{2^8}$ too; i.e., there is a significant amount of available studies, codes, and optimizations on the operations over $\mathbb{F}_{2^8}$.

On the other hand, a possible advantage of 24×24 MDS matrices over $\mathbb{F}_{2^7}$ and over $\mathbb{F}_{2^6}$ is the following: It is possible to construct $\mathbb{F}_{2^7}$ and $\mathbb{F}_{2^6}$ using irreducible polynomials $x^7 + x + 1$ and $x^6 + x + 1$ over $\mathbb{F}_2$, respectively. Hence, the arithmetic operations may be less costly since both polynomials are more lightweight (the number of terms is the smallest and the gap is the maximum) when we compare with the most lightweight irreducible polynomial $x^8 + x^4 + x^3 + x + 1$ over $\mathbb{F}_2$ of degree 8. (Recall that we require modular reduction with an irreducible polynomial of degree n to run arithmetic operations in $\mathbb{F}_{2^n}$.)

It is of course possible to separate 32 as $6 + 6 + 6 + 6 + 8$ and hence use 24×24 MDS matrices over $\mathbb{F}_{2^8}$ and over $\mathbb{F}_{2^6}$ on 5 suitable subcolumns. The possibilities can be increased by applying suitable separations such as $7+8+8+9$ or $10 + 10 + 12$, depending on the capabilities and requirements. This versatility shows a kind of algebraic richness and prospective trade-offs of the generalized subfield construction.

3.4   Security and Arithmetization Complexity Analyses

Note that the direct multiplication by an MDS matrix and the generalized subfield construction are both linear operations, and their unique purpose is to provide the maximum possible diffusion. They are both successful from this point of view, see Propositions 1 and 5. Also, it is interesting to examine whether any attacks can exploit generalized subfield construction and gain any advantage. We conjecture that no attacks obtain any advantage when we replace the direct MDS matrix multiplication with the generalized subfield construction.

The multiplication by an MDS matrix is a scalar operation. Therefore, using a different MDS matrix or the generalized subfield construction does not change the arithmetization complexity (see also [2, Section 4.1.5]).

3.5   Applicability to Other ZK-Friendly Hash Functions

The generalized subfield construction is applicable only when the finite field is not prime. Therefore, the ZK-friendly hash functions using large prime fields (such as Poseidon, MiMC, and Tip5) are disadvantageous than the ones using large binary finite fields (such as Vision, Starkad, and Vision Mark-32) from this perspective.

4   Final Remarks and Future Work

In conclusion, we observe that the generalized subfield construction provides the following advantages:

- **Efficiency:** There is a significant reduction on the number of XORs and FPGA implementation complexities.
- **Simplicity:** It is easy to implement and there is no need for additional optimization methods such as NTT.
- **Versatility:** Multiplication for each subcolumn can be implemented serially or in a parallel way, hence we can obtain a time-memory trade-off. Also, we can select the smaller fields freely (algebraic richness).
- **No security compromise:** We still keep the MDS diffusion feature. Also, there are no known attacks exploiting the properties of the (generalized) subfield construction.
- **No other efficiency compromises:** Arithmetization complexity does not increase.

Therefore, the generalized subfield construction is a powerful alternative, especially to higher-dimensional MDS matrices over larger finite fields.

It is also natural that several questions arise to understand and improve the generalized subfield construction method. We can list some of them below as future work:

- It is worth studying the applicability of the generalized subfield construction method (or similar ideas) when the base field is a prime field of a large prime size. In general, are there any (not necessarily linear but) efficient methods to satisfy the MDS diffusion property when the field is a (large) prime field?
- Investigation of different MDS matrix construction methods when the field is large and dimensions are high is another interesting question. For example, do 24×24 circulant MDS matrices exist over $\mathbb{F}_{2^8}$?
- Can generic methods (such as Cauchy MDS matrices) be improved for efficiency when the dimensions are high? For example, are there any probabilistic or deterministic methods to provide lighter (i.e., more efficient) 12×12 Cauchy MDS matrices over $\mathbb{F}_{2^6}$?
- We conjecture that no attacks obtain any advantage when we replace the direct MDS matrix multiplication with the generalized subfield construction. Note that it is not easy to prove such an assertion; however, can any attacks exploit the generalized subfield construction and gain any advantage?

References

1. Albrecht, M., Grassi, L., Rechberger, C., Roy, A., Tiessen, T.: MiMC: efficient encryption and cryptographic hashing with minimal multiplicative complexity. In: Cheon, J.H., Takagi, T. (eds.) ASIACRYPT 2016. LNCS, vol. 10031, pp. 191–219. Springer, Heidelberg (2016). https://doi.org/10.1007/978-3-662-53887-6_7
2. Aly, A., Ashur, T., Ben-Sasson, E., Dhooghe, S., Szepieniec, A.: Design of symmetric-key primitives for advanced cryptographic protocols. IACR Trans. Symmetric Cryptol. **2020**(3), 1–45 (2020). https://doi.org/10.13154/TOSC.V2020.I3.1-45
3. Ashur, T., Kindi, A., Mahzoun, M.: XHash8 and XHash12: efficient STARK-friendly hash functions. IACR Cryptology ePrint Archive, p. 1045 (2023). https://eprint.iacr.org/2023/1045
4. Ashur, T., Mahzoun, M., Posen, J., Sijacic, D.: Vision mark-32: ZK-friendly hash function over binary tower fields. IACR Cryptology ePrint Archive, p. 633 (2024). https://eprint.iacr.org/2024/633
5. Barreto, P.S.L.M., Nikov, V., Nikova, S., Rijmen, V., Tischhauser, E.: Whirlwind: a new cryptographic hash function. Des. Codes Crypt. **56**(2–3), 141–162 (2010). https://doi.org/10.1007/S10623-010-9391-Y
6. Bertoni, G., Daemen, J., Peeters, M., Van Assche, G.: Keccak. In: Johansson, T., Nguyen, P.Q. (eds.) EUROCRYPT 2013. LNCS, vol. 7881, pp. 313–314. Springer, Heidelberg (2013). https://doi.org/10.1007/978-3-642-38348-9_19
7. Boyar, J., Find, M.G., Peralta, R.: Small low-depth, low-size circuits for cryptographic applications. Cryptogr. Commun. **11**, 109–127 (2019). https://doi.org/10.1007/S12095-018-0296-3
8. Boyar, J., Matthews, P., Peralta, R.: On the shortest linear straight-line program for computing linear forms. In: Ochmański, E., Tyszkiewicz, J. (eds.) MFCS 2008. LNCS, vol. 5162, pp. 168–179. Springer, Heidelberg (2008). https://doi.org/10.1007/978-3-540-85238-4_13
9. Boyar, J., Matthews, P., Peralta, R.: Logic minimization techniques with applications to cryptology. J. Cryptol. **26**(2), 280–312 (2013). https://doi.org/10.1007/S00145-012-9124-7

10. Boyar, J., Peralta, R.: A new combinational logic minimization technique with applications to cryptology. In: Festa, P. (ed.) SEA 2010. LNCS, vol. 6049, pp. 178–189. Springer, Heidelberg (2010). https://doi.org/10.1007/978-3-642-13193-6_16

11. Daemen, J., Rijmen, V.: The Design of Rijndael - The Advanced Encryption Standard (AES). Information Security and Cryptography, 2nd Edn. Springer (2020). https://doi.org/10.1007/978-3-662-60769-5

12. Gauravaram, P., et al.: Grøstl - A SHA-3 candidate. In: Handschuh, H., Lucks, S., Preneel, B., Rogaway, P. (eds.) Symmetric Cryptography, 11.01.–16.01.2009. Dagstuhl Seminar Proceedings, vol. 09031. Schloss Dagstuhl - Leibniz-Zentrum für Informatik, Germany (2009). http://drops.dagstuhl.de/opus/volltexte/2009/1955/

13. Grassi, L., Khovratovich, D., Lüftenegger, R., Rechberger, C., Schofnegger, M., Walch, R.: Monolith: circuit-friendly hash functions with new nonlinear layers for fast and constant-time implementations. IACR Trans. Symmetric Cryptol. **2024**(3), 44–83 (2024). https://doi.org/10.46586/TOSC.V2024.I3.44-83

14. Grassi, L., Khovratovich, D., Rechberger, C., Roy, A., Schofnegger, M.: POSEIDON: a new hash function for zero-knowledge proof systems. In: Bailey, M.D., Greenstadt, R. (eds.) 30th USENIX Security Symposium, USENIX Security 2021, 11–13 August 2021, pp. 519–535. USENIX Association (2021). https://www.usenix.org/conference/usenixsecurity21/presentation/grassi

15. Gupta, K.C., Pandey, S.K., Ray, I.G., Samanta, S.: Cryptographically significant MDS matrices over finite fields: a brief survey and some generalized results. Adv. Math. Commun. **13**(4), 779–843 (2019). https://doi.org/10.3934/AMC.2019045

16. Ha, J., Hwang, S., Lee, J., Park, S., Son, M.: Polocolo: A ZK-friendly hash function based on S-boxes using power residues (full version). IACR Cryptology ePrint Archive, p. 926 (2025). https://eprint.iacr.org/2025/926

17. Jean, J., Peyrin, T., Sim, S.M., Tourteaux, J.: Optimizing implementations of lightweight building blocks. IACR Trans. Symmetric Cryptol. **2017**(4), 130–168 (2017). https://doi.org/10.13154/TOSC.V2017.I4.130-168

18. Khoo, K., Peyrin, T., Poschmann, A.Y., Yap, H.: FOAM: searching for hardware-optimal SPN structures and components with a fair comparison. In: Batina, L., Robshaw, M. (eds.) CHES 2014. LNCS, vol. 8731, pp. 433–450. Springer, Heidelberg (2014). https://doi.org/10.1007/978-3-662-44709-3_24

19. Kranz, T., Leander, G., Stoffelen, K., Wiemer, F.: Shorter linear straight-line programs for MDS matrices. IACR Trans. Symmetric Cryptol. **2017**(4), 188–211 (2017). https://doi.org/10.13154/TOSC.V2017.I4.188-211

20. Kurt-Pehlivanoğlu, M., Sakallı, M.T., Akleylek, S., Duru, N., Rijmen, V.: Generalisation of Hadamard matrix to generate involutory MDS matrices for lightweight cryptography. IET Inf. Secur. **12**(4), 348–355 (2018). https://doi.org/10.1049/IET-IFS.2017.0156

21. Li, S., Sun, S., Li, C., Wei, Z., Hu, L.: Constructing low-latency involutory MDS matrices with lightweight circuits. IACR Trans. Symmetric Cryptol. **2019**(1), 84–117 (2019). https://doi.org/10.13154/TOSC.V2019.I1.84-117

22. Lidl, R., Niederreiter, H.: Introduction to Finite Fields and Their Applications. Cambridge University Press, Cambridge, UK (1994)

23. Lin, S.J., Chung, W.H., Han, Y.S.: Novel polynomial basis and its application to Reed-Solomon erasure codes. In: 2014 IEEE 55th Annual Symposium on Foundations of Computer Science, pp. 316–325 (2014). https://doi.org/10.1109/FOCS.2014.41

24. Liu, M., Sim, S.M.: Lightweight MDS generalized circulant matrices. In: Peyrin, T. (ed.) FSE 2016. LNCS, vol. 9783, pp. 101–120. Springer, Heidelberg (2016). https://doi.org/10.1007/978-3-662-52993-5_6
25. Liu, Y., Rijmen, V., Leander, G.: Nonlinear diffusion layers. Des. Codes Cryptogr. **86**(11), 2469–2484 (2018). https://doi.org/10.1007/S10623-018-0458-5
26. MacWilliams, F.J., Sloane, N.J.A.: The Theory of Error Correcting Codes. North-Holland Publishing Co., Amsterdam-New York-Oxford (1977)
27. Otal, K.: A generalization of the subfield construction. Int. J. Inf. Secur. Sci. **11**(2), 1–11 (2022). https://dergipark.org.tr/en/pub/ijiss/issue/70915/1104896
28. Paar, C.: Optimized arithmetic for Reed-Solomon encoders. In: IEEE International Symposium on Information Theory (ISIT) 1997, p. 250. IEEE (1997)
29. Reed, I.S., Solomon, G.: Polynomial codes over certain finite fields. J. Soc. Ind. Appl. Math. **8**(2), 300–304 (1960). https://doi.org/10.1137/0108018
30. Roth, R.M.: Introduction to Coding Theory. Cambridge University Press (2006)
31. Roth, R.M., Lempel, A.: On MDS codes via Cauchy matrices. IEEE Trans. Inf. Theory **35**(6), 1314–1319 (1989). https://doi.org/10.1109/18.45291
32. Roth, R.M., Seroussi, G.: On generator matrices of MDS codes. IEEE Trans. Inf. Theory **31**(6), 826–830 (1985). https://doi.org/10.1109/TIT.1985.1057113
33. Sim, S.M., Khoo, K., Oggier, F., Peyrin, T.: Lightweight MDS involution matrices. In: Leander, G. (ed.) FSE 2015. LNCS, vol. 9054, pp. 471–493. Springer, Heidelberg (2015). https://doi.org/10.1007/978-3-662-48116-5_23
34. Szepieniec, A., Lemmens, A., Sauer, J.F., Threadbare, B.: The Tip5 hash function for recursive STARKs (2023). https://eprint.iacr.org/2023/107
35. Visconti, A., Schiavo, C.V., Peralta, R.: Improved upper bounds for the expected circuit complexity of dense systems of linear equations over GF(2). Inf. Process. Lett. **137**, 1–5 (2018). https://doi.org/10.1016/J.IPL.2018.04.010

Hardware and Architecture Security

ARCHER: Architecture-Level Simulator for Side-Channel Analysis in RISC-V Processors

Asmita Adhikary[1]([✉]) [ID], Abraham Basurto-Becerra[1] [ID], Lejla Batina[1] [ID], Ileana Buhan[1] [ID], Durba Chatterjee[1] [ID], Senna van Hoek[1] [ID], and Eloi Sanfelix Gonzalez[2]

[1] Radboud University, Nijmegen, The Netherlands
{asmita.adhikary,abraham.basurto,lejla.batina,ileana.buhan,
durba.chatterjee,senna.vanhoek}@ru.nl
[2] Nijmegen, The Netherlands

Abstract. Side-channel attacks pose a serious risk to cryptographic implementations, particularly in embedded systems. While current methods, such as test vector leakage assessment (TVLA), can identify leakage points, they do not provide insights into their root causes. We propose ARCHER, an architecture-level tool designed to perform side-channel analysis and root cause identification for software cryptographic implementations on RISC-V processors. ARCHER has two main components: (1) Side-Channel Analysis to identify leakage using TVLA and its variants, and (2) Data Flow Analysis to track intermediate values across instructions, explaining observed leaks. Taking the binary file of the target implementation as input, ARCHER generates interactive visualizations and a detailed report highlighting execution statistics, leakage points, and their causes. It is the first architecture-level tool tailored for the RISC-V architecture to guide the implementation of cryptographic algorithms resistant to power side-channel attacks. ARCHER is algorithm-agnostic, supports pre-silicon analysis for both high-level and assembly code, and enables efficient root cause identification. We demonstrate ARCHER's effectiveness through case studies on unprotected and protected AES and unprotected Ascon implementations, where it accurately traces the source of side-channel leaks. We report previously undocumented vulnerabilities due to architectural register usage in the ShiftRows operation of the protected AES implementation. For the Ascon implementation, we report leaks both in the substitution layer and in the diffusion layer, thus reflecting its susceptibility to data-dependent side-channel leakage.

Keywords: Side-Channel Analysis · RISC-V · Pre-silicon · Data Flow Analysis · Qiling · AES · Ascon

1 Introduction

Analyzing assembly language code often poses challenges due to its difficulty in readability and maintenance, and its dependency on specific architectures.

E. Savas et al. (Eds.): LightSec 2025, LNCS 16216, pp. 157–177, 2026.
https://doi.org/10.1007/978-3-032-15541-2_9

Despite these challenges, disassembling an executed binary file to examine low-level code is essential when investigating side-channel leaks in cryptographic software implementations.

Side-channel leaks stem from two sources: 1) improper implementation of the cryptographic scheme, which leads to undesirable interactions of sensitive data within architectural registers, and 2) data interactions from microarchitectural optimizations like pipelining, use of shadow registers, speculative execution, or caching. Two factors complicate the identification of the cause of side-channel leaks. Firstly, the lack of access to cycle-accurate information obscures the precise timing and sequence of events, which we need to pinpoint the instructions that triggered the leak. Secondly, understanding whether the component that caused the side-channel leakage is architectural or microarchitectural is crucial for developing effective remedies. *Best design practices advocate for a top-down approach, which suggests addressing architectural leaks before tackling microarchitectural ones. Differentiating between the two types of leaks requires a detailed analysis to isolate the microarchitectural components effectively.*

Solutions for architectural-level leaks involve reallocating or clearing registers [26,31]. Conversely, fixes for microarchitectural leaks typically target the specific components involved, such as employing fence instructions for speculative executions [25] or adopting constant-time programming to mitigate cache timing attacks [5]. With the advent of open hardware, the appeal of developing cryptographic algorithms for RISC-V architectures has increased [16,24,33], while the tools to support secure cryptographic implementations are few [9,13]. Leakage simulators are one such class of tools aimed at evaluation of side-channel vulnerabilities. While the literature includes several power-based leakage simulators for ARM [8,10,15,22,30,31], tools for RISC-V are geared towards verifying hardware implementations [12,13,29].

Contributions. We propose ARCHER, a design tool that focuses on architecture-level leakages for RISC-V cryptographic implementations. ARCHER acts as the first step for evaluating the side-channel leakage for any software cryptographic implementation. It assists with the analysis of the binary files using powerful data-flow visualization features. The core contributions of this work are:

1. We propose ARCHER, which to the best of our knowledge is the first power side-channel simulator for RISC-V, that isolates architectural side-channel leakage effects, thereby enabling users to focus on the implementation-level vulnerabilities.
2. ARCHER can simulate and analyze the *exact* binary file executed by the target device. This avoids the variability of compiler output that could occur otherwise.
3. The integrated *side-channel analysis* module has three leakage models and a built-in leakage assessment module that supports fixed-vs-random and fixed-vs-fixed TVLA tests.
4. The *flow analysis* module aids the data flow visualization and is a valuable tool when determining the root cause of side-channel leaks. We provide the

tool, **ARCHER**, the visualizations and reports generated by **ARCHER** in the URL: https://gitlab.science.ru.nl/cesca/archer.

5. We demonstrate the working of the tool and the derived insights using unprotected and protected AES and unprotected Ascon as case studies.

Target audience. We develop **ARCHER** for designers/developers who optimize cryptographic implementations and security evaluators who evaluate the impact of a side-channel leak.

2   Related Work

The landscape of cryptographic verification tools is fragmented. At high abstraction levels, tools such as MaskVerif [4], EasyCrypt [6], or Tamarin [7] assist in creating security proofs. Secure compilers like Jasmin [2] can produce low-level assembly; however, the supported architectures are limited. Once an implementation is proven to follow the desired security proof, it must also withstand side-channel attacks. Consequently, the interest in tools to detect, verify, and mitigate side-channel leaks is significant [9]. Papagiannopoulos et al. [27] were among the first to discuss the microarchitectural effects when analyzing side-channel leaks for software implementations. De Meyer et al. [23] and Arora et al. [3] continue their work and discuss additional microarchitecture leakage effects on different target devices.

McCann et al. [22] introduced ELMO, a side-channel leakage simulator which models the power consumption of a software implementation as a linear combination of values and transitions. Shelton et al. [31] improve the leakage model in ELMO by capturing data interactions across multiple cycles. As ELMO models (part of) the microarchitecture of the target device *it can only be used for ARM Cortex-M0* platforms. Abby [8] streamlines the profiling of the target device, which enables the use of machine learning models for capturing (parts of) the microarchitecture, for the *ARM Cortex M0 and M3*. Marshall et al. [21] propose MIRACLE, a generic set of microbenchmarks, which *can detect microarchitecture optimizations* to improve leakage models but does not examine their application in the context of side-channel attacks. In contrast, **ARCHER** *targets the architectural layer for modeling the data dependencies at the architecture level* with a goal to perform side-channel analysis. The closest tool to **ARCHER** is MAMBO [36], which captures architecture-specific *timing* leaks for RISC-V for creating constant-time code. In contrast, **ARCHER** is aimed at addressing *power side-channel leaks*. MAMBO-V uses dynamic binary instrumentation to generate execution traces, which are analyzed in parts to identify leakage. In contrast, execution traces generated in **ARCHER** include a sequence of assembly instructions along with the register contents capturing the processed data.

3   Preliminaries

This section presents the notations followed in this paper and briefly describes the basic concepts required in this work.

Notation. We denote an architectural register as r_i, where i is a number from the set $\{1, \ldots, m\}$. We denote with I an assembly instruction executed by the target. For all instructions, the instruction mnemonic (I) is specified first, followed by the destination register (RD), the first operand (OP1, also known as source register), and the second operand (OP2). An *execution trace* contains the sequence of executed instructions, $\{I_1, \ldots, I_N\}$ for a given input, where N represents the total number of executed instructions. For each instruction I_j we store the state of all architectural registers $\{r_1^j, \ldots, r_m^j\}^1$.

Test Vector Leakage Assessment (TVLA) [14] is one of the most popular leakage detection methods based on statistical hypothesis tests. It comes in two flavors: *specific* and *non-specific*. The 'fixed-vs-random' is the most common non-specific test and compares a set of traces acquired with a fixed plaintext with another set of traces acquired with random plaintext. In the case of a specific test, commonly known as 'fixed-vs-fixed', the traces are divided according to a known intermediate value tested for leakage. Welch's two-sample t-test for equality of means is applied for all trace samples in both cases. An absolute difference between two sets larger than the standard threshold of 4.5 is taken as evidence of a leak's presence.

RISC-V is an open-source ISA and follows a LOAD/STORE architecture. Due to the LOAD/STORE architecture, operations can not be performed directly on memory, and data must be first moved to registers. This implies that any data-dependent activity is visible in the register state.

Next, we briefly describe the algorithms chosen for analysis.

AES-128 is a symmetric-key cryptographic algorithm that transforms a 128-bit plaintext into a 128-bit ciphertext using a 128-bit key [11]. Its execution spans 10 rounds, with each round consisting of AddRoundKey, SubBytes (S-box), ShiftRows, and MixColumns operations, except for the last round, which has only AddRoundKey, SubBytes, and ShiftRows operations.

Byte-Masked AES is a first-order Boolean-masked implementation of AES based on the masking scheme described in [20], which applies masking to plaintext, key schedule, and round functions using six independent masks: $m, m', m_1, m_2, m_3,$ and m_4, which are propagated and updated across AES operations:

1. *AddRoundKey.* The key bytes are XOR-ed with the masked state. Each byte of the state is masked with a common mask m, and this step maintains this masking by XOR-ing the masked state with the (unmasked) key.
2. *SubBytes.* It is the only non-linear operation in AES and is implemented as a masked table lookup. A masked S-box s^m is precomputed as:

$$s^m(x \oplus m) = s(x) \oplus m'$$

   This operation uses a different mask byte m' to XOR with the S-box output, ensuring that the output remains first-order secure under the new mask.

---

^{1} In our case, the input is a pair (P_j, K_j), where P_j constitutes the plaintext and K_j represents the key. Depending on the specifics of the implementation, it is possible that other inputs, such as nonce, masks, may need to be provided.

3. *ShiftRows.* This operation rearranges the positions of the bytes in the state. Since each byte is still masked with the same m', the ShiftRows operation does not alter the masking scheme or introduce any mask mismatches.
4. *MixColumns.* To preserve masking security across the linear MixColumns transformation, the four rows of the state matrix are assigned independent masks: m_1, m_2, m_3, and m_4. These masks are derived from m' (the output mask of SubBytes) and applied such that each input byte to MixColumns is masked independently. The transformation outputs are masked with m'_1, m'_2, m'_3, and m'_4, which are reused as the input masks for the next round.
5. *Final Round.* The final AddRoundKey step includes a mask removal process that cancels the active masks and yields the correct unmasked ciphertext.

For AES and Masked AES, we analyze an open-source implementation, wherein enable/disable macros are used to compile the protected/unprotected implementation respectively[2].

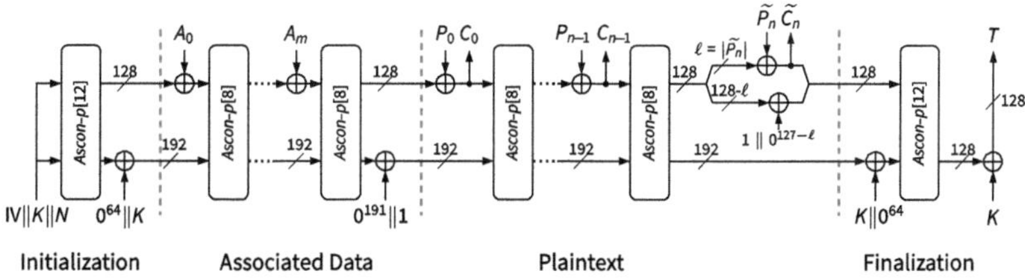

Fig. 1. Schematic representation of Ascon encryption [32].

Ascon-128 AEAD (Authenticated Encryption with Associated Data) [32], bit-sliced by design, processes a 320-bit state comprising a 128-bit key, 128-bit nonce, 64-bit associated data, and 64-bit plaintext to produce an authenticated cipher-text of the same length as the plaintext, along with a 128-bit tag. The algorithm applies a 12-round permutation p^a ($a = 12$) during Initialization and Finalization and a 6-round permutation p^b ($b = 6$) during associated data and plaintext processing as shown in Fig. 1. Each round consists of:

1. *Addition of round constant (p_C):* Adds c_i to the 64-bit register x_2 in round i, where the state S stores the initialization vector, the key and the nonce:

$$S = x_0||x_1||x_2||x_3||x_4 = IV||K||N = IV||K0||K1||N0||N1$$

2. *Substitution layer (p_S):* A 5-bit S-box ($S(x)$) is applied to each bit-slice of the five state registers $x_0, \dots, x_4$.
3. *Linear diffusion layer (p_L):* Adds diffusion via a 64-bit linear function $\Sigma_i(x_i)$.

Key points of interest include the first S-box outputs and linear diffusion layer outputs, as this is where the algorithm processes the key and nonce to start Initialization [19]. As shown in [28,35], these intermediates facilitate successful retrieval of key.

---

[2] https://github.com/CENSUS/masked-aes-c.

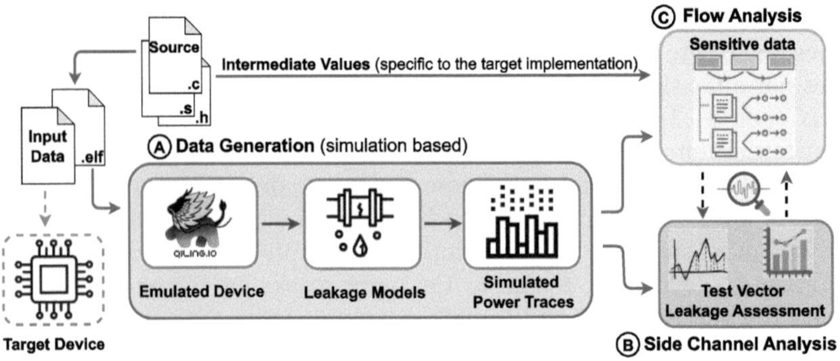

Fig. 2. Overview of side-channel architecture level simulator for RISC-V (ARCHER).

4   ARCHER: Side-Channel Architecture Level Simulator for RISC-V

ARCHER takes a binary file along with the input data (such as plaintext, nonce, keys, and other initialization data) and generates instruction-level interactive visualizations and statistical results pertaining to side-channel leaks. The end-to-end toolflow and component interactions depicted in Fig. 2 are described:

4.1   Data Generation

This module generates simulated power traces for input sets using the Qiling framework[3], executing the binary file with provided data. The number and size of inputs are determined by the cryptographic algorithm, as specified by the user. For leakage evaluation, we adhere to standard data generation guidelines (Sect. 5.1 of [1]) for creating keys, nonces, plaintexts, associated data and masks. These inputs are used consistently for both simulated and real trace collection. During measurements on the target device, inputs from the two datasets (for TVLA) are interleaved to reduce systematic bias. Execution traces are transformed via leakage models to produce simulated/hypothetical power traces, which are then used for side-channel and data flow analysis. The data generation process for each component is detailed separately in the next section.

4.2   Side-Channel Analysis (SCA)

This component is responsible for the identification of side-channel leakages in an implementation. ARCHER uses TVLA as a statistical test to identify leaks. The steps in this process are described as follows:

1. *Generate input data.* This module generates cryptographic inputs (e.g., plaintext, key, associated data, nonce) based on user-specified parameters, such as the number of input bytes and total inputs.

---

[3] https://qiling.io/.

2. *Generate execution traces.* The `.elf` file is executed with the generated inputs, and execution traces are saved in a `.csv` file, capturing all executed instructions and the register states after each instruction.
3. *Create simulation traces.* For each instruction recorded in the `.csv` trace file, we apply a transformation function called *leakage model*, which takes in the values of all the registers and produces an estimate for the data-dependent power consumption incurred by the target instruction (also referred to as hypothetical power trace). ARCHER supports three commonly used leakage models in side-channel analysis, namely Identity (ID), Hamming Weight (HW) (for identifying value-based leaks), and Hamming Distance (HD) (for identifying transition-based leaks). We describe the three models as follows:
   - ID: computes the summation of the contents of all the registers (Eq. 1). For an execution trace of length N, the resultant trace also contains N values.
   - HW: Computes the summation of HW of all the register contents after each instruction resulting in a trace of length N (Eq. 2).
   - HD: Calculates the sum of HD between the contents of all registers for each consecutive pair of instructions, resulting in a trace of length $N-1$. For computing the jth value in the simulated power trace, we take the HD between the register content at the end of j and $j+1$ instructions (Eq. 3).

$$L_{ID}(I_j) = \sum_{i=1}^{m} r_i^j, \qquad j = 1, \ldots, N \tag{1}$$

$$L_{HW}(I_j) = \sum_{i=1}^{m} HW(r_i^j), \qquad j = 1, \ldots, N \tag{2}$$

$$L_{HD}(I_j, I_{j+1}) = \sum_{i=1}^{m} HD(r_i^j, r_i^{j+1}), \qquad j = 1, \ldots, N-1 \tag{3}$$

4. *TVLA Analysis.* ARCHER uses TVLA for detecting leaks in two modes:
   Fixed-vs-Random: This mode compares traces generated with fixed and random plaintexts for the same key, providing quick leakage detection.
   Fixed-vs-Fixed: This mode compares traces where only one or more plaintext bytes vary, enabling detailed root-cause analysis.

ARCHER provides us with two kinds of TVLA graphs:

1. *Classic TVLA plot:* A plot with the sequence of instructions on the x-axis and the *t-score* on the y-axis, featuring red lines at 4.5 and -4.5 to indicate the threshold for side-channel leakage. Sample points that exceed these thresholds suggest the presence of side-channel information leakage (Fig. 4).
2. *Interactive plot:* A plot displaying the sequence of instructions along the x-axis and the different registers on the y-axis, where leaky instructions are

highlighted in red and non-leaky instructions are shown in grey. This visualization is appended with intermediate values obtained from *data flow analysis* to identify the root cause of the leakage (Fig. 5 and Fig. 8). This interactive visualization is browser-integrated. The HTML file can be viewed and operated standalone on any browser. It includes interactive features such as zoom and hover-text to aid the developer.

4.3   Flow Analysis

This component tracks sensitive data bytes in different registers across various instructions. The module takes as input the simulated power traces and intermediate values (such as the output of the substitution layer, a combination of plaintext and keys). Optionally, TVLA results can be added as input to generate interactive, annotated visualizations as depicted in Fig. 5 and Fig. 8. These figures provide information about i) the distribution of leaky instructions across different registers, ii) the content of registers after every instruction execution, iii) redundant entries of bytes in different registers, and the remanence of bytes across several instructions (which may potentially lead to leakage), iv) the usage pattern of registers for each algorithm execution. These features enable designers to identify the root cause of leakage. To aid designers in identifying and explaining the source of leakage, this component generates i) interactive visualizations incorporating the TVLA leakage along with the intermediate bytes and ii) a detailed report on the execution, register usage, and side-channel leaks. The steps involved in this component are described as follows:

1. *Generate intermediate values (to track).* For cryptographic implementations, the key bytes and sensitive intermediate data (e.g., S-box outputs, round results, etc.) typically form the focus of SCA. **ARCHER** extracts these intermediate values through a separate execution of the cryptographic algorithm. Since only the data values are relevant, this process remains platform-independent.
2. *Generate execution traces.* This step generates detailed execution traces with additional information, such as instruction mnemonics, operators, and machine code, to pinpoint the location of intermediates.
3. *Generate interactive visualizations.* In this step, the tool places markers in the interactive plots to highlight the presence of intermediate/sensitive bytes in the architectural registers through the execution. To locate markers, multiple execution traces are generated with different values for the sensitive data. The correct marker positions are found by intersecting the respective markers across the different traces.
4. *Visualize markers.* The intermediate bytes are plotted on top of the TVLA plots using different marker symbols as depicted in Fig. 5. The y coordinate of each marker is determined from the destination register holding the value.
5. *Generate report.* A document is generated based on the execution traces and TVLA results. It highlights information such as frequently executed leaking instructions and their locations in the source code and details the distribution of instruction types contributing to leakage.

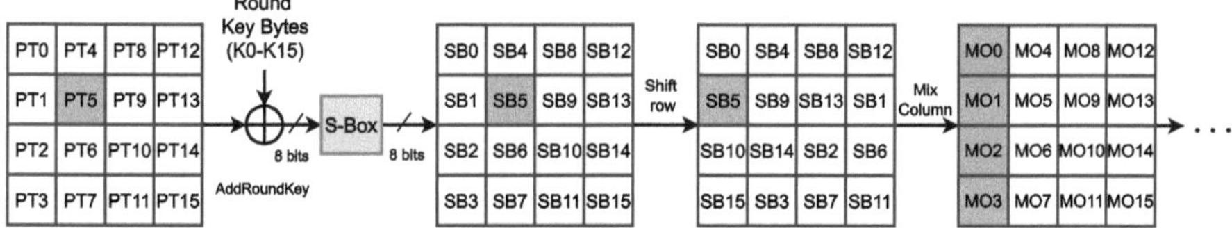

Fig. 3. Sequence of AES operations highlighting the bytes impacted on modifying 6th byte of plaintext.

5   ARCHER Implementation Details

This section describes the implementation details of ARCHER, followed by its workflow using the example of an unprotected AES implementation compiled for a RISC-V core, PicoRV32[4]. The tool is implemented in Python3.

Target Device Setup. ARCHER takes the binary file of the target cryptographic implementation as input. To obtain the compiled binary, i.e., the .elf file, we cross-compile the AES implementation with the RISC-V GNU Compiler Toolchain (version 2023.11.20). The C source code is cross-compiled for the RV32I architecture using the $-Os$ optimization level, as it reduces the size of the executable and is a popular choice for embedded systems. The leakage results reported are specific to the compiler version and the optimization level.

Simulation Setup. The simulation component of ARCHER takes the .elf file and the number of traces to be generated as input parameters. It retrieves the memory address of the essential elements of the compiled binary, such as the addresses of *key*, *plaintext*, *masks*, depending on the target implementation. After extraction of the addresses, ARCHER leverages the Qiling emulation framework [18,34] to run the same binary as would be flashed to a target board. Qiling uses Unicorn for CPU emulation, single-stepping through each instruction while Unicorn handles execution and reports results back to Qiling for state tracking. To support more architectures, Qiling includes its modifications to Unicorn. A callback is configured to be executed for every emulated instruction (code hook). The code hook collects the register states and disassembles the instruction using Capstone. These traces, consisting of assembly instructions and register states, are stored in .csv files. ARCHER using the Qiling engine, can capture the architectural register content at every instruction. The leakage models simulate the data-dependent power consumption at the architectural level. No microarchitectural feature (pipeline, caching, etc.) is supported.

Data Generation for Side-channel Analysis. In the example, we compute the *fixed-vs-fixed* TVLA wherein we want to highlight leakage caused by a one-byte change in the plaintext. For this, two datasets are generated, differing only in the 6th byte of the plaintext (referred to as PT5 in Fig. 3). The first dataset consists of a single fixed plaintext and key, while the second includes 500 inputs where all plaintext bytes remain the same except for byte 6, which is randomly

---

[4] https://github.com/YosysHQ/picorv32.

varied. These inputs are provided to Qiling along with the AES `.elf` file, which generates one execution trace for the fixed input and 500 traces for the varied inputs. We choose HD model for our analysis.

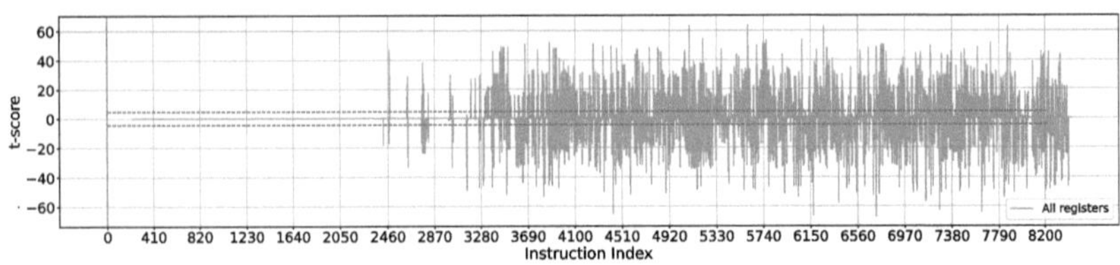

Fig. 4. t-score of unprotected AES obtained from HD simulated traces.

TVLA Analysis. Next, we compute the TVLA for the two sets of power traces and plot the t-score for each instruction. Figure 4 depicts the classic TVLA graph that indicates leakage throughout the algorithm's execution. The interactive visualization plots the TVLA leaks spread across different registers. Figure 5 depicts a zoomed portion illustrating the leakage points in the first round of AES. The horizontal dotted lines correspond to different registers denoted on the left end. The vertical lines represent the executed instructions. The x coordinate of a vertical bar denotes the instruction index (in the execution trace), and the y position denotes the destination register of the executed instruction. The leaky instructions are highlighted in red. To explain the source of the leaky points, we proceed to the flow analysis module.

Flow Analysis. This component involves generating intermediates for tracking and overlapping them with TVLA results. The performed steps are:

Generation of Intermediate Values. For AES, we track individual bytes of the plaintext (denoted by PT0 - PT15), key (denoted by K0 - K15), S-box output (denoted by SB0 - SB15), MixColumn output (denoted by MC0 - MC15), round keys (denoted by RK0 - RK15). These are obtained by executing the C implementation independently. Since we are tracking individual bytes, we might encounter some byte values in unexpected instruction indices. We refer to these unexpected byte appearances as *ghost* values that can be attributed to other byte operations. To remove such *ghost* values, we preprocess the intermediate byte locations before generating the visualizations.

Pre-processing. We work with three distinct inputs (randomly generated plaintext and key). We compute the instruction sequence of all the intermediate bytes for these inputs. An instruction sequence of a byte contains a mapping of the registers where the byte value occurs, along with the list of instruction indices when it appears in the particular register. We then compute the intersection of instruction sequences for each tracked byte across the inputs. The indices that appear in the intersection represent the legitimate points where the intermediate bytes are actually present. This step filters out illegitimate instruction indices where the intermediate byte might appear due to unrelated or independent computations. The final visualizations are generated using the filtered indices.

Though we demonstrate ARCHER on an RV32I architecture, it can be readily extended to 64-bit implementations, by: ① compiling for a 64-bit target architecture, and ② updating the Qiling script to emulate the resulting 64-bit binary. The leakage models will require adaptation to accommodate 64-bit registers. The root cause analysis of leakage is based on the relationship between internal data and observed leakage, independent of the underlying word size.
Visualizations. We utilize the `plotly` library in Python3 to generate interactive visualizations. A snapshot of the visualization for the first round of AES execution is shown in Fig. 5. The red lines indicate the leaky instructions identified by TVLA under the HD leakage model. The legend provides details of the various markers used to represent different intermediate values, with each byte shown in a distinct color and each intermediate output denoted by a unique marker, as seen in the legend. Hovering over a vertical line reveals the executed instruction, program counter (PC), and instruction index, while hovering over the colored markers displays the corresponding byte. For enhanced clarity, we annotate the plot with labels indicating the outputs of various operations. While the TVLA results (Fig. 4) identify the leaky instructions, these visualizations allow us to trace the leakage back to specific intermediate bytes during execution. Key insights derived from these visualizations are discussed in the subsequent section.

6   Insights from ARCHER

We evaluate ARCHER on AES (unprotected and protected) and an unprotected Ascon. The total instruction count for unprotected and masked AES, and unprotected Ascon is 8433, 14784, and 8629, respectively, demonstrating ARCHER's scalability. Each simulated trace size for unprotected AES, masked AES and unprotected Ascon is 4.6kB, 59.13kB and 7.1kB respectively. Simulated trace generation takes 2–3 hours per implementation, and capturing real masked AES measurements takes 34 min 45 s. We present our insights as follows:

6.1   Case Study: Unprotected AES

We examine an unprotected implementation of AES-128 [11], using the TVLA results obtained in Fig. 4. To understand the source of leakage, we first identify the bytes impacted by randomizing PT5 and track them via the visualizations. We restrict our analysis to the first round as the difference is propagated to all bytes in subsequent rounds. Figure 3 depicts the bytes impacted on randomizing PT5 during the first round of AES. From Fig. 5, we obtain the following insights:

– The registers used by each AES operation are localized for this implementation. For instance, S-box outputs are always stored in a2 (labeled C), and plaintext bytes always appear in register t3 (labeled B). Thus, the red lines atop the horizontal line a2 indicate leakage in the S-box operation.

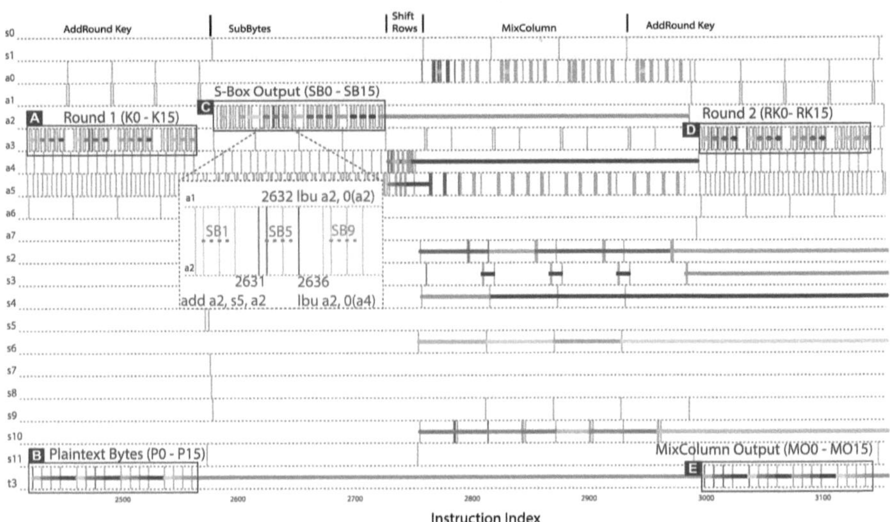

Fig. 5. Visualization of interim AES bytes over TVLA results computed using HD simulated traces.

– *Leakage in C:* From the intermediates, we gather that instructions in the range 2583 to 2624 (labeled C) correspond to S-box operation. TVLA reports leaks at three instruction indices, 2631, 2632, and 2636 (marked in red). The cause of these leakages can be understood by observing the contents of **a2** and **a4** registers at these instructions, illustrated as follows. Here, & is used to denote addresses.

```
2631  add a2,s5,a2    # a2=&(S-box mapping); s5=&state[5]
2632  lbu a2, 0(a2)   # a2=SB5
...
2636  lbu a2, 0(a4)   # a2=state[9]; a4=&state[9]
```

At instruction 2631, **s5** stores the pointer to the S-box mapping in memory, and **a2** stores the 6th byte of input to the S-box. The **add** operation computes the pointer to the resultant S-box output (&**state**[5]), and the value is loaded in **a2** in instruction 2632. In all three instructions, **a2** stores a value that is impacted by a change in PT5, thus explaining the TVLA leaks.

– *Leakage in B,E:* The leaky instructions in B correspond to instruction 0x9bc **lbu t3, 0(a4)** that load PT5 in **t3**. **a4** stores the pointer to the state array, iterates over each byte, and stores the content to **t3**. In E, we observe leaks for the same instruction. The reason for leaks is the loading of MixColumn outputs (MO0 - MO4), precisely the bytes impacted by a change in PT5 (Fig. 3).

– *Leakage in D:* The leaks correspond to instructions 0x9cc **xor a3,a3,t3** and 0x9b8 **add a3, a6, a5**, that constitute the AddRoundKey operation (Round 2). The reason for leaks is MO bytes, which are impacted by change in PT5.

```
3005  add a3,a6,a5    # a6=&state; a5=1 (index)
3010  xor a3,a3,t3    # t3=MO1; a3=RK1
```

```
3018  xor  a3,a3,t3      # t3=M02;  a3=RK2
3026  xor  a3,a3,t3      # t3=M03;  a3=RK3
```

6.2 Case Study: Masked AES

In this case study, we analyze a byte masked implementation of AES, compiled on a PicoRV32 core with -Os optimization level. In particular, we focus on the `ShiftRows` function of the implementation as described in 3. As a result of the `ShiftRows` operation, the first state row $(s_0^m, s_4^m, s_8^m, s_{12}^m)$ remains unchanged. Each byte of the state of the second row $(s_1^m, s_5^m, s_9^m, s_{13}^m)$ is left-shifted by one position to produce $(s_5^m, s_9^m, s_{13}^m, s_1^m)$. Similarly, the state bytes of the third $(s_2^m, s_6^m, s_{10}^m, s_{14}^m)$ row are left-shifted by two yielding $(s_{10}^m, s_{14}^m, s_2^m, s_6^m)$. Finally, the state bytes on the fourth row $(s_3^m, s_7^m, s_{11}^m, s_{15}^m)$ are shifted by three resulting in the byte order $(s_{15}^m, s_3^m, s_7^m, s_{11}^m)$. Figure 6 illustrates the register usage pattern involved in the execution of the generated assembly code. This operation is implemented via a series of load-store operations where the value to be shifted is first loaded into a register. Then, a store operation overwrites the state byte corresponding to the desired shift. The rows in the figure correspond to the registers used in this operation, and the columns correspond to the program counters (PCs).

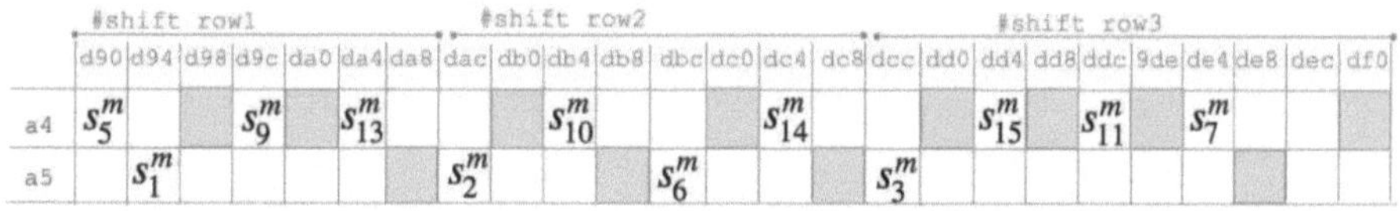

	#shift row1							#shift row2								#shift row3									
	d90	d94	d98	d9c	da0	da4	da8	dac	db0	db4	db8	dbc	dc0	dc4	dc8	dcc	dd0	dd4	dd8	ddc	9de	de4	de8	dec	df0
a4	s_5^m			s_9^m		s_{13}^m				s_{10}^m				s_{14}^m				s_{15}^m		s_{11}^m		s_7^m			
a5		s_1^m						s_2^m				s_6^m				s_3^m									

Fig. 6. Visual representation of compiler-generated assembly for the ShiftRows operation in Masked AES at level -Os, where s_i^m denotes the ith byte of S-box output. At each PC index, we show the content of the destination registers (**a4, a5**). Blank boxes indicate the value is retained till the next load instruction. Grey boxes represent a store operations. Corresponding assembly snippets are in Appendix A.

As shown in Fig. 6, only two registers **a4** and **a5** are used. Register **a4** stores temporary variables, while **a5** loads the byte value being shifted. The values s_5^m, s_9^m, and s_{13}^m share the same mask[5]. When loading byte s_9^m in the register containing s_5^m, the effect, shown in eq 4, removes the mask.

$$s_i^m \oplus s_j^m = (s_i \oplus m') \oplus (s_j \oplus m') = s_i \oplus s_j \tag{4}$$

As a result, the code will leak $HD(s_5, s_9)$ and $HD(s_9, s_{13})$. The same effect can be observed when shifting the third row of the state, where the code will leak $HD(s_{10}, s_{14})$, $HD(s_2, s_6)$ and when shifting the fourth row of the state,

---

[5] As all S-box output boxes share the same mask.

$HD(s_{15}, s_{11})$, $HD(s_{11}, s_7)$. The code will also leak $HD(s_{13}, s_{10})$, $HD(s_{14}, s_{15})$, $HD(s_1, s_2)$, $HD(s_6, s_3)$. With these leaks, an adversary can recover 12 of the 16 bytes of the total AES key[6].

Side-Channel and Root Cause Analysis. We perform a correlation to illustrate the HD leaks predicted from architectural register usage (Fig. 6). Figure 7 depicts the correlation results performed on simulated power traces of masked AES implementation. We have annotated the results to indicate the duration of each AES operation. This experiment aims to testify to the side-channel leaks in the ShiftRows operation of masked AES, a protected implementation. Herein, we correlate the instruction-granular power values with the HD of 6th byte and 10th byte of the SubBytes output. From Fig. 6 and Fig. 7, we observe a correlation peak of 1 is observed during the ShiftRows operation at instruction `lbu a4, 9(a5)`, which loads SubBytes 10th byte into register `a4`. Since the 6th byte remains in the same register from a prior operation, it leads to an overwrite. It is to be noted that despite considering the content of all registers in the simulated power value, the correlation peak reveals the effect of this overwrite. This is due to the reuse of the same architectural register used in the ShiftRow operation as depicted in Fig. 6. We refer the reader to Appendix A for the assembly instructions involved.

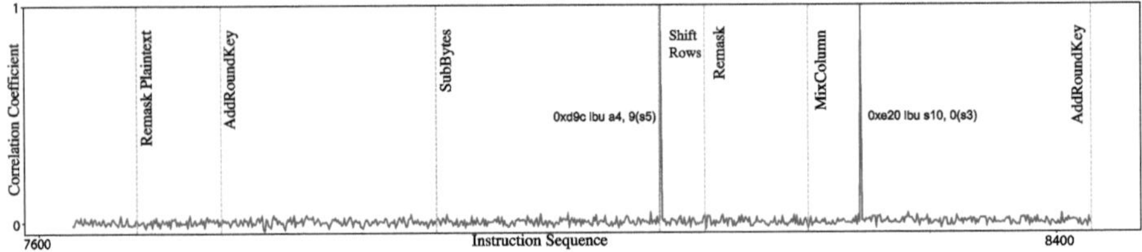

Fig. 7. Correlation results with $HD(s_5^m, s_9^m)$ for the masked AES implementations over 5000 traces where plaintext byte 9 is randomly selected, and all other bytes are fixed. We see a clear leak in the ShiftRow operation.

6.3   Case Study: Unprotected Ascon

We illustrate the functionalities of `ARCHER` using an open-source unprotected Ascon implementation[7] compiled on the Ibex core[8] with $-$`Os` optimization level. `ARCHER` retrieves addresses of *key*, *plaintext*, *nonce*, and *associated data*.

Side-Channel Analysis. We perform a fixed-vs-fixed TVLA by fixing all the bytes of the nonce except the 0th byte, while the key, associated data, and plaintext are kept fixed. Figure 8 illustrates the visualization depicting TVLA results, highlighting the leaky instructions in red if they leak as per the HD model. The instructions marked in grey does not leak side-channel information.

---

[6] The remaining bytes correspond to the first ShiftRow operation s_0, s_4, s_8, s_{12}.

[7] https://github.com/ascon/ascon-c.

[8] https://github.com/lowRISC/ibex-demo-system.

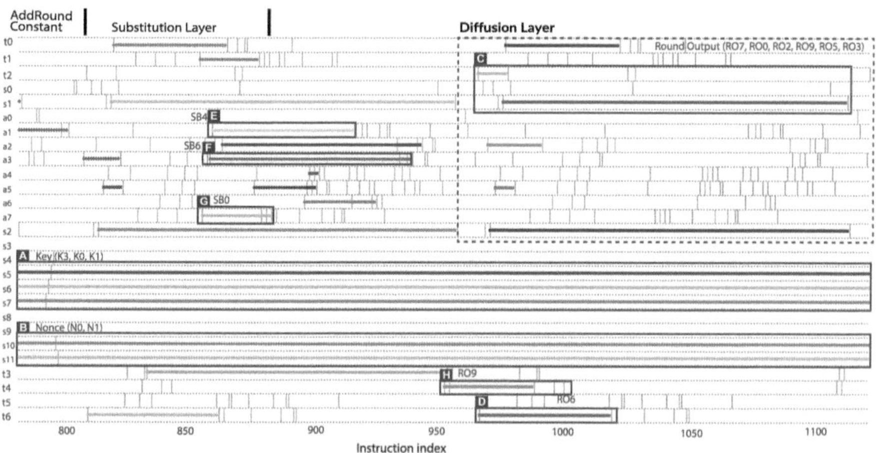

Fig. 8. Visualization of interim bytes of Ascon over TVLA results for HD model.

Data Flow Analysis. For Ascon, we track bytes of the key (denoted by K0-K4), nonce (denoted by N0-N4), S-box outputs (denoted by SB0-SB9), round outputs (denoted by RO0-RO9), associated data (denoted by A0-A1), and plaintext (denoted by M0-M1). We get the following insights from Fig. 8 showing the first four intermediates, of Round 1 of Initialization:

- The key bytes, K3, K0 and K1 (at A), are loaded into s5, s6 and s7 registers where they remain until completion, while the nonce, N1 and N0 (at B), loaded at s10 and s11 remain until the completion of p^a of Initialization. The rest of the intermediates are spread across 21 out of the 32 RISC-V registers. Unlike the first S-box output, which is present within the range of Round 1 of p^a (instruction index 809 to 905), the round output extends into Round 2 (starting from index 906) for most of its bytes.
- *Leakage at C, D, E, F, and G :* The intermediates RO0 and RO2 (at C), RO3, RO5, RO6 (at D) and SB4 (at E) exhibit leakage for the HD model, when they are either loaded into registers or are overwritten by other values in the registers. In the case of SB6 (at F) and SB0 (at G) in registers a3 and a7, the S-box values get overwritten by RO6 and RO0. For RO0, we see leakage because the value stored in t2 changes:

```
869 slli t2,a7,4        # t2=Shifted SB0 -> R0 ; a7=SB0
...
966 lw t2,0x4(a0)       # t2=R0; a0=0x18(sp), sp=&Ascon_state
967 lw t6,0x1c(a0)      # t2=&N0; t6=R06
```

- *Leakage at H:* The intermediate RO9 (at H) leaks for the HD model. In register t4, RO9 is plotted, coinciding with leaks at L: xor t4,a4,t4. Just after the completion of RO9, at N: not t4,s0, the HD leaks. The leakage at L and

N can be attributed to the change of value in t4 at $i^{th} + 1$ instruction with respect to i^{th} instruction. The disassembled code from Capstone shows that instruction at indices i and $i + 1$ updates the state S.x[4], i.e., the output of the linear diffusion layer applied on the nonce, N1, for L. Similarly, at N, using execution trace, we can identify that these instructions correspond to the S-box operation on the IV, K0, K1 and N0. Illustrating N:

```
953 xor  t4,a4,t4   #t4=R09; a4=intermediate results
...
989 not  t4,s0      # t4=R09
990 and  t3,t3,s1   # t4=not(s0); t4=R0(S.x[4]=N1)
```

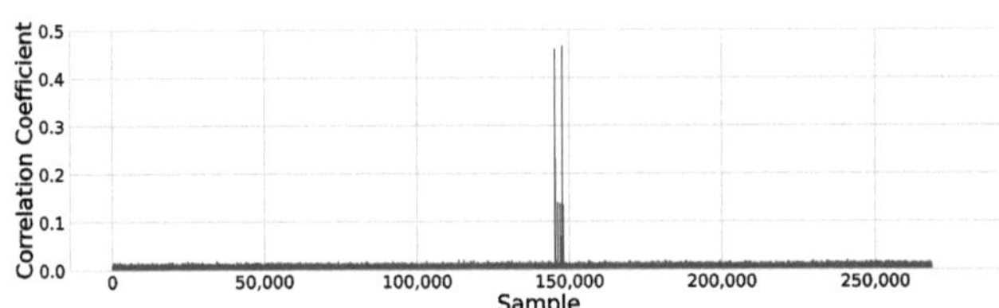

Fig. 9. Correlation results for masked AES using over 10000 power traces.

7   Experimental Validation

To validate the findings in 6.2, we analyze measured power traces collected from an ASIC implementation of the PicoRV32 core. The experiments presented in this section focus on highlighting the side-channel leakage on power traces collected from a real target. The details of our target/hardware setup are as follows:

7.1   Hardware Setup

PicoRV32 is a CPU core that implements the RISC-V RV32IMC Instruction Set. We use the ASIC implementation of the PICO chip on the Saidoyoki board [17] as our target. For power trace collection, a ChipWhisperer-Husky[9] is used, set up on a machine equipped with an Intel Core i7-6700 CPU running Ubuntu 22.04 operating system. The ChipWhisperer-Husky uses synchronous sampling and generates a 5 MHz clock signal for the target while the capture ADC clock frequency is set to 20 MHz. To provide the key, plaintext, and mask to the target device and to receive the corresponding ciphertext, the SimpleSerial[10] v1.1 communication protocol is used via the UART bus.

Test Vectors. We built 10,000 test vectors consisting of a fixed 128-bit key, a 128-bit plaintext with 6th and 10th byte randomized, and a random 48-bit mask.

---

[9] https://rtfm.newae.com/Capture/ChipWhisperer-Husky/.
[10] https://chipwhisperer.readthedocs.io/en/latest/simpleserial.html.

The key and plaintext are generated according to the guidelines for random dataset (in Sect. 5.1 of [1]). The mask is obtained using urandom entropy pool, its 48 bits translate to m_1, m_2, m_3, m_4, m, and m', each 1 byte in length.
Power Traces. For the masked implementation, 10,000 power traces—one per test vector—of the entire encryption operation are captured.

7.2   Experimental Validation of ShiftRow Leaks

To validate the leakage in `ShiftRows` operation of masked AES described in 6.2, we correlate the real power value with the Hamming distance between the 6th and 10th byte of the first round S-box output. It is noteworthy that in this experiment, we do not use any information related to the masks.

Figure 9 depicts the correlation plot where we observe two clear peaks with a correlation coefficient around 0.45. This clearly demonstrates that, despite masking being theoretically secure, implementation factors such as register usage can introduce vulnerabilities like byte overwrites. These overwrites effectively cancel the masking, rendering it ineffective in practice. This result is particularly significant given the presence of noise and constant power components (P_{noise} and P_{const}) in the real power traces, (as described in the power consumption model in [20]), highlighting that the architectural component of power leakage remains detectable even in real-world traces.

8   Conclusion and Future Directions

This paper presents `ARCHER`, an architecture-level simulator for analyzing side-channel vulnerabilities in RISC-V processors. `ARCHER` integrates binary, side-channel, and data-flow analysis, empowering developers to identify and understand leakage sources at the architecture level. Operating on binary cryptographic implementations independent of specific target hardware, it serves as a foundational tool for early-stage side-channel evaluation. We present case studies using unprotected and protected AES and unprotected Ascon, highlighting the capability of ARCHER to uncover the root causes of side-channel leaks. `ARCHER` identifies the root cause of a previously undocumented vulnerability in the ShiftRows operation of masked AES, caused by repeated register usage to store sensitive intermediate variables. This leakage is detected by `ARCHER` and linked to specific instructions and registers, validating the tool's diagnostic utility. As future work, we plan to incorporate advanced side-channel assessment methods, such as mutual information-based techniques, and extend `ARCHER` to analyze a broader range of implementations. Additionally, automating the identification of leakage causes from visualizations, by detecting patterns in data modifications, is another key research direction.

Acknowledgments. This work was (in part) supported by Dutch Research Council (NWO) through the PROACT project (NWA.1215.18.014), TTW PREDATOR project 19782, TTW BASES project 20858 and the CiCS project of the research programme Gravitation under the grant 024.006.037.

Disclosure of Interests. The authors have no competing interests to declare that are relevant to the content of this article.

A   Appendix: Architectural Register Leaks of ShiftRow Operation of Masked AES

```
0xd8c bne    a5,a3,LAB_00000d54
# shift row 1 of state
0xd90 lbu    a4,0x5(s5) #load in a4, state(5)
0xd94 lbu    a5,0x1(s5) #load in a5, state(1)
0xd98 sb     a4,0x1(s5) #store the content of a4 to state(1)
0xd9c lbu    a4,0x9(s5) #load in a4, state(9)
0xda0 sb     a4,0x5(s5) #store the content of a4 to state(5)
0xda4 lbu    a4,0xd(s5) #load in a4, state(13)
0xda8 sb     a5,0xd(s5) #store the content of a5 to state(13)
# shift row 2 of state
0xdac lbu    a5,0x2(s5) #load in a5, state(2)
0xdb0 sb     a4,0x9(s5) #store the content of a4 to state(9)
# finish row 1
0xdb4 lbu    a4,0xa(s5) #load in a4, state(10)
0xdb8 sb     a5,0xa(s5) #store the content of a5 to state(10)
0xdbc lbu    a5,0x6(s5) #load in a5, state(6)
0xdc0 sb     a4,0x2(s5) #store the content of a4 to state(2)
0xdc4 lbu    a4,0xe(s5) #load in a4, state(14)
0xdc8 sb     a5,0xe(s5) #store the content of a5 to state(14)
# shift row 3 of state
0xdcc lbu    a5,0x3(s5) #load in a5, state(3)
0xdd0 sb     a4,0x6(s5) #store the content of a4 to state(6)
# finish row 2
0xdd4 lbu    a4,0xf(s5) #load in a4, state(15)
0xdd8 sb     a4,0x3(s5) #store the content of a4 to state(3)
0xddc lbu    a4,0xb(s5) #load in a5, state(11)
0x9de sb     a4,0xf(s5) #store the content of a4 to state(15)
0xde4 lbu    a4,0x7(s5) #load in a5, state(7)
0xde8 sb     a5,0x7(s5) #store the content of a5 to state(7)
0xdec li     a5,0xa     # load value 0xa to a5
0xdf0 sb     a4,0xb(s5) #store the content of a4 to state(11)
```

Listing 1.1. Assembly snippet of Shift-Row operation in Masked AES compiled with optimization level -Os.

References

1. Test Vector Leakage Assessment (TVLA) Derived Test Requirements (DTR) with AES (2015). https://www.rambus.com/test-vector-leakage-assessment-tvla-derived-test-requirements-dtr-with-aes/

2. Almeida, J.B., et al.: Jasmin: High-assurance and high-speed cryptography. In: ACM CCS 2017, pp. 1807–1823. ACM (2017). https://doi.org/10.1145/3133956.3134078

3. Arora, V., Buhan, I., Perin, G., Picek, S.: A tale of two boards: on the influence of microarchitecture on side-channel leakage. In: CARDIS 2021. LNCS, vol. 13173, pp. 80–96. Springer (2021). https://doi.org/10.1007/978-3-030-97348-3_5

4. Barthe, G., Belaïd, S., Fouque, P., Grégoire, B.: MaskVerif: a formal tool for analyzing software and hardware masked implementations. IACR Cryptol. ePrint Arch., p. 562 (2018). https://eprint.iacr.org/2018/562

5. Barthe, G., et al.: Testing side-channel security of cryptographic implementations against future microarchitectures. In: ACM CCS 2024, pp. 1076–1090. ACM (2024). https://doi.org/10.1145/3658644.3670319

6. Barthe, G., Dupressoir, F., Grégoire, B., Kunz, C., Schmidt, B., Strub, P.: Easycrypt: a tutorial. In: FOSAD 2012/2013 Tutorial Lectures. LNCS, vol. 8604, pp. 146–166. Springer (2013). https://doi.org/10.1007/978-3-319-10082-1_6

7. Basin, D.A., Cremers, C., Dreier, J., Sasse, R.: Tamarin: verification of large-scale, real-world, cryptographic protocols. IEEE S&P **20**(3), 24–32 (2022). https://doi.org/10.1109/MSEC.2022.3154689

8. Bazangani, O., Iooss, A., Buhan, I., Batina, L.: ABBY: automating leakage modelling for side-channel analysis. In: ACM ASIA CCS 2024. ACM (2024). https://doi.org/10.1145/3634737.3637665

9. Buhan, I., Batina, L., Yarom, Y., Schaumont, P.: SOK: design tools for side-channel-aware implementations. In: ASIA CCS, pp. 756–770 (2022). https://doi.org/10.1145/3488932.3517415

10. Corre, Y.L., Großschädl, J., Dinu, D.: Micro-architectural power simulator for leakage assessment of cryptographic software on ARM cortex-M3 processors. In: COSADE 2018. LNCS, vol. 10815, pp. 82–98. Springer (2018). https://doi.org/10.1007/978-3-319-89641-0_5

11. Daemen, J., Rijmen, V.: The design of Rijndael: AES - the advanced encryption standard. Information Security and Cryptography, Springer (2002). https://doi.org/10.1007/978-3-662-04722-4

12. F, M.A.K., Ganesan, V., Bodduna, R., Rebeiro, C.: PARAM: A microprocessor hardened for power side-channel attack resistance. In: 2020 IEEE HOST 2020. pp. 23–34. IEEE (2020). https://doi.org/10.1109/HOST45689.2020.9300263

13. Gigerl, B., Hadzic, V., Primas, R., Mangard, S., Bloem, R.: COCO: Co-design and CO-verification of masked software implementations on CPUS. In: USENIX Security 2021, pp. 1469–1468. USENIX Association (2021)

14. Goodwill, G., Jun, J., P.Rohatgi: A testing methodology for side channel resistance validation. NIST non-invasive attack testing workshop (2018)

15. de Grandmaison, A., Heydemann, K., Meunier, Q.L.: ARMISTICE: microarchitectural leakage modeling for masked software formal verification. IEEE Trans. Comput. Aided Des. Integr. Circuits Syst. **41**(11), 3733–3744 (2022). https://doi.org/10.1109/TCAD.2022.3197507

16. Karl, P., Schupp, J., Fritzmann, T., Sigl, G.: Post-quantum signatures on RISC-V with hardware acceleration. ACM TECS **23**(2), 30:1–30:23 (2024). https://doi.org/10.1145/3579092

17. Kiaei, P., Liu, Z., Eren, R.K., Yao, Y., Schaumont, P.: SaidoYoki: evaluating side-channel leakage in pre- and post-silicon setting. IACR Cryptol. ePrint Arch., p. 1235 (2021). https://eprint.iacr.org/2021/1235

18. Liu, Q., et al.: FirmGuide: boosting the capability of rehosting embedded Linux kernels through model-guided kernel execution. In: ASE 2021, pp. 792–804. IEEE (2021). https://doi.org/10.1109/ASE51524.2021.9678653
19. Liu, Z., Schaumont, P.: Root-cause analysis of the side channel leakage from ascon implementations (2023)
20. Mangard, S., Oswald, E., Popp, T.: Power Analysis Attacks. Springer, Boston, MA (2007). https://doi.org/10.1007/978-0-387-38162-6
21. Marshall, B., Page, D., Webb, J.: MIRACLE: micro-architectural leakage evaluation a study of micro-architectural power leakage across many devices. IACR TCHES **2022**(1), 175–220 (2022). https://doi.org/10.46586/TCHES.V2022.I1.175-220
22. McCann, D., Oswald, E., Whitnall, C.: Towards practical tools for side channel aware software engineering: 'grey box' modelling for instruction leakages. In: USENIX Security 2017, pp. 199–216. USENIX Association (2017)
23. Meyer, L.D., Mulder, E.D., Tunstall, M.: On the effect of the (micro)architecture on the development of side-channel resistant software. IACR Cryptol. ePrint Arch., p. 1297 (2020). https://eprint.iacr.org/2020/1297
24. Miteloudi, K., Bos, J.W., Bronchain, O., Fay, B., Renes, J.: PQ.V.ALU.E: post-quantum RISC-V custom ALU extensions on Dilithium and Kyber. In: CARDIS 2023. LNCS, vol. 14530, pp. 190–209. Springer (2023). https://doi.org/10.1007/978-3-031-54409-5_10
25. Olmos, S.A., Barthe, G., Blatter, L., Grégoire, B., Laporte, V.: Preservation of speculative constant-time by compilation. Proc. ACM Program. Lang. **9**(POPL), 1293–1325 (2025). https://doi.org/10.1145/3704880
26. Olmos, S.A., et al.: High-assurance zeroization. IACR TCHES **2024**(1), 375–397 (2024). https://doi.org/10.46586/TCHES.V2024.I1.375-397
27. Papagiannopoulos, K., Veshchikov, N.: Mind the gap: towards secure 1st-order masking in software. In: Guilley, S. (ed.) COSADE 2017. LNCS, vol. 10348, pp. 282–297. Springer, Cham (2017). https://doi.org/10.1007/978-3-319-64647-3_17
28. Samwel, N., Daemen, J.: DPA on hardware implementations of ascon and keyak. In: Proceedings of the Computing Frontiers Conference, pp. 415–424. ACM (2017)
29. Sehatbakhsh, N., Yilmaz, B.B., Zajic, A.G., Prvulovic, M.: EMSIM: a microarchitecture-level simulation tool for modeling electromagnetic side-channel signals. In: IEEE HPCA 2020, pp. 71–85. IEEE (2020). https://doi.org/10.1109/HPCA47549.2020.00016
30. Shelton, M.A., Chmielewski, L., Samwel, N., Wagner, M., Batina, L., Yarom, Y.: Rosita++: automatic higher-order leakage elimination from cryptographic code. In: ACM CCS 2021, pp. 685–699. ACM (2021). https://doi.org/10.1145/3460120.3485380
31. Shelton, M.A., Samwel, N., Batina, L., Regazzoni, F., Wagner, M., Yarom, Y.: Rosita: towards automatic elimination of power-analysis leakage in ciphers. In: NDSS 2021. The Internet Society (2021)
32. Sönmez Turan, M., McKay, K., Chang, D., Kang, J., Kelsey, J.: Ascon-based lightweight cryptography standards for constrained devices: authenticated encryption, hash, and extendable output functions. Tech. rep, NIST (2024)
33. Stoffelen, K.: Efficient cryptography on the RISC-V architecture. In: Progress in Cryptology - LATINCRYPT 2019. LNCS, vol. 11774, pp. 323–340. Springer (2019). https://doi.org/10.1007/978-3-030-30530-7_16
34. Vouvoutsis, V., Casino, F., Patsakis, C.: On the effectiveness of binary emulation in malware classification. J. Inf. Secur. Appl. **68**, 103258 (2022). https://doi.org/10.1016/J.JISA.2022.103258

35. Weissbart, L., Picek, S.: Lightweight but not easy: side-channel analysis of the ascon authenticated cipher on a 32-bit microcontroller. IACR Cryptol. ePrint Arch, p. 1598 (2023). https://eprint.iacr.org/2023/1598
36. Wichelmann, J., Peredy, C., Sieck, F., Pätschke, A., Eisenbarth, T.: MAMBO-V: dynamic side-channel leakage analysis on RISC-V. In: DIMVA 2023. LNCS, vol. 13959, pp. 3–23. Springer (2023). https://doi.org/10.1007/978-3-031-35504-2_1

MIDSCAN: Investigating the Portability Problem for Cross-Device DL-SCA

Lizzy Grootjen[(✉)] [iD], Zhuoran Liu [iD], and Ileana Buhan [iD]

Digital Security Group, Radboud University, Nijmegen, The Netherlands
`{lizzy.grootjen,zhuoran.liu,ileana.buhan}@ru.nl`

Abstract. In deep learning side-channel analysis, a neural network is employed to develop a profile of our target device. Data from a similar dummy device is used to construct the profile. However, when the profiling device differs from the target device, the profile may not be accurate enough for a successful attack. This study examines the effect of manufacturing-induced inter-device discrepancies across 14 identical 32-bit STM32F303 devices. To map the manufacturing discrepancies for these devices, we create a tool called MIDSCAN - Manufacturing-Induced Discrepancies SCAN. Our analysis revealed that the 14 Chip-Whisperer 32-bit devices have limited manufacturing discrepancies. Only in a multilayer perceptron setup, the manufacturing discrepancies between the profiling and target devices affected the attack performance. In this case, devices that showed more discrepancies based on correlation and difference than the profiling device need additional traces for a successful attack. Manufacturing discrepancies between profiling and attack devices do not affect attack performance for convolutional neural network architectures. No additional attack traces were needed to perform a successful attack. Our findings indicate that statistical metrics, as implemented by MIDSCAN, can estimate inter-device discrepancies for identical devices. Finally, we found that manufacturing discrepancies are limited for 32-bit STM32F303 ChipWhisperer targets, eliminating the need for additional measures for cross-device deep learning attacks.

Keywords: Side-channel analysis · Deep learning · Portability problem · Inter-device variations · Cross-device attacks

1 Introduction

Today, communication is secured with the use of cryptographic algorithms. However, side-channel attacks form a realistic threat against embedded devices. These attacks can obtain keys from mathematically secure cryptographic implementations [14,23]. An attacker utilises leakage omitted by the physical properties of the device, *side-channels*, such as timing, power, and electromagnetic emanation, to obtain secret information. There are two main types of side-channel attacks: non-profiled and profiled attacks. In non-profiled attacks, many traces are collected from the target device to perform a statistical analysis, while in

E. Savas et al. (Eds.): LightSec 2025, LNCS 16216, pp. 178–197, 2026.
https://doi.org/10.1007/978-3-032-15541-2_10

profiled attacks, the attacker creates a profile from the target device to leverage such an attack [21]. Device profiles can be created in various ways. The most famous attack is the template attack, which assumes the leakage follows a multivariate Gaussian distribution and is considered one of the strongest attacks in an information-theoretic sense [6,23]. Another option is to create a profile based on power traces from a similar device. A greater similarity between the profiling device and the target device simplifies the success of an attack [27].

Even with similar profiling and target devices, certain differences, such as manufacturing discrepancies, environmental factors, and measurement setup, can result in an inaccurate template, possibly causing the attack to fail. This gap between the profile and the target device is called the *portability problem* [21]. Device and key variations can influence device portability and, therefore, attack performance [4]. These discrepancies occur not only between homogeneous and heterogeneous devices, but also between identical devices [27].

Various works have investigated the portability problem on identical devices for deep learning. Cao et al. explored how unsupervised domain adaptation, a type of transfer learning, facilitates cross-device attacks on 8-bit XMEGA devices [5], which are otherwise unfeasible without transfer learning. Golder et al. reported similar findings as Cao et al., demonstrating that additional measures were necessary to execute a cross-device attack on 30 chipWhisperer ATMEGA 8-bit devices, introducing their DTW-PCA-MLP solution [9]. Wang et al. reported the same results as Golder et al. on two other 8-bit ATMEGA devices where a cross-device attack was not directly possible [25]. Ninan et al. demonstrated that a cross-device attack is feasible on a 32-bit ChipWhisperer using EM traces without additional measures if the location of the probe is consistent [18]. This poses the question whether a cross-device is also possible in 32-bit devices with power traces, which are generally less noisy, easier to capture, and contain more circuit activity compared to EM traces [1]. Additionally, power traces are often used within the SCA community, as they do not require special equipment [23]. Finally, the potential for a cross-device attack varies between 8-bit and 32-bit devices.

The effect of manufacturing discrepancies among identical 32-bit devices on deep learning performance has not been studied, and it is unclear whether such variations should be considered. Therefore, we aim to answer the research question: How do manufacturing discrepancies influence the portability gap of 32-bit identical ChipWhisperer devices for cross-device deep learning attacks? To answer this question, first, we explore the variability arising from manufacturing discrepancies between 14 identical STM32F ChipWhisperer devices equipped with a Cortex-M4 chip. Second, we explore the impact of these discrepancies on the portability issue in deep learning profiling attacks. Lastly, we open-source our MIDSCAN tool to make it usable for any group of identical devices to examine manufacturing discrepancies[1]. In short, our main contributions are as follows.

---

[1] https://gitlab.science.ru.nl/lgrootjen/midscan.

1. Design a framework to compare our 14 identical 32STMF303 ChipWhisperer devices with each other on manufacturing discrepancies;
2. Create a tool (MIDSCAN) which implements the proposed framework;
3. Demonstrate that statistical metrics can assess manufacturing discrepancies in devices and indicate the impact on deep-learning model performance;
4. Show that deep learning architectures can handle identical device discrepancies of these 32-bit devices;

2   Background

2.1   Profiled Side-Channel Analysis and Leakage

A profiling side-channel attack assumes the attacker has complete access to a profiling device. Here, the attacker controls the plaintext and key input, enabling the collection of device traces to form a profile. Subsequently, the attacker collects traces of the target device containing unknown plaintexts and keys. The constructed profile is used to attack the target device to recover the keys. To analyze the leakage, a leakage model and a sensitive intermediate value y are selected. In AES, the sensitive value is selected as the s-box output.

$$y = Sbox(P \oplus k) \tag{1}$$

This value relies on plaintext and key, and its byte-wise characteristic within the AES algorithm enables a divide-and-conquer attack. Several approaches are available to model the value of y. The Hamming weight or the Hamming distance is a commonly used leakage model, resulting in a 9-class leakage model. Another option is the identity model, where we use a 256-class leakage model, one class for each possible value of y. In the Hamming weight model, the complexity of analysis is reduced because of the reduced classes. However, the Hamming weight leakage model does not guarantee that all classes are evenly balanced. For the identity leakage model, there is a uniform distribution in all 256 classes. Depending on the technique used for analysis, one leakage model might be more suitable than the other.

2.2   The Portability Problem

The portability issue refers to the difference in the leakage distribution between profiling and attacking devices, which is affected by how similar these devices are. In this work, we refer to manufacturing discrepancies *as the difference in the results in the set of metrics used to compare two devices.* The relationship between the profiling device and the target device based on their discrepancies can be sorted into four categories [27]:

1. **Same device**: When the same device is used for both profiling and attack, only variations in the measurement setup impact the leakage distribution. There are no manufacturing discrepancies, as the device used is the same for profiling and attacking. Practically speaking, this attack scenario is unrealistic.

2. **Identical/clone devices**: When the profiling device and target device are the same, they are identical or clone devices. This indicates that the architecture, microarchitecture, configurations, and manufacturer are the same. Differences in measurement setups and PCB manufacturing lead to variations between identical devices, as noted in [25]. This scenario is often used in lab setups.
3. **Homogeneous devices**: In a homogeneous device relationship, the profiling and attacking devices share the same architecture and manufacturer, yet differ in microarchitecture and configurations.
4. **Heterogeneous devices**: Here, the profiling and target devices vary entirely, encompassing both diverse manufacturers and architectures. Leakage through side channels is influenced by the microarchitecture of a device [3], resulting in different leakage distributions between heterogeneous devices.

2.3   Evaluation of Power Trace Signal Quality

Collected power traces can contain noise. Manufacturing discrepancies, measurement setup, and countermeasures can cause this noise. Countermeasures reduce the signal-to-noise (SNR) ratio to make side-channel attacks harder. The signal-to-noise ratio can be used to estimate the amount of signal in a trace compared to the noise. The signal-to-noise ratio is based on the variance of the signal and the variance of the noise [17].

$$SNR = \frac{Var(Signal)}{Var(Noise)} \tag{2}$$

2.4   Deep Learning

Neural networks have been applied in various domains, such as image classification and speech recognition. There are different architectures available, but they all perform a similar task: try to find the minimum in the landscape of a function. Gradient descent is the most commonly used technique for iteratively finding this minimum. For a supervised learning problem, the dataset consists of data points and their labels. The data used to find this optimum is divided into three parts: the training set, the validation set, and the test set. The most commonly used neural network architectures in deep learning side-channel analysis are the multilayer perceptron and the convolutional neural network [11,21,22].

Multilayer Perceptron. The multi-layer perceptron is composed of an input layer, one or more hidden layers, and an output layer, with nodes in each layer. Each layer in a fully-connected neural network links every node to the subsequent layer's nodes. The output of a neuron k in a layer is the sum of the weighted inputs n of the prior layer plus a bias b. This is typically represented in a matrix.

$$z_k = \sum_{i=1}^{n} w_i \cdot x_i + b = W \cdot x + b \tag{3}$$

An activation function can be applied to make the multilayer perceptron able to deal with non-linearity. This is usually the ReLU function, as it only keeps positive values within the network.

$$f_{relu}(x) = \max(0, x) \tag{4}$$

In a classification problem, the last layer is the number of classes in the problem. Each node denotes the score for each class. The softmax layer ensures that the output neuron values total 1, representing a probability distribution.

$$f(x)_i = \frac{e_i^x}{\sum_j e^{x_j}} \tag{5}$$

Convolutional Neural Networks. Created initially for image processing, convolutional neural networks, the convolutional layers are inspired by the animal visual cortex [2]. Later, they proved beneficial for 1D data like audio processing [12]. Within the side-channel research field, convolutional neural networks based on the VGG16 architecture are noted for their robustness against desynchronised power traces [11]. Convolutional neural networks share a similar structure to multilayer perceptrons: they consist of an input layer, at least one hidden layer, and an output layer. Hidden layers generally comprise blocks, each containing a convolutional layer and a subsequent pooling layer. CNNs feature a final fully-connected layer for classification. Every convolutional layer includes a kernel determining the window size and a stride specifying how far the window moves. In convolutional layers, the linear layers share weights across a plane. The core convolution between the signal and the weight matrix is as follows:

$$s(t) = (x * w)(t) = \sum_{a=-\infty}^{\infty} x(a)w(t - a) \tag{6}$$

The convolutional layers are often followed by a pooling layer. Pooling layers decrease dimensionality, thus needing fewer neurons in the subsequent network layers. The pooling layer downsamples a segment of the feature map. Average-Pooling computes the mean of the values within the receptive field of the feature map, while MaxPooling selects the maximum value of the feature map. The following equation represents the output of a MaxPooling layer.

$$MaxPool_k = \max(\{x_{k'} | k' \text{ in the receptive field of } k\}) \tag{7}$$

2.5   Evaluation of a DL-SCA

In deep learning, accuracy is commonly used to assess model performance. For image classification, each predicted label of a new image is correct or incorrect. The label is derived from the probability vector - a vector containing the probability for each class -, selecting the class with the highest probability. For side-channel analysis, accuracy is less suitable as a metric for model performance [20]. In a probability vector, even if the correct key ranks second, it can still facilitate a successful attack because the attacker can have multiple attack traces available. The community frequently uses *key rank* or *guessing entropy*, which are plotted against the number of required attack traces. Where the key rank is usually used for a known-key analysis, the guessing entropy is used to estimate the remaining workload after a side-channel attack [19]. In this work, the key rank is used as we perform a manufacturing discrepancies comparison for a cross-device attack. The key rank is based on the key guessing vector g on a T_a number of timesamples. The key guessing vector is calculated based on the log-likelihood principle, where $\hat{p_{ij}}$ is the estimated probability of a key candidate i using the sample j.

$$g_i = \sum_{j=1}^{T_a} log(\hat{p}_{ij}) \tag{8}$$

$$rank_{guess} = \text{position of } guess\text{'s score in } g \tag{9}$$

3   Related Work

Kocher et al. are the first to introduce a side-channel attack, where RSA is attacked using Simple Power Analysis (SPA) and Differential Power Analysis (DPA) [13]. After that, various other attacks are developed, such as Correlational Power Analysis (CPA) and Template Attacks [6,23]. In a Template Attack, the attacker creates a profile by assuming that the leakage follows a multivariate Gaussian distribution. Later, deep learning techniques were applied to learn the profile based on a similar device [10,15,16]. In recent work, the multilayer perceptron and the convolutional neural network are the most promising architectures in deep learning for side-channel analysis [11,22].

Using a similar device for profiling and attacking implicitly assumes they share the same leakage distribution [21]. This may not always be true due to inter-device differences [4]. Side-channel leakage is greatly influenced by a device's micro-architecture [3]. Current research aims to bridge the portability gap by introducing new solutions. For example, Das et al. [7] investigated how data augmentation from different identical profiling devices improves performance for a deep learning cross-device attack. Bhasin et al. [4] conducted research on the effect of inter-device and inter-key variations for attack performance. They suggested a similar solution as Das et al., the Multiple Device Model, which improves the training dataset by incorporating traces from different devices to address for these variations. Zhang et al. [27] showed in different device families how inter-device variations influence attack performance and proposed a pre-processing method, FL-PA, to deal with device variations of homogeneous and heterogeneous devices. Several studies have explored how transfer learning can help bridge the portability gap. Thapar et al. developed TranSCA, a transfer learning tool to address the portability gap in heterogeneous traces from simulated FPGA implementations [24]. Yu et al. similarly applied Meta-Transfer learning to enhance a cross-device attack on homogeneous 32STMFx devices and a cross-device attack involving the heterogeneous ATMEGA 8-bit device and 32STMFx 32-bit devices [26]. Genevey-Metat et al. applied transfer learning by retraining the network during the fine-tuning stage to target 32-bit homogeneous devices [8]. Cao et al. conducted a cross-device attack on identical 8-bit XMEGA devices utilizing unsupervised domain adaptation, discovering that this transfer learning technique enhances cross-device attack performance [5].

Most of the previous research has focused on covering the portability gap caused by the measurement setup, measurement domain, and architectural differences of devices. Few works have investigated the portability gap on identical devices. Ninan et al. focused on the variability in measurement setup and showed that the variation between devices increases when different probe locations are used compared to the profiling device [18]. They also found that for their 32-bit STM32F3 devices with the same probe location, their deep learning model, a convolutional neural network, was able to recover the keys without any additional pre-processing. For their 8-bit devices, it was feasible but required more attack traces. According to Golder et al. [9], for 30 identical 8-bit devices, inter-device variations affect attack performance. They used a convolutional neural network as a benchmark and compared it to their proposed solution, DTW-PCA-MLP, to account for the inter-device variations. Both authors showed different results on the portability gap between identical devices. The main difference between these two works is the target devices (8-bit vs. 32-bit) and their measurement technique (ChipWhisperer power consumption vs. EM probes). Interestingly, Ninan et al. found that a cross-device attack with EM-probes is possible without adjustments if the probe is positioned in the same area. However, when dealing with 8-bit ChipWhisperer devices, Golder et al. found that adjustments were needed for a cross-device deep learning attack. This suggests that manufacturing discrepancies can have an influence on attack performance, depending on the architecture of the devices and the chosen deep learning architecture. Table 1 provides an overview of related work concerning cross-device deep learning attacks on identical devices. This table shows that no other study has been conducted on a large set of 32-bit devices.

4   Capturing Manufacturing Discrepancies

4.1   Components Within a Power Trace

The device's power trace is connected to the algorithm in use. There are different approaches on how to determine the components of a power trace. In this study, we follow the definition of Mangard et al. [17], which is repeated below:

> "Each point in a power trace can be modelled as the sum of an operation-dependent component P_{op}, a data-dependent component P_{data}, electronic noise $P_{elnoise}$, and a constant component P_{const}."

Table 1. Overview of the related work on the portability issue for identical devices for a cross-device deep learning attack.

Reference	Device	Arch.	Nr. devices	Neural network	Side-channel
Das et al. [7]	XMEGA	8-bit	8	MLP	Power
Golder et al. [9]	XMEGA	8-bit	30	MLP & CNN	Power
Cao et al. [5]	XMEGA	8-bit	8	CNN	Power
Wang et al. [25]	XMEGA	8-bit	2	MLP & CNN	Power
Ninan et al. (1/2) [18]	XMEGA	8-bit	2	MLP & CNN	EM
Ninan et al. (2/2) [18]	STM32F3	32-bit	2	MLP & CNN	EM
Our work	STM32F303	32-bit	14	MLP & CNN	Power

$$P_{total} = P_{op} + P_{data} + P_{elnoise} + P_{const} \tag{10}$$

P_{const} is considered the constant power supply for a device and remains consistent across identical devices. If the devices are homogeneous instead of identical, P_{const} may vary. P_{data} is the component of the power trace influenced by the data, affecting overall power usage. P_{op} refers to the power required to execute operations on the device. These operations may rely on the data, depending on the op optimizations used within the chip. If clone devices have the same data input, their operations are equal. Bhasin et al. demonstrated that inter-key variations significantly influence the profiling phase [4]. $P_{elnoise}$ refers to the manufacturing process and measurement setup discrepancies.

A profile has to accommodate all of these variables, depending on the relationship between the two devices. Earlier studies have shown that extra steps might be necessary to address inter-device variations caused by differences in measurement setups, manufacturing, and the devices themselves [7,9].

To isolate the impact of device manufacturing discrepancies, we believe it is essential to accurately assess the electrical noise component $P_{elnoise}$. To achieve this, we keep P_{const}, P_{data}, and P_{op} uniform between devices. With identical ChipWhisperer boards used in all setups, P_{const} remains stable. Employing fixed keys and seeded plaintext data ensures P_{op} and P_{data} remain consistent across devices. This yields a single variable, $P_{elnoise}$, which reflects the manufacturing variations among the devices. To our knowledge, this work is the first to model manufacturing discrepancies by isolating $P_{elnoise}$.

4.2 MIDSCAN: Manufacturing-Induced Discrepancies SCAN

To facilitate the evaluation of $P_{elnoise}$, as described in Sect. 4.1, we developed a tool called MIDSCAN (Manufacturing-Induced Discrepancies SCAN). This tool includes scripts in three categories: data collection, device analysis, and deep learning attack. A schematic overview of MIDSCAN is visualised in Fig. 1. The data collection category consists of two scripts to collect data from ChipWhisperer: one script collects traces for the profiling device, and the other collects traces from the target devices. We use seeded random plaintext for our target devices to maintain a consistent P_{data} across all devices. We also collect 500 traces from a fixed plaintext and key to conduct a cross-device analysis of manufacturing-induced variations. The device analysis component includes the analysis of the point of interest between the profiling device and target devices, as well as a cross-device analysis.

The cross-device analysis calculates manufacturing discrepancies based on correlation, difference, standard deviation, time sample distribution, timesample outliers, and signal-to-noise ratio. The deep learning component assists in executing a deep learning side-channel attack. The initial script trains three deep learning models chosen from the literature on our profiling device. The second script executes the cross-device deep learning attack and determines the key rank for each device. This key rank is then used as an additional metric to assess cross-device attack performance when dealing with device discrepancies. This tool has been designed for use with our 14 available devices, but it is extendable to other (ChipWhisperer) devices.

MIDSCAN

Fig. 1. Schematic overview of MIDSCAN.

5   Experimental Setup

We gathered data from 14 ChipWhisperer Lite boards, each featuring a 32-bit STM32F303 ARM Cortex M4 target. These chips use NewAE Solutions' tinyAES-128 implementation. Among these 14 devices, one is randomly selected as the profile device; in this study, it is device A. As this work focuses on the effect of manufacturing differences, no countermeasures were implemented to protect against side-channel attacks.

5.1   Dataset Generation

The study is divided into two sections: device analysis and deep learning attack, with a dataset collected for each part. All devices share an identical, fixed key in this study. During the device analysis part, we collected 500 traces with fixed plaintext input, each trace consisting of 12,000 timesamples. Throughout the remainder of the paper, this dataset is called CW_{fixed}. In the deep learning part, we collected 10,000 traces with seeded plaintexts, each trace again consisting of 12,000 timesamples. This set of plaintexts is used on all devices, maintaining consistency in P_{op} and P_{data}. For the remainder of the paper, this dataset is referred to as CW_{seeded}. Figure 2 illustrates the structure of the dataset. Due to the size of the datasets, it is not publicly available. However, MIDSCAN as well as this paper offer all the information needed on the datasets.

	A	A	B	C	D	E	F	G	H	I	J	K	L	N	O
CW_fixed	-	500	500	500	500	500	500	500	500	500	500	500	500	500	500
CW_seeded	50k	10k	10k	10k	10k	10k	10k	10k	10k	10k	10k	10k	10k	10k	10k

Legend: Device analysis   ML_train   ML_test

Fig. 2. Overview of the ChipWhisperer dataset with the number of traces gathered for each device.

5.2 Point of Interest

In this work, we focused on attacking target byte 0 of the first AES round. For a comprehensive overview of inter-device discrepancies, we concentrated on three aspects of our power traces: the discrepancies across all 12,000 samples, the discrepancies within the defined point of interest window, and the discrepancies in a 10-sample window zoomed in on our target byte 0. The point of interest window is identified by calculating the correlation between the timesamples and the Hamming weight leakage model. For this, the dataset CW_{seeded} is used.

5.3 Deep Learning Architectures

The cross-device attack performance is evaluated for each device using three different deep learning architectures. The first model, the multilayer perceptron (MLP), introduced by Das et al. [7], is named `mlp_das` in this work. The second model, a deep convolutional neural network, was proposed by Kim et al. [11] and is called `cnn_kim` in this work. The third model, a shallow convolutional neural network, was proposed by Golder et al. [9] and is named `cnn_golder` in this work. The architectures of these networks are shown in Table 2.

In these models, no additional measures are taken to facilitate a cross-device attack. For the deep learning attack, the identity leakage model is used, resulting in a 256-bit classifier. To evaluate attack performance, the key rank metric is used as described by [19,22]. The architectures are the same as those proposed by the authors. The epochs, batch size, optimiser, and learning rate are adjusted to our dataset. For the convolutional neural networks, those happen to be the same as the original authors. In Table 3, these parameters are highlighted for each of these architectures. The aim is to investigate how discrepancies in manufacturing affect attack performance on identical 32-bit devices.

Table 2. Overview of the deep learning architectures. All Dense and Conv1D layers have a ReLU activation function, unless stated otherwise.

	`mlp_das` [7]	`cnn_kim` [11]	`cnn_golder` [9]
Input Layer		BatchNormalization()	
First block	Dense(200) BatchNormalization() Dropout(0.1)	Conv1D(8,3) MaxPooling1D(2) BatchNormalization()	Conv1D(70,60)
Second block	Dense(200) BatchNormalization()	Conv1D(16,3) MaxPooling1D(2)	Conv1D(70,60) MaxPooling1D(3)
Third block		Conv1D(32,3) MaxPooling1D(2) BatchNormalization()	
Fourth block		Conv1D(64,3) MaxPooling1D(2)	
Fifth block		Conv1D(64,3) MaxPooling1D(2) BatchNormalization()	
Sixth block		Conv1D(128,3) MaxPooling1D(2)	
Seventh block		Conv1D(256,3) MaxPooling1D(2) BatchNormalization()	
Eighth block		Conv1D(256,3) Dropout(0.5)	
Classification block	Dense(256, softmax)	Flatten() Dense(512) Dropout(0.5) Dense(256, softmax)	Flatten() Dropout(0.2) Dense(150) BatchNormalization() Dropout(0.1) Dense(256, softmax)

Table 3. Overview of the parameters for the neural network architectures

	`mlp_das`	`cnn_kim`	`cnn_golder`
epochs	20	75	20
batch size	256	256	256
optimizer	Adam	Adam	Adam
learning rate	0.00001	0.001	0.001

5.4   Evaluation Metrics

To investigate manufacturing discrepancies, the dataset CW_{fixed} is used. The metrics are computed on all three intervals as discussed in the previous section. The first two evaluation metrics are the difference and the correlation between the average power trace across the devices. This results in a heatmap showing which devices are more similar based on these metrics and how these similarities vary over different intervals. The hypothesis is that for devices more similar and more correlating to the training device, it is easier to perform a cross-device attack. Then, the standard deviation and the boxplot distribution for each device is calculated. This metric is used to determine outliers between our devices. Finally, we visualise the number of timesamples that fall in the extremes of a normal distribution, also known as 3σ, for the three intervals. This statistical measure has been taken from the research of Golder et al. and is used to detect outliers on a timesample view. Before performing the cross-device attack, the signal-to-noise ratio is calculated for each device. To perform the signal-to-noise ratio analysis, the dataset CW_{seeded} is used. We aim to explore whether discrepancies in manufacturing can affect the signal-to-noise ratio. Lastly, the key rank as introduced in Sect. 2.5 is used to determine the attack performance.

6   Results and Discussion

6.1   Device Analysis

Before starting the device analysis, we determine the point of interest. In line with other studies, we choose a window of 700 samples. We use the Hamming weight leakage model to associate s-box values with power traces, identifying leakage and thus the point of interest. Our POI analysis shows the s-box calculation for target byte 0 at timesample 1326 and for byte 15 at 1973. These results

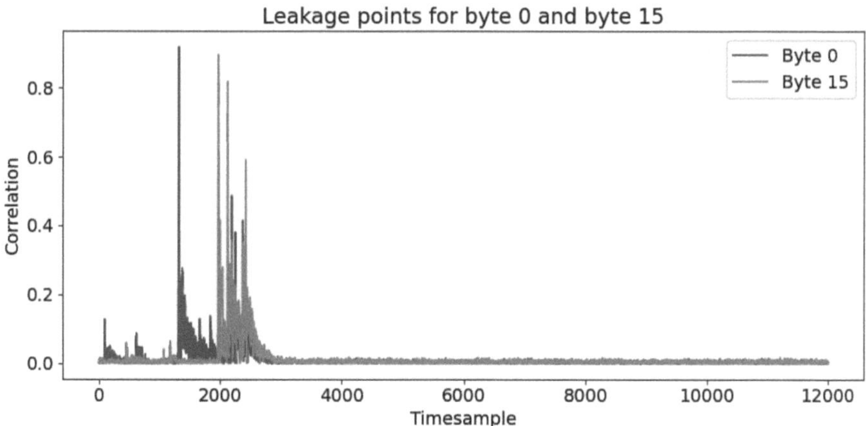

Fig. 3. Graph of leaky points on byte 0 and byte 15 for training device A.

are shown in Fig. 3. We investigate whether all test devices share the same leakage points. The results of this experiment are shown in Fig. 5. Devices G and O are unique in having a leaky point other than the training device A, differing by only a single timesample. Thus, we conclude that the point-of-interest window for all devices spans from timesample 1300 to 2000 (Fig. 4).

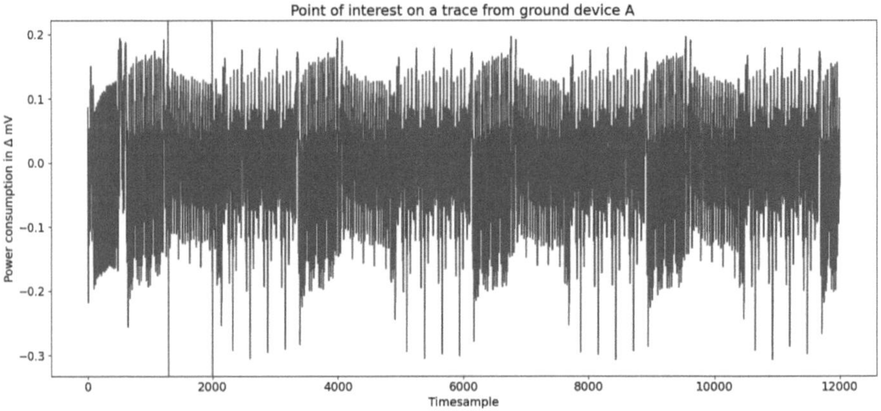

Fig. 4. The chosen POI based on the location of the leakage of byte 0 and byte 15.

Determining point of interest for target byte 0: correlating timesamples

	A	B	C	D	E	F	G	H	I	J	K	L	N	O
Highest correlation	1326	1326	1326	1326	1326	1326	1325	1326	1326	1326	1326	1326	1326	1325
Second highest correlation	1327	1325	1325	1325	1325	1325	1326	1325	1325	1327	1325	1325	1325	1326
Third highest correlation	1325	1327	1327	1327	1327	1327	1327	1327	1327	1325	1327	1327	1327	1327

Fig. 5. The timesample showing the most leakage correlated to byte 0 for each device.

For each combination of devices, the correlation and differences are computed. The results are shown in Figs. 6 and 7. Across the whole trace, device E shows the weakest correlation with our training device A, followed by devices C and O. These results remain the same when taking our POI into account. Zooming in on the target byte 0, device O shows more correlation with our training device. When evaluating the differences across devices, again device E shows to have the biggest difference compared to device A across the whole trace. Device H also shows a larger difference compared to device A. When zooming in on our POI, these findings remain roughly the same compared to our entire trace. Finally, zooming in at the byte level, device E shows less difference compared to the other two timesample windows. The heatmap for correlation varies only 0.2%, indicating that the devices are very similar. Without any feedback loop to the manufacturing process, it is not possible to investigate why these devices are so similar. A possible hypothesis could be that the variations within the data, which are kept constant in this study, have a greater influence on the device similarities compared to the manufacturing discrepancies.

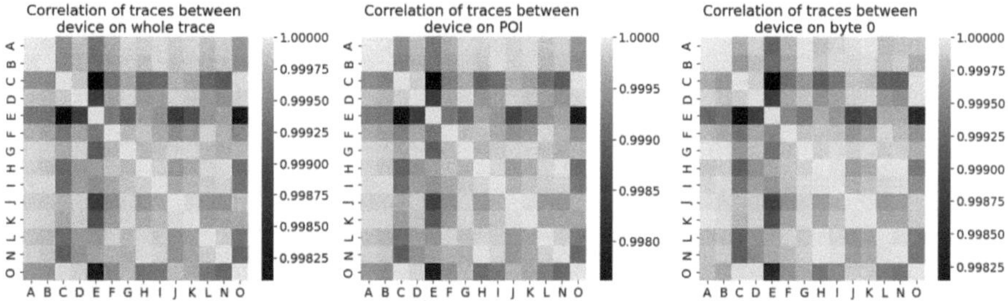

Fig. 6. Heatmap displaying the correlation between the devices on different timesample intervals.

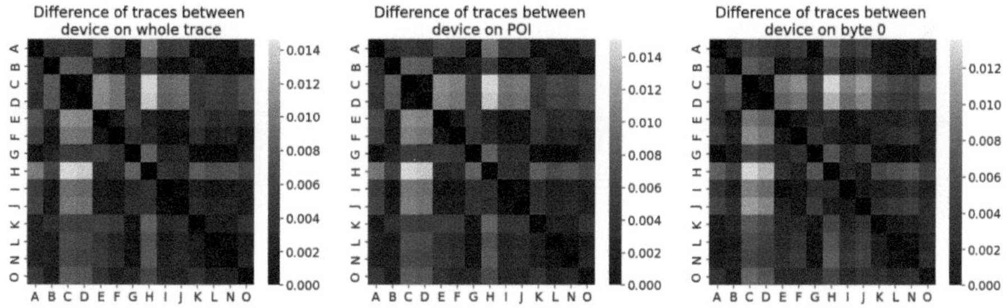

Fig. 7. Heatmap displaying the difference between the devices on different timesample intervals.

For each device, we calculated the standard deviation. The results of this experiment are shown in Fig. 8. The standard deviation is relatively small, and all the devices have a similar standard deviation. The pattern remains the same across different timesample windows. Figure 9 shows that each device has a similar power distribution. Across the whole trace, the points below the value -0.2 catch attention. These appear to be outliers, but this behaviour is the same across all devices. Interestingly, timesamples that are outliers do not occur in the windows of POI and byte 0, parts where the s-box computation takes place. From these two figures, we can conclude that there are no devices that have a different behaviour based on the power distribution or standard deviation.

Figure 10 shows the count of timesamples in the power traces that lie in the extremes of a normal distribution, that is, 3σ. This measure is adapted from

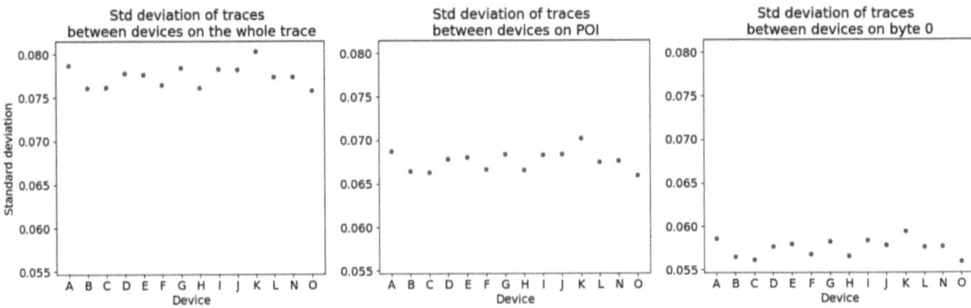

Fig. 8. Scatter plots showing the standard deviation of the devices on different time-sample intervals.

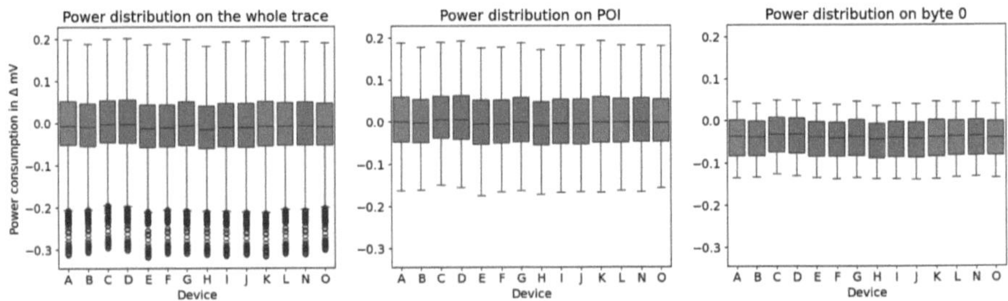

Fig. 9. Boxplot of the power consumption of the devices.

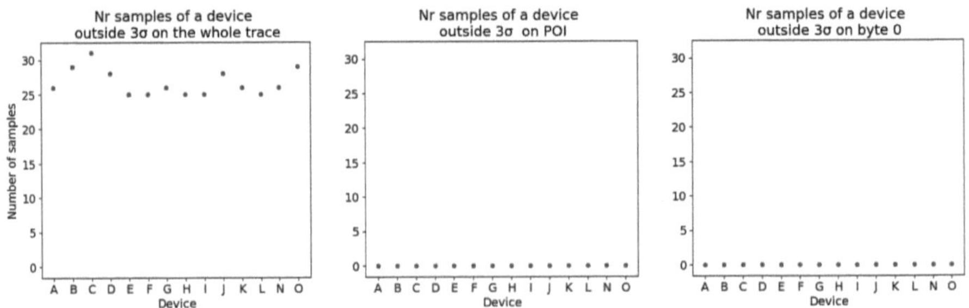

Fig. 10. Scatterplot displaying the number of timesamples outside 3σ on different timesample intervals.

Golder et al. [9]. As can be seen, the outliers in the power trace do not lie within our point of interest. This is in line with the observations in Fig. 9. Again, from this plot, we conclude that there is no device that is an apparent outlier.

Finally, Fig. 11 shows the signal-to-noise ratio of each device. Device G has the highest signal-to-noise ratio, and devices H and I have the lowest signal-to-noise ratio. The pattern in the signal-to-noise ratio is roughly the same for all devices. From this section, we conclude that the manufacturing discrepancies of these 14 ChipWhisperers are limited.

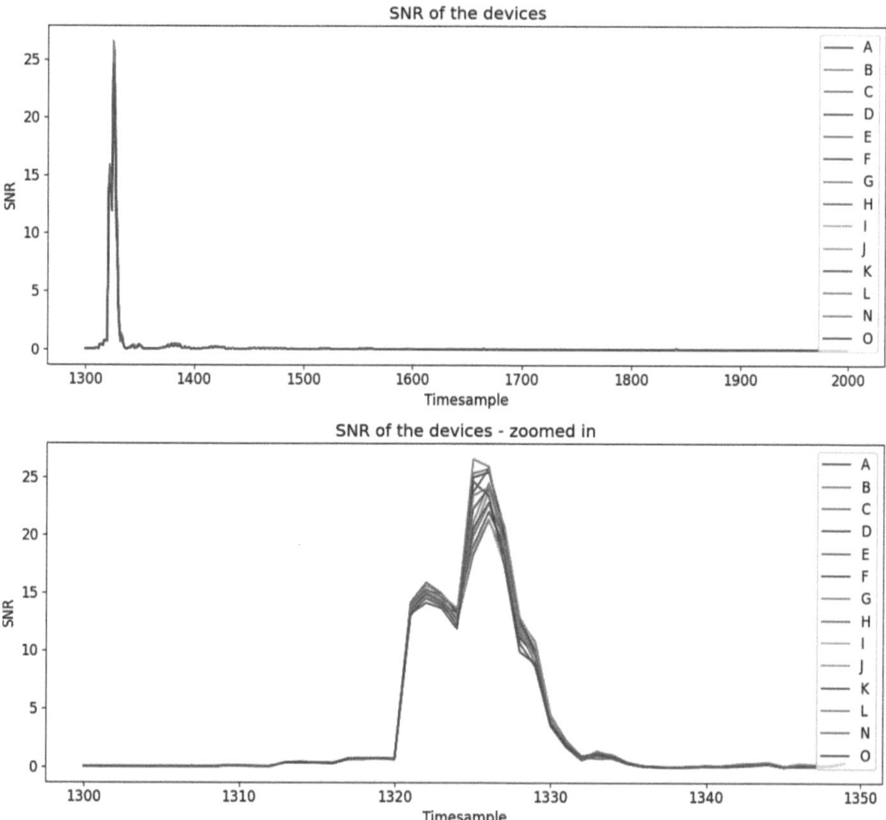

Fig. 11. Signal-to-noise ratio for each device.

6.2   Deep Learning Attack

This experiment was performed with the CW_{seeded} dataset. Firstly, three neural network architectures were trained on device A. Then, all devices were attacked using the three trained models. The results of this cross-device attack are shown in Fig. 12. Both convolutional neural networks, `cnn_kim` and `cnn_golder`, effectively handled the manufacturing discrepancies among the 14 devices. For the `mlp_das` multilayer perceptron, additional attack traces are required to successfully recover the key. In particular, devices E and H needed more attack traces for a successful key recovery.

These are the same devices that had larger interdevice discrepancies compared to training device A, based on the difference and correlation. There is no visible effect on the differences between the signal-to-noise ratio for a cross-device attack. This is most likely because the signal-to-noise ratio is already high, indicating more signal than noise. This also shows that the traces captured by the ChipWhisperer board are very clean.

Key ranks for cross-device side-channel attacks

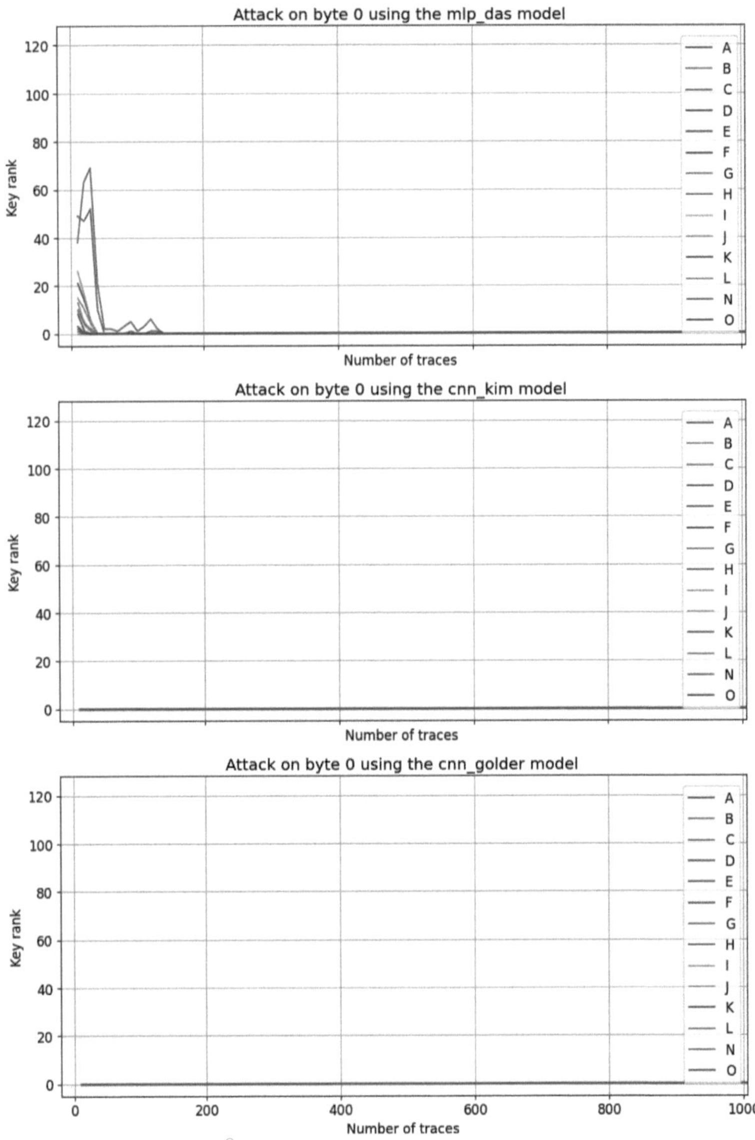

Fig. 12. The key ranks for three different neural network architectures, cross-device attacked.

7   Conclusions and Future Work

This research presented a tool with evaluation metrics to assess manufacturing discrepancies. From the experiments, we conclude that manufacturing discrepancies hardly influence attack performance for 32-bit 32STM303 ChipWhisperer devices. For MLP, more attack traces were needed for a successful key recovery. However, the amount of additional traces needed was only roughly 75 traces in a worst-case scenario. Devices with larger discrepancies compared to the training device were also devices that required more attack traces. This indicates that a cross-device attack using a multilayer perceptron without additional measures is still possible, at the cost of a few extra attack traces. The high signal-to-noise ratio of the ChipWhisperer devices did not make up for the inter-device variations. Using a convolutional neural network, one attack trace is required for identical 32-bit 32STMF303 devices in a cross-device attack, eliminating the need to consider additional measures to account for inter-device variations.

Our results align with those of Ninan et al., who demonstrated that a 32-bit cross-device attack is feasible with the same probe location. Research by Golder et al., Wang et al., and Cao et al. demonstrated that direct cross-device attacks are not successful for 8-bit identical devices. The analysis by Golder et al. revealed higher inter-device variations and wider power distributions between devices, indicating that a cross-device attack might not be feasible. Based on our work and similar previous work, we conclude that a cross-device deep-learning attack without additional measures to cover the portability gap is possible for 32-bit devices but not necessarily for 8-bit devices. In conclusion, our analysis reveals that manufacturing discrepancies detected by MIDSCAN minimally impact the deep learning attack performance of the multilayer perceptron.

For future work, a side-by-side comparison between 8-bit and 32-bit devices for a cross-device attack using the power side-channel can verify this hypothesis. In addition, transformer models can be evaluated for the effectiveness of cross-device attacks. Another aspect to investigate is whether manufacturing discrepancies between identical devices play a greater role if the signal-to-noise ratio of the devices is lower. Finally, the effect of data variations compared to manufacturing discrepancies can be investigated when doing a cross-device attack.

Acknowledgments. This work was (in part) supported by Dutch Research Council (NWO) through the PROACT project (NWA.1215.18.014), TTW PREDATOR project 19782, TTW BASES project 20858 and the CiCS project of the research programme Gravitation under the grant 024.006.037. We thank the reviewers for their suggestions and ideas to improve the paper.

Disclosure of Interests. The authors have no competing interests to declare that are relevant to the content of this article.

References

1. Amar, M., Navanesan, L., Sayakkara, A.P., Oren, Y.: Waves of knowledge: a comparative study of electromagnetic and power side-channel monitoring in embedded systems. In: Chen, Y., Lin, C.W., Chen, B., Zhu, Q. (eds.) Security and Privacy in Cyber-Physical Systems and Smart Vehicles. LNICST, pp. 158–170. Springer, Cham (2024). https://doi.org/10.1007/978-3-031-51630-6_11
2. Arbib, M.A. (ed.): The Handbook of Brain Theory and Neural Networks. The MIT Press (2002). https://doi.org/10.7551/mitpress/3413.001.0001
3. Arora, V., Buhan, I., Perin, G., Picek, S.: A tale of two boards: on the influence of microarchitecture on side-channel leakage. In: Grosso, V., Pöppelmann, T. (eds.) Smart Card Research and Advanced Applications. LNCS, vol. 13173, pp. 80–96. Springer, Cham (2022). https://doi.org/10.1007/978-3-030-97348-3_5
4. Bhasin, S., Chattopadhyay, A., Heuser, A., Jap, D., Picek, S., Shrivastwa, R.R.: Mind the portability: a warriors guide through realistic profiled side-channel analysis. In: Proceedings 2020 Network and Distributed System Security Symposium, San Diego, CA. Internet Society (2020). https://doi.org/10.14722/ndss.2020.24390
5. Cao, P., Zhang, C., Lu, X., Gu, D.: Cross-device profiled side-channel attack with unsupervised domain adaptation. TCHES, 27–56 (2021). https://doi.org/10.46586/tches.v2021.i4.27-56
6. Chari, S., Rao, J.R., Rohatgi, P.: Template attacks. In: Kaliski, B.S., Koç, K., Paar, C. (eds.) CHES 2002. LNCS, vol. 2523, pp. 13–28. Springer, Heidelberg (2003). https://doi.org/10.1007/3-540-36400-5_3
7. Das, D., Golder, A., Danial, J., Ghosh, S., Raychowdhury, A., Sen, S.: X-DeepSCA: cross-device deep learning side channel attack. In: Proceedings of the 56th Annual Design Automation Conference 2019, Las Vegas NV USA, pp. 1–6. ACM (2019).https://doi.org/10.1145/3316781.3317934
8. Genevey-Metat, C., Gérard, B., Heuser, A.: On what to learn: train or adapt a deeply learned profile? (2020). https://eprint.iacr.org/2020/952
9. Golder, A., Das, D., Danial, J., Ghosh, S., Sen, S., Raychowdhury, A.: Practical approaches toward deep-learning-based cross-device power side-channel attack. IEEE Trans. VLSI Syst. **27**(12), 2720–2733 (2019). https://doi.org/10.1109/TVLSI.2019.2926324
10. Hospodar, G., Gierlichs, B., De Mulder, E., Verbauwhede, I., Vandewalle, J.: Machine learning in side-channel analysis: a first study. J. Cryptogr. Eng. **1**(4), 293–302 (2011). https://doi.org/10.1007/s13389-011-0023-x
11. Kim, J., Picek, S., Heuser, A., Bhasin, S., Hanjalic, A.: Make some noise. unleashing the power of convolutional neural networks for profiled side-channel analysis. TCHES, 148–179 (2019). https://doi.org/10.46586/tches.v2019.i3.148-179
12. Kim, T., Lee, J., Nam, J.: Sample-level CNN architectures for music auto-tagging using raw waveforms (2018). https://doi.org/10.48550/arXiv.1710.10451
13. Kocher, P., Jaffe, J., Jun, B.: Differential power analysis. In: Wiener, M. (ed.) CRYPTO 1999. LNCS, vol. 1666, pp. 388–397. Springer, Heidelberg (1999). https://doi.org/10.1007/3-540-48405-1_25
14. Le, T.H., Canovas, C., Clédière, J.: An overview of side channel analysis attacks. In: Proceedings of the 2008 ACM Symposium on Information, Computer and Communications Security, Tokyo, Japan, pp. 33–43. ACM (2008). https://doi.org/10.1145/1368310.1368319
15. Lerman, L., Bontempi, G., Markowitch, O.: Power analysis attack: an approach based on machine learning. Int. J. Appl. Crypt. **3**(2), 97 (2014). https://doi.org/10.1504/IJACT.2014.062722

16. Lerman, L., Poussier, R., Markowitch, O., Standaert, F.X.: Template attacks versus machine learning revisited and the curse of dimensionality in side-channel analysis: extended version. J. Cryptogr. Eng. **8**(4), 301–313 (2017). https://doi.org/10.1007/s13389-017-0162-9

17. Mangard, S.: Hardware countermeasures against DPA – a statistical analysis of their effectiveness. In: Okamoto, T. (ed.) CT-RSA 2004. LNCS, vol. 2964, pp. 222–235. Springer, Heidelberg (2004). https://doi.org/10.1007/978-3-540-24660-2_18

18. Ninan, M., et al.: A second look at the portability of deep learning side-channel attacks over EM traces. In: The 27th International Symposium on Research in Attacks, Intrusions and Defenses, Padua Italy, pp. 630–643. ACM (2024). https://doi.org/10.1145/3678890.3678900

19. Papagiannopoulos, K., Glamočanin, O., Azouaoui, M., Ros, D., Regazzoni, F., Stojilović, M.: The side-channel metrics cheat sheet. ACM Comput. Surv. **55**(10), 1–38 (2023). https://doi.org/10.1145/3565571

20. Picek, S., Heuser, A., Jovic, A., Bhasin, S., Regazzoni, F.: The curse of class imbalance and conflicting metrics with machine learning for side-channel evaluations. Trans. Crypt. Hardware Embed. Syst. IACR, 209–237 (2019). https://doi.org/10.13154/tches.v2019.i1.209-237

21. Picek, S., Perin, G., Mariot, L., Wu, L., Batina, L.: SoK: deep learning-based physical side-channel analysis. ACM Comput. Surv. **55**(11), 1–35 (2023). https://doi.org/10.1145/3569577

22. Prouff, E., Strullu, R., Benadjila, R., Cagli, E., Dumas, C.: Study of deep learning techniques for side-channel analysis and introduction to ASCAD database (2018). https://doi.org/10.1007/s13389-019-00220-8

23. Randolph, M., Diehl, W.: Power side-channel attack analysis: a review of 20 years of study for the layman. Cryptography **4**(2), 15 (2020). https://doi.org/10.3390/cryptography4020015

24. Thapar, D., Alam, M., Mukhopadhyay, D.: TranSCA: cross-family profiled side-channel attacks using transfer learning on deep neural networks (2020). https://eprint.iacr.org/2020/1258

25. Wang, H., Brisfors, M., Forsmark, S., Dubrova, E.: How diversity affects deep-learning side-channel attacks. In: 2019 IEEE Nordic Circuits and Systems Conference (NORCAS): NORCHIP and International Symposium of System-on-Chip (SoC), Helsinki, Finland, pp. 1–7. IEEE (2019). https://doi.org/10.1109/NORCHIP.2019.8906945

26. Yu, H., Shan, H., Panoff, M., Jin, Y.: Cross-device profiled side-channel attacks using meta-transfer learning. In: 2021 58th ACM/IEEE Design Automation Conference (DAC), San Francisco, CA, USA, pp. 703–708. IEEE (2021). https://doi.org/10.1109/DAC18074.2021.9586100

27. Zhang, F., et al.: From homogeneous to heterogeneous: leveraging deep learning based power analysis across devices. In: 2020 57th ACM/IEEE Design Automation Conference (DAC), San Francisco, CA, USA, pp. 1–6. IEEE (2020). https://doi.org/10.1109/DAC18072.2020.9218693

Protecting AES-128 Against First-Order Side-Channel Analysis in Micro-Architectures by Enforcing Threshold Implementation Principles

Charles-Antoine De Paepe, John Gaspoz[iD], Dilara Toprakhisar[iD], and Svetla Nikova[(✉)][iD]

COSIC, KU Leuven, Leuven, Belgium
`ca.depaepe@gmail.com`,
`{John.Gaspoz,Dilara.Toprakhisar,Svetla.Nikova}@esat.kuleuven.be`

Abstract. As embedded systems become increasingly pervasive, ensuring cryptographic security against side-channel attacks has emerged as a critical challenge. While masking schemes are a well-established countermeasure, micro-architectural features inherent to modern processors can introduce unintended leakages that fall outside the scope of classical leakage models. This work presents a first-order masked software implementation of AES-128, including the key schedule, targeting the ARM Cortex-M4 platform. The design adheres to software-specific threshold implementation principles, enforcing horizontal and vertical non-completeness as well as register-uniform masking. A bitsliced representation is adopted, with each share computed at a distinct index and cross-products evaluated independently to preserve security guarantees. The AES S-box is decomposed using a tower field representation, limiting the need to secure only 2- and 4-bit multiplications. Secure Toffoli gate constructions are employed to ensure that cross-domain multiplications adhere to TI constraints. The *"changing of the guards"* principle is applied to enable randomness reuse, thereby reducing the demand for fresh randomness. In contrast to prior work that prioritizes performance, this research emphasizes real-world side-channel security, validated through extensive practical evaluation using a Test Vector Leakage Assessment. The results demonstrate that secure software implementations are feasible without hardware changes, though this comes with associated performance trade-offs.

Keywords: masking · micro-architectures · side-channel analysis · threshold implementations

1 Introduction

Embedded systems are now ubiquitous across application domains, many of which depend on cryptographic operations to ensure confidentiality, integrity,

© The Author(s), under exclusive license to Springer Nature Switzerland AG 2026
E. Savas et al. (Eds.): LightSec 2025, LNCS 16216, pp. 198–211, 2026.
https://doi.org/10.1007/978-3-032-15541-2_11

and authentication. These systems frequently rely on symmetric-key cryptographic algorithms like AES-128. However, real-world implementations are vulnerable to side-channel analysis (SCA) [17], particularly power analysis attacks.

Masking is a widely adopted countermeasure that randomizes intermediate values to statistically decorrelate them from sensitive data. In a dth-order masking, each sensitive value is split into $d+1$ random shares. Yet, even well-designed masked algorithms can leak when deployed on modern micro-controllers [12,23].

To counter such effects, Threshold Implementations (TI) [22], originally devised for hardware, have been adapted for micro-architectures [11] to enforce security properties like non-completeness and uniformity. Recent works demonstrate such implementations for 4- and 5-bit S-boxes [11], but not for the AES S-box.

This work presents a first-order masked software implementation of AES-128, including both the encryption and key schedule, on an ARM Cortex-M4. It employs a bitsliced representation and a secure Toffoli gate construction to prevent both vertical and horizontal leakage. Each share is processed independently, and cross-products are computed at isolated indices to minimize unintended interactions. The *"Changing of the Guards"* [6] technique is applied to reuse randomness to have low fresh randomness requirements. Additionally, a masked bitsliced implementation of the key schedule is included, which also satisfies software specific TI properties.

While prior work has prioritized performance [1,16,25], many existing AES implementations fail practical Test Vector Leakage Assessments (TVLA) [2]. This work prioritizes leakage resilience over speed, showing that a secure software AES implementation is achievable without hardware changes.

In summary, this work makes the following contributions:

- A secure software masking of 2- and 4-bit Toffoli gates, satisfying software specific TI principles, is proposed. They form the foundation for a secure AES S-box.
- First-order masked software implementation of AES-128 that has been validated by doing a TVLA with one million measurements.
- A masked and bitsliced implementation of the AES-128 key schedule, satisfying the software specific TI principles. Similar to the encryption algorithm, it is validated by doing a TVLA with one million measurements.

2   Preliminaries

This section introduces the notation used in this paper, boolean masking, Canright's implementation of the AES S-box and TVLA.

2.1   Notation

In this paper, variables are split into two shares, unless otherwise stated. Given a variable x, its share is represented as $\bar{x} = (x_0, x_1)$. A share consisting of m bits is represented as $x_0 = \{x_0^{m-1}, x_0^{m-2}, \ldots, x_0^0\}$. A finite field with order p^n is denoted as $\mathbb{F}_{p^n}$. Toffoli gates will be used as a building block in the actual implementation. A Toffoli gate is a function that maps three variables (a, b, c) to $(a + b \cdot c, b, c)$. The Toffoli gate over $\mathbb{F}_{2^n}$ will be denoted as $p_T^n(a, b, c)$ with $a, b, c \in \mathbb{F}_{2^n}$ and the multiplication and addition over $\mathbb{F}_{2^n}$ denoted by $\cdot$ and $+$, respectively. The first-order masking of a Toffoli gate is denoted as $p_{TS}^n(a_0, a_1, b_0, b_1, c_0, c_1)$ and is given by:

$$a_0' \leftarrow a_0 + b_0 \cdot c_1 + b_0 \cdot c_0$$
$$a_1' \leftarrow a_1 + b_1 \cdot c_1 + b_1 \cdot c_0$$

2.2 Boolean Masking

Boolean masking [5,15] is a widely adopted countermeasure against SCA. It aims to conceal sensitive key-dependent variables by decomposing them into multiple random shares. Specifically, in a dth-order Boolean masking scheme, a sensitive variable $x \in \mathbb{F}_{2^k}$ is split into $d + 1$ shares $\bar{x} = (x_0, x_1, \ldots, x_d)$. The shares $x_1, \ldots, x_d$ are independently sampled from a uniform distribution, and the final share x_0 is computed such that the original value is preserved, i.e., $x = \bigoplus_{i=0}^{d} x_i$. When the shares are uniformly distributed in this way, the scheme is referred to as uniform masking.

2.3 Canright's AES S-box Implementation

The AES S-box is defined based on inversion over $\mathbb{F}_{2^8}$. Canright [4] proposed a compact implementation based on a tower field representation with normal bases. Figure 1 shows a circuit diagram for the inversion over $\mathbb{F}_{2^8}$. Instead of operations over $\mathbb{F}_{2^8}$, they are decomposed into operations over $\mathbb{F}_{2^2}$ and $\mathbb{F}_{2^4}$ where the inversion over $\mathbb{F}_{2^2}$ can be realized with a simple bit swap. This AES S-box implementation will be used as a foundation for the actual implementation.

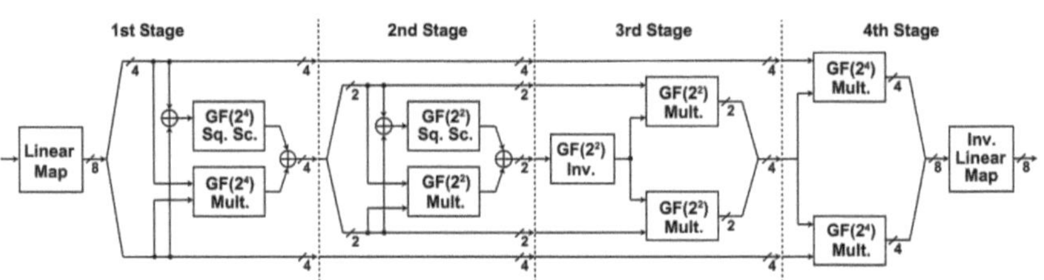

Fig. 1. Inversion over $\mathbb{F}_{2^8}$ in four stages [28].

2.4 Test Vector Leakage Assessment

Implementing side-channel countermeasures is not sufficient without rigorous validation. TVLA [14] is a widely adopted, cost-effective method for evaluating whether sensitive intermediate values leak information during cryptographic operations. While it does not provide exhaustive security guarantees, TVLA offers a reproducible and practical means to detect leakages.

TVLA applies Welch's t-test to compare two sets of power traces: one where the input is fixed, and another where it varies randomly. The null hypothesis assumes both sets are drawn from the same distribution i.e., no leakage occurs. The alternative hypothesis implies the sets are drawn from different distributions, suggesting potential leakage.

The t-statistic is computed for each time sample across the trace. A t value exceeding ± 4.5 at any time point indicates a statistically significant leakage with a 99.999% confidence level. A leakage result is confirmed if the same leakage occurs at the same sample index for another independent experiment.

3   Addressing Micro-architectural Leakage Sources

This section covers sources of micro-architectural leakage and software specific TI principles.

3.1   Transition Leakages

Dynamic power consumption in CMOS depends on signal transitions, leaking the Hamming Distance (HD) when values change. In first-order masking, overwriting one share with another in registers leaks the secret's Hamming Weight ("overwrite effect") [23]. Pipeline registers can similarly recombine shares during operand forwarding or speculative execution [10,18,23,26]. Even simple cores like Cortex-M exhibit this leakage [18]. The load-store unit (LSU) buffers recent data, and overwriting it with shares can leak information ("memory remnant effect") [23]. Additionally, memory writes may leak the HD between old and new values, further compromising security.

3.2   Glitch Related Leakage

Glitches, temporary signal changes from varying propagation delays, can cause side-channel leakage, similar to transition effects.

In the register file, glitches in the address decoder can expose the HD between nearby registers holding masked shares ("neighbor leakage effect") [12,23]. Memory address decoders are similarly vulnerable [12]. Accessing misaligned memory causes the LSU to buffer fetched data, which can glitch and recombine with other values, leaking sensitive information [12].

3.3   Bit-Interaction Leakage

The Independent Leakage Assumption (ILA) [24], which assumes operand bits leak independently, can fail due to micro-architectural effects [9].

A primary source is the ALU. To support instructions like ADD, SUB, and SHIFT, ALUs often compute all results in parallel, selecting the correct one afterward. Such components are referred to as always-active components [12]. The barrel shifter component is responsible for the SHIFT operation. Additionally, it enables a single-cycle computation on a shifted version of one operand. Specifically, it is the barrel shifter that is responsible for possible leakages when a complete set of the shares reside in one register. As it is an always active component, it shifts the bits inside a register for every clock cycle, leaking the HD of bits within the register.

3.4   Software Specific TI Properties

As discussed in the previous paragraphs, transition, glitch related and bit-interaction leakages can effectively reduce the security of an implementation. Gaspoz and Dhooghe [11] adapted TI principles to be software specific and therefore provide a robust foundation for secure implementations on micro-architectures. They provide the following three properties that must be satisfied for the entire duration of the computation:

"***Property 1 (Horizontal non-completeness)*** [11]. *A masked operation with input registers $R0$-Rl is horizontal non-complete when the set of all values in $R0$-Rl do not contain all shares of a variable.*" [11]

For first-order implementations, this property enforces that both shares cannot reside within the same register. Satisfying this property ensures the bit-interaction leakage will not be effective.

"***Property 2 (Vertical non-completeness)*** [11]. *A masked operation computing on m-bit registers $R0$-Rl is vertical non-complete when the set of all values at index $0 \leq i \leq m$ of $R0$-Rl do not contain all shares of a variable.*" [11]

For first-order implementations, this property enforces both shares to not be aligned at the same index. Cross-products must be computed at an independent index such that each index contains a non-complete set of the shares at all times.

"***Property 3 (Register uniform masking)*** [11]. *Given a masking in s shares, a set of $l+1$ registers $R0$-Rl are a register uniform masking when for every set of s-1 indices the set of shares at those indices jointly act as uniform random variables. Similarly, for every set of s-1 registers, the shares in those registers jointly act as uniform random variables.*" [11]

Essentially, the shares must be distributed evenly across the registers, while also being evenly distributed across the bit indices. However, for sequential operations on micro-controllers, it is not possible to comply with the three properties at all times when implementing non-linear functions. Therefore, it is sufficient that the overall function, composed of multiple instructions, is register uniform.

4   Implementation

This section covers the design choices for the encryption and key schedule.

4.1   Bitslicing

Bitslicing [3] is a technique that processes data bit-by-bit. By distributing bits of the AES state across multiple registers, bitslicing enables computations to be performed concurrently.

Since AES operates on 8-bit state elements, the bits of each byte of the AES state are distributed across 8 registers, with each register holding a specific bit index of all processed bytes. Given the 32-bit width of the registers, up to 32 bytes can be processed in parallel, allowing for two AES blocks (each 16 bytes) to be computed concurrently. However, this introduces complexity related to the handling of the mode of operation, which must be carefully managed to avoid security pitfalls.

This implementation processes a two-shared, masked version of AES, effectively doubling the size of the state to 32 bytes. In theory, both shares could be processed in parallel. However, the horizontal non-completeness property prohibits two shares of the same secret from residing in the same register.

Table 1 shows the bitsliced representation, which is based on [25]. Half of the bits are zero since only one 128-bit block is processed at a time. The bits from share 0 are located on the odd indices of the registers. To satisfy the vertical non-completeness property, the bits from share 1 are also represented by the same structure, but all registers are rotated one to the right.

Table 1. Bitsliced Representation based on [25].

	row 3								...	row 0							
	col 0		col 1		col 2		col 3		...	col 0		col 1		col 2		col 3	
R_0	b_0^{24}	0	b_0^{56}	0	b_0^{88}	0	b_0^{120}	0	...	b_0^{0}	0	b_0^{32}	0	b_0^{64}	0	b_0^{96}	0
$\vdots$	$\vdots$	$\vdots$	$\vdots$	$\vdots$	$\vdots$	$\vdots$	$\vdots$	$\vdots$	...	$\vdots$	$\vdots$	$\vdots$	$\vdots$	$\vdots$	$\vdots$	$\vdots$	$\vdots$
R_7	b_0^{31}	0	b_0^{63}	0	b_0^{95}	0	b_0^{127}	0	...	b_0^{7}	0	b_0^{39}	0	b_0^{71}	0	b_0^{103}	0

To reduce the number of clock cycles required for the change of representation, an assembly function is created which utilizes the **SWAPMOVE** instruction [19]. The function is based on the findings in [1] and results to an improvement in performance of 93% compared to an implementation in C.

The complete implementation can be split in two parts: one that is subject to the security evaluation and one that is not. As the shares are not vertical-non complete before the change of representation, the transformation is not considered in the security evaluation.

4.2   AES Linear Layers

The representation in Table 1 is designed to ensure a fast computation of the MixColumns operation. The implementation of [1] is adopted, which requires only 27 single-cycle instructions when using the barrel-shifter.

This representation is less favorable for the computation of the `ShiftRows` operation, as it requires byte-wise shifts. Two possible implementations require 104 single-cycle instructions [1,25]. However, in [1] it is shown that a more efficient implementation is possible when using the `SWAPMOVE` instruction [19]. This suggestion is implemented and requires only 66 single-cycle instructions.

Since both functions are linear, no cross-products have to be computed. To satisfy the software specific TI properties, both shares simply have to be computed at their respective index.

4.3   AES S-box

Daemen *et al.* [7] build upon Canright's foundation (see Sect. 2.3) by replacing the multiplications over $\mathbb{F}_{2^n}$ in his description by Toffoli gates over $\mathbb{F}_{2^n}$. This work uses their two-shared masked implementation of the AES S-box as a foundation [7].

The shared Toffoli gates over $\mathbb{F}_{2^2}$ and $\mathbb{F}_{2^4}$ are used to compute the cross-products. As elements of two shares have to be combined, these computations require special care to ensure a secure computation. Gaspoz and Dhooghe [11] propose a method to compute a secure Toffoli gate over $\mathbb{F}_2$. Their methodology is expanded for $\mathbb{F}_{2^2}$ and $\mathbb{F}_{2^4}$. Table 2 shows how to compute p_{TS}^2 step-by-step. The addition over $\mathbb{F}_{2^2}$ is a bitwise `XOR` while the multiplication is described in [7]. The security of this computation is based on two principles: cross-products are computed at index 2 to ensure vertical non-completeness and a_0 or a_1 are used to mask the cross-products before returning back to the original index. Gaspoz and Dhooghe [11] have proven that these principles are secure by evaluating it with the robust probing model [8] and a TVLA.

A similar methodology is applied to p_{TS}^4, which is shown in Table 3. The addition over $\mathbb{F}_{2^4}$ is a bitwise `XOR` and multiplication over $\mathbb{F}_{2^4}$ is described in [7]. In Table 3, $+$ and $\cdot$ denote the addition and multiplication over $\mathbb{F}_{2^2}$, respectively. Instead of generating fresh randomness for every round of AES, intermediate results from the previous computation can be used as new randomness. Sugawara [28] modifies the *"changing of the guards"* technique [6] for it to be applicable to Canright's AES S-box implementation [4]. Daemen *et al.* [7] adopt this technique for two-shared masking. This requires the copying of the randomness from share 0 to share 1 at the beginning of the S-box computation. However, this does not satisfy the vertical non-completeness property. Therefore, the randomness from share 1 is interpreted as fresh randomness for share 0 for the subsequent S-box. The randomness at index 2 will then be used as randomness for share 1. This guarantees vertical non-completeness throughout the entire encryption.

4.4   AES Key Schedule

The AES key schedule is one part of the algorithm that is often times forgotten while securing an implementation, as shown in [13]. Therefore, a first-order bitsliced implementation of the key schedule is presented. It follows the same

Table 2. Secure Computation of p_{TS}^2.

# Operation	Reg.	Index
0 push R14	R14	
1 $b_0^0 \oplus b_0^1$	R12	0
2 $c_0^0 \oplus c_0^1$	R14	0
3 $(b_0^0 \oplus b_0^1) \odot (c_0^0 \oplus c_0^1)$	R14	0
4 $a_0^0 \oplus (b_0^0 \oplus b_0^1) \odot (c_0^0 \oplus c_0^1)$	R0	0
5 $a_0^1 \oplus (b_0^0 \oplus b_0^1) \odot (c_0^0 \oplus c_0^1)$	R1	0
6 $c_1^0 \oplus c_1^1$	R14	1
7 shift $b_0^0 \oplus b_0^1$	R12	2
8 shift 14 & $(b_0^0 \oplus b_0^1) \odot (c_1^0 \oplus c_1^1)$	R12	2
9 shift R0 & $a_0^0 \oplus (b_0^0 \oplus b_0^1) \odot (c_0^0 \oplus c_0^1)$ $\oplus (b_0^0 \oplus b_0^1) \odot (c_1^0 \oplus c_1^1)$	R0	2
10 shift R1 & $a_0^0 \oplus (b_0^0 \oplus b_0^1) \odot (c_0^0 \oplus c_0^1)$ $\oplus (b_0^0 \oplus b_0^1) \odot (c_1^0 \oplus c_1^1)$	R1	2
11 shift b_0^0	R6	2
12 shift R8 & $b_0^0 \odot c_1^0$	R12	2
13 shift back b_0^0	R6	0
14 $a_0^0 \oplus (b_0^0 \oplus b_0^1) \odot (c_0^0 \oplus c_0^1)$ $\oplus (b_0^0 \oplus b_0^1) \odot (c_1^0 \oplus c_1^1) \oplus (b_0^0 \odot c_1^0)$	R0	2
15 $b_0^0 \odot c_0^0$	R12	0
16 shift back R0 & $a_0^0 \oplus (b_0^0 \oplus b_0^1) \odot (c_0^0 \oplus c_0^1) \oplus (b_0^0 \odot c_1^0)$ $\oplus (b_0^0 \oplus b_0^1) \odot (c_1^0 \oplus c_1^1) \oplus (b_0^0 \odot c_0^0)$	R0	0
17 shift b_0^1	R7	2
18 shift R9 & $b_0^1 \odot c_1^1$	R12	2
19 shift back b_0^1	R7	0
20 $a_0^1 \oplus (b_0^0 \oplus b_0^1) \odot (c_0^0 \oplus c_0^1)$ $\oplus (b_0^0 \oplus b_0^1) \odot (c_1^0 \oplus c_1^1) \oplus (b_0^1 \odot c_1^1)$	R1	2
21 $b_0^1 \odot c_0^1$	R12	0
22 shift back R1 & $a_0^1 \oplus (b_0^0 \oplus b_0^1) \odot (c_0^0 \oplus c_0^1) \oplus (b_0^1 \odot c_1^1)$ $\oplus (b_0^0 \oplus b_0^1) \odot (c_1^0 \oplus c_1^1) \oplus (b_0^1 \odot c_0^1)$	R1	0
23 $b_1^0 \oplus b_1^1$	R12	1
$\vdots$		
44 pop PC	R14	

Table 3. Secure Computation of p_{TS}^4.

Step	Operation	Reg.	Index
1	load c_1 and b_1	R2-R9	1
2	$c_1 \cdot b_1$	R0-R3	1
3	load a_1	R4, R5, R10, R11	1
4	$a_1 + c_1 \cdot b_1$	R0-R3	1
5	push $a_1 + c_1 \cdot b_1$	R0-R3	1
6	load c_0	R2-R5	0
7	shift c_0 and b_1	R2-R9	2
8	$c_0 \cdot b_1$	R0-R3	2
9	pop $a_1 + c_1 \cdot b_1$	R4-R7	1
10	shift $a_1 + c_1 \cdot b_1$ & $a_1 + c_1 \cdot b_1 + c_0 \cdot b_1$	R0-R3	2
11	shift back $a_1 + c_1 \cdot b_1 + c_0 \cdot b_1$	R0-R3	1
12	load c_0 and b_0	R2-R9	0
13	$c_0 \cdot b_0$	R0-R3	0
14	load a_0	R4, R5, R10, R11	0
15	$a_0 + c_0 \cdot b_0$	R0-R3	0
16	push $a_0 + c_0 \cdot b_0$	R0-R3	0
17	load c_1	R2-R5	1
18	shift c_1 and b_0	R2-R9	2
19	$c_1 \cdot b_0$	R0-R3	2
20	pop $a_0 + c_0 \cdot b_0$	R4-R7	0
21	shift $a_0 + c_0 \cdot b_0$ & $a_0 + c_0 \cdot b_0 + c_1 \cdot b_0$	R0-R3	2
22	shift back $a_0 + c_0 \cdot b_0 + c_1 \cdot b_0$	R0-R3	0

designs decisions as for the encryption: each share is computed at their respective index and the same S-box is used.

For the encryption it makes sense to use a bitsliced representation, as two blocks can be computed concurrently. However, for the key schedule only 4 bytes per block have to be transformed by the `RotWord`, `SubWord` and `Rcon` operations. Hence, the inherent concurrency potential of bitslicing remains largely underutilized.

5   Evaluation

This section discusses the measurement setup, a performance comparison against other first-order bitsliced implementations and the TVLA results.

5.1   Measurement Setup

The target platform is a CW308T-STM32F target board [21] which embeds a STM32F415RG [27] Cortex-M4 micro-controller using an internal 24 MHz operating frequency. The acquisition was performed using a NewAE CW308 UFO board [20] and a Tektronix DPO70404C oscilloscope with a sample rate of 625MS/s. The Cortex-M4 assembly implementation is compiled using the Arm GNU[1] toolchain with the compiler optimization flag -O0.

5.2   Performance Comparison

The implementation is benchmarked against three other first-order bitsliced implementations of AES-128: *All the AES You Need on Cortex-M3 and M4* [25], *First-Order Masking with Only Two Random Bits* [16] and the fully fixsliced implementation of *Fixslicing AES-like Ciphers* [1]. Beckers *et al.* [2] reported their cycle counts on a similar measurement setup, with only the used toolchain and compiler optimization flag to differ. Therefore, their reported cycle counts will be used. The required clock cycles for the encryption is shown in Table 4. For this work, that also includes the change of representations, generation of randomness and recombination of shares.

Table 4. Comparing Performance Results for AES-128 per Iteration. An asterisk indicates a real-world insecure implementation.

Implementation Encryption	Speed [cycles]	ROM [bytes]	RAM [bytes]
This Work	20,795	10,720	12
[25]*	17,500	39,900	1,600
[16]*	6,800	25,200	188
[1]*	6,200	22,100	188

The main reason behind the difference of clock cycles can be attributed to the S-box. References [16] and [1] use a compact S-box implementation that requires significantly less clock cycles. However, Beckers *et al.* [2] have shown that the three other implementations do not prove to be real-world secure when evaluated by TVLA.

Table 5 compares the different key schedule implementations. Similarly, the differences can be attributed to the S-box implementation and the inefficiency of the bitsliced representation for the key schedule, as discussed in Sect. 4.4.

---

[1] gcc-arm-11.2-2022.02-x86_64-arm-none-eabi.

Table 5. Comparing Performance Results for AES-128 Key Schedule. An asterisk indicates a real-world insecure implementation.

Implementation Key Schedule	Speed [cycles]
This work	23,677
[25]*	1,000
Unmasked [1]*	3,500
Masked [1]*	7,300

5.3   Results

To assess the security of the implementation, a TVLA is performed. To demonstrate the effectiveness of the evaluation method, the encryption and key schedule are tested without masking for 10,000 measurements. The results are shown in Fig. 2a and 2b, respectively. It is clear that there is leakage since the t-statistic exceeds the threshold. The encryption and key schedule evaluation for one million measurements is shown in Figs. 2c and d, respectively. For both the encryption and the key schedule two rounds are evaluated. Evaluating all rounds would be

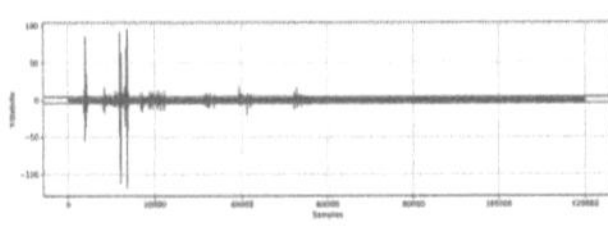

(a) Not Masked Encryption.

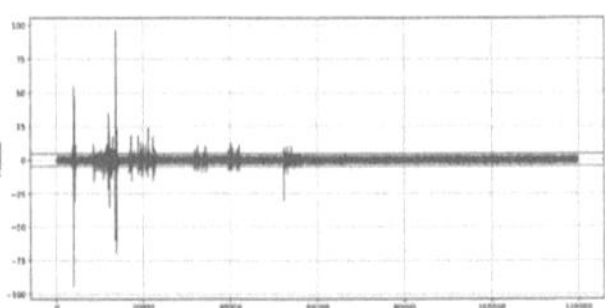

(b) Not Masked Key Schedule.

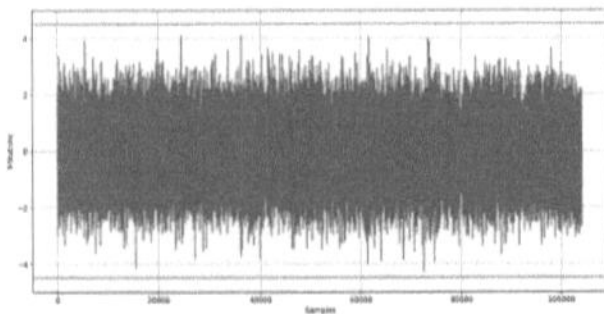

(c) TVLA Results Encryption.

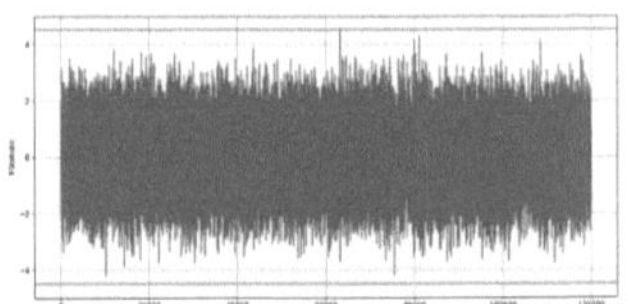

(d) TVLA Results Key Schedule.

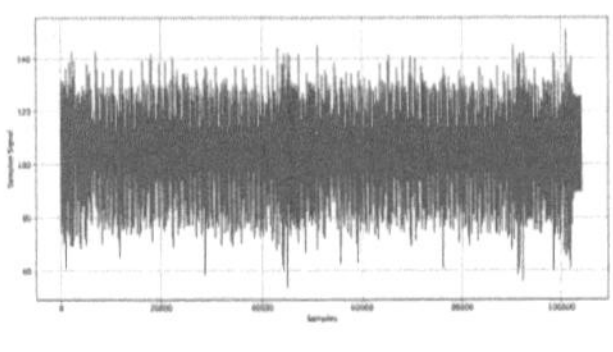

(e) Mean Encryption.

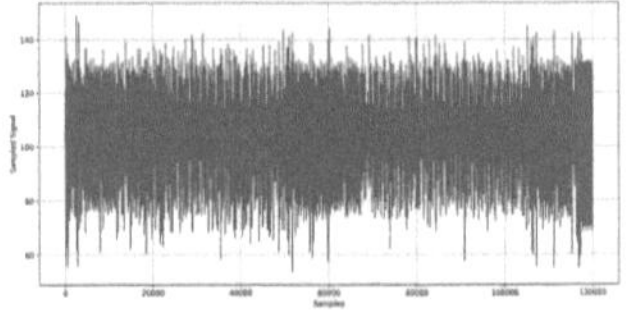

(f) Mean Key Schedule.

Fig. 2. First-order t-test results of two rounds of AES-128. The ±4.5 threshold is marked by red lines. (Color figure online)

prohibitively time-consuming, while limiting the analysis to a single round would not adequately capture the effectiveness of the changing of the guards technique. As the t-statistic does not exceed the ± 4.5 threshold, the implementation can be considered to be first-order secure. For reference, Figs. 2e and f show the average power consumption of the encryption and key schedule, respectively.

6 Conclusion

This work examined micro-architectural leakages in masked implementations, which compromises the theoretical security that masking provides. To counter these threats, a first-order secure AES-128 implementation was developed using software-oriented TI principles, ensuring properties like register-uniformity and non-completeness. A bitsliced design and secure Toffoli gates enabled both performance and security. TVLA confirmed no first-order leakage after one million traces for both the encryption and the key schedule.

Future directions include adapting the approach to other architectures, improving performance (e.g., via fixslicing), and extending to higher-order masking.

Overall, this work provides an example for building leakage-resilient cryptographic software, a critical need as embedded systems secure sensitive information.

Acknowledgements. This work was supported by CyberSecurity Research Flanders with reference number VR20192203.

References

1. Adomnicai, A., Peyrin, T.: Fixslicing AES-like ciphers: new bitsliced AES speed records on ARM-Cortex M and RISC-V. Cryptology ePrint Archive, Paper 2020/1123 (2020). https://eprint.iacr.org/2020/1123
2. Beckers, A., Wouters, L., Gierlichs, B., Preneel, B., Verbauwhede, I.: Provable secure software masking in the real-world. Cryptology ePrint Archive, Paper 2022/327 (2022). https://eprint.iacr.org/2022/327
3. Biham, E.: A fast new DES implementation in software. In: Biham, E. (ed.) FSE 1997. LNCS, vol. 1267, pp. 260–272. Springer, Heidelberg (1997). https://doi.org/10.1007/BFb0052352
4. Canright, D.: A very compact S-box for AES. In: Rao, J.R., Sunar, B. (eds.) CHES 2005. LNCS, vol. 3659, pp. 441–455. Springer, Heidelberg (2005). https://doi.org/10.1007/11545262_32
5. Chari, S., Jutla, C.S., Rao, J.R., Rohatgi, P.: Towards sound approaches to counteract power-analysis attacks. In: Wiener, M. (ed.) CRYPTO 1999. LNCS, vol. 1666, pp. 398–412. Springer, Heidelberg (1999). https://doi.org/10.1007/3-540-48405-1_26
6. Daemen, J.: Changing of the guards: a simple and efficient method for achieving uniformity in threshold sharing. In: Fischer, W., Homma, N. (eds.) CHES 2017. LNCS, vol. 10529, pp. 137–153. Springer, Cham (2017). https://doi.org/10.1007/978-3-319-66787-4_7

7. Daemen, J., Dobraunig, C., Eichlseder, M., Groß, H., Mendel, F., Primas, R.: Protecting against statistical ineffective fault attacks. IACR Trans. Cryptogr. Hardware Embed. Syst., 508–543 (2020)
8. Faust, S., Grosso, V., Pozo, S.M.D., Paglialonga, C., Standaert, F.X.: Composable masking schemes in the presence of physical defaults and the robust probing model. Cryptology ePrint Archive, Paper 2017/711 (2017). https://eprint.iacr.org/2017/711
9. Gao, S., Marshall, B., Page, D., Oswald, E.: Share-slicing: friend or foe? IACR Trans. Cryptogr. Hardware Embed. Syst. **2020**(1), 152–174 (2019). https://doi.org/10.13154/tches.v2020.i1.152-174, https://tches.iacr.org/index.php/TCHES/article/view/8396
10. Gao, S., Oswald, E., Page, D.: Reverse engineering the microarchitectural leakage features of a commercial processor (2021). https://eprint.iacr.org/2021/794
11. Gaspoz, J., Dhooghe, S.: Threshold implementations in software: microarchitectural leakages in algorithms. Cryptology ePrint Archive, Paper 2022/1546 (2022). https://eprint.iacr.org/2022/1546
12. Gigerl, B., Hadzic, V., Primas, R., Mangard, S., Bloem, R.: Coco: co-design and co-verification of masked software implementations on CPUs. In: USENIX Security Symposium, January 2021 (2021). https://www.usenix.net/system/files/sec21fall-gigerl.pdf
13. Gohr, A., Jacob, S., Schindler, W.: CHES 2018 side channel contest CTF - solution of the AES challenges. Cryptology ePrint Archive, Paper 2019/094 (2019). https://eprint.iacr.org/2019/094
14. Goodwill, G., Jun, B., Jaffe, J., Rohatgi, P.: A testing methodology for side channel resistance validation (2011). https://csrc.nist.gov/csrc/media/events/non-invasive-attack-testing-workshop/documents/08_goodwill.pdf. Retrieved 18 Apr 2025
15. Goubin, L., Patarin, J.: DES and differential power analysis the "duplication" method. In: Koç, Ç.K., Paar, C. (eds.) CHES 1999. LNCS, vol. 1717, pp. 158–172. Springer, Heidelberg (1999). https://doi.org/10.1007/3-540-48059-5_15
16. Gross, H., Stoffelen, K., Meyer, L.D., Krenn, M., Mangard, S.: Masking the AES with only two random bits. Cryptology ePrint Archive, Paper 2018/1007 (2018). https://eprint.iacr.org/2018/1007
17. Kocher, P.C.: Timing attacks on implementations of Diffie-Hellman, RSA, DSS, and other systems. In: Koblitz, N. (ed.) CRYPTO 1996. LNCS, vol. 1109, pp. 104–113. Springer, Heidelberg (1996). https://doi.org/10.1007/3-540-68697-5_9
18. Marshall, B., Page, D., Webb, J.: Miracle: Micro-architectural leakage evaluation. IACR Trans. Cryptogr. Hardware Embed. Syst., 175–220 (2021).https://doi.org/10.46586/tches.v2022.i1.175-220
19. May, L., Penna, L., Clark, A.: An implementation of bitsliced DES on the Pentium MMX^{TM} processor. In: Dawson, E.P., Clark, A., Boyd, C. (eds.) ACISP 2000. LNCS, vol. 1841, pp. 112–122. Springer, Heidelberg (2000). https://doi.org/10.1007/10718964_10
20. NewAE: CW308 UFO. https://rtfm.newae.com/Targets/CW308%20UFO/. Accessed 24 May 2025
21. NewAE: CW308T-STM32F. https://rtfm.newae.com/Targets/UFO%20Targets/CW308T-STM32F/. Accessed 24 May 2025
22. Nikova, S., Rechberger, C., Rijmen, V.: Threshold implementations against side-channel attacks and glitches. In: Ning, P., Qing, S., Li, N. (eds.) ICICS 2006. LNCS, vol. 4307, pp. 529–545. Springer, Heidelberg (2006). https://doi.org/10.1007/11935308_38

23. Papagiannopoulos, K., Veshchikov, N.: Mind the gap: towards secure 1st-order masking in software. Cryptology ePrint Archive, Paper 2017/345 (2017). https://eprint.iacr.org/2017/345
24. Renauld, M., Standaert, F.-X., Veyrat-Charvillon, N., Kamel, D., Flandre, D.: A formal study of power variability issues and side-channel attacks for nanoscale devices. In: Paterson, K.G. (ed.) EUROCRYPT 2011. LNCS, vol. 6632, pp. 109–128. Springer, Heidelberg (2011). https://doi.org/10.1007/978-3-642-20465-4_8
25. Schwabe, P., Stoffelen, K.: All the AES you need on Cortex-M3 and M4. In: Avanzi, R., Heys, H. (eds.) SAC 2016. LNCS, vol. 10532, pp. 180–194. Springer, Cham (2017). https://doi.org/10.1007/978-3-319-69453-5_10
26. Shelton, M.A., Samwel, N., Batina, L., Regazzoni, F., Wagner, M., Yarom, Y.: ROSITA: towards automatic elimination of power-analysis leakage in ciphers. Cryptology ePrint Archive, Paper 2019/1445 (2019). https://doi.org/10.14722/ndss.2021.23137, https://eprint.iacr.org/2019/1445
27. STMicroelectronics: STM32F415RG. https://www.st.com/en/microcontrollers-microprocessors/stm32f415rg.html. Accessed 19 May 2025
28. Sugawara, T.: 3-share threshold implementation of AES S-box without fresh randomness. IACR Trans. Cryptogr. Hardware Embed. Syst., 123–145 (2019)

On Advancing Pre-silicon Hardware Trojan Detection Against Lightweight Block Ciphers

Charilaos Memeletzoglou, Evangelia Konstantopoulou$^{(\boxtimes)}$ (iD), and Nicolas Sklavos (iD)

SCYTALE Group, Computer Engineering and Informatics Department, University of Patras,
Patras, Greece
`{c.memeletzoglou,e.konstanto}@ac.upatras.gr, nsklavos@upatras.gr`

Abstract. The growing integration of embedded cryptographic systems in smart city infrastructure, from connected traffic sensors to smart grids, has heightened the threat of stealthy Hardware Trojans. Lightweight block ciphers, favored for efficiency in such resource-constrained devices, remain susceptible to malicious modification during early design stages. This paper explores Register Transfer Level (RTL)-level Hardware Trojan design and detection through the insertion of nine lightweight Trojans into a Field Programmable Gate Array (FPGA) implementation of the PRESENT lightweight block cipher. The Trojans employ diverse triggering mechanisms based on internal and external system conditions, with payloads ranging from data corruption and information leakage to Denial of Service (DoS) attacks. A Functional Analysis (FA)-based detection method is applied using pseudorandom inputs at the logic simulation level, treating the system as a black-box. Results show that even RTL Trojans with very low triggering probabilities can be detected, albeit with increased simulation time. Hardware overhead remains minimal, with Look-Up Table (LUT) usage rising by just 0.24% to 1.31%.

Keywords: Hardware Trojans · Hardware Security · Hardware Trojan Detection · PRESENT · Lightweight Cryptography · Functional Analysis

1 Introduction

Smart cities rely heavily on interconnected embedded systems to provide essential services such as traffic control, environmental monitoring, smart metering, and public safety [1]. These systems often incorporate hardware-accelerated cryptographic cores to ensure data confidentiality and device authentication. However, their constrained nature makes them ideal candidates for deploying lightweight ciphers selected for their small area, low power, and high throughput characteristics. At the same time, this efficiency comes at a cost: such designs have limited redundancy and verification margin, leaving them particularly vulnerable.

At the same time, influenced by software development practices, the global semiconductor industry increasingly reuses Intellectual Property (IP) cores, whether developed in-house or obtained from external sources [2]. While Third-Party IP (3PIP) cores enable rapid and cost-effective Integrated Circuit (IC) development, they also introduce the risk

E. Savas et al. (Eds.): LightSec 2025, LNCS 16216, pp. 212–230, 2026.
https://doi.org/10.1007/978-3-032-15541-2_12

of malicious modifications embedded within or added beyond the specified functionality. Additionally, stealthy Hardware Trojans may be inserted during IC manufacturing, where untrusted foundries can subtly alter transistor-level parameters (e.g., doping material) to exploit process variation effects [3].

A Hardware Trojan typically consists of: a) a trigger, activated under rare internal or external conditions, and b) a payload, which performs a malicious action once activated [4]. Trigger logic is often placed in low-controllability nodes, while payloads target low-observability ones. Upon activation, a Trojan can disrupt system functionality, launch Denial of Service (DoS) attacks, drain power, leak sensitive data (e.g., cryptographic keys) through side channels, or weaken the randomness of embedded number generators [4].

The contributions of this work are:

1. Presentation of nine low-overhead Register-Transfer Level (RTL) Hardware Trojans targeting Lightweight Block Ciphers such as PRESENT [5], commonly used in resource-constrained embedded systems.
2. The Trojans exploit internal or external system conditions for triggering and cause effects including data corruption, information leakage, altered system behavior, and Denial of Service (DoS) attacks. Such RTL-level modifications could be introduced by a rogue employee or third-party design house embedding a malicious cryptographic core as a Third-Party IP (3PIP) within a System-on-Chip.
3. A rapid pre-silicon detection method based on Functional Analysis (FA) is proposed, using self-checking testbenches that apply pseudorandom input stimuli to the Design Under Test (DUT) to expose functional anomalies.

To the best of our knowledge, this is the first work demonstrating a broad class of Trojans against lightweight block ciphers, like PRESENT, and relying on self-checking testbenches for Trojan detection in such ciphers.

2 Security and Privacy in Smart Cities

The deployment of smart cities has led to an environment of pervasive sensing, communication, and decision-making. Supporting connected traffic systems and smart meters to autonomous infrastructure, such technologies rely heavily on embedded devices that are often constrained in terms of power, area, and cost. The complex and heterogenous environment of smart cities results in a security landscape with various vulnerabilities. Smart city systems face a wide spectrum of cybersecurity threats [6], including:

- Denial of Service (DoS): These attacks aim to compromise a system's availability by overwhelming it with excessive requests, rendering core services inoperable.
- Malware: Exploiting system vulnerabilities, malware can grant unauthorized access to attackers, allowing them to steal, alter, or destroy sensitive information.
- Eavesdropping: Interception of unencrypted or weakly secured data transmissions threatens network confidentiality by enabling unauthorized data retrieval.
- Tampering: Malicious modifications to messages or control signals can delay operations or create system bottlenecks, undermining data integrity.

- Traffic Analysis: By monitoring communication patterns, attackers may infer operational details or identify high-value targets without directly intercepting content.
- Spoofing: Adversaries impersonate trusted entities to extract sensitive information or manipulate system behavior.

Given these diverse and evolving threats, there is an undeniable need for robust security mechanisms tailored for smart city contexts. Security mechanisms and policies based on confidentiality, integrity, and access control are employed to mitigate such concerns. These systems are based on popular encryption methods including block ciphers such as PRESENT [5]. First of all, because smart devices usually have limited resources, solutions need to be adaptable and low-area. At the same time, it is critical to maintain a high enough throughput to satisfy the demands of the application while also meeting certain performance requirements. For efficient realization, hardware solutions are often adopted [7].

However, even cryptographic cores can be compromised by low-level attacks such as the insertion of RTL-level Hardware Trojans when being supplied by a third-party vendor. The increasingly global and opaque hardware supply chain opens the door to malicious modifications at early stages of the design cycle. The very mechanisms intended to provide data protection and system integrity thus become focal points for adversarial exploitation. This paper explores the feasibility of such Trojans within PRESENT and investigates functional pre-silicon detection techniques that can protect smart city systems before deployment.

3 Hardware Trojan Detection

The increasing magnitude of the threat posed by Hardware Trojans has paved the way for extensive research in both the academic and the industrial domain, where defenders often assume the role of the attacker. In order to better understand the nature of the security issues posed by Hardware Trojans, detailed Trojan taxonomies have been proposed in literature [8], categorizing Trojans based on their characteristics. At the same time open-source repositories, like Trust-Hub [9], allow researchers to use Trojan-infected benchmark circuits, not only to evaluate the effectiveness of known detection techniques but to develop new ones as well. In this work, we focus on RTL-level Hardware Trojans, which are malicious modifications introduced at the RTL of the design. Such Trojans are favored by attackers due to the flexibility of behavioral modeling and ease of integration before synthesis.

Current Hardware Trojan detection methods can be coarsely split into two categories [10], depending on the stage of the IC design flow in which they are used:

a) <u>Pre-silicon detection techniques:</u> Structural Analysis uses metrics to flag suspicious netlist nodes, while Code Coverage Analysis identifies RTL lines not exercised during Functional Verification. Functional Analysis applies pseudorandom inputs to compare system responses against a golden reference. Recently, Formal Verification with Proof-carrying Codes has been proposed to check 3PIP cores against security properties defined by the purchaser [11].

b) <u>Post-silicon detection techniques:</u> These can be classified into destructive and non-destructive methods, based on the DUT's state after inspection. Destructive techniques involve comparing the golden IC layout to the manufactured one via complex reverse engineering. Non-destructive methods include Side Channel Analysis, which compares physical parameters to detect leakage-based Trojans. However, this requires a golden IC and is vulnerable to process variation. Another method, Functional Testing, treats Trojans as manufacturing defects detectable via ATPG, but often misses non-functional or externally triggered Trojans.

4 Related Work

The increasing complexity of modern ICs enables adversaries to embed Trojans capable of executing diverse malicious payloads. This, combined with the high cost of Trojan removal at later design stages, drives ongoing research in pre-silicon Hardware Trojan detection. Notable techniques include Unused Circuit Identification (UCI), a code coverage method that flags nodes with no effect on primary outputs [13], and FA for Nearly-unused Circuit Identification (FANCI), which uses controllability metrics under random stimuli to identify nearly-unused logic potentially related to triggers [14].

The PRESENT lightweight block cipher has served as a frequent test case for Trojan insertion, emphasizing the need for detection in resource-constrained systems [5]. In [15], PCA-based side-channel fingerprinting detected externally triggered Trojans that leaked the last round key after specific inputs. Other works introduced delay-based Trojans against ASICs by subtly altering transistor characteristics [16], and similar routing-based variants on FPGAs [17]. Malicious PRESENT implementations have also been used for fault injection attacks [18], key leakage via side channels using added LUTs [19], and detection using Multiple Input Signature Register -based Built-In Self-Test logic [20]. Device aging has further been explored as a Trojan detection factor [21].

In contrast to structural or formal approaches, we propose a functional testing strategy using randomized testbenches to detect behavioral deviations caused by rarely triggered RTL-level Trojans, a lightweight solution suitable for early-stage validation.

5 Our Approach

5.1 Functional Detection Strategy for RTL-Level Trojans

The detection strategy of this paper uses Functional Analysis with self-checking testbenches that apply pseudorandom input blocks and cryptographic keys to compare the outputs of the Trojan-infected and golden systems. Chosen for its simplicity and effectiveness, this approach contrasts with structural methods like FANCI or UCI by focusing on behavioral deviations. To aid observability during simulation, internal signals were added, though such visibility is unavailable in real-world black-box IP verification due to time-to-market constraints and the globalization of the semiconductor industry. Additionally, since minor modifications in FPGA designs can alter placement and routing, we also compare resource usage between the golden and Trojan-infected implementations targeting the same device. While this assumes access to the original design, which is uncommon in commercial IP, it provides an extra detection vector in academic or controlled settings.

While we introduce new RTL-level Trojans for evaluation purposes, our main contribution lies in demonstrating the effectiveness of a lightweight functional detection strategy that exposes their behavior under constrained simulation setups.

5.2 Proposed System Architecture

Cryptographic cores are prime Trojan targets due to their handling of sensitive, long-lived data like cryptographic keys. We selected the PRESENT lightweight block cipher [5], implemented in VHSIC Hardware Description Language, as the target system due to its hardware efficiency and relevance in resource-constrained applications. PRESENT operates on 64-bit blocks, supports 80- and 128-bit keys, and performs 32 rounds of substitution-permutation with a distinct 64-bit round key per round. To reduce power, round keys are precomputed and stored in Look-Up Table Random Access Memory (LUTRAM), avoiding on-the-fly recomputation after a 32-cycle initialization phase. In many resource-constrained embedded systems, like Radio-Frequency Identification (RFID) tags, the key is either used for multiple cryptographic operations or never changes. This assumption underpins some of the Trojans designed in this work, such as Trojan #5, which triggers based on a fixed key value. While such Trojans may appear either always-on or never-on depending on the specific key used, a carefully chosen triggering condition can still be applicable across multiple devices sharing commonly used or default keys.

As shown in Fig. 1, the architecture includes a Control Unit, Key Schedule unit, memory for round keys, and separate encryption and decryption datapaths. A 2-bit mode_sel signal selects key size and operation mode, while output is provided via a 64-bit data bus and a 1-bit done flag.

PRESENT's regular structure, compact datapath, and minimal control logic facilitate Trojan insertion through predictable trigger points, though its constrained resources also raise the risk of detection from even slight overhead.

5.3 Hardware Trojans Against Lightweight Block Ciphers

The flexibility of RTL code makes it an ideal insertion point for Hardware Trojans in lightweight cipher implementations. We present nine practical Trojans targeting the PRESENT cipher, summarized in Table 1, each with distinct triggers and payloads. Rather than exhaustively covering all attack vectors, these Trojans were selected to span a range of trigger types and payloads. The focus was on designing rarely triggered, low-overhead Trojans, making detection harder while minimizing hardware impact.

Each Trojan's trigger, payload, hardware overhead (excluding LUTRAM for round keys), and activation/detection complexity is detailed. The baseline PRESENT coprocessor uses 588 LUTs and 423 Flip-Flops, with all overheads reported relative to this. Also, the Trojan circuitry is illustrated (highlighted in red color) inside the system's block diagram, where unaffected parts of the original design are omitted to allow for a closer examination of the Trojan at hand.

4. Trojan #1:

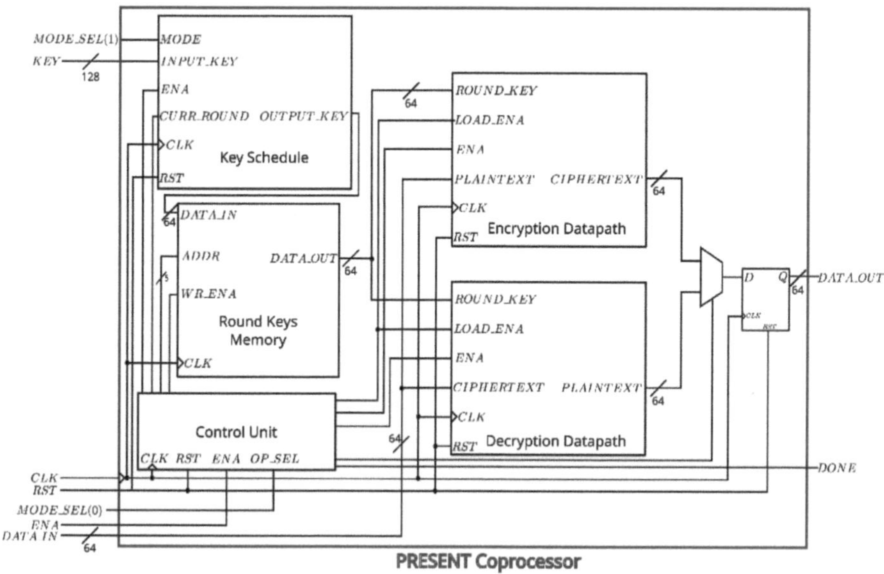

Fig. 1. PRESENT coprocessor architecture.

Table 1. Implemented Hardware Trojans

Trojan	Trigger	Payload
#1	Predefined input block	Flip round key K_i LSB
#2	data_in(47:44) = K_{13}(17:14)	Disable encryption unit
#3	data_in(3:0) = 1011	Drive output data bus with erroneous data
#4	key(7:0) = data_in(7:0)	Disable done flag
#5	key(7:0) = 0x1A & mode_sel(1) = 0	Replace key with a predefined key
#6	Completion of 2^{10} operations	Disallow computed data forwarding to output bus
#7	2^{10} mode changes	Flip data_in LSB
#8	2^{12} times: data_in(59:56) = ciph(43:40) & mode_sel(0) = 0	Overwrite output bus with data_in
#9	2^{15} times: ciph(63) = 0	DoS: raise rst signal

a) <u>Trigger and payload:</u> The first Trojan monitors the input data block and activates upon detecting an attacker-defined value, flipping the Least Significant Bit (LSB) of each of the 32 round keys. This injects faults into the encryption/decryption process, producing incorrect ciphertext or plaintext. As shown in Fig. 2, the trigger consists of a comparator using a simple XOR-based design, which is efficient due to the fixed input, and a Flip-Flop (FF) to store the Trojan's state, keeping it active even if the input changes mid-operation. The payload is executed by a single XOR gate, controlled by the stored Trojan state, which selectively inverts the current round key's LSB.

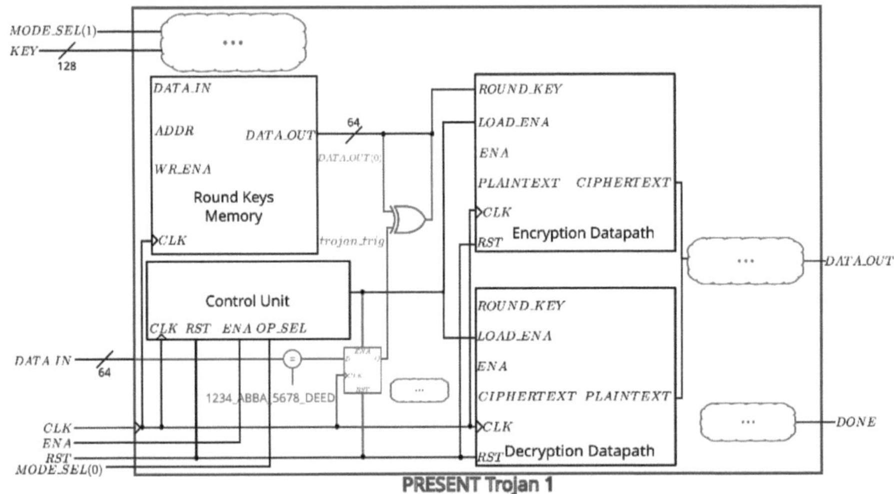

Fig. 2. Hardware Trojan #1.

b) <u>Hardware overhead:</u> The resources necessary to support the Trojan's infrastructure are 603 LUTs and 424 FFs, which result in a 0.4% increase in the number of LUTs and a 0.01% increase in the number of FFs required for the golden design, respectively.

c) <u>Ease of activation and detection:</u> Triggered by a specific 64-bit input block, this Trojan can be easily activated by an attacker with input access, while a remote attacker must rely on the legitimate user to unknowingly enter the trigger. Although its effect resembles known fault models (e.g., stuck-at faults), the extremely low activation probability allows it to evade both pre- and post-silicon detection unless all 2^{64} input blocks are tested. Detection in both cases also depends on access to a golden response set. Finally, if the defending party does not have access to the exact number of LUTs and FFs used by the original design, the small hardware overhead caused by the Trojan, can be overlooked as a different result of the place and route process.

5. Trojan #2:

   a) <u>Trigger and payload:</u> The second Trojan triggers when bits [47:44] of the input block match bits [17:14] of the 13th round key, a rarely satisfied condition involving both internal and external values, selected randomly to minimize detection likelihood. Upon activation, it disables the encryption unit at the start of round 14, causing a partially encrypted block to be output. The decryption unit is left untouched, as PRESENT is often deployed in encryption-only configurations for area efficiency and counter-mode decryption [5, 12], making this payload especially disruptive.

As shown in Fig. 3, the trigger consists of two comparators—one for the input/key match and one for detecting round 13, along with a 1-bit FF to store the Trojan's state. This ensures persistent activation and restricts the payload to the correct round. The payload effect is carried out through an AND gate whose one input is the complement of the Trojan's current state. While the Trojan is inactive, the FF's output is 0, thus forwarding the proper enable signal to the encryption unit. When the Trojan is successfully triggered, the encryption unit's enable signal is inverted as the FF's output transitions to a logic 1.

b) <u>Hardware overhead:</u> The resources necessary to support the Trojan's infrastructure are 603 LUTs and 424 FFs, which result in a 0.4% increase in the number of LUTs and a 0.01% increase in the number of FFs, respectively.

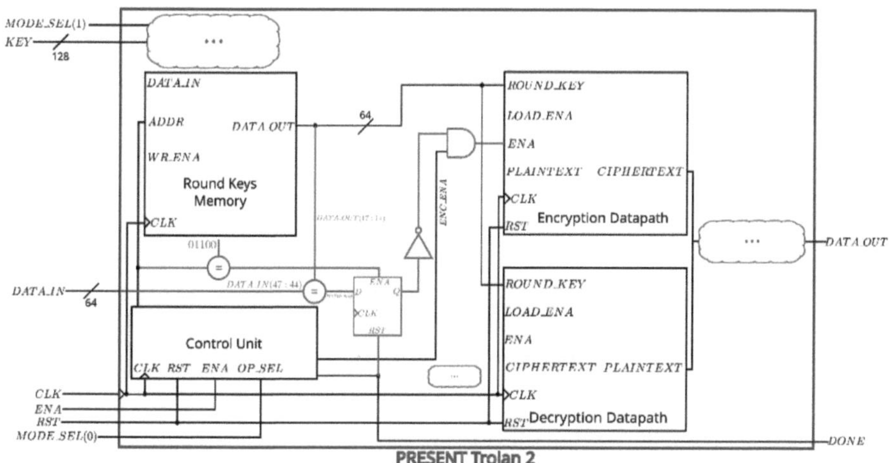

Fig. 3. Hardware Trojan #2.

Ease of activation and detection: Even with physical access, triggering this Trojan is challenging, as it depends on both the input block and the 13th round key. It assumes a non-fixed key, which is realistic in systems with dynamic key provisioning, such as test/debug modes or session-based encryption. In such cases, an attacker familiar with the PRESENT key schedule can craft input-key pairs to meet the condition. Since the trigger compares only 4 bits from the input and key, its activation probability is low (2^{-4}). When triggered, the cipher halts at round 13, leaking the internal state as valid ciphertext, detectable only with a golden response set. Due to its minimal overhead, resource-based detection would likely fail.

6. Trojan #3:

a) <u>Trigger and payload:</u> The third Trojan discussed, drives the system's output data bus with faulty data, when the 4 LSBs of the input data block are equal to 1011. As shown in Fig. 4, a similar structure is used for the Trojan's triggering mechanism comprised of a comparator and a FF. A XOR gate is used to execute the malicious payload of inverting the select signal of the multiplexer driving the

FF that stores the output data. While the Trojan is dormant, either the output data of the encryption or decryption unit are forwarded to the system's output, based on the cryptographic operation selected. After activation, the Trojan causes the output data of the deactivated cryptographic unit to be used as an input to the output data register.

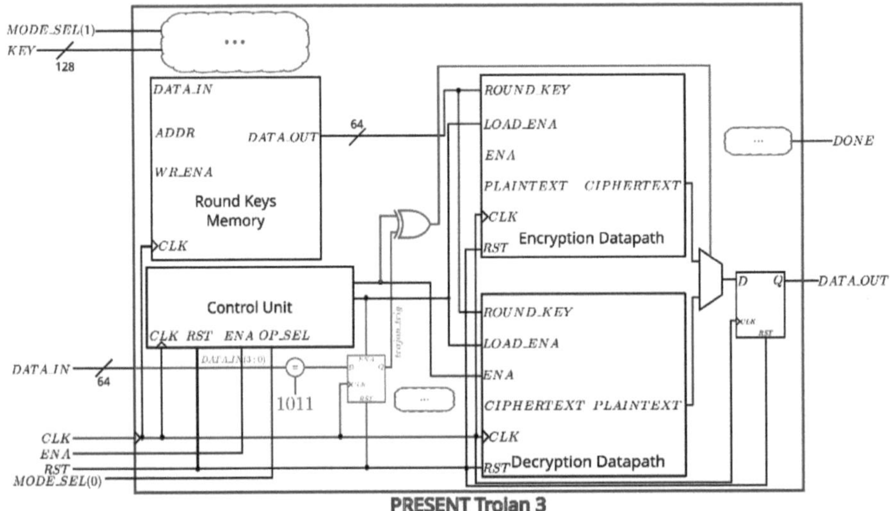

Fig. 4. Hardware Trojan #3.

b) <u>Hardware overhead</u>: In total, 627 LUTs and 424 FFs are required to implement the Trojan-infected system, resulting in a 1.04% and 0.01% increase in the respective resources necessary for the original design.

c) <u>Ease of activation and detection</u>: As was the case for Trojan #1, a remote attacker has to rely on the system's legitimate user to use an input block that satisfies the malicious circuit's triggering condition. The Trojan at hand is easier to detect compared to the aforementioned ones, as its triggering probability is equal to 2^{-4} due to the fact that the 4 LSBs of the input data block need to be equal to the attacker-predefined value. Even so, a defending party without access to input data-expected output data pairs, cannot detect such a Trojan. However, the increase in number of LUTs could result in higher power consumption, thus raising suspicion and leading to the detection of the Trojan.

7. Trojan #4:

a) <u>Trigger and payload</u>: This Trojan activates when the 8 LSBs of the input block match those of the cryptographic key, disabling the system's done signal upon triggering. As shown in Fig. 5, its trigger resembles previous designs, and the payload is implemented via an AND gate that outputs the inverted done signal once the Trojan is active. While inactive, the original done signal from the Control Unit is preserved. In systems where a main processor relies on a coprocessor for encryption/decryption, this payload can lead to data loss during off-chip transmission or internal post-processing.

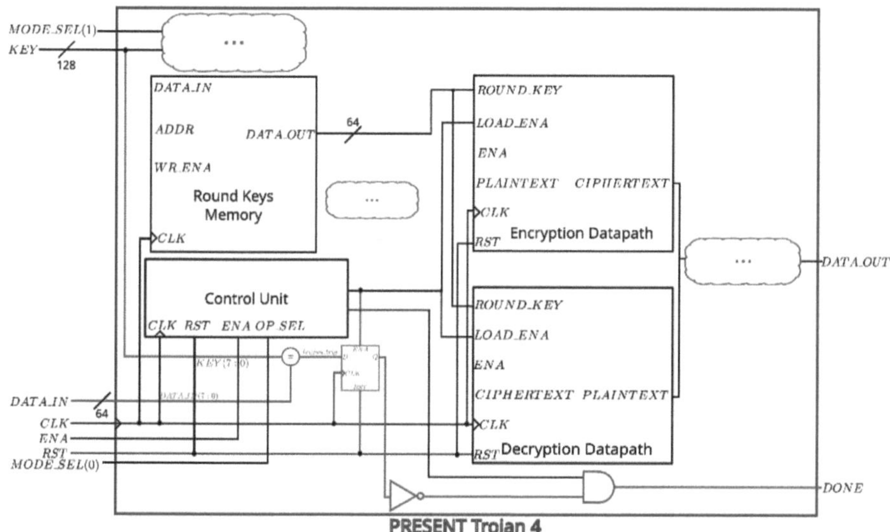

Fig. 5. Hardware Trojan #4.

b) <u>Hardware overhead:</u> In total, 627 LUTs and 424 FFs are required to implement the Trojan-infected system, which corresponds to a 1.04% and 0.01% increase in the resources necessary for the original design, respectively.

c) <u>Ease of activation and detection:</u> With a trigger similar to the previous Trojan, this one can also be easily activated by an attacker with input access. Its low activation probability (2^{-8}) helps it evade detection unless all input-key pairs are exhaustively tested. Unlike earlier Trojans, it does not alter the computed data but disables an auxiliary output signal (done), making it invisible to detection methods relying on output correctness. Instead, a resource-based detection approach may be more effective for uncovering such logic.

8. Trojan #5:

a) <u>Trigger and payload:</u> The last Functional Trojan presented, is triggered upon observing a specific value on the cryptographic key's least significant Byte when the 80-bit mode of the PRESENT cipher is selected. As a result, the legitimate cryptographic key is replaced with an attacker-predefined one. As shown in Fig. 6, the Trojan's triggering mechanism differs from the previous Trojans discussed as no FF is necessary to store the malicious circuit's state. A comparator is used to detect the predefined Byte at the original cryptographic key's least significant part. The malicious payload is executed by an AND gate controlling an extraneous multiplexer's select signal, thus allowing the replacement of the input key with the attacker predefined one.

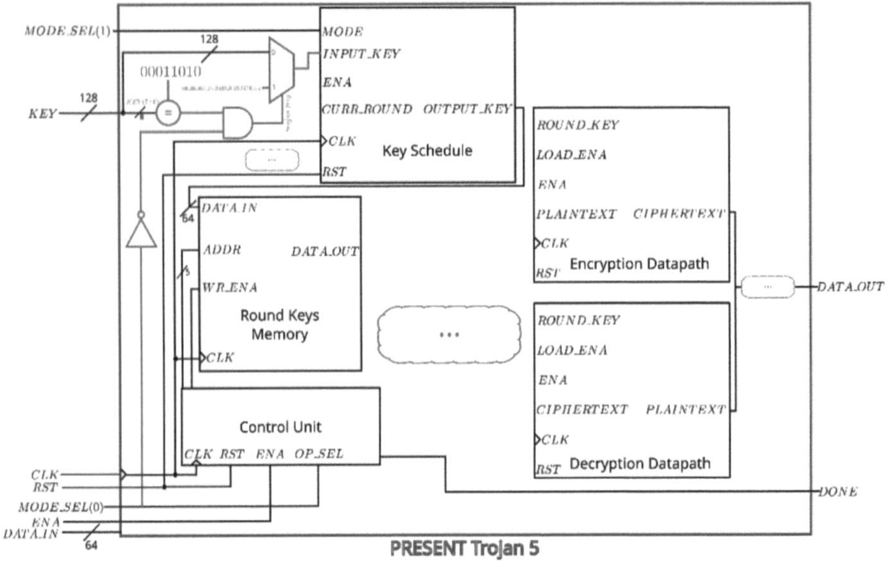

Fig. 6. Hardware Trojan #5.

b) <u>Hardware overhead:</u> Overall, 603 LUTs and 423 FFs are required for the tampered version of the system, resulting in a 0.4% increase in the LUT usage and no increase in the number of FFs used, compared to the golden design.

c) <u>Ease of activation and detection:</u> This Trojan is easily activated by an attacker with input access by selecting the 80-bit mode via mode_sel and providing a key with the desired least significant byte. A remote attacker, however, must rely on the user to input such a key and select the correct mode. Once triggered, the Trojan replaces the key, causing the system to output ciphertexts or plaintexts based on the attacker-defined key. In encryption scenarios, this leads to garbage upon decryption by the user, allowing the attacker to decrypt captured ciphertexts using the known key. This is true provided they know the least significant Byte or can infer message contents to validate decryption results.

The trigger condition has a low probability (2^{-8}) in 80-bit mode, aiding stealth. If a golden response set is available and the right key is tested, the Trojan can be detected through output mismatch. However, due to its low hardware overhead, resource-based detection is unlikely to catch it.

9. Trojan #6:

a) <u>Trigger and payload:</u> The next Trojan presented is the first of the 4 in total Timebomb Trojans (TTs) designed. TTs were designed as well, due to their inability to predict their activation. A TT triggers after a predefined number of rare events, with its counter width determining the delay, at the cost of added FFs. This Trojan is triggered asynchronously after 2^{10} cryptographic operations, disabling the output data register and preventing computed data from reaching the output bus. As shown in Fig. 7, the trigger uses a 10-bit counter incremented on each done signal. When the counter reaches its threshold, a comparator output drives a NOT gate, which controls the AND gate responsible for disabling the output register's enable signal.

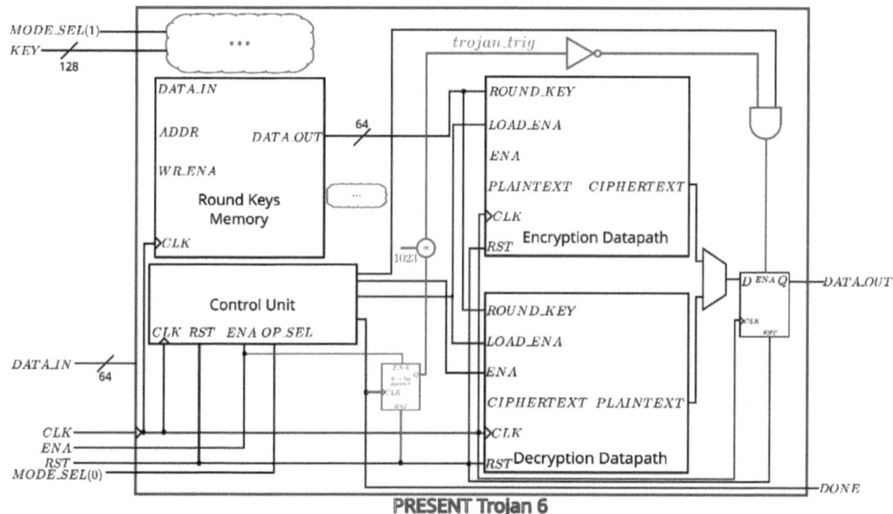

Fig. 7. Hardware Trojan #6.

b) <u>Hardware overhead:</u> To implement the Trojan infected design, 597 LUTs and 433 FFs are required, resulting in a 0.24% and 0.13% increase of the respective resources necessary for the original design. As expected, the increase in number of FFs is equal to the bit width of the counter used for the triggering circuitry.

c) <u>Ease of activation and detection:</u> By design, as an asynchronous Timebomb triggered by internal events, this Trojan cannot be activated on demand. Instead, it passively monitors rare events, giving the attacker an advantage by spreading activation over a long interval, reducing detection likelihood. However, its impact is easily observed: after 1024 operations, the output data bus stops updating. Thus, a defender testing the system over several thousand encryptions/decryptions can detect the Trojan, either via a golden response set or by simply monitoring output activity.

10. Trojan #7:

a) <u>Trigger and payload:</u> This asynchronous Timebomb Trojan activates after 2^{10} changes between encryption and decryption modes. Once triggered, it corrupts computations by inverting the LSB of the input block. As shown in Fig. 8, a Flip-Flop (FF) stores the previous value of mode_sel(0) and compares it with the current one via an XOR gate, which enables a counter upon mode change. When the counter reaches its threshold, a second XOR gate inverts the input block's LSB, injecting faults into the system's operation.

a) <u>Hardware overhead:</u> Overall, 637 LUTs and 434 FFs are required, which correspond to a 1.31% and 0.15% increase in the resources necessary to implement the original design, respectively. The increase in the number of FFs required is

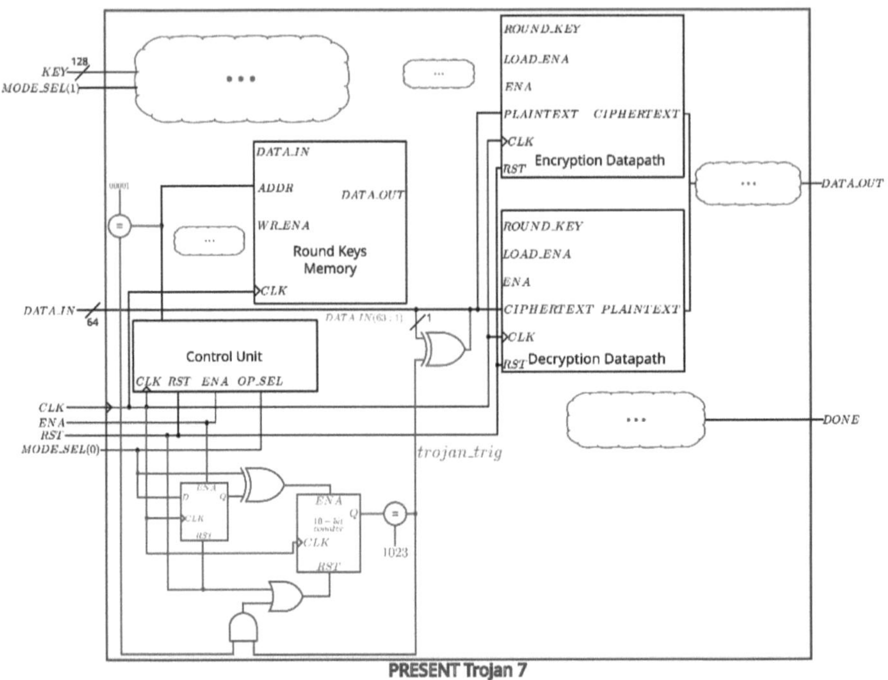

Fig. 8. Hardware Trojan #7.

equal to the bit width of the Timebomb's triggering mechanism's counter plus the one FF used to detect a change in the mode select bit, while the increase in the number of LUTs required is the highest compared to the previous Trojans.

b) <u>Ease of activation and detection:</u> An attacker with input access can activate the Trojan by repeatedly switching between encryption and decryption to meet its trigger condition. A remote attacker, however, must wait for the system to perform the required mode changes. In encryption-only cipher variants, the Trojan is ineffective, as its payload remains dormant. Detection is possible by comparing system output to a golden response set, since activation results in erroneous ciphertext/plaintext every 1024 cryptographic operations. The attacker may extend the counter width to increase activation intervals and hinder detection. Still, the Trojan's higher LUT usage may reveal its presence if resource data from the original design is available.

11. Trojan #8:

a) <u>Trigger and payload:</u> This TT is triggered when a complex condition, which is matching 4 specific bits of the input data block with 4 specific bits of the computed ciphertext, is satisfied 2^{12} times. Upon activation, it replaces the output with the input data block, leaking sensitive information during encryption. The trigger circuitry includes a comparator to detect the bit-match condition and a 12-bit counter to track occurrences (see Fig. 9). The payload is executed via an additional multiplexer, controlled by a comparator that checks if the counter has reached its maximum value.

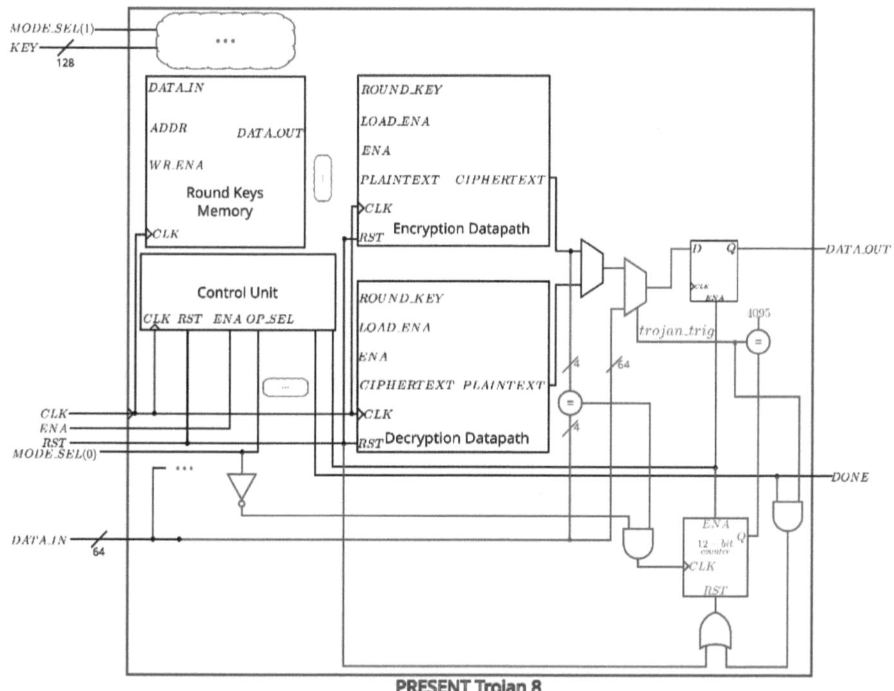

Fig. 9. Hardware Trojan #8.

b) <u>Hardware overhead</u>: In total, 637 LUTs and 435 FFs are required, which correspond to a 1.31% and 0.16% increase in the resources necessary to implement the original design, respectively. The increase in the number of FFs required is equal to the bit width of the TT's triggering mechanism's counter, and the increase in the number of LUTs required is the highest one, along with Trojan #7.

c) <u>Ease of activation and detection</u>: Activating the Trojan during system operation is difficult, even with input access, unless precomputed input blocks that meet the trigger condition are used. The attacker must also monitor the system's output to capture the leaked input, and knowledge of expected plaintext formats helps determine whether captured data is encrypted. Defenders can detect the Trojan using a golden response set, but even without one, repeated matches between input and output every 4096 encryption operations can indicate its presence. Monitoring resource usage may also aid detection.

12. Trojan #9:

a) <u>Trigger and payload</u>: The final Trojan is an asynchronous Timebomb triggered after 2^{15} occurrences where the ciphertext's Most Significant Bit (MSB) is zero. Upon activation, it launches a DoS attack by permanently asserting the system's reset signal, making it unusable. As shown in Fig. 10, the trigger mechanism includes a 15-bit counter incremented when the ciphertext's MSB is zero, and a comparator to detect when the counter reaches its maximum. The payload uses an XOR gate to invert the original reset signal, activating the reset of the Control Unit, both cryptographic units, and the output data FF.

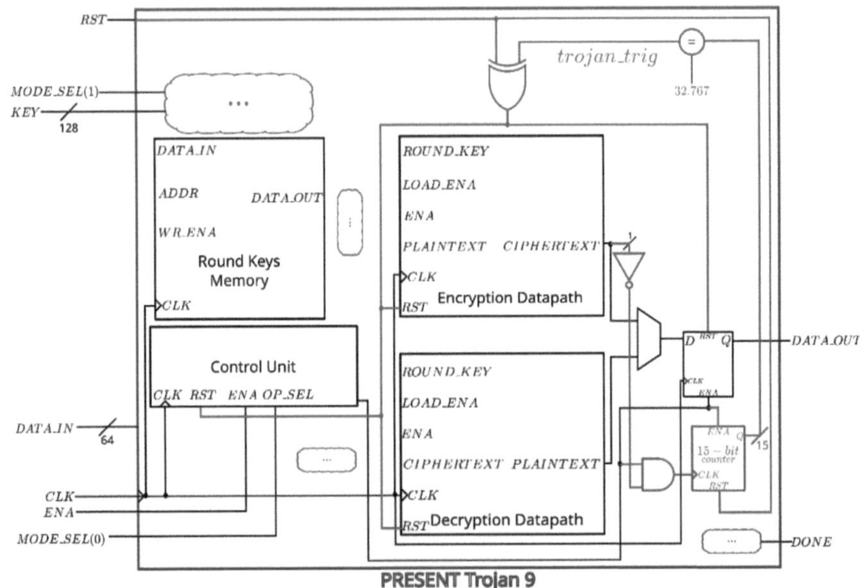

Fig. 10. Hardware Trojan #9.

b) <u>Hardware overhead:</u> Overall, 600 LUTs and 438 FFs are required, which correspond to a 0.32% and 0.2% increase in the resources necessary to implement the unaltered design, respectively. The increase in the number of FFs required is equal to the bit width of the Timebomb's triggering mechanism's counter.

c) <u>Ease of activation and detection:</u> Though not a trivial task, an attacker with input access can apply data blocks known to yield ciphertexts with an MSB of zero. Since the payload is a DoS attack, the attacker need not observe activation. By increasing the trigger counter's bit width, the Trojan can delay activation, helping it evade both pre-silicon verification and post-silicon testing. This underscores the severe threat DoS-based Trojans pose in critical or military systems, where even brief downtime can cause environmental damage or loss of life.

Unlike other Trojans, detecting a DoS-based TT doesn't require a golden response set, as it targets system availability, not functionality. Defenders can monitor for a persistent all-zero output following a cryptographic operation. Resource usage analysis is possible but less effective than output observation.

6 Trojan Implementation Results

The number of LUTs required to implement the golden system as well as each Trojan-infected version, is graphically represented in Fig. 11, which allows for a closer examination of the hardware overhead imposed onto the reference design by each malicious modification. The number of extraneous FFs is not taken into consideration as such storage elements constitute a less valuable hardware resource than LUTs in FPGA devices. As an example, an N-bit TT typically only causes an increase in the number of FFs by N, which can be discarded as negligible overhead.

Based on the results presented above, it can be concluded that small Functional Trojans triggered either by internal conditions or external inputs, bear a lower hardware overhead compared to the more complex TTs, designed around a k-bit wide counter incremented at each occurrence of a predefined rare event. In order to further decrease a TT's triggering probability, an adversary has to significantly increase the number of FFs used which could raise suspicions in the context of a lightweight system like the one proposed in this paper. The same would not be true for large and complex designs utilizing a significant part of the FPGA's fabric, as even an increase in the number of FF used by an order of 5% would be overlooked as a different Place and Route result. In addition, it is worth mentioning that a careful attacker could employ logic sharing by using the resources already occupied by the original design as part of the Trojan infrastructure, to further bury a Trojan inside the system's logic. However, even then, the cost of optimizing a TT might be greater than the attacker's gain, if a simpler Trojan triggered by a specific input block (like Trojan #1) or a part of it (like Trojan #2), was used instead. The implementation results of Trojan #1, show that Trojans with similar input-based triggering conditions not only have an extremely low activation probability but are easier to design, impose a lower hardware overhead on the original system and therefore are hard to detect unless the defender resorts to the time-consuming process of exhaustively applying all possible input blocks to the system's inputs.

The obtained implementation results indicate the possibility of designing and inserting Hardware Trojans in compact cryptographic systems, as the LUT overhead is between 0.24% and 1.31%, a negligible overhead when a system, like the PRESENT coprocessor presented, is embedded into a larger design as a 3PIP core.

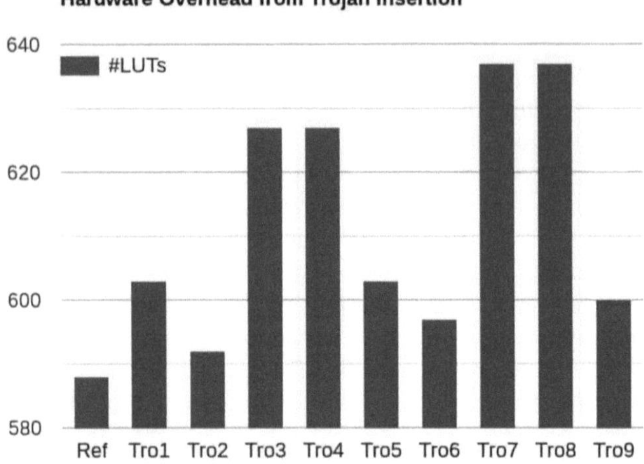

Fig. 11. LUT overhead from Trojan insertion.

7 Trojan Detection Results

As listed in Table 2, our Trojan detection approach allowed the detection of all of the presented Trojans, except for Trojan #1, where the number of input blocks applied to the system are limited in order to reduce simulation time. It is evident that if all of the 2^{64} possible input blocks were exhaustively enumerated, that such a Trojan would be successfully activated and thus detected. Therefore, Trojans relying on the occurrence of a specific, attacker-predefined input block can be successfully detected by such a technique, if the simulation time is increased.

The high number of pseudorandom input blocks necessary to detect TTs, like Trojans #7, #8, #9, indicates the Trojan designer's capability of significantly hardening detection by simply increasing the bit width of the triggering mechanism's counter. At this point it should be mentioned that, the process of Trojan detection was based on access to a golden responses set which allowed us to compare each Trojan-infected version's response to each input stimuli, to that of the reference design. In real case scenarios, access to such a set might not be available, especially if the system is a 3PIP designed by a third organization. However, if the design under Trojan test implements a cipher, the organization attempting to detect any malicious circuitry can gain access to a golden responses set by using software implementations of the cipher. Finally, in this study, the FPGA resource usage of the reference design was readily available, thus allowing the usage of a different detection approach based around the comparison of the resources needed to implement the original and a potentially tampered design.

Despite promising results, the proposed detection method cannot identify performance-degrading Trojans or those leaking information via side channels. Since side-channel Trojans, that are common in cryptographic systems for extracting assets like keys, pose significant risks, such techniques should be seen as tools for quickly detecting Trojans affecting functional behavior, not as comprehensive solutions. This highlights the need for multiple detection methods, as no single approach can detect all

Trojan types. While lacking the mathematical rigor of formal verification, the proposed method enables fast functional Trojan detection when a golden response set is available.

Table 2. Hardware Trojan detection results.

Trojan	# Random TVs	# Triggers
#1	2^{20} input blocks with 1 key	none
#2	2048 input blocks with 4 keys	multiple
#3	4096 input blocks (enc) with 1 key multiple 4096 input blocks (dec) with 1 key	multiple
#4	8192 input blocks with 1 key	few
#5	256 80-bit keys with 256 input blocks each	one
#6	4096 input blocks (enc) with 1 key 4096 input blocks (dec) with 1 key	few
#7	2^{10} mode changes	one
#8	2^{15} input blocks with 1 key	one
#9	2^{15} input blocks with 1 key	one

8 Conclusion and Outlook

In this paper, Hardware Trojan design against Lightweight Block Ciphers was explored, by inserting nine both internally and externally triggered RTL-level Trojans executing a broad range of disruptive payloads, in an FPGA implementation of the PRESENT block cipher. The implementation results obtained confirm the lightweight nature of all nine Trojans, as the LUT overhead is between 0.24% and 1.31%, drawing attention to both the attacker's freedom of attacking resource constrained cryptographic systems and the defending party's need for rapid pre-silicon detection techniques. Towards this direction, we propose a FA-based detection approach relying on self-checking testbenches to generate pseudorandom input stimuli to be applied on the DUT, whose responses are compared with expected ones. The possibility of detecting all of the proposed Trojans is highlighted by the detection results, even for Trojans depending on the occurrence of a specific input block or complex Timebomb Trojans whose detection requires a significant increase in the total verification time. Future work will focus on exploiting logic sharing to further reduce the circuitry required to implement the triggering mechanisms, while maximizing the payload's effect on the system.

References

1. Sklavos, N., Chaves, R., Di Natale, G., Regazzoni, F.: Hardware Security and Trust. Springer, Cham (2017)
2. Becker, G.T., Regazzoni, F., Paar, C., Burleson, W.P.: Stealthy dopant-level hardware trojans. In: Bertoni, G., Coron, J.S. (eds.) CHES 2013, LNCS, vol. 8086, pp. 197–214. Springer, Heidelberg (2013). https://doi.org/10.1007/978-3-642-40349-1_12

3. Bhunia, S., Tehranipoor, M.M.: Hardware Security: A Hands-on Learning Approach. Morgan Kaufmann, Cambridge (2018)

4. Martin, H., Peris-Lopez, P., Tapiador, J.E., San Millan, E., Sklavos, N.: Hardware trojans in TRNGs. In: Trustworthy Manufacturing and Utilization of Secure Devices Workshop, DATE 2015, Grenoble, France (2015)

5. Bogdanov, A., et al.: PRESENT: an ultra-lightweight block cipher. In: Paillier, P., Verbauwhede, I. (eds.) CHES 2007, LNCS, vol. 4727, pp. 450–466. Springer, Heidelberg (2007). https://doi.org/10.1007/978-3-540-74735-2_31

6. Al-Turjman, F., Zahmatkesh, H., Shahroze, R.: An overview of security and privacy in smart cities' IoT communications. Trans. Emerg. Telecommun. Technol. **33**, 3 (2022)

7. Konstantopoulou, E., Athanasiou, G., Sklavos, N.: Securing 5G/6G communications in smart cities: novel SNOW-V/ZUC-256 multimode architectures. In: Proceedings of the 2023 Int'l Conf. on Security and Management (SAM 2023), Las Vegas, NV, USA (2023)

8. Karri, R., Rajendran, J., Rosenfeld, K., Tehranipoor, M.: Trustworthy hardware: Identifying and classifying hardware trojans. Computer **43**(10), 39–46 (2010)

9. Trust-Hub: https://trust-hub.org/. Accessed 25 Oct 2023

10. Xiao, K., Forte, D., Jin, Y., Karri, R., Bhunia, S., Tehranipoor, M.: Hardware trojans: lessons learned after one decade of research. ACM Trans. Des. Autom. Electron. Syst. **22**(1), 1–23 (2016)

11. Love, E., Jin, Y., Makris, Y.: Proof-carrying hardware intellectual property: apathway to trusted module acquisition. IEEE Trans. Inf. Forensics Secur. **7**(1), 25–40 (2011)

12. Hicks, M., Finnicum, M, King, S.T., Martin, M.M., Smith, J.M.: Overcoming an untrusted computing base: Detecting and removing malicious hardware automatically. In: 2010 IEEE Symposium on Security and Privacy, pp. 159–172. IEEE (2010)

13. Waksman, A., Suozzo, M., Sethumadhavan, S.: FANCI: identification of stealthy malicious logic using Boolean functional analysis. In: Proceedings of the 2013 ACM SIGSAC Conference on Computer & Communications Security, pp. 697–708 (2013)

14. Kutzner, S., Poschmann, A.Y., Stöttinger, M.: Hardware trojan design and detection: a practical evaluation. In: Proceedings of the Workshop on Embedded Systems Security, pp. 1–9 (2013)

15. Ghandali, S., Moos, T., Moradi, A., Paar, C.: Side-channel hardware trojan for provably-secure SCA-protected implementations. IEEE Trans. VLSI Syst. **28**(6), 1435–1448 (2020)

16. Ender, M., Ghandali, S., Moradi, A., Paar, C.: The first thorough side-channel hardware trojan. In: Takagi, T., Peyrin, T. (eds.) ASIACRYPT 2017, LNCS, vol. 10624, pp. 755–780. Springer, Heidelberg (2017). https://doi.org/10.1007/978-3-319-70694-8_26

17. Breier, J., He, W.: Multiple fault attack on PRESENT with a hardware trojan implementation in FPGA. In: 2015 International Workshop on Secure Internet of Things (SIoT), pp. 58–64 (2015)

18. Kutzner, S., Poschmann, A., Stöttinger, M.: Trojanus: an ultra-lightweight side-channel leakage generator for FPGAs. In: 2013 International Conf. on Field-Programmable Technology (FPT), pp. 160–167. IEEE (2013)

19. Gbade-Alabi, A., Keezer, D., Mooney, V., Poschmann, A.Y., Stöttinger, M., Divekar, K.: A signature based architecture for trojan detection. In: Proceedings of the 9th Workshop on Embedded Systems Security, pp. 1–10 (2014)

20. Karimi, N., Danger, J.-L., Guilley, S.: On the effect of aging in detecting hardware trojan horses with template analysis. In: 2018 IEEE International Symposium on On-Line Testing and Robust System Design (IOLTS), pp. 281–286. IEEE (2018)

21. Rolfes, C., Poschmann, A., Leander, G., Paar, C.: Ultra-lightweight implementations for smart devices–security for 1000 gate equivalents. In: Grimaud, G., Standaert, F.X. (eds.) CARDIS 2008, LNCS, vol. 5189, pp. 89–103. Springer, Heidelberg (2008). https://doi.org/10.1007/978-3-540-85893-5_7

Hardware Circuits for the Legendre PRF

Subhadeep Banik[1(✉)] and Francesco Regazzoni[1,2]

[1] Universita della Svizzera Italiana, Lugano, Switzerland
`subhadeep.banik@usi.ch`
[2] University of Amsterdam, Amsterdam, Netherlands
`f.regazzoni@uva.nl`

Abstract. Linear Legendre pseudorandom functions were introduced in 1988 by Damgård, and higher degree generalizations were introduced by Russell and Shparlinski in 2004. To the best of our knowledge, there exists no efficient hardware circuit that accelerates the computation of the Legendre PRF in hardware. In this work, we try to address the issue of constructing a hardware accelerator for this task. We show that the most challenging part of constructing such a circuit is computing a sub-circuit that computes the modular reduction $p \bmod a$, when both operands a, p are variable. We propose two ideas for solving this problem. The first uses a number from the equivalence class $a \bmod p$ which is easier to compute than the modular reduction itself. We show that this circuit also computes the Legendre symbol correctly, but takes few additional clock cycles to do so. The second uses a sequential circuit for constructing modular reduction, for which we can additionally upper bound the number of clock cycles it takes to finish the computation. We verify our algorithm by synthesizing both circuits using three different standard cell libraries.

1 Introduction

The construction of pseudorandom function (PRF) using Legendre symbols was proposed by Damgård [Dam88]. The idea was extended by using higher degree polynomials were by Russell and Shparlinski [RS04]. In both cases a prime p is a public parameter and the Legendre PRF is defined as an oracle $\mathcal{O}$ that on input x outputs the Legendre symbol $\left(\frac{f(x)}{p}\right)$, where $f(x) \in \mathbb{F}_p[x]$ is a secret key. It was Damgård's conjectured that when f is linear, given a sequence of Legendre symbols of consecutive elements it is hard to predict the next one. Similar problems conjectured to be hard were also proposed [GRR+16], such as finding the secret polynomial while being given access to O and distinguishing O from a random function. So far no polynomial time algorithms have been found for either of these problems and it is believed that they are hard.

It was shown in [GRR+16] that the linear Legendre PRF was suitable as a multiparty computation (MPC) friendly pseudorandom generator. This is mainly due to the homomorphic property of the Legendre symbol and the possibility of evaluating it with only three modular multiplications in arithmetic circuit multiparty computations, which makes it a very efficient MPC friendly PRF candidate. Besides this, the linear Legendre PRF was also proposed to be used in the Ethereum 2.0 proof-of-custody mechanism.

© The Author(s), under exclusive license to Springer Nature Switzerland AG 2026
E. Savas et al. (Eds.): LightSec 2025, LNCS 16216, pp. 231–243, 2026.
https://doi.org/10.1007/978-3-032-15541-2_13

1.1 Contribution and Organization

In this paper, we present the first hardware circuits that accelerate the computation of the Legendre PRF. In Sect. 2, we present the mathematical preliminaries required to read this paper. In Sect. 3, we first present the algorithm used to compute the Legendre symbol, and explain why the $p \bmod a$, is the most challenging computation in hardware. We present two circuits to address this issue: in the first we use $p + a$ in place of $p \bmod a$, which is also in the same equivalence class. We prove that this modified algorithm also converges, but we are unable to prove an upper bound to the number of steps taken for the algorithm to converge, although through numerical simulations, it appears as if the circuit does not take more cycles than 5 times the size of the prime p in bits. In the second circuit, we take a schoolbook approach to long division to compute the modular reduction. We additionally are able to prove that the circuit certainly converges. Section 4, presents results of the synthesis of the circuits using three cell libraries. Section 5 concludes the paper.

2 Preliminaries

Recall that, given a prime p, for any $a \in \mathbb{F}_p^*$, we have that the Legendre Symbol $\left(\frac{a}{p}\right)$ is defined as:

$$\left(\frac{a}{p}\right) = \begin{cases} 1 & \text{if } \exists\, b \; st \; a = b^2 \mod p \\ 0 & \text{if } a = 0 \\ -1 & \text{othewise} \end{cases}$$

In other words $\left(\frac{a}{p}\right)$ evaluates to 1 iff a is a quadratic residue modulo p. Note that we can alternatively define $\left(\frac{a}{p}\right) = a^{\frac{p-1}{2}} \bmod p$. Damgård conjectured the following sequence may be pseudorandom

$$\left(\frac{k}{p}\right), \left(\frac{k+1}{p}\right), \left(\frac{k+2}{p}\right), \ldots$$

Also, by the Weil Bound, the number of occurrences of a fixed pattern of ℓ symbols in

$$T = \left(\frac{1}{p}\right), \left(\frac{2}{p}\right), \ldots, \left(\frac{p-1}{p}\right) \;\approx\; \frac{p}{2^\ell} + O(\sqrt{p}) \text{ as } p \to \infty$$

The Jacobi symbol is a generalization of the Legendre Symbol (for $n = \prod_i p_i$):

$$\left(\frac{a}{n}\right) = \prod_i \left(\frac{a}{p_i}\right)$$

The linear Legendre Pseudorandom function was defined in [GRR+16] as:

$$L_k(x) = \left\lfloor \frac{1}{2}\left(1 - \left(\frac{k+x}{p}\right)\right) \right\rfloor$$

The function $\left\lfloor \frac{1}{2}(1-t) \right\rfloor$ essentially maps $\{0,1\}$ to 0 and -1 to 1. Note that for the degenerate case that $a \equiv 0 \bmod p$, the Legendre symbol $\left(\frac{a}{p}\right)$ evaluates to 0. $L_k(x)$ maps this degenerate case also to 0. We outline some properties of the Legendre/Jacobi symbol:

1 Moduarity: $\left(\frac{a}{p}\right) = \left(\frac{b}{p}\right)$ iff $a \equiv b \bmod p$

2 Multiplicative: $\left(\frac{ab}{p}\right) = \left(\frac{a}{p}\right) \cdot \left(\frac{b}{p}\right)$

3 If numerator is 2: $\left(\frac{2}{p}\right) = (-1)^{\frac{p^2-1}{8}} = \begin{cases} 1 & \text{if } p \equiv 1 \text{ or } 7 \ (\bmod\ 8) \\ -1 & \text{if } p \equiv 3 \text{ or } 5 \ (\bmod\ 8). \end{cases}$

4 Reciprocity: $\left(\frac{q}{p}\right)\left(\frac{p}{q}\right) = (-1)^{\frac{p-1}{2} \cdot \frac{q-1}{2}} = \begin{cases} -1 & \text{if 2nd LSB of } p \textbf{ and } q \text{ are both 1} \\ 1 & \text{otherwise}\ . \end{cases}$

The following algorithm is well known for computing the Legendre/Jacobi symbol: The correctness of the above algorithm is easy to verify: if a is even it uses

---

Algorithm 1: Recursive algorithm for Legendre Symbol

---

1   Calculate $\left(\frac{a}{p}\right)$

---

2   **if** $a = 0$ *or* 1 **then**
3 | Return 1;
4   **end**
5   **if** a *is even* **then**
6
7 | **if** $p \equiv 1$ *or* 7   mod 8 **then** $t \leftarrow 1$ **else** $t \leftarrow -1$;
8 | **Return** $t \times \left(\frac{a/2}{p}\right)$
9   **end**
10   **if** a *is odd* **then**
11
12 | **if** *2nd LSB of* a, p *are both* $= 1$ **then** $t \leftarrow -1$ **else** $t \leftarrow 1$;
13 | **Return** $t \times \left(\frac{p \bmod a}{a}\right)$
14   **end**

---

the multiplicative property of the symbol to decompose $\left(\frac{a}{p}\right) = \left(\frac{2}{p}\right) \times \left(\frac{a/2}{p}\right)$. And $\left(\frac{2}{p}\right)$ is deduced from property 3 in the above list. If a is odd, it uses the reciprocity (and modularity) rule to express $\left(\frac{a}{p}\right) = \left(\frac{p \bmod a}{a}\right)(-1)^{\frac{p-1}{2} \cdot \frac{q-1}{2}}$, which can be deduced easily according as the 2nd LSB of a and p are both 1 or not. It is easy to verify that the above algorithm calculates $\left(\frac{a}{p}\right)$ in atmost $O(\log_2 p)$ steps, i.e. size in bits of p.

3   Circuit for $\left(\frac{a}{p}\right)$

The most difficult computation in hardware for Algorithm 1 is obviously the modular reduction $p \bmod a$, outlined in red. Note that there exist numerous algorithms/circuits to perform modular reduction if number with respect to which modular reduction is to be performed is a constant. However this is not the case here: both a, p vary in course of evaluating the algorithm and thus we ought to think of a solution that computes $p \bmod a$, where both p, a are variable.

3.1   Solution 1

One of the easiest ways of tackling the above problem is to get rid of the modular reduction altogether. The reciprocity law says that:

$$\left(\frac{a}{p}\right) = \left(\frac{p \bmod a}{a}\right)(-1)^{\frac{p-1}{2} \cdot \frac{q-1}{2}}$$

In stead of $p \bmod a$, we can replace it with any number that is also in the equivalence class defined by $p \bmod a$. One of the easiest ways to do this is use $p - a$. In other words, the following formula is also true:

$$\left(\frac{a}{p}\right) = \left(\frac{p - a}{a}\right)(-1)^{\frac{p-1}{2} \cdot \frac{q-1}{2}}$$

Of course, this will take additional clock cycles to compute, but since computer science literature is already rife with state of the art designs for adder/subtractor circuits we can certainly construct a HW circuit for this algorithm. Next observe that p is always odd throughout the runtime of Algorithm 1 and hence $p - a$ is surely even, so in the next step, the algorithm invokes the decomposition $\left(\frac{p-a}{a}\right) = \left(\frac{2}{a}\right) \times \left(\frac{(p-a)/2}{a}\right)$. Thus we can combine both steps in clock cycle, i.e.

$$\left(\frac{a}{p}\right) = \left(\frac{2}{p}\right) \times \left(\frac{(p-a)/2}{a}\right)(-1)^{\frac{p-1}{2} \cdot \frac{q-1}{2}} = \left(\frac{(p-a)/2}{a}\right)(-1)^{\frac{p^2-1}{8}}(-1)^{\frac{p-1}{2} \cdot \frac{q-1}{2}}$$

3.2   Solution 2

In the above sub-section we replace $p \bmod a$ with $p-a$. To construct such circuits, we have to deal with negative numbers, and thus we have an additional issue of having to deal with representation of negative numbers, allocating sign bits etc. We can easily side step this by choosing to replace $p \bmod a$ with $p + a$ in stead of $p - a$. Since $p + a$ also belongs to the equivalence class $p \bmod a$, this also works. Using numerical simulations with primes a large number of varying sizes, we found that, on average, using $p + a$, in stead of $p - a$ will only take a handful of additional cycles to compute, and so we can present the following Algorithm 2 to compute $\left(\frac{a}{p}\right)$ in HW. Note that the decomposition

$$\left(\frac{a}{p}\right) = \left(\frac{2}{p}\right) \times \left(\frac{(p+a)/2}{a}\right)(-1)^{\frac{p-1}{2} \cdot \frac{q-1}{2}} = \left(\frac{(p+a)/2}{a}\right)(-1)^{\frac{p^2-1}{8}}(-1)^{\frac{p-1}{2} \cdot \frac{q-1}{2}}$$

also holds in this case.

Algorithm 2: Second recursive algorithm for Legendre Symbol

---

15 Calculate $\left(\frac{a}{p}\right)$

---

16 **if** $a = 0$ *or* 1 **then**
17 | Return 1;
18 **end**
19 **if** a *is even* **then**
20 |
21 | **if** $p \equiv 1$ *or* $7 \mod 8$ **then** $t \leftarrow 1$ **else** $t \leftarrow -1$;
22 | **Return** $t\times\left(\frac{a/2}{p}\right)$
23 **end**
24 **if** a *is odd* **then**
25 |
26 | **if** $2nd\ LSB\ of\ a, p\ are\ both = 1$ **then** $t \leftarrow -1$ **else** $t \leftarrow 1$;
27 | **if** $a \equiv 1$ *or* $7 \mod 8$ **then** $u \leftarrow 1$ **else** $u \leftarrow -1$;
28 | **Return** $t \times u\times\left(\frac{(p+a)/2}{a}\right)$
29 **end**

Proof that the Algorithm Converges. The above algorithm brings into consideration the following recursive integer sequence

$$a_{t+1} = \begin{cases} a_t/2 & \text{if } a_t \bmod 2 \equiv 0 \\ (p_t + a_t)/2 & \text{otherwise.} \end{cases} \qquad p_{t+1} = \begin{cases} p_t & \text{if } a_t \bmod 2 \equiv 0 \\ a_t & \text{otherwise.} \end{cases}$$

with $a_0 = a$ and $p_0 = p$. Note this is how the variables a, p update themselves as the Algorithm 2 runs. The algorithm stops when $a_t = 1$ for some t. To prove that this happens eventually note the following lemma.

Lemma 1. *The sequence $\langle 2a_t + p_t \rangle$, for $t = 0, 1, 2, \ldots$ is non-increasing.*

Proof. If a_t is even then $2a_{t+1} + p_{t+1} = 2 \cdot (a_t/2) + p_t = a_t + p_t < 2a_t + p_t$. If a_t is odd then $2a_{t+1} + p_{t+1} = 2 \cdot ((a_t + p_t)/2) + a_t = 2a_t + p_t$. Thus the lemma follows. $\qquad\square$

This lemma shows that over increasing t, the algorithm does bring down the collective values of a_t, p_t, but this alone does not prove that the algorithm converges. Because it is possible that if a_t is odd for an infinite consecutive t, the value of $2a_t + p_t$ may remain constant forever and the algorithm may never reach $a_t = 1$. Therefore, lets see what happens when a_t is odd.

Lemma 2. *Let a_t be odd. Then $|a_{t+1} - p_{t+1}| = |a_t - p_t|/2$.*

Proof. This is easy to see. $a_{t+1} - p_{t+1} = (p_t + a_t)/2 - a_t = (p_t - a_t)/2$, and thus the lemma follows. $\qquad\square$

This means that if a_t is odd for T consecutive cycles then the value of $|a_t - p_t|$ decreases by a factor of 2 every cycle, until such time as $|a_t - p_t|$ is odd and so a_t becomes even. In the next cycle the value of a_t must decrease by a factor of 2 and so the value of $2a_t + p_t$ must therefore strictly decrease. The two lemmas prove that the algorithm must converge eventually but does not specify how many clock cycles it takes on average to do so. Nor does it upper bound this figure. In fact it is quite difficult to prove mathematically an upper bound for this figure. We did numerical simulations with primes of increasing sizes from 8 to 64, with 10000 randomly generated a, p. As shown in Fig. 1, in all cases the average number of steps needed to converge is less than $4\lceil \log_2 p \rceil$, and the maximum number of steps needed to converge is less than $5\lceil \log_2 p \rceil$.

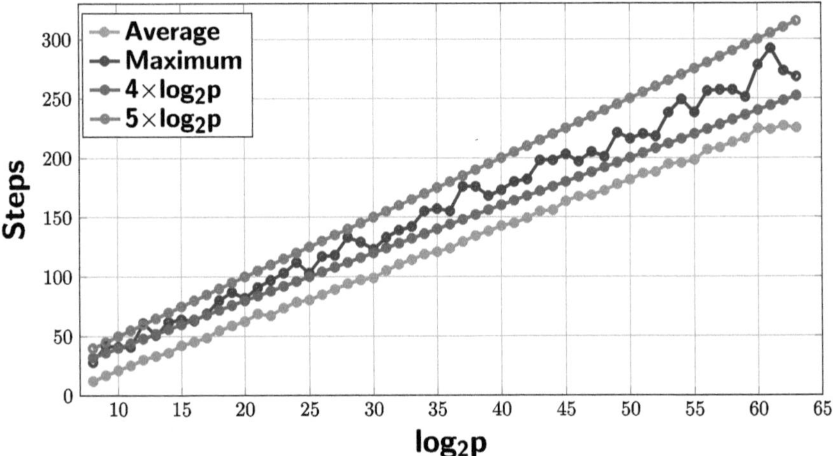

Fig. 1. Average/maximum number of steps taken for Algorithm 2 to converge.

Circuit for Algorithm 2. The circuit in hardware for Algorithm 2 is more or less self explanatory. We have two registers for a, p which update as per the rule given above. And additionally a single bit result flip-flop that keeps track of the current value Legendre symbol. So as to not have to deal with negative values, we use the map $f(t) = \lfloor \frac{1}{2}(1 - t) \rfloor$ as above that maps $\{0, 1\}$ to 0 and -1 to 1. Under this map, the multiplicative property of the Legendre Symbol becomes related by xor, i.e.

$$f\left(\left(\frac{ab}{p}\right)\right) = f\left(\left(\frac{a}{p}\right)\right) \oplus f\left(\left(\frac{b}{p}\right)\right)$$

This means that each recursion step is accompanied by update of the result flip-flop by an xor instead of multiplication i.e. $t \times \left(\frac{a}{p}\right)$ changes to $f(t) \oplus f\left(\left(\frac{a}{p}\right)\right)$. Figure 2 gives an overview of the circuit. The salient features of the circuit are as follows:

Interchangeability We have two registers marked **Areg** and **Preg** storing the current updated value of a, p respectively. When a is odd, the entire content

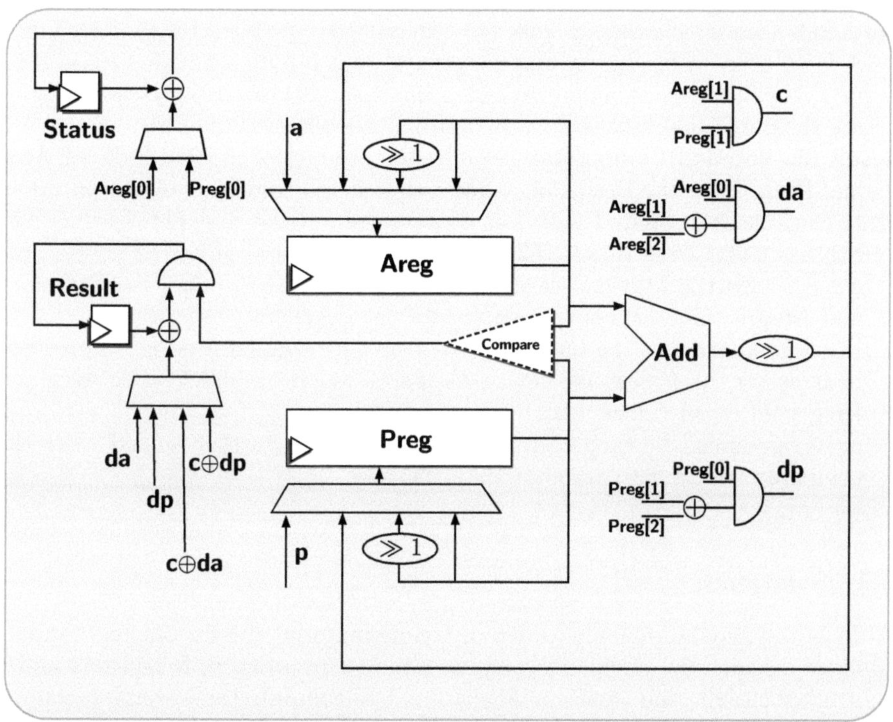

Fig. 2. Overview of circuit for Algorithm 2.

of **Areg** gets written to **Preg** in the next cycle (since $p_{t+1} = a_t$), and **Areg** gets written the result of the adder circuit right shifted by 1 (since $a_{t+1} = (p_t + a_t)/2$). This costs additional energy expenditure due to the register write operation. Instead, we could choose to retain the content of **Preg** as is, and write the adder result to **Areg**, thus saving energy required for one register write operation. To keep track of this, one could have a single bit **Status** flip-flop that would flip when such an event occurs. Thus the **Status** bit is set to '1' whenever **Areg** plays the role of storing p_t values in the circuit and vice-versa.

Note that one of the reasons that this can be done efficiently, is that the only other circuits of significant size that the two registers interact with, are the adder and comparator, which are symmetric in the order of its operands. For example, it makes no difference to the outcome of the adder if p_t is stored in **Areg** and a_t is stored in **Preg** or vice versa.

4:1 Muxes Since the registers are required to play the role of either variable a, p during the running of the circuit: each has to be able to accept four input values: **(1)** The value of a or p during initialization, **(2)** retain its previous value, **(3)** retain its previous value divided by 2, and **(4)** the result of $(p_t + a_t)/2$.

Modulo 8 Finding whether a signal x is either in the equivalence class 3 or 5 mod 8, is efficient in hardware. One just needs to compute the signal $d_x = x[0] \cdot (x[1] \oplus x[2])$ (corresponding to last 3 bits being 011 or 101). Here the $x[i]$'s are the individual bits of x, starting from $x[0]$ which is the LSB.

Result flip-flop and Comparator Let c be the product of the 2nd LSBs of **Areg** and **Preg**. Note the Result bit is reset to 0 at the beginning of computation. It needs to be updated with xor of its current value and **(1)** d_a when the **Status**=0 and **Areg** is even, **(2)** d_p when the **Status**=1 and **Preg** is even, **(3)** $c \oplus d_p$ when the **Status**=0 and **Areg** is odd, **(4)** $c \oplus d_a$ when the **Status**=1 and **Areg** is odd. This is true except for the degenerate case when $a = p$. In the degenerate case the output of the Legendre computation is supposed to be 0, as per the f map. We have a comparator that outputs 0 when **Areg** and **Preg** hold equal values, and 1 otherwise (this makes it symmetric wrt order of its operands). So each update to the result bit is further "anded" with the comparator output to accommodate this case.

3.3   Solution 3

Although it may be difficult to design a combinatorial circuit, but one can can think of a sequential circuit to compute p mod a by using shift registers and a subtractor circuit, and then use Algorithm 1 to compute the Legendre symbol. We can use the following example to explain how such a circuit would work.

Example 1. Let us say we need to compute 73 mod 13, i.e. $p_0 = 73, a_0 = 13$. Note that a_0 is always odd to begin with. In this event **Preg** has 1001001 and **Areg** has 0001101 at $t = 0$. We use a subtractor circuit to compute $p_t - a_t$. If the final "Borrow" produced by the circuit is '0', then we deduce that $p_t > a_t$ and in the next cycle we update **Preg** with $p_t - a_t$.

Step 1 Thus in the this step **Preg** is updated with $p_1 = p_0 - a_0 = 60$ =0111100. Since in the previous step the borrow was 0, **Areg** is left-shifted by 1, i.e. $a_1 = 2a_0 = 26$ =0011010. Since $p_1 > a_1$, in this step too, the subtractor produces 0 borrow.

Step 2 Since the previous step produced 0 borrow, we repeat the computations, i.e. $p_2 = p_1 - a_1 = 34$ =0100010, and $a_2 = 2a_1 = 52$ =0110100. This time the borrow produced by the subtractor is 1. So in the next step we do not update **Preg**.

Step 3 We have that $p_3 = p_2 = 34$=0100010, and we start right shifting **Areg**. Now we have $a_3 = a_2 \gg 1 = 26$ =0011010. The borrow in this step is now 0 again.

Step 4 Since the borrow was 0 in the previous step, we do $p_4 = p_3 - a_3 = 8$ =0000100. Since we have already started right shifting **Areg**, we continue the process and set $a_4 = a_3 \gg 1 = 13$= 0001101. Since **Areg** is odd again, this signals that the computation is nearing end. Since $p_t < a_t$ here, we terminate the modulo computation and deduce that 8 is the resulting answer. If however we had started with $p_0 = 79$, a_4 would have been equal to 14 at this stage, and we would need to do the subtraction for one more cycle to get 1 as the answer.

The above process mimics the schoolbook shift and subtract process of long division and therefore is guaranteed to work. The process takes a maximum of $2(1 + |\lceil \log_2 p \rceil - \lceil \log_2 a \rceil|)$ cycles, i.e. to shift **Areg** by $|\lceil \log_2 p \rceil - \lceil \log_2 a \rceil|$ steps in the left and right directions Note that even if a, p are of same size the circuit takes 2 cycles if $p > a$.

Upper Bound on the Number of Steps. Using this kind of an architecture, one can upper bound the number of steps taken by the circuit. The size of a_t decreases by 1 bit if it is even, else it gets replaced by $p_t \bmod a_t$ which at worse is of same size as a_t. Lets denote $s = \lceil \log_2 p \rceil$ to be the size in bits of p, and suppose a is also of the same size. The worst case number of steps this algorithm takes, if the following degenerate events happen

- a_0 is odd and if replaced in next step by $a_1 = p_0 \bmod a_0$ of same size. This needs at least 2 cycles.
- Since $a_1 = p \bmod a$ is even, it is replaced by $a_2 = a_1/2$, which takes 1 cycle. The size of a_2 is now $s - 1$, and the size of $p_2 = p_1 = a_0$ is s.
- Hereafter for every $t \geq 1$, we assume the induction hypothesis that a_{2t} is odd and of size $s - t$, and p_{2t} of size $s - t + 1$. We have $a_{2t+1} = p_{2t} \bmod a_{2t}$ of same size. Computing this takes 4 cycles in the worst case. After this the size of both a_{2t+1} and p_{2t+1} is $s - t$. In the next cycle, since a_{2t+1} is even, we have $a_{2t+2} = a_{2t+1}/2$ which is of size $s - t - 1$ and size of $p_{2t+2} = p_{2t+1}$ is $s - t$, which satisfies the induction hypothesis. So it takes 5 cycles for the size of a_t to reduce by 1 bit.
- Since the computation ends, when $a_t = 1$, the above estimate suggests that the maximum number of steps to get from size s to 1 should be $5(s - 2) + 3 = 5s - 7 \approx 5\lceil \log_2 p \rceil$ which is same as the circuit proposed in Solution 2.

To see why this sequence represents the worst case time. Consider the case when size of a_t equals size of $p_t = s'$ and it goes from s' to $s' - u$: using the sequence above where it is odd and even in successive takes around $5u$ clock cycles, and the size of p_t after these $5u$ cycles is same or one less than a_t. However, when a_t goes from s' to $s' - u$, by being even for u successive steps, and then odd in the next step, this would take $u + 2 \cdot (u + 1) \approx 3u$ clock cycles. Thus even/odd sequence represents worst case time complexity.

   We verified this by doing numerical simulations with primes of increasing sizes from 8 to 64, with 10000 randomly generated a, p. As shown in Fig. 3, in all cases the average number of steps needed to converge is less than $3\lceil \log_2 p \rceil$, and the maximum number of steps needed to converge is between $3\lceil \log_2 p \rceil$ and $5\lceil \log_2 p \rceil$ for all prime sizes.

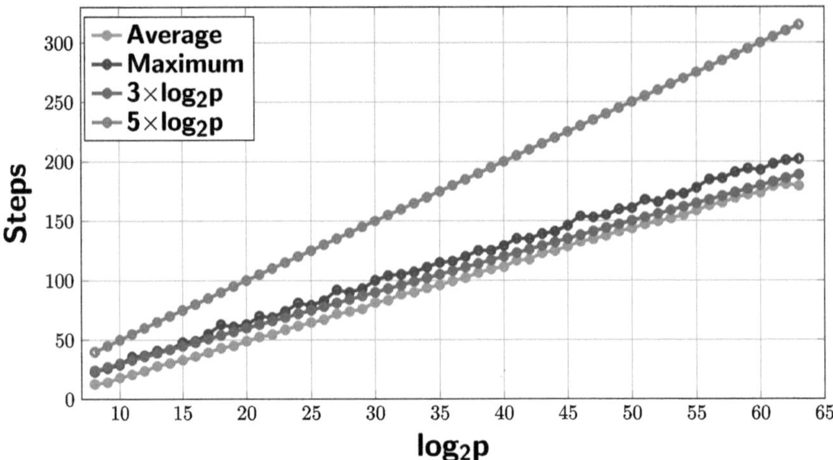

Fig. 3. Average/maximum number of cycles taken for the shift register based Legendre circuit using Algorithm 1.

Circuit Description. We present the circuit diagram for the algorithm in Fig. 4. Since we use a subtractor circuit, which is not symmetric wrt th eorder of its operands we can no longer use the registers in dual roles. Also the use of a subtractor obviates the need of having an extra comparator circuit to check equality between the two registers. A simple bitwise "or" operation performed on the subtractor output will do, i.e. when the signals are equal the or gate produces 0, and 1 otherwise. Sone salient features of the circuit are as follows:

Areg The register **Areg** is initially loaded with the value of a. thereafter it must be able to shift-left (during modular-reduction) or shift-right (to compute $a_{t+1} = a_t/2$ and during modular reduction) by one bit. Or it may also be required to retain its value during the last step of modular reduction (as in the example of $p_0 = 79, a_0 = 13$ above). After the modular reduction is completed, the result from **Preg** is written back to it.

Preg The register **Preg** is initially loaded with the value of p. It is mainly required to either store intermediate values during modular reduction from the output of the subtractor. After the modular reduction is completed, the value of a from **Areg** is written to it.

Or gate The bitwise or operation on the subtractor output serves as the comparator output. A single bit flip-flop, initialized to 1, handles the degenerate case when $a = p$. Once the or-gate output goes to 0, the zero value is permanently written on to the flip-flop which zeroes the content of the **Result** flip-flop permanently.

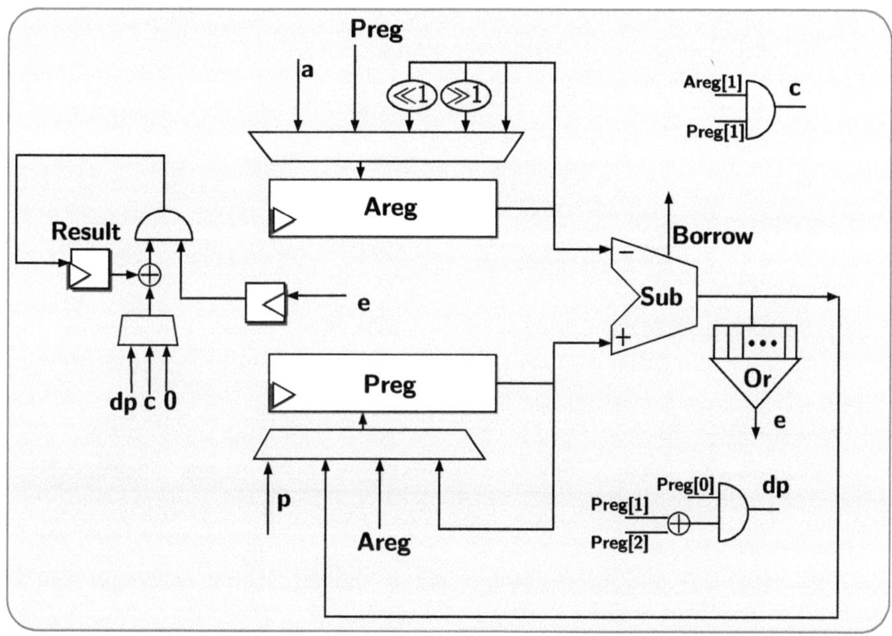

Fig. 4. Overview of circuit for Algorithm 1 using Shift register based modular reduction.

4   Synthesis Results

We synthesized all the ciphers using the NanGate 15nm, TSMC 65 nm and UMC 40nm standard cell libraries. All the designs were initially implemented in VHDL their functionality has been verified using Mentor Graphics ModelSim SE. The designs were synthesized using the Synopsys Design Compiler using the `compile_ultra` command. The switching activity was collected while performing a timing simulation on the synthesized netlist using Synopsys VCS. The switching activity was then back annotated to estimate the power consumption using Synopsys Power Compiler. Table 1, reports the result of our implementations.

We used the Brent-Kung [BK82] architecture for constructing the adder and subtractor circuits, which is known to have logarithmic depth. From the results in Table 1, we can see that the circuit can be reasonably hardware efficient, especially when compared to **AES-128** circuits. Using the same standard cell library (Nangate 15nm OCL), the smallest circuit for **AES-128** was reported in [BCB21]: it occupies 2247 GE and it takes 1408 cycles to map 128 bits of input to output. Using the Solution 2 circuit, for example if we map $x, x + 1, \ldots, x_{63}$ to $L_k(x), L_k(x + 1), \ldots, L_k(x + 63)$, then this 64-bit map would take around $180 \times 64 = 11520$ cycles on average, around 10 times slower than **AES-128** while taking the similar circuit area. However, the comparison is not quite accurate, since much faster circuits for **AES-128** by only around 4 or 5 times this circuit

Table 1. Synthesis results for the two circuits for the Legendre Symbol. Note that power has been evaluated at 10 MHz.

#	Architecture	Area		$\lceil \log_2 p \rceil$	Avge #Cycles	Power	Energy
		(μm^2)	(GE)	Bits		(μW)	(μJ)
Nangate 15 nm							
1	Solution 2	407.2	2071	64	230	12.283	282.51
	Solution 3	420.4	2138		180	12.829	230.92
TSMC 65 nm							
2	Solution 2	2762.3	1918		230	75.621	1739.28
	Solution 3	2794.3	1940		180	90.988	1637.78
UMC 40 nm							
3	Solution 2	1098.4	2001		230	16.346	375.96
	Solution 3	1122.2	2045		180	19.983	359.69

area, whereas it is not immediately clear if the same kind of circuit can be constructed for the Legendre map.

4.1   Some Thoughts on Side Channel Resistance

There are two main issues in constructing circuits for the Legendre symbol that offer some resistance to side channel attacks. First is designing a constant/fixed time circuit. To do this one can do the following. We can use the circuit in Solution 3, for which there exists an upper bound of $T = 5\lceil \log_2 p \rceil$ cycles. We run the circuit for T cycles, but stop updating the **Result** bit once **Areg** becomes 1. This is likely to leak no more than the bit-size of p.

The second is the issue of masking: and one can take advantage of the fact that $\left(\frac{r^2}{p}\right) = 1, \forall\, r$. Which means that $\left(\frac{a}{p}\right) = \left(\frac{ar}{p}\right) \cdot \left(\frac{r}{p}\right)$, for any random mask $r \in \mathbb{F}_p^*$. Therefore to compute $\left(\frac{k+x}{p}\right)$, we select a random r and use the masked input $s_1 = (k + x) \cdot r$ as the first share and $s_2 = r$ as the second share. We can compute $\left(\frac{s_1}{p}\right)$ and $\left(\frac{s_2}{p}\right)$ using two parallel circuits and multiply the result in the end. This should mask effectively all information leaking through the power side channel.

5   Conclusion

In this work we look at possible solutions to constructing a circuit for the Legendre PRF. The principal difficulty in constructing such a circuit lies in computing the modular reduction when both operands are variable. We looked at two solutions to overcome this difficulty, one using another number in the same equivalence class and second using a sequential circuit for constructing modular reduction. We verify our algorithm by synthesizing both circuits using three standard cell libraries.

References

[BCB21] Balli, F., Caforio, A., Banik, S.: The area-latency symbiosis: towards improved serial encryption circuits. IACR Trans. Cryptogr. Hardw. Embed. Syst. **2021**(1), 239–278 (2021)

[BK82] Brent, R.P., Kung, H.T.: A regular layout for parallel adders. IEEE Trans. Comput. (3), 260–264 (1982)

[Dam88] Damgård, I.: On the randomness of Legendre and Jacobi sequences. In: Goldwasser, S., (ed) Advances in Cryptology - CRYPTO '88, 8th Annual International Cryptology Conference, Santa Barbara, California, USA, August 21–25, 1988, Proceedings, volume 403 of Lecture Notes in Computer Science, pp. 163–172. Springer (1988)

[GRR+16] Grassi, L., Rechberger, C., Rotaru, D., Scholl, P., Smart, N.P.: MPC-friendly symmetric key primitives. In: Weippl, E.R., Katzenbeisser, S., Kruegel, C., Myers, A.C., Halevi, S., (eds) Proceedings of the 2016 ACM SIGSAC Conference on Computer and Communications Security, Vienna, Austria, October 24-28, 2016, pp. 430–443. ACM (2016)

[RS04] Russell, A., Shparlinski, I.E.: Classical and quantum function reconstruction via character evaluation. J. Complex. **20**(2–3), 404–422 (2004)

Lightweight Fault Detection Architecture for Modular Exponentiation in Cryptography on ARM and FPGA

Saeed Aghapour[1], Kasra Ahmadi[1], Mehran Mozaffari Kermani[1(✉)], and Reza Azarderakhsh[2]

[1] College of AI, Cybersecurity, and Computing, University of South Florida, Tampa, FL 33620, USA
{aghapour,ahmadi1,mehran2}@usf.edu
[2] Department of Electrical Engineering and Computer Science, Florida Atlantic University, Boca Raton, FL 33431, USA
razarderakhsh@fau.edu

Abstract. Whether stemming from malicious intent or natural occurrences, faults and errors can significantly undermine the reliability of lightweight architectures. In response to this challenge, fault detection plays a pivotal role in ensuring the secure deployment of cryptosystems. Even when a cryptosystem boasts mathematical security, its practical implementation may remain susceptible to exploitation through side-channel attacks. In this paper, we propose a lightweight fault detection architecture tailored for modular exponentiation, a building block of numerous cryptographic applications spanning from classical cryptography to post-quantum cryptography (PQC). Based on our simulations on ARM Cortex-A72 processor, our approach achieves an error detection ratio close to 100%, all while introducing a modest computational overhead of approximately 14%. Moreover, implementing our design on AMD/Xilinx Artix Ultrascale+ FPGA reported a minimal area and modest delay overhead compared to the unprotected design.

Keywords: ARM processor · Cryptography · Fault detection · FPGA · Modular exponentiation

1 Introduction

In today's era of online communication, cryptography plays an essential role in ensuring secure interactions. It has been established within cryptography research community that besides pure mathematical analysis, cryptographic algorithms can be threatened by exploitation of their implementation, known as side-channel attacks. It is well-known that one variant of side-channel attacks is denoted as fault analysis which was introduced in [1]. In fault attacks, adversaries intentionally induce malfunctions in a cryptosystem, with the potential

E. Savas et al. (Eds.): LightSec 2025, LNCS 16216, pp. 244–260, 2026.
https://doi.org/10.1007/978-3-032-15541-2_14

intention that these faults will reveal secret values within the system. Additionally, natural faults, which could arise due to various factors such as aging or environmental changes, if left unaddressed, may disrupt the functionality of an algorithm. The work in [2] provides a comprehensive study on different fault injection methods that do not require expensive equipment.

As a countermeasure to fault attacks, fault detection schemes have been developed. Various fault detection techniques have been introduced for different sub-blocks in cryptosystems. For instance, the research work in [3] presented fault detection schemes for the AES with very high error coverage, and the work in [4] proposed fault detection schemes for RSA. Moreover, addressing fault detection in elliptic curve cryptography, with a particular focus on the elliptic curve scalar multiplication (ECSM) module has been studied for years. In the research work conducted in [5], a novel fault detection scheme based on recomputation for ECSM is presented. Additionally, the works in [6,7] have proposed highly efficient fault detection methods for ECSM and τNAF conversion, capable of detecting transient and permanent errors. Moreover, the work in [8] introduces a novel compiler that resists adaptive fault attacks using polynomial masking. In [9], a fully automated software is presented, enabling designers to develop fault-tolerant circuits without requiring expert knowledge of hardware implementation.

Additionally, the work in [10] presents the first fault attack against secure inference implementations. The authors successfully executed a laser fault attack on existing solutions that were previously considered secure. Furthermore, the work in [11] introduced a systematic countermeasure for fault sensitivity analysis (FSA), focusing on different AES S-Box architecture implementations. The work in [12] demonstrated that EdDSA is vulnerable to fault attacks, showing that a single successful fault injection through voltage glitching or electromagnetic injections on WolfSSL EdDSA implementation can reveal the secret key. The authors of [13] proposed a hardware-only scheme to prevent fault attacks on general-purpose microprocessors, using value prediction while maintaining performance efficiency. The work in [14] introduced a fault attack on signature schemes like DSA and Schnorr, where faults injected during the signing process allowed the reconstruction of the correct signature and deduction of secret key bits. Additionally, the work in [15] targeted pairing-based cryptosystems, showing the vulnerability of several of such schemes to fault attacks. Moreover, the work in [16] proposed a technique for protecting RISC processor registers against multiple-bit upsets, demonstrating that their method could detect and correct up to eight faults in AES. The work in [17] presented a framework for Feistel ciphers, applied to three Feistel-based designs, showing that secret key could be efficiently obtained. Finally, [18] provided a quantitative analysis of security of hardware circuits against fault injection attacks.

The advent of practical quantum computers, forces us to shift to new standard PQC schemes. Consequently, significant research efforts have been directed toward proposing fault detection mechanisms for the newly NIST standardized schemes. The new standard schemes are categorized into Key Encapsulation

Mechanism (KEM) schemes and Digital Signature (DSA) schemes, with ML-KEM (Module Lattice-Based KEM) and ML-DSA (Module Lattice-Based Signature) being among the most efficient and promising families. In that regard, Sarker et al. [19] proposed an error detection algorithm for number theoretic transform (NTT), which could be deployed on many lattice based schemes. Additionally, the work in [20] proposes fault attack countermeasures for error samplers which are employed within lattice-based schemes to introduce noise to the secret information, thereby concealing direct computations on that sensitive data. The work in [21] presents two new key recovery fault attacks on the randomized FIPS 204 ML-DSA (Dilithium). These new attacks can efficiently bypass several traditional countermeasures. Additionally, the work in [22] focuses on FIPS 204 ML-DSA (Dilithium) and FIPS 206 FN-DSA (FALCON) and proposes a new fault attack capable of forging valid signatures for any arbitrary message for both schemes. The work in [23] introduces a new fault attack on cryptosystems which are based on the group action proposed in [24]. Their attack can successfully retrieve the secret key with a modest number of successful fault injections and computational effort. The work in [25] presented four attacks on the hardware implementation of FIPS 203 ML-KEM (Kyber), which either weakened the design's security or recovered the message. Additionally, the work in [26] proposed a fault attack targeting Learning With Error (LWE)-based PQC schemes, showing its effectiveness in extracting sensitive information. The attack was validated on the open-source STM32 implementation of FIPS 203 ML-KEM (Kyber).

Our Motivations and Contributions: Having discussed the previous research, limited attention has been given to fault detection solely for the modular exponentiation module. The significance of such work lies in its applicability across a wide range of applications employing this module, rather than being limited to a single cryptosystem. In this paper, we present a recomputation-based fault detection scheme tailored for modular exponentiation. Although using recomputation for fault detection is a known method, to the best of our knowledge, our work is the first to use partial recomputation efficiently for such an architecture. Extensive error simulations, along with hardware and software implementations, demonstrate high error coverage and an acceptable overhead of 14% in the number of clock cycles in software, and an increase of approximately 5% in LUTs and 16% in FFs in hardware.

2   Preliminaries

One of the most efficient techniques for computing modular exponentiation is called Right-to-Left algorithm which is also known as square and multiply. To calculate the value of $x^y \bmod N$, first y is represented in binary form as $y = \sum_{i=0}^{n-1} a_i 2^i$. Therefore, $x^y \bmod N$ can be expressed as $\prod_{i=0}^{n-1} x^{a_i 2^i} \bmod N$. Now, starting from $i = 0$, if $a_i = 0$, the base is squared, and we proceed to the next bit, but if $a_i = 1$, the intermediate result must be multiplied by x before squaring the base. Algorithm 1 presents this approach.

Algorithm 1. Right-to-Left Exponentiation Algorithm

Input: base x, exponent y, and modulus N
Output: $Result = x^y \bmod N$
1: $result = 1$
2: $x = x \bmod N$
3: **while** $(y > 0)$
4:     **if** $(y \bmod 2 == 1)$
5:         $Result = (Result \times x) \bmod N$
6:     $y = y >> 1$
7:     $x = (x \times x) \bmod N$
8: **return** $Result$

---

3 Proposed Fault Detection Architecture

In this section, we present our approach to detecting faults in the modular exponentiation operation of $x^y \bmod N$ through the right-to-left exponentiation algorithm. Our method relies on recomputation and the output is considered valid only if the results of the two calculations match. We introduce two fault detection schemes. The first scheme involves a full recomputation, which, while providing very high error coverage, consumes significant resources and is not suitable for resource-constrained devices. The second scheme makes a trade-off between overhead and error coverage by employing a partial recomputation approach, effectively reducing computational overhead.

An essential aspect of recomputation-based schemes is input encoding. Without input encoding, permanent faults and identical transient errors on both computation stages remain undetected, as they would generate the same outputs in both computations. The encoding module is responsible for generating distinct input values for the recomputation stage. After performing computations on these modified inputs, the decoding algorithm should produce the same result for both the main and recomputation stages. Additionally, efficient encoding and decoding algorithms should minimize computational overhead.

3.1 Scheme 1: Costly Full Recomputation

In this scheme, the entire output is computed twice, compared, and accepted only if both results match. To encode the inputs, we take advantage of the group properties and propose modifying the base and exponent as $x_2 = x + k_1 N$ and $y_2 = y + k_2 \phi(N)$ where $\phi(N)$ is the Euler's totient function. Since $(x + k_1 N)^{y + k\phi(N)} \equiv x^y \bmod N$, the two outputs, computed through different computational branches, must be identical if no fault is injected.

This full recomputation approach provides near 100% error coverage. However, despite the lightweight nature of the input encoding and the absence of a decoding algorithm, based on the method of implementation, it almost doubles either the run-time (if implemented sequentially) or area (if implemented parallel) of the design. Therefore, a more efficient design is required.

3.2   Scheme 2: Lightweight Partial Recomputation

In this approach, rather than recomputing the entire $x^y \bmod N$, we perform recomputation on a much smaller subset of the exponent as $y_{partial} = \sum_{i=0}^{l-1} 2^i y[i]$. We show that this subset can still effectively detect faults with a high probability.

Algorithm 2. Proposed Modular Exponentiation Module

Input: base x, exponent y, modulus N, and l
Output: $Result$ **and** $flag$
// Main computation
1: $Result = 1$, $x_1 = x$, $counter = 0$, **and** $HM_1 = 0$
2: **while** $(y > 0)$
3:    **if** $(y \bmod 2 == 1)$
4:        $Result = (Result \times x_1) \bmod N$
5:    $y = y >> 1$
6:    $x_1 = (x_1 \times x_1) \bmod N$
7:    $counter + +$
8:    **if** $(counter == l)$
9:        $Result_{part_1} = Result$
10: **if** $(counter > l)$
11:        $HM_1 = HM_1 + y \bmod 2$
// Recomputation with encoded inputs.
12: Random k_1, $Result_{part2} = 1$, **and** $HM_2 = 0$
13: $x_2 = x + k_1 N$ **and** $y_2 = \tilde{y}[length - l]||(y[l : 0] + mask)$
14: **for** $(i = 0 \text{ to } l)$
15:    **if** $(y_2 \bmod 2 == 1)$
16:        $Result_{part_2} = (Result_{part_2} \times x_2) \bmod N$
17:    $y_2 = y_2 >> 1$
18:    $x_2 = (x_2 \times x_2) \bmod N$
19: **for** $(i = l \text{ to } length)$
20:    $HM_2 = HM_2 + y_2 \bmod 2$
// Decoding and Comparison.
21: Random k_2 **and** $Result_{decode} = 1$
22: $x_3 = x + k_2 N$
23: **for** $(i = 0 \text{ to } l)$
24:    **if** $(mask \bmod 2 == 1)$
25:        $Result_{decode} = (Result_{decode} \times x_3) \bmod N$
26:    $mask = mask >> 1$
27:    $x_3 = (x_3 \times x_3) \bmod N$
28: **if** $(HM_1 == HM_2 \ \& \ (Result_{part_1})(Result_{decode}) \equiv Result_{part_2} \bmod N)$
29:    $flag = 1$
30: **return** $Result$ **and** $flag$

With more details, at time t_1, besides computing $Q_1 \equiv x^y \bmod N$ a partial result $Q_{1,partial} \equiv x^{y_{partial}} \bmod N$ where $y_{partial} = \sum_{i=0}^{l-1} 2^i y[i]$ is stored. Crucially, since $Q_{1,partial}$ is an intermediate value in the computation of Q_1, it does not require any additional computation.

At t_2, after encoding the inputs, $Q_{2,partial} \equiv x_2^{y_2,partial} \bmod N$ is computed and after decoding, it will be compared to $Q_{1,partial}$. Increasing l increases the computational overhead; however, it also provides a better detection rate, especially when the number of injections is low. For a high number of injections, even a low value of l is sufficient. Therefore, l can be selected adaptively based on the application, environment, and specific scenario in which the design is used. In applications where the likelihood of a low number of injections exists, a higher l is preferable, whereas in other scenarios, a lower l is sufficient.

To enhance the error coverage rate even with low values of l, we also calculate and compare the Hamming weight of the exponent at t_1 and t_2. That being said, while we can still encode the base as $x_2 = x + k_1 N$, we cannot encode the exponent as $y_2 = y + k_2 \phi(N)$. Because, the effect of the term $k_2 \phi(N)$ cancels out in the final result but remains present in the intermediate result $y_{partial}$. Hence, the partial results do not match.

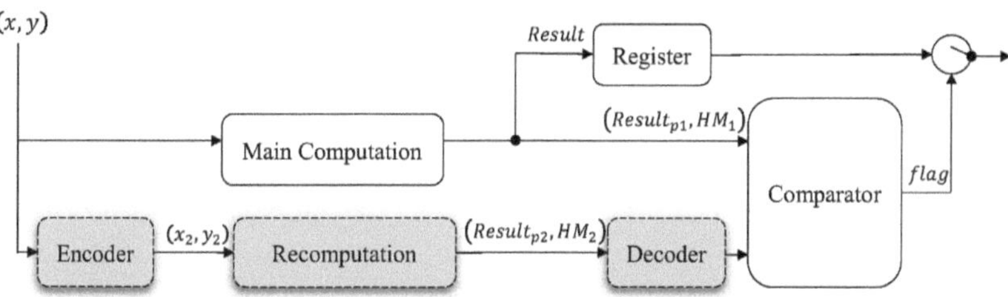

Fig. 1. Proposed scheme for error detection of modular exponentiation.

To encode the exponent, we mask the first l bits, and scramble the remaining bits to maintain the same Hamming weight. To mask the first l bits, we add a random number, $mask$, to y, ensuring that no carry occurs. For scrambling the remaining bits, various well-known scrambler algorithms could be used, but in this case, we simply reposition the remaining bits. Consequently, the overall encoded exponent is computed as $y_2 = \tilde{y}[length - l] \| (y[l : 0] + mask)$, where $\tilde{y}$ refers to the scrambled version of y. Based on these input encoding in this approach, the second partial result is computed as follows:

$$Q_{2,partial} \equiv x^{y_2,partial} \bmod N \equiv x^{y_1,partial + mask} \bmod N.$$

For decoding, we first compute $Q_{decode} = x_3^{mask} \bmod N$ where $x_3 = x + k_2 N$ is the encoded base, further adding a level of complexity for adversaries to perform a successful injection. Finally, the output $Q_1 \equiv x_1^{y_1} \bmod N$ is accepted only if the two conditions $Q_{2,partial} \equiv Q_{1,partial} \times Q_{decode} \bmod N$ and $HM_1 = HM_2$ hold. Figure 1 and Algorithm 2 illustrate the schematic and details of our design. Gray modules in Fig. 1 represent the recomputation stage. Note that the main computation, recomputation, and decoding stages can be performed either sequentially or in parallel. We prioritized area over delay and implemented them sequentially.

4   Error Coverage and Simulation Results

In this section, we begin by discussing the theoretical detection rate of our design. After providing a detailed explanation of our simulation methodology and fault model, we conduct various simulations to evaluate the error coverage of our design under different realistic scenarios. Finally, we report our results in a comprehensive table.

4.1   Theory

In theory, input encoding not only aids in the detection of permanent faults but also serves as a masking method to enhance the design's security against side-channel attacks. Also, due to the encoding, injecting faults that would produce the same impact for both computation stages becomes a challenging task. However, there are some fault injection scenarios where our design may fail to detect which we categorize into two groups.

In the first category, faults occur solely during the main computation stage. In this case, if a fault in x creates a new x' where $x^{y_l} \equiv x'^{y_l} \bmod N$ but $x^y \neq x'^y$ $\bmod N$, an error has occurred, and the fault remains undetected. Additionally, if faults occur in y, and the injected faults produce y' where $HM(y) = HM(y')$ and $x^{y_l} \equiv x^{y_l'} \bmod N$, but $x^y \neq x^{y'} \bmod N$, the faults introduce errors that go undetected. However, because of the Hamming weight check, odd number of fault injections will always be detected.

In the second category, faults may be injected in both the main and recomputation stages or even the decoding stage. If the injected faults result in identical effects in both computations, the faults will remain undetected. However, since the inputs are encoded, the likelihood of fault injections having the same effect in both stages is low. We demonstrate this through comprehensive simulations in the following subsections. Additionally, if faults occur only during the recomputation or decoding stages, they can be efficiently detected, even if they do not produce output errors.

4.2   Simulation Methodology and Settings

To perform our simulations, we implemented our design in Python. To comply with current security constraints, we selected 2048-bit numbers for N, x, and y. Moreover, the recomputation index is $l = 128$ meaning 6.25% recomputation. Additionally, the coefficients k_i used in the input encoders were set to 8 and 4, allowing the multiplication $k_i N$ to be efficiently performed using simple shifts. For each simulation case, we executed the algorithm 1,000 times and reported the average detection rate. For each run, a new random value for N, x, y, and *mask* are selected.

To cover a wide range of real-world scenarios, we have simulated six different fault models: random flip, random stuck-at-0, random stuck-at-1, burst flip, burst stuck-at-0, and burst stuck-at-1. The difference between these models lies in how the faulty bits are selected and altered. In the random flip fault model, the adversary selects a specified number of bits at random and flips their values ("XOR" with 1). Conversely, in the random stuck-at-0 (or stuck-at-1) model, after selecting the target bits randomly, the adversary forces them to 0 (or 1) using an "AND" with 0 (or using "OR" with 1).

Table 1. Our Comprehensive Simulation Results

Fault Model	fault #	Target					
		Main		(Main, Recomp)		(Main, Recomp, Decode)	
		x_1	y_1	(x_1, x_2)	(y_1, y_2)	(x_1, x_2, x_3)	$(y_1, y_2, mask)$
Random flip	1	100	100	100	75.1	100	100
	10	100	87.7	100	95.1	100	100
	15	100	100	100	99.5	100	100
	20	100	99.4	100	100	100	100
Random Stuck at 0	1	100	100	100	78.3	100	100
	10	100	100	100	99.4	100	100
	15	100	100	100	99.7	100	100
	20	100	100	100	100	100	100
Random Stuck at 1	1	100	100	100	78.7	100	100
	10	100	100	100	98.9	100	100
	15	100	100	100	99.2	100	100
	20	100	100	100	100	100	100
Burst flip	5	100	100	100	86.2	100	100
	10	100	85.3	100	94.8	100	100
	15	100	100	100	98.4	100	100
	20	100	88.8	100	99.7	100	100
Burst stuck at 0	5	100	100	100	87	100	100
	10	100	100	100	95.1	100	100
	15	100	100	100	100	100	100
	20	100	100	100	100	100	100
Burst stuck at 1	5	100	100	100	86.7	100	100
	10	100	100	100	94.6	100	100
	15	100	100	100	99.8	100	100
	20	100	100	100	100	100	100

Unlike the random models, the burst fault models do not select all faulty bits independently. Instead, after choosing an initial random bit, the next consecutive bits (determined by the intended number of injections) are either flipped or forced to 0 or 1 according to the injection model, simulating localized fault propagation. The burst fault model is crucial because injecting a single fault is often complex in practice, and even when a single fault is intended to be injected, it often affects multiple adjacent bits.

Furthermore, since our design is based on recomputation, we have considered three places for fault injections: (1) only at the main computation stage, (2) at both the main and recomputation stages, and (3) at the main, recomputation, and decoding stages. This is because an adversary might attempt to inject faults in a way that produces identical effects in both computation stages. but, due to input encoding, these faults can be detected effectively.

Moreover, any fault injection affecting only the recomputation stage, the decoding stage, or both will not lead to a faulty output. Although our design efficiently detects such anomalies, for sake of brevity we have omitted these injection scenarios. Finally, we have analyzed different fault targets based on each of the specified fault placements.

In this study, we assumed that the comparators are hardened and fault-free, with faults injected only into the inputs. However, comparator hardening can be achieved through various schemes, such as redundancy with majority voting. Since the computational overhead of the comparator is significantly lower than that of other sub-blocks in the design, the overall scheme remains lightweight.

4.3   Error Coverage

Table 1 presents the results of our comprehensive fault detection simulations. As mentioned earlier, the cases where the injections do not change the output are omitted.

Table 2. Total number of clock cycles in 1000 iterations on Cortex-A72 ARM processor

l	Unprotected	Our method	Overhead
5	39,218,317,844	39,990,918,705	1.97%
10		40,304,665,248	2.77%
25		40,896,861,847	4.28%
64		42,312,643,121	7.89%
128		44,669,664,024	13.9%

5   Implementation Results

To assess the performance of our design, we benchmarked it on ARM Cortex-A72 and Artix UltraScale+ FPGA. We note that the choice of platforms family does not limit us in using our approach.

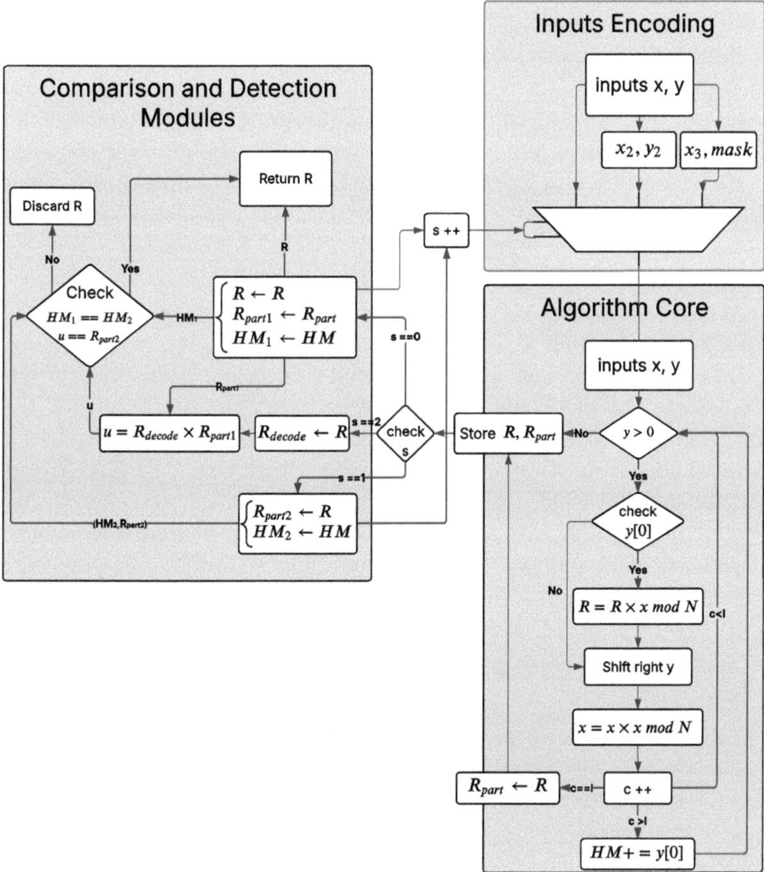

Fig. 2. Block diagram of the proposed architecture.

5.1 Software Implementation

In theory, in terms of computational overhead, since the encoding are executed only once, the most resource-intensive process is the partial recomputation and the decoding module, which directly correlate with the parameter l. As l increases, the total computational cost is primarily influenced by this step, overshadowing other components. In theory, for large values of l, it is expected that the total computational overhead to be close to the ratio of $\frac{2l}{|y|}$.

To measure the computational overhead of our design in practice, we have implemented it on a Raspberry Pi-4, and used Clang Version 11 as our compiler and leveraged the GMP library [27] designed for big numbers arithmetic. To calculate the number of clock cycles, we employed the Performance Application Programming Interface (PAPI) [28]. Furthermore, despite the ARM Cortex A72's capability of accommodating four cores, we intentionally chose not to leverage multi-core processing, and our design executes both the main computation and recomputation sequentially on a single core.

The results of the Cortex-A72 implementation are presented in Table 2. In this table, the overhead of the unprotected design is independent of l; however, since the algorithm does not run in constant time, the number of clock cycles slightly varies for different inputs. Therefore, the reported number is the average of 5 runs (each run includes 1000 different modular exponentiations).

5.2 Hardware Implementation

In theory, the additional circuitry in our design includes, shifting for encoding of x, an l-bit adder and an scrambler for encoding of y, and comparators. Figure 2 depicts the block diagram of the proposed architecture. For the hardware implementation, we used Verilog and AMD/Xilinx Vivado tool to analyze area, delay, and power of our design on Artix UltraScale+ FPGA. We used the default "Vivado synthesis" and "Vivado implementation" settings for both the unprotected design and our own. We employed the SchoolBook method and Barrett reduction for multiplication and modular reduction. To stay within the available IO limits, we used a bus that loads 128 bits of the inputs per clock cycle. Moreover, we implemented our design sequentially, where the decoding and recomputation states occur after the main computation is completed.

Table 3. Implementation results on Artix UltraScale+ xcau15p-ffvb676-1LV-i FPGA

Period Constraint		20 (*ns*)		25 (*ns*)		50 (*ns*)	
Design		Unprotected	Ours	Unprotected	Ours	Unprotected	Ours
Area	LUT	12938	13640	12894	13553	12893	13553
	FF	9355	10887	9355	10887	9355	10887
	DSP	50	50	50	50	50	50
Clock Cycles		67,020	74,979	67,020	74,979	67,020	74,979
Total Time (μs)		1340.4	1499.58	1675.5	1874.47	3351	3748.95
Max Freq (MHz)		50.91	50.11	43.72	42.23	35.48	34.72
Power (W)		0.052	0.063	0.041	0.049	0.021	0.026
Energy (μJ)		67.7	94.47	68.675	91.84	70.37	97.47

Table 3 presents the results of our implementation on the Artix UltraScale+ FPGA for three different period constraints. The values x, y, and N are each considered to be 512 bits, and l is set to 25. While our design can be easily extended to larger inputs, due to limitations in the Vivado simulation, we were unable to fully verify the soundness of our implementation. Therefore, we report results only for the 512-bit inputs. Nonetheless, percentage-wise, we observed relatively lower overhead for larger input sizes, demonstrating the effectiveness of our method for large numbers used in cryptography.

Table 4. Comparison of the proposed design with related works in terms of system overhead

Design	Implementation	Overhead			
		Theory	SW (%)	HW (%)	
				Area	Time
	Unprotected right-to-left exponentiation	$\simeq 6n \cdot m^2$			
	Unprotected Montgomery ladder	$\simeq 8n \cdot m^2$			
[29]	Montgomery ladder	$\simeq 12n \cdot m^2$		NA	
[31]	Right-to-left exponentiation	$\simeq 8n \cdot m^2$		NA	
[30]	CRT-RSA	$\simeq 4n(m + w)^2$	18.8	NA	
[32]	CRT-RSA	$\simeq 4n \cdot m^2$	12.5	NA	
Ours	Right-to-left exponentiation	$\simeq 6.7n \cdot m^2$	13.9	5.11 (LUT) 16.3 (FF)	11.87

5.3 Comparison

To the best of our knowledge, the first work proposing a generic fault-resistant method for modular exponentiation is [29]. However, as demonstrated in [30], the proposed method is insecure against fault attacks when applied to RSA-CRT (RSA using Chinese Remainder Theorem). Furthermore, the work in [31] presented a new approach which besides resisting fault attacks, could also resist against power analysis attacks. Moreover, a fast fault resistant method for RSA signature generation is proposed in [32] that could also resist simple power analysis attacks, but their work lacks fault simulation.

The work in [40] demonstrated that the right-to-left modular exponentiation algorithm is vulnerable to fault attacks. They showed that a single faulty signature can reveal a secret bit of the exponent with high probability. Furthermore, the work in [41] describes a simple yet effective method to verify each step of the modular exponentiation algorithm, stopping the process whenever a transient fault is detected. Moreover, [42] proposes a new countermeasure based on self-secure methods for modular exponentiation and the RSA scheme.

Table 4 provides a comparison of our work with related work. In this table, n, $2m$, and w refer to the sizes of the exponent, modulus, and word size, respectively. Moreover, the overhead of one modular multiplication (or squaring) with an m-bit modulus is considered to be m^2. Additionally, the reported software overheads for works [30, 32] are measured relative to the unprotected CRT-RSA implementation, whereas in our case, the comparison is made against the unprotected right-to-left exponentiation algorithm. However, our design is fully applicable to CRT-based implementations of RSA. In other words, in CRT-RSA, instead of computing $m = c^d \bmod pq$ directly, the values $m_1 = c^d \bmod p$ and $m_2 = c^d \bmod q$ are computed, and then m is reconstructed from m_1 and m_2. Therefore, our design can be applied to each exponentiation computation of m_1

and m_2 to detect injected faults. In theory, the overhead of our design when implemented on CRT-RSA would be approximately $\simeq 3.3\ n \cdot m^2$.

Comparing our design with prior works [29–32] highlights that our approach stands out as the sole design encompassing simulation, software, and hardware implementations, all while imposing minimal computational overhead.

6   Discussions

Our design is directly applicable to a wide range of public key cryptosystems which are based on modular exponentiation, including Diffie-Hellman key exchange, RSA, Shamir's secret sharing, etc. Additionally, the concept of partial recomputation can be extended to other applications such as Montgomery modular multiplication [33], signal processing tools [34], and the CSIDH scheme [24]. Moreover, although PQC is expected to eventually replace classical cryptography, this transition will not happen in the near future. Thus, fault detection in classical cryptography remains a crucial consideration.

6.1   Applicability to Other Cryptosystems

CSIDH is a PQC key exchange scheme which is based on isogenies between elliptic curves. In this scheme, both the public key and the shared key are obtained through a group action which takes a private key and an initial curve as inputs and outputs another curve after applying multiple isogeny maps with different degrees to the initial curve. Our approach involves storing the intermediate curve after l isogeny maps, and recomputing, these l isogenies later. For encoding the private key, since the group action is commutative, changing the order of performing the isogeny maps does not affect the result. For encoding the curve, we leverage the property of isomorphism, which states that applying the same isogeny map to two isomorphic curves will result in curves with the same j-invariant. Therefore, in the recomputation phase, we start with another curve that shares the same j-invariant as the initial curve. After performing l isogenies in a different order, we compare the j-invariant of the resulting curve with that of the partial curve obtained from the main computation.

6.2   Using Dedicated Tools

Rather than simulating custom fault injection scenarios, the use of dedicated tools such as ARCHIE [35] for software, and VerFI [36] and FIVER [37] for hardware implementations is encouraged. These tools provide a universal framework, enabling fair evaluation of countermeasures. However, using these tools is beyond the scope of this paper and is considered for future work.

6.3   Side-Channel and Fault Attack Protection in One Design

Past research endeavors have extensively scrutinized the security of purportedly protected designs against specific attacks, as evidenced by studies [38,39]. It has been observed that countermeasures designed to mitigate one threat may inadvertently introduce vulnerabilities, or conversely, bolster security against other side-channel and fault attacks. Thus, one of our future studies will be analyzing the efficacy of our approach against other side-channel attacks.

7   Conclusion

Fault and error detection play a pivotal role in ensuring the integrity and reliability of any algorithms. In this paper, we have introduced a new fault detection approach designed for modular exponentiation, a critical component in various cryptographic systems. Our approach achieves remarkably high error detection rates while imposing only a minimal computational burden to the underlying algorithm. Through comprehensive simulations and implementation on Cortex-A72 ARM processor, we showed that our method, with less than 14% increase in computational cost can provide high error coverage in software. Moreover, implementing our design on Artix UltraScale+ FPGA reported a modest overhead increase of 5.11% and 16.37% in number of LUTs and FFs while increasing the total time close to 11.8%. We observed that the area overhead became even less significant as the input sizes increased, making our design well-suited for cryptographic purposes.

References

1. Boneh, D., DeMillo, R., Lipton, R.: On the importance of eliminating errors in cryptographic computations. J. Cryptology **14** (2001)
2. Barenghi, A., Breveglieri, L., Koren, I., Naccache, D.: Fault injection attacks on cryptographic devices: theory, practice, and countermeasures. Proc. IEEE **100**(11) (2012)
3. Mozaffari-Kermani, M., Reyhani-Masoleh, A.: Concurrent structure independent fault detection schemes for the Advanced Encryption Standard. IEEE Trans. Computers **59**(5), 608–622 (2010)
4. Koylu, T. C., Reinbrecht, C. R. W., Hamdioui, S., Taouil, M.: RNN-based detection of fault attacks on RSA. In: Proceedings of the IEEE International Symposium on Circuits and Systems (ISCAS), pp. 1–5 (2020)
5. Dominguez-Oviedo, A., Hasan, M.: Error detection and fault tolerance in ECSM using input randomization. IEEE Trans. Dependable Secure Comput. **6**(3), 175–187 (2009)
6. Ahmadi, K., Aghapour, S., Mozaffari-Kermani, M., Azarderakhsh, R.: Efficient error detection schemes for ECSM window method benchmarked on FPGAs. IEEE Trans. Very Large Scale Integr. (VLSI) Syst. **32**(3), 592–596 (2024)
7. Ahmadi, K., Aghapour, S., Kermani, M.M., Azarderakhsh, R.: Error detection schemes for τ-NAF conversion within Koblitz curves benchmarked on various ARM processors. TechRxiv, Preprint (2023). https://doi.org/10.36227/techrxiv.24168654.v1

8. Berndt, S., et al.: Combined fault and leakage resilience: composability, constructions and compiler. In: Handschuh, H., Lysyanskaya, A. (eds.) CRYPTO 2023, Santa Barbara, CA, USA. LNCS, vol. 14083, pp. 377–409. Springer (2023)

9. Müller, N., Moradi, A.: Automated generation of fault-resistant circuits. IACR Trans. Cryptogr. Hardware Embedded Syst. **2024**(3), 136–173 (2024)

10. Hashemi, M., Mehta, D., Mitard, K., Tajik, S., Ganji, F.: FaultyGarble: fault attack on secure multiparty neural network inference. In: 2024 Workshop on Fault Detection and Tolerance in Cryptography (FDTC), pp. 53–64. IEEE (2024)

11. Ghalaty, N., Aysu, A., Schaumont, P.: Analyzing and eliminating the causes of fault sensitivity analysis. In: Proceedings of the Design, Automation and Test in Europe Conference and Exhibition, pp. 1–6 (2014)

12. Samwel, N., Batina, L.: Practical fault injection on deterministic signatures: the case of EdDSA. In: Joux, A., Nitaj, A., Rachidi, T. (eds.) AFRICACRYPT 2018. LNCS, vol. 10831, pp. 306–321. Springer, Cham (2018). https://doi.org/10.1007/978-3-319-89339-6_17

13. Cammarota, R., Sheikh, R.: Vpsec: countering fault attacks in general-purpose microprocessors with value prediction. In: Proceedings of the 15th ACM International Conference on Computing Frontiers (CF'18). ACM (2018)

14. Mus, K., Doroz, Y., Tol, M.C., Rahman, K., Sunar, B.: Jolt: Recovering TLS Signing Keys via Rowhammer Faults. In: IEEE S and P 2023, pp. 1719–1736 (2023)

15. Chatterjee, S., Karabina, K., Menezes, A.: Fault attacks on pairing-based protocols revisited. IEEE Trans. Comput. **64**(6), 1707–1714 (2015)

16. Ustaoglu, B., Yalcin, B.O.: Fault tolerant register file design for MIPS AES-crypto microprocessor. In: 2015 IEEE International Conference on Electronics, Circuits, and Systems (ICECS), pp. 442–445. IEEE (2015)

17. Bagheri, N., Sadeghi, S., Ravi, P., Bhasin, S., Soleimany, H.: SIPFA: Statistical ineffective persistent faults analysis on Feistel ciphers. IACR Trans. Cryptogr. Hardware Embedded Syst. **2022**(3), 367–390 (2022)

18. Feldtkeller, J., Guneysu, T., Schaumont, P.: Quantitative fault injection analysis. In: Guo, J., Steinfeld, R. (eds.) ASIACRYPT 2023, Guangzhou, China. LNCS, vol. 14441, pp. 302–336. Springer (2023)

19. Sarker, A., Canto, A.C., Kermani, M.M., Azarderakhsh, R.: Error detection architectures for hardware/software co-design approaches of number-theoretic transform. IEEE Trans. Comput. Aided Des. Integr. Circ. Syst. **42**(7), 2418–2422 (2023)

20. Howe, J., Khalid, A., Martinoli, M., Regazzoni, F., Oswald, E.: Fault attack countermeasures for error samplers in lattice-based cryptography. In: Proceedings of the IEEE International Symposium on Circuits and Systems (ISCAS), pp. 1–5. IEEE (2019)

21. Krämer, E., Pessl, P., Land, G., Guneysu, T.: Correction fault attacks on randomized CRYSTALS-Dilithium. Cryptology ePrint Archive, Paper 2024/138 (2024). https://eprint.iacr.org/2024/138

22. Bauer, S., De Santis, F.: Forging Dilithium and Falcon signatures by single fault injection. In: Workshop on Fault Detection and Tolerance in Cryptography (FDTC 2023), Prague, Czech Republic, September 10, 2023, pp. 81–88. IEEE (2023)

23. Banegas, G., et al.: Disorientation faults in CSIDH. In: Advances in Cryptology–EUROCRYPT 2023, part V, pp. 310–342. Springer Nature Switzerland (2023). https://doi.org/10.1007/978-3-031-30589-4_11.

24. Castryck, W., Lange, T., Martindale, C., Panny, L., Renes, J.: CSIDH: an efficient post-quantum commutative group action. In: Advances in Cryptology–ASIACRYPT 2018, pp. 395–427

25. Ni, Z., Khalid, A., Liu, W., O'Neill, M.: Bitstream fault injection attacks on CRYS-TALS Kyber implementations on FPGAs. In: Design, Automation and Test in Europe Conference and Exhibition, DATE 2024, pp. 1–6. IEEE (2024)

26. Kundu, S., et al.: Carry your fault: a fault propagation attack on side-channel protected LWE-based KEM. IACR Trans. Cryptogr. Hardw. Embed. Syst. 844–869 (2024)

27. The GNU Multiple Precision Arithmetic Library (GMP). https://gmplib.org/ Accessed March 2025

28. Terpstra, D., Jagode, H., You, H., Dongarra, J.: Collecting performance data with PAPI-C. In: Proceedings of Tools for High Performance Computing, Springer, pp. 157–173 (2010)

29. Fumaroli, G., Vigilant, D.: Blinded fault-resistant exponentiation. In: Proceedings of the Workshop on Fault Diagnosis and Tolerance in Cryptography (FDTC), pp. 62–70 (2006)

30. Kim, C.H., Quisquater, J.J.: How can we overcome both side-channel analysis and fault attacks on RSA-CRT? In: Proceedings of the Workshop on Fault Diagnosis and Tolerance in cryptography (FDTC), pp. 21–29 (2007)

31. Boscher, A., Handschuh, H., Trichina, E.: Blinded fault resistant exponentiation revisited. In: Proceedings of the Workshop on Fault Diagnosis and Tolerance in Cryptography (FDTC), pp. 3–9 (2009)

32. Giraud, C.: An RSA implementation resistant to fault attacks and to simple power analysis. IEEE Trans. Comput. 1116–1120 (2006)

33. Aghapour, S., Ahmadi, K., Mozaffari-Kermani, M., Azarderakhsh, R.: Partial Recomputation fault detection architecture for multiple-precision montgomery modular multiplication. IEEE Trans. Comput. Aided Des. Integr. Circ. Syst. (2025). https://doi.org/10.1109/TCAD.2025.3592590

34. Aghapour, S., Ahmadi, K., Mozaffari-Kermani, M. and Azarderakhsh, R.: Efficient partial recomputation-based fault detection approaches for z-transform. IEEE Trans. Very Large Scale Integr. (VLSI) Syst. **33**(7) 1983–1993 (2025). https://doi.org/10.1109/TVLSI.2025.3560154

35. Hauschild, F., Garb, K., Auer, L., Selmke, B., Obermaier, J.: ARCHIE: a QEMU-based framework for architecture-independent evaluation of faults. In: Proceedings of the Workshop on Fault Detection and Tolerance in Cryptography (FDTC), Italy, pp. 20–30 (2021)

36. Arribas, V., Wegener, F., Moradi, A., Nikova, S.: Cryptographic fault diagnosis using VerFI. In: Proceedings of the 2020 IEEE International Symposium on Hardware Oriented Security and Trust (HOST), pp. 229–240. IEEE (2020)

37. Richter-Brockmann, J., Shahmirzadi, A.R., Sasdrich, P., Moradi, A., Guneysu, T.: FIVER - Robust verification of countermeasures against fault injections. IACR Trans. Cryptogr. Hardw. Embed. Syst. (2021)

38. Regazzoni, F., Breveglieri, L., Ienne, P., Koren, I.: Interaction between fault attack countermeasures and the resistance against power analysis attacks. In: Proceedings of the Fault Analysis Cryptography, pp. 257–272 (2012)

39. Dofe, J., Pahlevanzadeh, H., Yu, Q.: A comprehensive FPGA-based assessment on fault-resistant AES against correlation power analysis attack. J. Electron. Test. **32**(5), 611–624 (2016)

40. Boreale, M.: Attacking right-to-left modular exponentiation with timely random-faults. In: International Workshop on Fault Diagnosis and Tolerance in Cryptography, pp. 24–35. Berlin, Heidelberg: Springer Berlin Heidelberg (2006)

41. Gueron, S.: Data and computational fault detection mechanism for devices that perform modular exponentiation. In: International Workshop on Fault Diagnosis and Tolerance in Cryptography, pp. 80–87. Berlin, Heidelberg: Springer Berlin Heidelberg (2006)
42. Rivain, M.: Securing RSA against fault analysis by double addition chain exponentiation. In: Proceedings of the The Cryptographers' Track at the RSA Conference 2009 on Topics in Cryptology, pp. 459–480, Berlin, Heidelberg (2009)

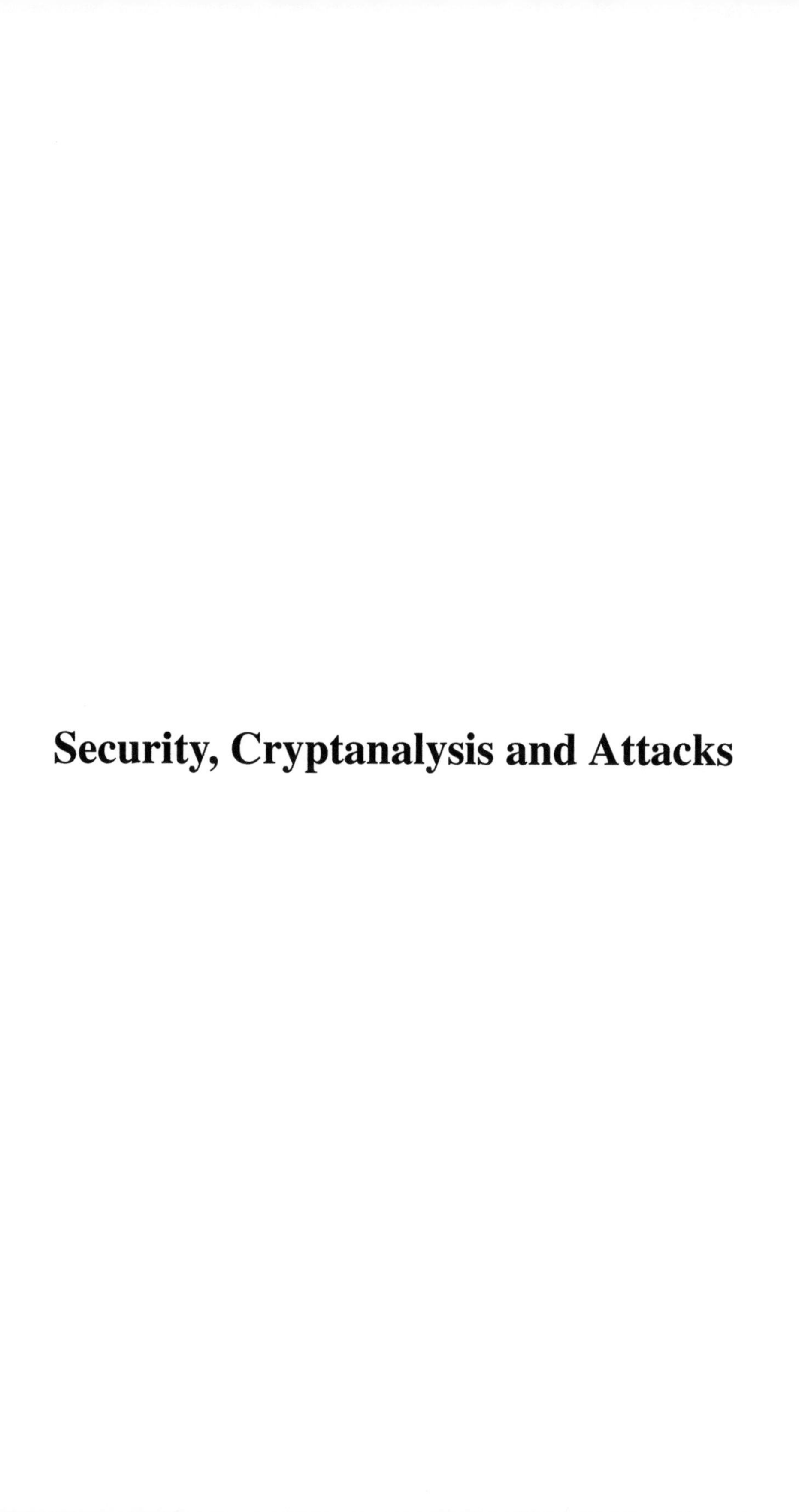

Security, Cryptanalysis and Attacks

Cube-Attack-Like Cryptanalysis of Keccak-Based Constructions Exploiting State Differences

Mohammad Vaziri$^{(\boxtimes)}$ and Vesselin Velichkov

The University of Edinburgh, Edinburgh, UK
{mohammad.vaziri,vvelichk}@ed.ac.uk

Abstract. This paper presents an enhancement to cube-attack-like cryptanalysis by minimizing output-bit dependency on related key bits, thereby improving attack complexity. We construct two distinct initial states differing exclusively in predetermined bit positions. Through independent cube summation and state difference analysis, we observed reduced related key bits dependency for specific output bits. We validate our approach by targeting three Keccak keyed variants Ketje Minor, Keccak-MAC-512 and Keccak-MAC-384, developing a dedicated tool to recover all output-bit superpolies. Using our computational resources, we successfully attacked 4-round of Ketje Minor and 5-round of other variants, confirming both the method's validity and practical applicability. While the best known attacks on these structures reach 7-round, our results improve upon the 5-round.

We construct our initial state configurations based on the automated method proposed by Bi et al. in *Design, Codes and Cryptography* (2019), and compare our results with theirs. For the 4-round Ketje Minor, we reduce the time complexity from 2^{20} to $2^{16.8}$; for 5 round Keccak-MAC-512, from 2^{34} to $2^{31.2}$; and for 5 round Keccak-MAC-384, from $2^{27.6}$ to $2^{26.5}$.

Keywords: cube attack · Keccak Keyed Variants · Cube-Attack-Like Cryptanalysis

1 Introduction

Following collision attacks on MD5 and SHA-1 proposed by Wang et al.'s [WY05, WYY05], the U.S. National Institute of Standards and Technology (NIST) held a public competition in 2007 to choose a new cryptographic hash function standard (SHA-3). After five years of careful review, NIST picked Keccak [BDP+11] as the winner in 2012.

Besides being used as a regular hash function, Keccak can also work in keyed modes like message authentication codes (MAC) and stream ciphers. Additionally, the Keccak permutation has been used in other cryptographic designs, including authenticated encryption schemes such as Keyak [BDP+16b], Ketje [BDP+16a], and the pseudorandom function Kravatte [BDH+17].

E. Savas et al. (Eds.): LightSec 2025, LNCS 16216, pp. 263–284, 2026.
https://doi.org/10.1007/978-3-032-15541-2_15

With the growing use of lightweight devices, the demand for efficient cryptographic algorithms has increased substantially. In response, the National Institute of Standards and Technology (NIST) [Nat23] initiated a competition to standardize lightweight authenticated encryption with associated data (AEAD) and hashing schemes. On February 7, 2023, NIST selected Ascon [DEMS21] winning algorithm. Another notable cryptographic algorithm submitted to NIST, is Xoodyak [DHP+20], which is designed based on [DHAK18] permutation. Xoodyak is designed by the Keccak team and has been one of the finalist of the NIST competition.

The first adaptation of cube attack [DS09] to Keccak keyed modes was developed by [DMP+15], who introduced cube-attack-like cryptanalysis where cube variables do not multiply in the first round. This key modification enables linearization of Keccak's first round and provided the first security evaluation of Keccak's keyed modes. Subsequent work by [HWX+17] proposed the conditional cube attack, exploiting Keccak's large state degree of freedom to identify conditional cube variables that avoid multiplication with ordinary cube variables through both first and second rounds.

To address the limited degrees of freedom in certain Keccak keyed modes and improve attack efficiency, researchers have pursued automated approaches for both cube-attack-like cryptanalysis and conditional cube attacks. Initial work by [BDL+19, SG18] independently developed mixed integer linear programming (MILP) model for cube-attack-like methods, while [LBDW17, SGSL18] advanced MILP modeling to improve conditional cube attacks. Subsequent innovations include [LDB+19]'s refined conditional attack variant and applications to Xoodyak by [ZLD+20, VV23], collectively expanding the framework's capabilities against Keccak based constructions.

Our Contributions. This paper focuses on enhancing cube-attack-like cryptanalysis by reducing output-bit dependency on related key bits, thereby improving attack complexity. Building on configurations from [BDL+19], we construct two initial states that differ exclusively in predetermined bit positions. Through independent cube summation on both states and exploiting state differences, we observed reduced dependency on related key bits for specific output bits. We verify our approach by targeting three Keccak keyed variants Ketje Minor, Keccak-MAC-512, and Keccak-MAC-384, using by developing a tool[1] that recovers all output-bit superpolies.

Using our computational resources, we successfully attacked 4-round of Ketje Minor and 5-round of other variants. These results verify both the correctness and practical applicability of our method. However, due to the faster diffusion of variables in Ketje Minor a lightweight design, extending the attack to 5 rounds proved infeasible, as our computational resources encountered memory limitations.

---

[1] The tool has been fully implemented, and all attacks have been empirically validated. The tool is available at: https://github.com/mohammadvaziri/Cube-Attack-Like-Cryptanalysis-of-Keccak-Based-Constructions-Exploiting-State-Differences.

It is worth mentioning that while the best known-attacks on our target structures reach 7 rounds, we specifically compare our results with the 5-round attacks from [BDL+19] for equivalent evaluation. Enhanced computational resources or tool optimizations could potentially extend our approach to 6-round attacks. The best achieved complexities (to the best of our knowledge) for each variant are:

- Ketje Minor: Using conditional cube attack, 2^{113} time complexity, targeting 7-round, proposed by [SGSL18].
- Keccak-MAC-512: Using cube-attack-like, 2^{111} time complexity, targeting 7-round, proposed by [SG18].
- Keccak-MAC-384: Using conditional cube attack, 2^{75} time complexity, targeting 7-round, proposed by [LBDW17].

Table 1 presents a comparative analysis of our results against the results achieved by the [BDL+19] technique.

Table 1. Complexity comparison between our technique and [BDL+19] for 4-round attack on Ketje Minor and 5-round attacks on Keccak-MAC-512 and Keccak-MAC-384.

Target	$|K|$	Degree of freedom	Rounds	Time	Memory	Data	Reference
Ketje Minor	128	654	4	$2^{16.8}$	2^1	2^{10}	Sect. 5.3
				2^{20}	$2^{7.3}$	$2^{15.3}$	[BDL+19]
Keccak-MAC-512	128	447	5	$2^{31.2}$	2^7	2^{28}	Sect. 5.1
				2^{34}	2^{15}	2^{31}	[BDL+19]
Keccak-MAC-384	128	703	5	$2^{26.5}$	$2^{3.5}$	$2^{21.5}$	Sect. 5.2
				$2^{27.4}$	2^7	2^{24}	[BDL+19]

Outline. The paper is organized as follows. Section 2 details the Keccak sponge construction and the specific keyed variants under evaluation. Section 3 systematically reviews cube attack variants, focusing on cube-attack-like cryptanalysis and its MILP-based automation. Section 4 presents our core technical contribution: a state difference propagation control method. Finally, Sect. 5 demonstrates practical cryptanalysis, applying our technique to three keyed Keccak variants (Ketje Minor, Keccak-MAC-512 and Keccak-MAC-384).

1.1 Notations

Throughout the paper, we will use the following notations:

A_0 — initial state of the Keccak permutation,

$A_{i,\theta}$ — internal state of Keccak after θ in the $(i+1)$-th round,

$A_{i,\rho}$ — internal state of Keccak after ρ in the $(i+1)$-th round,

$A_{i,\pi}$ — internal state of Keccak after π in the $(i+1)$-th round,

$A_{i,\chi}$ — internal state of Keccak after χ in the $(i+1)$-th round,

A_i — output state of Keccak of the $(i+1)$-th round,

$(i, *, k)$ — index of a column,

$(*, j, k)$ — index of a row,

$(i, j, *)$ — index of a lane,

(i, j, k) — index of a bit,

$A[i][j]$ — the lane indexed by $(i, j, *)$ of state A,

$A[i][j][k]$ — the bit indexed by (i, j, k) of state A.

2 Preliminaries

In the section, we will briefly introduce some necessary background for this paper.

2.1 The Keccak-p Permutations

The Keccak-p permutations, denoted as Keccak-$p[b, n]$, are defined by two parameters: the width of the permutation in bits $b = 25 \times 2^l$ (where $l = 0, \ldots, 6$) and the number of rounds n. The state of Keccak-$p[b, n]$ is represented as a three-dimensional array of bits $a[5][5][w]$, with $w = 2^l$. Each bit is indexed by coordinates (x, y, z), where x and y are modulo 5 and z is modulo w.

The state can be visualized in several ways:

- A **slice** is a two-dimensional part $a[*][*][z]$.
- A **row** is a one-dimensional part $a[*][y][z]$.
- A **column** is $a[x][*][z]$.
- A **lane** is $a[x][y][*]$, also written as $a[x][y]$ for simplicity. At the lane level, the state becomes a 5×5 array.

The round function of Keccak-$p[b, n]$ consists of five steps: θ, ρ, π, χ, and ι ($R = \iota \circ \chi \circ \pi \circ \rho \circ \theta$). These steps perform operations such as XOR, bitwise rotations, lane reordering, and nonlinear transformations. The round Function can be formalized as follows:

$$\theta : A[x][y] = A[x][y] \oplus \sum_{j=0}^{4}(A[x-1][j] \oplus (A[x+1][j] \lll 1)).$$

$$\rho : A[x][y] = A[x][y] \lll r[x,y].$$

$$\Pi : A[y][2x+3y] = A[x][y]. \tag{1}$$

$$\chi : A[x][y] = A[x][y] \oplus ((\neg A[x+1][y]) \wedge A[x+2][y]).$$

$$\iota : A[0][0] = A[0][0] \oplus RC_{i_r}, \text{ where } RC_{i_r} \text{ is the } i_r\text{-th round constant.}$$

The operation θ is used for the state diffusion. If the variables in each column of the state has even parity, they bypass the diffusion to other columns caused by θ. This property is called column-parity-like kernel (CP-like kernel), and for the first time was exploited by [DMP+15] to control the diffusion of the cube variables through the first round of Keccak.

In the round function of Keccak, the only nonlinear operation is χ, with an algebraic degree of 2. As a result, following an r-round Keccak internal permutation, the maximum algebraic degree of the output polynomial is bounded by 2^r.

Due to the structure of the χ operation, any two variables placed in adjacent positions before χ will be multiplied together. To prevent variable multiplication in the first round, we strategically position variables in the initial state such that they avoid adjacent placement prior to χ. This approach, employed in previous cube attacks on Keccak constructions, ensures that the resulting polynomials maintain a degree of 1 with respect to the cube variables.

The operation ι is not considered in our analysis, as it does not influence the described attacks.

2.2 Keccak-MAC

A MAC mode of Keccak is constructed by prefixing the message/nonce with the key. For Keccak-MAC-n, the input consists of the key concatenated with the message, where n represents half of the capacity length. Additional details can be found in [BDP+11].

2.3 Ketje

Ketje is one of the 16 candidates in the 3rd round CAESAR competition. In Ketje V2, Ketje Minor and Ketje Major are introduced, where a twisted version of Keccak-p, denoted Keccak-p* is used. It reorders lanes before and after applying the original permutation to simplify certain operations. More details can be found in [BDP+16a].

3 Related Works

3.1 Cube Attacks

The cube attack is a key-recovery technique that uses chosen plaintexts. It was formally introduced in [DS09] and builds upon earlier methods such as higher-order differential cryptanalysis [Lai94].

This attack treats the output bits of a cipher as a Boolean polynomial $f : X^n \rightarrow \{0, 1\}$ over the input bits. The main idea is that if f has a low algebraic degree d, then summing over all 2^{d-1} inputs of a specific subset of variables (called a cube), while keeping the other variables fixed, gives a function that is linear in the secret variables.

Theorem 1 (Dinur, Shamir [DS09]). *Given a Boolean polynomial $f : X^n \rightarrow \{0, 1\}$ of degree d, let $t = x_0 x_1 \cdots x_{k-1}$ be a monomial with $0 < k < d$. Then f can be written as*

$$f(x) = t \cdot P_t(x) + Q_t(x) \tag{2}$$

where $Q_t(x)$ contains no terms divisible by t, and $\deg(P_t) \leq d - k$. $P_t(x)$ is called superpoly of t. If we take the sum over the cube C_t defined by the k variables in t, we obtain

$$\sum_{x' \in C_t} f(x', x) = P_t(1, \ldots, 1, x_k, \ldots, x_{n-1})$$

which has a degree of at most $d - k$. In particular, when $k = d - 1$, the result is linear.

Cube attack is divided into two preprocessing and online phases.

3.2 Dinur et al.'s Cube-Attack-Like Cryptanalysis on Keccak

In traditional cube attacks, the cipher's structure is treated as a black-box system. Since the actual degree of the polynomial in the cube variables in higher rounds is unknown, the cube variables are typically selected at random. However, in the case of Keccak, the degree of the cube variables is explicitly known (for the r-th round, it is 2^r). This knowledge allows for a simplification of the cube attack procedure.

In [DMP+15], Dinur et al.'s. observe that by carefully selecting the positions of the cube variables in the initial state and utilizing the CP-like kernel property, they can prevent the multiplication of cube variables in the first round.

Consequently, for an attack on r-round of the Keccak keyed mode, the complexity of the cube attack depends solely on $S = 2^{r-1}$ cube variables and T key bits that multiply with the cube variables in the first round.

In the preprocessing phase, for each possible value of the T key bits, the cube summation over S cube variables is computed and stored in a list L, indexed by the cube sum values. During the online phase, while the secret key bits remain fixed, a cube summation over the S cube variables is calculated. For each match found in L, the corresponding candidate values for the T related key bits are retrieved.

Therefore, the time complexity of the attack is 2^{S+T} for the preprocessing phase and 2^S for the online phase. Additionally, the overall memory and data complexity of the attack are 2^T and 2^S, respectively.

Trade-Off Between Preprocessing and Online Phases. The basic attack described above involves an expensive preprocessing phase that dominates its time complexity. As presented in [DMP+15], Dinur *et al.* propose a complexity trade-off between the preprocessing and online phases, resulting in a more efficient attack.

For the specific case of 6-round reduced Keccak-MAC, their approach introduces 32-bit auxiliary variables during the preprocessing phase. These variables are constrained to equal the key bits in $A[0][0]$ within the same column. This constraint places half of $A[0][0]$ (a 32-bit key bits) along with the auxiliary variables set in the CP-like kernel.

This configuration provides two key advantages:

- Cube variables avoid multiplication with these key bits and auxiliary variables in the first round
- Only 32 key bits interact with cube variables after the first round

Consequently, just these 32 key bits affect the cube sums of the output after six rounds in the preprocessing phase.

In the online phase, this trade-off requires computing the cube sum for each possible value of the auxiliary variables. This technique modifies the time complexity of both preprocessing and online phases to $2^{S+T/2}$ and reduces the memory complexity to $2^{T/2}$. To calculate the data complexity, since the cube summation is performed over $T/2$ auxiliary variables in the online phase, the overall complexity increases to $2^{S+T/2}$.

Now let us formally define the following two key concepts:

Definition 1 (Related Key Bits). *The subset of secret key bits that multiply with cube variables during the first round.*

Definition 2 (Auxiliary Variables). *Variables constrained to equal specific key bits during the preprocessing phase, used to control their diffusion through the first θ operation.*

3.3 Automating Dinur et al.'s Technique with MILP

As discussed in Sect. 3.2, the complexity of the cube-attack-like cryptanalysis depends only on two parameters: the number of cube variables and the number of related key bits. To optimize the attack complexity while keeping the number of cube variables fixed, one can strategically select the positions of cube variables in the initial state. This careful positioning may reduce the number of related key bits, thereby improving the overall attack efficiency.

In the method proposed by [DMP+15], the selected cube variables are not optimal, which consequently leads to a non-optimal number of related key bits. To minimize the number of related key bits in cube-attack-like cryptanalysis, the works of [BDL+19] and [SG18] independently propose automated techniques based on MILP modeling.

The method presented in [BDL+19] enforces constraints by requiring all cube variables to be limited within the CP-like kernel. In contrast, the model introduced in [SG18] adopts a more flexible approach, permitting cube variable placement anywhere in the initial state without restriction to the CP-like kernel. This broader selection typically yields superior results.

In our attack framework presented in Sect. 4, we employ the MILP technique introduced by [BDL+19], primarily due to the availability of their implementation. We subsequently compare our results with their findings.

4   Cube-Attack-Like Cryptanalysis Exploiting State Differences

In this section, we introduce our approach to improve cube-attack-like cryptanalysis. We explain how the dependency on related key bits in the superpolies of output bits can be reduced by exploiting state differences.

4.1   Basic Idea

As established in Sect. 3, optimizing the complexity of cube-attack-like cryptanalysis requires minimizing the number of related key bits involved in the attack. One potential research direction involves examining the superpolies of each output bit in the cube summation to identify whether certain output bits depend on fewer related key bits. However, this approach proves ineffective for higher-round analysis due to the strong diffusion properties of the Keccak permutation.

Using our automated tool, we have systematically analyzed the superpolies of all output bits in several keyed variants of Keccak constructions. Our experiments demonstrate that after 5 rounds (requiring 16 cube variables for the attack), nearly all output bits exhibit dependence on almost every related key bit. To be more specific, the polynomial expression of each superpoly contains all related key bits

To obtain superpolies in the output bits that depend on fewer related key bits following cube summation, we observed that when considering two distinct configurations sharing identical cube variables and consequently the same related key bits, differing only in specific predetermined positions of the initial state, the following holds: By performing cube summation separately for each configuration and then computing their difference, the structural similarity between the two configurations causes cancellation of common terms in the superpolies. This differential analysis reveals that certain output bits depend on fewer related key bits compared to their counterparts in the non-differentiated case.

In the following, we present our methodology. To illustrate our technique, we focus on attacking 3-round Keccak-MAC-512.

For visualization clarity, the 3 dimensional state of the Keccak provided in Figure ?? is replaced with the figure presented in the Fig. 1.

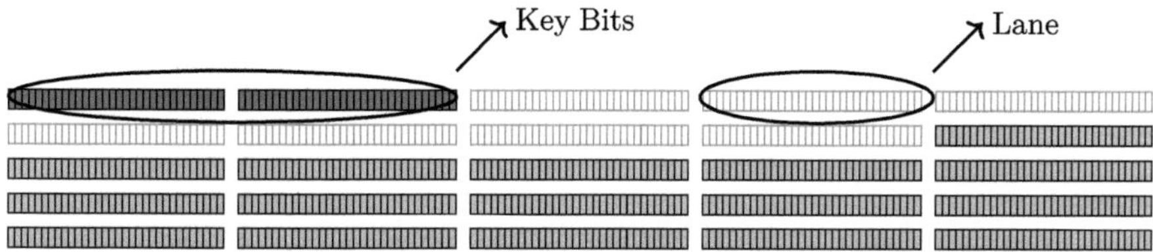

Fig. 1. Visualization of Keccak-MAC-512 state with key bits (red), padding (gray), and lane structure highlighted. The cube variable should be placed in white lanes. Each small square presents 2 bits. (Color figure online)

We begin by outlining the attack procedure for 3-round Keccak-MAC-512. The attack requires 4 cube variables and employs the MILP model from [BDL+19], which identifies 9 related key bits.

The first state in Fig. 2 illustrates the initial state configuration, where cube variables are uniquely colored for identification, and Related key bits are marked in red. As shown in Fig. 2, state (b) demonstrates the spatial relationship between related key bit k_{42} and cube variable v_1 prior to the first χ operation. Their adjacent positioning ensures multiplication during the χ step, as highlighted in the figure.

State (c) in Fig. 2, identifies the bit positions dependent on key bits after cube summation for 3-round Keccak-MAC-512. The 3-round attack serves as an illustrative example due to the limited number of cube variables and related key bits. As can be seen, there are just some limited bit positions with non-zero superpolies and also they depend on specific subsets of related key bits. This simplicity facilitates tracing the attack mechanism, though we emphasize that higher-round scenarios exhibit considerably more complex behavior. We present this simplified case to demonstrate our technique's core principles.

To exploit state differences between two configurations, we proceed as follows. Let first configuration be defined by the initial state shown in Fig. 2. For second configuration, we maintain the same initial state structure and introduce a constant difference at bit position $A_0[0][1][42]$ along with the same column containing related key bit k_{42}. For clarity, we set $A_0[0][1][42] = 0$ in Configuration 1 and $A_0[0][1][42] = 1$ in Configuration 2 (see Fig. 3). This controlled modification enables precise analysis of state propagation differences.

After the θ operation, the constant 1 in Configuration 2 propagates to produce $k_{42} + 1$ in specific bit positions, replacing the original k_{42} term. This modification results in the multiplication of v_1 with $k_{42} + 1$ rather than k_{42} during the subsequent χ operation.

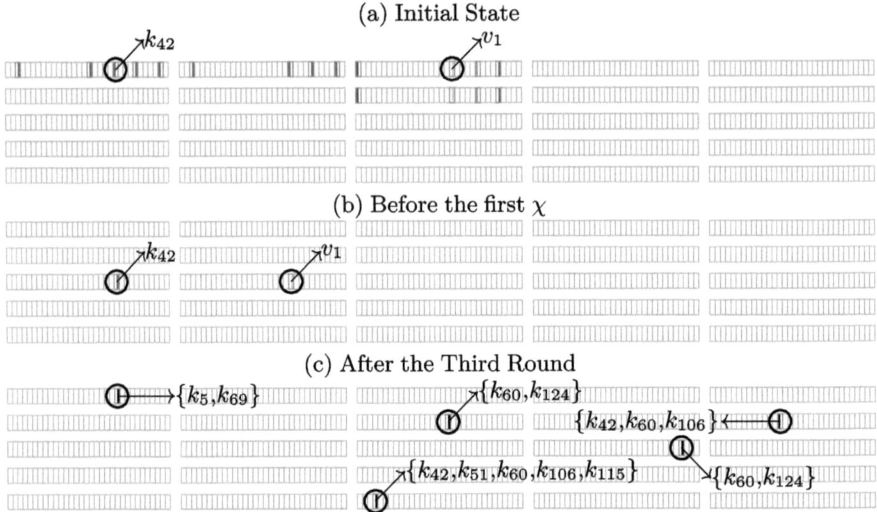

Fig. 2. (a) Initial state configuration for attacking 3-round Keccak-MAC-512. (b) Detailed view of the interaction between k_{42} and v_1. (c) Related key bits in non-zero superpolies in output bit positions after 3-round

Fig. 3. Initial state of second configuration.

By analyzing state differences after the first χ operation, we observe that only the cube variable v_1 appears at bit position $A_0[4][2][43]$. Figure 4 traces these state differences through multiple operations until the final round. The last state of Fig. 4 specifically demonstrates how the non-zero superpolies depend on subsets of related key bits.

As shown in Fig. 4, the superpolies for output bit positions $A_2[4][1][26]$ and $A_2[2][4][7]$ depend only on k_{60} and $\{k_{51}, k_{60}, k_{115}\}$, respectively, whereas in the first case (Fig. 2), these superpolies depend on $\{k_{42}, k_{60}, k_{106}\}$ and $\{k_{42}, k_{51}, k_{60}, k_{106}, k_{115}\}$. Additionally, the superpolies for bit positions $A_2[0][0][43]$, $A_2[2][1][35]$, and $A_2[3][2][57]$ are canceled after state difference exploitation, as they originally depend on $\{k_5, k_{69}\}$, $\{k_{60}, k_{124}\}$, and $\{k_{60}, k_{124}\}$ without such exploitation.

The limited number of cube variables in this analysis enables straightforward verification using computational algebra tools such as SageMath.

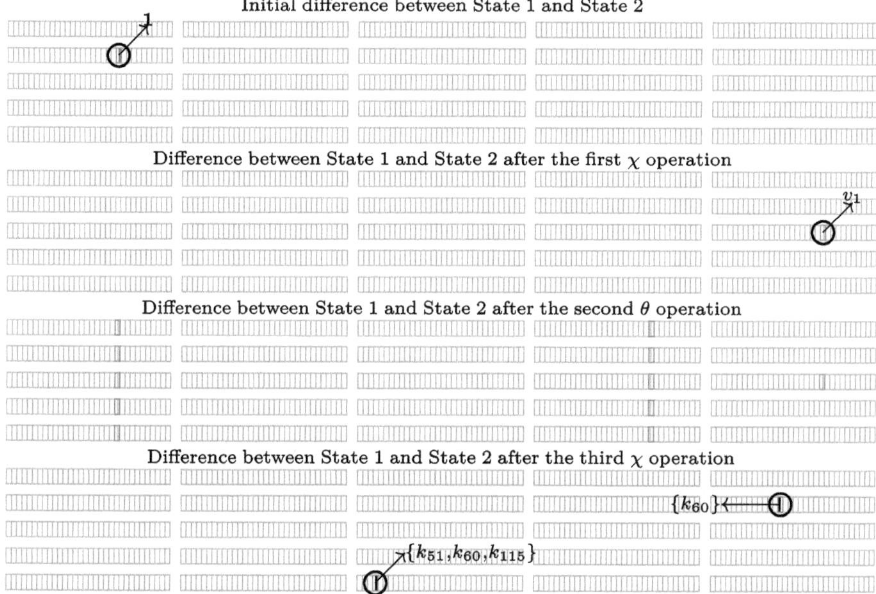

Fig. 4. State difference propagation between Configuration 1 (Fig. 2) and Configuration 2 (Fig. 3) across all rounds.

It should be noted that in our demonstrated examples, we exclusively include terms that contribute to the final superpolies in the cube summation. This focused representation eliminates non-essential components.

To further develop our analysis, we introduce two key concepts central to understanding state differences in our technique:

Definition 3 (Axis Cube Variable). *A cube variable that persists in the state difference pattern following the first χ operation.*

Definition 4 (Axis Related Key). *A related key bit that only multiplies with an axis cube variable after the first χ operation, and differs (one of them is negated in the states after passing θ) in two states for performing the state differences.*

In our proposed technique, the key strategy involves generating two distinct states that, while not identical, are as similar as possible. By doing so, when we compute the difference after independently performing the cube summation on each state, a significant number of terms in the corresponding superpolies cancel out. Consequently, the dependency of the superpolies on a smaller number of related key bits is expected.

As can be observed, the presence of axis cube variables introduces differences between the states. Consequently, the similarity between the two states depends on the propagation of these axis cube variables. This implies that better control over the propagation of axis cube variables leads to greater similarity between the generated states. In the next section, we present a method to control the propagation of axis cube variables during the second round.

It should be noted that our technique employs only a single axis cube variable. This design choice stems from the observation that introducing additional axis cube variables would increase the dissimilarity between the two states.

4.2 Controlling the Propagation of Axis Cube Variable with Modifying the MILP Model Proposed by [BDL+19]

In the configuration setting described in Sect. 4.1, the axis cube variable is generated only at position $A_0[4][2][6]$ at the output of the first round. Therefore, the θ operation in the second round propagates this axis cube variable to 10 additional positions (see Fig. 4). However, leveraging the CP-like kernel property of the θ operation, we can control the propagation by ensuring that axis cube variables remain within the same column after the χ operation at the first round. This configuration allows us to bypass the diffusion effect of θ in the second round. Below, we detail the methodology for achieving this.

To ensure the axis cube variable appears in two bit positions of the same column after the first round, we first analyze the initial positioning of v_0. The Keccak structure guarantees that when axis cube variables are placed in four specific bit positions of the initial state with each pair located in the same column (i.e., $A_0[x_0][y_0][z_0]$, $A_0[x_0][y_1][z_0]$, $A_0[x_1][y_2][z_1]$, and $A_0[x_1][y_3][z_1]$), two axis cube variables will appear in the same column after the first χ operation $(A_{0,\chi}[x_2][y_4][z_2], A_{0,\chi}[x_2][y_5][z_2])$.

As a concrete example, when v_0 is initialized at positions $A_0[2][0][0]$, $A_0[2][1][0]$, $A_0[3][0][34]$, and $A_0[3][1][34]$, it propagates to multiple positions including $A_{0,\chi}[3][1][62]$ and $A_{0,\chi}[3][4][62]$ after the first round. In this configuration, the related key bit k_{65} multiplies with v_0 at position $A_{0,\chi}[3][1][62]$, while k_{60} multiplies with v_0 at $A_{0,\chi}[3][4][62]$. We designate k_{60} and k_{65} as axis related keys.

Crucially, to maintain v_0 exclusively in these output positions after the first round, we must prevent multiplication of axis related keys with any other cube variables. This constraint necessitates modifications to the MILP model proposed by [BDL+19]. The following outlines the key steps in implementing these modifications.

1. Add the following constraints to the MILP model:

$$A_0[x_0][y_0][z_0] = A_0[x_0][y_1][z_0] = A_0[x_1][y_2][z_1] = A_0[x_1][y_3][z_1] = 1$$

2. Modify the constraint from Equation (6) in [BDL+19]:

$$\sum_{x,y,z} A_0[x][y][z] - \sum_{x,z} d[x][z] = 2^{n-1} - 1$$

by excluding the variables $A_0[x_0][y_0][z_0]$, $A_0[x_0][y_1][z_0]$, $A_0[x_1][y_2][z_1]$, $A_0[x_1][y_3][z_1]$, $d[x_0][z_0]$, and $d[x_1][z_1]$.

3. Solve the MILP model to obtain the solution file.
4. Implement the obtained configuration by:
   - Loading the configuration onto a state
   - Applying the transformation $\chi \circ \pi \circ \rho \circ \theta$
5. Verify whether the axis related keys multiply with any non-axis cube variables.
6. If such multiplication occurs:
   - Identify the initial position of the interfering cube variable (e.g., $A_0[x_3][y_6][z_3]$)
   - Add the constraint $A_0[x_3][y_6][z_3] = 0$ to the MILP model
   - Return to Step 3
   Otherwise, output the obtained configuration as the final result.

The modified MILP model typically results in a greater number of related key bits compared to the conventional approach. Nevertheless, despite this increase in related key bits, our experiments reveal significant outcomes.

To clarify our technique, we present a concrete example for 4-round Keccak-MAC-512. We focus on the 4-round case because, in the 3-round scenario, our controlled propagation of the axis cube variable results in complete cancellation of all terms in the superpolies of the output bits. Consequently, for the 3-round case our technique becomes independent of any related key bits, making the 4-round case more illustrative for demonstrating our key-dependent approach.

Fig. 5 illustrates the initial states of the two configurations obtained from our modified MILP model following the aforementioned steps. For these configurations, the model yields a minimum of 19 related key bits, which represents a 3-fold increase compared to the conventional attack proposed by [BDL+19].

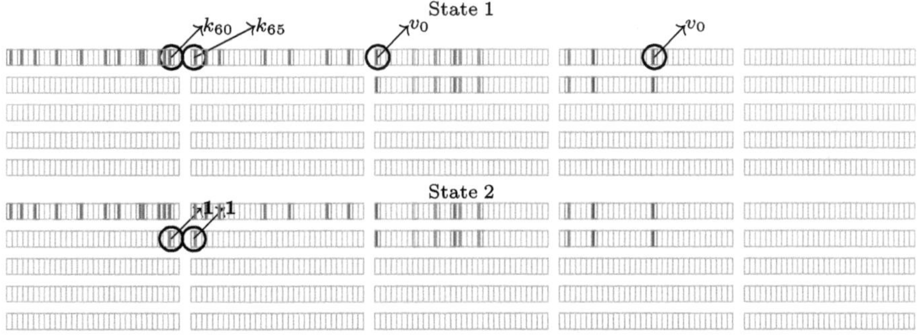

Fig. 5. Initial states of the two configurations to attack 4-round of Keccak-MAC-512, the axis cube variable is v_0 and the axis related key bits are k_{60} and k_{65}.

Figure 6 traces the evolution of state differences for the configurations shown in Fig. 5 through successive rounds of operations. The final state of Fig. 6 specifically illustrates how the non-zero superpolies depend on particular subsets of

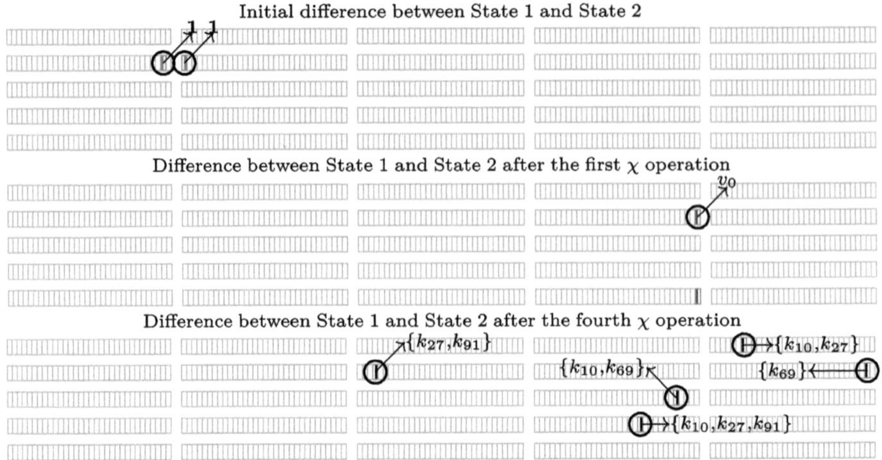

Fig. 6. State difference propagation between Configurations in (Fig. 5) across some rounds.

related key bits, demonstrating the controlled propagation achieved by our technique.

As shown in the final state of Fig. 6, several state positions demonstrate particularly efficient key dependence. Specifically, the superpolies for positions $A_{3,\chi}[4][0][12]$, $A_{0,\chi}[2][1][7]$, $A_{0,\chi}[4][1][60]$, $A_{0,\chi}[3][2][55]$, and $A_{0,\chi}[3][3][41]$ each depend on no more than three related key bits: $\{k_{10}, k_{27}\}$, $\{k_{27}, k_{91}\}$, $\{k_{69}\}$, $\{k_{10}, k_{69}\}$, and $\{k_{10}, k_{27}, k_{91}\}$ respectively. This constrained key dependence highlights a significant advantage of our technique.

To clarify our technique, we summarize the procedure in the Algorithm 1:

4.3   Compute Limitations

In the technique we present, we have computationally verified the improvements. This required developing a dedicated tool capable of recovering all terms in all superpolies.

As evident, the number of terms grows exponentially with additional rounds, making superpoly recovery computationally infeasible beyond 4-round given our available computing server. However, we observed that tracking all terms is unnecessary and a significant portion can be eliminated to reduce computational overhead.

Algorithm 1: Automated cube-attack-like Cryptanalysis with Exploiting State Differences

---

    Input: : Initialized keyed Keccak construction
    Output:: Candidate secret key values

1 Initialization Phase;
2   Load initial state with cube variables and related keys obtained from MILP model in [BDL+19];
3   Designate axis cube variable and axis related key based on Section 1.;
4   Configure auxiliary variables:;
5   Align in same columns as related keys;
6   Enforce non-multiplication with cube variables in first round;

7 Analysis Phase;
8   Configure two different initial states;
9   Identify non-zero superpolies with minimal key dependency using proposed tool;
10   Initialize sets:;
11 $G \leftarrow$ All guessing key values;
12 $A \leftarrow$ All auxiliary variable values;

13 Preprocessing Phase;
14 for *each* $g \in G$ **do**
15   Compute differential cube summation for both initial states;
16   Store result in lookup table L indexed by summation value;

17 Online Phase;
18 for *each* $a \in A$ **do**
19   Compute differential cube summation S_a;
20   **if** S_a *exists in* L **then**
21   Retrieve candidate (g, a) pairs where $L[g] = S_a$;

According to Eq. 2, computing the superpoly requires only the polynomial expression of $t \cdot P_t(x)$. As this section explains, this includes exclusively terms containing the term t. More precisely, recovering $t \cdot P_t(x)$ requires only terms containing all cube variables; other terms cancel out during cube summation.

The χ operation's algebraic structure implies that the degree at round r is 2^r. Since in cube-attack-like cryptanalysis the first round is linearized, we only need to retain terms containing 2^{r-1} cube variables in round r. Terms with fewer variables do not contribute to $t \cdot P_t(x)$. To be more specific, the Boolean Algebraic Normal Form of χ can be represented as Eq. 3, where b_i represents the output bit corresponding to input a_i:

$$b_i = a_i + (a_{i+1} + 1) \cdot a_{i+2} \tag{3}$$

As evident from Eq. 3, only the product term $a_{i+1} \cdot a_{i+2}$ generates terms containing 2^{r-1} cube variables in the r-th round. Consequently, for rounds beyond the first (which is linearized), the χ operation can be simplified to $b_i = a_{i+1} \cdot a_{i+2}$ while maintaining analytical precision. The original χ formulation must be retained for the first round.

By implementing these optimizations, we significantly reduced the computational complexity of our tool. This enabled successful recovery of superpolies for all output bits up to 5-round in structures like Keccak-MAC-512, leveraging the available degree of freedom and our computing resources.

5   Applications

In this section, we evaluate our technique on four Keccak-based constructions: Keccak-MAC-512, Keccak-MAC-384 and Ketje Minor. For Ketje Minor, we successfully verify the improvements up to 4 rounds, while for the other variants the improvements extend to 5 rounds.

In the following, we provide detailed evaluation results for keyed Keccak variants: Keccak-MAC-512, Keccak-MAC-384 and Ketje Minor. In Fig. 7 red positions represent key bits; light gray areas indicate capacity bits for MAC structures and padded or encoded bits for Ketje structures; white positions correspond to nonce or message bits. This color scheme explicitly determines that cube variables must be placed exclusively in white areas.

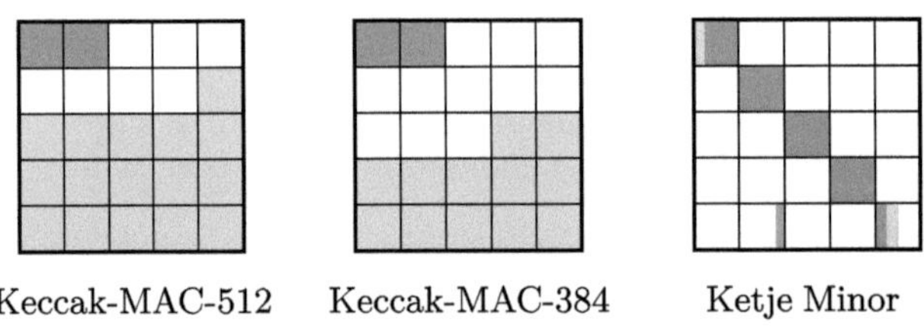

Fig. 7. The degrees of freedom in Keccak-MAC-512, Keccak-MAC-384, Ketje Minor.

All computations were performed on a server with the following specifications: **CPU:** Dual AMD EPYC 7302 processors (32 physical cores, 64 threads) operating at 3.0 GHz base frequency with 256 MB shared L3 cache, **Memory:** 503 GB of system RAM, **Storage:** 455 GB NVMe scratch disk, Operating System: Ubuntu 22.04 LTS, Compiler: g++ version 11.4.0 with -O3 optimization. We have implemented our tool in C++.

5.1   Application to 5-Round Keccak-MAC-512

Applying the automated technique from [BDL+19] to 5-round Keccak-MAC-512 yields 30 related key bits, requiring guessing of 15 key bits during preprocessing phase and 15 auxiliary variables in online phase. The time complexity for recovering these 30 related key bits is $2^{15} \times 2^{16} = 2^{31}$ for both preprocessing and online phases, with a total complexity of 2^{32} and memory complexity of 2^{15}.

For complete key recovery, we exploit the symmetric property of the permutation along the z-axis. By considering all i-bit rotations ($0 \leq i < 64$) in the z-axis, we focus on the case where $0 \leq i < 4$. This allows recovery of 120 independent key bits out of the total 128-bit key, leaving the remaining 8 bits for exhaustive search (2^8 complexity). Consequently, the total time complexity for full 128-bit key recovery becomes $4 \times 2^{32} + 2^8 \approx 2^{34}$, with memory complexity 2^{15}. The data complexity, because of doing cube summation over 15 auxiliary variables is $2^{15} \times 2^{16} = 2^{31}$.

To implement our technique, we first select the bit positions $A_0[2][0][0]$, $A_0[2][1][0]$, $A_0[3][0][34]$, and $A_0[3][1][34]$ to place the axis cube variable v_0. We designate k_{60} (located at $A_0[0][0][60]$) and k_{65} (located at $A_0[1][0][1]$) as the axis related keys. Following the methodology outlined in Sect. 4.2, our MILP model generated a configuration involving 33 related key bits.

For correct state difference computation in both preprocessing and online phases, we maintain fixed positions for the axis related keys across both phases. We partition the remaining related key bits into two distinct sets 18 guessed key bits for the preprocessing phase and 17 auxiliary variables for the online phase as follows:

$$\begin{aligned}
\text{guessed keys} &= \{k_{60}, k_{65}, k_5, k_{18}, k_{25}, k_{27}, k_{33}, k_{41}, k_{43}, \\
&\quad k_{50}, k_{68}, k_{76}, k_{84}, k_{92}, k_{106}, k_{114}, k_{122}, k_{124}\} \\
\text{keys corresponding to auxiliary variables} &= \{k_{60}, k_{65}, k_{10}, k_{19}, k_{26}, \\
&\quad k_{28}, k_{34}, k_{42}, k_{49}, k_{58}, k_{66}, k_{69}, k_{83}, k_{91}, k_{98}, k_{107}, k_{121}\}
\end{aligned} \tag{4}$$

Our analysis of state differences reveals distinct key dependencies in each phase in the preprocessing phase the bit position $A_{4,\chi}[4][3][15]$ exhibits dependence on only four key bits: $\{k_{27}, k_{76}, k_{92}, k_{106}\}$ and in the online Phase the corresponding bit position shows dependence on eight key bits corresponding to auxiliary variables: $\{k_{19}, k_{26}, k_{28}, k_{34}, k_{42}, k_{66}, k_{98}, k_{121}\}$.

Our cube summation process, operating on two similar states, incurs a computational cost of 2^{17} (compared to 2^{16} for single-state summation). The preprocessing phase requires $2^4 \times 2^{17} = 2^{21}$ operations for the 4 key bits. The online phase follows the same principle as the preprocessing phase. This results in a base of $2^8 \times 2^{17} = 2^{25}$ operations for testing all combinations of the 8 key bits.

Since the lookup table in the preprocessing phase is constructed for a single bit ($A_{4,\chi}[4][3][15]$), false positives are mitigated by repeating the cube summation over 2^4 distinct plaintexts. Given that the bit $A_{4,\chi}[4][3][15]$ depends on four key bits in the preprocessing phase and eight key bits in the online phase, the process must be repeated for eight distinct plaintexts, with the corresponding results stored in the lookup table. Consequently, the time complexity in the preprocessing phase is $8 \times 2^{21} = 2^{24}$, while in the online phase it is $8 \times 2^{25} = 2^{28}$.

The described process recovers 12 related key bits initially. Through 9 rotations in the z-axis, we extend this to recover 108 key bits, with the remaining 20 bits determined via exhaustive search (2^{20} complexity). The complete attack requires:

- Time complexity: $9 \times (2^{24} + 2^{28}) + 2^{20} \approx 2^{31.2}$
- Memory complexity: $8 \times 2^4 \approx 2^7$
- Data complexity: $8 \times 2^8 \times 2^{17} \approx 2^{28}$

We emphasize that this process admits multiple optimization opportunities through different configurations. Systematic examination of alternative axis cube variable placements in the initial state may yield improved complexity results. Table 2 presents the configuration parameters used in our 5-round attack on Keccak-MAC-512.

Table 2. Configuration to attack on 5-round Keccak-MAC-512

Axis cube variable

$A_0[2][0][0] = A_0[2][1][0] = A[3][0][34] = A[3][1][34] = v_0$

Axis related Keys

$A[0][0][60] = k_{60}, A[1][0][1] = k_{65}$

Bit positions that differ in two states

$A_0[0][1][60], A_0[1][1][1]$

Cube variables

$A_0[2][0][14] = A_0[2][1][14] = v_1, A_0[2][0][22] = A_0[2][1][22] = v_2, A_0[2][0][23] = A_0[2][1][23] = v_3,$

$A_0[2][0][29] = A_0[2][1][29] = v_4, A_0[2][0][37] = A_0[2][1][37] = v_5, A_0[2][0][38] = A_0[2][1][38] = v_6,$

$A_0[2][0][45] = A_0[2][1][45] = v_7, A_0[2][0][53] = A_0[2][1][53] = v_8, A_0[3][0][3] = A_0[3][1][3] = v_9,$

$A_0[3][0][11] = A_0[3][1][11] = v_{10}, A_0[3][0][12] = A_0[3][1][12] = v_{11}, A_0[3][0][19] = A_0[3][1][19] = v_{12}$

$A_0[3][0][26] = A_0[3][1][26] = v_{13}, A_0[3][0][27] = A_0[3][1][27] = v_{14}, A_0[3][0][35] = A_0[3][1][35] = v_{15}$

Other Related key bits

$k_{19}, k_{26}, k_{27}, k_{28}, k_{34}, k_{42}, k_{66}, k_{76}, k_{92}, k_{98}, k_{106}, k_{121}$

Guessed Key bits

$k_{27}, k_{76}, k_{92}, k_{106}$

Auxiliary variables

$A_0[0][1][19] = a_0, A_0[0][1][26] = a_1, A_0[0][1][28] = a_2, A_0[0][1][34] = a_3, A_0[0][1][42] = a_4,$

$A_0[1][1][2] = a_5, A_0[1][1][34] = a_6, A_0[1][1][57] = a_7,$

5.2 Application to 5-Round Keccak-MAC-384

Applying the automated MILP technique from [BDL+19] to 5-round Keccak-MAC-384 yields a configuration with 15 related key bits.

The preprocessing phase requires $2^7 \times 2^{16} = 2^{23}$ operations, while the online phase needs $2^8 \times 2^{16} = 2^{24}$ computations, yielding a combined time complexity of $2^{24.5}$. For full 128-bit key recovery, we employ 8 rotational variants to extract 120 bits plus 2^8 exhaustive search, achieving the time complexity $7 \times 2^{24.5} + 2^{23} \approx 2^{27.4}$, the memory complexity 2^7 and the data complexity $2^{8+16} = 2^{24}$.

Following Sect. 4.2's methodology, our MILP model generated a 19 related key bits configuration. The preprocessing phase revealed the bit position $A_{4,\chi}[3][1][22]$ dependents on $\{k_3, k_{118}\}$, resulting in a preprocessing cost of $2^2 \times 2^{17} = 2^{19}$ operations.

In the online phase, the corresponding bit position depends on k_{39}, k_{96}, k_{106}, resulting in a computational cost of $2^3 \times 2^{17} = 2^{20}$ operations. Following the explanation in Sect. 5.1, the total time complexity for recovering 5 key bits is $3 \times (2^{19} + 2^{20}) \approx 2^{22.1}$. For full key recovery, the complexity increases to $22 \times 2^{22.1} + 2^{18} \approx 2^{26.5}$, with a memory complexity of $3 \times 2^2 = 2^{3.5}$ and a data complexity of $3 \times 2^{3+17} = 2^{21.5}$.

Table 3 summarizes the configuration parameters for our 5-round attack on Keccak-MAC-384.

Table 3. Configuration to attack on 5-round Keccak-MAC-384

Axis cube variable
$A_0[1][1][59] = A_0[1][2][59] = A[4][0][19] = A[4][1][19] = v_0$
Axis related Keys
$A[1][0][35] = k_{99}, A[1][0][60] = k_{124}$
Bit positions that differ in two states
$A_0[1][1][35], A_0[1][1][60]$
Cube variables
$A_0[2][1][1] = v_1, A_0[2][2][1] = v_1, A_0[2][0][4] = v_2, A_0[2][1][4] = v_3, A_0[2][2][4] = v_2 + v_3,$
$A_0[2][0][7] = v_4, A_0[2][1][7] = v_5, A_0[2][2][7] = v_4 + v_5, A_0[2][0][10] = v_6, A_0[2][2][10] = v_6,$
$A_0[2][0][13] = v_7, A_0[2][2][13] = v_7, A_0[2][1][37] = v_8, A_0[2][2][37] = v_8, A_0[2][0][40] = v_9,$
$A_0[2][2][40] = v_9, A_0[2][0][43] = v_{10}, A_0[2][2][43] = v_{10}, A_0[4][0][0] = v_{11}, A_0[4][1][0] = v_{11}$
$A_0[4][0][16] = v_{12}, A_0[4][1][16] = v_{12}, A_0[4][0][22] = v_{13}, A_0[4][1][22] = v_{13}, A_0[4][0][26] = v_{14},$
$A_0[4][1][26] = v_{14}, A_0[4][0][42] = v_{15}, A_0[4][1][42] = v_{15}$
Other Related key bits
$k_3, k_{39}, k_{42}, k_{96}$
Guessed Key bits
k_3, k_{42}
Auxiliary variables
$A_0[0][1][39] = a_0, A_0[1][1][32] = a_1$

5.3 Application to 4-Round Ketje Minor

For Ketje Minor, our computational resources were insufficient to recover 5-round superpolies due to RAM limitations. When applying the automated MILP technique from [BDL+19] to 4-round Ketje Minor, we obtained a configuration involving 21 related key bits. Through analysis, we identified output bit positions with reduced key-bit dependencies, most notably $A_{4,\chi}[1][3][4]$, which depends on only 10 key bits: $\{k_6, k_{43}, k_{56}, k_{59}, k_{65}, k_{68}, k_{69}, k_{77}, k_{78}, k_{106}\}$.

By dividing the 10 related key bits into 5 guessing key bits and 5 auxiliary variables, both preprocessing and online phases require $5 \times 2^5 \times 2^8 \approx 2^{15.3}$ operations each, resulting in a combined time complexity of $2^{16.3}$. For complete 128-bit key recovery, we utilize 12 rotational variants to recover 120 key bits combined with a 2^8 exhaustive search, yielding final complexities of: time $12 \times 2^{16.3} + 2^8 \approx 2^{20}$, memory $5 \times 2^5 \approx 2^{7.3}$, and data $5 \times 2^{5+8} = 2^{15.3}$.

For 4-round, we followed the technique proposed in Sect. 4 and observed that the bit position $A_{4,\chi}[3][3][7]$ dependents only on $\{k_{65}, k_{69}\}$. The preprocessing complexity to recover 1 guessing-key is $2 \times 2^9 = 2^{10}$, also the same for recovering 1 auxiliary variable in the online phase.

The total complexity for full key recovery is $58 \times (2^{10} + 2^{10}) + 2^{12} \approx 2^{16.8}$. The memory and data complexities are 2 and data $2^{1+9} = 2^{10}$, respectively.

Table 4 summarizes the configuration parameters for our 4-round attack on Ketje Minor.

Table 4. Configuration to attack on 4-round Ketje Minor

Axis cube variable
$A_0[2][0][0] = A_0[2][1][0] = v_0$
Axis related Key
$A[2][2][18] = k_{74}$
Bit positions that differ in two states
$A_0[2][0][18]$
Cube variables
$A_0[2][1][9] = v_1, A_0[2][3][9] = v_1, A_0[2][1][28] = v_2, A_0[2][3][28] = v_2, A_0[2][1][31] = v_3,$ $A_0[2][3][31] = v_3, A_0[4][0][29] = v_4, A_0[4][1][29] = v_5, A_0[4][2][29] = v_6,$ $A_0[4][3][29] = v_4 + v_5 + v_6, A_0[4][1][30] = v_7, A_0[4][3][30] = v_7$
Other Related key bits
k_{65}, k_{69}
Guessed Key bits
k_{65}
Auxiliary variables
$A_0[2][0][13] = a_0$

6   Conclusion and Future Works

In this paper, we have presented an improved cube-attack-like cryptanalysis technique that reduces output-bit dependency on related key bits, leading to more efficient attacks against Keccak-based constructions. Our method, building upon [BDL+19], demonstrates practical advantages through comprehensive attacks on 5-round versions of Keccak-MAC-512, Keccak-MAC-384 and 4-round of Ketje Minor. While current implementations are limited to 5-round, the technique shows potential for extension to 6-round given enhanced computational resources or tool improvement.

Future work may focus on:

- Extending the attack to higher rounds through tool optimizations and enhanced computational resources;
- Theoretical analysis of superpoly independence from specific key bits to establish formal security bounds, As the experiments suggest, complexity improvement on a higher number of rounds is expected;
- In all of our experiments, we also observed that none of the superpolies depend on axis related keys. Theoretically proving this or understanding the underlying logic may open a new research direction.

References

BDH+17. Bertoni, G., Daemen, J., Hoffert, S., Peeters, M., Assche, G.V., Keer, R.V.: Farfalle: parallel permutation-based cryptography. IACR Trans. Symmetric Cryptol. **2017**(4), 1–38 (2017). https://tosc.iacr.org/index.php/ToSC/article/view/801, https://doi.org/10.13154/tosc.v2017.i4.1-38

BDL+19. Bi, W., Dong, X., Li, Z., Zong, R., Wang, X.: MILP-aided cube-attack-like cryptanalysis on keccak keyed modes. Des. Codes Cryptogr. **87**(6), 1271–1296 (2019). https://doi.org/10.1007/S10623-018-0526-X

BDP+11. Berton, G., Daemen, J., Peeters, M., Assche, G.V., Keer, R.V.: The keccak reference (2011). http://keccak.noekeon.org

BDP+16a. Berton, G., Daemen, J., Peeters, M., Assche, G.V., Keer, R.V.: Ketje v2: A Submission to the CAESAR Competition (2016). CAESAR Competition Round 3 Submission (2016). http://competitions.cr.yp.to/round3/ketjev2.pdf

BDP+16b. Berton, G., Daemen, J., Peeters, M., Assche, G.V., Keer, R.V.: Keyak v2: A Submission to the CAESAR Competition (2016). CAESAR Competition Round 3 Submission (2016). https://keccak.team/files/Keyakv2-doc2.2-diff.pdf

DEMS21. Dobraunig, C., Eichlseder, M., Mendel, F., Schläffer, M.: Ascon v1.2: lightweight authenticated encryption and hashing. J. Cryptol. **34**(3), 1–42 (2021). https://doi.org/10.1007/s00145-021-09398-9

DHAK18. Daemen, J., Hoffert, S., Assche, G.V., Keer, R.V.: The design of Xoodoo and Xoofff. IACR Trans. Symmetric Cryptol. **2018**, 1–38 (2018). https://doi.org/10.13154/tosc.v2018.i4.1-38

DHP+20. Daemen, J., Hoffert, S., Peeters, M., Assche, G.V., Keer, R.V.: Xoodyak: a lightweight cryptographic scheme. IACR Trans. Symmetric Cryptol. **2020**(S1), 60–87 (2020). https://doi.org/10.13154/tosc.v2020.iS1.60-87

DMP+15. Dinur, I., Morawiecki, P., Pieprzyk, J., Srebrny, M., Straus, M.: Cube attacks and cube-attack-like cryptanalysis on the round-reduced keccak sponge function. In: Oswald, E., Fischlin, M. (eds.) EUROCRYPT 2015. LNCS, vol. 9056, pp. 733–761. Springer, Heidelberg (2015). https://doi.org/10.1007/978-3-662-46800-5_28

DS09. Dinur, I., Shamir, A.: Cube attacks on tweakable black box polynomials. In: Joux, A. (ed.) EUROCRYPT 2009. LNCS, vol. 5479, pp. 278–299. Springer, Heidelberg (2009). https://doi.org/10.1007/978-3-642-01001-9_16

HWX+17. Huang, S., Wang, X., Xu, G., Wang, M., Zhao, J.: Conditional cube attack on reduced-round keccak sponge function. In: Coron, J.-S., Nielsen, J.B. (eds.) EUROCRYPT 2017. LNCS, vol. 10211, pp. 259–288. Springer, Cham (2017). https://doi.org/10.1007/978-3-319-56614-6_9

Lai94. Lai, X.: Higher order derivatives and differential cryptanalysis. In: Communications and Cryptography: Two Sides of One Tapestry, pp. 227–233. Springer, Cham (1994). https://doi.org/10.1007/978-1-4615-2694-0_23

LBDW17. Li, Z., Bi, W., Dong, X., Wang, X.: Improved conditional cube attacks on keccak keyed modes with MILP method. In: Takagi, T., Peyrin, T. (eds.) ASIACRYPT 2017. LNCS, vol. 10624, pp. 99–127. Springer, Cham (2017). https://doi.org/10.1007/978-3-319-70694-8_4

LDB+19. Li, Z., Dong, X., Bi, W., Jia, K., Wang, X., Meier, W.: New conditional cube attack on Keccak keyed modes. IACR Trans. Symmetric Cryptol. **2019**(2), 94–124 (2019). https://doi.org/10.13154/tosc.v2019.i2.94-124

Nat23. National Institute of Standards and Technology (NIST): Lightweight Cryptography Standardization Process: NIST Selects Ascon. NIST Website, 07 February 2023. https://csrc.nist.gov/News/2023/lightweight-cryptography-nist-selects-ascon

SG18. Song, L., Guo, J.: Cube-attack-like cryptanalysis of round-reduced keccak using MILP. IACR Trans. Symmetric Cryptol. **2018**(3), 182–214 (2018). https://doi.org/10.13154/tosc.v2018.i3.182-214

SGSL18. Song, L., Guo, J., Shi, D., Ling, S.: New MILP modeling: improved conditional cube attacks on keccak-based constructions. In: Peyrin, T., Galbraith, S. (eds.) ASIACRYPT 2018. LNCS, vol. 11273, pp. 65–95. Springer, Cham (2018). https://doi.org/10.1007/978-3-030-03329-3_3

VV23. Vaziri, M., Velichkov, V.: Conditional cube key recovery attack on round-reduced Xoodyak. In: Zhou, J., et al. (eds.) ACNS 2023. LNCS, vol. 13907, pp. 43–62. Springer, Cham (2023). https://doi.org/10.1007/978-3-031-41181-6_3

WY05. Wang, X., Yu, H.: How to break MD5 and other hash functions. In: Cramer, R. (ed.) EUROCRYPT 2005. LNCS, vol. 3494, pp. 19–35. Springer, Heidelberg (2005). https://doi.org/10.1007/11426639_2

WYY05. Wang, X., Yin, Y.L., Yu, H.: Finding collisions in the full SHA-1. In: Shoup, V. (ed.) CRYPTO 2005. LNCS, vol. 3621, pp. 17–36. Springer, Heidelberg (2005). https://doi.org/10.1007/11535218_2

ZLD+20. Zhou, H., Li, Z., Dong, X., Jia, K., Meier, W.: Practical key-recovery attacks on round-reduced Ketje Jr, Xoodoo-AE and Xoodyak. Comput. J. **63**(8), 1231–1246 (2020). https://doi.org/10.1093/comjnl/bxz152

Differential and Linear Analyses of DIZY Through MILP Modeling

Murat Burhan İlter[1]([envelope]) [iD], Onur Koçak[2], Orhun Kara[2,3] [iD], and Fatih Sulak[4] [iD]

[1] Aselsan Inc., Ankara, Turkey
`ilter.muratb@gmail.com`
[2] TÜBİTAK BİLGEM, Gebze, Kocaeli, Turkey
`onur.kocak@tubitak.gov.tr`, `orhunkara@iyte.edu.tr`
[3] Department of Mathematics, İzmir Institute of Technology (IZTECH),
İzmir, Turkey
[4] Department of Mathematics, Atılım University, Ankara, Turkey
`fatih.sulak@atilim.edu.tr`

Abstract. In this work, we present the first independent security analysis of DIZY, a recently proposed ultra-lightweight stream cipher with two variants: DIZY-80 and DIZY-128. Our analysis focuses on DIZY's resistance to linear and differential cryptanalysis. We employ a formal technique known as Mixed Integer Linear Programming (MILP), which enables us to model the internal structure of DIZY and search for characteristics that describe how XOR differences or linear masks propagate through the cipher. Specifically, we construct such characteristics to evaluate how many S-boxes become "active" during keystream generation, as this number directly affects the cipher's resistance to these attacks. Contrary to the designers' claim that any linear or differential characteristic over 8 rounds must involve at least 20 active S-boxes in DIZY-80 and 22 in DIZY-128, we identify characteristics with only 18 differentially or linearly active S-boxes and 20 linearly active S-boxes, respectively.

We mount two distinguishing attacks on each cipher. Our 3-round linear distinguishing attack requires 2^{23} bits of keystream, while the 4-round version requires 2^{35} bits for DIZY-128 and DIZY-80, respectively. Our 2-round differential resynchronization attacks succeed using only the first four bytes of keystream data from approximately 2^{30} and 2^{26} different initializations with chosen initialization vectors (IVs) for DIZY-128 and DIZY-80, respectively. While these attacks do not compromise the full 15-round version of the cipher, they provide valuable insights into the design of DIZY and contribute to a deeper understanding of the security requirements of its diffusion layer.

Keywords: Differential attack · Cryptanalysis · Linear attack · Stream Cipher · DIZY · Mixed Integer Linear Programming (MILP) · Block Cipher

O. Kara and F. Sulak—The authors are partially supported by TÜBİTAK 1001 Project under the grant number 124F270.

E. Savas et al. (Eds.): LightSec 2025, LNCS 16216, pp. 285–305, 2026.
https://doi.org/10.1007/978-3-032-15541-2_16

1 Introduction

Block ciphers are widely favored in ultra-lightweight applications, due to their relatively higher resistance to cryptanalytic attacks compared to stream ciphers, as demonstrated in the literature. Several ultra-lightweight stream ciphers, such as Lizard [1], Sprout [2], and Fruit-80 [3], have been subject to successful attacks. Lizard is broken by an internal state recovery attack with a total complexity of 2^{54} [4]. Sprout is proposed to resist internal state recovery trade-off attacks [5–7] but it has undergone extensive cryptanalysis, including practical attacks [8–11], and its successor, Plantlet [12], has also faced multiple cryptanalytic efforts [13–16]. Fruit-80 inherits some of these vulnerabilities as well [13,14]. Other notable additions to the family of ultra-lightweight stream ciphers include LILLE, introduced in 2018 [17], and DIZY, introduced in 2023 [18]. A keystream distinguishing attack has been reported on LILLE [19], whereas no independent cryptanalysis of DIZY has been published to date, not even for reduced-round versions.

DIZY comes in two variants: DIZY-80 and DIZY-128, with key sizes of 80 and 128 bits, respectively. Both versions use a 15-round state update function and are notable for their extremely compact hardware implementation. For instance, DIZY-80 and DIZY-128 require only 1010 and 1297 gate equivalents (GE), respectively, when implemented using the TSMC 65 nm CMOS process, and just 791 and 920 GE in a 45 nm setting [18,20], making DIZY one of the smallest symmetric ciphers available. Given this minimal hardware footprint, assessing DIZY's security is essential, especially in light of the absence of any previously published independent cryptanalysis.

In this work, we analyze the DIZY variants using *Mixed Integer Linear Programming (MILP)* to construct linear and differential characteristics. MILP has been widely used in the cryptanalysis of lightweight ciphers [21–23]. By modeling the cipher's internal structure as a system of linear constraints, we use Gurobi [24] to search for optimal characteristics. In the context of DIZY, this corresponds to finding the minimum number of active S-boxes with respect to both linear cryptanalysis [25] and differential cryptanalysis [26].

Due to DIZY's relatively large internal state and the use of 5×5 S-boxes per round, the MILP models contain more constraints and variables in bitwise formulations compared to those for typical lightweight ciphers. To address this issue, we adopt the XOR modeling technique proposed in [27], along with the generalized form introduced in [28], which we adapt to reduce the number of variables.

Using our MILP models, we construct new *linear and differential characteristics* for the state permutation reduced to 8 rounds of DIZY. To the best of our knowledge, these are the first characteristics reported for the 8-round DIZY.

DIZY-80: Our differential and linear characteristics involve only 18 active S-boxes, thereby contradicting the designers' claim that there are at least 20 active S-boxes over 8 rounds in both types of attacks [18]. Our linear characteristic has a bias of approximately 2^{-37}, and our differential characteristic has a probability of approximately 2^{-72}. These characteristics are illustrated in Tables 8 and 10.

DIZY-128: The linear characteristic involves only 20 active S-boxes, which contradicts the designers' claim of having at least 22 active S-boxes over 8 rounds. Our differential characteristic involves 22 active S-boxes, thereby aligning with the designers' claim over 8 rounds. The corresponding characteristics are detailed in Tables 9 and 11, respectively.

We also present two distinguishing attacks for each variant of DIZY.

- **3- and 4-round linear distinguishing attacks:** We restrict our characteristics to input and output bits of linear masks that directly appear in the keystream, ensuring all involved bits lie within consecutive 32-bit keystream words. Our 3-round and 4-round linear distinguishing attacks require 2^{23} and 2^{35} bits of keystream with biases 2^{-9} and 2^{-15} for DIZY-128 and DIZY-80, respectively.
- **2-round differential resynchronization attacks:** We construct a 4-round differential characteristic with probability 2^{-24}, enabling a 2-round resynchronization attack on DIZY-80 with chosen IVs using approximately 2^{26} initializations to distinguish it from a random generator. Similarly, for DIZY-128, we derive a 4-round differential characteristic with probability 2^{-28} and mount a 2-round resynchronization attack by incorporating suitable differences into the IV, requiring about 2^{30} initializations.

Although our distinguishers demonstrate non-random behavior in reduced-round DIZY-80 and DIZY-128, extending them into full key-recovery or internal-state recovery attacks remains an open challenge, primarily due to DIZY's specialized keystream generation mode [18].

The rest of the paper is organized as follows. Section 2 describes the DIZY-80 and DIZY-128 ciphers. Section 3 presents our MILP modeling approach. The characteristics are described in Sect. 4, followed by distinguishing attacks in Sect. 5. Section 6 provides a discussion about the matrices of DIZY. We conclude the paper in Sect. 7.

2   Brief Description of DIZY

The DIZY stream cipher, introduced in [18], has two variants: DIZY-80 and DIZY-128, which use 80-bit and 128-bit keys, respectively[1].

Although DIZY is a stream cipher, its design philosophy is rooted in the Substitution-Permutation Network (SPN) structure commonly used in block ciphers. It incorporates round constants instead of round key additions. The state update function operates over 15 such rounds. Table 1 summarizes the sizes and counts of the core components used in the cipher.

TPP (Truncated Pseudorandom Permutation) mode is a method of keystream generation [18]. In general, the process of extracting a portion of the

---

[1] The original paper contains an erroneous entry in the matrix for the 80-bit version of DIZY, which was later corrected in [29]. In this work, we present the corrected version of the matrix used in DIZY-80.

Table 1. The building blocks of DIZY

Version	DIZY-80	DIZY-128
State Size	120 bit	160 bit
Number of S-boxes	24	32
Sizes of M_{30} & M_{40}	30×30	40×40
Number of Matrices	4	4
Subblock size	15 bit	20 bit

internal state as the output after updating the previous internal state via a bijective function is referred to as the TPP mode. This mode is used for keystream generation, where the internal state is updated through a permutation, typically constructed using an SPN structure. After each update, an output function selects specific bits from the internal state to produce the current keystream word.

Formally, let the update function of the keystream be an s-bit permutation $\mathcal{P}$. That is, the next state is given by $S_i = \mathcal{P}(S_{i-1})$, where S_i denotes the internal state at step i. The output is generated by truncating certain bits of S_i. In this sense, the TPP mode can be viewed as the composition of the permutation $\mathcal{P}$ and a truncation function. The permutation $\mathcal{P}$ can be regarded as a secure block cipher without a key schedule.

DIZY operates in TPP mode. After completing 15 iterations of its SPN-based round function, 32 bits are extracted from the internal state to produce the keystream word. Specifically, the output consists of the least significant bit of the $3i$-th bit of the internal state, for $i = 0, \ldots, 31$. Then, 15 additional rounds are applied to the updated state before the next 32 bits are extracted, and the process repeats.

Each round consists of 24 or 32 parallel 5×5 S-boxes (given in Table 2), followed by a fixed permutation of eight subblocks over a 120-bit or 160-bit internal state for DIZY-80 and DIZY-128, respectively. The round concludes with linear diffusion, implemented as bitwise matrix multiplication using the matrices M_{30} and M_{40}, applied independently to each 30-bit and 40-bit group for DIZY-80 and DIZY-128, respectively. The overall round structure of DIZY-80 is illustrated in Fig. 1; the structure for DIZY-128 is similar. The maximum total length of the keystream generated with a single key is limited to 2^{32} blocks, corresponding to 2^{37} bits. Therefore, we restrict ourselves to using at most 2^{37} bits of keystream in our attacks.

In the round function, first a round constant is added, that is the least significant four bits of each $s = 5$-bit word are XORed with the i-th round constant, where $i = 1, \ldots, 15$. The round constants are generated by a linear feedback shift register (LFSR) whose characteristic polynomial is $x^4 + x + 1$, with the initial state $(1, 0, 0, 0)$ and the LFSR is clocked i times. Recall that the next step is the parallel S-box operations and it is given in Table 2. The permutation of the eight subblocks is performed according to the pattern $(0, 4, 1, 5, 2, 6, 3, 7)$. The

Table 2. S-box of DIZY. The first row lists the output values corresponding to input values 0âĂŞ15, and the second row lists the outputs for input values 16âĂŞ31, in order.

00	04	0e	09	0d	0b	1e	1b	1c	14	13	18	17	1d	05	0c
0f	11	08	15	03	1f	19	06	10	02	16	07	1a	0a	01	12

final operation is the matrix multiplication using the matrix M_{30} for DIZY-80, and the matrix M_{40} for DIZY-128.

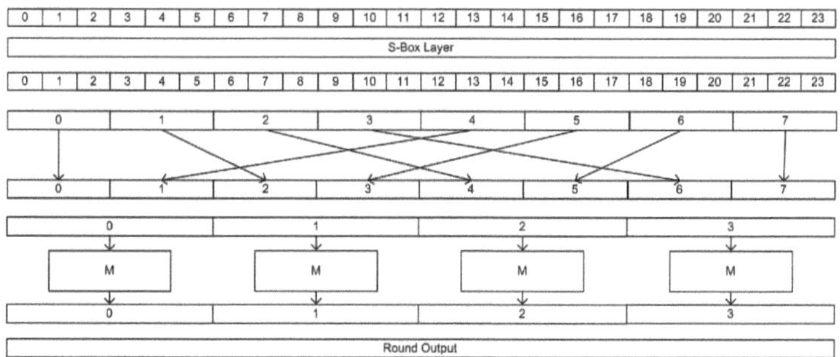

Fig. 1. DIZY Round Function for 80-bit. DIZY-128 is very similar. Only the state sizes, the matrices, and the S-box numbers are different.

The M_{30} Matrix: Table 3 displays the 30×30 binary matrix used in DIZY-80. The design incorporates four parallel instances of M_{30}, each receiving the outputs of six S-boxes coming from two distinct subblocks.

The M_{40} Matrix: Table 4 presents the 40×40 binary matrix employed in DIZY-128. Similarly, there are four parallel instances of M_{40}, and the outputs of eight S-boxes from two subblocks are fed into each M_{40}.

Table 3. M_{30} used in DIZY-80. The input vector is $(y_0, \ldots, y_{29})$, and the table displays the 5-bit segments of the 30-bit output resulting from the M_{30} multiplication. For example, the most significant bit of the last output word is computed as $y_{12} \oplus y_{25}$.

$y_6 \oplus y_{22}$	$y_{16} \oplus y_8$	$y_0 \oplus y_{18}$	y_{15}	y_1
$y_7 \oplus y_{27}$	$y_{20} \oplus y_{13}$	$y_2 \oplus y_{23}$	y_{21}	y_{11}
$y_{12} \oplus y_{17}$	$y_{26} \oplus y_3$	$y_{10} \oplus y_{28}$	y_{25}	y_5
$y_2 \oplus y_{27}$	$y_{21} \oplus y_9$	$y_{11} \oplus y_{24}$	y_{16}	y_0
$y_7 \oplus y_{17}$	$y_{15} \oplus y_{14}$	$y_1 \oplus y_{29}$	y_{20}	y_{10}
$y_{12} \oplus y_{25}$	$y_{22} \oplus y_4$	$y_5 \oplus y_{19}$	y_{26}	y_6

Table 4. M_{40} used in DIZY-128, with the same format as M_{30} shown in Table 3. The input vector is $(y_0, \ldots, y_{39})$

$y_{22} \oplus y_2$	$y_{35} \oplus y_8$	$y_{16} \oplus y_{28}$	y_{10}	y_{31}
$y_{20} \oplus y_7$	$y_{27} \oplus y_{13}$	$y_1 \oplus y_{33}$	y_{15}	y_{36}
$y_{25} \oplus y_{12}$	$y_{32} \oplus y_{18}$	$y_6 \oplus y_{38}$	y_0	y_{21}
$y_{37} \oplus y_{17}$	$y_{26} \oplus y_3$	$y_{11} \oplus y_{23}$	y_5	y_{30}
$y_{27} \oplus y_{17}$	$y_{30} \oplus y_9$	$y_0 \oplus y_{24}$	y_{11}	y_{35}
$y_{32} \oplus y_2$	$y_{36} \oplus y_{14}$	$y_5 \oplus y_{29}$	y_{16}	y_{20}
$y_{37} \oplus y_7$	$y_{21} \oplus y_{19}$	$y_{10} \oplus y_{34}$	y_1	y_{25}
$y_{22} \oplus y_{12}$	$y_{31} \oplus y_4$	$y_{15} \oplus y_{39}$	y_6	y_{26}

Initialization Phase: Initially, the internal state is all zero. The process begins by XORing the 48 most significant bits of the key with a 48-bit segment of the internal state for DIZY-80. This segment is formed by sequentially collecting the two most significant bits from each 5-bit word. The result of each XOR operation is then used to update the internal state, replacing the most significant two bits of the corresponding 5-bit word.

Next, the round function is applied once. Following this, the remaining 32 least significant bits of the key are introduced. These bits are grouped in pairs and XORed with the most significant two bits of each 5-bit word in the upper 120 bits of the internal state.

After that, the round function is executed 14 additional times without any further input, completing the key initialization process at the end of the 15th round. Next, the initialization vector (IV) is integrated in a similar manner over another 15 rounds. In total, 30 rounds are performed during the initialization phase, after which the initial internal state is fully established. The round and output functions are then applied repeatedly: after every 15 iterations of the SPN-based round function, 32 bits are extracted from the internal state to form a keystream word. Therefore, including the initialization, the round function is called 45 times in total before the first keystream word is output.

The initialization of DIZY-128 is almost the same, with the only difference being that the key or IV is XORed in 64-bit chunks.

3   A MILP Model for DIZY

In this section, we present the MILP-based differential and linear models for DIZY. As described in Sect. 2, each round of DIZY comprises an S-box layer, a permutation layer, and a matrix multiplication step, applied in sequence. To construct MILP formulations for identifying differential and linear characteristics, we represent each of these components through sets of linear constraints. Specifically, the cipher's building blocks are encoded as systems of linear inequalities over binary variables, enabling automated exploration of valid characteristics through MILP solvers [24]. Our MILP models for DIZY, along with the corresponding solution files and implementation codes, are available at: https://github.com/murat-ilter/dizy.

DIZY-80: The state vector of DIZY-80 consists of 120 bits. We denote the input of each round by x_{r_i} where $0 \leq i \leq 119$ and r indicates the round number.

DIZY-128: The state vector of DIZY-128 consists of 160 bits. We denote the input of each round by x_{r_i} where $0 \leq i \leq 159$ and r indicates the round number.

3.1   Differential Model

In differential cryptanalysis, we construct models for the S-box layer, the permutation layer, and the matrix multiplication by M_{30} and M_{40} for DIZY-80 and DIZY-128, respectively.

3.1.1   Objective Function

For DIZY-80, the minimum number of differentially active S-boxes is determined by the following objective function:

$$\min \sum_{i=1}^{r} \sum_{j=0}^{23} A_{i_j}$$

where r denotes the number of rounds, and A_{i_j} represents the differential activity of the S-box at position j in round i, with $1 \leq i \leq r$ and $0 \leq j \leq 23$.

For DIZY-128, the range is updated to $0 \leq j \leq 31$ to reflect the state size.

3.1.2   S-Box Layer

DIZY uses 5×5 S-boxes. Let $(x_{0_0}, x_{0_1}, x_{0_2}, x_{0_3}, x_{0_4})$ be the input and $(y_{0_0}, y_{0_1}, y_{0_2}, y_{0_3}, y_{0_4})$ be the output of the first S-box of the first round. The following constraints are added to the MILP model to determine whether each S-box is active.

$$x_{0_0} \leq A_{0_0}$$
$$x_{0_1} \leq A_{0_0}$$
$$x_{0_2} \leq A_{0_0}$$
$$x_{0_3} \leq A_{0_0}$$
$$x_{0_4} \leq A_{0_0}$$
$$x_{0_0} + x_{0_1} + x_{0_2} + x_{0_3} + x_{0_4} \geq A_{0_0}$$
$$5(x_{0_0} + x_{0_1} + x_{0_2} + x_{0_3} + x_{0_4}) - (y_{0_0} + y_{0_1} + y_{0_2} + y_{0_3} + y_{0_4}) \geq 0$$
$$5(y_{0_0} + y_{0_1} + y_{0_2} + y_{0_3} + y_{0_4}) - (x_{0_0} + x_{0_1} + x_{0_2} + x_{0_3} + x_{0_4}) \geq 0.$$

Let $(x_{0_0}, x_{0_1}, x_{0_2}, x_{0_3}, x_{0_4}) \rightarrow (y_{0_0}, y_{0_1}, y_{0_2}, y_{0_3}, y_{0_4})$ denote a possible differential denote a possible differential transition over the S-box. There are 497 non-zero entries in the difference distribution table. The transition $(0, 0, 0, 0, 0) \rightarrow (0, 0, 0, 0, 0)$ occurs with probability 1, while all the other non-zero transitions occur with probability 2^{-4}. The differential behavior of the S-box is modeled using the method proposed by Sun et al. [30].

The H-representation of

$$(x_{i_j}, x_{i_{j+1}}, x_{i_{j+2}}, x_{i_{j+3}}, x_{i_{j+4}}, y_{i_j}, y_{i_{j+1}}, y_{i_{j+2}}, y_{i_{j+3}}, y_{i_{j+4}})$$

where i denotes the round number for $0 \leq i \leq r$, and j satisfies $j \equiv 0 \pmod 5$ and $0 \leq j \leq 115$ is computed using SageMath [31]. This representation initially includes redundant equations. To eliminate them, the method proposed by Sasaki and Todo [32] is applied, resulting in a reduced set of 164 equations that accurately capture the differential behavior of the S-box.

3.1.3 Permutation and Matrix Multiplication Layer DIZY-80:

This layer of DIZY-80 consists of a bitwise permutation followed by multiplication with the matrix M_{30} is given in Table 3. In the MILP model, these two operations are merged into a single step. For DIZY-80, the input to the first S-box in the second round is modeled with the following equalities:

$$x_{1_0} + y_{0_6} + y_{0_{67}} - 2d_{0_0} = 0$$
$$x_{1_1} + y_{0_8} + y_{0_{61}} - 2d_{0_1} = 0$$
$$x_{1_2} + y_{0_0} + y_{0_{63}} - 2d_{0_2} = 0$$
$$x_{1_3} - y_{0_{60}} = 0$$
$$x_{1_4} - y_{0_1} = 0.$$

in which $d_{0_0}, d_{0_1}, d_{0_2}$ are binary dummy variables. The permutation layer is modeled using 120 equations, involving 72 dummy variables for one round of DIZY-80.

DIZY-128: We use the matrix M_{40}, given in Table 4, and merge the permutation operations into a single step. The permutation layer is modeled using 160 equations and involves 96 dummy variables for one round of DIZY-128.

3.2 Linear Model

In the linear cryptanalysis, we model the S-box, the permutation layer, and the inverse of the matrix multiplication by M_{30}^{-1} and M_{40}^{-1} for DIZY-80 and DIZY-128, respectively.

3.2.1 Objective Function

The same objective function, as given in Sect. 3.1.1, is used for DIZY-80 and DIZY-128.

3.2.2 S-Box Layer

Let $(x_{0_0}, x_{0_1}, x_{0_2}, x_{0_3}, x_{0_4}) \rightarrow (y_{0_0}, y_{0_1}, y_{0_2}, y_{0_3}, y_{0_4})$ denote a possible linear transition over the S-box of the first-round, first S-box, S_0. There are 497 non-zero elements in the linear approximation table. The transition $(0, 0, 0, 0, 0) \rightarrow (0, 0, 0, 0, 0)$ occurs with probability 1, while all other non-zero elements have a bias of 2^{-3}. As indicated in Sect. 3.1.2, the same approach is applied, resulting in 77 equations that represent the linear behavior of the S-box.

3.2.3 Our XOR Model Let "n-XOR" represent the XOR operation involving $n + 1$ binary variables. As an example, $y = x_0 \oplus x_1 \oplus x_2 \oplus x_3 \oplus x_4$ is a 4-XOR operation.

In [28], the authors generalize the idea of [27] to model "n-XOR" operation, providing a general formula that depends on whether n is even or odd. As an example, the 4-XOR operation can be modeled as follows:

$$y + x_0 + x_1 + x_2 + x_3 + x_4 - 6d_0 + 4d_1 + 2d_2 = 0,$$

in which $y, x_0, x_1, x_2, x_3, x_4$ are binary variables and d_0, d_1, d_2 are dummy binary variables.

In this work, we present a refined approach in which this operation is modeled using fewer dummy variables, as follows:

$$y + x_0 + x_1 + x_2 + x_3 + x_4 - 4d_0 - 2d_1 = 0.$$

We generalize this approach to model the n-XOR operation

$$y = x_0 \oplus x_1 \oplus \cdots \oplus x_n$$

as:

$$x_0 + x_1 + \cdots + x_n + y = 2^b d_0 + 2^{b-1} d_1 + \cdots + 2d_{b-1}$$

where b equals $\lceil \log_2(n + 1) \rceil$.

A comparison of the number of variables in existing models, up to 10-XOR, is provided in Table 5.

Table 5. Number of variables required to represent an n- XOR operation

	[28]	This work
n-XOR	Number of Variables	Number of Variables
4	9	8
5	10	9
6	12	11
7	13	12
8	15	13
9	16	14
10	18	15

3.2.4 Permutation and Matrix Multiplication Layer Similar to the differential case, we model permutation and matrix multiplications simultaneously. Let β and γ be the input and output masks of the matrix multiplication, respectively. As also given in [28], the linear characteristic can be modeled as follows:

$$\gamma^T = \beta^T M^{-1}$$

where $\cdot^T$ denotes the transpose of the vector. In other words, the transpose of the input mask multiplied by M^{-1} determines the transpose of the output mask. As a result, in the linear case, we need to model the matrix multiplication using M_{30}^{-1} and M_{40}^{-1}, which are given in Table 6 and Table 7, respectively.

Table 6. M_{30}^{-1} in DIZY-80. The input vector is $(y_0, \ldots, y_{29})$. The table shows the 5-bit chunks of the 30-bit output after the matrix multiplication.

$y_4 \oplus y_{22}$	y_8	y_{18}	$y_{14} \oplus y_{15}$	$y_1 \oplus y_{29}$
$y_2 \oplus y_{23} \oplus y_{27}$	y_{13}	y_{23}	$y_9 \oplus y_{21}$	$y_{11} \oplus y_{24}$
$y_2 \oplus y_7 \oplus y_{17} \oplus y_{23} \oplus y_{27}$	y_3	y_{28}	$y_2 \oplus y_7 \oplus y_{12} \oplus y_{17} \oplus y_{23} \oplus y_{25} \oplus y_{27}$	$y_5 \oplus y_{19}$
$y_2 \oplus y_{23}$	y_9	y_{24}	$y_8 \oplus y_{16}$	$y_0 \oplus y_{18}$
$y_2 \oplus y_7 \oplus y_{23} \oplus y_{27}$	y_{14}	y_{29}	$y_{13} \oplus y_{20}$	$y_{10} \oplus y_{28}$

Table 7. M_{40}^{-1} in DIZY-128. The input vector is $(y_0, \ldots, y_{39})$. The table shows the 5-bit chunks of the 40-bit output after the matrix multiplication.

$y_2 \oplus y_{18} \oplus y_{32}$	y_8	y_{28}	$y_{10} \oplus y_{34}$	$y_4 \oplus y_{31}$
$y_7 \oplus y_{13} \oplus y_{17} \oplus y_{27} \oplus y_{37}$	y_{13}	y_{33}	$y_{15} \oplus y_{39}$	$y_{14} \oplus y_{36}$
$y_2 \oplus y_{12} \oplus y_{18} \oplus y_{22} \oplus y_{32}$	y_{18}	y_{38}	$y_0 \oplus y_{24}$	$y_{19} \oplus y_{21}$
$y_{13} \oplus y_{17} \oplus y_{27}$	y_3	y_{23}	$y_5 \oplus y_{29}$	$y_9 \oplus y_{30}$
$y_{13} \oplus y_{27}$	y_9	y_{24}	$y_{11} \oplus y_{23}$	$y_8 \oplus y_{35}$
$y_{18} \oplus y_{32}$	y_{14}	y_{29}	$y_{16} \oplus y_{28}$	$y_7 \oplus y_{13} \oplus y_{17} \oplus y_{20} \oplus y_{27} \oplus y_{37}$
$y_{13} \oplus y_{17} \oplus y_{27} \oplus y_{37}$	y_{19}	y_{34}	$y_1 \oplus y_{33}$	$y_2 \oplus y_{12} \oplus y_{18} \oplus y_{22} \oplus y_{25} \oplus y_{32}$
$y_2 \oplus y_{18} \oplus y_{22} \oplus y_{32}$	y_4	y_{39}	$y_6 \oplus y_{38}$	$y_3 \oplus y_{26}$

DIZY-80: In the MILP model, each round of this layer requires up to 6-XOR operations, modeled using 120 linear constraints and 100 dummy variables.

DIZY-128: In the MILP model, each round of this layer requires up to 5-XOR operations, modeled using 160 linear constraints and 128 dummy variables.

4   New Linear and Differential Characteristics for DIZY

In this section, using the models from Sect. 3, we construct linear and differential characteristics for DIZY. Both characteristics contain fewer active S-boxes than the claimed lower bound in [18] for 8-round DIZY-80.

For DIZY-128, the linear characteristic exhibits 20 active S-boxes, falling short of the designers' stated minimum of 22. In contrast, the observed differential characteristic with 22 active S-boxes is consistent with the designers' security claim over 8 rounds.

All nonzero entries in the Linear Approximation Table (LAT) have a bias of 2^{-3}. This implies that any input mask can lead to a probable output mask with a bias of 2^{-3}. All nonzero entries in the Difference Distribution Table (DDT) have probability 2^{-4}.

4.1   A Linear Characteristic for DIZY-80

In this section, we present an 8-round linear characteristic for DIZY-80.

For simplicity, we omit the individual biases of the S-box transitions in the following description and instead compute the overall bias based on the total number of active S-boxes. The values in `typewriter` font represent 5-bit binary

Table 8. An 8-round linear characteristic of DIZY-80. The subscript i denotes the input to an S-box, and o denotes the output.

R	00	01	02	03	04	05	06	07	08	09	10	11	12	13	14	15	16	17	18	19	20	21	22	23
0_i	00	00	00	00	00	00	00	04	00	00	00	00	00	00	00	00	00	00	00	10	00	00	00	00
0_o	00	00	00	00	00	00	00	01	00	00	00	00	00	00	00	00	00	00	00	08	00	00	00	00
1_i	00	00	00	00	00	00	00	00	00	00	00	00	00	00	00	08	00	00	00	00	00	00	00	00
1_o	00	00	00	00	00	00	00	00	00	00	00	00	00	00	00	10	00	00	00	00	00	00	00	00
2_i	00	00	00	00	00	00	02	00	00	00	00	00	00	00	00	00	00	00	00	00	00	00	00	00
2_o	00	00	00	00	00	00	09	00	00	00	00	00	00	00	00	00	00	00	00	00	00	00	00	00
3_i	00	00	00	00	00	00	00	00	00	00	00	00	11	00	00	00	00	09	00	00	00	00	00	00
3_o	00	00	00	00	00	00	00	00	00	00	00	00	08	00	00	00	00	08	00	00	00	00	00	00
4_i	00	00	00	02	00	00	00	00	00	00	00	02	00	00	00	00	00	00	00	00	00	00	00	00
4_o	00	00	00	09	00	00	00	00	00	00	00	12	00	00	00	00	00	00	00	00	00	00	00	00
5_i	00	00	00	00	00	00	11	00	00	00	00	09	00	00	00	00	00	00	00	08	00	00	03	00
5_o	00	00	00	00	00	00	04	00	00	00	00	08	00	00	00	00	00	00	00	0A	00	00	11	00
6_i	00	00	00	00	00	00	00	00	00	00	00	00	00	06	00	00	00	00	00	00	00	04	02	00
6_o	00	00	09	00	00	00	00	00	00	00	00	00	00	08	00	00	00	00	00	00	00	08	09	00
7_i	00	02	00	00	00	00	00	00	00	00	00	00	00	00	00	00	00	00	00	03	00	06	00	00
7_o	00	09	00	00	00	00	00	00	00	00	00	00	00	00	00	00	00	00	00	03	00	01	00	00
8_i	00	02	00	08	00	01	00	00	00	00	00	00	00	15	12	14	10	10	00	00	01	00	00	04

Table 9. An 8-round linear characteristic of DIZY-128. The subscript i denotes the input to an S-box, while o represents the output.

R	00	01	02	03	04	05	06	07	08	09	10	11	12	13	14	15	16	17	18	19	20	21	22	23	24	25	26	27	28	29	30	31
0_i	00	04	00	00	04	00	00	00	00	00	00	00	00	00	00	00	00	00	00	08	00	10	00	00	00	00	00	00	00	00	00	00
0_o	00	02	00	00	02	00	00	00	00	00	00	00	00	00	00	00	00	00	00	10	00	08	00	00	00	00	00	00	00	00	00	00
1_i	08	00	00	00	00	00	00	00	00	00	00	08	00	00	00	00	00	00	00	00	00	00	00	00	00	00	08	00	00	00	00	00
1_o	10	00	00	00	00	00	00	00	00	00	00	10	00	00	00	00	00	00	00	00	00	00	00	00	00	00	10	00	00	00	00	00
2_i	00	00	02	00	00	00	00	00	00	00	00	00	00	00	00	00	00	02	00	00	00	00	00	00	00	00	00	00	00	00	00	00
2_o	00	00	06	00	00	00	00	00	00	00	00	00	00	00	00	00	00	14	00	00	00	00	00	00	00	00	00	00	00	00	00	00
3_i	00	08	10	00	00	00	00	00	00	00	00	00	00	00	00	00	00	00	00	00	00	00	00	00	00	00	08	10	00	00	00	00
3_o	00	08	08	00	00	00	00	00	00	00	00	00	00	00	00	00	00	00	00	00	00	00	00	00	00	00	08	08	00	00	00	00
4_i	00	00	00	00	02	00	00	02	00	00	00	00	00	00	00	00	00	00	00	00	00	00	00	00	00	00	00	00	02	00	00	00
4_o	00	00	00	00	14	00	00	0A	00	00	00	00	00	00	00	00	00	00	00	00	00	00	00	00	00	00	00	00	00	00	00	00
5_i	00	00	00	00	00	00	00	00	00	00	0A	00	00	12	00	00	00	00	00	00	00	00	00	00	00	00	00	00	00	00	00	00
5_o	00	00	00	00	00	00	00	00	00	00	08	00	00	08	00	00	00	00	00	00	00	00	00	00	00	00	00	00	00	00	00	00
6_i	00	00	00	00	00	00	02	00	00	00	00	00	00	00	00	00	00	00	00	00	02	00	00	00	00	00	00	00	00	00	00	02
6_o	00	00	00	00	00	00	09	00	00	00	00	00	00	00	00	00	00	00	00	00	09	00	00	00	00	00	00	00	00	00	00	09
7_i	00	00	00	00	00	00	00	00	00	00	03	00	04	00	00	00	00	00	00	00	00	00	00	00	00	03	00	00	00	00	00	04
7_o	00	00	00	00	00	00	03	00	00	00	0F	00	03	00	00	00	00	00	00	00	00	00	00	00	00	0F	00	00	00	00	00	03
8_i	00	00	00	00	00	00	00	00	00	00	00	00	00	00	00	00	04	09	10	02	02	0E	01	01	01	02	04	08	00	00	00	0F

values in little-endian format for the input and output masks of the S-boxes. As an illustrative example, the first two rounds are explained below.

Let the input mask be active at the 37th and 95th bits. These bits correspond to the S-boxes S_7 and S_{19} in the first round. The input masks 00100 and 10000 are transformed by S_7 and S_{19} into 00001 and 01000, respectively.

After passing through the permutation and matrix multiplication layers, the active bits propagate to the 76th bit. In the S-box layer of the second round, this activates S_{15}, whose output mask becomes 10000, corresponding to the 75th bit.

The 8-round linear characteristic is summarized in Table 8.

The linear input mask at bits $(37, 95)$ has a linear correlation with the output mask at bits $(8, 16, 29, 65, 67, 69, 70, 73, 75, 77, 80, 85, 104, 117)$ with an overall bias of

$$2^{17} \cdot 2^{-3 \cdot 18} = 2^{-37}.$$

4.2 A Linear Characteristic for DIZY-128

The 8-round linear characteristic:

$$(7, 22, 96, 105) \xrightarrow{\text{8-Rounds}} (82, 86, 89, 90, 98, 103, 106, 107, 108, 114$$
$$119, 124, 128, 132, 136, 156, 157, 158, 159).$$

has been derived and is presented in Table 9.

This characteristic includes 20 active S-boxes, resulting in an overall bias given by

$$2^{19} \cdot 2^{-3 \cdot 20} = 2^{-41}.$$

4.3 A Differential Characteristic for DIZY-80

Table 10 shows an 8-round differential characteristic for DIZY-80 with 18 active S-boxes and probability 2^{-72}: $(15, 16, 24) \xrightarrow{\text{8-Rounds}} (14, 27, 104, 106, 117)$.

Table 10. An 8-round differential characteristic of DIZY-80. The subscript i denotes the input to an S-box, while o represents the output.

R	00	01	02	03	04	05	06	07	08	09	10	11	12	13	14	15	16	17	18	19	20	21	22	23
0_i	00	00	00	18	01	00	00	00	00	00	00	00	00	00	00	00	00	00	00	00	00	00	00	00
0_o	00	00	00	01	0A	00	00	00	00	00	00	00	00	00	00	00	00	00	00	00	00	00	00	00
1_i	00	00	00	00	00	00	18	00	00	00	00	09	00	00	00	00	00	00	00	00	00	00	00	00
1_o	00	00	00	00	00	00	01	00	00	00	00	01	00	00	00	00	00	00	00	00	00	00	00	00
2_i	00	00	00	08	00	00	00	00	00	00	00	00	00	00	00	00	00	08	00	00	00	00	08	00
2_o	00	00	00	00	00	00	00	00	00	00	00	00	00	00	00	00	00	18	00	00	00	00	10	00
3_i	00	00	00	00	00	00	00	00	0A	00	00	12	00	00	00	00	00	00	00	08	00	00	02	00
3_o	00	00	00	00	00	00	00	00	03	00	00	03	00	00	00	00	00	00	00	10	00	00	10	00
4_i	00	00	00	00	00	00	00	00	00	00	00	00	00	00	00	00	0A	00	00	00	00	00	0A	00
4_o	00	00	00	00	00	00	00	00	00	00	00	00	00	00	00	00	02	00	00	00	00	00	02	00
5_i	00	00	00	00	00	00	00	04	00	00	00	00	00	00	00	00	00	00	00	04	00	00	00	00
5_o	00	00	00	00	00	00	00	09	00	00	00	00	00	00	00	00	00	00	00	0E	00	00	00	00
6_i	00	00	00	00	00	00	00	00	00	00	00	00	00	06	00	00	00	09	00	00	00	00	00	00
6_o	00	00	00	00	00	00	00	00	00	00	00	00	00	02	00	00	00	01	00	00	00	00	00	00
7_i	00	04	00	00	00	00	00	00	00	00	04	00	00	00	00	00	00	00	00	00	00	00	00	00
7_o	00	10	00	00	00	00	00	00	00	00	11	00	00	00	00	00	00	00	00	00	00	00	00	00
8_i	00	00	01	00	04	04	00	00	00	00	00	00	00	00	00	00	00	00	00	00	01	08	00	04

4.4 A Differential Characteristic for DIZY-128

Table 11 gives an 8-round DIZY-128 differential characteristic with 22 active S-boxes and probability 2^{-88}: $(39, 107, 108, 109) \xrightarrow{\text{8-Rounds}} (1, 24, 120, 142, 155)$.

Table 11. An 8-round differential characteristic of DIZY-128. The subscript i denotes the input to an S-box, while o represents the output.

R	00	01	02	03	04	05	06	07	08	09	10	11	12	13	14	15	16	17	18	19	20	21	22	23	24	25	26	27	28	29	30	31
0_i	00	00	00	00	00	00	00	01	00	00	00	00	00	00	00	00	00	00	00	00	00	07	00	00	00	00	00	00	00	00	00	00
0_o	00	00	00	00	00	00	00	09	00	00	00	00	00	00	00	00	00	00	00	00	00	02	00	00	00	00	00	00	00	00	00	00
1_i	00	00	00	00	00	00	00	00	00	00	00	00	00	02	08	00	00	00	00	00	00	00	00	00	00	00	00	00	00	00	00	00
1_o	00	00	00	00	00	00	00	00	00	00	00	00	00	06	12	00	00	00	00	00	00	00	00	00	00	00	00	00	00	00	00	00
2_i	00	00	00	00	00	00	00	00	00	00	00	00	00	00	00	00	00	00	00	00	00	00	00	00	0A	18	00	00	00	00	14	00
2_o	00	00	00	00	00	00	00	00	00	00	00	00	00	00	00	00	00	00	00	00	00	00	00	00	02	02	00	00	00	00	02	00
3_i	00	00	00	00	00	00	00	00	00	00	00	00	00	00	00	00	04	00	00	04	00	00	00	00	00	04	00	00	00	00	00	00
3_o	00	00	00	00	00	00	00	00	00	00	00	00	00	00	00	00	10	00	00	08	00	00	00	00	00	08	00	00	00	00	00	00
4_i	00	11	00	00	00	09	00	00	00	00	00	00	00	00	00	00	00	00	08	00	00	00	01	00	00	00	00	00	00	00	00	00
4_o	00	02	00	00	00	03	00	00	00	00	00	00	00	00	00	00	00	00	00	11	00	00	00	10	00	00	00	00	00	00	00	00
5_i	00	00	00	00	01	00	00	04	00	00	00	00	09	00	00	00	00	00	00	00	00	00	00	00	00	00	00	00	00	00	00	00
5_o	00	00	00	00	04	00	00	08	00	00	00	00	01	00	00	00	00	00	00	00	00	00	00	00	00	00	00	00	00	00	00	00
6_i	00	00	00	00	00	00	00	00	14	00	00	00	00	12	00	00	00	00	00	00	00	00	00	00	00	00	00	00	00	00	00	08
6_o	00	00	00	00	00	00	00	00	02	00	00	00	00	03	00	00	00	00	00	00	00	00	00	00	00	00	00	00	00	00	00	10
7_i	00	00	00	00	00	00	00	00	00	00	00	00	00	00	00	00	00	00	08	00	00	00	00	00	00	00	00	00	09	00	00	00
7_o	00	00	00	00	00	00	00	00	00	00	00	00	00	00	00	00	00	00	00	10	00	00	00	00	00	00	00	00	05	00	00	00
8_i	08	00	00	00	01	00	00	00	00	00	00	00	00	00	00	00	00	00	00	00	00	00	00	00	10	00	00	00	04	00	00	10

5   Distinguishing Attacks on DIZY

In this section, we present linear and differential characteristics, which we subsequently exploit to construct distinguisher attacks on keystreams generated by DIZY-80 and DIZY-128. As in the previous section, we omit the individual probabilities and biases of each S-box operation during the description of the characteristics, and instead provide the overall probability and bias at the end of the analysis.

5.1   A Linear Distinguishing Attack on DIZY-80

We present a 4-round linear characteristic with 7 active S-boxes, resulting in a bias of 2^{-15}. A key constraint in constructing this characteristic is that the input and output bits involved in the linear mask must correspond to bits from the previous and current 32-bit keystream words, respectively. This special characteristic ensures that the linear mask value can be computed, and given a sufficient amount of keystream output, an attacker can estimate the bias empirically. Consequently, this enables a distinguishing attack that separates the DIZY-80 keystream from a truly random sequence when enough data is available, which is roughly 2^{30} 32-bit keystream words. The 4-round characteristic $(15, 51, 87) \xrightarrow{\text{4-Rounds}} (33, 39, 51)$ is given in Table 12.

Table 12. A 4-round linear characteristic of DIZY-80. The subscript i denotes the input to an S-box, while o represents the output.

R	00	01	02	03	04	05	06	07	08	09	10	11	12	13	14	15	16	17	18	19	20	21	22	23
0_i	00	00	00	10	00	00	00	00	00	00	08	00	00	00	00	00	00	04	00	00	00	00	00	00
0_o	00	00	00	02	00	00	00	00	00	00	10	00	00	00	00	00	00	08	00	00	00	00	00	00
1_i	00	00	00	00	00	00	00	00	08	00	00	00	00	00	00	00	00	00	00	00	01	00	00	00
1_o	00	00	00	00	00	00	00	00	10	00	00	00	00	00	00	00	00	00	00	00	12	00	00	00
2_i	00	00	00	00	00	00	00	00	00	00	00	00	00	00	06	00	00	00	00	00	00	00	00	00
2_o	00	00	00	00	00	00	00	00	00	00	00	00	00	00	08	00	00	00	00	00	00	00	00	00
3_i	00	00	00	00	00	02	00	00	00	00	00	00	00	00	00	00	00	00	00	00	00	00	00	00
3_o	00	00	00	00	00	09	00	00	00	00	00	00	00	00	00	00	00	00	00	00	00	00	00	00
4_i	00	00	00	00	00	00	02	01	00	00	08	00	00	00	00	00	00	00	00	00	00	00	00	00

5.2 A Linear Distinguishing Attack on DIZY-128

We present a 3-round linear characteristic with 4 active S-boxes, resulting in a bias of 2^{-9}. The 3-round characteristic $(0, 87) \xrightarrow{\text{3-Rounds}} (45, 69, 78)$ is given in Table 13.

Table 13. An 3-round differential characteristic of DIZY-128. The subscript i denotes the input to an S-box, while o represents the output.

R	00	01	02	03	04	05	06	07	08	09	10	11	12	13	14	15	16	17	18	19	20	21	22	23	24	25	26	27	28	29	30	31
0_i	10	00	00	00	00	00	00	00	00	00	00	00	00	00	00	00	00	04	00	00	00	00	00	00	00	00	00	00	00	00	00	00
0_o	02	00	00	00	00	00	00	00	00	00	00	00	00	00	00	00	00	08	00	00	00	00	00	00	00	00	00	00	00	00	00	00
1_i	00	00	00	08	00	00	00	00	00	00	00	00	00	00	00	00	00	00	00	00	00	00	00	00	00	00	00	00	00	00	00	00
1_o	00	00	00	08	00	00	00	00	00	00	00	00	00	00	00	00	00	00	00	00	00	00	00	00	00	00	00	00	00	00	00	00
2_i	00	00	00	00	00	02	00	00	00	00	00	00	00	00	00	00	00	00	00	00	00	00	00	00	00	00	00	00	00	00	00	00
2_o	00	00	00	00	00	0C	00	00	00	00	00	00	00	00	00	00	00	00	00	00	00	00	00	00	00	00	00	00	00	00	00	00
3_i	00	00	00	00	00	00	00	00	00	10	00	00	00	01	00	02	00	00	00	00	00	00	00	00	00	00	00	00	00	00	00	00
3_o	00	00	00	00	00	00	00	00	00	00	00	00	00	00	00	00	00	00	00	00	00	00	00	00	00	00	00	00	00	00	00	00
4_i	00	00	00	00	00	00	00	00	00	00	00	00	00	00	00	00	00	00	00	00	00	00	00	00	00	00	00	00	00	00	00	00

5.3 A Differential Distinguishing Attack on DIZY-80

In a resynchronization attack, the keystream generator is initialized with several chosen IVs, and the first few words of the resulting keystreams are collected. A statistical distinguisher between the keystream words and their corresponding IVs is then exploited as a weakness.

We construct a 4-round differential characteristic to mount our resynchronization attack on DIZY-80. The input difference is restricted to the positions where the IV bits are injected, while the output difference is limited to the bits that contribute to the first 32-bit keystream word.

The attack proceeds as follows: we introduce a specific difference into the first 48-bit segment of the IV such that it aligns with the input difference of the characteristic. We assume that the initialization phase consists of 4 rounds, where the first two rounds are dedicated to key incorporation. The IV difference then propagates through the remaining two initialization rounds and diffuses further during the first two rounds of the keystream generation phase.

The overall effect is equivalent to a 4-round differential characteristic observable in the keystream output. Since two of these rounds occur during initialization and two during keystream production, the resulting resynchronization attack effectively targets 2-round DIZY. Our differential characteristic $(10, 71) \xrightarrow{\text{4-Rounds}} (12, 24, 42, 54)$, which holds with probability 2^{-24}, is presented in Table 14.

If DIZY-80 is initialized with IV pairs whose differences match the input difference of this characteristic, then among approximately 2^{25} such IV pairs, we expect the output difference to appear about twice in the first 32 bits of the corresponding keystream outputs. In contrast, we would expect such an event to occur with negligible probability in sequences generated by a truly random number generator since its probability is 2^{-32}.

Table 14. A 4-round differential characteristic of DIZY-80. The subscript i denotes the input to an S-box, while o represents the output.

R	00	01	02	03	04	05	06	07	08	09	10	11	12	13	14	15	16	17	18	19	20	21	22	23
0_i	00	00	10	00	00	00	00	00	00	00	00	00	00	00	08	00	00	00	00	00	00	00	00	00
0_o	00	00	04	00	00	00	00	00	00	00	00	00	00	00	12	00	00	00	00	00	00	00	00	00
1_i	00	00	16	00	00	00	00	00	00	00	00	00	00	00	00	00	00	00	00	00	00	00	00	00
1_o	00	00	02	00	00	00	00	00	00	00	00	00	00	00	00	00	00	00	00	00	00	00	00	00
2_i	00	08	00	00	00	00	00	00	00	00	00	00	00	00	00	00	00	00	00	00	00	00	00	00
2_o	00	10	00	00	00	00	00	00	00	00	00	00	00	00	00	00	00	00	00	00	00	00	00	00
3_i	00	00	01	00	00	04	00	00	00	00	00	00	00	00	00	00	00	00	00	00	00	00	00	00
3_o	00	00	10	00	00	10	00	00	00	00	00	00	00	00	00	00	00	00	00	00	00	00	00	00
4_i	00	00	04	00	01	00	00	00	04	00	01	00	00	00	00	00	00	00	00	00	00	00	00	00

5.4   A Differential Distinguishing Attack on DIZY-128

Our resynchronization attack on DIZY-128 is quite similar to the one on DIZY-80. Our differential characteristic for DIZY-128 is $(15, 16, 90,$

$91, 135, 136) \xrightarrow{\text{4-Rounds}} (45, 69)$, which holds with probability 2^{-28}. It is given in Table 15.

Table 15. An 4-round differential characteristic of DIZY-128. The subscript i denotes the input to an S-box, while o represents the output.

R	00	01	02	03	04	05	06	07	08	09	10	11	12	13	14	15	16	17	18	19	20	21	22	23	24	25	26	27	28	29	30	31
0_i	00	00	00	18	00	00	00	00	00	00	00	00	00	00	00	00	00	00	18	00	00	00	00	00	00	00	00	18	00	00	00	00
0_o	00	00	00	01	00	00	00	00	00	00	00	00	00	00	00	00	00	00	01	00	00	00	00	00	00	00	00	01	00	00	00	00
1_i	00	00	00	00	00	00	0C	00	00	00	00	00	00	00	00	00	00	00	00	00	00	00	00	04	00	00	00	00	00	00	00	00
1_o	00	00	00	00	00	00	03	00	00	00	00	00	00	00	00	00	00	00	00	00	00	00	00	08	00	00	00	00	00	00	00	00
2_i	00	00	00	00	00	00	00	00	00	09	00	00	00	00	00	00	00	00	00	00	00	00	00	00	00	00	00	00	00	00	00	00
2_o	00	00	00	00	00	00	00	00	00	01	00	00	00	00	00	00	00	00	00	00	00	00	00	00	00	00	00	00	00	00	00	00
3_i	00	00	00	00	00	00	00	00	00	00	00	00	00	00	00	00	00	00	00	00	08	00	00	00	00	00	00	00	00	00	00	00
3_o	00	00	00	00	00	00	00	00	00	00	00	00	00	00	00	00	00	00	00	00	10	00	00	00	00	00	00	00	00	00	00	00
4_i	00	00	00	00	00	00	00	00	00	10	00	00	00	01	00	00	00	00	00	00	00	00	00	00	00	00	00	00	00	00	00	00

6 Discussion on the Designs

The main motivation of the work in [18] is to introduce a new construction method for keystream generators based on utilizing SPN structures in TPP mode. One of the limitations of using an SPN structure in a keystream generator is its relatively large block size. To address this issue, the authors propose a new criterion for diffusion layers and refer to the binary matrices satisfying this criterion as matrices providing SDD (Second Degree Diffusion).

Roughly speaking, a matrix $\mathcal{M}$ that provides SDD has two main properties. First, it must be a 2×2 MDS (Maximum Distance Separable) matrix over its subblocks. Moreover, each of its word-size submatrices must be nonzero and contain at most one 1 in each row or column. If these submatrices are permutation matrices, then $\mathcal{M}$ is said to provide SDD perfectly. Additionally, the authors define a matrix as providing SDD completely if, whenever one of the output subblocks is passive, the other subblock contains at least two active S-boxes with respect to a differential or linear attack [18]. Then, they prove several properties about the SPN constructions whose diffusion layers consist of four matrices providing SDD and a permutation defined over the subblocks.

For the sake of illustrating the keystream construction in TPP mode, the authors of [18] present an example of a lightweight keystream generator called DIZY. One of their additional goals is to minimize the hardware cost of the construction. To achieve this, they forgo the full benefits of matrices providing SDD in favor of reducing the number of XOR operations. Indeed, neither M_{30} nor M_{40} provides SDD, but they require only 18 and 24 XORs, respectively.

On the other hand, to retain some of the security advantages offered by SDD-providing matrices, the authors introduce certain properties that mimic their behavior. Some of these properties are listed below [18]:

- The first three bits of each 5-bit word are duplicated, while the last two bits remain single. Moreover, no single bit is XORed with another single bit.
- M_{30} and M_{40} provide complete SDD for characteristics in which the single bits of each 5-bit word are either both active or both passive.
- The single bits of a 5-bit word are mapped to and from different subblocks. Additionally, the four input bits of any two XORs originate from at least three different S-boxes.

It is clear that none of our characteristics would hold if both M_{30} and M_{40} provided SDD. In this work, we have shown that the properties stated above are not sufficient to fully exploit the security guarantees offered by matrices satisfying the SDD criterion. Moreover, we observed that the assumption in the second property is fulfilled by neither M_{30} nor M_{40}. Specifically, we identified characteristics in which only one of the two single bits is active, which clearly violates the MDS property of the matrices over the subblocks. As a result, only one subblock can be active in each of two consecutive rounds, making it possible to construct characteristics that span two rounds with only a single active S-box.

We suspect that this case may have escaped the authors' notice. It appears they assumed that the second property, where the two single bits in a word are either both active or both passive, always holds, and likely based their security analysis on this assumption.

7   Conclusion

In this work, we have analyzed the number of active S-boxes in DIZY with respect to both differential and linear cryptanalysis using MILP modeling. To this end, we used the XOR modeling technique from [27, 28] and adapted it to reduce the number of variables, which is particularly effective in the linear case.

Utilizing our model, we have constructed both a differential and a linear characteristic for 8-round DIZY-80, each involving only 18 active S-boxes. These characteristics serve as counterexamples to the designers' claim that any differential or linear characteristic over 8 rounds of DIZY-80 must involve at least 20 active S-boxes [18]. Similarly, for 8-round DIZY-128, we have constructed one differential characteristic with 22 active S-boxes and one linear characteristic with 20 active S-boxes. While the differential characteristic aligns with the designers' claim, the linear characteristic contradicts their assertion that at least 22 active S-boxes are required for a linear attack on 8-round DIZY-128 [18]. Furthermore, based on our findings, we have presented two distinguishing attacks on reduced-round versions of each variant of DIZY.

The DIZY cipher generates keystreams using a specialized mode of operation known as TPP mode, for which security proofs are provided under the assumption that the underlying permutation is random [18]. If DIZY were structured as a conventional SPN-based block cipher with round keys XORed between rounds, the 8-round state update permutation of DIZY could be distinguished from a random permutation using both our linear and differential characteristics. These characteristics could be readily exploited in a 1-round key recovery attack by appending one additional round. However, due to the unique structure of the TPP mode, such characteristics cannot be directly applied for key or internal state recovery.

This raises an important question: how does the security of the TPP mode change when the underlying permutation is not truly random? To answer this, new cryptanalysis methods might be needed, beyond the usual first-round or last-round key recovery attacks, that are designed specifically for the TPP mode.

Acknowledgment. We want to thank the anonymous reviewers for their invaluable comments. In particular, we are grateful to the reviewer who has shepherded our paper.

References

1. Hamann, M., Krause, M., Meier, W.: LIZARD - a lightweight stream cipher for power-constrained devices. IACR Trans. Symmetric Cryptol. **2017**(1), 45–79 (2017)
2. Armknecht, F., Mikhalev, V.: On lightweight stream ciphers with shorter internal states. In: Leander, G. (ed.) FSE 2015. LNCS, vol. 9054, pp. 451–470. Springer, Heidelberg (2015). https://doi.org/10.1007/978-3-662-48116-5_22
3. Ghafari, V.A., Hu, H.: Fruit-80: a secure ultra-lightweight stream cipher for constrained environments. Entropy **20**(3), 180 (2018)
4. Dalai, D.K., Pal, S., Sarkar, S.: A state bit recovery algorithm with TMDTO attack on lizard and grain-128a. Des. Codes Cryptogr. **90**(3), 489–521 (2022)
5. Biryukov, A., Shamir, A.: Cryptanalytic time/memory/data tradeoffs for stream ciphers. In: Okamoto, T. (ed.) ASIACRYPT 2000. LNCS, vol. 1976, pp. 1–13. Springer, Heidelberg (2000). https://doi.org/10.1007/3-540-44448-3_1
6. Babbage, S.: Improved "exhaustive search" attacks on stream ciphers. In: European Convention on Security and Detection, pp. 161–166. IET (1995)
7. Golić, J.D.: Cryptanalysis of alleged a5 stream cipher. In: Fumy, W. (ed.) EUROCRYPT 1997. LNCS, vol. 1233, pp. 239–255. Springer, Heidelberg (1997). https://doi.org/10.1007/3-540-69053-0_17
8. Lallemand, V., Naya-Plasencia, M.: Cryptanalysis of full sprout. In: Gennaro, R., Robshaw, M. (eds.) CRYPTO 2015. LNCS, vol. 9215, pp. 663–682. Springer, Heidelberg (2015). https://doi.org/10.1007/978-3-662-47989-6_32
9. Maitra, S., Sarkar, S., Baksi, A., Dey, P.: Key recovery from state information of sprout: application to cryptanalysis and fault attack. IACR Cryptol. ePrint Arch. **2015**, 236 (2015)
10. Zhang, B., Gong, X.: Another tradeoff attack on sprout-like stream ciphers. In: Iwata, T., Cheon, J.H. (eds.) ASIACRYPT 2015. LNCS, vol. 9453, pp. 561–585. Springer, Heidelberg (2015). https://doi.org/10.1007/978-3-662-48800-3_23
11. Esgin, M.F., Kara, O.: Practical cryptanalysis of full sprout with TMD tradeoff attacks. In: Dunkelman, O., Keliher, L. (eds.) SAC 2015. LNCS, vol. 9566, pp. 67–85. Springer, Cham (2016). https://doi.org/10.1007/978-3-319-31301-6_4

12. Mikhalev, V., Armknecht, F., Müller, C.: On ciphers that continuously access the non-volatile key. IACR Trans. Symmetric Cryptol. **2016**(2), 52–79 (2016)
13. Todo, Y., Meier, W., Aoki, K.: On the data limitation of small-state stream ciphers: correlation attacks on fruit-80 and plantlet. In: Paterson, K.G., Stebila, D. (eds.) SAC 2019. LNCS, vol. 11959, pp. 365–392. Springer, Cham (2020). https://doi.org/10.1007/978-3-030-38471-5_15
14. Wang, S., Liu, M., Lin, D., Ma, L.: Fast correlation attacks on grain-like small state stream ciphers and cryptanalysis of Plantlet, Fruit-v2 and Fruit-80. IACR Cryptol. ePrint Arch. **2019**, 763 (2019)
15. Banik, S., Barooti, K., Isobe, T.: Cryptanalysis of Plantlet. IACR Trans. Symmetric Cryptol. **2019**(3), 103–120 (2019)
16. Copeland, J., Simpson, L.: Finding slid pairs for the Plantlet stream cipher. In: Jayaraman, P.P., Georgakopoulos, D., Sellis, T.K., Forkan, A. (es.) Proceedings of the Australasian Computer Science Week, ACSW 2020, Melbourne, VIC, Australia, 3-7 February 2020, pp. 7:1–7:7. ACM (2020)
17. Banik, S., Isobe, T., Morii, M.: On design of robust lightweight stream cipher with short internal state. IEICE Trans. Fundam. Electron. Commun. Comput. Sci. **101-A**(1), 99–109 (2018)
18. Gül, Ç., Kara, O.: A new construction method for keystream generators. IEEE Trans. Inf. Forensics Secur. **18**, 3735–3744 (2023)
19. Amin-Ghafari, V., Orumiehchiha, M.A., Rostami, S.: An attack on the LILLE stream cipher. Cryptology ePrint Archive, Paper 2023/111 (2023)
20. Schmid, M., Arul, T., Kavun, E.B., Regazzoni, F., Kara, O.: Robust and energy-efficient hardware architectures for DIZY stream cipher. In: 2024 IEEE Asia Pacific Conference on Circuits and Systems (APCCAS), pp. 461–465 (2024)
21. Sun, S., Hu, L., Song, L., Xie, Y., Wang, P.: automatic security evaluation of block ciphers with s-bp structures against related-key differential attacks. In: Lin, D., Xu, S., Yung, M. (eds.) Inscrypt 2013. LNCS, vol. 8567, pp. 39–51. Springer, Cham (2014). https://doi.org/10.1007/978-3-319-12087-4_3
22. Zhu, B., Dong, X., Yu, H.: MILP-based differential attack on round-reduced GIFT. In: Matsui, M. (ed.) CT-RSA 2019. LNCS, vol. 11405, pp. 372–390. Springer, Cham (2019). https://doi.org/10.1007/978-3-030-12612-4_19
23. Ji, F., Zhang, W., Zhou, C., Ding, T.: Improved (related-key) differential cryptanalysis on GIFT. In: Dunkelman, O., Jacobson, Jr., M.J., O'Flynn, C. (eds.) SAC 2020. LNCS, vol. 12804, pp. 198–228. Springer, Cham (2021). https://doi.org/10.1007/978-3-030-81652-0_8
24. Gurobi Optimization, LLC. Gurobi Optimizer Reference Manual (2024). https://www.gurobi.com
25. Matsui, M.: Linear cryptanalysis method for DES cipher. In: Helleseth, T. (ed.) EUROCRYPT 1993. LNCS, vol. 765, pp. 386–397. Springer, Heidelberg (1994). https://doi.org/10.1007/3-540-48285-7_33
26. Biham, E., Shamir, A.: Differential cryptanalysis of the full 16-round DES. In: Brickell, E.F. (ed.) CRYPTO 1992. LNCS, vol. 740, pp. 487–496. Springer, Heidelberg (1993). https://doi.org/10.1007/3-540-48071-4_34
27. Fu, K., Wang, M., Guo, Y., Sun, S., Hu, L.: MILP-based automatic search algorithms for differential and linear trails for speck. In: Peyrin, T. (ed.) FSE 2016. LNCS, vol. 9783, pp. 268–288. Springer, Heidelberg (2016). https://doi.org/10.1007/978-3-662-52993-5_14
28. Murat Burhan Ilter and Ali Aydın Selçuk: MILP modeling of matrix multiplication: cryptanalysis of KLEIN and PRINCE. Turk. J. Electr. Eng. Comput. Sci. **32**(1), 183–197 (2024)

29. Gül, Ç., Kara, O.: Correction to A new construction method for keystream generators. IEEE Trans. Inf. Forensics Secur. **19**, 4198–4198 (2024)
30. Sun, S., Hu, L., Wang, P., Qiao, K., Ma, X., Song, L.: Automatic security evaluation and (related-key) differential characteristic search: application to SIMON, PRESENT, LBlock, DES(L) and other bit-oriented block ciphers. In: Sarkar, P., Iwata, T. (eds.) ASIACRYPT 2014. LNCS, vol. 8873, pp. 158–178. Springer, Heidelberg (2014). https://doi.org/10.1007/978-3-662-45611-8_9
31. The Sage Developers. SageMath, the Sage Mathematics Software System (Version 10.6) (2025). https://www.sagemath.org
32. Sasaki, Yu., Todo, Y.: New algorithm for modeling S-box in milp based differential and division trail search. In: Farshim, P., Simion, E. (eds.) SecITC 2017. LNCS, vol. 10543, pp. 150–165. Springer, Cham (2017). https://doi.org/10.1007/978-3-319-69284-5_11

Automated Tool for Meet-in-the-Middle Attacks with Very Low Data and Memory Complexity

Mohammad Vaziri$^{(\boxtimes)}$

The University of Edinburgh, Edinburgh, UK
`mohammad.vaziri@ed.ac.uk`

Abstract. In this paper, we present a simple meet-in-the-middle attack that requires low data and memory resources. To evaluate the complexity of the attack, we also propose an automated tool that calculates the time, data, and memory complexities based on the suggested matching points. Our method operates at the bit level and employs a known-plaintext attack, with no constraints on the attacker's choice of data. We apply our tool on various lightweight block ciphers, including CRAFT, Midori, WARP, PRESENT, and ARADI. For CRAFT, our tool successfully identified an attack targeting 15 rounds using 3 known plaintexts. In the case of Midori64 and Midori128, the tool proposed attacks on 5 rounds with 16 known plaintexts and 7 rounds with 3 known plaintexts, respectively. For WARP, the tool discovered an attack on 18 rounds utilizing 7 known plaintexts. Additionally, for PRESENT80, the tool identified an attack on 6 rounds with 18 known plaintexts, and for ARADI, an attack on 5 rounds with 28 known plaintexts was determined.

Keywords: MITM Attacks · Automated Tools · Lightweight Cryptography · Key-recovery Attacks

1 Introduction

In the field of symmetric key cryptanalysis, meet-in-the-middle (MITM) attacks have drawn significant attention. Since the introduction of MITM by Diffie and Hellman [DH77], numerous MITM techniques have been developed to analyze the security of various cryptographic primitives, such as block ciphers, stream ciphers, and hash functions. MITM attacks involve identifying internal states in the middle of the primitive as matching points. The values at these matching points are computed independently in the forward and backward directions. By doing so, the attacker can retain partial key candidates that satisfy the matching conditions while discarding all others.

MITM attacks have been effectively applied to numerous designs using increasingly sophisticated techniques. Some of these techniques include Sieve-in-the-Middle [BC13], splice-and-cut [GLRW10], guess-and-determine [DSP07], bicliques [KRS12], 3-subset MITM [BR10], differential MITM [BDD+23] and Demirci-Selçuk [DS08].

E. Savas et al. (Eds.): LightSec 2025, LNCS 16216, pp. 306–327, 2026.
https://doi.org/10.1007/978-3-032-15541-2_17

MITM techniques have also been automated by some researchers. In [DF16], the Demirci-Selçuk MITM attack was automated using general constraint programming. In [SS23], a new MITM technique was proposed using Mixed Integer Linear Programming (MILP), which can be applied to lightweight Substitution-Permutation-Network (SPN) ciphers with a simple key schedule. Additionally, in [Sas18], Sasaki used MILP to optimize the 3-subset MITM attack on GIFT-64.

Since the US National Institute of Standards and Technology (NIST) announced a call for a new lightweight cryptographic standard in 2018 [oSN18], many lightweight cryptographic ciphers have been proposed. In lightweight ciphers, to make them suitable for lightweight platforms, the key schedule is often designed with slow diffusion or none at all. This design choice makes MITM attacks more feasible on such structures.

Our contributions. In this paper, we present a simple automated MITM attack which is easy to follow and implement. This technique is based on the relationship of the key bits at the matching points. The matching points depend only on the key bits that are nonlinearly involved, while the linearly involved key bits are canceled out by performing the differential in each direction. We introduce a tool[1] that models every bit and determines the relationship of key bits to each other.

Our proposed meet-in-the-middle attack introduces a notable balance between simplicity and efficiency, setting it apart from other complex techniques. While it may not achieve the highest number of rounds for key recovery, the simplicity of our approach results in exceptionally low data and memory complexity, making it highly accessible and easy to implement. Unlike many existing methods, our technique operates under a known-plaintext setting, eliminating the need for a chosen-plaintext attack and thus broadening its practical applicability. Despite its straightforward nature, which might limit its capability, the advantages in terms of data efficiency and ease of deployment position our technique as a valuable tool in cryptographic analysis.

We apply our tool to the block ciphers CRAFT [BLMR19], Midori [BBI+15], WARP [BBI+20], PRESENT [BKL+07], and ARADI [GMW24]. The complexities obtained using our tool are summarized in Table 1.

Outline. The paper is organized as follows. In Sect. 2, we provide details about our attack methodology, outline our MITM algorithm, and explain how the time data and memory complexities are computed. Next, in Sect. 3, we describe how the operations in the round functions are modeled and how the nonlinearly and linearly dependent key bits are calculated for each bit. Additionally, we present an algorithm that summarizes the operation of our tool, where the output includes the suggested matching points as well as the time, memory, and data complexities. In Sect. 4, we apply our technique to perform key recovery attacks on CRAFT, Midori, WARP, PRESENT80 and ARADI. We conclude the paper in Sect. 5.

---

[1] The tool has been fully implemented, and all attacks have been empirically validated. The tool is available at: https://github.com/mohammadvaziri/Automated-Meet-in-the-Middle-Attacks-Tool.

Table 1. Attacks overview. KP stands for Known Plaintext attack, and CP stands for Chosen Plaintext attack.

Target	Rounds	Data	Time(log_2)	Memory(log_2)	Attack Type	Reference
CRAFT	15/31	**3**	126.5/128	4	**KP**	Sect. 4.1
	20/31	2^{56}	126.9/128	109	CP	[MLC23]
Midori64	5/16	**16**	77/128	48	**KP**	Sect. 4.2
	12/16	$2^{55.5}$	125.5/128	106	CP	[LW17]
Midori128	7/20	**3**	126.3/128	0	**KP**	Sect. 4.2
WARP	18/41	**7**	125/128	6	**KP**	Sect. 4.3
	19/41	16	124.48/128	4	CP	[ZLW+23]
PRESENT80	6/31	**18**	68.2/80	15	**KP**	Sect. 4.4
	9/31	2^{12}	77/80	16	CP	[SS23]
ARADI	5/16	**28**	234.8/256	19	**KP**	Sect. 4.5

1.1 Notations

Throughout the paper, we will use the following notations:

$\mathcal{K}$	The set of all key bits.
K_f	The set of key bits involved in the forward direction at the matching points.
K_b	The set of key bits involved in the backward direction at the matching points.
K_u	The union of the set of all key bits in K_f and K_b ($K_u = K_f \cup K_b$).
K_c	The set of common key bits between K_f and K_b ($K_c = K_f \cap K_b$).
K_r	The set of key bits that are not included in K_u ($K_r = \mathcal{K} - K_u$).
$\mathcal{P}(\mathcal{K})$	The power set of the set $\mathcal{K}$.
$+$	The bitwise XOR operation.
$\parallel$	concatenation.

2 Background

In this section, we present a comprehensive overview of our MITM attack, along with the related formulas for time, data and memory complexities. In our approach, the meeting occurs at the bit level. Each bit within the internal rounds of the cipher algorithm retains crucial data, including the sets of key bits that are linearly and nonlinearly involved in the bit. Hereafter, the term *bit address* refers to the position of such encoded information. For the i-th bit of the internal state in round r, denoted as $x^r[i]$, we define the corresponding bit address as $X^r[i]$. In our methodology, essential information within each bit address is extracted using our automated tool in both forward and backward directions. The process of identifying the sets of linearly and nonlinearly dependent key bits at each bit address will be discussed in Sect. 3.

2.1   Description of Our MITM Approach

Our attack methodology is based on a known plaintext attack. To prepare the data for the attack, a set of pairs $D = \{(P_0, C_0), \ldots, (P_{d-1}, C_{d-1})\}$ of plaintext/ciphertext are randomly selected. The initial pair is designated as the primary pair. For each direction, the difference between the primary pair and the other pairs is computed at the matching points. These difference values are then used to check for a match. The purpose of calculating the differences at the matching points is to cancel the effect of linearly dependent key bits in both the forward and backward directions. The matching points may consist of a single bit or multiple bits. The selection of a bit address as a matching point depends on several factors, which will be discussed in Sect. 3.

As discussed, each bit depends on specific key bits in both the forward and backward directions. It is essential that the bit addresses chosen as matching points depend on the same set of key bits in the forward direction and the same set of key bits in the backward direction.

To illustrate the rationale behind performing the difference at the matching points to eliminate the effect of linearly involved key bits, consider the cipher structure in Fig. 1. Assume that the set of bit addresses $X = \{X[0], \ldots, X[m-1]\}$ is chosen as the matching points. For a given pair of plaintext and ciphertext (P, C), and the key bits in the forward and backward directions, $k_f \in K_f$ and $k_b \in K_b$, we define the forward and backward path functions as $F_f(P, k_f)$ and $F_b(C, k_b)$, respectively. Assume that the sets of nonlinearly dependent key bits in K_f and K_b are denoted by K_f^n and K_b^n, and the sets of linearly dependent key bits are represented by K_f^l and K_b^l. In the following, we discuss why the difference between pairs at the matching points within the set $D = \{(P_0, C_0), \ldots, (P_{d-1}, C_{d-1})\}$ remains unaffected by any key bits in the sets K_f^l and K_b^l.

Assume that the Boolean function $F_f(P, k_f)$ in the forward direction at the matching points X is divided into two sub-functions, $G_n(P, k_f^n)$ and $G_l(k_f^l)$, such that $F_f(P, k_f) = G_n(P, k_f^n) + G_l(k_f^l)$, where $k_f^n \in K_f^n$ and $k_f^l \in K_f^l$. According to Relations 1, the differential between two plaintexts P_0 and P_1 at the matching points, cancels out the effect of the function $G_l(k_f^l)$. A similar conclusion can be drawn for the backward direction.

$$\begin{aligned}
Xf_0 &= G_n(P_0, k_f^n) + G_l(k_f^l) \\
Xf_1 &= G_n(P_1, k_f^n) + G_l(k_f^l) \\
Xf_0 + Xf_1 &= G_n(P_0, k_f^n) + G_n(P_1, k_f^n)
\end{aligned} \tag{1}$$

It is important to note that the sub-function $G_l(k_f^l)$ can be derived independently of the plaintext vector P. Let $P = (p_0, \ldots, p_{n-1})$ represent the plaintext bits and $K = (k_0, \ldots, k_{n-1})$ the key bits introduced through a key schedule during the key addition phase. Since key addition is a linear operation, there exists no nonlinear interaction between bits, such as terms of the form $p_i k_j$ for $0 \leq i, j < n$. Consequently, unless a nonlinear operation is applied to the bit addresses, the plaintext and key bits remain linearly dependent. In such cases, the sub-function $G_l(k_f^l)$ remains derivable. For a detailed discussion on the identification of linearly and nonlinearly dependent key bit sets, refer to Sect. 3.

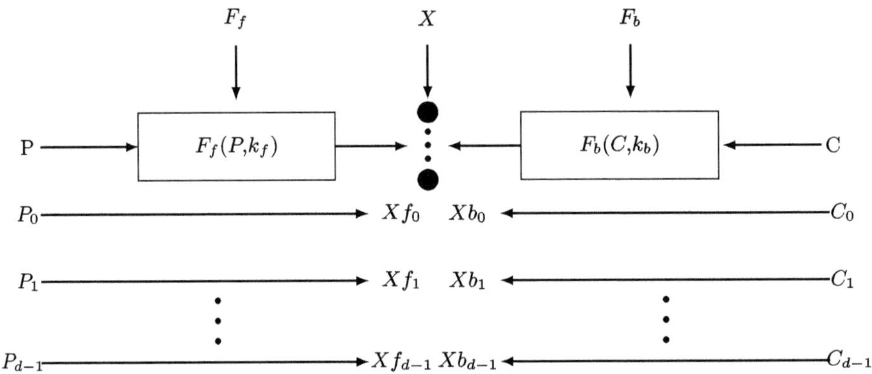

Fig. 1. General structure of the attack, where the forward and backward paths meet at the bit addresses $X = \{X[0], \ldots, X[m-1]\}$. By taking the differences between the pairs $(Xf_0, Xf_1), \ldots, (Xf_0, Xf_{d-1})$ and $(Xb_0, Xb_1), \ldots, (Xb_0, Xb_{d-1})$, the effect of the linearly dependent key bits in both directions can be canceled.

Consequently, the matching point difference is just influenced by the nonlinearly dependent key bits involved in both the forward and backward directions. Hereafter, for simplicity, the sets K_f and K_b denote the sets of nonlinearly dependent key bits in the forward and backward directions, respectively, for the given bit address $X^r[i]$.

It is important to note that if we denote the differences of (Xf_0, Xf_1), (Xf_0, Xf_2), and (Xf_1, Xf_2) as ΔXf_{01}, ΔXf_{02}, and ΔXf_{12} respectively at the matching points, the difference ΔXf_{12} contains no useful information. This is because we have already utilized the differences ΔXf_{01} and ΔXf_{02} to filter certain candidates. Additionally, since the difference ΔXf_{12} can be derived from ΔXf_{01} and ΔXf_{02}, it cannot effectively filter key candidates. Hence, we designate one pair as the primary pair and compute the differences of other pairs in comparison to the primary one.

The attack is divided into two phases. In the first phase a table H is generated to store whole of the possible values of the differentials of the pairs in one of the directions and in the second phase, whole of the possible values of the other direction is computed and the found matches are evaluated. The role of the forward and backward directions can be interchanged. To minimize memory complexity, the direction with the smaller size of key bits involved should be selected for generating the H table.

It is notable that optimizing memory complexity can be achieved by considering the set of key bits K_c shared between the forward and backward directions. In this approach, for each $k_c \in K_c$, the computations for both phases can be performed independently, allowing the memory to be reset afterward.

In order to recover the remaining key bits K_r in our attack, during the second phase, once a match is found in the table H, a set of $T = \{(P_0', C_0'), \ldots, (P_{t-1}', C_{t-1}')\}$ data pairs, encrypted with the main master key, is required to verify the correctness of the guessed key bits. This means that each plaintext in T is encrypted using the guessed key bits $k_c\|k_f\|k_b\|k_r$, where $k_c \in K_c$, $k_f \in K_f - K_c$, $k_b \in K_b - K_c$, and $k_r \in K_r$. If the resulting ciphertext does not match the corresponding ciphertext in the pair, the guessed key bits are incorrect. The size of the set T depends on the size of the block cipher and the main master key. For example, if the block cipher size is 64 bits and the master key size is 128 bits, the size of the set T should be 2.

To perform the attack, assume we have d random pairs of data represented as $D = \{(P_0, C_0), \ldots, (P_{d-1}, C_{d-1})\}$, with (P_0, C_0) designated as the primary pair. A set of m bit addresses, $X = \{X[0], \ldots, X[m-1]\}$, is selected as the matching points. For the given pair of data (P, C), with $k_f \in K_f$ and $k_b \in K_b$, assume the Boolean functions used in the forward and backward directions are $F_f(P, k_f)$ and $F_b(C, k_b)$, respectively. The forward direction is used to generate the table H. The steps of the attack proceed as follows:

For each $k_c \in K_c$, perform the following steps:

1. Initialize the hash table H, which is indexed by the differentials of all matching point values in the forward direction. Since there are m matching points and $d-1$ differences, the table H contains $2^{m(d-1)}$ indices. Therefore, assuming the cipher behaves similarly to a random function, we expect to have an average of $2^{|K_f|-|K_c|-m(d-1)}$ values for each index in the table H.

2. a. For each $k_f \in K_f - K_c$, and for each P_i, where $0 \le i \le d-1$ in $D = \{(P_0, C_0), \ldots, (P_{d-1}, C_{d-1})\}$, compute the values of all Xf_i, where $Xf_i = F_f(P_i, k_c\|k_f)$.

   b. Compute the values $\Delta Xf_{0i} = Xf_0 + Xf_i$ for $1 \le i \le d-1$. Using the obtained value, update the corresponding index in the table H with $k_c\|k_f$.

3. a. For each $k_b \in K_b - K_c$, and for each C_i, where $0 \le i \le d-1$ in $D = \{(P_0, C_0), \ldots, (P_{d-1}, C_{d-1})\}$, compute the values of all Xb_i, where $Xb_i = F_b(C_i, k_c\|k_b)$.

   b. Compute the values $\Delta Xb_{0i} = Xb_0 + Xb_i$ for $1 \le i \le d-1$, and search for a match for $\Delta Xb_{01}\|\ldots\|\Delta Xb_{0d-1}$ in the table H.

   c. i. For each value k_f in $H[\Delta Xb_{01}\|\ldots\|\Delta Xb_{0d-1}]$ proceed to the following steps.

      ii. A. For each $k_r \in K_r$, set a Flag to true, and perform the following steps.

          B. For each (P_t', C_t') in the set T, encrypt the plaintext P_t' using the guessed key bits $k_c\|k_f\|k_b\|k_r$ as $C_t = F(P_t', k_c\|k_f\|k_b\|k_r)$. If $C_t \ne C_t'$, set the Flag to false. If the Flag is false, this indicates that the guessed key is incorrect, and a different k_r should be tried. In this case, return to step A.

C. If the Flag remains true, return the guessed key $k_c\|k_f\|k_b\|k_r$ as the master key.

Based on the aforementioned algorithm, where the forward direction is selected to generate the table H, the time complexity of the attack is given by:

$$2^{|K_c|}\left(d \cdot 2^{|K_f|-|K_c|} + 2^{|K_b|-|K_c|} \cdot \left(d + 2^{|K_f|-|K_c|-(d-1)m} \cdot 2^{|K_r|} \cdot t\right)\right) \tag{2}$$

The time complexity formula in Eq. (2) can be simplified as follows:

$$\tau = d \cdot 2^{|K_f|} + d \cdot 2^{|K_b|} + t \cdot 2^{|K_f|+|K_b|+|K_r|-|K_c|-(d-1)m} \tag{3}$$

As seen in Eq. (3), all terms are precomputed and fixed except for the data complexity d. Therefore, to achieve optimal time and data complexity, Eq. (3) can be regarded as a function with one variable d, where the goal is to find the minimum value of d such that $\tau < 2^{|\mathcal{K}|}$. The obtained d should then be rounded to the nearest integer.

Algorithm 1: Our meet in the middle algorithm

Input   : d random pairs of data as $D = \{(P_0, C_0), ..., (P_{d-1}, C_{d-1})\}$,
The bit addresses $X[0], \ldots, X[m-1]$ as the chosen matching points,
t extra pairs of data as $T = \{(P'_0, C'_0), ..., (P'_{t-1}, C'_{t-1})\}$

Output: A value for the key bits in the set $\mathcal{K}$ as candidate

1 **for** *each k_c in K_c* **do**

2   Initialize the hash table H indexed by the differences of the values at the matching points in the forward direction;

3   **for** *each k_f in $K_f - K_c$* **do**

4          $Xf_i = F_f(P_i, k_c\|k_f), \quad 0 \le i \le d-1$;

5          $\Delta Xf_{0i} = Xf_0 \oplus Xf_i, \quad 1 \le i \le d-1$;

6          $H[\Delta Xf_{01}\|\ldots\|\Delta Xf_{0d-1}] \leftarrow H[\Delta Xf_{01}\|\ldots\|\Delta Xf_{0d-1}] \cup \{k_f\}$;

7   **for** *each k_b in $K_b - K_c$* **do**

8          $Xb_i = F_b(C_i, k_c\|k_b), \quad 0 \le i \le d-1$;

9          $\Delta Xb_{0i} = Xb_0 \oplus Xb_i, \quad 1 \le i \le d-1$;

10   **for** *each k_f in $H[\Delta Xb_{01}\|\ldots\|\Delta Xb_{0d-1}]$* **do**

11   **for** *each k_r in K_r* **do**

12   Flag = True;

13   **for** *each (P'_t, C'_t) in T* **do**

14                      $C_t = F(P'_t, k_c\|k_f\|k_b\|k_r)$;

15   **if** $C_t \neq C'_t$ **then**

16   Flag = False;

17   Go back to line 11

18   **if** *Flag is True* **then**

19   Return $k_c\|k_f\|k_b\|k_r$ as the master key;

Based on the algorithm, the memory complexity can be calculated as follows:

$$\min(2^{|K_f|-|K_c|}, 2^{|K_b|-|K_c|}) \tag{4}$$

The process of the algorithm is summarized in Algorithm 1.

3   Overview of Our Automatic Tool

In this section, we provide details of our modeling method. As discussed in Sect. 2, the set of key bits that are nonlinearly involved at the bit addresses determine the complexity. Therefore, the key question is how to calculate the sets of linearly and nonlinearly dependent key bits for each bit address and determine which bits are suitable to be chosen as matching points. The answers to these questions are elaborated below.

3.1   Modeling the Operations

In our technique, all key bits in the sets of linearly and nonlinearly dependent bits for each bit address, whether in the forward or backward direction, must be determined. It is important to note that the intersection of the linearly and nonlinearly dependent sets for each direction in each bit address must be empty.

The information regarding each bit address in the internal rounds, which includes the set of nonlinearly and linearly dependent key bits, relies on the boolean functions $F_i : \mathbb{F}_2^n \rightarrow \mathbb{F}_2$ in $F = (F_0, F_1, \ldots, F_{n-1})$ applied to the corresponding bit. Let $x = (x_0, x_1, \ldots, x_{n-1})$ represent the input bits of F, and $x' = (x_0', x_1', \ldots, x_{n-1}')$ represent the corresponding output bits of F. Let the associated bit addresses for the input and output vectors be $(X[0], \ldots, X[n-1])$ and $(X'[0], \ldots, X'[n-1])$ respectively.

Each bit address $X[i]$ $(X'[i])$, where $i \in \{0, 1, \ldots, n-1\}$, is a tuple (N_i, L_i) (N_i', L_i'), where N_i (N_i') and L_i (L_i') denote the sets of nonlinearly and linearly dependent key bits, respectively, and $N_i \subseteq \mathcal{K}$ $(N_i' \subseteq \mathcal{K})$ and $L_i \subseteq \mathcal{K}$ $(L_i' \subseteq \mathcal{K})$, with $N_i \cap L_i = \emptyset$ $(N_i' \cap L_i' = \emptyset)$.

Assume that all of the tuples (N_i, L_i), where $i \in \{0, 1, \ldots, n-1\}$, for the bit addresses $X[i]$ are already determined, and we aim to calculate the tuples (N_i', L_i') for the bit addresses $X'[i]$. For each bit address $X'[i]$, which is the output of the function F_i, we define two sets of dependency indices I_i and J_i, where $I_i \cap J_i = \emptyset$, based on certain properties of F_i (explained in the following). The set I_i contains the indices of the bit addresses $X[u]$ $(u \in \mathbb{Z}_n)$ on which $X'[i]$ nonlinearly depends, and similarly, J_i contains the indices of the bit addresses $X[v]$ $(v \in \mathbb{Z}_n)$ on which $X'[i]$ linearly depends. Therefore, we have:

$$\begin{aligned}
I_i &= \{u \mid u \in \mathbb{Z}_n \text{ and } X'[i] \text{ nonlinearly depends on } X[u]\} \\
J_i &= \{v \mid v \in \mathbb{Z}_n \text{ and } X'[i] \text{ linearly depends on } X[v]\} \\
I_i &\cap J_i = \emptyset
\end{aligned} \tag{5}$$

Given the algebraic normal form of F_i, where $i \in \{0, 1, \ldots, n-1\}$, the dependency sets I_i and J_i for the given bit address $X'[i]$ can be calculated. To clarify, consider the block cipher PRESENT [BKL+07] as an example. In PRESENT, if the vector (x_3, x_2, x_1, x_0) represents the input and the vector (x_3', x_2', x_1', x_0') represents the output of the S-box function, the algebraic normal form of the PRESENT S-box is expressed as follows:

$$
\begin{aligned}
x_3' &= x_1 x_2 + x_0 + x_2 + x_3 \\
x_2' &= x_0 x_1 x_2 + x_0 x_1 x_3 + x_0 x_2 x_3 + x_1 x_3 + x_2 x_3 + x_1 + x_3 \\
x_1' &= x_0 x_1 x_3 + x_0 x_2 x_3 + x_0 x_1 + x_0 x_3 + x_1 x_3 + x_2 + x_3 + 1 \\
x_0' &= x_0 x_1 x_2 + x_0 x_1 x_3 + x_0 x_2 x_3 + x_1 x_2 + x_0 + x_1 + x_3 + 1
\end{aligned}
\tag{6}
$$

As shown in Eq. (6), the first (x_0'), second (x_1'), and third (x_2') output bits nonlinearly depend on all four input bits. However, the fourth (x_3') output bit nonlinearly depends on the second and third input bits and linearly depends on the first and fourth input bits. Therefore, the corresponding sets of dependencies I_i and $J_i, 0 \le i \le 3$ can be represented as follows:

$$
\begin{aligned}
I_0 &= I_1 = I_2 = \{0, 1, 2, 3\}, \quad J_0 = J_1 = J_2 = \emptyset \\
I_3 &= \{1, 2\} \quad J_3 = \{0, 3\}
\end{aligned}
\tag{7}
$$

Without loss of generality, to compute (N_i', L_i') for $i \in \{0, \dots, n-1\}$ at bit address $X'[i]$, we define two functions N_{F_i} and L_{F_i}. The function N_{F_i} (L_{F_i}) is designed to establish N_i' (L_i'). N_{F_i} takes as input a set of bit addresses at the input of F_i, indexed by I_i and J_i, and returns a subset of $\mathcal{K}$. On the other hand, L_{F_i} only takes as input a set of bit addresses indexed by J_i and returns a subset of $\mathcal{K}$. It is essential to note that the intersection of the outputs of N_{F_i} and L_{F_i} must be empty. Therefore, N_{F_i} and L_{F_i} are formulated as follows:

$$
\begin{aligned}
&N_{F_i} : \left(\prod_{j \in I_i} (N_j, L_j) \times \prod_{j \in J_i} (N_j, L_j) \right) \to \mathcal{P}(\mathcal{K}) \\
&N_{F_i}(\{X[j] \mid j \in I_i\}, \{X[j] \mid j \in J_i\}) \to \bigcup_{j \in I_i} (N_j \cup L_j) \cup \bigcup_{j \in J_i} N_j = N_i'
\end{aligned}
\tag{8}
$$

$$
\begin{aligned}
&L_{F_i} : \left(\prod_{j \in J_i} (N_j, L_j), N_i' \right) \to \mathcal{P}(\mathcal{K}) \\
&L_{F_i}(\{X[j] \mid j \in J_i\}, N_i') \to \bigcup_{j \in J_i} L_j \setminus N_i' = L_i'
\end{aligned}
$$

As shown in Eq. (8), the functions N_{F_i} and L_{F_i} are used to determine the dependency of each key bit at each bit address $X'[i]$. Therefore, for the S-box of the PRESENT, if we assume that the bit addresses $X[i] = (N_i, L_i), 0 \le i \le 3$ correspond to the vector (x_3, x_2, x_1, x_0) as the input of the S-box, for calculating the data in the bit addresses $X'[i]$, we have:

$$
\begin{aligned}
N_u' &= \bigcup_{i \in I_u} (N_i \cup L_i), \quad L_u' = \emptyset \quad u \in \{0, 1, 2\} \\
N_3' &= \bigcup_{i \in I_3} (N_i \cup L_i) \cup \bigcup_{i \in J_3} N_i \quad L_3' = \bigcup_{i \in J_3} L_i \setminus N_3'
\end{aligned}
\tag{9}
$$

It is noteworthy that linear operations in cryptographic primitives, such as MixColumn and XOR, can be represented using the same formula introduced in Eq. (8). However, it should be noted that the dependency sets I_i, where $i \in \{0, 1, \ldots, n-1\}$, are $\emptyset$ for these operations. Before proceeding to the next section, we introduce the following definition:

Definition 1. *Permissible matching points: Permissible matching points are those bits whose corresponding bit addresses contain information that leads to a successful attack.*

3.2   Algorithm to Find the Matching Points

In this section, we elucidate the functionality of our automated tool for implementing MITM attacks. Specifically, we delve into computing the time, data, and memory complexities and also the process of selecting matching points. To illustrate this, we refer to Fig. 2, which depicts the structure of a cipher.

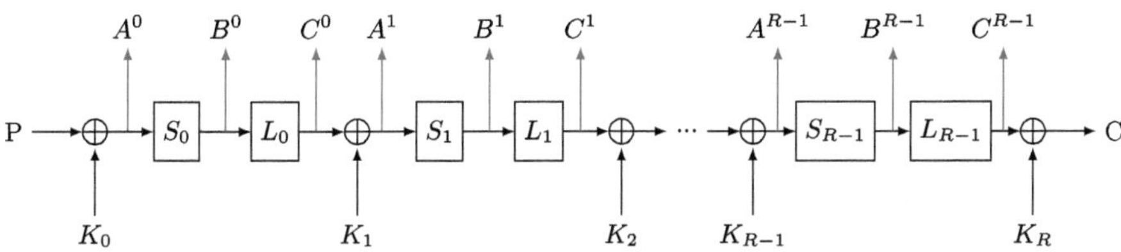

Fig. 2. Illustration of a cipher, where the positions $A^r[i]$, $B^r[i]$, and $C^r[i]$ (for $0 \leq r < R$ and $0 \leq i < n$) are designated as the bit addresses.

In Fig. 2, assume that the cipher has a block size of n and comprises R rounds. The round keys K_i, $0 \leq i \leq R$, are derived using the key schedule algorithm from the set of all key bits $\mathcal{K}$. Our goal is to target the maximum number of rounds feasible, while ensuring that the time complexity remains lower than exhaustive search.

To model the cipher with our tool, we first determine which positions are suitable to be considered as bit addresses. Each position is selected based on the operations applied in the cipher. Specifically, positions after operations that modify the arrangement of nonlinearly dependent key bits are ideal candidates for bit addresses. In Fig. 2, the positions $A^r[i]$, $B^r[i]$, and $C^r[i]$, where $0 \leq r < R$ and $0 \leq i < n$, are chosen as the bit addresses, and each bit address is modeled according to the method described in Sect. 3.1. For each bit address, the tool then computes the sets of linearly and nonlinearly dependent key bits in both the forward and backward directions. Once these sets are established, the cardinality of each set of nonlinearly dependent key bits is calculated based on the key schedule[2]. This enables the computation of the time complexity required to recover the key bits at each bit address.

---

[2] There may exist dependencies among the key-bits due to the key schedule. For instance, refer to the details of PRESENT80 in Sect. 4.4.

It is evident that as the number of rounds increases, the size of the set of nonlinearly dependent key bits in both the forward and backward directions also increases, until it reaches a point where the time complexity for all bit addresses becomes greater than or equal to $2^{|\mathcal{K}|}$. This indicates that the attack is no longer faster than an exhaustive search, and no permissible matching points can be found among the bit addresses. Therefore, to find the maximum number of rounds possible to perform the attack, the number of rounds R is increased as long as the time complexity remains lower than $2^{|\mathcal{K}|}$.

The following provides an explanation of how our automatic tool operates. For simplicity, we define the following terms for a given bit address $X^r[i]$:

$XK_f^r[i]$	The set of nonlinearly dependent key bits in the forward direction.
$XK_b^r[i]$	The set of nonlinearly dependent key bits in the backward direction.
$XK_u^r[i]$	$XK_u^r[i] = XK_f^r[i] \cup XK_b^r[i]$.
$XK_c^r[i]$	$XK_c^r[i] = XK_f^r[i] \cap XK_b^r[i]$.
$XK_r^r[i]$	$XK_r^r[i] = \mathcal{K} - XK_u^r[i]$.
$XT^r[i]$	the time complexity to recover the master key if $X^r[i]$ is a matching point.
$XD^r[i]$	the data complexity to recover the master key if $X^r[i]$ is a matching point.
$XM^r[i]$	the memory complexity to recover the master key if $X^r[i]$ is a matching point.
$XT'^r[i]$	$XT'^r[i] = \max\left(|XK_f^r[i]|, |XK_b^r[i]|\right)$.
$XM'^r[i]$	$XM'^r[i] = \min\left(|XK_f^r[i]|, |XK_b^r[i]|\right)$.

For each bit address $X^r[i]$, our automatic tool first forms the sets $XK_f^r[i]$ and $XK_b^r[i]$, and then derives the values $|XK_f^r[i]|$, $|XK_b^r[i]|$, $|XK_c^r[i]|$, and $|XK_r^r[i]|$ from these sets. According to relations 3 and 4, $XT'^r[i]$ determines the time complexity, while $XM'^r[i]$ determines the memory complexity.

After calculating $XT'^r[i]$ for each bit address $X^r[i]$, the bit addresses with the minimum value of $XT'^r[i]$ are selected as candidates for the matching points. If this minimum value equals $|\mathcal{K}|$, it indicates that no permissible matching point exists, and the attack is no longer faster than exhaustive search.

By using the values $XM'^r[i]$ and $XK_c^r[i]$ for each bit address $X^r[i]$ selected as a candidate, the memory complexity $XM^r[i]$ can be calculated. Therefore, among these candidates, those with the minimum $XM^r[i]$ value are selected as the new candidates for the matching points, and the minimum value is returned as the memory complexity.

According to Eq. (3), to achieve better time and data complexity, the number of matching points m should be as large as possible. Therefore, among the list of candidates, those that share the same set of nonlinearly dependent key bits in the forward direction and also same set of nonlinearly dependent key bits in the backward direction are grouped into distinct sets. Among these sets, the one with the maximum size is randomly selected as the final set of candidates for the matching points. It should be noted that the size of this final set represents the number of matching points m.

At this stage, all values $|K_f|, |K_b|, |K_c|, |K_r|$, and m have been computed, and according to Eq. (3), the value of the function τ depends only on the variable d. Therefore, the data complexity d is determined to minimize the time complexity τ. If the obtained value is greater than or equal to $2^{|\mathcal{K}|}$, it indicates that there is no permissible matching point for the given round R. Algorithm 2, summarizes the functioning of our automatic tool.

Algorithm 2: The algorithm used in our automatic tool.

Input   : Given cipher with size n and round R, with the set of its master key $\mathcal{K}$ and its key schedule

Output: Time complexity T, Memory complexity M, Data complexity D, set of bit addresses as the matching points

1 **for** *each r in R* **do**
2   -Model each $X^r[i]$ and form the sets $XK_f^r[i]$ and $XK_b^r[i]$;
3   -For each $X^r[i]$, derive the values $|XK_f^r[i]|, |XK_b^r[i]|, |XK_c^r[i]|, |XK_r^r[i]|, XT'^r[i]$ and $XM'^r[i]$.;
4   -Select the bit addresses that have minimum value for $XT'^r[i]$ as candidates and name the minimum value T';
5   **if** $T' = |\mathcal{K}|$ **then**
6   Terminate the algorithm;
7   **else**
8   -For each $X^r[i]$ in the list of candidates, calculate $XM^r[i]$;
9   -Update the list of candidates by selecting the bit addresses that have minimum value for $XM^r[i]$ and name the minimum value M;
10   -**Return** M as the memory complexity;
11   -For the candidates, categorize them, by inserting those that share the same set of keys in the forward and backward direction in a set;
12   -Name the maximum size of the sets m (number of the matching points);
13   -Randomly select one of the sets with the size of m and name the set S;
14   -Minimize the function τ, by carefully selecting a value for d, in the Equation 3;
15   -Name the obtained value for τ, T and name d as D;
16   **if** $T \geq 2^{|\mathcal{K}|}$ **then**
17   Terminate the algorithm;
18   **else**
19   **Return** T as the time complexity;
20   **Return** D as the data complexity;
21   **Return** S as the set of matching points;

---

4 Applications

In this section, we illustrate how our tool can be applied to various lightweight block ciphers. Specifically, for the ciphers CRAFT [BLMR19] and the Midori family [BBI+15], which employ MixColumn in their design, we introduce two attack strategies. The first approach is the "regular technique", while the second leverages what we term the "equivalent key technique."

In the equivalent key technique, during backward analysis, we do not guess a key bit in its original position post-MixColumn. Instead, we guess an equivalent key bit before the MixColumn, where the MixColumn establishes a linear relationship between the key bits and their equivalent counterparts. This method, initially introduced by [IS13], was developed to perform key recovery attacks on Feistel structures, aiming to reduce the number of guessed key bits by substituting original key bits with equivalent ones. By applying the equivalent key technique to CRAFT, we were able to enhance the key recovery attack; however, no improvement was observed for the Midori family.

All experiments were conducted on a personal computer running Ubuntu 22.04.3 LTS, equipped with an Intel Core i5-10210U CPU (4 cores, 2 threads) and 16 GB of RAM. The code was implemented in Python 3.10. The tool demonstrated high computational efficiency: for example, the CRAFT regular technique required approximately 3 s to complete, while the equivalent technique took 52 s.

4.1   Application to CRAFT

CRAFT is a lightweight tweakable SPN block cipher devised by Beierle et al. In this section, we present our results on CRAFT. We conducted regular and equivalent key attacks on CRAFT. With the regular attack, we successfully attacked to 14 rounds, while employing the equivalent key technique enabled us to reach 15 rounds. For the complete specification of CRAFT, we refer to [BLMR19].

In order to utilize our tool, the initial step involves determining the bits within the round functions that are to be regarded as the bit addresses, along with describing the operations at the bit level. Figure 3 illustrates the CRAFT structure and highlights the positions designated as the bit addresses in the regular technique.

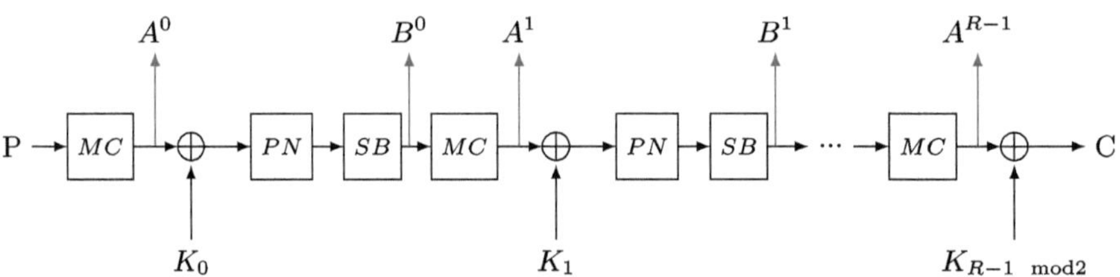

Fig. 3. Regular attack on CRAFT. The positions $A^r, B^r, 0 \leq r < R$ are considered as the bit Addresses.

Next, to illustrate the S-box, we must establish the dependency sets as described in Sect. 3.1. Based on the structure of the CRAFT S-box, the dependency sets are as follows:

$$I_0 = I_1 = I_3 = \{0,1,2,3\}, \quad J_0 = J_1 = J_3 = \emptyset$$
$$I_2 = \{0,1,3\} \quad J_2 = \emptyset \tag{10}$$

Since the S-box is involutory, the dependency sets for the forward and backward directions remain the same.

We represent the set of all key bits as $\mathcal{K} = \{k_0, \ldots, k_{127}\}$. The round keys K_0 and K_1, derived from $\mathcal{K}$ based on the key schedule and used alternately in the round functions of CRAFT, are as follows:

$$K_0 = \{k_0, k_1, \ldots, k_{63}\}$$
$$K_1 = \{k_{64}, k_{65}, \ldots, k_{127}\} \tag{11}$$

To clarify how our automatic tool works, based on Fig. 3, the method by which the sets of nonlinearly dependent key bits $XN^r[i]$, where $0 \le i < 64$ and $0 \le r < 32$, and linearly dependent key bits $XL^r[i]$ for a given bit address $X^r[i]$ are formed is explained in Table 2. The process begins by forming the sets at bit addresses $A^0[i]$ in the forward direction and $A^{r-1}[i]$ in the backward direction, continuing until the set of all nonlinearly dependent key bits for all bit addresses equals $|\mathcal{K}|$.

In the regular attack, we managed to attack 14 rounds with time, data, and memory complexities of $2^{126.5}$, 3 and 2^4, respectively. The bit addresses identified as matches by our tool are $A^6[16], A^6[17], A^6[18]$ and $A^6[19]$. The parameters obtained using our tool are $K_f = K_b = 124$, $K_u = 128$, $K_c = 120$, $K_r = 0$, and $m = 4$. According to the structure of the cipher, we have $t = 2$.

In the equivalent technique case, the positions chosen as bit addresses are shown in Fig. 4.

Table 2. The process by which the set of key bits is formed in CRAFT in the forward and backward directions.

$A^r[0]$	$A^r[1]$	$A^r[2]$	$\ldots$ $A^r[63]$
Forward Direction			
$AN^0[0] = \emptyset$ $AL^0[0] = \emptyset$	$AN^0[1] = \emptyset$ $AL^0[1] = \emptyset$	$AN^0[2] = \emptyset$ $AL^0[2] = \emptyset$	$\ldots$ $AN^0[63] = \emptyset$ $AL^0[63] = \emptyset$
$BN^0[0] = \{k_{60}, k_{61}, k_{62}, k_{63}\}$ $BL^0[0] = \emptyset$	$BN^0[1] = \{k_{60}, k_{61}, k_{62}, k_{63}\}$ $BL^0[1] = \emptyset$	$BN^0[2] = \{k_{60}, k_{62}, k_{63}\}$ $BL^0[2] = \emptyset$	$\ldots$ $BN^0[63] = \{k_0, k_1, k_2, k_3\}$ $BL^0[63] = \emptyset$
$\vdots$	$\vdots$	$\vdots$	$\ddots$ $\vdots$
$AN^8[0] = \mathcal{K}$ $AL^8[0] = \emptyset$	$AN^8[1] = \mathcal{K}$ $AL^8[1] = \emptyset$	$AN^8[2] = \mathcal{K}$ $AL^8[2] = \emptyset$	$\ldots$ $AN^8[63] = \mathcal{K}$ $AL^8[63] = \emptyset$
Backward Direction			
$AN^{r-1}[0] = \emptyset$ $AL^{r-1}[0] = k_{64}$	$AN^{r-1}[1] = \emptyset$ $AL^{r-1}[1] = k_{65}$	$AN^{r-1}[2] = \emptyset$ $AL^{r-1}[2] = k_{66}$	$\ldots$ $AN^{r-1}[63] = \emptyset$ $AL^{r-1}[63] = k_{127}$
$BN^{r-2}[0] = \emptyset$ $BL^{r-2}[0] = \{k_{64}, k_{96}, k_{112}\}$	$BN^{r-2}[1] = \emptyset$ $BL^{r-2}[1] = \{k_{65}, k_{97}, k_{113}\}$	$BN^{r-2}[2] = \emptyset$ $BL^{r-2}[2] = \{k_{66}, k_{98}, k_{114}\}$	$\ldots$ $BN^{r-2}[63] = \emptyset$ $BL^{r-2}[63] = \{k_{127}\}$
$\vdots$	$\vdots$	$\vdots$	$\ddots$ $\vdots$
$BN^{r-9}[0] = \mathcal{K}$ $BL^{r-9}[0] = \emptyset$	$BN^{r-9}[1] = \mathcal{K}$ $BL^{r-9}[1] = \emptyset$	$BN^{r-9}[2] = \mathcal{K}$ $BL^{r-9}[2] = \emptyset$	$\ldots$ $BN^{r-9}[63] = \mathcal{K}$ $BL^{r-9}[63] = \emptyset$

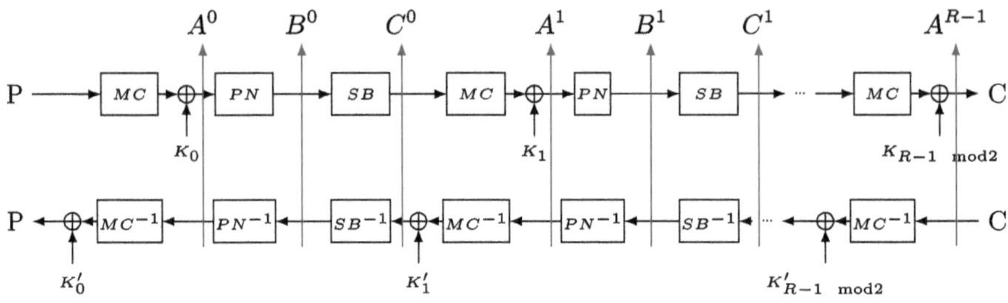

Fig. 4. Equivalent key attack on CRAFT. the positions A^r, B^r, C^r, $0 \leq i < R$ are considered as the bit Addresses. In the backward direction the key addition is moved prior to Mixcolumn

As explained earlier, in the equivalent key technique, the round keys in the backward direction are shifted prior to the MixColumn operation. As a result, the round keys are represented as $K'_0 = \{k'_0, \dots, k'_{63}\}$ and $K'_1 = \{k'_{64}, \dots, k'_{127}\}$, where each k'_i ($0 \leq i \leq 127$) is obtained by applying the inverse of the Mix-Column operation to the original k_i values[3]. Consequently, each k'_i is a linear combination of the original k_i values. Specifically, based on the structure of the CRAFT MixColumn, we have:

$$k'_0 = k_0 + k_{32} + k_{48}$$
$$k'_1 = k_1 + k_{33} + k_{49}$$
$$k'_2 = k_2 + k_{34} + k_{50} \tag{12}$$
$$\vdots$$

Based on the output of the tool, we successfully attacked 15 rounds with time, data and memory complexities of $2^{126.5}$, 3 and 2^4, respectively. The bit addresses identified as the matching points by our tool are $A^6[16]$, $A^6[17]$, $A^6[18]$ and $A^6[19]$. The parameters are the same as those derived in the regular attack.

To the best of our knowledge, there is one other reported MITM attack on CRAFT, proposed by [MLC23]. Their attack targets 20 rounds with time, data and memory complexities of $2^{126.94}$, 2^{56} and 2^{109}, respectively. Although their attack covers more rounds, it is based on a chosen-plaintext attack and requires significantly more data and memory compared to our approach.

4.2 Application to Midori

Midori is an SPN variant designed by Banik et al. It comprises two block ciphers: Midori64 and Midori128. In this section, we detail our results on the Midori family. In both th regular and equivalent key technique, we successfully attacked

---

[3] Since the MixColumn of CRAFT is involutory, the MixColumn and its inverse are identical.

5 and 7 rounds for Midori64 and Midori128, respectively. The full specification of Midori can be found in [BBI+15].

Figure 5 illustrates the structure of Midori along with the designated bit address positions utilized in the regular approach.

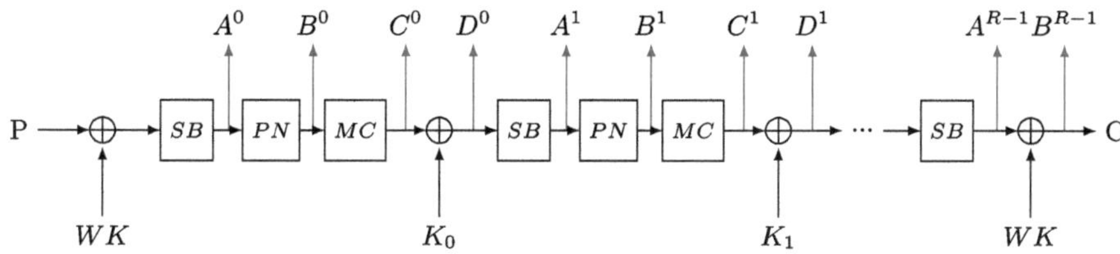

Fig. 5. Regular attack on Midori. the positions $A^r, B^r, C^r, D^r, 0 \leq r < R$ are considered as the bit Addresses.

The S-box utilized in Midori64 is identical to CRAFT. However, for Midori128, a different S-box is used and the dependency sets for its S-box are as follows:

$$I_0 = I_1 = I_2 = I_3 = \{0, 1, 2, 3\}, \quad J_0 = J_1 = J_2 = J_3 = \emptyset \tag{13}$$

If we represent the set of all key bits as $\mathcal{K} = \{k_0, \ldots, k_{127}\}$. The round keys WK, K_0 and K_1, derived from $\mathcal{K}$ based on the key schedule and used alternately in the round functions of Midori64, are as follows:

$$\begin{aligned}
WK &= \{k_0 + k_{64}, k_1 + k_{65}, \ldots, k_{63} + k_{127}\} \\
K_0 &= \{k_0, k_1, \ldots, k_{63}\} \\
K_1 &= \{k_{64}, k_{65}, \ldots, k_{127}\}
\end{aligned} \tag{14}$$

For Midori128 we have $WK = K_0 = K_1 = \{k_0, k_1, \ldots, k_{127}\}$.

For Midori64 in the regular technique, we were able to attack 5 rounds with the time, data and memory complexity of $2^{77}, 16$ and 2^{48}, respectively, with matching points are $C^1[20], C^1[21], C^1[22]$ and $C^1[23]$. Using our tool, we derived the following parameters: $K_f = K_b = 72$, $K_u = 120$, $K_c = 24$, $K_r = 8$, and $m = 4$. Based on the cipher's structure, this implies $t = 2$.

For Midori128, we were able to attack 7 rounds with the time, data and memory complexity of $2^{126.3}, 3, 2^0$, respectively, with the matching points are $C^2[40], C^2[43], C^2[45]$ and $C^2[46]$. Our tool yields the parameter values $K_f = K_b = 124$, $K_u = 124$, $K_c = 124$, $K_r = 4$, and $m = 4$. According to the cipher design, the corresponding value of t is 1.

For the equivalent key technique, we used Fig. 6 for reference.

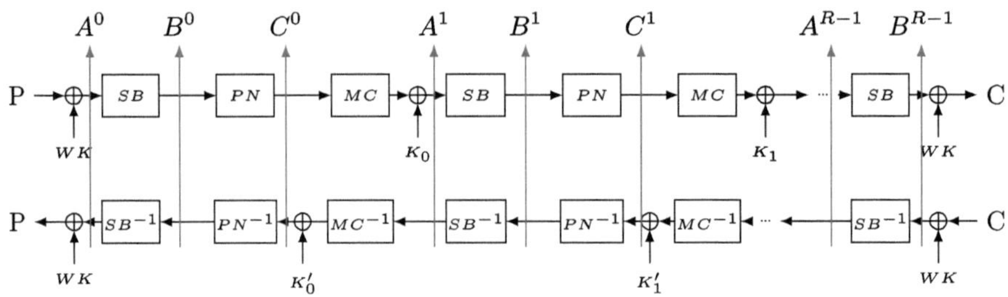

Fig. 6. Equivalent key attack on Midori. the positions A^r, B^r, C^r, $0 \leq r < R$ are considered as the bit Addresses. In the backward direction the key addition is moved prior to Mixcolumn.

For Midori64, we were able to attack 5 rounds with the time, data and memory complexity of $2^{86.6}, 49$ and 2^{39} respectively. The bit address that our tool returned as the matching point is $B^2[6]$. The analysis performed by our tool produces the parameters $K_f = 76$, $K_b = 81$, $K_u = 120$, $K_c = 37$, $K_r = 8$, and $m = 1$, with the cipher's structure indicating that $t = 2$.

For Midori128, we were able to attack 6 rounds with the time, data and memory complexity of $2^{125.5}, 3$ and 2^4, respectively. The matching points are $A^3[32], A^3[34], A^3[37]$ and $A^3[39]$. According to the results from our tool, the parameters are set as $K_f = 124$, $K_b = 88$, $K_u = 128$, $K_c = 84$, $K_r = 0$, and $m = 4$. The structure of the cipher further determines $t = 1$.

As far as we know, only one other MITM attack on Midori64 has been documented, as introduced by [LW17]. This attack focuses on 12 rounds and has time, data and memory complexities of $2^{125.5}$, $2^{55.5}$ and 2^{106}, respectively.

4.3 Application to WARP

The lightweight block cipher WARP, proposed by Banik et al. [BBI+20], is a variant of the 32-nibble Type-2 Generalized Feistel Network (GFN). In this section, we present our results on WARP. We were able to attack 18 rounds of WARP. The complete specification of WARP can be found in [BBI+20].

The S-box utilized in WARP is identical to those used in Midori and CRAFT. As WARP's structure does not incorporate MixColumn operations, we exclusively executed a regular attack. The round keys K_0 and K_1 used in WARP are as the same as used in CRAFT 11.

Leveraging our tool, we successfully attacked 18 rounds with time, data and memory complexities of 2^{125}, 7, and 2^6, respectively. The matching point is the single bit $B^8[2]$. Our tool computes the parameters as follows: $K_f = 122$, $K_b = 118$, $K_u = 128$, $K_c = 112$, $K_r = 0$, and $m = 1$. From the structural characteristics of the cipher, it follows that $t = 1$.

4.4   Application to **PRESENT80**

PRESENT80 is an ultra-lightweight block cipher designed as an SP-network, operating through 31 rounds. It has a block size of 64 bits and supports a key size of 80 bits. Each of the 31 rounds includes an XOR operation to add a round key K_r for $1 \leq r \leq 32$, with K_{32} used for post-whitening. Additionally, each round involves a linear bitwise permutation and a nonlinear substitution layer. The nonlinear layer utilizes a single 4-bit S-box S, which is applied 16 times in parallel during each round. The complete specification of PRESENT80 is provided in [BKL+07].

Although the most effective key-recovery attacks on the block cipher PRESENT are based on linear cryptanalysis, they require high data complexity. In contrast, MITM attacks offer the benefit of lower data complexity.

The dependency sets for the S-box of PRESENT80 are defined in Eq. 7. However, it should be noted that in the backward direction, the inverse of the S-box is applied. The dependency sets for the backward direction are as follows:

$$I_0 = I_1 = I_2 = \{0, 1, 2, 3\}, \quad J_0 = J_1 = J_2 = \emptyset$$
$$I_3 = \{0, 2\} \quad J_3 = \{1, 3\} \tag{15}$$

According to the key schedule of PRESENT80, each round of key scheduling applies an S-box, resulting in the definition of 4 new key variables for each round. Therefore, if we represent the set of all key bits as $\mathcal{K} = \{k_0, \ldots, k_{79}\}$, the round keys K_r, $0 \leq r \leq R$, derived from $\mathcal{K}$ based on the key schedule, are as follows:

$$K_0 = \{k_{79}, k_{78}, k_{77}, k_{76}, \ldots, k_{16}\}$$
$$K_1 = \{k_{83}, k_{82}, k_{81}, k_{80}, \ldots, k_{35}\}$$
$$K_2 = \{k_{87}, k_{86}, k_{85}, k_{84}, \ldots, k_{54}\} \tag{16}$$
$$\vdots$$

The way the round keys are defined creates dependencies among the key bits, making it complex to compute the cardinality of the key bit set for each bit address. To address this issue, we use the Autoguess tool proposed by [HE22]. We form the set of nonlinearly dependent key bits for each bit address, provide it to the Autoguess tool as input, and obtain the cardinality of the set. In Fig. 7, we describe the round functions of PRESENT80 and show how the bit addresses are defined.

For PRESENT80, we were able to attack 6 rounds with time, data and memory complexities of $2^{68.2}$, 18, and 2^{15}, respectively, with the matching point being the bit $A^2[63]$. The values $K_f = 56$, $K_b = 64$, $K_u = 79$, $K_c = 41$, $K_r = 1$, and $m = 1$ were determined by our tool, while the cipher's structure necessitates that $t = 2$.

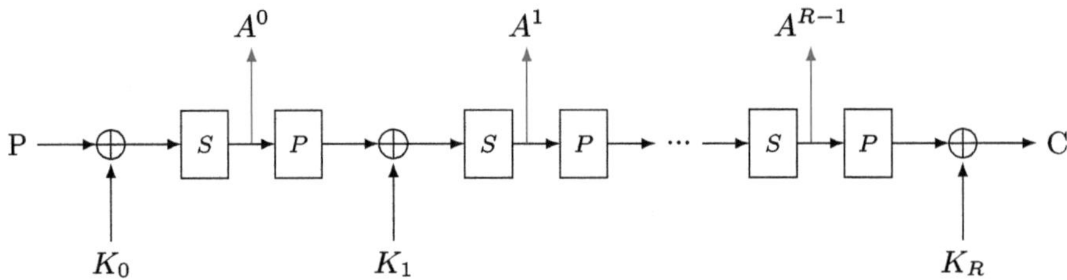

Fig. 7. Attack on PRESENT80. the positions A^r, $\quad 0 \leq r < R$ are considered as the bit Addresses.

4.5 Application to ARADI

ARADI is a block cipher designed with low-latency, introduced by Greene et al. [GMW24] from the US National Security Agency. This section details our findings on ARADI, where our tool attacked 5 rounds of the cipher. The specification of ARADI is provided in [GMW24].

In Fig. 8, we outline the positions designated as bit addresses in the structure of ARADI.

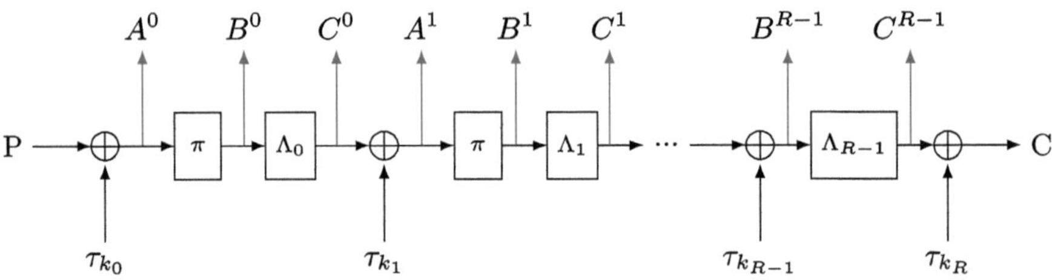

Fig. 8. Attack on ARADI. The positions $A^r, B^r, C^r \quad 0 \leq r < R$ are considered as bit addresses.

As shown in the structure of ARADI, the S-box π is applied to each bit of the 4 words (w, x, y, z). Based on this, a look-up table for the S-box π can be produced as follows:

Table 3. The look-up table for the ARADI's S-box π.

x	0	1	2	3	4	5	6	7	8	9	A	B	C	D	E	F
$S(x)$	0	1	2	3	4	D	F	6	8	B	5	E	C	7	A	9

Based on the component function of the look-up table in Table 3, the dependency sets for the forward direction are as follows:

$$I_0 = I_2 = \{0, 1, 2, 3\}, \quad J_0 = J_2 = \emptyset$$
$$I_1 = \{0, 2\}, \quad J_1 = \{1\} \tag{17}$$
$$I_3 = \{0, 1, 2\}, \quad J_3 = \{3\}$$

For the backward direction, we have:

$$I_0 = \{1, 3\}, \quad J_0 = \{0\}$$
$$I_1 = I_3 = \{0, 1, 2, 3\}, \quad J_1 = J_3 = \emptyset \tag{18}$$
$$I_2 = \{0, 1, 3\}, \quad J_2 = \{2\}$$

Representing the set of all key bits as $\mathcal{K} = \{k_0, \ldots, k_{256}\}$, the round keys τ_{k_r} for $0 \leq r \leq R$, derived from $\mathcal{K}$ based on the key schedule and used alternately in the round functions of ARADI, are defined as follows:

$$\tau_{k_0} = \{k_{160}, k_{159}, \ldots, k_{225}\}$$
$$\tau_{k_i} = \{k_{31} + k_{64}, k_{30} + k_{63}, \ldots, k_{88} + k_{97} + k_{101}\} \tag{19}$$

$$\vdots$$

For ARADI, our tool was able to suggest an attack on 5 rounds with time, data, and memory complexities of $2^{234.8}$, 28, and 2^{19}, respectively, with the matching point being the bits $B^3[22]$. According to the output of our tool, the parameters are $K_f = 171$, $K_b = 230$, $K_u = 249$, $K_c = 152$, $K_r = 7$, and $m = 1$. Given the cipher's structure, the value of t is set to 2.

5   Conclusion and Future Works

In this paper, we presented MITM key recovery attack that requires minimal data and memory resources. Additionally, we proposed an automated tool that optimally measures the complexity of the attack and suggests suitable bits to be used as matching points. We applied our tool to the lightweight block ciphers CRAFT, Midori, WARP, PRESENT80, and ARADI.

Although our proposed MITM technique does not cover the higher number of rounds, it has significant advantages, including low data and memory requirements, and it is not restricted by the type of data used, making it effective with any random data. One notable benefit of our automated tool is its ability to quickly measure the complexity of the attack and suggest matching points, in contrast to other automated techniques that require the code to run for several hours or even days before returning the attack's complexity.

A potential direction for future work is to apply this technique to other ciphers. Additionally, in the proposed technique, the cancellation of key bits that are nonlinearly involved through the linear layers is not considered. Modeling such events could improve the complexity of the attack or extend its coverage to additional rounds.

References

BBI+15. Banik, S., et al.: A block cipher for low energy. In: Advances in Cryptology – ASIACRYPT 2015, vol. 9453 of LNCS, pp. 411–436. Springer (2015). https://doi.org/10.1007/978-3-662-48800-3_17

BBI+20. Banik, S., et al.: WARP: Revisiting GFN for lightweight 128-bit block cipher. In: Selected Areas in Cryptography (SAC), vol. 12804 of LNCS, pp. 535–564. Springer (2020). https://doi.org/10.1007/978-3-030-81652-0_21

BC13. Boura, C., Canteaut, A.: A new criterion for avoiding the propagation of linear relations through an Sbox. In: Fast Software Encryption (FSE), vol. 8424 of LNCS, pp. 585–604. Springer (2013). https://doi.org/10.1007/978-3-662-43933-3_30

BDD+23. Boura, C., David, N., Derbez, P., Leander, G., Naya-Plasencia, M.: Differential meet-in-the-middle cryptanalysis. In: Adv. in Cryptology – CRYPTO, vol. 14083 LNCS, pages 240–272. Springer (2023). https://doi.org/10.1007/978-3-031-38548-3_9

BKL+07. Bogdanov, A., et al.: PRESENT: an ultra-lightweight block cipher. In: Cryptographic Hardware and Embedded Systems (CHES), vol. 4727 LNCS, pages 450–466. Springer (2007). https://doi.org/10.1007/978-3-540-74735-2_31

BLMR19. Beierle, C., Leander, G., Moradi, A., Rasoolzadeh, S.: CRAFT: lightweight tweakable block cipher with efficient protection against DFA attacks. IACR Trans. Symmetric Cryptol., 2019(1):5–45 (2019). https://doi.org/10.13154/tosc.v2019.i1.5-45

BR10. Bogdanov, A., Rechberger., C.: A 3-subset meet-in-the-middle attack: cryptanalysis of the lightweight block cipher KTANTAN. In: Selected Areas in Cryptography, vol. 6544 of Lecture Notes in Computer Science, pp. 229–240. Springer (2010). https://doi.org/10.1007/978-3-642-19574-7_16

DF16. Derbez, P., Fouque, P.-A.: Automatic search of meet-in-the-middle and impossible differential attacks. In: Advances in Cryptology – CRYPTO 2016, vol. 9815 of LNCS, pp. 157–184. Springer (2016). https://doi.org/10.1007/978-3-662-53008-5_6

DH77. Diffie, W., Hellman, M.E.: Special feature: exhaustive cryptanalysis of the NBS data encryption standard. Computer 10(6), 74–84 (June 1977). https://doi.org/10.1109/c-m.1977.217750

DS08. Demirci, H., Selçuk, A.A.: A meet-in-the-middle attack on 8-round AES. In: Fast Software Encryption (FSE) volume 5086 of LNCS, pp. 116–126. Springer (2008). https://doi.org/10.1007/978-3-540-71039-4_7

DSP07. Dunkelman, O., Sekar, G., Preneel, B.: Improved meet-in-the-middle attacks on reduced-round DES. In: Progress in Cryptology – INDOCRYPT 2007, vol. 4859 of LNCS, pp. 86–100. Springer (2007). https://doi.org/10.1007/978-3-540-77026-8_8

GLRW10. Guo, J., Ling, S., Rechberger, C., Wang, H.: Advanced meet-in-the-middle preimage attacks: first results on full Tiger, and improved results on MD4 and SHA-2. In: Advances in Cryptology – ASIACRYPT 2010, vol. 6477 of LNCS, pp. 56–75. Springer (2010). https://doi.org/10.1007/978-3-642-17373-8_4

GMW24. Greene, P., Motley, M., Weeks, B.: Aradi and llama: Low-latency cryptography for memory encryption. IACR Cryptol. ePrint Arch. (2024)

HE22. Hadipour, H., Eichlseder, M.: AutoGuess: A tool for finding guess-and-determine attacks and key bridges. In: Applied Cryptography and Network Security (ACNS), vol. 13269 of LNCS pp. 230–250. Springer (2022). https://doi.org/10.1007/978-3-031-09234-3_12

IS13. Isobe, T., Shibutani, K.: Generic key recovery attack on feistel scheme. In: Advances in Cryptology – ASIACRYPT 2013, vol. 8269 of LNCS, pp. 464–485. Springer (2013). https://doi.org/10.1007/978-3-642-42033-7_24

KRS12. Khovratovich, D., Rechberger, C., Savelieva, A.: Bicliques for preimages: Attacks on Skein-512 and the SHA-2 family. In: Fast Software Encryption (FSE), vol. 7549 of LNCS, pp. 244–263. Springer (2012). https://doi.org/10.1007/978-3-642-34047-5_15

LW17. Lin, L., Wu, W.: Meet-in-the-middle attacks on reduced-round Midori64. IACR Trans. Symmetric Cryptol., **2017**(1), 215–239 (2017). https://doi.org/10.13154/tosc.v2017.i1.215-239

MLC23. Ma, Z., Li, M., Chen, S.: Meet-in-the-middle attacks on round-reduced CRAFT based on automatic search. IET Inf. Secur. **17**(3), 534–543 (2023). https://doi.org/10.1049/ise2.12114

oSN18. National Institute of Standards and Technology (NIST). Lightweight cryptography (2018)

Sas18. Sasaki, Y.: Integer linear programming for three-subset meet-in-the-middle attacks: application to GIFT. In: Advances in Information and Computer Security (IWSEC), vol. 11049 of Lecture Notes in Computer Science, pp. 227–243. Springer (2018). https://doi.org/10.1007/978-3-319-97916-8_15

SS23. Schrottenloher, A., Stevens, M.: Simplified modeling of MITM attacks for block ciphers: new (quantum) attacks. IACR Trans. Symmetric Cryptol. (3), 146–183 (2023). https://doi.org/10.46586/tosc.v2023.i3.146-183

ZLW+23. Zhang, K., et al.: Meet-in-the-middle attack with splice-and-cut technique and a general automatic framework. Des. Codes Cryptogr. **91**(9):2845–2878 (2023). https://doi.org/10.1007/s10623-023-01226-4

JWT Back to the Future on the (Ab)use of JWTs in IoT Transactions

Alberto Battistello[(✉)] [ID], Guido Bertoni [ID], Filippo Melzani [ID],
and Maria Chiara Molteni [ID]

Security Pattern, Milan, Italy
{a.battistello,g.bertoni,f.melzani,m.molteni}@securitypattern.com

Abstract. The use of JSON Web Token (JWT)s has become ubiquitous in the Internet of Things (IoT) for the secure exchange of messages between the things and the Cloud. However, the standard that describes the JWT is fragmented, and interpretations may pave the way for abuses. In this work we show a supply chain attack that exploits a weakness in the JWT standard. In particular an attacker that takes control of one device during production, may be able to create a series of valid JWTs, that may be used further after the deployment, to impersonate the device when accessing the Cloud infrastructure. Among the advantages of the attack is that the network is completely unaware about the JWTs created in the supply chain by the attacker.

We show that the use of JWTs in the context of the Google Cloud IoT Core [15] infrastructure paves the way for a subtle attack, and that quite unexpectedly, the presence of an Secure Element (SE) on the connecting device does not allow to thwart the problem, but instead seems to make a solution harder to reach. We showcase our attack on the - now retired - Google Cloud IoT Core, in order to avoid malicious use of our findings, but our discovery can be applied to other services that provide token-based authentication. For example we further show that the same weaknesses applies to other tokens like the Concise Binary Object Representation Web Token (CWT) and the Entity Attestation Token (EAT) [23, 26], and to platforms like HiveMQ and EMQX [13, 17] providing a much wider attacker scope then merely a single token type or Cloud provider. Furthermore, our attack also applies to the Open Charge Metering Format (OCMF) standard, used for recording meter readings from charging station for Electric Vehicles (EV) [33].

In order to thwart the presented attack we provide a few countermeasures that can be applied, depending on the IoT infrastructure at hand.

This work was partially funded by the European Union under grant agreement no. 101070008 (ORSHIN project). Views and opinions expressed are however those of the author(s) only and do not necessarily reflect those of the European Union. Neither the European Union nor the granting authority can be held responsible for them.

1   Introduction

The JWT standard described in RFC 7519 [21] specifies how to securely represent claims between two parties. It is one of the building blocks of the OAuth protocol [24], which allows authorization grants to be exchanged between services. For example, applications on computers, phones, TVs, printers etc. can use Google OAuth 2.0 to authorize access to Google's APIs [15]. This means for example that once you are logged in your phone, you can get access to your Google Drive documents without the need to input your credentials again.

JWT's have been developed in order to reduce both development complexity and friction in user's adoption. Developers can use a single API to create and validate JWTs for different services. At the same time the user experience is simplified by requiring a Single-Sign-On (SSO) to use different services. While the user experience has effectively been improved, the same is not completely true for developers. The main problem lies in the versatility of JWTs which can be declined in several different forms, use many different cryptographic algorithms and solve many different problems.

Lately, Google Cloud IoT Core adopted the use of JWTs to authenticate the requests coming from devices in the field. The idea is that the JWT token is much more lightweight to produce than a Transport Layer Security (TLS) authentication, thus improving the efficiency of the "things", as described in [13,14].

The present work stems from the fact that the JWT standard does not require the inclusion of a nonce in the token construction, thus the server receiving the token cannot validate its freshness. Despite a claim named "nonce" was defined and register with IANA for JWT (see [16]), none of the JWT claims are mandatory, thus in practice such nonces are never used. This remark is the starting point for replay attacks and also for a more subtle attack that we describe in this work as *JWT Back to the future*. We show an abuse of the JWTs in the supply chain, where a malicious attacker that can manipulate the time perceived by the IoT device under production can obtain a set of valid JWTs that she can use in the future to authenticate custom messages sent to the Cloud. After the malicious JWTs are produced, the device has no recollection or logs of the happening, and so the abuse cannot be detected. Naively, without an SE, an attacker may simply steal the signing key by accessing the microcontroller internal memory in debug mode, during production. One of our main contributions is to show that the presence of an SE does not necessarily thwart the attack, and we present the few options currently available to protect a system against our finding in Sect. 6.

In the following, we showcase our work by using the Arduino MKR 1010 and the Google Cloud IoT Core. This example is illustrated by Google in [19]. We specifically opted to use a now retired platform in order to avoid the abuse of our attack in real world scenarios. However, this work straightforward applies to other uses of the JWT, like for example HiveMQ or the EMQX platforms [13,17], and also to other token standards, for example the CWT [23], described by the Object Security for Constrained RESTful Environments (OSCORE) IETF working group [6,25,31] in the context of the RESTful environments for Authentication and Authorization for Constrained Environments (ACE) project. CWTs were used for example in the EU Digital Covid certificate, or in EAT tokens from [26]. Finally, we remark that our work also applies to the emerging technology of EVs as the standard used to transfer charge information to the station is based on the JWT and CWT standard and is described in [33].

Recently, Shingala [34] published an interesting comparison between the use of JWTs versus the use of the mutual authentication from the TLS [32] protocol for authentications of the things on the Internet. Interested by such work and from the internet discussions on-going, we decided to contribute with our findings concerning the use of JWTs for IoT.

Interestingly, we remark that our work does not apply to the ARM PSA tokens [5], as such tokens include a *mandatory* nonce coming from the caller, to demonstrate freshness of the generated token (see [5] Sect. 4.1.1).

The rest of this work is organized as follows: we introduce the concepts of JSON Web Tokens and related structures and security in Sect. 2. Then Sect. 3 describe the general IoT architecture that we use in the rest of the paper, while Sect. 4 the different phases of the life of an IoT device in order to illustrate our threat model. In Sect. 5 we present our attack Back2TheFuture and possible countermeasures in Sect. 6. Finally Sect. 7 concludes this work.

2   JWTs, JWSs and JWEs

In this section we present in more details the different aspects of the JWT, JSON Web Signature (JWS) and JSON Web Encryption (JWE) standards, which collectively goes under the JOSE acronym (for JSON Object Signing and Encryption), described respectively in RFC 7519, RFC 7515, and RFC 7516 [20–22]. Then we describe other token types, as the CWT, and EAT, defined by the ACE group [25], and the RATS (Remote ATtestation procedureS) working group [26], respectively.

2.1   JWT

A JWT, described in RFC 7519 [21], is a compact, URL-safe means of representing claims to be transferred between two parties. The claims in a JWT are encoded as a JSON object that is used as the payload of a JWS structure or as the plaintext of a JWE structure, enabling the claims to be digitally signed or integrity protected with a Message Authentication Code (MAC) and/or encrypted. A JWT is divided into three fields: header, payload, and signature.

The header provides information about the content of the JWT, like the cryptographic algorithms used in the other blocks. The payload contains the actual claims: a set of statements about an entity. Claims can be public or private and standardized by the IANA Web Token Registry or not. Finally the latter field consists of the signature of the previous blocks, encoded in Base64. These three fields, encoded in Base64, and separated by dots, compose the JWT.

An example JWT from the site [30] is provided in Fig. 1. The public key used to validate JWT in this work is the one indicated in Subsect. 5.1.

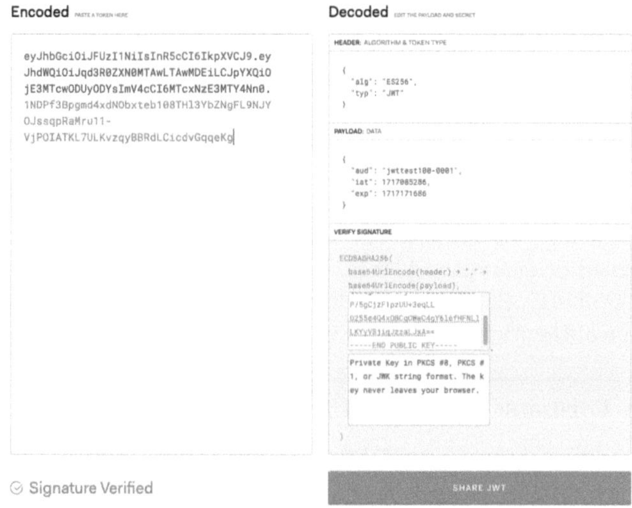

Fig. 1. Example of a legitimate JWT obtained by using an Arduino MKR WiFi 1010 and and decoded thanks to the https://jwt.io website. On the left is presented the base64 encoded value, while on the right are presented the decoded header and payload and the signature verification.

2.2 JWS

A JWS, described in RFC 7515 [20], allows the creation of a digital signature or Message Authentication Code (MAC) over a JSON-based data structure to ensure data integrity and authenticity. Cryptographic algorithms and identifiers for use with this specification are described in the separate JSON Web Algorithms (JWA) specification and an IANA registry defined by that specification.

The JWS does NOT protect the confidentiality of the data. Anyone who can get a hold of the JWS can decode and read the bytes that were signed. Related encryption capabilities are described in the separate JSON Web Encryption (JWE) specification.

2.3 JWE

A JWE, described in RFC 7516 [22], is a JSON-based data structure which protects the confidentiality of the payload by encrypting it and can sometimes ensure integrity of the payload data (depending on the algorithm chosen). A JWE can be used to store/transport sensitive data.

2.4 Sign Then Encrypt

JWTs can be signed then encrypted to provide confidentiality of the claims. While it is technically possible to perform the operations in any order to create a nested JWT, senders should first sign the JWT, then encrypt the resulting message. So, sign-then-encrypt is the preferred order for the following reasons: it prevents attacks in which the signature is stripped, leaving just an encrypted message; it provides privacy for the signer; finally, signatures over encrypted text are not considered valid in some jurisdictions. Certain papers advocate applying a second signature after the encryption [9]. This is not required with standard JWE algorithms due to their use of authenticated encryption [7].

In the following, we will use the term JWT to denote a JWT being it in plaintext, signed or encrypted (JWE, JWS). In particular, we will focus on the authenticity property, thus on JWSs, for which we demonstrate that the attacker can bypass the authenticity of some of the fields contained in the claims in Sect. 5.

2.5 Other Formats: CWTs and EATs

The ACE working group from IETF [25] is the responsible for the standard-ization of a solution framework to enable the protection of exchanges between a client and a server in a constrained environment. The method chosen by the working group to protect the exchanges uses tokens similar to the JWTs, but based on the CBOR format [8,11], called CWTs. A Go implementation for CWTs can be found for example in [1]. Furthermore, the RATS IETF working group developed a draft [26] in which they describe the EAT token [26] as a JWT or CWT token, with some attestation-oriented claims. Such tokens are used by a relying party, server or service to determine the type and degree of trust placed in the entity, like a smartphone, IoT device, network equipment and so on.

3 The IoT Generic Architecture

We consider a generic IoT environment, composed of a device which connects to the Cloud in order to securely send and receive data from the attached sen-sors. The device itself is composed of a micro-controller, which implements the application, and various modules in charge of different tasks. For example the micro-controller may implement the connectivity itself, or delegate it to an WiFi, BLE, or GSM module. Similarly, the micro-controller may use the cryptographic functionalities exposed by an SE.

In our scenario, we assume that the cryptographic primitives necessary for the security operations are provided by an SE module connected to the MCU, for example by the Inter-Integrated Circuit (I2C) channel [29], and not operated by the MCU itself. Such a situation is usually depicted as more secure, thanks to the presence of the SE and the assurance provided by it (see for example [14]). Then a WiFi module, for example connected to Serial Peripheral Interface (SPI) bus [27], is in charge of establishing the TLS connection to Cloud endpoint. This architecture is commonly realized by many IoT devices (e.g.: [12,28,35]).

As described in [14], the use of JWTs works as follows. The device will establish a secure connection to the global Cloud endpoint using TLS by using the WiFi module, but instead of triggering the mutual authentication it will generate a very simple JWT, sign it with its private key and pass it as authenticator. The JWT is received by the Cloud, the public key for the device is retrieved and used to verify the JWT signature. If valid, the mutual authentication is effectively established. As the SE offers the possibility to sign JWTs securely without ever exposing the private key, this scenario is generally considered more secure than in the absence of an SE.

We depict the two different architectures described above in Fig. 2b and Fig. 2a.

The latter architecture is realized for example by the Arduino MKR WiFi 1010, depicted in Fig. 3. We use it in the following by connecting it to the Google IoT Core. Such a combination has been suggested in [2,14].

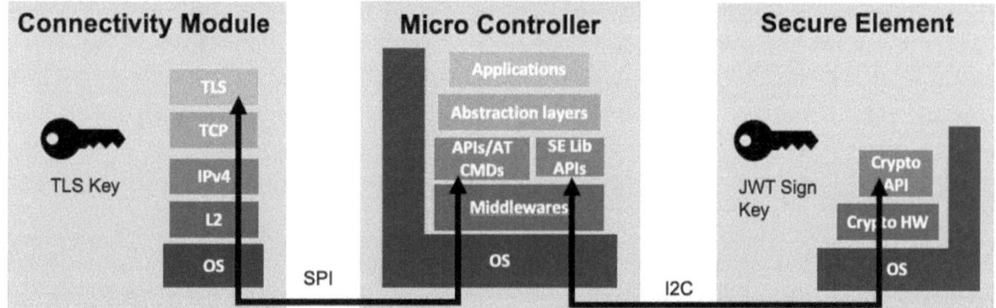

(a) Modular architecture with different modules for the connectivity and security.

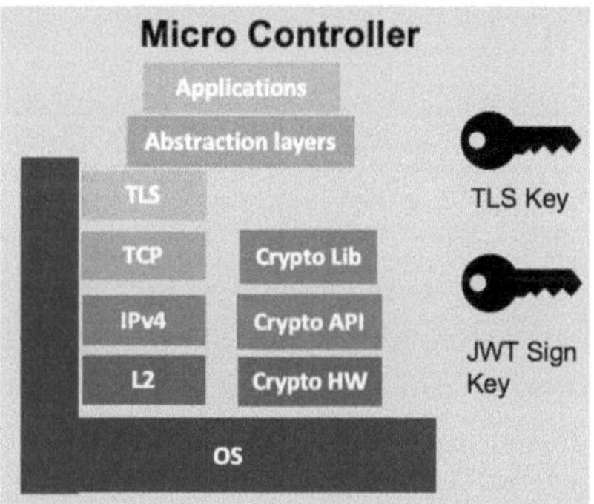

(b) Monolithic architecture with the connectivity and security on the MCU.

Fig. 2. Example of an IoT hardware and software stack architectures.

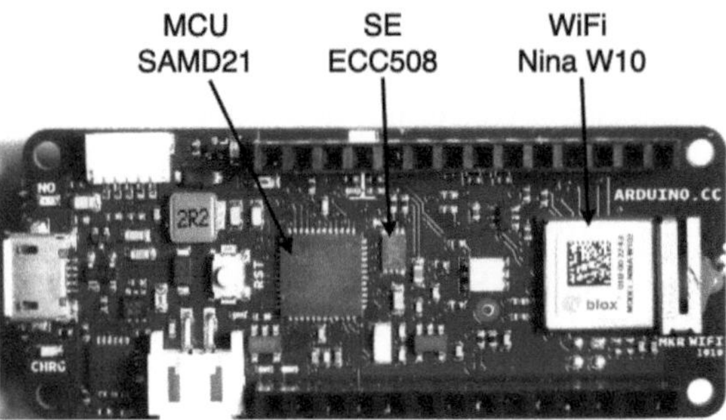

Fig. 3. Modules organization of the Arduino MKR WiFi 1010.

4 Device's Lifecycle

This section presents an example life-cycle of an IoT device that we will use to illustrate the attack. The life-cycle of an IoT device is split into two main parts: manufacturing and deployment. Such splitting is useful to distinguish those steps which needs to be performed before and after the device is deployed in the field.

4.1 Manufacturing

During the first stages of life, the device is assembled, in particular all sub-modules are soldered together, the SE is connected to the micro-controller which is itself connected to the Wi-Fi module for communication. Afterwards, tests are performed on the complete device to verify all connections and functionalities. This step in general involves the generation of a cryptographic private key inside the SE on-boarded with the device, and the publication of the associated public key, together with an ID of the device, onto the Cloud Provider's fleet management system. Alternatively, it is possible that the SE comes pre-provisioned by the founder. For Google Cloud IoT Core, the instructions for device on-boarding can be found on different sources [10,18,28]. The final firmware is then loaded onto the micro-controller and thus the device is ready to go in the field. It is quite common that the manufacturing process is performed by a dedicated third-party company, where the use of secure manufacturing lines are not guaranteed. So the personnel having access to the devices during the manufacturing could be malicious and may try tampering, in particular, with the cryptographic assets. This aspect is commonly referred to as *supply chain attacks*, since it extends to all the steps of the supply chain, from component acquisition to manufacturing up to last mile shipping. During manufacturing, a supply chain attack can be problematic because the malicious attacker can act on the complete population of produced devices. Loading malicious firmware is the most naive supply chain attack. In such an environment, a *remote attestation* can be used to prove the device's software and hardware integrity to a remote party, providing cryptographic evidence that it is running as expected and has not been tampered with. However there are attacks, such as the one we present here, that leave no evidence on the final device, and thus are hard to detect.

4.2 Deployment

After manufacturing is finished, the device is deployed in the field. From that moment on, every time the device needs to connect to the cloud to transfer data, the micro-controller connects to the Wi-Fi module trough the SPI channel, and requests the current time to a network time server. The current time thus retrieved is used to prepare a JWT. Claims in the JWT are generated by the micro-controller and signed by the SE. The signature generation is requested and returned through the I2C channel. The micro-controller then requires the opening of a TLS session with the cloud service to the Wi-Fi module, the interconnection between the micro-controller and the Wi-Fi module is ensured by the SPI channel. After the TLS session is established the micro-controller passes the signed JWT to the Wi-Fi module, to be sent to the Cloud service. Once the Cloud receives the JWT, it validates it and acts accordingly.

We want to stress that since the SPI and I2C channels are not protected, the micro-controller and the SE are not capable of understanding if the input data are coming from legitimate sources. This is true in particular for the signature request and data to be signed from the SE perspective, or time/date incoming from the SPI in the case of the micro-controller perspective.

4.3 Threat Model

This work considers a typical IoT device production scenario where a designer provides a factory with the hardware design and firmware. The factory's role is to manufacture a specified number of devices, each loaded with the designer's chosen firmware and secrets. It is assumed that the designer uses an SE to protect sensitive information and employs JWTs to ensure message authenticity between the IoT device and the Cloud after production.

For the purpose of this work, we can assume that the private key used for signing messages is the only secret, generated and accessible exclusively to the SE on the device. A key assumption is that factory employees are untrusted and could potentially tamper with devices during production to extract sensitive information like the signing key, by accessing the micro-controller internal memory in debug mode.

Specifically, attackers are assumed to be capable of eavesdropping and manipulating data on exposed communication channels (buses) before, during, and after firmware installation, to retrieve all secret material. However, the model excludes physical attacks on devices, such as side-channel or fault injection attacks.

In this context, the attacker's goal is to generate valid communication that the Cloud provider will accept, effectively impersonating legitimate IoT devices. The authors highlight that while JWTs are intended to provide authentication, they fail to protect against attackers who gain access to the private key. This also implies that JWTs cannot protect against attackers who have access to the private key at any time, but also that even if the attacker cannot access the secret, the JWT construction fails to protect the communications that use the secret key.

In this perspective we want to remark two main aspects. First, if the SE is not present, then the attacker may simply steal the signing key by accessing the micro-controller internal memory in debug mode. Second, in order to thwart such a naive attack, an SE is usually mounted on the device. Although very surprisingly, using an SE in this context opens a new attack scenario (described in Sect. 5) which was not identified by the manufacturer nor the Cloud platform [14].

5   Back to the Future

In this section we show that JWTs used in such context creates a security threat to the system. The JWT is created by the device based on its own time representation, while the Cloud side has no interaction in the generation of the JWT. This means that a JWT can be created at any time by the device or by anyone having access to the private key associated with the device. This represents a weakness in the authentication protocol, it can be used for example to mount replay attacks, by sending twice the same JWT.

We found a more subtle attack than a replay, and show in this section how to generate custom JWTs that will be valid in the future.

Our attack applies when the device is provided with an SE, being it pre-provisioned or not. An attacker having access to the device during manufacturing can interact with the SE and require the signature of a JWT for whatever moment in time. This is possible since the I2C between the micro-controller and the SE is not protected. Despite the possibilities for commercial SEs to establish a secure channel over the I2C with the micro-controller, we observe that this is not a sufficient countermeasure to thwart the attack presented in this work. As the key used to protect the I2C channel needs to be exchanged/rotated on the very same I2C channel on first boot, then an attacker that can eavesdrop such a communication would know the key and would thus be able to observe/modify all further communications.

Similarly, since the SPI connection between the micro-controller and the Wi-Fi module is not encrypted, an attacker can tamper with the time communicated by the Wi-Fi module as well. The attacker eavesdrops on the SPI channel and waits for the micro-controller to connect to a network time server. The attacker then alters the response, setting the time to some moment in the future. The micro-controller then receives the modified time and requests the signature on a JWT with a wrong time, to the SE. In this way, the micro-controller obtains a signed JWT with a custom time field ("iat"), which is controlled by the attacker, and can be used in the future.

We observe that by targeting the Wi-Fi channel, only the JWT "iat" can be misused, and the attack is limited with respect to the one targeting the micro-controller-SE connection.

5.1   Attack

We present our attack by using the Arduino MKR WiFi 1010 [2] as victim's board. The attacker uses a second Arduino, the Arduino MKR 1000 WiFi, which is not provided of an SE, to abuse the SE of the victim's and make it generate a JWT for authenticating to the Cloud. As showed in Fig. 3, the SE on the MKR WiFi 1010 is easily accessible. The experiment setup is depicted in Fig. 4. It shows that the ground (GND), Serial DAta (SDA) and Serial CLock (SCL) signals are connected from the PINs of the attacker to the corresponding PINs on the victim' SE. In particular, from the SE's datasheet we can observe that the GDN, VCC, SCL, and SDA PINs are respectively PINs 4,8,6 and 7 on the SE. In order to ease the probes' positioning, we followed the SCL and SDA PINs to the nearest resistors, and connected the probes to them.

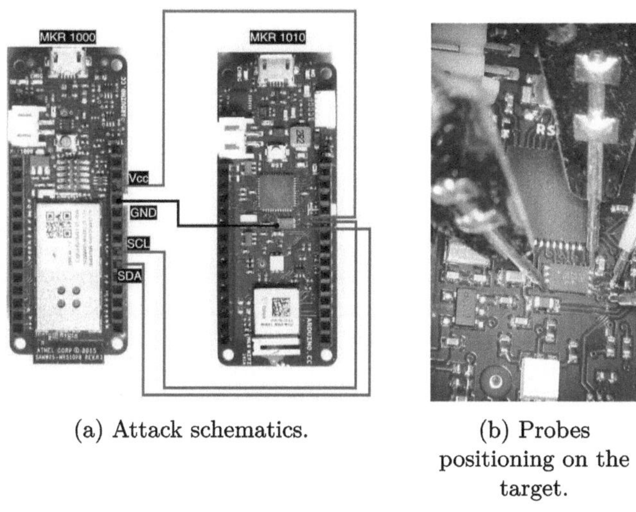

(a) Attack schematics.

(b) Probes positioning on the target.

Fig. 4. Attack schematics (a) and experimental setup (b).

We demonstrate our attack by using the sketch given by Arduino in [2] to connect the MKR to the Cloud Provider, in particular the version for the Google IoT Cloud. In order to emulate a pre-provisioned keypair, on the victim board we first load the Arduino ECCX08JWSPublicKey sketch [3] to generate the cryptographic material inside the SE. Further instructions on these procedures can be found in [4].

The obtained public key (necessary to validate the signature of the JWT) is:

```
-----BEGIN PUBLIC KEY-----
MFkwEwYHKoZIzj0CAQYIKoZIzj0DAQcDQgAEoEPtFj
VHxvodsOKutQilCP/5gCjzF1pzUU+3eqLLD255e4Q4
xOBCqOWwC4gY6l6fHFNLlLKYyV8jiqJzzaLJxA==
-----END PUBLIC KEY-----
```

After registering the corresponding public key on the Cloud provider, we load the Arduino GCP_IoT_Core_WiFi [2] sketch to authenticate the node to the Cloud. This sketch executes the following steps: connects to the WiFi, retrieves the time information from the network, sign a JWT that contains the retrieved timing information in the "iat" claim, then use the signed JWT to authenticate to the MQTT server to publish and retrieve information. An example of a legitimate JWT generated by the victim is provided in Fig. 1.

The attacker's board performs the same actions, but it cannot authenticate to the server as it has no SE connected. So it needs to "steal" it from the victim's board. In order to do so, she disconnects the power from the victim, and wire the two boards as depicted in Fig. 4 (a). With the GND and VCC from the attacker to the victim' SE PINs, and the SDA and SCL signals to the corresponding signals of the victim's board.

Once this is done, the attacker can use the SE to sign any JWT of her choice, as if the SE was on its own board. So what she can do for example is creating a set of signed JWTs for the future, by manipulating the time, and store them for further use. We have performed such an attack, and edited the "iat" claim by setting it to a date far away in the future: 2077-12-02 17:26:22. The corresponding obtained JWT is depicted in Fig. 5.

We would like to stress that once the attacker obtains the JWTs, she doesn't need the devices anymore, and the JWTs can be used on any other device, i.e. a software tool executing an MQTT [36] client. Finally, as far as we know, if the attack is detected by the Cloud backend, the only possibility to mitigate it is to revoke all of the devices' keys. Alternatively, if the devices' private key can't be changed, dispose of all the devices.

5.2 A JWT Weakness

JWTs were initially conceived to be used to authenticate users between interconnected servers, where all servers were controlled by the same entity and no (or little) clock skew was possible between them. The attack described above is the result of the use of the JWTs in a different context, where the token producer and the token consumer are different devices, under control of different entities. Thus, probably, the JWTs mechanism would require some adaptation in order to be securely applied to such use cases. Alternatively, one can argue that the problem is present due to a weakness in the JWT standards. Such weakness can be identified in the lack of communication between the Cloud and the device

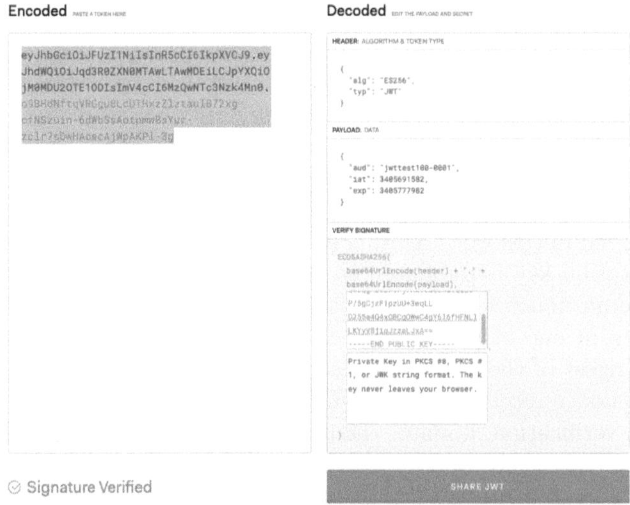

Fig. 5. Example of a JWT generated by the attacker with "iat" claim set to a date far in the future: 2077-12-02 17:26:22. Image taken from https://jwt.io website.

during the JWT generation. One of the building blocks of many security protocols is a random nonce generated by the party that verifies the claims and included in the signature by the party that wants to prove its identity. The lack of such nonce in the JWT specification makes difficult to prove the protocol security, and opens the way to attacks as the one demonstrated in this work.

6   Countermeasures

In this section we present possible countermeasures that can be applied to thwart our attack. The applicability of the countermeasure obviously depends on the particular setup, device at hand, supply chain condition, resources, etc.

6.1   Use the TLS Authentication

One simple solution is to use the TLS authentication mechanism instead of the JWT one. This has the obvious drawback that not all Cloud providers allows it, and of a heavier authentication mechanism. However it allows to thwart the attack as the nonces included in the TLS handshake prevents attackers to reuse previous commitments or generate JWTs valid in the future.

6.2   Pre-provisioned Keys

A second solution would be to take advantage of the presence of pre-provisioned private-keys inside the SE.

For example, many commercial SEs contains a private key pre-provisioned by the founder (commonly referred to as *attestation key*). This countermeasure assumes that such pre-provisioned keys are installed by a trusted party, in a trusted environment. The attestation key can only be used to sign data internal to the SE or data internal to the SE and some additional external bytes. The module also provides slots to store additional self generated private keys, which can be used to sign external data. We suggest the following protocol to thwart the attack described in this work. During provisioning, the public key corresponding to the attestation key is published to the Cloud. After deployment, the Cloud sends a random nonce to the SE. After receiving the nonce, the SE generates a private key in one of the free slots. Then, the SE uses the attestation key to sign the digest of the public key corresponding to the private self-generated key, and the nonce received from the Cloud. The signature is sent to the Cloud, which, upon verification, updates the public key to use during JWT verification with the one just received. The signature of subsequent JWTs can be signed by the self-generated private key. In such a way the Cloud can trust that the JWTs have been generated only after the nonce communication. This solution has the advantages of avoiding the need to implement a TLS stack on the micro-controller, and offering a robust mechanism to update the device's private keys in the field. The drawback of this solution is that a new step needs to be implemented in the Cloud provider's back-end, and the device must implement the new protocol. Another advantage of such countermeasure is that compromised keys can be revoked and compromised devices can be re-provisioned, simply by generating another signing key inside the SE and repeating the *nonce* procedure.

6.3   Use the Nonce Claim

A fourth solution to thwart the attack is similar to the previous one, but does not require the use of pre-provisioned keys in the SE module. It simply requires the Cloud to send the nonce to the device after deployment, prior to creating JWTs. Once received, the device includes the Cloud's nonce into the JOSE header of the JWTs. Afterwards, each JWT must contain the signed JOSE header containing the nonce, thus providing an assurance to the cloud concerning the generation time of the JWT. The main advantage of such solution is that it is the simplest solution to implement. The drawbacks involve a new step to be implemented in the Cloud's provider's back-end. Similarly to the solution with pre-provisioned keys, a further advantage is that compromised keys can be revoked and compromised devices can be re-provisioned by generating new sign keys and refreshing the *nonce* step.

6.4   Key Use Limit

A fifth solution takes advantage of the presence of monotonic counters in the SE, paired with a private key slot. Each time the key in the paired slot is used, the counter is incremented. By using an additional JWT field, the micro-controller can include the value of the counter in the JWT. The Cloud then verifies that the value in the counter is monotonic increasing, in order to mitigate the attack described in this work. The advantage of this solution is that it is simple and does not require a TLS stack on the micro-controller. On the other hand, a new step is to be implemented in the Cloud provider's back-end, and a new field needs to be implemented in the JWT. Furthermore, differently from the solutions proposed in Subsect. 6.2 and Subsect. 6.3, this solution does not allow to revoke the used key if it is compromised.

6.5   Trusted Supply Chain

One final mention have to go to the simplest solution of all, at least from the technological point of view, which is of having a secure supply chain, or at least partially secure supply chain. Definition of a trusted supply chain is out of scope of this work, however we consider a supply chain to be trusted if it consists of a comprehensive and verifiable system encompassing all stages of an IoT device's lifecycle – from design and component sourcing to manufacturing, distribution, deployment, operation, maintenance, and eventual disposal – that ensures the security, integrity, and resilience of the device and its associated data throughout its entire existence. This would allow the first steps of the personalization of the SE to be performed in a trusty environment. The following steps, where the attack can not be mounted anymore, can be delegated to an untrusty supply chain. This solution, however have an intrinsic drawback of dividing the production into two different sites, the secure and insecure one, with obvious costs and troubles.

7   Conclusions

This work presents *JWT Back to the future*, the possibility of (ab)using an IoT device during production for preparing credential claims (JWTs) that will be later used by the malicious actor to connect to the Cloud service. A malicious user in the supply chain might have the possibility to collect a large number of JWTs for mounting a massive attack in the future.

The flaw is related to the lack of a mandatory nonce in the JWT standard. We show that it is possible to take advantage of such a flaw to abuse the authentication of IoT devices in the field, when JWT are used. In particular we show that an attacker in the supply chain may be able to make the IoT device generate some JWTs which are valid in the future and use them afterwards to impersonate the device with respect to the Cloud Provider.

Interestingly, we describe our attack against devices with different architectures. Showing that an SE attached to the micro-controller cannot protect from such an attack. We present a practical attack against an off-the-shelf IoT device by Arduino [2] and the mechanism used by the Google Cloud IoT Core to authenticate the devices. We demonstrate that an attacker on the production line can request a number of signatures on self generated JWTs, from the SE connected to the micro-controller, to be used in the future to connect to the Cloud.

We showcase our attack on the - now retired - Google Cloud IoT Core, in order to avoid malicious use of our findings, but our discovery can be applied to other services that provide token-based authentication. For example we further show that the same weaknesses applies to other tokens like the CWT and the EAT, and to platforms like HiveMQ and EMQX [13,17,23,26] providing a much wider attacker scope then merely a single token type or Cloud provider. Furthermore, our attack also applies to the OCMF standard, used for recording meter readings from charging station for EV [33].

In order to thwart the presented attack we provide a few countermeasures that can be applied, depending on the IoT infrastructure at hand. The simplest countermeasure is to use TLS authentication, while other countermeasures involve implementing a nonce-like mechanism in the JWTs or the authentication itself.

References

1. Keys, Algorithms, COSE and CWT in Go. https://github.com/ldclabs/cose
2. Arduino: Arduino cloud provider examples (2019). https://github.com/arduino/ArduinoCloudProviderExamples
3. Arduino: Arduino eccx08jwspublickey (2019). https://github.com/arduino-libraries/ArduinoECCX08/tree/master/examples/Tools/ECCX08JWSPublicKey
4. Arduino: Securely connecting a MKR GSM 1400 to google cloud IoT core (2024). https://docs.arduino.cc/tutorials/mkr-gsm-1400/securely-connecting-a-mkr-gsm-1400-to-google-cloud-iot-core/
5. ARM: ARM PSA. https://datatracker.ietf.org/doc/html/draft-tschofenig-rats-psa-token
6. Beltran, V., Skarmeta, A.F.: An overview on delegated authorization for CoAP: authentication and authorization for constrained environments (ACE). In: 2016 IEEE 3rd World Forum on Internet of Things (WF-IoT), pp. 706–710 (2016)
7. Black, J.: Authenticated encryption (2005)
8. Bormann, C., Hoffman, P.E.: Concise Binary Object Representation (CBOR). RFC 8949, December 2020
9. Davis, D.: Defective sign & encrypt in S/MIME, PKCS# 7, MOSS, PEM, PGP, and XML. In: USENIX Annual Technical Conference, General Track, pp. 65–78 (2001)
10. Analog Devices: How to create a secure Google to IoT core connection with MAXQ1065. https://www.analog.com/en/resources/app-notes/how-to-create-a-secure-google-iot-core-connection-with-maxq1065.html
11. Ericsson: ACE-OAuth – A new standard for lightweight authorization and access control. https://www.ericsson.com/en/blog/2023/7/ace-oauth-standard-for-lightweight-authorization
12. Espressif: ESP32-WROOM-32SE. https://docs.espressif.com/projects/esp-idf/en/release-v4.3/esp32/api-reference/peripherals/secure_element.html
13. HiveMQ GmbH: Step Up Your MQTT Security with JWT Authentication on HiveMQ Cloud Starter. https://www.hivemq.com/blog/step-up-mqtt-security-jwt-authentication/. Posted 18 Mar 2024
14. Google: Securing cloud-connected devices with cloud IoT and microchip (2018). https://cloud.google.com/blog/products/gcp/securing-cloud-connected-devices-with-cloud-iot-and-microchip

15. Google: GCP-IoT-core-examples (2023). https://cloud.google.com/iot/docs/how-tos/credentials/jwts
16. IANA: IANA JSON Web Token registered Claims. https://www.iana.org/assignments/jwt/jwt.xhtml
17. EMQ Technologies Inc.: Migrate Your Business from GCP IoT Core 03 Use JSON Web Token (JWT) to Verify Device Credentials. https://www.emqx.com/en/blog/migrate-your-business-from-gcp-iot-core-03. Posted 28 Nov 2022
18. Google Inc.: Best practices for running an IoT backend on google cloud. https://cloud.google.com/architecture/connected-devices/bps-running-iot-backend-securely
19. Google Inc.: Google cloud platform IoT Arduino examples (2020). https://github.com/GoogleCloudPlatform/google-cloud-iot-arduino
20. Jones, M., Bradley, J., Sakimura, N.: JSON Web Signature (JWS). RFC 7515, RFC Editor (2015)
21. Jones, M., Bradley, J., Sakimura, N.: JSON Web Token (JWT). RFC 7519, RFC Editor (2015)
22. Jones, M., Hildebrand, J.: JSON Web Encryption (JWE). RFC 7516, RFC Editor (2015)
23. Jones, M.B., Wahlstroem, E., Erdtman, S., Tschofenig, H.: CBOR Web Token (CWT). RFC 8392, May 2018
24. Lodderstedt, T., Richer, J., Campbell, B.: OAuth 2.0 Rich Authorization Requests. RFC 9396, RFC Editor (2023)
25. Hollebeek, T., Velvindron, L.: Authentication and authorization for constrained environments. Internet-Draft draft-ietf-ace-about, Internet Engineering Task Force (2018). Work in Progress
26. Lundblade, L., Mandyam, G., O'Donoghue, J., Wallace, C.: The entity attestation token (EAT). Internet-Draft draft-ietf-rats-eat-26, Internet Engineering Task Force, May 2024. Work in Progress
27. Motorola: Single-Chip Microcomputer Data (1984). https://archive.org/details/bitsavers_motoroladaSingleChipMicrocomputerData_68061538
28. NXP: A71CH for secure connection to Google cloud IoT core. https://www.nxp.com/docs/en/application-note/AN12199.pdf
29. NXP: I2C-bus specification and user manual, 1 October 2021. https://www.nxp.com/docs/en/user-guide/UM10204.pdf
30. Inc. Okta. JWT.io. https://jwt.io
31. Palombini, F., Tiloca, M.: Key provisioning for group communication using ACE. Internet-Draft draft-ietf-ace-key-groupcomm-19, Internet Engineering Task Force, April 2024. Work in Progress
32. Rescorla, E.: The Transport Layer Security (TLS) Protocol Version 1.3. RFC 8446, RFC Editor (2018)
33. SAFE-eV.   ECMF.   https://github.com/SAFE-eV/OCMF-Open-Charge-Metering-Format/blob/master/OCMF-en.md
34. Shingala, K.: JSON web token (JWT) based client authentication in message queuing telemetry transport (MQTT). CoRR, abs/1903.02895 (2019)
35. Arduino S.r.l. Arduino security primer (2020). https://blog.arduino.cc/2020/07/02/arduino-security-primer/
36. OASIS Standard: MQTT version 5.0 (2019). Retrieved 22 June 2020

Author Index

A
Adhikary, Asmita   157
Aghapour, Saeed   244
Ahmadi, Kasra   244
Aikata, Aikata   39
Alaybeyoğlu, Ersin   117
Arslan, Atakan   3
Aysu, Aydin   77
Ayyagari, Modini   77
Azarderakhsh, Reza   57, 244

B
Banik, Subhadeep   231
Basurto-Becerra, Abraham   157
Batina, Lejla   157
Battistello, Alberto   328
Bertoni, Guido   328
Buhan, Ileana   157, 178

C
Chatterjee, Durba   157

D
De Paepe, Charles-Antoine   198
Düzyol, Gökçe   138

F
Feussner, Martin   23

G
Gaspoz, John   198
Gönen, Mehmet Emin   3

Grootjen, Lizzy   178
Gündoğan, Muhammed Said   3

I
İlter, Murat Burhan   285

K
Kara, Orhun   285
Kavun, Elif Bilge   97
Kırbıyık, Selim   117
Koçak, Onur   285
Koçer, Emre   117
Konstantopoulou, Evangelia   212

L
Liu, Zhuoran   178

M
Magesh, Rahul   77
Manzoni, Giuseppe   97
Melzani, Filippo   328
Memeletzoglou, Charilaos   212
Molteni, Maria Chiara   328
Mozaffari Kermani, Mehran   57, 244
Mukherjee, Anisha   39

N
Neisarian, Shekoufeh   97
Nikova, Svetla   198

O
Otal, Kamil   138

P
Pendyala, Sharath   77

R
Regazzoni, Francesco   231

S
Sanfelix Gonzalez, Eloi   157
Saygan, Arda   3
Semaev, Igor   23

Sinha Roy, Sujoy   39
Sklavos, Nicolas   212
Sulak, Fatih   285

T
Taghavi, Bardia   57
Toprakhisar, Dilara   198
Tosun, Tolun   117

V
van Hoek, Senna   157
Vaziri, Mohammad   263, 306
Velichkov, Vesselin   263

If you have any concerns about our products,
you can contact us on
ProductSafety@springernature.com

In case Publisher is established outside the EU,
the EU authorized representative is:
**Springer Nature Customer Service Center GmbH
Europaplatz 3, 69115 Heidelberg, Germany**

Printed by Libri Plureos GmbH
in Hamburg, Germany